A Primer in Econometric Theory

A Primer in Econometric Theory

John Stachurski

The MIT Press
Cambridge, Massachusetts
London, England

This book was typeset in LaTeX by the author. Printed and bound in the United States of America.

Library of Congress Cataloging-in-Publication Data

Names: Stachurski, John, 1969- author.
Title: A primer in econometric theory / John Stachurski.
Description: Cambridge, MA : The MIT Press, 2016. | Includes bibliographical references and index.
Identifiers: LCCN 2016008483 | ISBN 9780262034906 (hardcover : alk. paper)
Subjects: LCSH: Economics–Mathematical models. | Economics–Statistical methods.
Classification: LCC HB135 .S668 2016 | DDC 330.01/5195–dc23 LC record available at http://lccn.loc.gov/2016008483

10 9 8 7 6 5 4 3 2 1

To my parents

Contents

Preface

This is a quick course on econometric theory and methods, along with the underlying ideas from probability, statistics and linear algebra that budding econometricians should know. The focus is on foundations and general principles. Although it was written to teach from, there are many solved exercises, making the text well suited to self-study. Worked examples and sample code are used to reinforce ideas.

The level of the text is calibrated towards the first year of graduate school—perhaps even to the first semester of the first year of graduate school—as an initial upper level course on econometrics and statistics. Those who work through the book will be well placed to take more specialized or applied quantitative courses in topics such as microeconometrics, time series analysis, or finance, to read graduate econometrics texts, and to begin to study papers from the econometrics literature and research from the wider world of statistics and data science.

One aim in writing the text was to link core topics in econometrics and statistics, identifying unifying principles and common themes. For example, the orthogonal projection theorem bestrides much of the technical material, from least squares to conditional expectation, while the concept of empirical risk minimization ties together most of our estimation theory. Another aim was to blend traditional econometrics with some of the theoretical ideas emanating from the data science and statistical learning communities.

I have emphasized the value of modern programming tools not only for data analysis but also for studying econometric theory. I'm certain that the best way to understand a result in econometric theory is to first work through the proof and then run a simulation that shows the theory in action. Sample code is provided in a mix of three programming languages: Julia, Python, and `R`. Python and `R` are the heavyweights of data science, and their popularity is now spilling over to econometrics. Julia is a new language for scientific programming with much to recommend it. All three are fun, high productivity languages. All three are open source. You can find the code for this course at

`johnstachurski.net/emet.html`

Programs are organized into Jupyter notebooks, including many figures along with the code listings.

Note that this text is not an encyclopedic treatment, nor a reference manual. I have tried to keep the book concise—suitable for a one semester course rather than anything longer. As a result, many well known econometric methods have been omitted or given only cursory treatments. As such, this book is intended as a complement or companion to the existing graduate level econometrics texts, most of which are cited in what follows.

I have freely borrowed ideas and results from a large number of sources. Some of these are listed in the "Further Reading" section at the end of each chapter. Doubtless some are missing. Many of the proofs in the text are "new" in the sense of being written from first principles, although they are certainly just remixes of what is already in the literature.

This book has benefited from the input of many students and colleagues. In particular, I wish to thank Blair Alexander, Frank Cai, Yiyong Cai, Tim Christensen, Bikramaditya Datta, Chenghan Hou, Takashi Kamihigashi, Paul Kitney, Qingyin Ma, Matthew McKay, Kieron Meagher, José L. Montiel Olea, Alex Olssen, Guanlong Ren, Tom Sargent, Stefan Webb, and Varang Wiriyawit. Extra thanks go to Cleo, my wife, for sharing the journey and helping with proofreading, and to Akshay Shanker, for reading the book so closely.

Common Symbols

$P \implies Q$	P implies Q
$P \iff Q$	$P \implies Q$ and $Q \implies P$
$a := 1$	a is defined as equal to 1
$\mathbb{R}$	all real numbers
$\mathbb{N}$	the natural numbers $\{1, 2, \ldots\}$
$\operatorname{rng} T$	range of function T
$\langle \mathbf{x}, \mathbf{y} \rangle$	inner product of $\mathbf{x}$ and $\mathbf{y}$
$\mathbf{e}_n$	nth canonical basis vector
$\|\mathbf{x}\|$	norm of $\mathbf{x}$
$\mathbf{x} \perp \mathbf{y}$	$\mathbf{x}$ and $\mathbf{y}$ are orthogonal
$S^\perp$	orthogonal complement of S
$\operatorname{proj} S$	orthogonal projection onto subspace S
$\mathbf{I}$	identity matrix
$\mathbf{A}^\intercal$	transpose of $\mathbf{A}$
$\operatorname{diag}(d_1, \ldots, d_N)$	diagonal matrix with diagonal elements $(d_1, \ldots, d_N)$
$\mathcal{L}(x)$	distribution (or law) of random variable x
$\mathscr{B}(\mathbb{R}^N)$	Borel sets
$\mathscr{B}$-measurable	Borel measurable
$\mathrm{N}(\mu, \sigma^2)$	normal distribution with mean μ and variance σ^2
Φ	standard normal CDF
ϕ	standard normal density
$\mathbb{1}_B$	indicator function of set B
IID	independent and identically distributed
$\mathbf{z}_{\mathcal{D}}$	data set
$Z_{\mathcal{D}}$	sample space

Chapter 1

Introduction

1.1 The Nature of Econometrics

Is econometrics just statistics applied to economic problems? To say so seems insulting. After all, econometricians have made many fundamental contributions to the theory and practice of quantitative modeling. At the same time, we do ourselves a disservice if we fail to link common principles from different fields.

So is the answer yes or no? And if no, what is econometrics?

We can probably agree that econometrics is concerned with quantitative analysis of economic problems using data. One of the idiosyncrasies of economic data is that most are observational, as opposed to experimental. The prevalence of observational data has been an ongoing challenge for econometricians, especially those concerned with causal inference. This challenge has certainly shaped what we call econometrics.

Another idiosyncrasy of econometrics is that it models the implications of choices made by people, and human beings have stubbornly refused to adopt the kinds of behavioral patterns that would make their choices easy to replicate consistently in quantitative models. Even the best economic models are only right along one or two dimensions. This fact has led to a relative emphasis on estimation methods that use partially specified models, such as the generalized method of moments.

A third notable feature of econometrics is that it tends to focus more on models that explain than models that predict. This is particularly so if you compare econometrics to fields like data science or machine learning. For example, consider the following quote from Vapnik (2006):

> I believe that something drastic has happened in computer science and machine learning. Until recently, philosophy was based on the idea that

> the world is simple. In machine learning, for the first time, we have examples where the world is not simple. For example, when we solve the "forest" problem [and] use data of size 15,000 we get 85%–87% accuracy. However, when we use 500,000 training examples we achieve 98% correct answers. This means that a good decision rule is not a simple one, it cannot be described by a very few parameters....
>
> So the question is, what is the real world? Is it simple or complex? Machine learning shows that there are examples of complex worlds. We should approach complex worlds from a completely different position than simple worlds. For example, in a complex world one should give up explainability (the main goal in classical science) to gain better predictability.

Putting aside the issue of whether economics should be modeled as a "complex world," the quote above nicely illustrates the trade-off between optimizing out-of-sample prediction versus fitting simple models where parameters have straightforward interpretations. Economists have traditionally focused on the latter, which is why topics such as identification are central to econometrics while at the same time largely ignored in fields like data science.

So far the discussion points to econometrics being relatively unique, and distinct from statistics. Let's look at the reverse claim. There's really only one argument running in this direction, but it's a good one. The fundamental problem of econometrics is exactly the same as the fundamental problem of statistics: a finite set of data is observed, and on the basis of these data, we seek to make *general statements*.

For example, suppose that a group of 100 pilot schools receive a treatment, such as a new reading program. The treatment is found to produce desired outcomes vis-à-vis some classification scheme in 95% of cases. On the basis of this test, it is claimed that the treatment is highly effective. The implication of this claim is that we can *generalize* to the wider population. The interest is not so much in what happened to the pilot schools but rather on what the outcome for the pilot schools implies *for other schools*. What we as econometricians/statisticians want to know is: to what extent is generalization valid in this and other instances?

Another word for generalization is *induction*. Inductive learning is where reasoning proceeds from the specific to the general—as opposed to deductive learning, which proceeds from general to specific. As researchers and scientists we often celebrate deductive reasoning, but the more you think about the human ability to generalize, the more striking and remarkable it seems. How is it that a 3 year old can determine that a dog it has never seen before is in fact a dog—rather than a cat, say, or a donkey? Surely most of this ability comes from induction rather than from following deductive rules. The child's brain has learned to generalize from examples.

At the same time, some problems are harder for our brains to generalize over.

While our ancestors best able to distinguish among types of wild creatures were certainly more successful in passing on their genes, little in the natural or social world of the past thousand or so millennia has prepared *Homo sapiens* for trying to back out the probabilistic structure behind firm size distributions, or to distinguish among diffusion processes most appropriate for tracking asset prices. Statistics and econometrics are ways for us to scale and codify our inductive learning abilities in order to confront these new problems.

This, then, is the fundamental problem of both econometrics and statistics: in the modern world we have lots of data, but still lack deep knowledge on how many systems work, or how different economic variables are related to one another. What is the process of extracting general knowledge from data—that is, from specific observations? What are the best techniques to use? Under what conditions will this process be successful?

1.2 Data versus Theory

One of the recurring issues in any form of statistical learning is the need to blend theory with data. To illustrate the idea, suppose that we observe inputs $\mathbf{x}_1, \ldots, \mathbf{x}_N$ to some system, as well as corresponding outputs $y_1, \ldots, y_N$. For example, the inputs might be a "treatment," such as the school reading program mentioned above. Outputs could be a measure of the effect of this treatment. Or inputs could be a mix of policy instruments such as spending and interest rates, with outputs being the response of quantities like inflation or unemployment. Given the observed input–output pairs, we seek a function f such that, given a new pair $(\mathbf{x}, y)$, the value $f(\mathbf{x})$ will accurately predict the corresponding output y.

If we knew the joint distribution of $(\mathbf{x}, y)$ pairs, then we could compute or approximate the conditional expectation $\mathbb{E}[y \mid \mathbf{x}]$, which, as we'll see, has a strong claim to being the best predictor of y given $\mathbf{x}$. Our problem lies in the fact that we don't know the distribution. Instead, we have the sample, which contains some but not all information about the joint distribution.

In problems such as this, our ability to generalize requires more than just data. Ideally, data are combined with a theoretical model that encapsulates our knowledge of the system we are studying. Data can be used to pin down parameter values for the model. If our model is good, then combining the model with data allows us to gain an understanding of how the system works.

Even when we have no formal model of how the system works, we cannot avoid assumptions if we want to generalize. Figure 1.1 helps illustrate this idea. Consider the regression setting described above, with scalar input x. Imagine that the dots shown in the figure are our data. Now make a guess as to the likely value of the

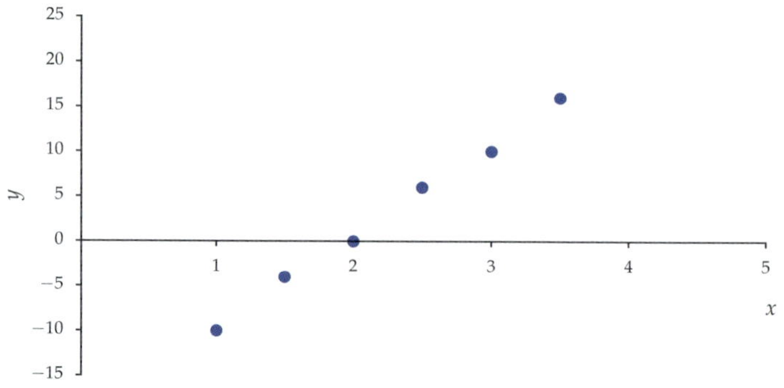

Figure 1.1 Generalization requires knowledge

output y, given new x value 4.

Did you select a y value close to 20? If so, this is because your brain picks up a pattern: the dots lie roughly on a straight line. Our brains have been trained or hardwired to notice these kinds of patterns. And even though this thought process is subconscious, in the end we are bringing our own assumptions into play.

Depending on the problem at hand, our assumption about the linear relationship could, of course, be completely wrong.[1] But the point is that we cannot forecast a new observation from the data alone. There is no free lunch. We have to take a stand and make *some* assumptions as to the functional relationship in order to guess a likely output given our new input. Those assumptions may come from knowledge of the system, or they might come from the customs of a particular academic community. Either way, we are adding something to the data in order to make inferences about likely outcomes.

We have spent some time on this point because it's essential that we are aware of what assumptions are being made in any given estimation problem, what justification is used for them, and what impact they might have. This process allows us to be critical. One of the aims of this book is to draw out assumptions behind different econometric procedures and their respective implications. You shouldn't treat any of these assumptions as sound without forming your own judgment.

1. For example, in 1929 the economist Irving Fisher famously declared "Stocks have reached what looks like a permanently high plateau." On that occasion linear extrapolation turned out to be a poor prediction rule.

1.3 Comments on the Literature

Much of the innovation in the field of statistics over the past few decades has been driven by the branch of research referred to above as machine learning, or data science. The term "statistical learning" is also used to describe this approach to inference. The field is distinguished by its use of flexible, high-dimensional models combined with large amounts of data. High-profile successes in applied problems have now been matched with important theoretical progress in the foundations of statistics.

These trends have had less impact on the field of econometrics. One reason is that microeconometrics has a long tradition of causal modeling using relatively simple models and a small number of covariates. Another is that structural modeling holds out the possibility of generating estimated macroeconomic models that are robust to the Lucas critique. It's not so clear how high-dimensional data-centric methods should be tied to these kinds of models.

Yet, economics does involve the study of highly complex relationships. Think first about the number of forces acting on the sail of a ship or a projectile fired from a gun. We can accurately model outcomes by considering only a few forces. But how many forces determine the price of US treasuries? How many forces determine educational outcomes across the United States for Hispanic males? Perhaps these are examples of Vapnik's "complex worlds," where relatively large amounts of data and flexible models are required.

While there are no definitive answers to these questions, the theory of statistical learning and the ever-expanding work of the machine learning community certainly offer important insights. Their ideas will shape our treatment of some fundamental econometric problems, including linear regression and model selection.

1.4 Further Reading

More extensive discussions of econometrics versus statistics can be found in Heckman (1992) and the early chapters of Hill et al. (2008), Wooldridge (2010), and Kennedy (2008). An overview of modern econometrics can be found in Geweke et al. (2006).

High-quality texts on the theory and applications of machine learning and statistical learning include Friedman et al. (2009), Bishop (2006), Vapnik (2000), and Abu-Mostafa et al. (2012). For some additional discussion of how machine learning techniques might be applied to econometric modeling, see Einav and Levin (2014), Varian (2014), Athey and Wager (2015), and Athey (2015).

Part I

Background

Chapter 2

Vector Spaces

Our first technical topic for this book is linear algebra, which is one of the foundation stones of applied mathematics in general, and econometrics and statistics in particular. Data ordered by observation are naturally stored in vectors. Related vectors are naturally grouped into matrices. Once our data are organized this way, we need to perform basic arithmetic operations or solve equations or quadratic minimization problems. In this chapter we cover the foundations of vector operations used in linear algebra. As we'll see, the conceptual aspects of linear algebra are clearest if we begin by stripping away details such as matrices and look instead at linear operations from a more abstract perspective.

2.1 Vectors and Vector Space

Let's begin with vector space and basic vector operations.

2.1.1 Vectors

For arbitrary $N \in \mathbb{N}$, the symbol $\mathbb{R}^N$ represents the set of all N-vectors, or vectors of length N. A typical element has the form

$$\mathbf{x} = \begin{pmatrix} x_1 \\ x_2 \\ \vdots \\ x_N \end{pmatrix} \qquad \text{where } x_n \in \mathbb{R} \text{ for each } n$$

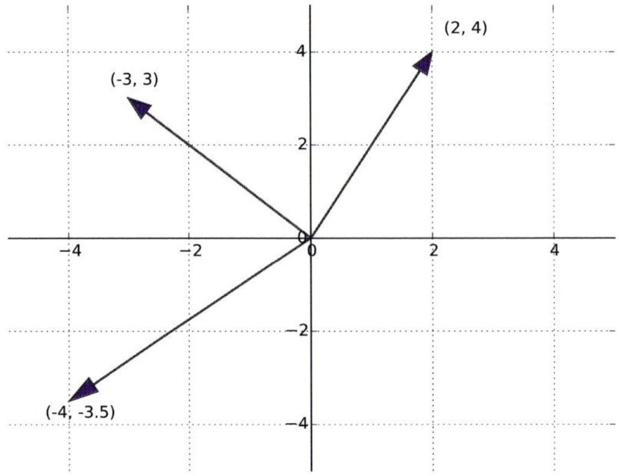

Figure 2.1 Three vectors in $\mathbb{R}^2$

($\mathbb{R} = \mathbb{R}^1$ represents the set of all real numbers, which is the union of the rational and irrational numbers.) While $\mathbf{x}$ has been written vertically, as a column of numbers, we could also write it horizontally as $\mathbf{x} = (x_1, \ldots, x_N)$. For now vectors are just a sequences of numbers, and it makes no difference whether we write them vertically or horizontally. (Only when we work with matrix multiplication does it become necessary to distinguish between column and row vectors.)

The vector of ones will be denoted $\mathbf{1}$ and the vector of zeros will be denoted $\mathbf{0}$:

$$\mathbf{1} := \begin{pmatrix} 1 \\ \vdots \\ 1 \end{pmatrix}, \qquad \mathbf{0} := \begin{pmatrix} 0 \\ \vdots \\ 0 \end{pmatrix}$$

Although vectors are infinitesimal points in $\mathbb{R}^N$, they are often represented visually as arrows from the origin to the point itself. Figure 2.1 gives an illustration for the case $N = 2$.

In vector space theory there are two fundamental algebraic operations: vector addition and scalar multiplication. For $\mathbf{x}, \mathbf{y} \in \mathbb{R}^N$, their **vector sum** is

$$\mathbf{x} + \mathbf{y} = \begin{pmatrix} x_1 \\ \vdots \\ x_N \end{pmatrix} + \begin{pmatrix} y_1 \\ \vdots \\ y_N \end{pmatrix} := \begin{pmatrix} x_1 + y_1 \\ \vdots \\ x_N + y_N \end{pmatrix}$$

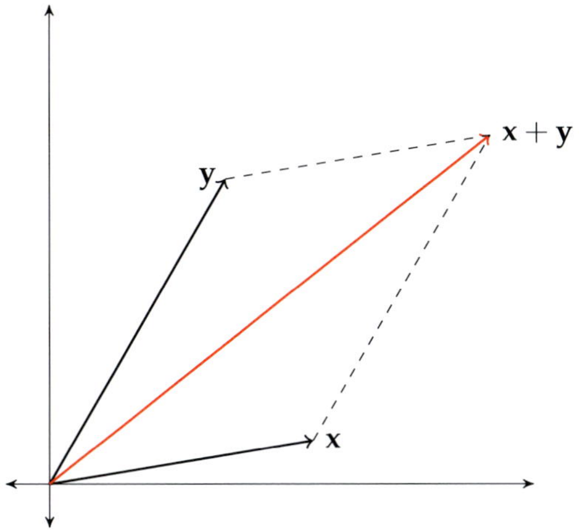

Figure 2.2 Vector addition

If $\alpha \in \mathbb{R}$, then the **scalar product** of α and $\mathbf{x}$ is defined to be

$$\alpha \mathbf{x} = \alpha \begin{pmatrix} x_1 \\ \vdots \\ x_N \end{pmatrix} := \begin{pmatrix} \alpha x_1 \\ \vdots \\ \alpha x_N \end{pmatrix}$$

Thus addition and scalar multiplication are defined in terms of ordinary addition and multiplication in $\mathbb{R}$, computed element by element, adding and multiplying respectively.[1] Figures 2.2 and 2.3 show examples of vector addition and scalar multiplication in the case $N = 2$.

Subtraction of two vectors is performed element by element, just like addition. Subtraction is not a primitive operation because the definition can be given in terms of addition and scalar multiplication: $\mathbf{x} - \mathbf{y} := \mathbf{x} + (-1)\mathbf{y}$. An illustration of subtraction is given in figure 2.4. One way to remember this operation is to draw a line from $\mathbf{y}$ to $\mathbf{x}$ and then shift it to the origin.

The **inner product** of two vectors $\mathbf{x}$ and $\mathbf{y}$ in $\mathbb{R}^N$ is denoted by $\langle \mathbf{x}, \mathbf{y} \rangle$, and defined

1. In some instances, the notion of scalar multiplication includes multiplication of vectors by complex numbers. In what follows we will work almost entirely with real scalars. Hence scalar multiplication means real scalar multiplication unless otherwise stated.

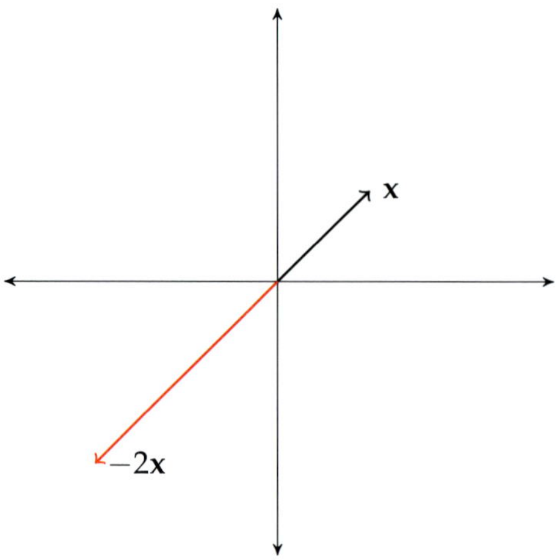

Figure 2.3 Scalar multiplication

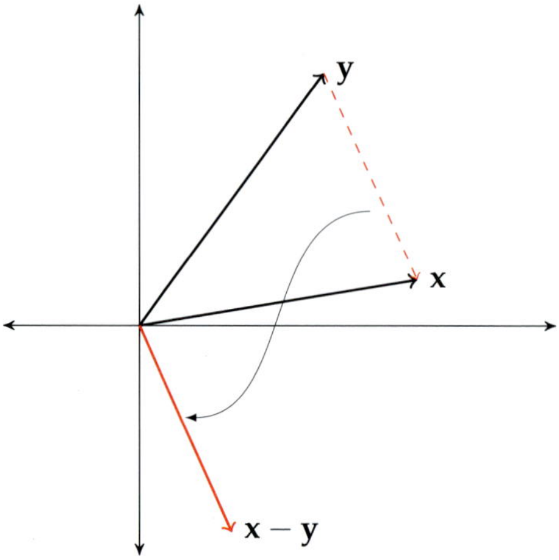

Figure 2.4 Difference between vectors

as the sum of the products of their elements:

$$\langle \mathbf{x}, \mathbf{y} \rangle := \sum_{n=1}^{N} x_n y_n \tag{2.1}$$

Fact 2.1.1 For any $\alpha, \beta \in \mathbb{R}$ and any $\mathbf{x}, \mathbf{y}, \mathbf{z} \in \mathbb{R}^N$, the following statements are true:

(i) $\langle \mathbf{x}, \mathbf{y} \rangle = \langle \mathbf{y}, \mathbf{x} \rangle$,

(ii) $\langle \alpha\mathbf{x}, \beta\mathbf{y} \rangle = \alpha\beta \langle \mathbf{x}, \mathbf{y} \rangle$, and

(iii) $\langle \mathbf{x}, \alpha\mathbf{y} + \beta\mathbf{z} \rangle = \alpha \langle \mathbf{x}, \mathbf{y} \rangle + \beta \langle \mathbf{x}, \mathbf{z} \rangle$.

These properties are easy to check from (2.1). For example, regarding the second equality, pick any $\alpha, \beta \in \mathbb{R}$ and any $\mathbf{x}, \mathbf{y} \in \mathbb{R}^N$. By the definitions of scalar multiplication and inner product respectively, we have

$$\langle \alpha\mathbf{x}, \beta\mathbf{y} \rangle = \sum_{n=1}^{N} \alpha x_n \beta y_n = \alpha\beta \sum_{n=1}^{N} x_n y_n = \alpha\beta \langle \mathbf{x}, \mathbf{y} \rangle$$

The (Euclidean) **norm** of a vector $\mathbf{x} \in \mathbb{R}^N$ is defined as

$$\|\mathbf{x}\| := \sqrt{\langle \mathbf{x}, \mathbf{x} \rangle} \tag{2.2}$$

and represents the length of the vector $\mathbf{x}$. (In the arrow representation of vectors in figures 2.2–2.4, the norm of the vector is equal to the length of the arrow.)

Fact 2.1.2 For any $\alpha \in \mathbb{R}$ and any $\mathbf{x}, \mathbf{y} \in \mathbb{R}^N$, the following statements are true:

(i) $\|\mathbf{x}\| \geqslant 0$ and $\|\mathbf{x}\| = 0$ if and only if $\mathbf{x} = \mathbf{0}$,

(ii) $\|\alpha\mathbf{x}\| = |\alpha|\|\mathbf{x}\|$,

(iii) $\|\mathbf{x} + \mathbf{y}\| \leqslant \|\mathbf{x}\| + \|\mathbf{y}\|$, and

(iv) $|\langle \mathbf{x}, \mathbf{y} \rangle| \leqslant \|\mathbf{x}\|\|\mathbf{y}\|$.

Properties (i) and (ii) you can verify yourself without difficulty. Proofs for (iii) and (iv) are a bit harder. Property (iii) is called the **triangle inequality**, while (iv) is called the **Cauchy–Schwarz inequality**. The proof of the Cauchy–Schwarz inequality is given as a solved exercise after we've built up some more tools (see ex. 3.5.33). If you're prepared to accept the Cauchy–Schwarz inequality for now, then the triangle inequality follows, because, by the properties of the inner product given in fact 2.1.1,

$$\|\mathbf{x} + \mathbf{y}\|^2 = \langle \mathbf{x} + \mathbf{y}, \mathbf{x} + \mathbf{y} \rangle = \langle \mathbf{x}, \mathbf{x} \rangle + 2 \langle \mathbf{x}, \mathbf{y} \rangle + \langle \mathbf{y}, \mathbf{y} \rangle \leqslant \langle \mathbf{x}, \mathbf{x} \rangle + 2|\langle \mathbf{x}, \mathbf{y} \rangle| + \langle \mathbf{y}, \mathbf{y} \rangle$$

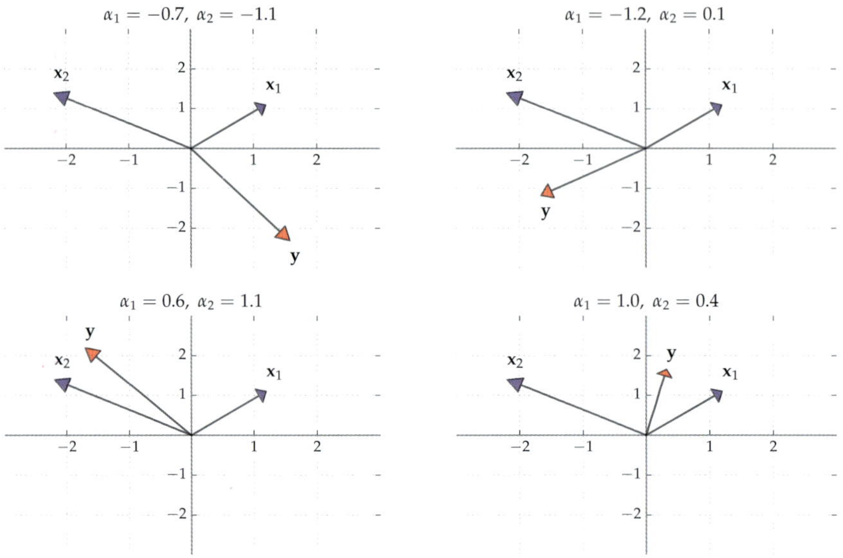

Figure 2.5 Linear combinations of $\mathbf{x}_1, \mathbf{x}_2$

Applying the Cauchy–Schwarz inequality leads to $\|\mathbf{x}+\mathbf{y}\|^2 \leqslant (\|\mathbf{x}\| + \|\mathbf{y}\|)^2$. Taking the square root gives the triangle inequality.

Given two vectors $\mathbf{x}$ and $\mathbf{y}$, the value $\|\mathbf{x}-\mathbf{y}\|$ has the interpretation of being the "distance" between these points. To see why, consult figure 2.4 again.

2.1.2 Linear Combinations and Span

One of the most elementary ways to work with vectors is to combine them using linear operations. Given vectors $\mathbf{x}_1, \ldots, \mathbf{x}_K$ in $\mathbb{R}^N$, a **linear combination** of these vectors is a new vector of the form

$$\mathbf{y} = \sum_{k=1}^{K} \alpha_k \mathbf{x}_k = \alpha_1 \mathbf{x}_1 + \cdots + \alpha_K \mathbf{x}_K \tag{2.3}$$

for some collection of scalars $\alpha_1, \ldots, \alpha_K$ (i.e., with $\alpha_k \in \mathbb{R}$ for all k). Figure 2.5 shows four different linear combinations $\mathbf{y} = \alpha_1 \mathbf{x}_1 + \alpha_2 \mathbf{x}_2$ where $\mathbf{x}_1, \mathbf{x}_2$ are fixed vectors in $\mathbb{R}^2$ and the scalars α_1 and α_2 are varied.

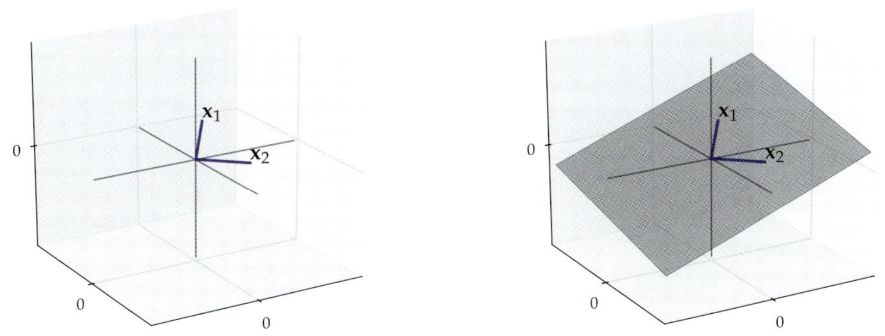

Figure 2.6 Span of $X = \{\mathbf{x}_1, \mathbf{x}_2\}$

Given any nonempty $X \subset \mathbb{R}^N$, the set of all vectors that can be made by (finite) linear combinations of elements of X is called the **span** of X, and denoted by span X. For example, the set of all linear combinations of $X := \{\mathbf{x}_1, \ldots, \mathbf{x}_K\}$ is

$$\operatorname{span} X := \left\{ \text{all vectors } \sum_{k=1}^{K} \alpha_k \mathbf{x}_k \text{ such that } \boldsymbol{\alpha} := (\alpha_1, \ldots, \alpha_K) \in \mathbb{R}^K \right\}$$

As will be discussed below, the span of certain collections of vectors turns out to have an intimate connection with existence of solutions to linear equations.

Example 2.1.1 By construction, the four vectors labeled $\mathbf{y}$ in figure 2.5 lie in the span of $X = \{\mathbf{x}_1, \mathbf{x}_2\}$. Looking at this picture might lead you to wonder whether *any* vector in $\mathbb{R}^2$ could be created as a linear combination of $\mathbf{x}_1, \mathbf{x}_2$. The answer is affirmative. We'll prove this in §2.1.5.

Example 2.1.2 Let $X = \{\mathbf{1}\} = \{(1,1)\} \subset \mathbb{R}^2$. The span of X is all vectors of the form $\alpha\mathbf{1} = (\alpha, \alpha)$ with $\alpha \in \mathbb{R}$. This constitutes a line in the plane. Since we can take $\alpha = 0$, it follows that the origin $\mathbf{0}$ is in span X. In fact span X is the unique line in the plane that passes through both $\mathbf{0}$ and the vector $\mathbf{1} = (1,1)$.

Example 2.1.3 Let $\mathbf{x}_1 = (3,4,2)$ and let $\mathbf{x}_2 = (3,-4,0.4)$. The span of $\{\mathbf{x}_1, \mathbf{x}_2\}$ is a plane in $\mathbb{R}^3$ that passes through both of these vectors and the origin, as shown in figure 2.6.

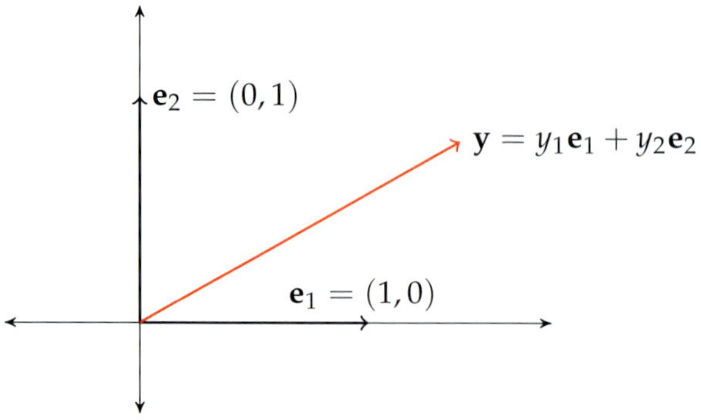

Figure 2.7 Canonical basis vectors in $\mathbb{R}^2$

Example 2.1.4 Consider the vectors $\{\mathbf{e}_1, \ldots, \mathbf{e}_N\} \subset \mathbb{R}^N$, where $\mathbf{e}_n$ has all zeros except for a 1 as the nth element:

$$\mathbf{e}_1 := \begin{pmatrix} 1 \\ 0 \\ \vdots \\ 0 \end{pmatrix}, \quad \mathbf{e}_2 := \begin{pmatrix} 0 \\ 1 \\ \vdots \\ 0 \end{pmatrix}, \quad \cdots, \quad \mathbf{e}_N := \begin{pmatrix} 0 \\ 0 \\ \vdots \\ 1 \end{pmatrix}$$

The case of $\mathbb{R}^2$ is illustrated in figure 2.7. The vectors $\mathbf{e}_1, \ldots, \mathbf{e}_N$ are called the **canonical basis vectors** of $\mathbb{R}^N$. One reason is that $\{\mathbf{e}_1, \ldots, \mathbf{e}_N\}$ spans all of $\mathbb{R}^N$. Here's a proof for $N = 2$: Observe that for any $\mathbf{y} \in \mathbb{R}^2$, we have

$$\mathbf{y} := \begin{pmatrix} y_1 \\ y_2 \end{pmatrix} = \begin{pmatrix} y_1 \\ 0 \end{pmatrix} + \begin{pmatrix} 0 \\ y_1 \end{pmatrix} = y_1 \begin{pmatrix} 1 \\ 0 \end{pmatrix} + y_2 \begin{pmatrix} 0 \\ 1 \end{pmatrix} = y_1\mathbf{e}_1 + y_2\mathbf{e}_2$$

Thus $\mathbf{y} \in \operatorname{span}\{\mathbf{e}_1, \mathbf{e}_2\}$. Since $\mathbf{y}$ is an arbitrary vector in $\mathbb{R}^2$, we have shown that $\{\mathbf{e}_1, \mathbf{e}_2\}$ spans $\mathbb{R}^2$.

Example 2.1.5 Consider the set $P := \{(x_1, x_2, 0) \in \mathbb{R}^3 : x_1, x_2 \in \mathbb{R}\}$. Graphically, P corresponds to the flat plane in $\mathbb{R}^3$, where the height coordinate is always zero. If we take $\mathbf{e}_1 = (1, 0, 0)$ and $\mathbf{e}_2 = (0, 1, 0)$, then given $\mathbf{y} = (y_1, y_2, 0) \in P$, we have $\mathbf{y} = y_1\mathbf{e}_1 + y_2\mathbf{e}_2$. In other words, any $\mathbf{y} \in P$ can be expressed as a linear combination of $\mathbf{e}_1$ and $\mathbf{e}_2$. Equivalently, $P \subset \operatorname{span}\{\mathbf{e}_1, \mathbf{e}_2\}$.

The next fact follows directly from the definition of span.

Fact 2.1.3 If X, Y are nonempty subsets of $\mathbb{R}^N$ and $X \subset Y$, then $\operatorname{span} X \subset \operatorname{span} Y$.

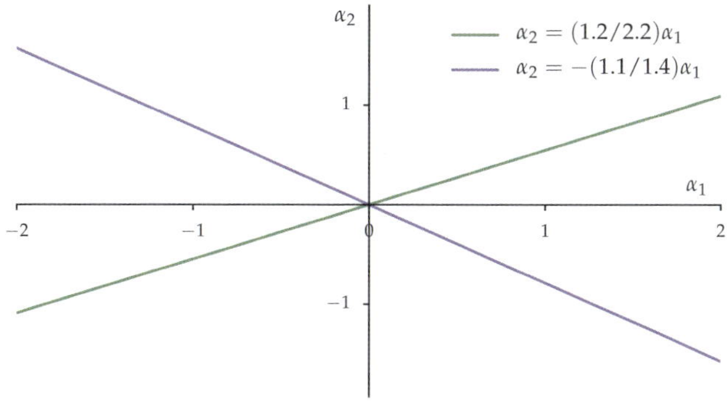

Figure 2.8 The only solution is $\alpha_1 = \alpha_2 = 0$

2.1.3 Linear Independence

Linear independence is an apparently simple concept with implications that stretch deep into many aspects of analysis. If you wish to understand when a matrix is invertible, or when a system of linear equations has a unique solution, or when a least squares estimate is uniquely defined, the most important foundational idea is linear independence of vectors.

Let's begin with the definition. Consider a set of vectors $X := \{\mathbf{x}_1, \ldots, \mathbf{x}_K\}$. We can surely realize the origin $\mathbf{0}$ as a linear combination of these vectors, just by setting all of the scalars α_k in $\sum_{k=1}^{K} \alpha_k \mathbf{x}_k$ to zero. The set X is called linearly independent when this is the only possibility. That is, $X \subset \mathbb{R}^N$ is called **linearly independent** if

$$\alpha_1 \mathbf{x}_1 + \cdots + \alpha_K \mathbf{x}_K = \mathbf{0} \quad \Longrightarrow \quad \alpha_1 = \cdots = \alpha_K = 0 \tag{2.4}$$

We call X **linearly dependent** if it is not linearly independent.

Example 2.1.6 In figure 2.5 on page 14, the two vectors are $\mathbf{x}_1 = (1.2, 1.1)$ and $\mathbf{x}_2 = (-2.2, 1.4)$. Suppose that α_1 and α_2 are scalars with

$$\alpha_1 \begin{pmatrix} 1.2 \\ 1.1 \end{pmatrix} + \alpha_2 \begin{pmatrix} -2.2 \\ 1.4 \end{pmatrix} = \mathbf{0}$$

This translates to the linear, two-equation system shown in figure 2.8, where the unknowns are α_1 and α_2. The only solution is $\alpha_1 = \alpha_2 = 0$. Hence $\{\mathbf{x}_1, \mathbf{x}_2\}$ is linearly independent.

Example 2.1.7 The set of N canonical basis vectors $\{\mathbf{e}_1, \ldots, \mathbf{e}_N\}$ is linearly independent in $\mathbb{R}^N$. To see this, let $\alpha_1, \ldots, \alpha_N$ be coefficients such that $\sum_{n=1}^N \alpha_n \mathbf{e}_n = \mathbf{0}$. Equivalently,

$$\alpha_1 \begin{pmatrix} 1 \\ 0 \\ \vdots \\ 0 \end{pmatrix} + \alpha_2 \begin{pmatrix} 0 \\ 1 \\ \vdots \\ 0 \end{pmatrix} + \cdots + \alpha_N \begin{pmatrix} 0 \\ 0 \\ \vdots \\ 1 \end{pmatrix} = \begin{pmatrix} \alpha_1 \\ \alpha_2 \\ \vdots \\ \alpha_N \end{pmatrix} = \begin{pmatrix} 0 \\ 0 \\ \vdots \\ 0 \end{pmatrix}$$

In particular, $\alpha_n = 0$ for all n.

Example 2.1.8 Consider the vectors $\{\mathbf{x}_1, \mathbf{x}_2\}$ as given in

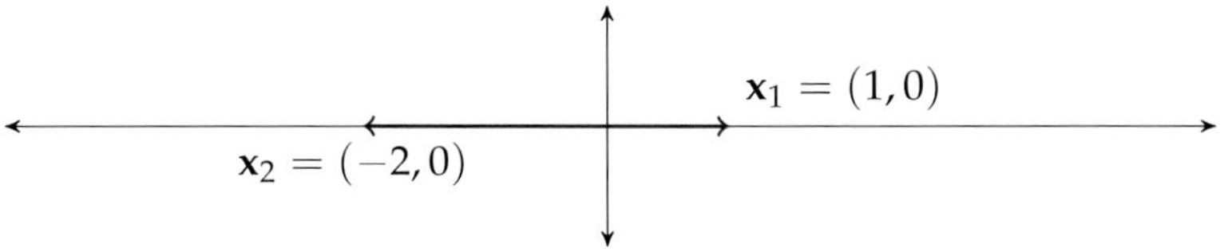

This pair fails to be linearly independent, since $\mathbf{x}_2 = -2\mathbf{x}_1$, and hence $2\mathbf{x}_1 + \mathbf{x}_2 = \mathbf{0}$.

How can we interpret linear independence? One way to understand it is as an indicator of the algebraic diversity of a given collection of vectors. In particular, in a linearly independent set, the span is relatively large, in the sense that every vector contributes to the span. Here's a formal statement of this idea.

Theorem 2.1.1 *Let* $X := \{\mathbf{x}_1, \ldots, \mathbf{x}_K\} \subset \mathbb{R}^N$. *For* $K > 1$, *the following statements are equivalent:*

(i) *X is linearly independent.*

(ii) *X_0 is a proper subset*[2] *of X* $\implies$ span X_0 *is a proper subset of* span X.

(iii) *No vector in X can be written as a linear combination of the others.*

Exercise 2.4.15 asks you to check these equivalences. For now let's just step through them in the context of two examples. First consider the pair of canonical basis vectors $\{\mathbf{e}_1, \mathbf{e}_2\}$ in $\mathbb{R}^2$, as depicted in figure 2.7. As we saw in examples 2.1.4 and 2.1.7, this pair is linearly independent, and its span is all of $\mathbb{R}^2$. Both vectors contribute to the span, since removing either one reduces the span to just a line in $\mathbb{R}^2$. (For example, the span of $\{\mathbf{e}_1\}$ is just the horizontal axis in $\mathbb{R}^2$.) Neither one of this pair can be written as a linear combination of the other.

2. A is a proper subset of B if $A \subset B$ and $A \neq B$.

Next, consider instead the pair $\{\mathbf{x}_1, \mathbf{x}_2\}$ in example 2.1.8. These vectors fail to be linearly independent, as shown in that example. It is also clear that dropping either one does not change the span—it remains the horizontal axis in any case. Finally, we saw in example 2.1.8 that $\mathbf{x}_2 = -2\mathbf{x}_1$, which means that each vector can be written as a linear combination of the other.

Fact 2.1.4 If $X := \{\mathbf{x}_1, \ldots, \mathbf{x}_K\}$ is linearly independent, then

(i) every subset of X is linearly independent,

(ii) X does not contain $\mathbf{0}$, and

(iii) $X \cup \{\mathbf{x}\}$ is linearly independent for all $\mathbf{x} \in \mathbb{R}^N$ such that $\mathbf{x} \notin \operatorname{span} X$.

The proof is a solved exercise (ex. 2.4.16 on page 36).

2.1.3.1 Linear Independence and Uniqueness

As we'll see below, the problem of existence of solutions to systems of linear equations comes down to whether or not a given point is contained in the span of a collection of vectors (which typically correspond to the columns of a matrix). This depends in general on the size of the span, and the size of the span in turn depends on whether or not the vectors are linearly independent.

Given that linear independence is the key condition for existence of solutions, it's surprising at first to learn that linear independence is the key condition for uniqueness as well. As we'll see, the connection between linear independence and uniqueness stems from the following result.

Theorem 2.1.2 *Let $X := \{\mathbf{x}_1, \ldots, \mathbf{x}_K\}$ be any collection of vectors in $\mathbb{R}^N$. The following statements are equivalent:*

(i) X is linearly independent.

(ii) For each $\mathbf{y} \in \mathbb{R}^N$ there exists at most one set of scalars $\alpha_1, \ldots, \alpha_K$ such that

$$\mathbf{y} = \alpha_1 \mathbf{x}_1 + \cdots + \alpha_K \mathbf{x}_K \tag{2.5}$$

Proof. ((i) $\implies$ (ii)) Let X be linearly independent and pick any $\mathbf{y} \in \mathbb{R}^N$. Suppose that there are two sets of scalars such that (2.5) holds. In particular, suppose that $\mathbf{y} = \sum_{k=1}^K \alpha_k \mathbf{x}_k = \sum_{k=1}^K \beta_k \mathbf{x}_k$. It follows from the second equality that $\sum_{k=1}^K (\alpha_k - \beta_k)\mathbf{x}_k = \mathbf{0}$. By linear independence, we then have $\alpha_k = \beta_k$ for all k. In other words, the representation is unique.

((ii) $\implies$ (i)) If (ii) holds, then there exists at most one set of scalars such that $\mathbf{0} = \sum_{k=1}^K \alpha_k \mathbf{x}_k$. Because $\alpha_1 = \cdots = \alpha_k = 0$ has this property, we conclude that no nonzero scalars yield $\mathbf{0} = \sum_{k=1}^K \alpha_k \mathbf{x}_k$. In other words, X is linearly independent. $\square$

2.1.4 Linear Subspaces

We will find it rewarding to study more closely the structure of spans generated by a collection of vectors. One of the defining features of the span of a set X is that it is "closed" under the linear operations of vector addition and scalar multiplication, in the sense that

(i) $\mathbf{x}, \mathbf{y} \in \operatorname{span} X \implies \mathbf{x} + \mathbf{y} \in \operatorname{span} X$, and

(ii) $\mathbf{y} \in \operatorname{span} X$ and $\gamma \in \mathbb{R} \implies \gamma \mathbf{y} \in \operatorname{span} X$.

For example, (i) holds because the sum of two linear combinations of elements of X is another linear combination of elements of X.

The notion of a set being closed under scalar multiplication and vector addition is important enough to have its own name: A nonempty subset S of $\mathbb{R}^N$ is called a **linear subspace** (or just **subspace**) of $\mathbb{R}^N$ if

$$\mathbf{x}, \mathbf{y} \in S \text{ and } \alpha, \beta \in \mathbb{R} \implies \alpha\mathbf{x} + \beta\mathbf{y} \in S \tag{2.6}$$

Example 2.1.9 It follows from the preceding discussion that if X is any nonempty subset of $\mathbb{R}^N$, then span X is a linear subspace of $\mathbb{R}^N$. For this reason, span X is often called the **linear subspace spanned by X.**

Example 2.1.10 Given any $\mathbf{a} \in \mathbb{R}^N$, the set $A := \{\mathbf{x} \in \mathbb{R}^N : \langle \mathbf{a}, \mathbf{x} \rangle = 0\}$ is a linear subspace of $\mathbb{R}^N$. To see this let $\mathbf{x}, \mathbf{y} \in A$ and let $\alpha, \beta \in \mathbb{R}$. We claim that $\mathbf{z} := \alpha\mathbf{x} + \beta\mathbf{y} \in A$, or, equivalently, that $\langle \mathbf{a}, \mathbf{z} \rangle = 0$. This is true because

$$\langle \mathbf{a}, \mathbf{z} \rangle = \langle \mathbf{a}, \alpha\mathbf{x} + \beta\mathbf{y} \rangle = \alpha \langle \mathbf{a}, \mathbf{x} \rangle + \beta \langle \mathbf{a}, \mathbf{y} \rangle = 0 + 0 = 0$$

Example 2.1.11 The entire space $\mathbb{R}^N$ is a linear subspace of $\mathbb{R}^N$ because any linear combination of N-vectors is an N-vector.

To visualize subspaces in $\mathbb{R}^3$, think of lines and planes that pass through the origin. Here are some elementary facts about linear subspaces:

Fact 2.1.5 If S is a linear subspace of $\mathbb{R}^N$, then

(i) $\mathbf{0} \in S$,

(ii) $X \subset S \implies \operatorname{span} X \subset S$, and

(iii) $\operatorname{span} S = S$.

There's also one deep result about linear subspaces we need to cover, which forms a cornerstone of many foundational results:

Theorem 2.1.3 *Let S be a linear subspace of $\mathbb{R}^N$. If S is spanned by K vectors, then any linearly independent subset of S has at most K vectors.*

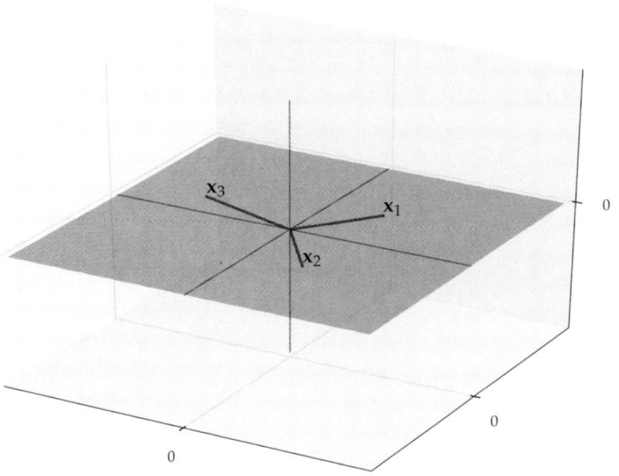

Figure 2.9 Any three vectors in P are linearly dependent

In other words, if there exists a set $X = \{\mathbf{x}_1, \ldots, \mathbf{x}_K\}$ with $S \subset \operatorname{span} X$, then any subset of S with more than K vectors will be linearly dependent. The proof can be found in most texts on linear algebra (e.g., §3.5 of Jänich 1994).

Example 2.1.12 We saw in example 2.1.4 that $\mathbb{R}^2$ is spanned by the pair $\{\mathbf{e}_1, \mathbf{e}_2\}$, where $\mathbf{e}_i$ is the ith canonical basis vector in $\mathbb{R}^2$. (See also figure 2.7.) It follows immediately from this fact and theorem 2.1.3 that the three vectors in $\mathbb{R}^2$ shown in figure 2.1 are linearly dependent.

Example 2.1.13 Consider the plane $P := \{(x_1, x_2, 0) \in \mathbb{R}^3 : x_1, x_2 \in \mathbb{R}\}$ from example 2.1.5. We saw in that example that P can be spanned by two vectors. As a consequence of theorem 2.1.3, we now know that any three vectors in this plane—such as the three shown in figure 2.9—are linearly dependent.

2.1.5 Bases and Dimension

Consider again the pair $\mathbf{x}_1, \mathbf{x}_2$ shown in figure 2.5 on page 14, and the four different vectors labeled $\mathbf{y}$ that we created from $\mathbf{x}_1, \mathbf{x}_2$ by way of linear combinations. Eyeballing the figure gives the impression that any $\mathbf{y} \in \mathbb{R}^2$ could be constructed as a linear combination of $\mathbf{x}_1, \mathbf{x}_2$ with suitable choice of the scalars α_1, α_2. Indeed this is true. The reason is that the pair $\{\mathbf{x}_1, \mathbf{x}_2\}$ is linearly independent (see example 2.1.6

on page 17), and any pair of linearly independent vectors in $\mathbb{R}^2$ spans $\mathbb{R}^2$. Here's a statement of this result for the general case:

Theorem 2.1.4 *Let $X := \{\mathbf{x}_1, \ldots, \mathbf{x}_N\}$ be any N vectors in $\mathbb{R}^N$. The following statements are equivalent:*

(i) $\operatorname{span} X = \mathbb{R}^N$.

(ii) X is linearly independent.

Proof. ((i) $\implies$ (ii)) Suppose that $\operatorname{span} X = \mathbb{R}^N$ but X is not linearly independent. Then, by theorem 2.1.1, there exists a proper subset X_0 of X with $\operatorname{span} X_0 = \operatorname{span} X$. Since X_0 is a proper subset of X it contains $K < N$ elements. We now have K vectors spanning $\mathbb{R}^N$. In particular, the span of K vectors contains the $N > K$ linearly independent vectors $\mathbf{e}_1, \ldots, \mathbf{e}_N$. This contradicts theorem 2.1.3.

((ii) $\implies$ (i)) Suppose that X is linearly independent and yet there exists an $\mathbf{x} \in \mathbb{R}^N$ with $\mathbf{x} \notin \operatorname{span} X$. By fact 2.1.4, it follows that the $N+1$ element set $X \cup \{\mathbf{x}\} \subset \mathbb{R}^N$ is linearly independent. Since $\mathbb{R}^N$ is spanned by the N canonical basis vectors, this statement also contradicts theorem 2.1.3. □

We now come to a key definition. Let S be a linear subspace of $\mathbb{R}^N$ and let $B \subset S$. The set B is called a **basis** of S if

(i) B spans S and

(ii) B is linearly independent.

The plural of basis is **bases**. In view of theorem 2.1.2, when B is a basis of S, each point in S has exactly one representation as a linear combination of elements of B.

It follows immediately from theorem 2.1.4 that any N linearly independent vectors in $\mathbb{R}^N$ form a basis of $\mathbb{R}^N$.

Example 2.1.14 The set of canonical basis vectors $\{\mathbf{e}_1, \ldots, \mathbf{e}_N\} \subset \mathbb{R}^N$ described in example 2.1.4 is linearly independent and spans all of $\mathbb{R}^N$. As a result, it provides a basis for $\mathbb{R}^N$—as anticipated by the name.

Example 2.1.15 The pair $\{\mathbf{x}_1, \mathbf{x}_2\}$ from figure 2.5 (page 14) forms a basis of $\mathbb{R}^2$.

Example 2.1.16 The pair $\{\mathbf{e}_1, \mathbf{e}_2\}$ is a basis for the set P defined in example 2.1.5.

Here are the two most fundamental results about bases:

Theorem 2.1.5 *If S is a linear subspace of $\mathbb{R}^N$ distinct from $\{\mathbf{0}\}$, then*

(i) S has at least one basis and

(ii) every basis of S has the same number of elements.

The proof of part (i) is not particularly hard. See, for example, section 3.2 of Jänich (1994). Part (ii) follows from theorem 2.1.3 and is left as an exercise (ex. 2.4.17).

If S is a linear subspace of $\mathbb{R}^N$, then the common number identified in theorem 2.1.5 is called the **dimension** of S, and written as $\dim S$.

Example 2.1.17 For $P := \{(x_1, x_2, 0) \in \mathbb{R}^3 : x_1, x_2 \in \mathbb{R}\}$ we have $\dim P = 2$ because $\{\mathbf{e}_1, \mathbf{e}_2\} \subset \mathbb{R}^3$ is a basis (see example 2.1.5) and $\{\mathbf{e}_1, \mathbf{e}_2\}$ has two elements.

Example 2.1.18 $\dim \mathbb{R}^N = N$ because $\{\mathbf{e}_1, \ldots, \mathbf{e}_N\} \subset \mathbb{R}^N$ is a basis.

Example 2.1.19 A line $\{\alpha \mathbf{x} \in \mathbb{R}^N : \alpha \in \mathbb{R}\}$ through the origin is one dimensional.

In $\mathbb{R}^N$ the singleton subspace $\{\mathbf{0}\}$ is said to have zero dimension.

If we take a set of K vectors, then how large will its span be in terms of dimension? The next theorem answers this question.

Theorem 2.1.6 *Let* $X := \{\mathbf{x}_1, \ldots, \mathbf{x}_K\} \subset \mathbb{R}^N$. *Then*

(i) $\dim \operatorname{span} X \leqslant K$ *and*

(ii) $\dim \operatorname{span} X = K$ *if and only if* X *is linearly independent.*

Exercise 2.4.19 asks you to prove these results.

Let's finish this section with facts that can be deduced from the preceding results.

Fact 2.1.6 The following statements are true:

(i) Let S and S' be K-dimensional linear subspaces of $\mathbb{R}^N$. If $S \subset S'$, then $S = S'$.

(ii) If S is an M-dimensional linear subspace of $\mathbb{R}^N$ and $M < N$, then $S \neq \mathbb{R}^N$.

Part (i) of fact 2.1.6 implies that the only N-dimensional linear subspace of $\mathbb{R}^N$ is $\mathbb{R}^N$ itself.

2.1.6 Linear Maps

The single most important class of functions in applied mathematics is the linear functions. In high school we are told that linear functions as those whose graph is a straight line. Here's a better definition: A function $T \colon \mathbb{R}^K \to \mathbb{R}^N$ is **linear** if

$$T(\alpha \mathbf{x} + \beta \mathbf{y}) = \alpha T \mathbf{x} + \beta T \mathbf{y} \quad \text{for any } \mathbf{x}, \mathbf{y} \in \mathbb{R}^K \text{ and } \alpha, \beta \in \mathbb{R} \tag{2.7}$$

(Following a common convention, we'll write linear functions with uppercase letters and omit the parenthesis around the argument where no confusion arises. This convention has come about because the action of linear maps is essentially isomorphic to multiplication of vectors by matrices. More on that topic soon.)

Example 2.1.20 The function $T\colon \mathbb{R} \to \mathbb{R}$ defined by $Tx = 2x$ is linear because, for any α, β, x, y in $\mathbb{R}$, we have $T(\alpha x + \beta y) = 2(\alpha x + \beta y) = \alpha 2x + \beta 2y = \alpha Tx + \beta Ty$.

Example 2.1.21 Given $\mathbf{a} \in \mathbb{R}^K$, the function $T\colon \mathbb{R}^K \to \mathbb{R}$ defined by $T\mathbf{x} = \langle \mathbf{a}, \mathbf{x} \rangle$ is linear. Indeed, by the rules for inner products on page 13, for any α, β in $\mathbb{R}$ and $\mathbf{x}, \mathbf{y}$ in $\mathbb{R}^K$ we have

$$T(\alpha \mathbf{x} + \beta \mathbf{y}) = \langle \mathbf{a}, \alpha \mathbf{x} + \beta \mathbf{y} \rangle = \alpha \langle \mathbf{a}, \mathbf{x} \rangle + \beta \langle \mathbf{a}, \mathbf{y} \rangle = \alpha T\mathbf{x} + \beta T\mathbf{y}$$

Example 2.1.22 The function $f\colon \mathbb{R} \to \mathbb{R}$ defined by $f(x) = x^2$ fails to be linear because, if $\alpha = \beta = x = y = 1$, then $f(\alpha x + \beta y) = 4$, while $\alpha f(x) + \beta f(y) = 2$.

Example 2.1.23 The function $f\colon \mathbb{R} \to \mathbb{R}$ defined by $f(x) = 1 + 2x$ is not linear because if $\alpha = \beta = x = y = 1$, then $f(\alpha x + \beta y) = f(2) = 5$, while $\alpha f(x) + \beta f(y) = 3 + 3 = 6$. This kind of function is called an **affine** function. We see that identifying linear functions with functions whose graph is a straight line is not correct.

The definition in (2.7) tells us directly that if T is linear then the exchange of order in $T[\sum_{k=1}^K \alpha_k \mathbf{x}_k] = \sum_{k=1}^K \alpha_k T\mathbf{x}_k$ will be valid whenever $K = 2$. A simple inductive argument extends this to arbitrary K. As an application of this fact, consider the following: As discussed in example 2.1.4, any $\mathbf{x} \in \mathbb{R}^K$ can be expressed in terms of the basis vectors as $\sum_{k=1}^K \alpha_k \mathbf{e}_k$, for some suitable choice of scalars. Hence, for a linear function T, its range, denoted $\operatorname{rng} T$, is the set of all points of the form

$$T\mathbf{x} = T\left[\sum_{k=1}^K \alpha_k \mathbf{e}_k\right] = \sum_{k=1}^K \alpha_k T\mathbf{e}_k$$

as we vary $\alpha_1, \ldots, \alpha_K$ over all scalar combinations. (See §15.2 for the definition of range.) In other words, the range of a linear map is the span of the image of the canonical basis functions. This will prove to be important later on. The next fact summarizes.

Fact 2.1.7 If $T\colon \mathbb{R}^K \to \mathbb{R}^N$ is a linear map, then

$$\operatorname{rng} T = \operatorname{span} V, \quad \text{where } V := \{T\mathbf{e}_1, \ldots, T\mathbf{e}_K\}$$

Soon we'll turn to the topic of determining when linear functions are bijections, an issue that is intimately related to invertibility of matrices. To this end it's useful to note that, for linear functions, the property of being one-to-one can be determined by examining the set of points it maps to the origin. To express this idea, for any $T\colon \mathbb{R}^K \to \mathbb{R}^N$, we define the **null space** or **kernel** of T as

$$\operatorname{null} T := \{\mathbf{x} \in \mathbb{R}^K : T\mathbf{x} = \mathbf{0}\}$$

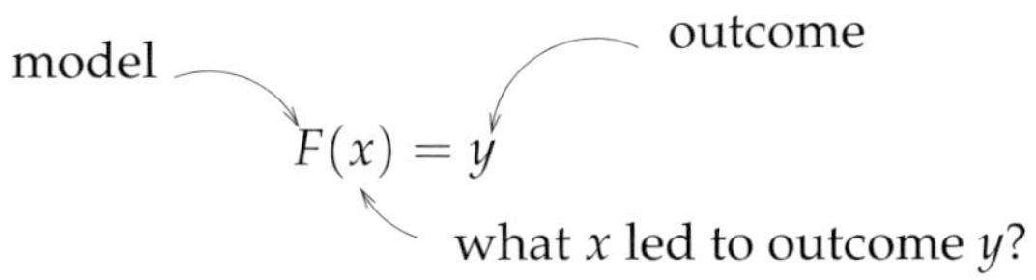

Figure 2.10 Inverse problem

Fact 2.1.8 If $T : \mathbb{R}^K \to \mathbb{R}^N$ is linear, then

(i) null T is a linear subspace of $\mathbb{R}^K$ and

(ii) null $T = \{\mathbf{0}\}$ if and only if T is one-to-one.

The proofs are straightforward. For example, if $T\mathbf{x} = T\mathbf{y}$ for some $\mathbf{x}, \mathbf{y} \in \mathbb{R}^K$, then $T(\mathbf{x} - \mathbf{y}) = \mathbf{0}$, and hence $\mathbf{x} - \mathbf{y} \in$ null T. So if null $T = \{\mathbf{0}\}$, then $T\mathbf{x} = T\mathbf{y}$ implies $\mathbf{x} = \mathbf{y}$, which means that T is one-to-one.

2.1.7 Linear Independence and Bijections

Many statistical problems are "inverse" problems, in the sense that we observe outcomes and wish to determine what generated them. For example, we might want to know what consumer preferences led to observed market behavior, or what kinds of expectations led to a given shift in exchange rates.

Consider the generic inverse problem in figure 2.10, where F and y are given, and we seek to obtain the unknown object x. Two immediate questions are: Does this problem have a solution? and Is it unique? To provide general answers to these questions, we need to know whether F is one-to-one, onto, etc. (see §15.2 for definitions and further discussion). The best case is when F is a bijection, for then we know that a unique solution x exists for every possible y.

In general, functions can be onto, one-to-one, bijections, or none of the above. However, for linear functions from $\mathbb{R}^N$ to $\mathbb{R}^N$, the first three properties are all equivalent! The next theorem gives details.

Theorem 2.1.7 *If T is a linear function from $\mathbb{R}^N$ to $\mathbb{R}^N$, then all of the following are equivalent:*

(i) T is a bijection.

(ii) T is onto.

(iii) T is one-to-one.

(iv) null $T = \{\mathbf{0}\}$.

(v) $V := \{T\mathbf{e}_1, \ldots, T\mathbf{e}_N\}$ is linearly independent.

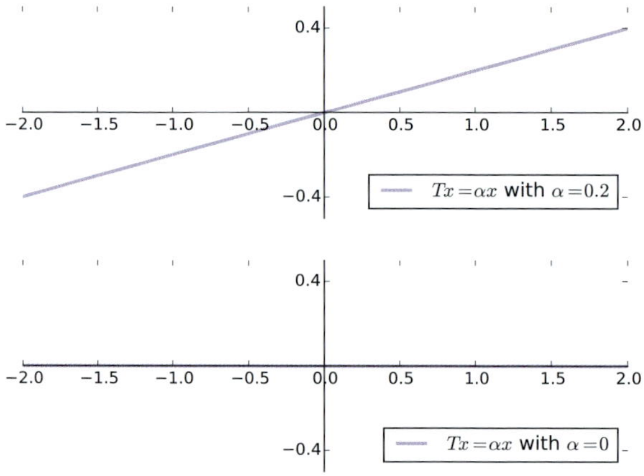

Figure 2.11 The case of $N = 1$, nonsingular and singular

(vi) *$V := \{T\mathbf{e}_1, \ldots, T\mathbf{e}_N\}$ forms a basis of $\mathbb{R}^N$.*

If any one of these conditions is true, then T is called **nonsingular**. (Equivalently, a nonsingular function is a linear bijection.) Otherwise T is called **singular**. The proof of theorem 2.1.7 is a solved exercise (ex. 2.4.21). Figure 2.11 provides intuition for the case of $N = 1$. In the top panel all conditions in theorem 2.1.7 are satisfied. In the lower panel none are. In particular, we can see that the condition for T to be one-to-one and onto is exactly the same (i.e., $\alpha \neq 0$).

If T is nonsingular, then, being a bijection, it must have an inverse function T^{-1} that is also a bijection (fact 15.2.1 on page 410). It turns out that this inverse function inherits the linearity of T (see ex. 2.4.20). In summary,

Fact 2.1.9 If $T \colon \mathbb{R}^N \to \mathbb{R}^N$ is nonsingular, then so is T^{-1}.

Theorem 2.1.7 only applies to linear maps between spaces of the *same* dimension. When linear functions map across distinct dimensions the situation changes:

Theorem 2.1.8 *For a linear map T from $\mathbb{R}^K \to \mathbb{R}^N$, the following statements are true:*

(i) *If $K < N$, then T is not onto.*

(ii) *If $K > N$, then T is not one-to-one.*

The most important implication is that if $N \neq K$, then we can forget about bijections. The proof of theorem 2.1.8 is a solved exercise (ex. 2.4.22).

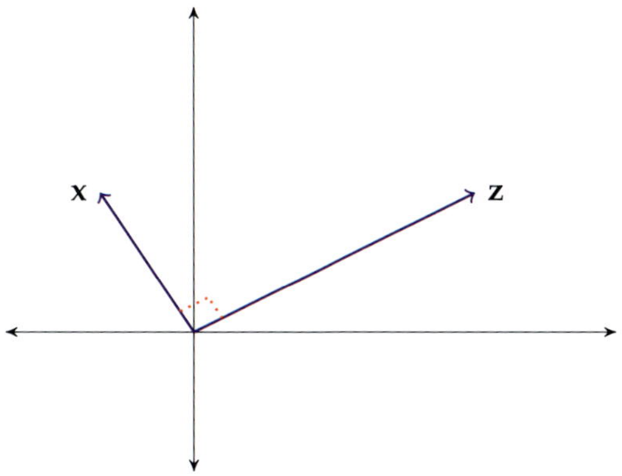

Figure 2.12 $\mathbf{x} \perp \mathbf{z}$

2.2 Orthogonality

One of the core concepts in this book is orthogonality, not just of vectors but also of more complex objects such as random variables. Let's begin with the vector definition and some key implications.

2.2.1 Definition and Basic Properties

Let $\mathbf{x}$ and $\mathbf{z}$ be vectors in $\mathbb{R}^N$. If $\langle \mathbf{x}, \mathbf{z} \rangle = 0$, then we write $\mathbf{x} \perp \mathbf{z}$ and call $\mathbf{x}$ and $\mathbf{z}$ **orthogonal**. In $\mathbb{R}^2$, $\mathbf{x}$ and $\mathbf{z}$ are orthogonal when they are perpendicular to one another, as in figure 2.12. For $\mathbf{x} \in \mathbb{R}^N$ and $S \subset \mathbb{R}^N$, we say that **$\mathbf{x}$ is orthogonal to S** if $\mathbf{x} \perp \mathbf{z}$ for all $\mathbf{z} \in S$ (figure 2.13), and we write $\mathbf{x} \perp S$. A set of vectors $\{\mathbf{z}_1, \ldots, \mathbf{z}_K\} \subset \mathbb{R}^N$ is called an **orthogonal set** if its elements are mutually orthogonal, that is, if $\mathbf{z}_j \perp \mathbf{z}_k$ whenever j and k are distinct.

Fact 2.2.1 (Pythagorian law) If $\{\mathbf{z}_1, \ldots, \mathbf{z}_K\}$ is an orthogonal set, then

$$\|\mathbf{z}_1 + \cdots + \mathbf{z}_K\|^2 = \|\mathbf{z}_1\|^2 + \cdots + \|\mathbf{z}_K\|^2$$

Orthogonal sets and linear independence are closely related. For example,

Fact 2.2.2 If $O \subset \mathbb{R}^N$ is an orthogonal set and $\mathbf{0} \notin O$, then O is linearly independent.

While not every linearly independent set is orthogonal, an important partial converse to fact 2.2.2 is given in §2.2.4.

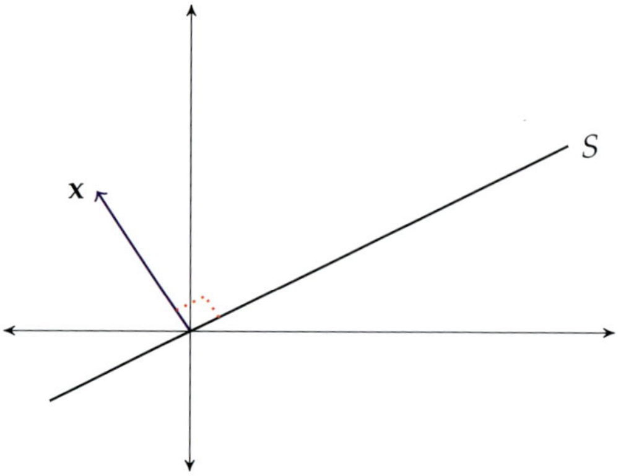

Figure 2.13 $\mathbf{x} \perp S$

An orthogonal set $O \subset \mathbb{R}^N$ is called an **orthonormal set** if $\|\mathbf{u}\| = 1$ for all $\mathbf{u} \in O$. An orthonormal set that lies in and spans a linear subspace S of $\mathbb{R}^N$ is called an **orthonormal basis** of S. It is, necessarily, a basis of S. (Why?) The standard example of an orthonormal basis for all of $\mathbb{R}^N$ is the canonical basis $\{\mathbf{e}_1, \ldots, \mathbf{e}_N\}$.

By definition, if $O = \{\mathbf{u}_1, \ldots, \mathbf{u}_K\}$ is any basis of S, then, for any $\mathbf{x} \in S$, we can find unique scalars $\alpha_1, \ldots, \alpha_K$ such that $\mathbf{x} = \sum_{k=1}^K \alpha_k \mathbf{u}_k$. While the values of these scalars are not always transparent, for an orthonormal basis they are easy to compute:

Fact 2.2.3 If $\{\mathbf{u}_1, \ldots, \mathbf{u}_K\}$ is an orthonormal set and $\mathbf{x} \in \text{span}\{\mathbf{u}_1, \ldots, \mathbf{u}_K\}$, then

$$\mathbf{x} = \sum_{k=1}^{K} \langle \mathbf{x}, \mathbf{u}_k \rangle \, \mathbf{u}_k \tag{2.8}$$

The proof is an exercise. Given $S \subset \mathbb{R}^N$, the **orthogonal complement** of S is defined as

$$S^\perp := \{\mathbf{x} \in \mathbb{R}^N : \mathbf{x} \perp S\}$$

Figure 2.14 gives an example in $\mathbb{R}^2$.

Fact 2.2.4 For any nonempty $S \subset \mathbb{R}^N$, the set $S^\perp$ is a linear subspace of $\mathbb{R}^N$.

Indeed, if $\mathbf{x}, \mathbf{y} \in S^\perp$ and $\alpha, \beta \in \mathbb{R}$, then $\alpha\mathbf{x} + \beta\mathbf{y} \in S^\perp$ because, for any $\mathbf{z} \in S$,

$$\langle \alpha\mathbf{x} + \beta\mathbf{y}, \mathbf{z} \rangle = \alpha \langle \mathbf{x}, \mathbf{z} \rangle + \beta \langle \mathbf{y}, \mathbf{z} \rangle = \alpha \times 0 + \beta \times 0 = 0$$

Fact 2.2.5 For $S \subset \mathbb{R}^N$, we have $S \cap S^\perp = \{\mathbf{0}\}$.

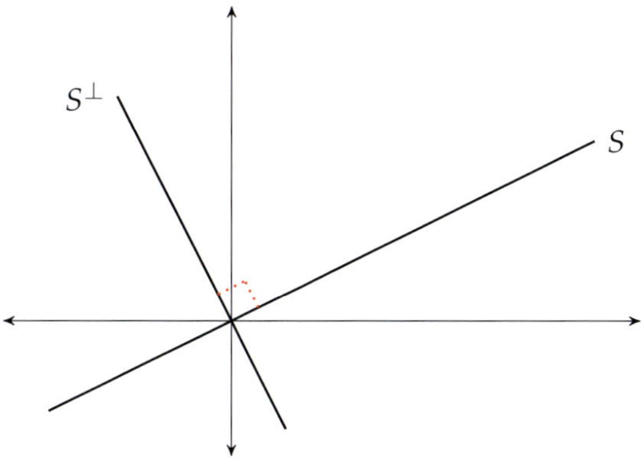

Figure 2.14 Orthogonal complement of S

2.2.2 The Orthogonal Projection Theorem

A central problem in linear regression and many other applications is approximation of some $\mathbf{y}$ of $\mathbb{R}^N$ by an element of a given subspace S of $\mathbb{R}^N$. Stated more precisely, the problem is, given $\mathbf{y}$ and S, to find the closest element $\hat{\mathbf{y}}$ of S to $\mathbf{y}$. Closeness is in terms of Euclidean norm, so $\hat{\mathbf{y}}$ is the minimizer of $\|\mathbf{y} - \mathbf{z}\|$ over all $\mathbf{z} \in S$:

$$\hat{\mathbf{y}} = \operatorname*{argmin}_{\mathbf{z} \in S} \|\mathbf{y} - \mathbf{z}\| \tag{2.9}$$

The next theorem tells us that a solution $\hat{\mathbf{y}}$ to this minimization problem always exists, as well as providing a means to identify it.

Theorem 2.2.1 (Orthogonal Projection Theorem I) *Let $\mathbf{y} \in \mathbb{R}^N$ and let S be any nonempty linear subspace of $\mathbb{R}^N$. The following statements are true:*

(i) The optimization problem (2.9) has exactly one solution.

(ii) $\hat{\mathbf{y}} \in \mathbb{R}^N$ solves (2.9) if and only if $\hat{\mathbf{y}} \in S$ and $\mathbf{y} - \hat{\mathbf{y}} \perp S$.

The unique solution $\hat{\mathbf{y}}$ is called the **orthogonal projection of y onto** *S.*

The intuition is easy to grasp from a graphical presentation. Figure 2.15 illustrates. Looking at the figure, we can see that the closest point to $\mathbf{y}$ in S is the one point $\hat{\mathbf{y}} \in S$ such that $\mathbf{y} - \hat{\mathbf{y}}$ is orthogonal to S.

For a full proof see, for example, theorem 5.16 of Çinlar and Vanderbei (2013). Let's just cover sufficiency of the conditions in part (ii): Let $\mathbf{y} \in \mathbb{R}^N$ and let S be a linear subspace of $\mathbb{R}^N$. Let $\hat{\mathbf{y}}$ be a vector in S satisfying $\mathbf{y} - \hat{\mathbf{y}} \perp S$. Let $\mathbf{z}$ be any other point

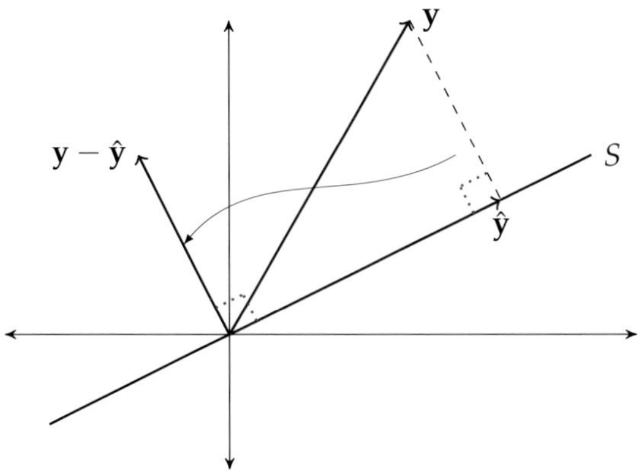

Figure 2.15 Orthogonal projection

in S. We have

$$\|\mathbf{y}-\mathbf{z}\|^2 = \|(\mathbf{y}-\hat{\mathbf{y}}) + (\hat{\mathbf{y}}-\mathbf{z})\|^2 = \|\mathbf{y}-\hat{\mathbf{y}}\|^2 + \|\hat{\mathbf{y}}-\mathbf{z}\|^2$$

The second equality follows from $\mathbf{y}-\hat{\mathbf{y}} \perp S$ (why?) and the Pythagorian law. Since $\mathbf{z}$ was an arbitrary point in S, we have $\|\mathbf{y}-\mathbf{z}\| \geqslant \|\mathbf{y}-\hat{\mathbf{y}}\|$ for all $\mathbf{z} \in S$. Hence (2.9) holds.

Example 2.2.1 Let $\mathbf{y} \in \mathbb{R}^N$ and let $\mathbf{1} \in \mathbb{R}^N$ be the vector of ones. Let S be the set of constant vectors in $\mathbb{R}^N$, meaning that all elements are equal. Evidently S is the span of $\{\mathbf{1}\}$. The orthogonal projection of $\mathbf{y}$ onto S is $\hat{\mathbf{y}} := \bar{y}\mathbf{1}$, where $\bar{y} := \frac{1}{N}\sum_{n=1}^{N} y_n$. To see this, note that $\hat{\mathbf{y}} \in S$ clearly holds. Hence we only need to check that $\mathbf{y}-\hat{\mathbf{y}}$ is orthogonal to S, for which it suffices to show that $\langle \mathbf{y}-\hat{\mathbf{y}}, \mathbf{1}\rangle = 0$ (see ex. 2.4.14 on page 36). This is true because

$$\langle \mathbf{y}-\hat{\mathbf{y}}, \mathbf{1}\rangle = \langle \mathbf{y}, \mathbf{1}\rangle - \langle \hat{\mathbf{y}}, \mathbf{1}\rangle = \sum_{n=1}^{N} y_n - \bar{y}\,\langle \mathbf{1}, \mathbf{1}\rangle = 0$$

2.2.3 Projection as a Mapping

In view of theorem 2.2.1, for each fixed linear subspace S in $\mathbb{R}^N$, the operation

$$\mathbf{y} \mapsto \text{the orthogonal projection of } \mathbf{y} \text{ onto } S$$

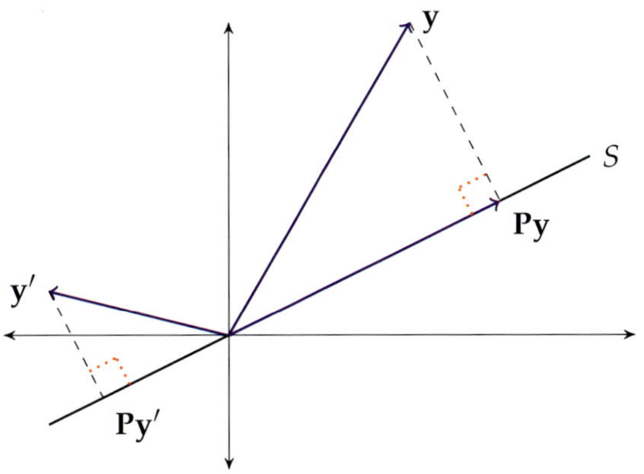

Figure 2.16 Orthogonal projection under $\mathbf{P}$

is a well-defined function from $\mathbb{R}^N$ to $\mathbb{R}^N$. The function is typically denoted by $\mathbf{P}$. For each $\mathbf{y} \in \mathbb{R}^N$, the symbol $\mathbf{Py}$ represents the image of $\mathbf{y}$ under $\mathbf{P}$, which is the orthogonal projection $\hat{\mathbf{y}}$. $\mathbf{P}$ is called the **orthogonal projection onto** S, and we write

$$\mathbf{P} = \operatorname{proj} S$$

Figure 2.16 illustrates the action of $\mathbf{P}$ on two different vectors.

Using this notation, we can restate the orthogonal projection theorem, as well as adding some properties of $\mathbf{P}$:

Theorem 2.2.2 (Orthogonal Projection Theorem II) *Let S be any linear subspace of $\mathbb{R}^N$, and let $\mathbf{P} = \operatorname{proj} S$. The following statements are true:*

(i) $\mathbf{P}$ *is a linear function.*

Moreover, for any $\mathbf{y} \in \mathbb{R}^N$, we have

(ii) $\mathbf{Py} \in S$,

(iii) $\mathbf{y} - \mathbf{Py} \perp S$,

(iv) $\|\mathbf{y}\|^2 = \|\mathbf{Py}\|^2 + \|\mathbf{y} - \mathbf{Py}\|^2$,

(v) $\|\mathbf{Py}\| \leqslant \|\mathbf{y}\|$,

(vi) $\mathbf{Py} = \mathbf{y}$ *if and only if* $\mathbf{y} \in S$, *and*

(vii) $\mathbf{Py} = \mathbf{0}$ *if and only if* $\mathbf{y} \in S^{\perp}$.

These results are not difficult to prove, given theorem 2.2.1. Linearity of $\mathbf{P}$ is left as an exercise (ex. 2.4.29). Parts (ii)–(iii) follow directly from theorem 2.2.1. To see (iv), observe that $\mathbf{y}$ can be decomposed as $\mathbf{y} = \mathbf{P}\mathbf{y} + \mathbf{y} - \mathbf{P}\mathbf{y}$. Now apply the Pythagorean law (page 27). Part (v) follows from part (iv). Part (vi) follows from the definition of $\mathbf{P}\mathbf{y}$ as the closest point to $\mathbf{y}$ in S. Part (vii) is an exercise.

Fact 2.2.6 If $\{\mathbf{u}_1, \ldots, \mathbf{u}_K\}$ is an orthonormal basis for S, then, for each $\mathbf{y} \in \mathbb{R}^N$,

$$\mathbf{P}\mathbf{y} = \sum_{k=1}^{K} \langle \mathbf{y}, \mathbf{u}_k \rangle \, \mathbf{u}_k \tag{2.10}$$

Fact 2.2.6 is a fundamental result. It's true because the right-hand side of (2.10) clearly lies in S (being a linear combination of basis functions) and, for any $\mathbf{u}_j$ in the basis set

$$\langle \mathbf{y} - \mathbf{P}\mathbf{y}, \mathbf{u}_j \rangle = \langle \mathbf{y}, \mathbf{u}_j \rangle - \sum_{k=1}^{K} \langle \mathbf{y}, \mathbf{u}_k \rangle \langle \mathbf{u}_k, \mathbf{u}_j \rangle = \langle \mathbf{y}, \mathbf{u}_j \rangle - \langle \mathbf{y}, \mathbf{u}_j \rangle = 0$$

This is enough to confirm that $\mathbf{y} - \mathbf{P}\mathbf{y} \perp S$ (see ex. 2.4.14).

Example 2.2.2 Recall example 2.2.1, where we showed that the projection of $\mathbf{y} \in \mathbb{R}^N$ onto $\operatorname{span}\{\mathbf{1}\}$ is $\bar{y}\mathbf{1}$, where $\bar{y}$ is the "sample mean" $\bar{y} := \frac{1}{N}\sum_{n=1}^{N} y_n$. We can see this from (2.10) too. To apply (2.10), we just need to find an orthonormal basis for $\operatorname{span}\{\mathbf{1}\}$. The obvious candidate is $\{N^{-1/2}\mathbf{1}\}$. Applying (2.10) now gives $\mathbf{P}\mathbf{y} = \left\langle N^{-1/2}\mathbf{1}, \mathbf{y} \right\rangle N^{-1/2}\mathbf{1}$. As before, this leads us to $\bar{y}\mathbf{1}$.

There's one more essential property of $\mathbf{P}$ that we need to make note of: Suppose that we have two linear subspaces S_1 and S_2 of $\mathbb{R}^N$, where $S_1 \subset S_2$. What then is the difference between (1) first projecting a point onto the bigger subspace S_2, and then projecting the result onto the smaller subspace S_1, and (2) projecting directly to the smaller subspace S_1? The answer is none—we get the same result:

Fact 2.2.7 Let S_i be a linear subspace of $\mathbb{R}^N$ for $i = 1, 2$ and let $\mathbf{P}_i = \operatorname{proj} S_i$. If $S_1 \subset S_2$, then

$$\mathbf{P}_1\mathbf{P}_2\mathbf{y} = \mathbf{P}_2\mathbf{P}_1\mathbf{y} = \mathbf{P}_1\mathbf{y} \quad \text{for all } \mathbf{y} \in \mathbb{R}^N$$

2.2.4 The Residual Projection

Consider the setting of the orthogonal projection theorem. Our interest is in projecting $\mathbf{y}$ onto S, where S is a linear subspace of $\mathbb{R}^N$. The closest point to $\mathbf{y}$ in S is $\hat{\mathbf{y}} := \mathbf{P}\mathbf{y}$ where $\mathbf{P} = \operatorname{proj} S$. Unless $\mathbf{y}$ was already in S, some error $\mathbf{y} - \mathbf{P}\mathbf{y}$ remains. Tracking and managing this residual will be important to us, so let's introduce an operator $\mathbf{M}$ that takes $\mathbf{y} \in \mathbb{R}^N$ and returns the residual. We can define it as

$$\mathbf{M} := \mathbf{I} - \mathbf{P} \tag{2.11}$$

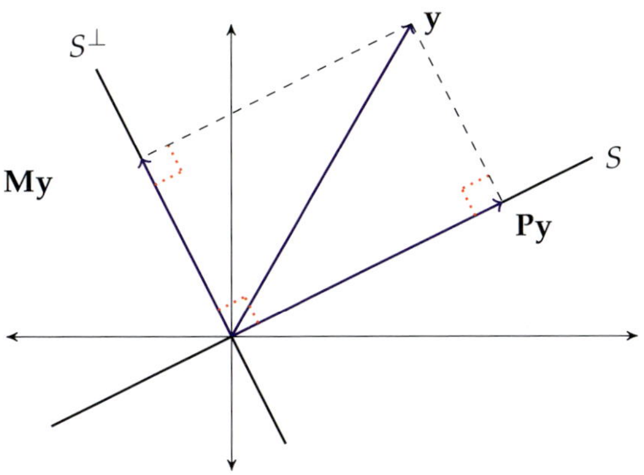

Figure 2.17 The residual projection

where $\mathbf{I}$ is the identity mapping on $\mathbb{R}^N$. For any $\mathbf{y}$ we have $\mathbf{My} = \mathbf{Iy} - \mathbf{Py} = \mathbf{y} - \mathbf{Py}$ as required. In regression analysis $\mathbf{M}$ shows up as a matrix called the "annihilator." This is a pretty cool name, but it's also not a great description of its function. In what follows we will refer to $\mathbf{M}$ as the **residual projection**.

Example 2.2.3 Recall example 2.2.1, where we found that the projection of $\mathbf{y} \in \mathbb{R}^N$ onto span$\{\mathbf{1}\}$ is $\bar{y}\mathbf{1}$. The residual projection is $\mathbf{M}_c\mathbf{y} := \mathbf{y} - \bar{y}\mathbf{1}$. In econometric applications, we'll view this as a vector of errors obtained when the elements of a vector are predicted by its sample mean. The subscript reminds us that $\mathbf{M}_c$ centers vectors around their mean.

Fact 2.2.8 Let S be a linear subspace of $\mathbb{R}^N$, let $\mathbf{P} = \operatorname{proj} S$, and let $\mathbf{M}$ be the residual projection as defined in (2.11). The following statements are true:

(i) $\mathbf{M} = \operatorname{proj} S^{\perp}$.

(ii) $\mathbf{y} = \mathbf{Py} + \mathbf{My}$ for any $\mathbf{y} \in \mathbb{R}^N$.

(iii) $\mathbf{Py} \perp \mathbf{My}$ for any $\mathbf{y} \in \mathbb{R}^N$.

(iv) $\mathbf{My} = \mathbf{0}$ if and only if $\mathbf{y} \in S$.

(v) $\mathbf{P} \circ \mathbf{M} = \mathbf{M} \circ \mathbf{P} = \mathbf{0}$.

Part (v) means that $\mathbf{PMy} = \mathbf{MPy} = \mathbf{0}$ for all $\mathbf{y} \in \mathbb{R}^N$. Figure 2.17 illustrates the action of $\mathbf{M}$. The results in fact 2.2.8 can be seen in the figure.

If S_1 and S_2 are two subspaces of $\mathbb{R}^N$ with $S_1 \subset S_2$, then $S_2^{\perp} \subset S_1^{\perp}$. This means that the result in fact 2.2.7 is reversed for $\mathbf{M}$.

Fact 2.2.9 Let S_1 and S_2 be two subspaces of $\mathbb{R}^N$ and let $\mathbf{y} \in \mathbb{R}^N$. Let $\mathbf{M}_1$ and $\mathbf{M}_2$ be the projections onto $S_1^\perp$ and $S_2^\perp$ respectively. If $S_1 \subset S_2$, then

$$\mathbf{M}_1\mathbf{M}_2\mathbf{y} = \mathbf{M}_2\mathbf{M}_1\mathbf{y} = \mathbf{M}_2\mathbf{y}$$

As an application of the ideas above, let's now discuss a procedure called Gram–Schmidt orthogonalization, which provides a fundamental link between the two major concepts discussed in this chapter: linear independence and orthogonality. It can be considered as a partial converse to fact 2.2.2 on page 27.

Theorem 2.2.3 *For each linearly independent set* $\{\mathbf{b}_1, \ldots, \mathbf{b}_K\} \subset \mathbb{R}^N$, *there exists an orthonormal set* $\{\mathbf{u}_1, \ldots, \mathbf{u}_K\}$ *with*

$$\text{span}\{\mathbf{b}_1, \ldots, \mathbf{b}_k\} = \text{span}\{\mathbf{u}_1, \ldots, \mathbf{u}_k\} \quad \textit{for } k = 1, \ldots, K$$

The proof of theorem 2.2.3 provides an important algorithm for generating the orthonormal set $\{\mathbf{u}_1, \ldots, \mathbf{u}_K\}$. The first step is to construct orthogonal sets $\{\mathbf{v}_1, \ldots, \mathbf{v}_k\}$ with span identical to $\{\mathbf{b}_1, \ldots, \mathbf{b}_k\}$ for each k. The construction of $\{\mathbf{v}_1, \ldots, \mathbf{v}_K\}$ uses the so called **Gram–Schmidt orthogonalization** procedure. First, for each $k = 1, \ldots, K$, let

(i) $B_k := \text{span}\{\mathbf{b}_1, \ldots, \mathbf{b}_k\}$,

(ii) $\mathbf{P}_k := \text{proj}\, B_k$ and $\mathbf{M}_k := \text{proj}\, B_k^\perp$,

(iii) $\mathbf{v}_k := \mathbf{M}_{k-1}\mathbf{b}_k$ where $\mathbf{M}_0$ is the identity mapping, and

(iv) $V_k := \text{span}\{\mathbf{v}_1, \ldots, \mathbf{v}_k\}$.

In step (iii) we map each successive element $\mathbf{b}_k$ into a subspace orthogonal to the subspace generated by $\mathbf{b}_1, \ldots, \mathbf{b}_{k-1}$. In the exercises you are asked to show that $\{\mathbf{v}_1, \ldots, \mathbf{v}_K\}$ is an orthogonal set and $V_k = B_k$ for all k (ex. 2.4.34). To complete the argument, we introduce the vectors $\mathbf{u}_k$ by $\mathbf{u}_k := \mathbf{v}_k / \|\mathbf{v}_k\|$ and confirm that this set of vectors $\{\mathbf{u}_1, \ldots, \mathbf{u}_k\}$ is orthonormal with span equal to V_k. These results are also (solved) exercises.

2.3 Further Reading

Good texts on vector spaces include Marcus and Minc (1988) and Jänich (1994).

2.4 Exercises

Ex. 2.4.1 Show that inner products of linear combinations satisfy the following rule:

$$\left\langle \sum_{k=1}^{K} \alpha_k \mathbf{x}_k, \sum_{j=1}^{J} \beta_j \mathbf{y}_j \right\rangle = \sum_{k=1}^{K} \sum_{j=1}^{J} \alpha_k \beta_j \langle \mathbf{x}_k, \mathbf{y}_j \rangle$$

Ex. 2.4.2 Show that the vectors $(1, 1)$ and $(-1, 2)$ are linearly independent.

Ex. 2.4.3 Use fact 2.1.2 on page 13 to show that if $\mathbf{y} \in \mathbb{R}^N$ is such that $\langle \mathbf{y}, \mathbf{x} \rangle = 0$ for every $\mathbf{x} \in \mathbb{R}^N$, then $\mathbf{y} = \mathbf{0}$.

Ex. 2.4.4 Fix nonzero $\mathbf{x} \in \mathbb{R}^N$. Consider the optimization problem

$$\max_{\mathbf{y}} \langle \mathbf{x}, \mathbf{y} \rangle \quad \text{subject to} \quad \mathbf{y} \in \mathbb{R}^N \text{ and } \|\mathbf{y}\| = 1$$

Show that the maximizer is $\hat{\mathbf{x}} := (1/\|\mathbf{x}\|)\mathbf{x}$.[3]

Ex. 2.4.5 Is $\mathbb{R}^2$ a linear subspace of $\mathbb{R}^3$? Why or why not?

Ex. 2.4.6 Show that if $T \colon \mathbb{R}^K \to \mathbb{R}^N$ is a linear function, then $\mathbf{0} \in \ker T$.

Ex. 2.4.7 Let $\{\mathbf{x}_1, \mathbf{x}_2\}$ be a linearly independent set in $\mathbb{R}^2$ and let γ be a nonzero scalar. Is it true that $\{\gamma\mathbf{x}_1, \gamma\mathbf{x}_2\}$ is also linearly independent?

Ex. 2.4.8 Is it true that

$$\mathbf{z} := \begin{pmatrix} -3.9 \\ 12.4 \\ -6.8 \end{pmatrix} \in \text{span}\{\mathbf{x}_1, \mathbf{x}_2, \mathbf{x}_3\} \quad \text{when} \quad \mathbf{x}_1 = \begin{pmatrix} -4 \\ 0 \\ 0 \end{pmatrix}, \ \mathbf{x}_2 = \begin{pmatrix} 0 \\ 2 \\ 0 \end{pmatrix}, \ \mathbf{x}_3 = \begin{pmatrix} 0 \\ 0 \\ -1 \end{pmatrix}$$

Why or why not?

Ex. 2.4.9 Show that if S and S' are two linear subspaces of $\mathbb{R}^N$, then $S \cap S'$ is also a linear subspace of $\mathbb{R}^N$.

Ex. 2.4.10 Prove fact 2.1.5 on page 20.

Ex. 2.4.11 Let $Q := \{(x_1, x_2, x_3) \in \mathbb{R}^3 : x_2 = x_1 + x_3\}$. Is Q a linear subspace of $\mathbb{R}^3$?

Ex. 2.4.12 Let $Q := \{(x_1, x_2, x_3) \in \mathbb{R}^3 : x_2 = 1\}$. Is Q a linear subspace of $\mathbb{R}^3$?

---

3. Hint: There's no need to go taking derivatives and setting them equal to zero. An easier proof exists. If you're stuck, consider the Cauchy–Schwarz inequality.

Ex. 2.4.13 Show that if $T\colon \mathbb{R}^N \to \mathbb{R}^N$ is a linear function and λ is any scalar, then $E := \{\mathbf{x} \in \mathbb{R}^N : T\mathbf{x} = \lambda\mathbf{x}\}$ is a linear subspace of $\mathbb{R}^N$.

Ex. 2.4.14 Show that if $B \subset S$ with $\operatorname{span} B = S$, then $\mathbf{x} \perp S$ if and only if $\mathbf{x} \perp \mathbf{b}$ for all $\mathbf{b} \in B$.

Ex. 2.4.15 Prove the equivalences in theorem 2.1.1 on page 18.

Ex. 2.4.16 Prove fact 2.1.4 on page 19.

Ex. 2.4.17 Show that if S is a linear subspace of $\mathbb{R}^N$ then every basis of S has the same number of elements.

Ex. 2.4.18 Prove fact 2.1.6 on page 23.

Ex. 2.4.19 Prove theorem 2.1.6 on page 23.

Ex. 2.4.20 Show that if $T\colon \mathbb{R}^N \to \mathbb{R}^N$ is nonsingular (i.e., a linear bijection), then T^{-1} is also linear.

Ex. 2.4.21 Prove theorem 2.1.7 on page 25.

Ex. 2.4.22 Prove theorem 2.1.8 on page 26.

Ex. 2.4.23 Find two unit vectors (i.e., vectors with norm equal to one) that are orthogonal to $(1, -2)$.

Ex. 2.4.24 Prove the Pythagorean law (fact 2.2.1 on page 27). See ex. 2.4.1 if you need a hint.

Ex. 2.4.25 Prove fact 2.2.2 on page 27.

Ex. 2.4.26 Prove fact 2.2.8 using theorems 2.2.1 and 2.2.2.

Ex. 2.4.27 Prove fact 2.2.5: If $S \subset \mathbb{R}^N$, then $S \cap S^{\perp} = \{\mathbf{0}\}$.

Ex. 2.4.28 Prove fact 2.2.7 on page 32.

Ex. 2.4.29 Let $\mathbf{P}$ be the orthogonal projection described in theorem 2.2.2 (page 31). Confirm that $\mathbf{P}$ is a linear function from $\mathbb{R}^N$ to $\mathbb{R}^N$.

Ex. 2.4.30 Let $S := \{(x_1, x_2, x_3) \in \mathbb{R}^3 : x_3 = 0\}$ and let $\mathbf{y} := \mathbf{1} := (1, 1, 1)$. Using the orthogonal projection theorem, find the closest point in S to $\mathbf{y}$.

Ex. 2.4.31 Let S be any linear subspace of $\mathbb{R}^N$ and let $\mathbf{P} = \operatorname{proj} S$ (see theorem 2.2.2 on page 31). Is $\mathbf{P}$ one-to-one as a function on $\mathbb{R}^N$?

Ex. 2.4.32 Prove the reverse triangle inequality. That is, given two vectors $\mathbf{x}$ and $\mathbf{y}$, show that $|\|\mathbf{x}\| - \|\mathbf{y}\|| \leqslant \|\mathbf{x} - \mathbf{y}\|$.[4]

Ex. 2.4.33 Show that $\mathbf{P}\mathbf{y} = \mathbf{0}$ implies $\mathbf{y} \in S^{\perp}$.

In the next three exercises, the notation is as given in theorem 2.2.3 and the discussion immediately afterwards.

Ex. 2.4.34 Show that $V_k = B_k$ for all k.

Ex. 2.4.35 Show that $\{\mathbf{v}_1, \ldots, \mathbf{v}_K\}$ is an orthogonal set.

Ex. 2.4.36 Show that $\{\mathbf{u}_1, \ldots, \mathbf{u}_k\}$ is an orthonormal set with span equal to V_k for all k.

2.4.1 Solutions to Selected Exercises

Solution to Ex. 2.4.4. Fix nonzero $\mathbf{x} \in \mathbb{R}^N$. Let $\hat{\mathbf{x}} := \mathbf{x}/\|\mathbf{x}\|$. Comparing this point with any other $\mathbf{y} \in \mathbb{R}^N$ satisfying $\|\mathbf{y}\| = 1$, the Cauchy–Schwarz inequality yields

$$\langle \mathbf{y}, \mathbf{x} \rangle \leqslant | \langle \mathbf{y}, \mathbf{x} \rangle | \leqslant \|\mathbf{y}\| \|\mathbf{x}\| = \|\mathbf{x}\| = \frac{\langle \mathbf{x}, \mathbf{x} \rangle}{\|\mathbf{x}\|} = \langle \hat{\mathbf{x}}, \mathbf{x} \rangle$$

Hence $\hat{\mathbf{x}}$ is the maximizer, as claimed. □

Solution to Ex. 2.4.5. This is a bit of a trick question. To solve it, you need to look carefully at the definitions (as always). A linear subspace of $\mathbb{R}^3$ is a subset of $\mathbb{R}^3$ with certain properties. $\mathbb{R}^3$ is a collection of 3-tuples (x_1, x_2, x_3) where each x_i is a real number. Elements of $\mathbb{R}^2$ are 2-tuples (pairs), and hence not elements of $\mathbb{R}^3$. Therefore $\mathbb{R}^2$ is not a subset of $\mathbb{R}^3$, and, in particular, not a linear subspace of $\mathbb{R}^3$. □

Solution to Ex. 2.4.6. Let T be as in the question. We need to show that $T\mathbf{0} = \mathbf{0}$. Here's one proof. We know from the definition of scalar multiplication that $0\mathbf{x} = \mathbf{0}$ for any vector $\mathbf{x}$. Let $\mathbf{x}$ and $\mathbf{y}$ be any vectors in $\mathbb{R}^K$ and apply the definition of linearity to obtain

$$T\mathbf{0} = T(0\mathbf{x} + 0\mathbf{y}) = 0T\mathbf{x} + 0T\mathbf{y} = \mathbf{0} + \mathbf{0} = \mathbf{0}$$ □

Solution to Ex. 2.4.7. The answer is yes. Suppose, to the contrary, that $\{\gamma\mathbf{x}_1, \gamma\mathbf{x}_2\}$ is linearly dependent. Then one element can be written as a linear combination of the others. In our setting with only two vectors, this translates to $\gamma\mathbf{x}_1 = \alpha\gamma\mathbf{x}_2$ for some α. Since $\gamma \neq 0$, we can multiply each side by $1/\gamma$ to get $\mathbf{x}_1 = \alpha\mathbf{x}_2$. This contradicts linear independence of $\{\mathbf{x}_1, \mathbf{x}_2\}$. □

4. Hint: Use the triangle inequality.

Solution to Ex. 2.4.8. There is an easy way to do this: We know that any linearly independent set of 3 vectors in $\mathbb{R}^3$ will span $\mathbb{R}^3$. Since $\mathbf{z} \in \mathbb{R}^3$, this will include $\mathbf{z}$. So all we need to do is show that the 3 vectors are linearly independent. To this end, take any scalars $\alpha_1, \alpha_2, \alpha_3$ with

$$\alpha_1 \begin{pmatrix} -4 \\ 0 \\ 0 \end{pmatrix} + \alpha_2 \begin{pmatrix} 0 \\ 2 \\ 0 \end{pmatrix} + \alpha_3 \begin{pmatrix} 0 \\ 0 \\ -1 \end{pmatrix} = \mathbf{0} := \begin{pmatrix} 0 \\ 0 \\ 0 \end{pmatrix}$$

Written as three equations, this says that $-4\alpha_1 = 0$, $2\alpha_2 = 0$, and $-1\alpha_3 = 0$. Hence $\alpha_1 = \alpha_2 = \alpha_3 = 0$, and therefore the set is linearly independent. □

Solution to Ex. 2.4.9. Let S and S' be two linear subspaces of $\mathbb{R}^N$. Fix $\mathbf{x}, \mathbf{y} \in S \cap S'$ and $\alpha, \beta \in \mathbb{R}$. We claim that $\mathbf{z} := \alpha\mathbf{x} + \beta\mathbf{y} \in S \cap S'$. To see this, note that since $\mathbf{x}, \mathbf{y} \in S$ and S is a linear subspace, we have $\mathbf{z} \in S$; and since $\mathbf{x}, \mathbf{y} \in S'$ and S' is a linear subspace, we have $\mathbf{z} \in S'$. It follows that $\mathbf{z} \in S \cap S'$, as was to be shown. □

Solution to Ex. 2.4.11. If $\mathbf{a} := (1, -1, 1)$, then Q is all $\mathbf{x}$ with $\langle \mathbf{a}, \mathbf{x} \rangle = 0$. This set is a linear subspace of $\mathbb{R}^3$, as shown in example 2.1.10. □

Solution to Ex. 2.4.15. We are asked to verify the equivalences in theorem 2.1.1 on page 18 for the set $X := \{\mathbf{x}_1, \ldots, \mathbf{x}_K\}$. We will prove the cycle (i) $\implies$ (ii) $\implies$ (iii) $\implies$ (i).

((i) $\implies$ (ii)) We aim to show that if (i) holds and X_0 is a proper subset of X, then span X_0 is a proper subset of span X. To simplify notation let's take $X_0 := \{\mathbf{x}_2, \ldots, \mathbf{x}_K\}$. Suppose, to the contrary, that span X_0 = span X. Since $\mathbf{x}_1 \in \operatorname{span} X$, we must then have $\mathbf{x}_1 \in \operatorname{span} X_0$, from which we deduce the existence of scalars $\alpha_2, \ldots, \alpha_K$ such that $\mathbf{0} = -\mathbf{x}_1 + \alpha_2\mathbf{x}_2 + \cdots + \alpha_K\mathbf{x}_K$. Since $-1 \neq 0$, this contradicts part (i).

((ii) $\implies$ (iii)) The claim is that when (ii) holds, no vector in X can be written as a linear combination of the others. Suppose, to the contrary, that $\mathbf{x}_1 = \alpha_2\mathbf{x}_2 + \cdots + \alpha_K\mathbf{x}_K$, say. Let $\mathbf{y} \in \operatorname{span} X$, so that $\mathbf{y} = \beta_1\mathbf{x}_1 + \cdots + \beta_K\mathbf{x}_K$. If we use the preceding equality to substitute out $\mathbf{x}_1$, we get $\mathbf{y}$ as a linear combination of $\{\mathbf{x}_2, \ldots, \mathbf{x}_K\}$ alone. In other words, any element of span X is in the span of the proper subset $\{\mathbf{x}_2, \ldots, \mathbf{x}_K\}$. Contradiction.

((iii) $\implies$ (i)) The final claim is that $\alpha_1 = \cdots = \alpha_K = 0$ whenever $\alpha_1\mathbf{x}_1 + \cdots + \alpha_K\mathbf{x}_K = \mathbf{0}$. Suppose, to the contrary, that there exist scalars with $\alpha_1\mathbf{x}_1 + \cdots + \alpha_K\mathbf{x}_K = \mathbf{0}$ and yet $\alpha_k \neq 0$ for at least one k. It follows immediately that $\mathbf{x}_k = (1/\alpha_k)\sum_{j \neq k} \alpha_j \mathbf{x}_j$. This contradicts (iii). □

Solution to Ex. 2.4.16. The aim is to prove fact 2.1.4 on page 19. Regarding the part (i), let's take X as linearly independent and show that the subset $X_0 := \{\mathbf{x}_1, \ldots, \mathbf{x}_{K-1}\}$ is linearly independent. (The argument for more general subsets is similar.) Suppose, to the contrary, that X_0 is linearly dependent. Then, by the definition, we can take $\alpha_1, \ldots, \alpha_{K-1}$ not all zero with $\sum_{k=1}^{K-1} \alpha_k \mathbf{x}_k = \mathbf{0}$. Letting $\alpha_K = 0$, we can write this as $\sum_{k=1}^{K} \alpha_k \mathbf{x}_k = \mathbf{0}$. Since not all coefficients are zero, we have contradicted linear independence of X.

Regarding (ii), let $X := \{\mathbf{x}_1, \ldots, \mathbf{x}_K\}$ be linearly independent and suppose that $\mathbf{x}_j = \mathbf{0}$. Then by setting $\alpha_k = 0$ for $k \neq j$ and $\alpha_j = 1$, we can form scalars not all equal to zero with $\sum_{k=1}^{K} \alpha_k \mathbf{x}_k = \mathbf{0}$.

Regarding (iii), let $X := \{\mathbf{x}_1, \ldots, \mathbf{x}_K\} \subset \mathbb{R}^N$ be linearly independent and let $\mathbf{x}_{K+1}$ be any point in $\mathbb{R}^N$ such that $\mathbf{x}_{K+1} \notin \operatorname{span} X$. The claim is that $X \cup \{\mathbf{x}_{K+1}\}$ is linearly independent. Suppose, to the contrary, that there exist $\alpha_1, \ldots, \alpha_K, \alpha_{K+1}$ not all zero such that $\sum_{k=1}^{K+1} \alpha_k \mathbf{x}_k = \mathbf{0}$. There are two possibilities for α_{K+1}, both of which lead to a contradiction: First, if $\alpha_{K+1} = 0$, then, since $\alpha_1, \ldots, \alpha_K, \alpha_{K+1}$ are not all zero, at least one of $\alpha_1, \ldots, \alpha_K$ are nonzero, and moreover $\sum_{k=1}^{K} \alpha_k \mathbf{x}_k = \sum_{k=1}^{K+1} \alpha_k \mathbf{x}_k = \mathbf{0}$. This contradicts our assumption of independence on X. Second, if $\alpha_{K+1} \neq 0$, then from $\sum_{k=1}^{K+1} \alpha_k \mathbf{x}_k = \mathbf{0}$ we can express $\mathbf{x}_{K+1}$ as a linear combination of elements of X. This contradicts the hypothesis that $\mathbf{x}_{K+1} \notin \operatorname{span} X$. □

Solution to Ex. 2.4.17. Let B_1 and B_2 be two bases of S, with K_1 and K_2 elements respectively. By definition, B_2 is a linearly independent subset of S. Moreover, S is spanned by the set B_1, which has K_1 elements. Applying theorem 2.1.3, we see that B_2 has at most K_1 elements. That is, $K_2 \leqslant K_1$. Reversing the roles of B_1 and B_2 gives $K_1 \leqslant K_2$. □

Solution to Ex. 2.4.18. The aim is to prove fact 2.1.6 on page 23. Suppose that S and S' are K-dimensional linear subspaces of $\mathbb{R}^N$ with $S \subset S'$. We claim that $S = S'$. To see this, observe that by the definition of dimension, S is equal to $\operatorname{span} B$ where B is a set of K linearly independent basis vectors $\{\mathbf{b}_1, \ldots, \mathbf{b}_K\}$. If $S \neq S'$, then there exists a vector $\mathbf{x} \in S'$ such that $\mathbf{x} \notin \operatorname{span} B$. In view of theorem 2.1.1 on page 18, the set $\{\mathbf{x}, \mathbf{b}_1, \ldots, \mathbf{b}_K\}$ is linearly independent. Moreover, since $\mathbf{x} \in S'$ and since $B \subset S \subset S'$, we now have $K + 1$ linearly independent vectors inside S'. At the same time, being K-dimensional, we know that S' is spanned by K vectors. This contradicts theorem 2.1.3 on page 20.

Regarding part (ii), suppose that S is an M-dimensional linear subspace of $\mathbb{R}^N$ where $M < N$ and yet $S = \mathbb{R}^N$. Then we have a space S spanned by $M < N$ vectors that also contains the N linearly independent canonical basis vectors. We are led to another contradiction of theorem 2.1.3. Hence $S = \mathbb{R}^N$ cannot hold. □

Solution to Ex. 2.4.19. Regarding part (i), let B be a basis of $\operatorname{span} X$. By definition, B is a linearly independent subset of $\operatorname{span} X$. Since $\operatorname{span} X$ is spanned by K vectors, theorem 2.1.3 implies that B has no more than K elements. Hence, $\dim \operatorname{span} X \leqslant K$.

Regarding part (ii), suppose first that X is linearly independent. Then X is a basis for span X. Since X has K elements, we conclude that $\dim \operatorname{span} X = K$. Conversely, if $\dim \operatorname{span} X = K$, then X must be linearly independent. If X were not linearly independent, then there would exist a proper subset X_0 of X such that $\operatorname{span} X_0 = \operatorname{span} X$. By part (i) of this theorem, we then have $\dim \operatorname{span} X_0 \leqslant \# X_0 \leqslant K - 1$. Therefore $\dim \operatorname{span} X \leqslant K - 1$, a contradiction. □

Solution to Ex. 2.4.20. Let $T\colon \mathbb{R}^N \to \mathbb{R}^N$ be nonsingular, and let T^{-1} be its inverse. To see that T^{-1} is linear, we need to show that for any pair $\mathbf{x}, \mathbf{y}$ in $\mathbb{R}^N$ (which is the domain of T^{-1}) and any scalars α and β, the following equality holds:

$$T^{-1}(\alpha \mathbf{x} + \beta \mathbf{y}) = \alpha T^{-1} \mathbf{x} + \beta T^{-1} \mathbf{y} \tag{2.12}$$

In the proof we will exploit the fact that T is by assumption a linear bijection.

Pick any vectors $\mathbf{x}, \mathbf{y} \in \mathbb{R}^N$ and any two scalars α, β. Since T is a bijection, we know that $\mathbf{x}$ and $\mathbf{y}$ have unique preimages under T. In particular, there exist unique vectors $\mathbf{u}$ and $\mathbf{v}$ such that $T\mathbf{u} = \mathbf{x}$ and $T\mathbf{v} = \mathbf{y}$. Using these definitions, linearity of T and the fact that T^{-1} is the inverse of T, we have

$$T^{-1}(\alpha \mathbf{x} + \beta \mathbf{y}) = T^{-1}(\alpha T \mathbf{u} + \beta T \mathbf{v}) = T^{-1}(T(\alpha \mathbf{u} + \beta \mathbf{v})) = \alpha \mathbf{u} + \beta \mathbf{v} = \alpha T^{-1} \mathbf{x} + \beta T^{-1} \mathbf{y}$$

This chain of equalities confirms (2.12). □

Solution to Ex. 2.4.21. A collection of equivalent statements such as this is usually proved via a cycle of implications, with the form (i) $\implies$ (ii) $\implies \cdots \implies$ (vi) $\implies$ (i). However, in this case the logic is clearer if we directly show that all statements are equivalent to linear independence of V.

First observe equivalence of the onto property and linear independence of V via

$$T \text{ onto} \iff \operatorname{rng} T = \mathbb{R}^N \iff \operatorname{span} V = \mathbb{R}^N$$

by fact 2.1.7. The last statement is equivalent to linear independence of V by theorem 2.1.4 on page 22.

Next let's show that $\operatorname{null} T = \{\mathbf{0}\}$ implies linear independence of V. To this end, suppose that $\operatorname{null} T = \{\mathbf{0}\}$ and let $\alpha_1, \ldots, \alpha_N$ be such that $\sum_{n=1}^N \alpha_n T \mathbf{e}_n = \mathbf{0}$. By linearity of T, we then have $T(\sum_{n=1}^N \alpha_n \mathbf{e}_n) = \mathbf{0}$. Since $\operatorname{null} T = \{\mathbf{0}\}$, this means that $\sum_{n=1}^N \alpha_n \mathbf{e}_n = \mathbf{0}$, which in view of independence of $\{\mathbf{e}_1, \ldots, \mathbf{e}_N\}$, implies $\alpha_1 = \cdots = \alpha_N = 0$. This establishes that V is linearly independent.

Now let's check that linear independence of V implies $\operatorname{null} T = \{\mathbf{0}\}$. To this end, let $\mathbf{x}$ be a vector in $\mathbb{R}^N$ such that $T\mathbf{x} = \mathbf{0}$. We can represent $\mathbf{x}$ in the form $\sum_{n=1}^N \alpha_n \mathbf{e}_n$ for suitable scalars $\{\alpha_n\}$. From linearity and $T\mathbf{x} = \mathbf{0}$, we get $\sum_{n=1}^N \alpha_n T \mathbf{e}_n = \mathbf{0}$. By linear independence of V, this implies that each $\alpha_n = 0$, whence $\mathbf{x} = \mathbf{0}$. Thus $\text{null}\, T = \{\mathbf{0}\}$ as claimed.

From fact 2.1.8 we have $\text{null}\, T = \{\mathbf{0}\}$ iff T is one-to-one, so we can now state the following equivalences

$$T \text{ onto} \iff V \text{ linearly independent} \iff T \text{ one-to-one} \tag{2.13}$$

If T is a bijection, then T is onto and hence V is linearly independent by (2.13). Conversely, if V is linearly independent then T is both onto and one-to-one by (2.13). Hence T is a bijection.

Finally, equivalence of linear independence of V and the statement that V forms a basis of $\mathbb{R}^N$ is immediate from the definition of bases and theorem 2.1.4 on page 22.

□

Solution to Ex. 2.4.22. Regarding part (i), let $K < N$ and let $T\colon \mathbb{R}^K \to \mathbb{R}^N$ be linear. T cannot be onto because, if T were onto, then we would have $\text{rng}\, T = \mathbb{R}^N$, in which case the vectors in $V = \{T\mathbf{e}_1, \ldots, T\mathbf{e}_K\}$ in fact 2.1.7 would span $\mathbb{R}^N$, despite having only $K < N$ elements. This is impossible. (Why?)

Regarding part (ii), let $T\colon \mathbb{R}^K \to \mathbb{R}^N$ be linear and let $K > N$. Seeking a contradiction, suppose in addition that T is one-to-one. Let $\{\alpha_k\}_{k=1}^K$ be such that $\sum_{k=1}^K \alpha_k T\mathbf{e}_k = \mathbf{0}$. By linearity, $T(\sum_{k=1}^K \alpha_k \mathbf{e}_k) = \mathbf{0}$, and since T is one-to-one and $T\mathbf{0} = \mathbf{0}$, this in turn implies $\sum_{k=1}^K \alpha_k \mathbf{e}_k = \mathbf{0}$. Since the canonical basis vectors are linearly independent, it must be that $\alpha_1 = \cdots = \alpha_K = 0$. From this we conclude that $\{T\mathbf{e}_1, \ldots, T\mathbf{e}_K\}$ is linearly independent. Thus $\mathbb{R}^N$ contains K linearly independent vectors, despite the fact that $N < K$. This is impossible by theorem 2.1.3 on page 20. □

Solution to Ex. 2.4.25. Let $O = \{\mathbf{x}_1, \ldots, \mathbf{x}_K\} \subset \mathbb{R}^N$ be an orthogonal set that does not contain $\mathbf{0}$. Let $\alpha_1, \ldots, \alpha_K$ be such that $\sum_{k=1}^K \alpha_k \mathbf{x}_k = \mathbf{0}$. We claim that $\alpha_j = 0$ for any j. To see that this is so, fix j and take the inner product of both sides of $\sum_{k=1}^K \alpha_k \mathbf{x}_k = \mathbf{0}$ with respect to $\mathbf{x}_j$ to obtain $\alpha_j \|\mathbf{x}_j\|^2 = 0$. Since $\mathbf{x}_j \neq \mathbf{0}$, we conclude that $\alpha_j = 0$. The proof is done. □

Solution to Ex. 2.4.27. Let $S \subset \mathbb{R}^N$. We aim to show that $S \cap S^\perp = \{\mathbf{0}\}$. Fix $\mathbf{a} \in S \cap S^\perp$. Since $\mathbf{a} \in S^\perp$, we know that $\langle \mathbf{a}, \mathbf{s} \rangle = 0$ for any $\mathbf{s} \in S$. Since $\mathbf{a} \in S$, we have in particular, $\langle \mathbf{a}, \mathbf{a} \rangle = \|\mathbf{a}\|^2 = 0$. As we saw in fact 2.1.2, the only such vector is $\mathbf{0}$. □

Solution to Ex. 2.4.29. Fix $\alpha, \beta \in \mathbb{R}$ and $\mathbf{x}, \mathbf{y} \in \mathbb{R}^N$. The claim is that

$$\mathbf{P}(\alpha\mathbf{x} + \beta\mathbf{y}) = \alpha\mathbf{P}\mathbf{x} + \beta\mathbf{P}\mathbf{y}$$

To verify this equality, we need to show that the right-hand side is the orthogonal projection of $\alpha\mathbf{x} + \beta\mathbf{y}$ onto S. Going back to theorem 2.2.1, we need to show that (i)

$\alpha \mathbf{Px} + \beta \mathbf{Py} \in S$ and (ii) for any $\mathbf{z} \in S$, we have

$$\langle \alpha \mathbf{x} + \beta \mathbf{y} - (\alpha \mathbf{Px} + \beta \mathbf{Py}), \mathbf{z} \rangle = 0$$

Here (i) is immediate, because $\mathbf{Px}$ and $\mathbf{Py}$ are in S by definition, and, moreover S is a linear subspace. To see that (ii) holds, just note that

$$\langle \alpha \mathbf{x} + \beta \mathbf{y} - (\alpha \mathbf{Px} + \beta \mathbf{Py}), \mathbf{z} \rangle = \alpha \langle \mathbf{x} - \mathbf{Px}, \mathbf{z} \rangle + \beta \langle \mathbf{y} - \mathbf{Py}, \mathbf{z} \rangle$$

By definition, the projections of $\mathbf{x}$ and $\mathbf{y}$ are orthogonal to S, so we have $\langle \mathbf{x} - \mathbf{Px}, \mathbf{z} \rangle = \langle \mathbf{y} - \mathbf{Py}, \mathbf{z} \rangle = 0$. We are done. □

Solution to Ex. 2.4.30. Let $\mathbf{x} = (x_1, x_2, x_3)$ be the closest point in S to $\mathbf{y}$. Note that $\mathbf{e}_1 \in S$ and $\mathbf{e}_2 \in S$. By the orthogonal projection theorem, we have (i) $\mathbf{x} \in S$ and (ii) $\mathbf{y} - \mathbf{x} \perp S$. From (i) we have $x_3 = 0$. From (ii) we have

$$\langle \mathbf{y} - \mathbf{x}, \mathbf{e}_1 \rangle = 0 \quad \text{and} \quad \langle \mathbf{y} - \mathbf{x}, \mathbf{e}_2 \rangle = 0$$

These equations can be expressed more simply as $1 - x_1 = 0$ and $1 - x_2 = 0$. We conclude that $\mathbf{x} = (1, 1, 0)$. □

Solution to Ex. 2.4.31. If $S = \mathbb{R}^N$, then $\mathbf{P}$ is the identity mapping (why?), which is one-to-one. If $S \neq \mathbb{R}^N$, then take any $\mathbf{x} \notin S$. By definition, $\mathbf{y} := \mathbf{Px}$ is in S, and hence $\mathbf{y}$ and $\mathbf{x}$ are distinct. But $\mathbf{P}$ maps elements of S to themselves, so $\mathbf{Py} = \mathbf{y} = \mathbf{Px}$. Hence $\mathbf{P}$ is not one-to-one. □

Solution to Ex. 2.4.32. From the triangle inequality we have

$$\|\mathbf{x}\| = \|\mathbf{x} - \mathbf{y} + \mathbf{y}\| \leqslant \|\mathbf{x} - \mathbf{y}\| + \|\mathbf{y}\|$$

It follows that $\|\mathbf{x}\| - \|\mathbf{y}\| \leqslant \|\mathbf{x} - \mathbf{y}\|$. A similar argument reversing the roles of $\mathbf{x}$ and $\mathbf{y}$ gives $\|\mathbf{y}\| - \|\mathbf{x}\| \leqslant \|\mathbf{x} - \mathbf{y}\|$. Combining the last two inequalities gives

$$-\|\mathbf{x} - \mathbf{y}\| \leqslant \|\mathbf{x}\| - \|\mathbf{y}\| \leqslant \|\mathbf{x} - \mathbf{y}\|$$

This is equivalent to $|\|\mathbf{x}\| - \|\mathbf{y}\|| \leqslant \|\mathbf{x} - \mathbf{y}\|$. □

Solution to Ex. 2.4.33. If $\mathbf{Py} = \mathbf{0}$, then $\mathbf{y} = \mathbf{Py} + \mathbf{My} = \mathbf{My}$. Hence $\mathbf{M}$ does not shift $\mathbf{y}$. If an orthogonal projection onto a subspace doesn't shift a point, that's because the point is already in that subspace (see theorem 2.2.2). In this case the subspace is $S^{\perp}$, and we conclude that $\mathbf{y} \in S^{\perp}$. □

Solution to Ex. 2.4.34. To see that $V_k = B_k$ for all k, fix k and consider the claim that $V_k \subset B_k$. By definition, $\mathbf{v}_k = \mathbf{b}_k - \mathbf{P}_{k-1}\mathbf{b}_k$, and the two terms on the right-hand side lie in B_k. Hence $\mathbf{v}_k \in B_k$. Since spans increase as we add more elements, it follows that $\mathbf{v}_j \in B_k$ for $j \leqslant k$. In other words, $\{\mathbf{v}_1, \ldots, \mathbf{v}_k\} \subset B_k$. Since B_k is a linear subspace, we have $V_k \subset B_k$.

An induction argument shows that $B_k \subset V_k$ also holds. Clearly it holds for $k = 1$. Suppose that it also holds for $k-1$. From the definition of $\mathbf{v}_k$, we have $\mathbf{b}_k = \mathbf{P}_{k-1}\mathbf{b}_k + \mathbf{v}_k$. The first term on the right-hand side lies in B_{k-1}, which, by our induction hypothesis, satisfies $B_{k-1} \subset V_{k-1} \subset V_k$. The second term on the right-hand side is $\mathbf{v}_k$, which obviously lies in V_k. Hence both terms are in V_k, and therefore $\mathbf{b}_k \in V_k$. Using arguments analogous to the end of the last paragraph leads us to $B_k \subset V_k$. □

Solution to Ex. 2.4.35. To show that $\{\mathbf{v}_1, \ldots, \mathbf{v}_K\}$ is an orthogonal set, it suffices to check that $\mathbf{v}_k \perp \mathbf{v}_j$ whenever $j < k$. To see this, fix any pair $j < k$. By construction, $\mathbf{v}_k \in B_{k-1}^{\perp}$. But, as shown in the solution to ex. 2.4.34, $\mathbf{v}_j \in B_{k-1}$ must hold. Hence $\mathbf{v}_k \perp \mathbf{v}_j$. □

Solution to Ex. 2.4.36. Since $\{\mathbf{v}_1, \ldots, \mathbf{v}_k\}$ is orthogonal, the family $\{\mathbf{u}_1, \ldots, \mathbf{u}_k\}$ will be orthonormal provided that the norm of each element is 1. This is true by construction, since $\mathbf{u}_k := \mathbf{v}_k / \|\mathbf{v}_k\|$. The only concern is that $\|\mathbf{v}_k\| = 0$ might hold for some k. But $\mathbf{v}_k = \mathbf{0}$ is impossible because, if it was to hold, then by (vii) of theorem 2.2.2 we would have $\mathbf{b}_k \in B_{k-1}$, contradicting linear independence of $\{\mathbf{b}_1, \ldots, \mathbf{b}_K\}$.

The proof that $\operatorname{span}\{\mathbf{u}_1, \ldots, \mathbf{u}_k\} = V_k$ is straightforward and left for you. □

Chapter 3

Linear Algebra and Matrices

The previous chapter was relatively abstract but it sets us up nicely to study the kinds of practical problems from linear algebra that we encounter in statistics and econometrics. This chapter treats many of the core problems in linear algebra, frequently relating them back to our analysis of vectors and linear maps in chapter 2.

3.1 Matrices and Linear Equations

Matrices provide a convenient way to organize data and algebraic operations. Let's start with definitions.

3.1.1 Basic Definitions

A $N \times K$ **matrix** is a rectangular array $\mathbf{A}$ of real numbers with N rows and K columns, written in the following way:

$$\mathbf{A} = \begin{pmatrix} a_{11} & a_{12} & \cdots & a_{1K} \\ a_{21} & a_{22} & \cdots & a_{2K} \\ \vdots & \vdots & & \vdots \\ a_{N1} & a_{N2} & \cdots & a_{NK} \end{pmatrix}$$

The symbol a_{nk} stands for the element in the nth row of the kth column. Often these elements represent coefficients in a system of linear equations, such as

$$\begin{aligned} a_{11}x_1 + a_{12}x_2 + \cdots + a_{1K}x_K &= b_1 \\ &\vdots \\ a_{N1}x_1 + a_{N2}x_2 + \cdots + a_{NK}x_K &= b_N \end{aligned} \tag{3.1}$$

For obvious reasons, $\mathbf{A}$ is also called a vector if either $N = 1$ or $K = 1$. In the former case, $\mathbf{A}$ is called a **row vector**, while in the latter case it is called a **column vector**. When convenient, we will use the notation $\text{row}_n \mathbf{A}$ to refer to the nth row of $\mathbf{A}$, and $\text{col}_k \mathbf{A}$ to refer to its kth column.

We extend the notation $\mathbf{0}$ and $\mathbf{1}$ from vectors to matrices, in the sense that these symbols will also represent matrices with all elements equal to zero and one respectively. Dimensions will be stated explicitly or clear from context.

If $\mathbf{A}$ is $N \times K$ and $N = K$, then $\mathbf{A}$ is called **square**. For an $N \times N$ matrix $\mathbf{A}$, the N elements of the form a_{nn} for $n = 1, \ldots, N$ are called the **principal diagonal**:

$$\begin{pmatrix} a_{11} & a_{12} & \cdots & a_{1N} \\ a_{21} & a_{22} & \cdots & a_{2N} \\ \vdots & \vdots & & \vdots \\ a_{N1} & a_{N2} & \cdots & a_{NN} \end{pmatrix}$$

The unique $N \times N$ matrix with ones on the principle diagonal and zeros elsewhere is called the **identity matrix**, and denoted by $\mathbf{I}$:

$$\mathbf{I} := \begin{pmatrix} 1 & 0 & \cdots & 0 \\ 0 & 1 & \cdots & 0 \\ \vdots & \vdots & & \vdots \\ 0 & 0 & \cdots & 1 \end{pmatrix}$$

Note that $\text{col}_n \mathbf{I} = \mathbf{e}_n$, the nth canonical basis vector in $\mathbb{R}^N$.

Just as was the case for vectors, a number of algebraic operations are defined for matrices. The first two, scalar multiplication and addition, are immediate generalizations of the vector case: For $\gamma \in \mathbb{R}$, we let

$$\gamma \begin{pmatrix} a_{11} & a_{12} & \cdots & a_{1K} \\ a_{21} & a_{22} & \cdots & a_{2K} \\ \vdots & \vdots & & \vdots \\ a_{N1} & a_{N2} & \cdots & a_{NK} \end{pmatrix} := \begin{pmatrix} \gamma a_{11} & \gamma a_{12} & \cdots & \gamma a_{1K} \\ \gamma a_{21} & \gamma a_{22} & \cdots & \gamma a_{2K} \\ \vdots & \vdots & & \vdots \\ \gamma a_{N1} & \gamma a_{N2} & \cdots & \gamma a_{NK} \end{pmatrix}$$

while

$$\begin{pmatrix} a_{11} & \cdots & a_{1K} \\ a_{21} & \cdots & a_{2K} \\ \vdots & \vdots & \vdots \\ a_{N1} & \cdots & a_{NK} \end{pmatrix} + \begin{pmatrix} b_{11} & \cdots & b_{1K} \\ b_{21} & \cdots & b_{2K} \\ \vdots & \vdots & \vdots \\ b_{N1} & \cdots & b_{NK} \end{pmatrix} := \begin{pmatrix} a_{11}+b_{11} & \cdots & a_{1K}+b_{1K} \\ a_{21}+b_{21} & \cdots & a_{2K}+b_{2K} \\ \vdots & \vdots & \vdots \\ a_{N1}+b_{N1} & \cdots & a_{NK}+b_{NK} \end{pmatrix}$$

Addition is only defined for matrices that have identical shape.

The **matrix product** $\mathbf{C} = \mathbf{AB}$ of matrices $\mathbf{A}$ and $\mathbf{B}$ is formed by taking as its i, jth element the inner product of the ith row of $\mathbf{A}$ and the jth column of $\mathbf{B}$. That is,

$$c_{ij} = \langle \text{row}_i\, \mathbf{A}, \text{col}_j\, \mathbf{B} \rangle = \sum_{k=1}^{K} a_{ik} b_{kj}$$

Here's the picture for $i = j = 1$:

$$\begin{pmatrix} a_{11} & \cdots & a_{1K} \\ a_{21} & \cdots & a_{2K} \\ \vdots & \vdots & \vdots \\ a_{N1} & \cdots & a_{NK} \end{pmatrix} \begin{pmatrix} b_{11} & \cdots & b_{1J} \\ b_{21} & \cdots & b_{2J} \\ \vdots & \vdots & \vdots \\ b_{K1} & \cdots & b_{KJ} \end{pmatrix} = \begin{pmatrix} c_{11} & \cdots & c_{1J} \\ c_{21} & \cdots & c_{2J} \\ \vdots & \vdots & \vdots \\ c_{N1} & \cdots & c_{NJ} \end{pmatrix}$$

Since inner products are only defined for vectors of equal length, we need the length of the rows of $\mathbf{A}$ to be equal to the length of the columns of $\mathbf{B}$. In other words, if $\mathbf{A}$ is $N \times K$ and $\mathbf{B}$ is $J \times M$, then we require $K = J$. The resulting matrix $\mathbf{AB}$ is $N \times M$. Here's the rule to remember:

$$\mathbf{A} \text{ is } N \times K \text{ and } \mathbf{B} \text{ is } K \times M \implies \mathbf{AB} \text{ is } N \times M$$

Matrix multiplication is not commutative: $\mathbf{AB}$ and $\mathbf{BA}$ are not in general equal. In most other ways it behaves like ordinary multiplication:

Fact 3.1.1 For conformable matrices $\mathbf{A}$, $\mathbf{B}$, $\mathbf{C}$ and scalar α, we have

(i) $\mathbf{A}(\mathbf{BC}) = (\mathbf{AB})\mathbf{C}$,

(ii) $\mathbf{A}(\mathbf{B} + \mathbf{C}) = \mathbf{AB} + \mathbf{AC}$,

(iii) $(\mathbf{A} + \mathbf{B})\mathbf{C} = \mathbf{AC} + \mathbf{BC}$,

(iv) $\mathbf{A}\alpha\mathbf{B} = \alpha\mathbf{AB}$, and

(v) $\mathbf{AI} = \mathbf{A}$ and $\mathbf{IA} = \mathbf{A}$, where $\mathbf{I}$ is the identity matrix.

Here and below we use the word **conformable** to indicate dimensions are such that the operation in question makes sense. For example, two matrices are conformable for addition if they have the same number of rows and columns.

The **kth power** of a square matrix $\mathbf{A}$ is defined as

$$\mathbf{A}^k := \underbrace{\mathbf{A} \cdots \mathbf{A}}_{k \text{ terms}}$$

If $\mathbf{B}$ is such that $\mathbf{B}^2 = \mathbf{A}$, then $\mathbf{B}$ is called the **square root** of $\mathbf{A}$ and written $\sqrt{\mathbf{A}}$.

Before going further, let's state the fundamental connection between matrix multiplication and the more elementary notion of linear combinations of vectors, as introduced in §2.1.2: Given $N \times K$ matrix $\mathbf{A}$ and $K \times 1$ column vector $\mathbf{x}$, the product $\mathbf{Ax}$ is an $N \times 1$ column vector formed as a linear combination of the columns of $\mathbf{A}$, with scalars $x_1, \ldots, x_K$. In symbols,

$$\begin{aligned}
\mathbf{Ax} &= \begin{pmatrix} a_{11} & a_{12} & \cdots & a_{1K} \\ a_{21} & a_{22} & \cdots & a_{2K} \\ \vdots & \vdots & & \vdots \\ a_{N1} & a_{N2} & \cdots & a_{NK} \end{pmatrix} \begin{pmatrix} x_1 \\ x_2 \\ \vdots \\ x_K \end{pmatrix} \\
&= x_1 \begin{pmatrix} a_{11} \\ a_{21} \\ \vdots \\ a_{N1} \end{pmatrix} + x_2 \begin{pmatrix} a_{12} \\ a_{22} \\ \vdots \\ a_{N2} \end{pmatrix} + \cdots + x_K \begin{pmatrix} a_{1K} \\ a_{2K} \\ \vdots \\ a_{NK} \end{pmatrix} \\
&= \sum_{k=1}^{K} x_k \operatorname{col}_k \mathbf{A}
\end{aligned}$$

3.1.2 Matrices as Maps

One of the most useful ways to think about matrices is as maps from one vector space to another. In particular, an $N \times K$ matrix $\mathbf{A}$ can be thought of as a map sending a vector $\mathbf{x} \in \mathbb{R}^K$ into a new vector $\mathbf{y} = \mathbf{Ax}$ in $\mathbb{R}^N$. As the next theorem shows, these maps are always linear. In fact, they are the *only* linear functions. In other words, the set of linear functions from $\mathbb{R}^K$ to $\mathbb{R}^N$ and the set of $N \times K$ matrices are in one-to-one correspondence:

Theorem 3.1.1 *Let T be a function from $\mathbb{R}^K$ to $\mathbb{R}^N$. The following are equivalent:*

(i) T is linear.

(ii) There exists an $N \times K$ matrix $\mathbf{A}$ such that $T\mathbf{x} = \mathbf{Ax}$ for all $\mathbf{x} \in \mathbb{R}^K$.

Proof. ((i) $\implies$ (ii)) Let $T \colon \mathbb{R}^K \to \mathbb{R}^N$ be linear. We aim to construct a matrix $\mathbf{A}$ such that $T\mathbf{x} = \mathbf{Ax}$ for all $\mathbf{x} \in \mathbb{R}^K$. As usual, let $\mathbf{e}_k$ be the kth canonical basis vector in

$\mathbb{R}^K$. Define an $N \times K$ matrix $\mathbf{A}$ by $\mathrm{col}_k\,\mathbf{A} = T\mathbf{e}_k$. Pick any $\mathbf{x} \in \mathbb{R}^K$. We can also write $\mathbf{x} = \sum_{k=1}^K x_k \mathbf{e}_k$, where x_k is the kth element of $\mathbf{x}$. By linearity, we have

$$T\mathbf{x} = \sum_{k=1}^K x_k T\mathbf{e}_k = \sum_{k=1}^K x_k \,\mathrm{col}_k\,\mathbf{A}$$

This is just $\mathbf{Ax}$, as shown in §3.1.1.

((ii) $\implies$ (i)) Fix $N \times K$ matrix $\mathbf{A}$ and consider the function $T\colon \mathbb{R}^K \to \mathbb{R}^N$ defined by $T\mathbf{x} = \mathbf{Ax}$. Pick any $\mathbf{x}$, $\mathbf{y}$ in $\mathbb{R}^K$, and any scalars α and β. The rules of matrix arithmetic (see fact 3.1.1) tell us that

$$T(\alpha\mathbf{x} + \beta\mathbf{y}) := \mathbf{A}(\alpha\mathbf{x} + \beta\mathbf{y}) = \mathbf{A}\alpha\mathbf{x} + \mathbf{A}\beta\mathbf{y} = \alpha\mathbf{Ax} + \beta\mathbf{Ay} =: \alpha T\mathbf{x} + \beta T\mathbf{y}$$

Hence T is linear. □

When we consider the problem of solving a system of linear equations such as $\mathbf{Ax} = \mathbf{b}$, the first issue we need to concern ourselves with is existence. Can we find an $\mathbf{x}$ that satisfies this equation, for any given $\mathbf{b}$? A bit of thought will convince you that this is the same question as: Is the corresponding linear map $T\mathbf{x} = \mathbf{Ax}$ an onto function? (See §15.2 for the definition.) Equivalently, is $\mathrm{rng}\,T$ equal to all of $\mathbb{R}^N$?

The range of T is all vectors of the form $T\mathbf{x} = \mathbf{Ax}$ where $\mathbf{x}$ varies over $\mathbb{R}^K$. We just saw in §3.1.1 that, for any $\mathbf{x} \in \mathbb{R}^K$, we have $\mathbf{Ax} = \sum_{k=1}^K x_k \,\mathrm{col}_k\,\mathbf{A}$. It follows that $\mathrm{rng}\,T$ is equal to the **column space** of $\mathbf{A}$, which is by definition the span of the columns of $\mathbf{A}$. We represent it by the symbol

$$\mathrm{colspace}\,\mathbf{A} := \mathrm{span}\{\mathrm{col}_1\,\mathbf{A}, \ldots, \mathrm{col}_K\,\mathbf{A}\} \tag{3.2}$$

To summarize the preceding discussion, we have

$$\mathrm{colspace}\,\mathbf{A} = \mathrm{rng}\,T = \{\mathbf{Ax} : \mathbf{x} \in \mathbb{R}^K\}$$

How large is the column space of a given matrix? To answer that question, we have to say what "large" means. In the context of linear algebra, size of subspaces is usually measured by dimension. The dimension of $\mathrm{colspace}\,\mathbf{A}$ is known as the **rank** of $\mathbf{A}$. That is,

$$\mathrm{rank}\,\mathbf{A} := \dim \mathrm{colspace}\,\mathbf{A}$$

$\mathbf{A}$ is said to have **full column rank** if $\mathrm{rank}\,\mathbf{A}$ is equal to K, the number of its columns. The reason we say "full" rank here is that, by definition, $\mathrm{colspace}\,\mathbf{A}$ is the span of K vectors. Hence, by part (i) of theorem 2.1.6 on page 23, we must have $\dim \mathrm{colspace}\,\mathbf{A} \leqslant K$. In other words, the rank of $\mathbf{A}$ is less than or equal to K. $\mathbf{A}$ is said to have full column rank when this maximum is achieved.

When is this maximum achieved? By part (ii) of theorem 2.1.6, this will be the case precisely when the columns of $\mathbf{A}$ are linearly independent. Let's state this as a fact:

Fact 3.1.2 Let $\mathbf{A}$ be an $N \times K$ matrix. The following statements are equivalent:

(i) $\mathbf{A}$ is of full column rank.

(ii) The columns of $\mathbf{A}$ are linearly independent.

(iii) $\mathbf{Ax} = \mathbf{0} \implies \mathbf{x} = \mathbf{0}$.

The last equivalence follows from theorem 2.1.1 on page 18.

3.1.3 Square Matrices and Invertibility

Perhaps the most common problem in linear algebra is solving systems of linear equations. A generic representation is $\mathbf{Ax} = \mathbf{b}$, where $\mathbf{x}$ contains the unknowns and $\mathbf{A}$ and $\mathbf{b}$ are given. There are a variety of scenarios depending on the properties of $\mathbf{A}$. For now let's consider the case where $\mathbf{A}$ is $N \times N$, and seek conditions on $\mathbf{A}$ under which, for every $\mathbf{b} \in \mathbb{R}^N$, there exists exactly one $\mathbf{x} \in \mathbb{R}^N$ such that $\mathbf{Ax} = \mathbf{b}$.

The best way to understand this problem is as follows. Let T be the linear map $T\mathbf{x} = \mathbf{Ax}$. The question we are asking here is: When does each point $\mathbf{b} \in \mathbb{R}^N$ have one and only one preimage under T? In other words, when is T a bijection?

To answer this question, we can refer back to the discussion in §2.1.7. We saw there that linear bijections are called nonsingular functions, and we discussed a number of equivalences for this property. The next fact replicates these equivalences in the language of matrices.

Fact 3.1.3 For $N \times N$ matrix $\mathbf{A}$, the following are equivalent:

(i) The columns of $\mathbf{A}$ are linearly independent.

(ii) The columns of $\mathbf{A}$ form a basis of $\mathbb{R}^N$.

(iii) $\operatorname{rank} \mathbf{A} = N$.

(iv) $\operatorname{colspace} \mathbf{A} = \mathbb{R}^N$.

(v) $\mathbf{Ax} = \mathbf{Ay} \implies \mathbf{x} = \mathbf{y}$.

(vi) $\mathbf{Ax} = \mathbf{0} \implies \mathbf{x} = \mathbf{0}$.

(vii) For each $\mathbf{b} \in \mathbb{R}^N$, the equation $\mathbf{Ax} = \mathbf{b}$ has a solution.

(viii) For each $\mathbf{b} \in \mathbb{R}^N$, the equation $\mathbf{Ax} = \mathbf{b}$ has a unique solution.

These results can all be verified using theorem 2.1.7 on page 25 by checking the corresponding implications for $T\mathbf{x} = \mathbf{Ax}$. For example, it's easy to see that if $\mathbf{e}_n$ is the

nth canonical basis vector of $\mathbb{R}^N$, then

$$T\mathbf{e}_n = \mathbf{A}\mathbf{e}_n = \operatorname{col}_n \mathbf{A}$$

and hence the condition of linear independence of $\{T\mathbf{e}_1, \ldots, T\mathbf{e}_N\}$ in theorem 2.1.7 translates to linear independence of the columns of $\mathbf{A}$.

Following common usage, if any of the equivalent conditions in fact 3.1.3 are true we will call not just the map T but also the underlying matrix $\mathbf{A}$ **nonsingular**. If any one—and hence all—of these conditions fail, then $\mathbf{A}$ is called **singular**.

Any bijection has an inverse (see §15.2). In fact any nonsingular map T has a nonsingular inverse T^{-1} (see fact 2.1.9 on page 26). In the present setting, where T is generated by a matrix $\mathbf{A}$, the inverse T^{-1} is also associated with a matrix, called the inverse of $\mathbf{A}$. The next theorem gives details:

Theorem 3.1.2 *For nonsingular* $\mathbf{A}$ *the following statements are true:*

(i) There exists a square matrix $\mathbf{B}$ *such that* $\mathbf{AB} = \mathbf{BA} = \mathbf{I}$, *where* $\mathbf{I}$ *is the identity matrix. The matrix* $\mathbf{B}$ *is called the* **inverse** *of* $\mathbf{A}$, *and written as* $\mathbf{A}^{-1}$.

(ii) For each $\mathbf{b} \in \mathbb{R}^N$, *the unique solution to* $\mathbf{Ax} = \mathbf{b}$ *is given by*

$$\mathbf{x} = \mathbf{A}^{-1}\mathbf{b} \tag{3.3}$$

For this reason, nonsingular matrices are also referred to as **invertible**. The proof of theorem 3.1.2 is a solved exercise (ex. 3.5.5).

Example 3.1.1 Consider the N good linear demand system

$$q_n = \sum_{k=1}^{N} a_{nk} p_k + b_n, \quad n = 1, \ldots, N$$

where q_n and p_n are quantity and price of the nth good respectively. We want to compute the inverse demand function, which gives prices in terms of quantities. To do so, we write our system in matrix form as $\mathbf{q} = \mathbf{Ap} + \mathbf{b}$. If the columns of $\mathbf{A}$ are linearly independent, then we can invert the system: a unique solution exists for each fixed $\mathbf{q}$ and $\mathbf{b}$. That solution is given by $\mathbf{p} = \mathbf{A}^{-1}(\mathbf{q} - \mathbf{b})$.

As stated in the next fact, to show that $\mathbf{A}$ is invertible and $\mathbf{B}$ is the inverse of $\mathbf{A}$, it suffices to show that $\mathbf{B}$ is either a **left inverse**, in the sense that $\mathbf{BA} = \mathbf{I}$, or a **right inverse**, in the sense that $\mathbf{AB} = \mathbf{I}$. A proof is given in §3.1.4.

Fact 3.1.4 Let $\mathbf{A}$ and $\mathbf{B}$ be $N \times N$ square matrices. If $\mathbf{B}$ is either a left or a right inverse of $\mathbf{A}$, then $\mathbf{A}$ is nonsingular and $\mathbf{B}$ is its inverse.

The next fact collects more useful results about inverse matrices.

Fact 3.1.5 If $\mathbf{A}$ and $\mathbf{B}$ are nonsingular and $\alpha \neq 0$, then

(i) $(\mathbf{A}^{-1})^{-1} = \mathbf{A}$,

(ii) $(\alpha\mathbf{A})^{-1} = \alpha^{-1}\mathbf{A}^{-1}$, and

(iii) $(\mathbf{AB})^{-1} = \mathbf{B}^{-1}\mathbf{A}^{-1}$.

The relation $(\mathbf{AB})^{-1} = \mathbf{B}^{-1}\mathbf{A}^{-1}$ is just a special case of the analogous rule for inversion of bijections (see fact 15.2.1 on page 410). But you can also prove the equality directly by confirming that $\mathbf{B}^{-1}\mathbf{A}^{-1}$ is a right inverse (or left inverse) of $\mathbf{AB}$.

3.1.4 Determinants

To each square matrix $\mathbf{A}$, we can associate a unique number $\det \mathbf{A}$ called the determinant of $\mathbf{A}$. To define it, let $S(N)$ be the set of all bijections from $\{1, \ldots, N\}$ to itself. For $\pi \in S(N)$ we define the **signature** of π as

$$\operatorname{sgn}(\pi) := \prod_{m<n} \frac{\pi(m) - \pi(n)}{m - n}$$

The **determinant** of $N \times N$ matrix $\mathbf{A}$ is then given as

$$\det \mathbf{A} := \sum_{\pi \in S(N)} \operatorname{sgn}(\pi) \prod_{n=1}^{N} a_{\pi(n)n}$$

We won't concern ourselves with the details of this definition. For now it's enough to know the following facts:

Fact 3.1.6 If $\mathbf{I}$ is the $N \times N$ identity, $\mathbf{A}$ and $\mathbf{B}$ are $N \times N$ matrices and $\alpha \in \mathbb{R}$, then

(i) $\det \mathbf{I} = 1$,

(ii) $\mathbf{A}$ is nonsingular if and only if $\det \mathbf{A} \neq 0$,

(iii) $\det(\mathbf{AB}) = \det(\mathbf{A}) \det(\mathbf{B})$,

(iv) $\det(\alpha\mathbf{A}) = \alpha^N \det(\mathbf{A})$, and

(v) $\det(\mathbf{A}^{-1}) = (\det(\mathbf{A}))^{-1}$.

In the 2×2 case one can show that the determinant satisfies

$$\det \begin{pmatrix} a & b \\ c & d \end{pmatrix} = ad - bc \tag{3.4}$$

As an example of how these results can be useful, let's go back and prove fact 3.1.4. Fix square matrix $\mathbf{A}$ and suppose that a right inverse $\mathbf{B}$ exists, in the sense that $\mathbf{AB} = \mathbf{I}$. This equality implies that both $\mathbf{A}$ and $\mathbf{B}$ are nonsingular, since applying det to both sides of $\mathbf{AB} = \mathbf{I}$ and using the rules in fact 3.1.6 gives $\det(\mathbf{A})\det(\mathbf{B}) = 1$. It follows that both $\det \mathbf{A}$ and $\det \mathbf{B}$ are nonzero. Hence both matrices are nonsingular.

To show that $\mathbf{B}$ is the inverse of $\mathbf{A}$, we just need to check that, in addition to $\mathbf{AB} = \mathbf{I}$, we have $\mathbf{BA} = \mathbf{I}$. To obtain the latter equality from the former, premultiply the former by $\mathbf{B}$ to get $\mathbf{BAB} = \mathbf{B}$ and then postmultiply by $\mathbf{B}^{-1}$ to get $\mathbf{BA} = \mathbf{I}$. The proof for the left inverse case is similar.

3.2 Properties of Matrices

Let's look at some special kinds of matrices and their role in linear algebra.

3.2.1 Diagonal and Triangular Matrices

A square matrix is called

- **lower triangular** if each element strictly above the principal diagonal is zero,
- **upper triangular** if every element strictly below the principal diagonal is zero, and
- **triangular** if it is either upper or lower triangular.

For example, if we define

$$\mathbf{L} := \begin{pmatrix} 1 & 0 & 0 \\ 2 & 5 & 0 \\ 3 & 6 & 1 \end{pmatrix} \quad \text{and} \quad \mathbf{U} := \begin{pmatrix} 1 & 2 & 3 \\ 0 & 5 & 6 \\ 0 & 0 & 1 \end{pmatrix}$$

then $\mathbf{L}$ and $\mathbf{U}$ are lower and upper triangular respectively. The great advantage of triangular matrices is that the associated linear equations are simple to solve using either forward or backward substitution. For example, with the system

$$\begin{pmatrix} 1 & 0 & 0 \\ 2 & 5 & 0 \\ 3 & 6 & 1 \end{pmatrix} \begin{pmatrix} x_1 \\ x_2 \\ x_3 \end{pmatrix} = \begin{pmatrix} x_1 \\ 2x_1 + 5x_2 \\ 3x_1 + 6x_2 + x_3 \end{pmatrix} = \begin{pmatrix} b_1 \\ b_2 \\ b_3 \end{pmatrix}$$

the top equation involves only x_1, so we can solve for its value directly. Plugging this value into the second equation, we can solve for x_2 and so on.

Fact 3.2.1 If $\mathbf{A} = (a_{mn})$ is triangular, then $\det \mathbf{A} = \prod_{n=1}^{N} a_{nn}$.

An even better situation arises when our matrix is *both* upper and lower triangular. These are the **diagonal** matrices. In other words, a square matrix $\mathbf{A}$ is diagonal if all entries off the principal diagonal are zero. For example, the identity matrix is diagonal.

The following notation is often used to define diagonal matrices:

$$\operatorname{diag}(d_1, \dots, d_N) := \begin{pmatrix} d_1 & 0 & \cdots & 0 \\ 0 & d_2 & \cdots & 0 \\ \vdots & \vdots & & \vdots \\ 0 & 0 & \cdots & d_N \end{pmatrix}$$

With diagonal matrices it is trivial to compute powers, roots, inverses and products:

Fact 3.2.2 Let $\mathbf{C} = \operatorname{diag}(c_1, \dots, c_N)$ and $\mathbf{D} = \operatorname{diag}(d_1, \dots, d_N)$. The following statements are true:

(i) $\mathbf{C} + \mathbf{D} = \operatorname{diag}(c_1 + d_1, \dots, c_N + d_N)$.

(ii) $\mathbf{CD} = \operatorname{diag}(c_1 d_1, \dots, c_N d_N)$.

(iii) $\mathbf{D}^k = \operatorname{diag}(d_1^k, \dots, d_N^k)$ for any $k \in \mathbb{N}$.

(iv) If $d_n \geqslant 0$ for all n, then $\sqrt{\mathbf{D}}$ exists and equals $\operatorname{diag}(\sqrt{d_1}, \dots, \sqrt{d_N})$.

(v) If $d_n \neq 0$ for all n, then $\mathbf{D}$ is nonsingular and $\mathbf{D}^{-1} = \operatorname{diag}(d_1^{-1}, \dots, d_N^{-1})$.

You can check parts (i) and (ii) directly. The other claims follow from (i) and (ii).

3.2.2 Trace, Transpose, and Symmetry

The **trace** of an $N \times N$ matrix $\mathbf{A}$ is the sum of the elements on its principal diagonal:

$$\operatorname{trace} \mathbf{A} = \sum_{n=1}^{N} a_{nn}$$

Fact 3.2.3 If $\mathbf{A}$ and $\mathbf{B}$ are $N \times N$ matrices and α and β are two scalars, then

$$\operatorname{trace}(\alpha \mathbf{A} + \beta \mathbf{B}) = \alpha \operatorname{trace}(\mathbf{A}) + \beta \operatorname{trace}(\mathbf{B})$$

Moreover, if $\mathbf{A}$ is $N \times M$ and $\mathbf{B}$ is $M \times N$, then $\operatorname{trace}(\mathbf{AB}) = \operatorname{trace}(\mathbf{BA})$.

The **transpose** of $N \times K$ matrix $\mathbf{A}$ is a $K \times N$ matrix $\mathbf{A}^\top$ such that $\operatorname{col}_n(\mathbf{A}^\top) =$

row_n **A**. For example,

$$\mathbf{A} := \begin{pmatrix} 10 & 40 \\ 20 & 50 \\ 30 & 60 \end{pmatrix} \implies \mathbf{A}^\top = \begin{pmatrix} 10 & 20 & 30 \\ 40 & 50 & 60 \end{pmatrix} \tag{3.5}$$

and

$$\mathbf{B} := \begin{pmatrix} 1 & 3 & 5 \\ 2 & 4 & 6 \end{pmatrix} \implies \mathbf{B}^\top = \begin{pmatrix} 1 & 2 \\ 3 & 4 \\ 5 & 6 \end{pmatrix}$$

A square matrix **A** is called **symmetric** if $\mathbf{A}^\top = \mathbf{A}$, or, equivalently, $a_{nk} = a_{kn}$ for every k and n. Note that $\mathbf{A}^\top \mathbf{A}$ and $\mathbf{A}\mathbf{A}^\top$ are always well-defined and symmetric.

Fact 3.2.4 For conformable matrices **A** and **B**, transposition satisfies

(i) $(\mathbf{A}^\top)^\top = \mathbf{A}$,

(ii) $(\mathbf{A}\mathbf{B})^\top = \mathbf{B}^\top \mathbf{A}^\top$,

(iii) $(\mathbf{A} + \mathbf{B})^\top = \mathbf{A}^\top + \mathbf{B}^\top$, and

(iv) $(c\mathbf{A})^\top = c\mathbf{A}^\top$ for any constant c.

Fact 3.2.5 For each square matrix **A**, we have

(i) $\text{trace}(\mathbf{A}) = \text{trace}(\mathbf{A}^\top)$ and

(ii) $\det(\mathbf{A}^\top) = \det(\mathbf{A})$.

(iii) If **A** is nonsingular, then so is $\mathbf{A}^\top$, and its inverse is $(\mathbf{A}^\top)^{-1} = (\mathbf{A}^{-1})^\top$.

Note that if **a** and **b** are $N \times 1$ vectors, then the matrix product $\mathbf{a}^\top \mathbf{b} = \mathbf{b}^\top \mathbf{a}$ is equal to $\sum_{n=1}^N a_n b_n$, which is the same as the inner product $\langle \mathbf{a}, \mathbf{b} \rangle$. In what follows we'll often work with column vectors and use matrix product rather than inner product notation.

3.2.3 Eigenvalues and Eigenvectors

Let **A** be $N \times N$. As in § 3.1.2, think of **A** as a linear map, so that $\mathbf{Ax}$ is the image of **x** under **A**. In general, **A** will map **x** to some arbitrary new location but sometimes **x** will only be *scaled*. That is,

$$\mathbf{Ax} = \lambda \mathbf{x} \tag{3.6}$$

for some scalar λ. If **x** and λ satisfy (3.6) and **x** is nonzero, then **x** is called an **eigenvector** of **A**, λ is called an **eigenvalue**, and $(\mathbf{x}, \lambda)$ is called an **eigenpair**.

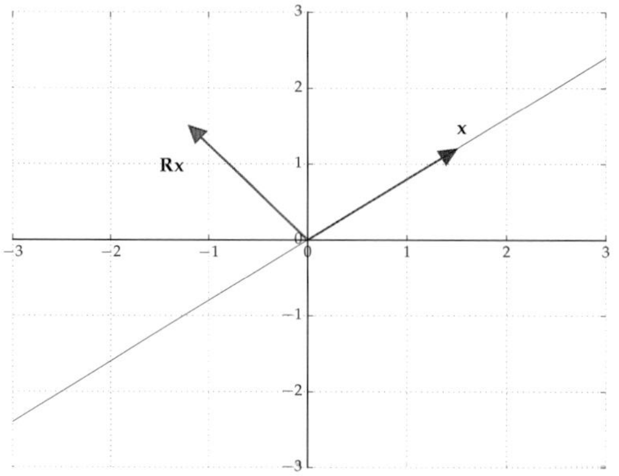

Figure 3.1 **R** rotates points by 90°

Example 3.2.1 If

$$\mathbf{A} := \begin{pmatrix} 1 & -1 \\ 3 & 5 \end{pmatrix}, \quad \mathbf{x} := \begin{pmatrix} 1 \\ -1 \end{pmatrix} \quad \text{and} \quad \lambda := 2$$

then $(\mathbf{x}, \lambda)$ is an eigenpair of **A**, since $\mathbf{x} \neq \mathbf{0}$ and

$$\mathbf{A}\mathbf{x} = \begin{pmatrix} 1 & -1 \\ 3 & 5 \end{pmatrix} \begin{pmatrix} 1 \\ -1 \end{pmatrix} = \begin{pmatrix} 2 \\ -2 \end{pmatrix} = 2 \begin{pmatrix} 1 \\ -1 \end{pmatrix} = \lambda \mathbf{x}$$

Example 3.2.2 If **I** is the $N \times N$ identity then $(\mathbf{x}, 1)$ is an eigenpair of **I** for every nonzero $\mathbf{x} \in \mathbb{R}^N$.

Consider now the matrix

$$\mathbf{R} := \begin{pmatrix} 0 & -1 \\ 1 & 0 \end{pmatrix}$$

that rotates any point counterclockwise by 90°, as shown in figure 3.1. This rotation causes the scaling in (3.6) to fail for any $\lambda \in \mathbb{R}$ and nonzero $\mathbf{x} \in \mathbb{R}^2$. If, however, we admit the possibility that λ and the elements of **x** can be complex, then (3.6) can hold. For example, direct calculation confirms that $\lambda = i$ and $\mathbf{x} = (1, -i)^\top$ is an eigenpair for **R**. It turns out that contemplation of complex eigenpairs is useful. Here eigenpairs are taken to be complex-valued unless explicitly stated to be real.

Fact 3.2.6 Given $N \times N$ matrix $\mathbf{A}$, the scalar λ is an eigenvalue of $\mathbf{A}$ if and only if

$$\det(\mathbf{A} - \lambda \mathbf{I}) = 0$$

Here $\mathbf{I}$ is the $N \times N$ identity. Exercise 3.5.17 asks you to confirm this important fact. For the 2×2 matrix in (3.4), the rule for the 2×2 determinant in (3.4), fact 3.2.6 and a little bit of algebra imply that its eigenvalues are given by the two roots of the polynomial expression

$$\lambda^2 - (a + d)\lambda + (ad - bc) = 0$$

More generally, given any $N \times N$ matrix $\mathbf{A}$, it can be shown via the fundamental theorem of algebra that there exist complex numbers $\lambda_1, \ldots, \lambda_N$, not necessarily distinct, such that

$$\det(\mathbf{A} - \lambda \mathbf{I}) = \prod_{n=1}^{N} (\lambda_n - \lambda) \tag{3.7}$$

It is clear that each λ_n satisfies $\det(\mathbf{A} - \lambda_n \mathbf{I}) = 0$ and hence is an eigenvalue of $\mathbf{A}$. In particular, $\lambda_1, \ldots, \lambda_N$ is the set of eigenvalues of $\mathbf{A}$, although it's worth repeating that these numbers are not necessarily distinct.

Fact 3.2.7 Let $\mathbf{A}$ be $N \times N$ and let $\lambda_1, \ldots, \lambda_N$ be the eigenvalues defined in (3.7). The following statements are true:

(i) $\det \mathbf{A} = \prod_{n=1}^{N} \lambda_n$.

(ii) $\operatorname{trace} \mathbf{A} = \sum_{n=1}^{N} \lambda_n$.

(iii) If $\mathbf{A}$ is symmetric, then $\lambda_n \in \mathbb{R}$ for all n.

(iv) If $\mathbf{A}$ is nonsingular, then the eigenvalues of $\mathbf{A}^{-1}$ are $1/\lambda_1, \ldots, 1/\lambda_N$.

(v) If $\mathbf{A}$ is triangular, then its eigenvalues coincide with the elements on the principle diagonal.

It is immediate from (i) that $\mathbf{A}$ is nonsingular $\iff$ all its eigenvalues are nonzero.

3.2.4 Quadratic Forms

In statistics and econometrics we often encounter quadratic expressions. In general, given symmetric $N \times N$ matrix $\mathbf{A}$, the **quadratic function** or **quadratic form** on $\mathbb{R}^N$ associated with $\mathbf{A}$ is the map Q defined by

$$Q(\mathbf{x}) := \mathbf{x}^\top \mathbf{A} \mathbf{x} = \sum_{j=1}^{N} \sum_{i=1}^{N} a_{ij} x_i x_j$$

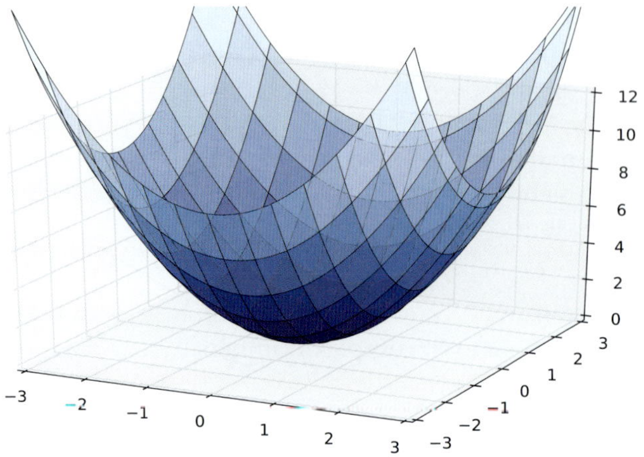

Figure 3.2 Quadratic function $Q(\mathbf{x}) = x_1^2 + x_2^2$

To give a simple illustration, let $N = 2$ and let $\mathbf{A}$ be the identity matrix $\mathbf{I}$. In this case,

$$Q(\mathbf{x}) = \|\mathbf{x}\|^2 = x_1^2 + x_2^2$$

A 3D graph of this function is shown in figure 3.2.

One thing you'll notice about this function is that its graph lies everywhere above zero, or $Q(\mathbf{x}) \geqslant 0$. In fact we know that $\|\mathbf{x}\|^2$ is nonnegative and will be zero only when $\mathbf{x} = \mathbf{0}$. Hence the graph touches zero only at the point $\mathbf{x} = \mathbf{0}$. Many other choices of $\mathbf{A}$ yield a quadratic form with this property. Such $\mathbf{A}$ are said to be positive definite. More generally, an $N \times N$ symmetric matrix $\mathbf{A}$ is called

- **nonnegative definite** if $\mathbf{x}^\top \mathbf{A} \mathbf{x} \geqslant 0$ for all $\mathbf{x} \in \mathbb{R}^N$,
- **positive definite** if $\mathbf{x}^\top \mathbf{A} \mathbf{x} > 0$ for all $\mathbf{x} \in \mathbb{R}^N$ with $\mathbf{x} \neq \mathbf{0}$,
- **nonpositive definite** if $\mathbf{x}^\top \mathbf{A} \mathbf{x} \leqslant 0$ for all $\mathbf{x} \in \mathbb{R}^N$, and
- **negative definite** if $\mathbf{x}^\top \mathbf{A} \mathbf{x} < 0$ for all $\mathbf{x} \in \mathbb{R}^N$ with $\mathbf{x} \neq \mathbf{0}$.

If $\mathbf{A}$ fits none of these categories, then $\mathbf{A}$ is called **indefinite**. Figure 3.3 shows the graph of a negative definite quadratic function. Now the function is hill-shaped, and $\mathbf{0}$ is the unique global maximum. Figure 3.4 shows an indefinite form.

The easiest case for detecting definiteness is when the matrix $\mathbf{A}$ is diagonal, since

$$\mathbf{A} = \operatorname{diag}(d_1, \ldots, d_N) \quad \text{implies} \quad Q(\mathbf{x}) = d_1 x_1^2 + \cdots + d_N x_N^2$$

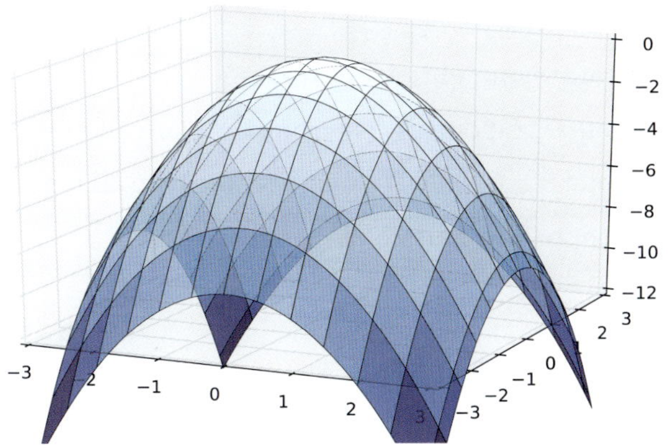

Figure 3.3 Quadratic function $Q(\mathbf{x}) = -x_1^2 - x_2^2$

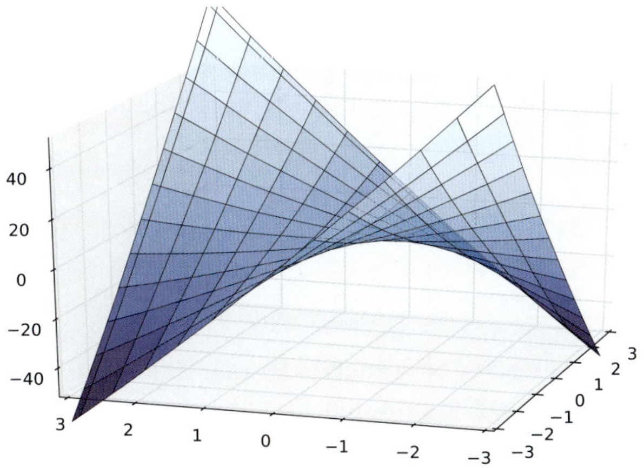

Figure 3.4 Quadratic function $Q(\mathbf{x}) = x_1^2/2 + 8x_1x_2 + x_2^2/2$

From the right-hand expression we see that a diagonal matrix is positive definite if and only if all diagonal elements are positive. Analogous statements are true for nonnegative, nonpositive and negative definite matrices. The next fact generalizes this idea and is proved in §3.3.4.

Fact 3.2.8 Let $\mathbf{A}$ be any symmetric matrix. $\mathbf{A}$ is

(i) positive definite if and only if its eigenvalues are all positive,

(ii) negative definite if and only if its eigenvalues are all negative,

and similarly for nonpositive and nonnegative definite.

It follows from fact 3.2.8 that

Fact 3.2.9 If $\mathbf{A}$ is positive definite, then $\mathbf{A}$ is nonsingular, with $\det \mathbf{A} > 0$.

Finally, here's a necessary (but not sufficient) condition for each kind of definiteness.

Fact 3.2.10 If $\mathbf{A}$ is positive definite, then each element a_{nn} on the principal diagonal is positive, and the same for nonnegative, nonpositive and negative.

3.3 Projection and Decomposition

This section collects some essential results on projection and decomposition of matrices. The projection material takes our abstract projection theory from §2.2 and translates it into the more concrete language of matrices.

3.3.1 Projection Matrices

As stated in theorem 2.2.2 on page 31, given any subspace S, the corresponding projection $\mathbf{P} = \operatorname{proj} S$ is a linear map from $\mathbb{R}^N$ to $\mathbb{R}^N$. In view of theorem 3.1.1 on page 48, it follows that there exists an $N \times N$ matrix $\hat{\mathbf{P}}$ such that $\mathbf{P}\mathbf{x} = \hat{\mathbf{P}}\mathbf{x}$ for all $\mathbf{x} \in \mathbb{R}^N$. In fact we've anticipated this in the notation $\mathbf{P}$, and from now on $\mathbf{P}$ will also represent the corresponding matrix. But what does this matrix look like?

Theorem 3.3.1 *Let S be a subspace of $\mathbb{R}^N$. If $\mathbf{P} = \operatorname{proj} S$, then*

$$\mathbf{P} = \mathbf{B}(\mathbf{B}^\top \mathbf{B})^{-1}\mathbf{B}^\top \tag{3.8}$$

for every matrix $\mathbf{B}$ such that the columns of $\mathbf{B}$ form a basis of S.

This result generalizes fact 2.2.6 on page 32, which pertains to projection onto the span of an orthonormal basis. The expression in (3.8) is more complex, but at the same time it applies to any basis, orthonormal or otherwise. We further explore the connection between the two results in §3.3.3. For the proof of theorem 3.3.1 see exercise 3.5.30 and its solution.

The construction of $\mathbf{P}$ in (3.8) implicitly assumes that $\mathbf{B}^\top \mathbf{B}$ is nonsingular. This is justified because $\mathbf{B}$ has full column rank (see ex. 3.5.28). As usual, we let $\mathbf{M} = \mathbf{I} - \mathbf{P}$ denote the residual projection (see page 32).

Example 3.3.1 Recall example 2.2.1 on page 30, where we found that the projection of $\mathbf{y} \in \mathbb{R}^N$ onto span$\{\mathbf{1}\}$ is $\bar{y}\mathbf{1}$. We can get this from (3.8) as well. Since $\mathbf{1}$ is a basis for span$\{\mathbf{1}\}$, we have

$$\mathbf{P} = \text{proj span}\{\mathbf{1}\} \implies \mathbf{P} = \mathbf{1}(\mathbf{1}^\top \mathbf{1})^{-1}\mathbf{1}^\top = \frac{1}{N}\mathbf{1}\mathbf{1}^\top \tag{3.9}$$

This leads us back to $\mathbf{P}\mathbf{y} = \bar{y}\mathbf{1}$, as expected. The corresponding residual projection is

$$\mathbf{M}_c = \mathbf{I} - \frac{1}{N}\mathbf{1}\mathbf{1}^\top \tag{3.10}$$

The reason for the subscripted c was discussed in example 2.2.3 on page 33.

Fact 3.3.1 In the setting of theorem 3.3.1, we have

(i) $\mathbf{M}\mathbf{B} = \mathbf{0}$

(ii) $\mathbf{P}\mathbf{B} = \mathbf{B}$

For example, it's easy to see that $\mathbf{M}_c$ in (3.10) maps $\mathbf{1}$ to $\mathbf{0}$. Exercise 3.5.31 asks you to prove fact 3.3.1.

A square matrix $\mathbf{A}$ is called **idempotent** if $\mathbf{A}\mathbf{A} = \mathbf{A}$.

Fact 3.3.2 Both $\mathbf{P}$ and $\mathbf{M}$ are symmetric and idempotent.

Idempotence of $\mathbf{P}$ and $\mathbf{M}$ can be checked by direct calculation. A better understanding is obtained by reflecting on the fact that projecting onto a subspace twice is the same as projecting once. After one projection the vector is already in the subspace. See fact 2.2.8 on page 33.

Fact 3.3.3 If $\mathbf{A}$ is any idempotent matrix, then rank $\mathbf{A}$ = trace $\mathbf{A}$.

For orthogonal projections, we can say more:

Fact 3.3.4 Let S be a linear subspace of $\mathbb{R}^N$. If $\mathbf{P} = \text{proj}\, S$ and $\mathbf{M}$ is the residual projection, then

(i) $\operatorname{rank} \mathbf{P} = \operatorname{trace} \mathbf{P} = \dim S$ and

(ii) $\operatorname{rank} \mathbf{M} = \operatorname{trace} \mathbf{M} = N - \dim S$.

To see why $\operatorname{rank} \mathbf{P} = \dim S$, recall that the rank of a linear map is the dimension of its range. When $\mathbf{P} = \operatorname{proj} S$, the range of $\mathbf{P}$ is exactly S.

To show that $\operatorname{trace} \mathbf{P} = \dim S$ also holds, we can appeal to fact 3.3.3. There's also a nice direct proof. See exercise 3.5.27 and its solution. Once we know that $\operatorname{trace} \mathbf{P} = \dim S$, it's clear that $\operatorname{trace} \mathbf{M} = N - \dim S$ because

$$\operatorname{trace} \mathbf{M} = \operatorname{trace}(\mathbf{I} - \mathbf{P}) = \operatorname{trace} \mathbf{I} - \operatorname{trace} \mathbf{P} = N - \dim S$$

3.3.2 Overdetermined Systems of Equations

In §3.1.3 we talked about solving equations of the form $\mathbf{A}\mathbf{x} = \mathbf{b}$ when $\mathbf{A}$ is square. In statistics and econometrics, we often work the case where $\mathbf{A}$ is $N \times K$ and $K \leqslant N$. When the inequality is strict, the system of equations is said to be **overdetermined**.

Consider the problem of whether or not there exists a vector $\mathbf{x}$ satisfying $\mathbf{A}\mathbf{x} = \mathbf{b}$ in this setting. Intuitively, when the number of equations is larger than the number of unknowns ($N > K$) we may not be able to find an $\mathbf{x}$ that satisfies all N equations. There are several equivalent ways to formalize this intuition. The linear map $T \colon \mathbb{R}^K \to \mathbb{R}^N$ corresponding to $\mathbf{A}$ is $T\mathbf{x} = \mathbf{A}\mathbf{x}$ (see 3.1.2). We know the following statements to be equivalent:

(i) there exists an $\mathbf{x} \in \mathbb{R}^K$ with $\mathbf{A}\mathbf{x} = \mathbf{b}$.

(ii) $\mathbf{b} \in \operatorname{colspace} \mathbf{A}$.

(iii) $\mathbf{b} \in \operatorname{rng} T$.

We also know from theorem 2.1.8 on page 26 that when $K < N$, the function T cannot be onto, and hence it's possible that $\mathbf{b}$ lies outside the range of T.

In fact we can say more than this. When $K < N$, the scenario $\mathbf{b} \in \operatorname{colspace} \mathbf{A}$ is in some sense very rare. The reason is that the dimension of $\operatorname{colspace} \mathbf{A}$, which is precisely the rank of $\mathbf{A}$, is less than or equal to K (see §3.1.2) and hence strictly less than N. There is a sense in which K-dimensional subspaces of $\mathbb{R}^N$ are negligible, and hence the "chance" of $\mathbf{b}$ happening to lie in this subspace is tiny.[1]

As a result the standard approach is to admit that an exact solution may not exist, and to focus instead on finding a $\mathbf{x} \in \mathbb{R}^K$ such that $\mathbf{A}\mathbf{x}$ is as close to $\mathbf{b}$ as possible. It's

1. Formally, K dimensional subspaces have measure zero in $\mathbb{R}^N$ whenever $K < N$. Hence every probability measure that is absolutely continuous with respect to Lebesgue measure puts zero mass on such a set. Less formally, consider the case where $N = 3$ and $K = 2$. Then $\operatorname{colspace} \mathbf{A}$ forms at most a 2-dimensional plane in $\mathbb{R}^3$. Intuitively, this set has no volume in $\mathbb{R}^3$ because planes have no "thickness." Similarly, while we might visualize $\mathbf{b}$ as a dot in $\mathbb{R}^3$, as a point it is in fact infinitesimally small. Hence the chance of a randomly chosen $\mathbf{b}$ lying in $\operatorname{colspace} \mathbf{A}$ is zero.

natural that "close to" is defined in terms of ordinary Euclidean norm, which leads us to the minimization problem

$$\min_{\mathbf{x} \in \mathbb{R}^K} \|\mathbf{b} - \mathbf{A}\mathbf{x}\| \tag{3.11}$$

This is called a **least squares problem** because solving (3.11) is the same as minimizing $\|\mathbf{b} - \mathbf{A}\mathbf{x}\|^2$ with respect to $\mathbf{x}$, and the squared norm is, by definition, a sum of squares. Assuming as before that $\mathbf{A}$ is $N \times K$ with $K \leqslant N$ and $\mathbf{b}$ is $N \times 1$, we can use the orthogonal projection theorem to solve (3.11) as follows:

Theorem 3.3.2 *If* $\mathbf{A}$ *has full column rank, then* (3.11) *has the unique solution*

$$\hat{\mathbf{x}} := (\mathbf{A}^\top \mathbf{A})^{-1} \mathbf{A}^\top \mathbf{b} \tag{3.12}$$

Proof. Let $\mathbf{A}$ and $\mathbf{b}$ be as in the statement of the theorem. Let $\hat{\mathbf{x}}$ be as in (3.12) and let $S :=$ colspace $\mathbf{A}$. By the full column rank assumption, the columns of $\mathbf{A}$ form a basis for S. Hence, applying theorem 3.3.1, the orthogonal projection of $\mathbf{b}$ onto S is

$$\mathbf{P}\mathbf{b} := \mathbf{A}(\mathbf{A}^\top \mathbf{A})^{-1} \mathbf{A}^\top \mathbf{b} = \mathbf{A}\hat{\mathbf{x}} \tag{3.13}$$

Moreover, since the orthogonal projection theorem gives a unique minimizer in terms of the closest point in S to $\mathbf{b}$, we must have

$$\|\mathbf{b} - \mathbf{A}\hat{\mathbf{x}}\| < \|\mathbf{b} - \mathbf{y}\| \quad \text{for all } \mathbf{y} \in S, \ \mathbf{y} \neq \mathbf{A}\hat{\mathbf{x}} \tag{3.14}$$

Pick any $\mathbf{x} \in \mathbb{R}^K$ such that $\mathbf{x} \neq \hat{\mathbf{x}}$. By the definition of S we have $\mathbf{A}\mathbf{x} \in S$. In addition, since $\mathbf{x} \neq \hat{\mathbf{x}}$, and since $\mathbf{A}$ has full column rank, it must be that $\mathbf{A}\mathbf{x} \neq \mathbf{A}\hat{\mathbf{x}}$ (ex. 3.5.4). Hence

$$\|\mathbf{b} - \mathbf{A}\hat{\mathbf{x}}\| < \|\mathbf{b} - \mathbf{A}\mathbf{x}\| \quad \text{for all } \mathbf{x} \in \mathbb{R}^K, \ \mathbf{x} \neq \hat{\mathbf{x}}$$

In other words, $\hat{\mathbf{x}}$ is the unique solution to (3.11). □

In the expression for $\hat{\mathbf{x}}$ in (3.12), the matrix $(\mathbf{A}^\top \mathbf{A})^{-1} \mathbf{A}^\top$ is called the **pseudoinverse** of $\mathbf{A}$. If $K = N$—that is, if $\mathbf{A}$ is in fact square—then, under our full rank assumption, the pseudoinverse reduces to the inverse $\mathbf{A}^{-1}$, and the least squares solution $\hat{\mathbf{x}}$ in (3.12) reduces to the expression given in (3.3) on page 51.

What happens if we drop the assumption that the columns of $\mathbf{A}$ are linearly independent? The set colspace $\mathbf{A}$ is still a linear subspace, and the orthogonal projection theorem still gives us a closest point $\mathbf{P}\mathbf{b}$ to $\mathbf{b}$ in colspace $\mathbf{A}$. Since $\mathbf{P}\mathbf{b} \in$ colspace $\mathbf{A}$, there still exists a vector $\hat{\mathbf{x}}$ such that $\mathbf{P}\mathbf{b} = \mathbf{A}\hat{\mathbf{x}}$. The problem is that now there exists an infinity of such vectors. Exercise 3.5.34 asks you to prove this.

3.3.3 QR Decomposition

The **QR decomposition** of a given matrix $\mathbf{A}$ is a product of the form $\mathbf{QR}$, where the first matrix has orthonormal columns and the second is upper triangular. This factorization has many applications, including least squares problems and the computation of eigenvalues. The decomposition is based on Gram–Schmidt orthogonalization.

Theorem 3.3.3 *If $\mathbf{A}$ is an $N \times K$ matrix with full column rank, then there exists a factorization $\mathbf{A} = \mathbf{QR}$ where*

(i) $\mathbf{R}$ is $K \times K$, upper triangular and nonsingular, and

(ii) $\mathbf{Q}$ is $N \times K$, with orthonormal columns.

Proof. Let $\mathbf{A}$ be as stated, and let $\mathbf{a}_k := \text{col}_k \mathbf{A}$. Theorem 2.2.3 gives us existence of an orthonormal set $\{\mathbf{u}_1, \ldots, \mathbf{u}_K\}$ such that the span of $\{\mathbf{u}_1, \ldots, \mathbf{u}_k\}$ equals that of $\{\mathbf{a}_1, \ldots, \mathbf{a}_k\}$ for $k = 1, \ldots, K$. In particular, $\mathbf{a}_k$ is in the span of $\{\mathbf{u}_1, \ldots, \mathbf{u}_k\}$, and hence, appealing to fact 2.2.3 on page 28, we can write

$$\begin{aligned}
\mathbf{a}_1 &= (\mathbf{a}_1^\top \mathbf{u}_1)\mathbf{u}_1 \\
\mathbf{a}_2 &= (\mathbf{a}_2^\top \mathbf{u}_1)\mathbf{u}_1 + (\mathbf{a}_2^\top \mathbf{u}_2)\mathbf{u}_2 \\
\mathbf{a}_3 &= (\mathbf{a}_3^\top \mathbf{u}_1)\mathbf{u}_1 + (\mathbf{a}_3^\top \mathbf{u}_2)\mathbf{u}_2 + (\mathbf{a}_3^\top \mathbf{u}_3)\mathbf{u}_3
\end{aligned}$$

and so on. Sticking to the 3×3 case to simplify expressions, we can stack these equations horizontally to get

$$\begin{pmatrix} | & | & | \\ \mathbf{a}_1 & \mathbf{a}_2 & \mathbf{a}_3 \\ | & | & | \end{pmatrix} = \begin{pmatrix} | & | & | \\ \mathbf{u}_1 & \mathbf{u}_2 & \mathbf{u}_3 \\ | & | & | \end{pmatrix} \begin{pmatrix} (\mathbf{a}_1^\top \mathbf{u}_1) & (\mathbf{a}_2^\top \mathbf{u}_1) & (\mathbf{a}_3^\top \mathbf{u}_1) \\ 0 & (\mathbf{a}_2^\top \mathbf{u}_2) & (\mathbf{a}_3^\top \mathbf{u}_2) \\ 0 & 0 & (\mathbf{a}_3^\top \mathbf{u}_3) \end{pmatrix}$$

or $\mathbf{A} = \mathbf{QR}$. This is our QR decomposition.

It remains to show that $\mathbf{R}$ is invertible. This will be so if each term $\mathbf{a}_k^\top \mathbf{u}_k$ is nonzero, since the determinant is the product of these elements (see fact 3.2.7 on page 57). Suppose, to the contrary, that $\mathbf{a}_k^\top \mathbf{u}_k = 0$ for some k. Then $\mathbf{a}_k$ lies in the span of $\{\mathbf{u}_1, \ldots, \mathbf{u}_{k-1}\}$, which, by construction, agrees with the span of $\{\mathbf{a}_1, \ldots, \mathbf{a}_{k-1}\}$. This contradicts linear independence of the columns of $\mathbf{A}$. □

Given the decomposition $\mathbf{A} = \mathbf{QR}$, the least squares solution $\hat{\mathbf{x}}$ defined in (3.12) can also be written as $\hat{\mathbf{x}} = \mathbf{R}^{-1}\mathbf{Q}^\top \mathbf{b}$ (ex. 3.5.32). Premultiplying by $\mathbf{R}$ converts this expression to $\mathbf{R}\hat{\mathbf{x}} = \mathbf{Q}^\top \mathbf{b}$, which is easy to solve because $\mathbf{R}$ is triangular (see §3.2.1).

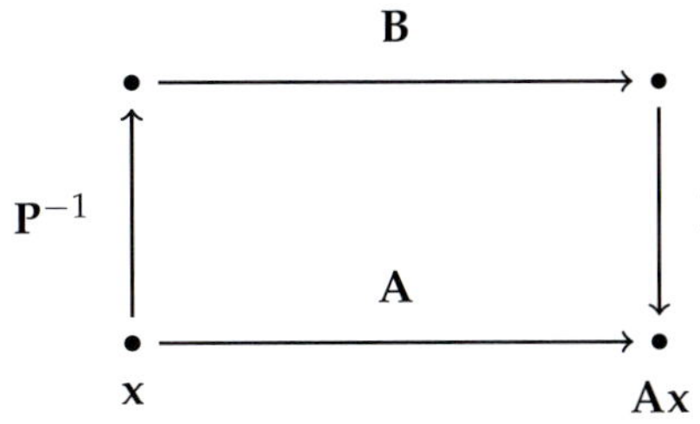

Figure 3.5 **A** is similar to **B**

3.3.4 Diagonalization and Spectral Theory

One important concept in dynamic systems and related fields is topological conjugacy. If $f : A \to A$ and $g : B \to B$, then g is said to be **topologically conjugate** to f whenever there exists a continuous bijection $\tau : B \to A$ such that $f = \tau \circ g \circ \tau^{-1}$. The idea is that the action of f can be replicated by transporting a point into the domain of g, applying g, and then transporting it back. This can be beneficial if g is somehow simpler than f.

In the case of linear maps—that is, matrices—it is natural to study conjugacy in a setting where the bijection is also required to be linear. In linear algebra this is called *similarity*. In particular, a square matrix $\mathbf{A}$ is said to be **similar** to another matrix $\mathbf{B}$ if there exists an invertible matrix $\mathbf{P}$ such that $\mathbf{A} = \mathbf{P}\mathbf{B}\mathbf{P}^{-1}$. Figure 3.5 shows the conjugate relationship of the two matrices when thought of as maps.

The next fact is a fun exercise.

Fact 3.3.5 If $\mathbf{A}$ is similar to $\mathbf{B}$, then $\mathbf{A}^t$ is similar to $\mathbf{B}^t$ for all $t \in \mathbb{N}$.

As discussed above, similarity of $\mathbf{A}$ to a given matrix $\mathbf{B}$ is most useful when $\mathbf{B}$ is somehow simpler than $\mathbf{A}$, or more amenable to a given operation. The simplest kind of matrices we work with are diagonal matrices, so similarity to a diagonal matrix is particularly desirable. If $\mathbf{A}$ is similar to a diagonal matrix, then $\mathbf{A}$ is called **diagonalizable**.

Example 3.3.2 Suppose that we want to calculate $\mathbf{A}^t$ for some given $t \in \mathbb{N}$. If $\mathbf{A} = \mathbf{P}\mathbf{\Lambda}\mathbf{P}^{-1}$ for some $\mathbf{\Lambda} = \operatorname{diag}(\lambda_1, \ldots, \lambda_N)$, then by fact 3.3.5 and fact 3.2.2 on page 54, we have $\mathbf{A}^t = \mathbf{P} \operatorname{diag}(\lambda_1^t, \ldots, \lambda_N^t)\mathbf{P}^{-1}$. Aside from mapping backward and forward with $\mathbf{P}$, the only effort required to take the tth power of $\mathbf{A}$ is to take the tth power of N scalars.

If $\mathbf{A} = \mathbf{P}\mathbf{\Lambda}\mathbf{P}^{-1}$ where $\mathbf{\Lambda}$ is diagonal, it follows immediately that the elements on the principal diagonal of $\mathbf{\Lambda}$ are the eigenvalues of $\mathbf{A}$, and that the columns of $\mathbf{P}$ are eigenvectors. To see this, observe that $\mathbf{A} = \mathbf{P}\mathbf{\Lambda}\mathbf{P}^{-1}$ implies $\mathbf{AP} = \mathbf{P}\mathbf{\Lambda}$. Equating the nth column on each side gives $\mathbf{A}\mathbf{p}_n = \lambda_n \mathbf{p}_n$, where $\mathbf{p}_n := \operatorname{col}_n \mathbf{P}$. Finally, $\mathbf{p}_n$ is not the zero vector because otherwise $\mathbf{P}$ would not be invertible. Let's summarize:

Fact 3.3.6 If $\mathbf{A} = \mathbf{P}\mathbf{\Lambda}\mathbf{P}^{-1}$ for some $\mathbf{\Lambda} = \operatorname{diag}(\lambda_1, \ldots, \lambda_N)$, then $(\operatorname{col}_n \mathbf{P}, \lambda_n)$ is an eigenpair of $\mathbf{A}$ for each n.

But when is $\mathbf{A}$ diagonalizable? The only thing we need to make the expression $\mathbf{A} = \mathbf{P}\mathbf{\Lambda}\mathbf{P}^{-1}$ work is for $\mathbf{P}$ to be invertible. This explains the next fact.

Fact 3.3.7 An $N \times N$ matrix $\mathbf{A}$ is diagonalizable if and only if it has N linearly independent eigenvectors.[2]

If $\mathbf{A}$ does have N linearly independent eigenvectors, then we are in good shape—diagonalization is possible. But can we do any better? The matrix $\mathbf{\Lambda}$ cannot really be simplified, but in some cases $\mathbf{P}$ can be. In particular, things are even nicer if $\mathbf{P}$ has orthonormal columns—that is, its columns form an orthonormal set, and hence an orthonormal basis of $\mathbb{R}^N$. These kinds of matrices are called **orthogonal matrices**. Here are some nice properties of such matrices.

Fact 3.3.8 If $\mathbf{Q}$ and $\mathbf{P}$ are $N \times N$ orthogonal matrices, then

(i) $\mathbf{Q}^\top$ is orthogonal and $\mathbf{Q}^{-1} = \mathbf{Q}^\top$,

(ii) $\mathbf{QP}$ is orthogonal, and

(iii) $\det \mathbf{Q} \in \{-1, 1\}$.

The first result tells us is that if $\mathbf{A} = \mathbf{Q}\mathbf{\Lambda}\mathbf{Q}^{-1}$ and $\mathbf{Q}$ has orthonormal columns, then $\mathbf{A} = \mathbf{Q}\mathbf{\Lambda}\mathbf{Q}^\top$. It's easy to see from this expression that $\mathbf{A}$ must be symmetric, so if we hope to diagonalize with this extra orthonormal property, then we shouldn't look beyond symmetric matrices. The following fundamental theorem tells us that this form of diagonalization is possible precisely when $\mathbf{A}$ is symmetric.

Theorem 3.3.4 *If $\mathbf{A}$ is symmetric, then $\mathbf{A}$ can be diagonalized as $\mathbf{A} = \mathbf{Q}\mathbf{\Lambda}\mathbf{Q}^\top$, where $\mathbf{Q}$ is an orthogonal matrix and $\mathbf{\Lambda}$ is the diagonal matrix formed from the eigenvalues of $\mathbf{A}$.*

This is one version of the **spectral decomposition theorem**. See, for example, §10.3 of Jänich (1994). $\mathbf{Q}\mathbf{\Lambda}\mathbf{Q}^\top$ is called the **symmetric eigenvalue decomposition** of $\mathbf{A}$. It's not hard to see that its action on a given $N \times 1$ vector $\mathbf{x}$ can be written as

$$\mathbf{A}\mathbf{x} = \sum_{n=1}^{N} \lambda_n (\mathbf{u}_n^\top \mathbf{x}) \mathbf{u}_n$$

2. If we permit the eigenvectors to be complex, then the requirement is that they form a basis of $\mathbb{C}^N$, the set of complex N-vectors. In this case there is a sense in which almost all matrices are diagonalizable.

where λ_n is the nth eigenvalue of $\mathbf{A}$ and $\mathbf{u}_n = \text{col}_n\, \mathbf{Q}$. Compare with $\mathbf{x} = \sum_{n=1}^{N} (\mathbf{u}_n^\top \mathbf{x}) \mathbf{u}_n$, which is true by fact 2.2.3 on page 28.

One nice application of the spectral theorem is a proof of fact 3.2.8 on page 60, which states among other things that symmetric matrix $\mathbf{A}$ is positive definite if and only if its eigenvalues are all positive. Exercise 3.5.23 and its solution step you through the arguments.

Fact 3.3.9 If $\mathbf{A}$ is nonnegative definite, then $\sqrt{\mathbf{A}}$ exists and equals $\mathbf{Q}\sqrt{\mathbf{\Lambda}}\mathbf{Q}^\top$. The matrix $\sqrt{\mathbf{\Lambda}}$ is given by $\text{diag}(\sqrt{\lambda_1}, \ldots, \sqrt{\lambda_N})$.

Here $\mathbf{Q\Lambda Q}^\top$ is the spectral decomposition of $\mathbf{A}$. To check that $\mathbf{Q}\sqrt{\mathbf{\Lambda}}\mathbf{Q}^\top$ is a square root just multiply. $\sqrt{\mathbf{\Lambda}}$ exists because $\mathbf{A}$ is nonnegative definite, and hence its eigenvalues are nonnegative (see fact 3.2.8 and fact 3.2.2).

By combining our results on spectral decomposition with the QR decomposition discussed in §3.3.3, we can prove the following well-known fact:

Fact 3.3.10 If $\mathbf{A}$ is positive definite, then there exists a nonsingular, upper triangular matrix $\mathbf{R}$ such that $\mathbf{A} = \mathbf{R}^\top \mathbf{R}$.

This decomposition is called the **Cholesky decomposition**. The proof is obtained by writing

$$\mathbf{A} = \mathbf{Q\Lambda Q}^\top = \mathbf{Q}\sqrt{\mathbf{\Lambda}}\sqrt{\mathbf{\Lambda}}\mathbf{Q}^\top = (\sqrt{\mathbf{\Lambda}}\mathbf{Q}^\top)^\top \sqrt{\mathbf{\Lambda}}\mathbf{Q}^\top$$

and applying the QR decomposition to $\sqrt{\mathbf{\Lambda}}\mathbf{Q}^\top$. This allows us to write $\sqrt{\mathbf{\Lambda}}\mathbf{Q}^\top = \tilde{\mathbf{Q}}\mathbf{R}$, where $\mathbf{R}$ is nonsingular and upper triangular, and $\tilde{\mathbf{Q}}$ has orthonormal columns. Because the columns of $\tilde{\mathbf{Q}}$ are orthonormal,

$$\mathbf{A} = (\tilde{\mathbf{Q}}\mathbf{R})^\top \tilde{\mathbf{Q}}\mathbf{R} = \mathbf{R}^\top \tilde{\mathbf{Q}}^\top \tilde{\mathbf{Q}}\mathbf{R} = \mathbf{R}^\top \mathbf{R}$$

Our decomposition has the properties stated in fact 3.3.10.

3.3.5 Norms and Continuity

Given vector sequence $\{\mathbf{x}_n\}$ in $\mathbb{R}^K$ and any point $\mathbf{x} \in \mathbb{R}^K$, we say that $\{\mathbf{x}_n\}$ **converges** to $\mathbf{x}$ and write $\mathbf{x}_n \to \mathbf{x}$ if, for any $\epsilon > 0$, there exists an $N \in \mathbb{N}$ such that $\|\mathbf{x}_n - \mathbf{x}\| < \epsilon$ whenever $n \geqslant N$. Another way to say this is that the real-valued sequence $z_n := \|\mathbf{x}_n - \mathbf{x}\|$ converges to zero in $\mathbb{R}$ as $n \to \infty$.

Fact 3.3.11 The following results hold:

(i) If $\mathbf{x}_n \to \mathbf{x}$ and $\mathbf{y}_n \to \mathbf{y}$, then $\mathbf{x}_n + \mathbf{y}_n \to \mathbf{x} + \mathbf{y}$.

(ii) If $\mathbf{x}_n \to \mathbf{x}$ and $\alpha \in \mathbb{R}$, then $\alpha\mathbf{x}_n \to \alpha\mathbf{x}$.

(iii) $\mathbf{x}_n \to \mathbf{x}$ if and only if $\mathbf{a}^\top \mathbf{x}_n \to \mathbf{a}^\top \mathbf{x}$ for all $\mathbf{a} \in \mathbb{R}^K$.

For econometrics it is helpful if we extend the notion of convergence to matrices. We can do this in a parallel fashion by defining norms over matrices. The **matrix norm** of $N \times K$ matrix $\mathbf{A}$ is defined as

$$\|\mathbf{A}\| := \max\left\{\|\mathbf{A}\mathbf{x}\| \,:\, \mathbf{x} \in \mathbb{R}^K,\ \|\mathbf{x}\| = 1\right\} \tag{3.15}$$

In this expression there are two different norms in play: The left-hand side is a matrix norm, while on the right we have the ordinary vector norm.

Given a sequence of $N \times K$ matrices $\mathbf{A}_n$ and an $N \times K$ matrix $\mathbf{A}$, we say that $\mathbf{A}_n$ **converges** to $\mathbf{A}$ if the matrix norm deviation $\|\mathbf{A}_n - \mathbf{A}\|$ converges to zero in $\mathbb{R}$.

While the value in (3.15) is not particularly easy to solve for in general, the definition is entirely standard, and one can show that the matrix norm behaves like the vector norm in many ways. For example,

Fact 3.3.12 For any conformable matrices $\mathbf{A}$ and $\mathbf{B}$, the matrix norm satisfies

(i) $\|\mathbf{A}\| \geqslant 0$ and $\|\mathbf{A}\| = 0$ if and only if all entries of $\mathbf{A}$ are zero,

(ii) $\|\alpha\mathbf{A}\| = |\alpha|\|\mathbf{A}\|$ for any scalar α,

(iii) $\|\mathbf{A} + \mathbf{B}\| \leqslant \|\mathbf{A}\| + \|\mathbf{B}\|$, and

(iv) $\|\mathbf{A}\mathbf{B}\| \leqslant \|\mathbf{A}\|\|\mathbf{B}\|$.

Compare these results with those of fact 2.1.2 on page 13.

Fact 3.3.13 For any $J \times K$ matrix $\mathbf{A}$ with elements a_{jk}, we have

$$\|\mathbf{A}\| \leqslant \sqrt{JK} \max_{jk} |a_{jk}|$$

This bound is handy. For example, it tells us that if every element of $\mathbf{A}$ is close to zero then $\|\mathbf{A}\|$ must also be close to zero.

3.3.5.1 Neumann Series

Let's look at an important result in analysis that uses matrix norms. Starting in chapter 7, we will investigate dynamic systems such as $\mathbf{x}_{t+1} = \mathbf{A}\mathbf{x}_t + \mathbf{b}$, where $\mathbf{x}_t$ represents the values of some variables of interest and $\mathbf{A}$ and $\mathbf{b}$ form the parameters in the law of motion for $\mathbf{x}_t$. One question we might ask in this setting is whether or not there exists a "stationary" vector $\mathbf{x} \in \mathbb{R}^N$, in the sense that $\mathbf{x}_t = \mathbf{x}$ implies $\mathbf{x}_{t+1} = \mathbf{x}$. In other words, we seek an $\mathbf{x} \in \mathbb{R}^N$ that solves the system of equations

$$\mathbf{x} = \mathbf{A}\mathbf{x} + \mathbf{b} \qquad (\mathbf{A} \text{ is } N \times N \text{ and } \mathbf{b} \text{ is } N \times 1) \tag{3.16}$$

We can get some insight by reflecting on the scalar case $x = ax + b$. If $|a| < 1$, then this equation has the unique solution

$$\bar{x} = \frac{b}{1-a} = b \sum_{k=0}^{\infty} a^k$$

The second equality follows from elementary results on geometric series.

It turns out that a similar result is true in $\mathbb{R}^N$ if we replace the condition $|a| < 1$ with an analogous result for matrices based around the matrix norm. We begin with the **Neumann series lemma**, which states the following:

Theorem 3.3.5 *If* $\mathbf{A}$ *is square and* $\|\mathbf{A}^j\| < 1$ *for some* $j \in \mathbb{N}$, *then* $\mathbf{I} - \mathbf{A}$ *is invertible, and*

$$(\mathbf{I} - \mathbf{A})^{-1} = \sum_{i=0}^{\infty} \mathbf{A}^i \tag{3.17}$$

Here $\mathbf{I}$ is the identity. The equality in (3.17) means that the matrix sum $\sum_{i=0}^{t} \mathbf{A}^i$ converges to the left-hand side in matrix norm as $t \to \infty$. The sum is called the **Neumann series** associated with $\mathbf{A}$. The condition in the theorem ensures that it converges. When the condition holds, (3.16) has the unique solution

$$\bar{\mathbf{x}} = (\mathbf{I} - \mathbf{A})^{-1}\mathbf{b} = \sum_{i=0}^{\infty} \mathbf{A}^i \mathbf{b}$$

How to test the condition in theorem 3.3.5? The most commonly used sufficient condition involves the **spectral radius** of $\mathbf{A}$, which is defined as

$$\varrho(\mathbf{A}) := \max\{|\lambda| : \lambda \text{ is an eigenvalue of } \mathbf{A}\} \tag{3.18}$$

In this definition, $|\lambda|$ is the **modulus** of the possibly complex number λ.[3]

Fact 3.3.14 If $\varrho(\mathbf{A}) < 1$, then $\|\mathbf{A}^j\| < 1$ for some $j \in \mathbb{N}$.

To understand why $\varrho(\mathbf{A}) < 1$ is sufficient for the result in the Neumann series lemma, consider theorem 3.3.5 in this light: The claim is that $\sum_{i=0}^{\infty} \mathbf{A}^i$ is the inverse of $\mathbf{I} - \mathbf{A}$, so $\sum_{i=0}^{t} \mathbf{A}^i(\mathbf{I} - \mathbf{A})$ should be close to $\mathbf{I}$ for large t. Evidently

$$\sum_{i=0}^{t} \mathbf{A}^i(\mathbf{I} - \mathbf{A}) = \sum_{i=0}^{t} \mathbf{A}^i - \sum_{i=0}^{t} \mathbf{A}^{i+1} = \mathbf{I} - \mathbf{A}^{t+1}$$

3. The modulus of $a + ib \in \mathbb{C}$ is $(a^2 + b^2)^{1/2}$. If the imaginary part is zero, this reduces to the usual notion of absolute value.

Hence, for the result to go through, we require $\mathbf{A}^t \to \mathbf{0}$ as $t \to \infty$. The case where $\mathbf{A}$ is diagonalizable gives the clearest insight here, so let's suppose, as in §3.3.4, that $\mathbf{A} = \mathbf{P}\mathbf{\Lambda}\mathbf{P}^{-1}$ where $\mathbf{\Lambda}$ is a diagonal matrix containing the eigenvalues $\lambda_1, \ldots, \lambda_N$ of $\mathbf{A}$ on its principal diagonal. As discussed in fact 3.3.5 on page 65, we then have

$$\mathbf{A}^t = \mathbf{P} \begin{pmatrix} \lambda_1^t & 0 & \cdots & 0 \\ 0 & \lambda_2^t & \cdots & 0 \\ \vdots & \vdots & & \vdots \\ 0 & 0 & \cdots & \lambda_N^t \end{pmatrix} \mathbf{P}^{-1}$$

If $\varrho(\mathbf{A}) < 1$, then $|\lambda_n| < 1$ for all n, and hence $\lambda_n^t \to 0$ as $t \to \infty$. It follows that $\mathbf{A}^t \to \mathbf{0}$ as required.

3.4 Further Reading

Good treatments of matrix and linear algebra include Jänich (1994) and Axler (2015).

3.5 Exercises

Ex. 3.5.1 Prove that the inverse of a nonsingular matrix is always nonsingular.

Ex. 3.5.2 Prove the claim in fact 3.2.9 on page 60 that if $\mathbf{A}$ is positive definite, then $\mathbf{A}$ is nonsingular. If you can, prove it without invoking positivity of its eigenvalues.

Ex. 3.5.3 Prove fact 3.2.10 on page 60.

Ex. 3.5.4 Let $\mathbf{A}$ be $N \times K$ and full column rank. Show that $\mathbf{x}, \mathbf{z} \in \mathbb{R}^K$ and $\mathbf{x} \neq \mathbf{z}$ implies $\mathbf{A}\mathbf{x} \neq \mathbf{A}\mathbf{z}$.

Ex. 3.5.5 Prove theorem 3.1.2 on page 51. Before doing so, you might like to review fact 2.1.9 on page 26 and theorem 3.1.1 on page 48.

Ex. 3.5.6 Let $\mathbf{A}$ be square. Assuming existence of the inverse $\mathbf{A}^{-1}$, show that $(\mathbf{A}^\top)^{-1} = (\mathbf{A}^{-1})^\top$.

Ex. 3.5.7 Show that if $\mathbf{e}_i$ and $\mathbf{e}_j$ are the ith and jth canonical basis vectors of $\mathbb{R}^N$ respectively, and $\mathbf{A}$ is an $N \times N$ matrix, then $\mathbf{e}_i^\top \mathbf{A} \mathbf{e}_j = a_{ij}$, the i, jth element of $\mathbf{A}$.

Ex. 3.5.8 Suppose that $\mathbf{A}$ is $N \times K$, the equation $\mathbf{A}\mathbf{x} = \mathbf{b}$ has a solution, and $K > N$. Show that the same equation has an infinity of solutions.[4]

4. This is the so-called "underdetermined" case, where the number of equations is less than the number of unknowns. Intuitively, we do not have enough restrictions to pin down values uniquely.

Ex. 3.5.9 Let

$$\mathbf{A} := \begin{pmatrix} 1 & -1 \\ -1 & 1 \end{pmatrix}, \quad \mathbf{B} := \begin{pmatrix} 1 & 2 \\ 2 & 1 \end{pmatrix}$$

Show that

(i) $\mathbf{A}$ is nonnegative definite.

(ii) $\mathbf{B}$ is *not* positive definite.

Ex. 3.5.10 Let $\mathbf{A}_1, \ldots, \mathbf{A}_J$ be invertible matrices. Use induction and fact 3.1.5 on page 52 to show that the product of these matrices is invertible, and, in particular, that

$$(\mathbf{A}_1 \mathbf{A}_2 \cdots \mathbf{A}_J)^{-1} = \mathbf{A}_J^{-1} \cdots \mathbf{A}_2^{-1} \mathbf{A}_1^{-1}$$

Ex. 3.5.11 Show that for any matrix $\mathbf{A}$, the matrix $\mathbf{A}^\top \mathbf{A}$ is well-defined (i.e., multiplication is possible), square, and nonnegative definite.

Ex. 3.5.12 Show that if $\mathbf{A}$ and $\mathbf{B}$ are positive definite and $\mathbf{A} + \mathbf{B}$ is well-defined, then $\mathbf{A} + \mathbf{B}$ is also positive definite.

Ex. 3.5.13 Let $\mathbf{A}$ be $N \times K$. Show that if $\mathbf{A}\mathbf{x} = \mathbf{0}$ for all $K \times 1$ vectors $\mathbf{x}$, then $\mathbf{A} = \mathbf{0}$ (i.e., every element of $\mathbf{A}$ is zero). Show as a corollary that if $\mathbf{A}$ and $\mathbf{B}$ are $N \times K$ and $\mathbf{A}\mathbf{x} = \mathbf{B}\mathbf{x}$ for all $K \times 1$ vectors $\mathbf{x}$, then $\mathbf{A} = \mathbf{B}$.

Ex. 3.5.14 Let $\mathbf{I}$ be the $N \times N$ identity matrix.

(i) Explain why $\mathbf{I}$ is full column rank.

(ii) Show that $\mathbf{I}$ is the inverse of itself.

(iii) Let $\mathbf{A} := \alpha \mathbf{I}$. Give a condition on α such that $\mathbf{A}$ is positive definite.

Ex. 3.5.15 Let $\mathbf{X} := \mathbf{I} - 2\mathbf{u}\mathbf{u}^\top$, where $\mathbf{u}$ is an $N \times 1$ vector with $\|\mathbf{u}\| = 1$. Show that $\mathbf{X}$ is symmetric and $\mathbf{X}\mathbf{X} = \mathbf{I}$.

Ex. 3.5.16 Recall the definition of similarity of matrices, as given in §3.3.4. Let's write $\mathbf{A} \sim \mathbf{B}$ if $\mathbf{A}$ is similar to $\mathbf{B}$. Show that $\sim$ is an **equivalence relation** on the set of $N \times N$ matrices. In particular, show that, for any $N \times N$ matrices $\mathbf{A}, \mathbf{B}$, and $\mathbf{C}$, we have (i) $\mathbf{A} \sim \mathbf{A}$, (ii) $\mathbf{A} \sim \mathbf{B}$ implies $\mathbf{B} \sim \mathbf{A}$ and (iii) $\mathbf{A} \sim \mathbf{B}$ and $\mathbf{B} \sim \mathbf{C}$ implies $\mathbf{A} \sim \mathbf{C}$.

Ex. 3.5.17 Confirm the claim in fact 3.2.6 on page 56.

Ex. 3.5.18 Show that $\mathbf{A}$ is nonsingular if and only if 0 is *not* an eigenvalue for $\mathbf{A}$.

Ex. 3.5.19 Show that the only nonsingular idempotent matrix is the identity matrix.

Ex. 3.5.20 Let $\mathbf{1}$ be $N \times 1$ and let $\mathbf{P} := \frac{1}{N}\mathbf{1}\mathbf{1}^\top$. Verify that $\mathbf{P}$ is idempotent.

Ex. 3.5.21 Show that, for conformable and suitably invertible matrices $\mathbf{A}$, $\mathbf{U}$ and $\mathbf{W}$, we have

$$(\mathbf{A}+\mathbf{U}\mathbf{W})^{-1} = \mathbf{A}^{-1} - \mathbf{A}^{-1}\mathbf{U}\left(\mathbf{I}+\mathbf{W}\mathbf{A}^{-1}\mathbf{U}\right)^{-1}\mathbf{W}\mathbf{A}^{-1}$$

Ex. 3.5.22 Let $\mathbf{Q}$ be an orthogonal matrix. Show that $\mathbf{Q}^{-1} = \mathbf{Q}^\top$ and $\det \mathbf{Q} \in \{-1, 1\}$ both hold.

Ex. 3.5.23 Use theorem 3.3.4 (page 66) to prove the following part of fact 3.2.8: A symmetric matrix $\mathbf{A}$ is positive definite if and only if its eigenvalues are all positive.

Ex. 3.5.24 Show that if $\mathbf{Q}$ is an $N \times N$ orthogonal matrix, then $\mathbf{Q}$ is an isometry on $\mathbb{R}^N$. That is, for any $\mathbf{x}, \mathbf{y} \in \mathbb{R}^N$, we have $\|\mathbf{Q}\mathbf{x} - \mathbf{Q}\mathbf{y}\| = \|\mathbf{x} - \mathbf{y}\|$.

Ex. 3.5.25 Let $\mathbf{P}$ be square, symmetric and idempotent. Let $S :=$ colspace $\mathbf{P}$. Show that $\mathbf{P} = \operatorname{proj} S$.

Ex. 3.5.26 Consider theorem 3.3.2 on page 63. If $N = K$, what does $\hat{\mathbf{x}}$ reduce to? Interpret.

Ex. 3.5.27 Let S be a linear subspace of $\mathbb{R}^N$ and let $\mathbf{P} = \operatorname{proj} S$. Show that trace $\mathbf{P} = \dim S$ without using the idempotence connection in fact 3.3.3.

Ex. 3.5.28 Show that when $N \times K$ matrix $\mathbf{B}$ is full column rank, the matrix $\mathbf{B}^\top\mathbf{B}$ is nonsingular.[5]

Ex. 3.5.29 Let $\mathbf{A}$ be an $N \times N$ matrix.

(i) Show that if $\mathbf{I} - \mathbf{A}$ is idempotent, then $\mathbf{A}$ is idempotent.

(ii) Show that if $\mathbf{A}$ is both symmetric and idempotent, then the matrix $\mathbf{I} - 2\mathbf{A}$ is orthogonal.

Ex. 3.5.30 Prove theorem 3.3.1 on page 60. (This takes a bit of work, of course.)

Ex. 3.5.31 Let $\mathbf{P} = \mathbf{B}(\mathbf{B}^\top\mathbf{B})^{-1}\mathbf{B}^\top$, as in theorem 3.3.1, and let $\mathbf{M}$ be the residual projection. Show that $\mathbf{M}\mathbf{B} = \mathbf{0}$ using matrix algebra.

Ex. 3.5.32 Let $\mathbf{A}$ be an $N \times K$ matrix with linearly independent columns and QR factorization $\mathbf{A} = \mathbf{Q}\mathbf{R}$ (see §3.3.3). Fix $\mathbf{b} \in \mathbb{R}^N$. Show that $\hat{\mathbf{x}}$ defined in (3.12) can also be written as $\hat{\mathbf{x}} = \mathbf{R}^{-1}\mathbf{Q}^\top\mathbf{b}$.

Ex. 3.5.33 Let's prove the Cauchy–Schwarz inequality $|\mathbf{x}^\top\mathbf{y}| \leqslant \|\mathbf{x}\|\|\mathbf{y}\|$ from fact 2.1.2 on page 13 via the orthogonal projection theorem. Let $\mathbf{y}$ and $\mathbf{x}$ be nonzero vectors in $\mathbb{R}^N$ (since if either equals zero then the inequality is trivial), and let span$\{\mathbf{x}\}$ be all vectors of the form $\alpha\mathbf{x}$ for $\alpha \in \mathbb{R}$.

5. Hint: In view of fact 3.2.9, it suffices to show that $\mathbf{B}^\top\mathbf{B}$ is positive definite.

(i) Letting $\mathbf{P}$ be the orthogonal projection onto $\operatorname{span}\{\mathbf{x}\}$, show that

$$\mathbf{P}\mathbf{y} = \frac{\mathbf{x}^\top \mathbf{y}}{\mathbf{x}^\top \mathbf{x}} \mathbf{x}$$

(ii) Using this expression and any relevant properties of orthogonal projections (see theorem 2.2.2 on page 31), confirm the Cauchy–Schwarz inequality.

Ex. 3.5.34 Prove the claim made after theorem 3.3.2 regarding failure of uniqueness without full column rank. In particular, let $\mathbf{A}$ be $N \times K$ with linearly *dependent* columns, and let $\mathbf{P}\mathbf{b}$ be the closest point to $\mathbf{b}$ in colspace $\mathbf{A}$. Prove that there are infinitely many $\mathbf{x} \in \mathbb{R}^K$ such that $\mathbf{P}\mathbf{b} = \mathbf{A}\mathbf{x}$.

Ex. 3.5.35 Let $\mathbf{A}$ be symmetric and idempotent. Show that every eigenvalue of $\mathbf{A}$ is either 0 or 1.

Ex. 3.5.36 Show that if $\mathbf{A}$ is positive definite, then there exists a symmetric matrix $\mathbf{C}$ such that $\mathbf{C}\mathbf{A}\mathbf{C} = \mathbf{I}$.[6]

3.5.1 Solutions to Selected Exercises

Solution to Ex. 3.5.1. Let $\mathbf{A}$ be a nonsingular matrix. Being nonsingular, $\mathbf{A}$ is invertible, with inverse $\mathbf{A}^{-1}$. By the definition of the inverse, we have $\mathbf{A}\mathbf{A}^{-1} = \mathbf{A}^{-1}\mathbf{A} = \mathbf{I}$, where $\mathbf{I}$ is the identity. This tells us directly that $\mathbf{A}$ is an inverse for $\mathbf{A}^{-1}$. Hence $\mathbf{A}^{-1}$ is invertible, which is equivalent to nonsingularity. □

Solution to Ex. 3.5.2. Let $\mathbf{A}$ be positive definite and consider the following: If $\mathbf{A}$ is singular, then there exists nonzero $\mathbf{x}$ with $\mathbf{A}\mathbf{x} = \mathbf{0}$ (see fact 3.1.3 on page 50). But then $\mathbf{x}^\top \mathbf{A}\mathbf{x} = 0$ for nonzero $\mathbf{x}$. Contradiction. □

Solution to Ex. 3.5.3. If $\mathbf{x} = \mathbf{e}_n$, then $\mathbf{x}^\top \mathbf{A}\mathbf{x} = a_{nn}$. The claim follows. □

Solution to Ex. 3.5.4. Let $\mathbf{A}$, $\mathbf{x}$ and $\mathbf{z}$ be as stated in the question. Suppose, to the contrary, that $\mathbf{A}\mathbf{x} = \mathbf{A}\mathbf{z}$. Then $\mathbf{A}(\mathbf{x} - \mathbf{z}) = \mathbf{0}$, which, by fact 3.1.2 on page 50, implies $\mathbf{x} - \mathbf{z} = \mathbf{0}$, or $\mathbf{x} = \mathbf{z}$. Contradiction. □

Solution to Ex. 3.5.5. Let $\mathbf{A}$ be a nonsingular matrix and let T be the linear map associated with $\mathbf{A}$ via $T\mathbf{x} = \mathbf{A}\mathbf{x}$. Since A is nonsingular, T is also, by definition, nonsingular and hence, by fact 2.1.9 on page 26, has a nonsingular inverse T^{-1}. Being nonsingular, T^{-1} is necessarily linear, and hence, by theorem 3.1.1 on page 48, there exists a matrix $\mathbf{B}$ such that $T^{-1}\mathbf{x} = \mathbf{B}\mathbf{x}$ for all $\mathbf{x}$. By the definition of the inverse, we

6. Hint: Look at fact 3.3.9 and the argument that follows it.

have $\mathbf{ABx} = T(T^{-1}(\mathbf{x})) = \mathbf{x} = \mathbf{Ix}$. Since this holds for any $\mathbf{x}$, we have $\mathbf{AB} = \mathbf{I}$ (see ex. 3.5.13). A similar argument shows that $\mathbf{BA} = \mathbf{I}$.

Regarding the second claim, $\mathbf{A}^{-1}\mathbf{b}$ is a solution to $\mathbf{Ax} = \mathbf{b}$, since $\mathbf{AA}^{-1}\mathbf{b} = \mathbf{Ib} = \mathbf{b}$. Uniqueness follows from fact 3.1.3 (and, in particular, the fact that nonsingularity of $\mathbf{A}$ includes the implication that the map $\mathbf{x} \mapsto \mathbf{Ax}$ is one-to-one). □

Solution to Ex. 3.5.8. Since the columns of $\mathbf{A}$ consist of K vectors in $\mathbb{R}^N$, the fact that $K > N$ implies that not all of the columns of $\mathbf{A}$ are linearly independent. (Recall theorem 2.1.3 on page 20.) It follows that $\mathbf{Az} = \mathbf{0}$ for some nonzero $\mathbf{z}$ in $\mathbb{R}^K$, and hence $\mathbf{A}\lambda\mathbf{z} = \mathbf{0}$ for any scalar λ. Now suppose that some $\mathbf{x}$ solves $\mathbf{Ax} = \mathbf{b}$. Then, for any $\lambda \in \mathbb{R}$, we have $\mathbf{Ax} + \mathbf{A}\lambda\mathbf{z} = \mathbf{A}(\mathbf{x} + \lambda\mathbf{z}) = \mathbf{b}$. This proves the claim. □

Solution to Ex. 3.5.14. The solutions are as follows: (1) $\mathbf{I}$ is full column rank because its columns are the canonical basis vectors, which are independent. (2) By definition, $\mathbf{B}$ is the inverse of $\mathbf{A}$ if $\mathbf{BA} = \mathbf{AB} = \mathbf{I}$. It follows immediately that $\mathbf{I}$ is the inverse of itself. (3) A sufficient condition is $\alpha > 0$. If this holds, then given $\mathbf{x} \neq \mathbf{0}$, we have $\mathbf{x}^\top \alpha \mathbf{I} \mathbf{x} = \alpha \|\mathbf{x}\|^2 > 0$. □

Solution to Ex. 3.5.15. First, $\mathbf{X}$ is symmetric because

$$\mathbf{X}^\top = (\mathbf{I} - 2\mathbf{uu}^\top)^\top = \mathbf{I} - 2(\mathbf{uu}^\top)^\top = \mathbf{I} - 2(\mathbf{u}^\top)^\top\mathbf{u}^\top = \mathbf{I} - 2\mathbf{uu}^\top = \mathbf{X}$$

Second, $\mathbf{XX} = \mathbf{I}$ because

$$\begin{aligned}\mathbf{XX} = (\mathbf{I} - 2\mathbf{uu}^\top)(\mathbf{I}^\top - 2\mathbf{uu}^\top) &= \mathbf{II} - 2\mathbf{I}2\mathbf{uu}^\top + (2\mathbf{uu}^\top)(2\mathbf{uu}^\top) \\ &= \mathbf{I} - 4\mathbf{uu}^\top + 4\mathbf{uu}^\top\mathbf{uu}^\top = \mathbf{I} - 4\mathbf{uu}^\top + 4\mathbf{uu}^\top = \mathbf{I}\end{aligned}$$

The second last equality is due to the assumption that $\mathbf{u}^\top\mathbf{u} = \|\mathbf{u}\|^2 = 1$. □

Solution to Ex. 3.5.17. Let $\mathbf{A}$ be $N \times N$ and let $\mathbf{I}$ be the $N \times N$ identity. We have

$$\begin{aligned}\det(\mathbf{A} - \lambda\mathbf{I}) = 0 &\iff \mathbf{A} - \lambda\mathbf{I} \text{ is singular} \\ &\iff \exists\, \mathbf{x} \neq \mathbf{0} \text{ s.t. } (\mathbf{A} - \lambda\mathbf{I})\mathbf{x} = \mathbf{0} \iff \exists\, \mathbf{x} \neq \mathbf{0} \text{ s.t. } \mathbf{Ax} = \lambda\mathbf{x}\end{aligned}$$

In other words, λ is an eigenvalue of $\mathbf{A}$. □

Solution to Ex. 3.5.19. Suppose that $\mathbf{A}$ is both idempotent and nonsingular. From idempotence we have $\mathbf{AA} = \mathbf{A}$. Premultiplying by $\mathbf{A}^{-1}$ gives $\mathbf{A} = \mathbf{I}$. □

Solution to Ex. 3.5.21. The claim is true because

$$\begin{aligned}(\mathbf{A}+\mathbf{UW})&\left[\mathbf{A}^{-1}-\mathbf{A}^{-1}\mathbf{U}\left(\mathbf{I}+\mathbf{WA}^{-1}\mathbf{U}\right)^{-1}\mathbf{WA}^{-1}\right]\\&=\mathbf{I}+\mathbf{UWA}^{-1}-(\mathbf{U}+\mathbf{UWA}^{-1}\mathbf{U})(\mathbf{I}+\mathbf{WA}^{-1}\mathbf{U})^{-1}\mathbf{WA}^{-1}\\&=\mathbf{I}+\mathbf{UWA}^{-1}-\mathbf{U}(\mathbf{I}+\mathbf{WA}^{-1}\mathbf{U})(\mathbf{I}+\mathbf{WA}^{-1}\mathbf{U})^{-1}\mathbf{WA}^{-1}\\&=\mathbf{I}+\mathbf{UWA}^{-1}-\mathbf{UWA}^{-1}=\mathbf{I}\end{aligned}$$

□

Solution to Ex. 3.5.22. Let $\mathbf{Q}$ be an orthogonal matrix with columns $\mathbf{u}_1,\ldots,\mathbf{u}_N$. By the definition of matrix multiplication, the m,nth element of $\mathbf{Q}^\top\mathbf{Q}$ is $\mathbf{u}_m^\top\mathbf{u}_n$, which is 1 if $m=n$ and zero otherwise. Hence $\mathbf{Q}^\top\mathbf{Q}=\mathbf{I}$. It follows from fact 3.1.4 on page 51 that $\mathbf{Q}^\top$ is the inverse of $\mathbf{Q}$.

To see that $\det\mathbf{Q}\in\{-1,1\}$, apply the results of fact 3.1.6 (page 52) and fact 3.2.5 (page 55) to the equality $\mathbf{Q}^\top\mathbf{Q}=\mathbf{I}$ to obtain $\det(\mathbf{Q})^2=1$. The claim follows. □

Solution to Ex. 3.5.23. Suppose that $\mathbf{A}$ is symmetric with eigenvalues $\lambda_1,\ldots,\lambda_N$. By theorem 3.3.4 we can decompose it as $\mathbf{A}=\mathbf{Q}\mathbf{\Lambda}\mathbf{Q}^\top$, where $\mathbf{\Lambda}$ is the diagonal matrix formed from eigenvalues and $\mathbf{Q}$ is an orthogonal matrix. Fixing $\mathbf{x}\in\mathbb{R}^N$ and letting $\mathbf{y}:=\mathbf{Q}^\top\mathbf{x}$, we have

$$\mathbf{x}^\top\mathbf{A}\mathbf{x}=(\mathbf{Q}^\top\mathbf{x})^\top\mathbf{\Lambda}(\mathbf{Q}^\top\mathbf{x})=\mathbf{y}^\top\mathbf{\Lambda}\mathbf{y}=\lambda_1y_1^2+\cdots+\lambda_Ny_N^2 \tag{3.19}$$

Suppose that all eigenvalues are positive. Take $\mathbf{x}$ to be nonzero. The vector $\mathbf{y}$ must be nonzero (why?), and it follows from (3.19) that $\mathbf{x}^\top\mathbf{A}\mathbf{x}>0$. Hence $\mathbf{A}$ is positive definite as claimed.

Conversely, suppose that $\mathbf{A}$ is positive definite. Fix $n\leqslant N$ and set $\mathbf{x}=\mathbf{Q}\mathbf{e}_n$. Evidently $\mathbf{x}$ is nonzero (why?). Hence $\mathbf{x}^\top\mathbf{A}\mathbf{x}>0$. Since $\mathbf{Q}^\top$ is the inverse of $\mathbf{Q}$, it follows that

$$\lambda_n=\mathbf{e}_n^\top\mathbf{\Lambda}\mathbf{e}_n=(\mathbf{Q}^\top\mathbf{x})^\top\mathbf{\Lambda}\mathbf{Q}^\top\mathbf{x}=\mathbf{x}^\top\mathbf{Q}\mathbf{\Lambda}\mathbf{Q}^\top\mathbf{x}=\mathbf{x}^\top\mathbf{A}\mathbf{x}>0$$

Since n was arbitrary, all eigenvalues are positive. □

Solution to Ex. 3.5.24. Fixing $\mathbf{x},\mathbf{y}\in\mathbb{R}^N$ and letting $\mathbf{z}:=\mathbf{x}-\mathbf{y}$ we have

$$\|\mathbf{Qx}-\mathbf{Qy}\|^2=\|\mathbf{Qz}\|^2=(\mathbf{Qz})^\top\mathbf{Qz}=\mathbf{z}^\top\mathbf{Q}^\top\mathbf{Qz}=\mathbf{z}^\top\mathbf{z}=\|\mathbf{z}\|^2=\|\mathbf{x}-\mathbf{y}\|^2$$

□

Solution to Ex. 3.5.26. If $N=K$, then, in view of the full column rank assumption and theorem 3.1.2 on page 51, the matrix $\mathbf{A}$ is nonsingular. By fact 3.2.5 on page 55, $\mathbf{A}^\top$ is likewise nonsingular. Applying the usual rule for inverse of products (fact 3.1.5

on page 52), we have

$$\hat{\mathbf{x}} = (\mathbf{A}^\top \mathbf{A})^{-1} \mathbf{A}^\top \mathbf{b} = \mathbf{A}^{-1} (\mathbf{A}^\top)^{-1} \mathbf{A}^\top \mathbf{b} = \mathbf{A}^{-1} \mathbf{b}$$

This is the solution to the system $\mathbf{A}\mathbf{x} = \mathbf{b}$ when $\mathbf{A}$ is square and invertible. □

Solution to Ex. 3.5.27. Let S and $\mathbf{P}$ be as in the statement of the exercise and let $K := \dim S$. We aim to show that $\operatorname{trace} \mathbf{P} = K$. Let $\mathbf{B}$ be a matrix such that its columns form a basis for S. By the definition of dimension, $\mathbf{B}$ has K columns. Applying (3.8), we have

$$\operatorname{trace} \mathbf{P} = \operatorname{trace}(\mathbf{B}(\mathbf{B}^\top \mathbf{B})^{-1} \mathbf{B}^\top)$$

Recalling fact 3.2.3, we rearrange to get

$$\operatorname{trace}[\mathbf{B}(\mathbf{B}^\top \mathbf{B})^{-1} \mathbf{B}^\top] = \operatorname{trace}[(\mathbf{B}^\top \mathbf{B})^{-1} \mathbf{B}^\top \mathbf{B}] = \operatorname{trace} \mathbf{I}$$

where $\mathbf{I}$ is the $K \times K$ identity. The claim follows. □

Solution to Ex. 3.5.28. Let $\mathbf{A} = \mathbf{B}^\top \mathbf{B}$. It suffices to show that $\mathbf{A}$ is positive definite, since this implies that its determinant is strictly positive, and any matrix with nonzero determinant is nonsingular. To see that $\mathbf{A}$ is positive definite, pick any $\mathbf{b} \neq \mathbf{0}$. We must show that $\mathbf{b}^\top \mathbf{A} \mathbf{b} > 0$. To see this, observe that

$$\mathbf{b}^\top \mathbf{A} \mathbf{b} = \mathbf{b}^\top \mathbf{B}^\top \mathbf{B} \mathbf{b} = (\mathbf{B}\mathbf{b})^\top \mathbf{B}\mathbf{b} = \|\mathbf{B}\mathbf{b}\|^2$$

By the properties of norms, the last term is zero only when $\mathbf{B}\mathbf{b} = \mathbf{0}$. But this is not true because $\mathbf{b} \neq \mathbf{0}$ and $\mathbf{B}$ is full column rank (see theorem 2.1.1). □

Solution to Ex. 3.5.30. Let S and $\mathbf{P}$ be as stated in theorem 3.3.1 and let $\mathbf{B}$ be a matrix such that the columns of $\mathbf{B}$ form a basis of S. Fix $\mathbf{y} \in \mathbb{R}^N$. The claim is that $\hat{\mathbf{y}} := \mathbf{B}(\mathbf{B}^\top \mathbf{B})^{-1} \mathbf{B}^\top \mathbf{y}$ is the orthogonal projection of $\mathbf{y}$ onto S. To verify this, we need to show that

(i) $\hat{\mathbf{y}} \in S$ and

(ii) $\mathbf{y} - \hat{\mathbf{y}} \perp S$.

Part (i) is true because $\hat{\mathbf{y}}$ can be written as $\hat{\mathbf{y}} = \mathbf{B}\mathbf{x}$ where $\mathbf{x} := (\mathbf{B}^\top \mathbf{B})^{-1} \mathbf{B}^\top \mathbf{y}$. The vector $\mathbf{B}\mathbf{x}$ is a linear combination of the columns of $\mathbf{B}$. Since these columns form a basis of S, they must lie in S. Hence $\hat{\mathbf{y}} \in S$ as claimed.

Regarding (ii), from the assumption that $\mathbf{B}$ gives a basis for S, all points in S have the form $\mathbf{B}\mathbf{x}$ for some $\mathbf{x} \in \mathbb{R}^K$. Thus (ii) translates to the claim that

$$\mathbf{y} - \mathbf{B}(\mathbf{B}^\top \mathbf{B})^{-1} \mathbf{B}^\top \mathbf{y} \perp \mathbf{B}\mathbf{x} \quad \text{for all } \mathbf{x} \in \mathbb{R}^K$$

This is true because if $\mathbf{x} \in \mathbb{R}^K$, then

$$(\mathbf{B}\mathbf{x})^\top[\mathbf{y} - \mathbf{B}(\mathbf{B}^\top\mathbf{B})^{-1}\mathbf{B}^\top\mathbf{y}] = \mathbf{x}^\top[\mathbf{B}^\top\mathbf{y} - \mathbf{B}^\top\mathbf{B}(\mathbf{B}^\top\mathbf{B})^{-1}\mathbf{B}^\top\mathbf{y}] = \mathbf{x}^\top[\mathbf{B}^\top\mathbf{y} - \mathbf{B}^\top\mathbf{y}] = 0 \quad \square$$

Solution to Ex. 3.5.31. These are straightforward. For example,

$$\mathbf{M}\mathbf{B} = \mathbf{B} - \mathbf{B}(\mathbf{B}^\top\mathbf{B})^{-1}\mathbf{B}^\top\mathbf{B} = \mathbf{0} \quad \square$$

Solution to Ex. 3.5.32. Let $\mathbf{A}$, $\mathbf{Q}$, $\mathbf{R}$ and $\mathbf{b} \in \mathbb{R}^N$ be as in the statement of the exercise. The claim is that $\hat{\mathbf{x}}$ defined in (3.12) is equal to $\tilde{\mathbf{x}} := \mathbf{R}^{-1}\mathbf{Q}^\top\mathbf{b}$. To show this, in view of linear independence of the columns of $\mathbf{A}$, it suffices to show that $\mathbf{A}\tilde{\mathbf{x}} = \mathbf{A}\hat{\mathbf{x}}$, or

$$\mathbf{A}(\mathbf{A}^\top\mathbf{A})^{-1}\mathbf{A}^\top\mathbf{b} = \mathbf{Q}\mathbf{R}\mathbf{R}^{-1}\mathbf{Q}^\top\mathbf{b}$$

After simplifying, we see it suffices to show that $\mathbf{A}(\mathbf{A}^\top\mathbf{A})^{-1}\mathbf{A}^\top = \mathbf{Q}\mathbf{Q}^\top$. Since $\mathbf{A}$ and $\mathbf{Q}$ have the same column space, this follows from theorem 3.3.1 on page 60. $\square$

Solution to Ex. 3.5.33. Regarding (i), the expression for $\mathbf{P}\mathbf{y}$ given in exercise 3.5.33 can also be written as $\mathbf{x}(\mathbf{x}^\top\mathbf{x})^{-1}\mathbf{x}^\top\mathbf{y}$. Since $\mathbf{x}$ is a basis for $\text{span}\{\mathbf{x}\}$, the validity of this expression as the projection onto $\text{span}\{\mathbf{x}\}$ follows immediately from theorem 3.3.1. Regarding (ii), recall that orthogonal projections contract norms, so that, in particular, $\|\mathbf{P}\mathbf{y}\| \leqslant \|\mathbf{y}\|$ must hold. Using our expression for $\mathbf{P}\mathbf{y}$ from (i) and rearranging gives the desired bound $|\mathbf{x}^\top\mathbf{y}| \leqslant \|\mathbf{x}\|\|\mathbf{y}\|$. $\square$

Solution to Ex. 3.5.34. By the definition of orthogonal projection, $\mathbf{P}\mathbf{b} \in \text{colspace}\,\mathbf{A}$, and hence there exists a vector $\mathbf{x}$ such that $\mathbf{P}\mathbf{b} = \mathbf{A}\mathbf{x}$. Since $\mathbf{A}$ has linearly dependent columns, there exists a nonzero vector $\mathbf{a}$ such that $\mathbf{A}\mathbf{a} = \mathbf{0}$. Hence $\mathbf{A}\lambda\mathbf{a} = \mathbf{0}$ for all $\lambda \in \mathbb{R}$. For each such λ we have $\mathbf{P}\mathbf{b} = \mathbf{A}\mathbf{x} = \mathbf{A}\mathbf{x} + \mathbf{A}\lambda\mathbf{a} = \mathbf{A}(\mathbf{x} + \lambda\mathbf{a})$. This proves the claim. $\square$

Solution to Ex. 3.5.35. By the spectral decomposition theorem (page 66), we know that $\mathbf{A} = \mathbf{Q}\mathbf{\Lambda}\mathbf{Q}^\top$ where $\mathbf{Q}$ is an orthogonal matrix and $\mathbf{\Lambda}$ is the diagonal matrix formed from the eigenvalues of $\mathbf{A}$. It follows (see page 65) that $\mathbf{A}^2 = \mathbf{Q}\mathbf{\Lambda}^2\mathbf{Q}^\top$ and, since $\mathbf{A}$ is idempotent, that $\mathbf{Q}\mathbf{\Lambda}\mathbf{Q}^\top = \mathbf{Q}\mathbf{\Lambda}^2\mathbf{Q}^\top$. From this we obtain $\mathbf{\Lambda} = \mathbf{\Lambda}^2$. For diagonal matrices, powers are obtained by taking powers of the diagonal elements, from which we get $\lambda_n = \lambda_n^2$ for any eigenvalue λ_n. Hence $\lambda_n \in \{0, 1\}$ as claimed. $\square$

Chapter 4

Foundations of Probability

Probability theory is one of the foundation stones of statistics and econometrics. We'll start at the basics but move relatively quickly.

4.1 Probabilistic Models

Probability is a technically demanding field. The main reason is that we want to assign probabilities to all manner of events. The set of possible events can be very large, and we need ways to manage this complexity. In this and the next few sections, we'll review the basic machinery involved and why this machinery is necessary. At the same time, we'll skip several details that would take us too far away from econometric theory. This will cost little in terms of understanding.

One concept worth mentioning before we start is countable and uncountable sets. In essence, a nonempty set S is called **countable** if it is either finite or can be represented as a sequence, and **uncountable** if is not countable. In probability theory this distinction is important. A quick review can be found in §15.3.

4.1.1 Sample Spaces and Events

In setting up a probabilistic model, we start with the notion of a **sample space**, which we think of as being a "list" of all possible outcomes in a given random experiment. In general, the sample space can be any nonempty set, and is usually denoted Ω. A typical element of Ω is denoted ω. The general idea is that a realization of uncertainty will lead to the selection of a particular $\omega \in \Omega$.

Example 4.1.1 In a random experiment that involves rolling a die once, the set of possible outcomes is naturally represented by $\Omega := \{1, \ldots, 6\}$.

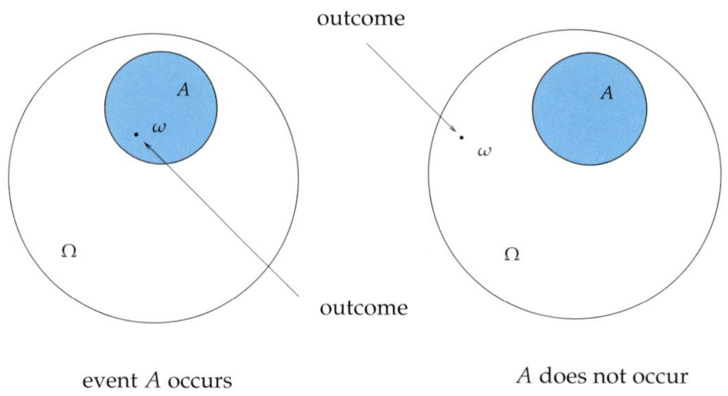

Figure 4.1 Outcomes and events

Example 4.1.2 Imagine that Burton Malkiel's blindfolded monkey throws darts at a dartboard of radius 1. To record the outcome we impose ordinary Cartesian coordinates with origin at the center of the board. Let (h, v) be a typical location measured on the horizontal and vertical coordinates respectively. A natural sample space is $\Omega := \{(h, v) \in \mathbb{R}^2 : \|(h, v)\| \leqslant 1\}$. This set is also called the **unit disk** in $\mathbb{R}^2$.

Example 4.1.3 Consider an experiment where we roll a die twice. A suitable sample space is the set of integer pairs (i, j) with $1 \leqslant i, j \leqslant 6$. The first element i represents the outcome of the first roll, while the second element j represents the outcome of the second roll. Thus $\Omega := \{(i, j) : i, j \in \{1, \ldots, 6\}\} = \{1, \ldots, 6\} \times \{1, \ldots, 6\}$.

Once we have a sample space in place we can start to think about events. In the language of probability theory, an **event** is just a subset of Ω (with some caveats that will be addressed below). An event A occurs whenever the individual $\omega \in \Omega$ selected in the random experiment happens to lie in A. Figure 4.1 illustrates.

4.1.1.1 Probabilities and Events

The next thing we need to do is to assign probabilities to outcomes. One idea is to start by assigning appropriate probabilities to every ω in Ω. We could then derive the probability of events by looking at the probabilities attached to points contained in those events. It turns out, however, that this is not the best approach, at least if we want to consider uncountable Ω. Rather, the standard approach is to *directly assign probabilities to subsets of* Ω *instead.*

To see why the first approach is problematic, consider the dart throwing model in example 4.1.2, where Ω is the unit disk in $\mathbb{R}^2$. Imagine that hitting any point in Ω is "equally likely." We can model this by assuming that the probability the dart lands in some region A of the dartboard (some $A \subset \Omega$) is simply proportional to the area of A.

Consider now the probability of hitting some individual point $\omega \in \Omega$. Intuitively, this should be less than the probability of hitting any region A containing ω. By choosing A to be sufficiently small in area, we can show that the probability of hitting ω is less than ϵ for any given $\epsilon > 0$. We are forced to conclude that the probability of hitting the individual point ω is zero.[1]

This example shows that in many sensible models the probability assigned to individual points in the sample space must be zero. If you reflect on this for even a moment you will agree that there is no way to build up a useful probabilistic model with such information alone. Hence we must assign probabilities directly to the events themselves.

4.1.1.2 Choosing the Set of Events

Should we assign probabilities to every possible event—that is, to every possible subset of Ω? In the dart model above, we could say that the probability the dart lands in any region $A \subset \Omega$ is equal to the area of A divided by the area of Ω itself, which is π. In symbols,

$$\mathbb{P}(A) = \frac{\lambda(A)}{\pi} \quad \text{where } \lambda(A) := \text{ the area of set } A \tag{4.1}$$

This seems sensible enough. For example, if $A = \Omega$, then $\mathbb{P}(A) = \pi/\pi = 1$, as it should be. If A is the top half of the dartboard then $\mathbb{P}(A) = 0.5$, and so on.

Unfortunately, if we think carefully about this approach, some cracks start to appear. What exactly do we mean by "area of A"? If A is a circle, then its area is π times the square of its radius. If A is a rectangle, then its area is the product of its two sides. But how about the area of more general subsets of Ω?

It turns out that assigning area to all subsets of Ω in a consistent way is problematic. The reason is that Ω contains an awful lot of subsets, and some of them can be manipulated to exhibit very strange phenomena. (If you are curious, look up the Banach–Tarski paradox for a hint of the problems that can occur when we try to assign notions like area or volume to arbitrary sets.) We can dream up all sorts of strange events that confound our ability to construct a sensible probabilistic model.

Because of this, when Ω is uncountable, we usually resist taking the set of events to be all subsets of Ω. Instead, we take them to be some family of "well-behaved" subsets of Ω, denoted below by $\mathscr{F}$, and only assign probabilities to elements of $\mathscr{F}$.

There is of course a trade-off here. If we restrict $\mathscr{F}$ to be a small fraction of the subsets of Ω, then assigning probabilities becomes easy and we can eliminate strange

1. If p is a nonnegative number satisfying $p \geqslant 0$ and $p \leqslant \epsilon$ for all $\epsilon > 0$, then $p = 0$ must hold.

behavior. But if we make $\mathscr{F}$ too small, then we might not be able to assign probabilities to events that we care about. For example, in the dartboard model, if we restrict $\mathscr{F}$ to be the set of rectangles, then we can easily measure area and hence assign probabilities via (4.1). But this excludes interesting events such as the dart landing in the top half of the board.

How can we ensure that $\mathscr{F}$ is large enough? To think about this in a systematic way, suppose that $A \in \mathscr{F}$, and that $\mathbb{P}(A)$ is well-defined and represents the "probability of event A." Now, given that we can assign a probability to the event A, it would be unfortunate if we couldn't assign a probability to the event "not A", which corresponds to A^c. So normally we require that if $A \in \mathscr{F}$, then $A^c \in \mathscr{F}$. When this is true, we say that $\mathscr{F}$ is "closed under the taking of complements."

Further, suppose that A and B are both in $\mathscr{F}$, and we can assign probabilities to these events. In this case, it would be natural to think about the probability of the event "A or B", which corresponds to $A \cup B$. So we also require that if A and B are in $\mathscr{F}$, then $A \cup B$ is likewise in $\mathscr{F}$. We say that $\mathscr{F}$ is "closed under the taking of unions." In fact for technical reasons it turns out that we prefer $\mathscr{F}$ to be closed under the taking of countable unions, which means that if $A_1, A_2, \ldots$ is a sequence of sets in $\mathscr{F}$, then its union is likewise in $\mathscr{F}$.

A set $\mathscr{F}$ of subsets of a given set Ω that satisfies all these properties is called a σ-algebra. Formally, $\mathscr{F}$ is a **σ-algebra** on Ω if

(i) $A \in \mathscr{F} \implies A^c \in \mathscr{F}$,

(ii) $A_1, A_2, \ldots \in \mathscr{F} \implies \cup_{n=1}^{\infty} A_n \in \mathscr{F}$, and

(iii) $\Omega \in \mathscr{F}$.

Note that (i) and (iii) together imply that $\emptyset \in \mathscr{F}$. In this context, the empty set $\emptyset$ is called the **impossible event**. In contrast, Ω is called the **certain event** because it always occurs (regardless of which outcome ω is selected, $\omega \in \Omega$ is true by definition).

The σ-algebra of events $\mathscr{F}$ we choose to pair with a given Ω can vary from problem to problem. There is however one particular σ-algebra that you should know at least something about, and that is the standard σ-algebra we use to pair with ordinary vector space $\mathbb{R}^N$. This σ-algebra is called the Borel sets.

To understand the idea, consider the following: The property of $\mathscr{F}$ being a σ-algebra seems to imply that $\mathscr{F}$ is a relatively rich class of sets. After all, we can take complements and unions (and intersections too—see ex. 4.4.1) without ever leaving $\mathscr{F}$. However, there are trivial examples of σ-algebras, such as $\mathscr{F} := \{\emptyset, \Omega\}$. So if we want to pin down a large and useful class of events, the best way to proceed is to assume not only that $\mathscr{F}$ is a σ-algebra, but also that $\mathscr{F}$ contains some fundamental sets that we are likely to want to attach probabilities to, such as intervals and rectangles.

In this connection, the **Borel subsets of $\mathbb{R}^N$** are defined as the smallest σ-algebra of subset of $\mathbb{R}^N$ that contains all rectangles in $\mathbb{R}^N$. (See §15.1 if you wish to learn more about rectangles.) This definition turns out to be highly successful: Restricting attention to Borel sets does a great job of excluding the kind of strange behavior found in the Banach-Tarski paradox, and, moreover, every subset of $\mathbb{R}^N$ we need to deal with in day to day analysis is a Borel set. These include planes and hyperplanes, circles, spheres, polygons, finite sets, and sequences of points. In what follows we use $\mathscr{B}(\mathbb{R}^N)$ to represent the Borel sets of $\mathbb{R}^N$.

4.1.2 Probabilities

Now let's take a σ-algebra of events as given and consider how to assign probabilities to elements of $\mathscr{F}$. For given event B, the symbol $\mathbb{P}(B)$ will be interpreted as representing "the probability that event B occurs." The way you should think about it is this:

> $\mathbb{P}(B)$ represents the probability that when uncertainty is resolved and some $\omega \in \Omega$ is selected by "nature," the statement $\omega \in B$ is true.

In order to make sure our model of probability is well behaved, we need to put certain restrictions on $\mathbb{P}$. For example, it wouldn't do to have a B with $\mathbb{P}(B) = -93$, since negative probabilities don't make sense. The standard restrictions are imposed in the next definition:

Let Ω be a nonempty set and let $\mathscr{F}$ be a σ-algebra of subsets of Ω. A **probability** $\mathbb{P}$ on $(\Omega, \mathscr{F})$ is a function from $\mathscr{F}$ to $[0,1]$ that satisfies

(i) $\mathbb{P}(\Omega) = 1$ and

(ii) $\mathbb{P}(\cup_{n=1}^{\infty} A_n) = \sum_{n=1}^{\infty} \mathbb{P}(A_n)$ for any disjoint sequence of sets $A_1, A_2, \ldots \in \mathscr{F}$.

In this context $\mathbb{P}$ is also called a **probability measure**. Together, the triple $(\Omega, \mathscr{F}, \mathbb{P})$ is called a **probability space**.

In the definition, axiom (i) is straightforward. We require $\mathbb{P}(\Omega) = 1$ because, by construction, every possible ω lies in the set Ω. Axiom (ii) is called **countable additivity**. The concept of disjointness in the statement of the axiom is pairwise: Any distinct pair A_i, A_j share no points in common. By taking some of the sets as empty, countable additivity can be shown to imply finite **additivity**, which requires that

$$\mathbb{P}(A_1 \cup \cdots \cup A_k) = \mathbb{P}(A_1) + \cdots + \mathbb{P}(A_k) \tag{4.2}$$

whenever $A_1, \ldots, A_k$ are disjoint.

The general notion of additivity is a natural requirement for probabilistic models. It says that to find the probability of a given event, we can determine all the different (think "disjoint") ways that the event could occur, and then sum their probabilities.

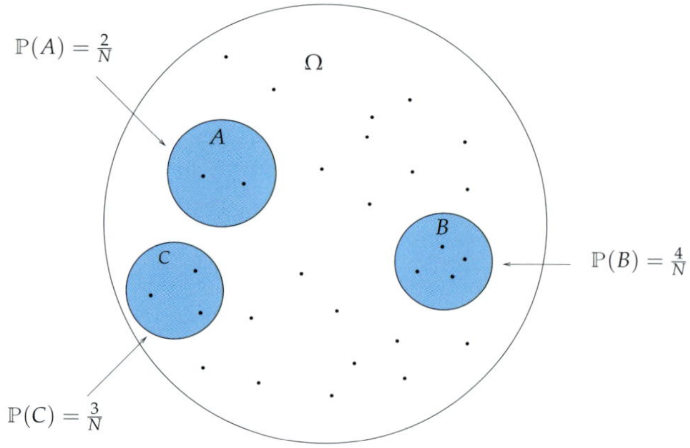

Figure 4.2 Each of the N dots occurs with probability $1/N$

Probabilists boost this up to countable additivity because it helps certain limiting arguments work smoothly.

Figure 4.2 gives an illustration of additivity. Suppose that the N dots in the figure are the only possible outcomes. Suppose that each of these occurs with probability $1/N$, and hence the probability of an event is the number of dots it contains divided by N. Hence $\mathbb{P}(A) = 2/N$, $\mathbb{P}(B) = 4/N$ and $\mathbb{P}(C) = 3/N$. In addition there are 9 dots in $A \cup B \cup C$, so

$$\mathbb{P}(A \cup B \cup C) = \frac{9}{N} = \mathbb{P}(A) + \mathbb{P}(B) + \mathbb{P}(C)$$

Notice how disjointness is important in making additivity work here: If the sets were not disjoint we would run the risk of double counting on the right hand side of this sum, breaking the equality.

Example 4.1.4 Let $\Omega := \{1, \ldots, 6\}$ represent the six different faces of a die, as in example 4.1.1. Since Ω is finite, we can and do take $\mathscr{F}$ to be the set of all subsets of Ω. We define a probability $\mathbb{P} \colon \mathscr{F} \to [0, 1]$ by

$$\mathbb{P}(A) := \frac{|A|}{6} \quad \text{where } |A| := \text{number of elements in set } A \tag{4.3}$$

For example, $\mathbb{P}\{2, 4, 6\} = 3/6 = 1/2$. It's easy to see that $0 \leqslant \mathbb{P}(A) \leqslant 1$ for any $A \in \mathscr{F}$, and that $\mathbb{P}(\Omega) = 1$. Regarding additivity, suppose that A and B are two disjoint subsets of $\{1, \ldots, 6\}$. Then $|A \cup B| = |A| + |B|$, since, by disjointness, the number of elements in the union is just the number contributed by A plus the number contributed by B. Hence

$$\mathbb{P}(A \cup B) = \frac{|A \cup B|}{6} = \frac{|A| + |B|}{6} = \frac{|A|}{6} + \frac{|B|}{6} = \mathbb{P}(A) + \mathbb{P}(B)$$

This proves additivity for pairs of sets. An analogous argument confirms additivity for any finite collection, in the sense that (4.2) holds. Finite additivity is in this case equivalent to countable additivity, since the total number of distinct events is finite.

Example 4.1.5 Continuing example 4.1.4, if we roll the die, the probability of getting an even number should be equal to the probability of getting a 2 plus that of getting a 4 plus that of getting a 6. This works because of additivity. Formally,

$$\mathbb{P}\{2,4,6\} = \mathbb{P}[\{2\} \cup \{4\} \cup \{6\}] = \mathbb{P}\{2\} + \mathbb{P}\{4\} + \mathbb{P}\{6\} = 1/2$$

Example 4.1.6 Imagine flipping a coin N times and recording the outcome of each flip. One sample space for this experiment is

$$\Omega_0 := \{(b_1, \dots, b_N) : b_n \in \{\text{heads, tails}\} \text{ for each } n\}$$

Letting zero represent tails and one represent heads yields the more practical space

$$\Omega := \{0,1\}^N := \{(b_1, \dots, b_N) : b_n \in \{0,1\} \text{ for each } n\}$$

Thus Ω is the set of all binary sequences of length N. Since Ω is again finite, we take $\mathscr{F}$ to be the set of all subsets of Ω. As our probability, we define

$$\mathbb{P}(A) := 2^{-N}|A|$$

where $|A|$ is again the number of distinct elements in A. This is a kind of uniform probability, where all outcomes are equally likely. Indeed, if $(b_1, \dots, b_N)$ is any complete sequence of flips and $A \in \mathscr{F}$ is the singleton set containing just this draw, then $\mathbb{P}(A) = 2^{-N}$. Hence all such sequences have the same probability under $\mathbb{P}$.

Regarding the axioms on page 83, it is not hard to check that $0 \leqslant \mathbb{P}(A) \leqslant 1$ for all $A \subset \Omega$ and $\mathbb{P}(\Omega) = 1$ (note that the number of distinct binary sequences of length N is 2^N). In addition $\mathbb{P}$ is additive. Exercise 4.4.8 asks you to confirm this.

Example 4.1.7 Consider again the dartboard model from example 4.1.2, where Ω is the unit disk in $\mathbb{R}^2$. For the event space, the set of all subsets of Ω is problematic (see §4.1.1), so we take instead $\mathscr{F}$ to be the set of Borel subsets of $\mathbb{R}^2$ that lie inside Ω. For $\mathbb{P}$ we follow the "uniform" probability assignment given in (4.1). That is, $\mathbb{P}(B) = \lambda(B)/\pi$ for every $B \in \mathscr{F}$. The function λ that assigns area to Borel sets is known to be countably additive, in that $\lambda(\cup_n A_n) = \sum_{n=1}^{\infty} \lambda(A_n)$ whenever these sets are disjoint. From this it follows that $\mathbb{P}$ is likewise countably additive. Evidently $\mathbb{P}(\Omega) = 1$.

The function λ from example 4.1.7 that maps Borel sets to their "area" is formally known as the **Lebesgue measure**. §15.3.1 provides a brief introduction to this concept.

4.1.2.1 Implications of the Axioms

Now let's go back to the general case, where $(\Omega, \mathscr{F}, \mathbb{P})$ is an arbitrary probability space. From the axioms on page 83, we can derive a surprising number of properties. Let's list the key ones, starting with the next fact.

Fact 4.1.1 Let $(\Omega, \mathscr{F}, \mathbb{P})$ be a probability space, and let $A, B \in \mathscr{F}$. If $A \subset B$, then

(i) $\mathbb{P}(B \setminus A) = \mathbb{P}(B) - \mathbb{P}(A)$,

(ii) $\mathbb{P}(A) \leqslant \mathbb{P}(B)$,

(iii) $\mathbb{P}(A^c) = 1 - \mathbb{P}(A)$, and

(iv) $\mathbb{P}(\emptyset) = 0$.

(Here $A^c = \Omega \setminus A$. See §15.1 for a review of set-theoretic operations.)

To prove fact 4.1.1, note that when $A \subset B$, we have $B = (B \setminus A) \cup A$. Since $B \setminus A$ and A are disjoint, additivity of $\mathbb{P}$ now gives

$$\mathbb{P}(B) = \mathbb{P}(B \setminus A) + \mathbb{P}(A) \qquad \text{(whenever } A \subset B\text{)}$$

This equality implies (i)–(iv) of fact 4.1.1. Rearranging gives (i), while nonnegativity of $\mathbb{P}$ gives (ii). Specializing to $B = \Omega$ gives (iii), and setting $B = A$ gives (iv).

The property $A \subset B \implies \mathbb{P}(A) \leqslant \mathbb{P}(B)$ is called **monotonicity**, and is both fundamental and intuitive: If $A \subset B$, then we know that B occurs whenever A occurs, since ω lands in B whenever it lands in A. Hence the probability of B should be no smaller. Many results in probability turn on this idea.

Fact 4.1.2 If A and B are any (not necessarily disjoint) events, then

$$\mathbb{P}(A \cup B) = \mathbb{P}(A) + \mathbb{P}(B) - \mathbb{P}(A \cap B)$$

Exercise 4.4.2 asks you to prove this. It follows from fact 4.1.2 that for any $A, B \in \mathscr{F}$, we have $\mathbb{P}(A \cup B) \leqslant \mathbb{P}(A) + \mathbb{P}(B)$. This inequality is called **subadditivity**. Thus probabilities are subadditive over arbitrary pairs of events and additive over disjoint pairs.

4.1.2.2 Dependence and Independence

If A and B are events, then the **conditional probability of A given B** is

$$\mathbb{P}(A \mid B) := \frac{\mathbb{P}(A \cap B)}{\mathbb{P}(B)} \tag{4.4}$$

It represents the probability that A will occur, given the information that B has occurred. For the definition to make sense, we need $\mathbb{P}(B) > 0$. Events A and B are called independent if $\mathbb{P}(A \cap B) = \mathbb{P}(A)\mathbb{P}(B)$. More generally, events $A_1, \ldots, A_N \in \mathscr{F}$ are called **independent** if

$$\mathbb{P}\left(\cap_{n=1}^{N} A_n\right) = \prod_{n=1}^{N} \mathbb{P}(A_n) \tag{4.5}$$

Note that if A and B are independent, then the conditional probability of A given B is just the probability of A.

Example 4.1.8 Recall example 4.1.3, where we roll a die twice. The sample space is $\Omega := \{(i,j) : i,j \in \{1,\ldots,6\}\}$. Since Ω is finite we can again take $\mathscr{F}$ to be the set of all subsets of Ω. For our probability, we define $\mathbb{P}(E) := |E|/36$. (Here elements of E are pairs, so $|E|$ is the number of pairs in E.) Now consider the events

$$A := \{(i,j) \in \Omega : i \text{ is even}\} \quad \text{and} \quad B := \{(i,j) \in \Omega : j \text{ is even}\}$$

In this case we have

$$A \cap B = \{(i,j) \in \Omega : i \text{ and } j \text{ are even}\}$$

The events A and B are independent under $\mathbb{P}$. To check this, recall the basic principle for counting ordered tuples: The total number of possible tuples is the product of the number of possibilities for each element. For example, the number of distinct tuples

$$(i,j,k) \text{ where } i \in I, j \in J \text{ and } k \in K$$

is $|I| \times |J| \times |K|$. Hence, the number of elements in A is $3 \times 6 = 18$, the number of elements in B is $6 \times 3 = 18$, and the number of elements in $A \cap B$ is $3 \times 3 = 9$. As a result

$$\mathbb{P}(A \cap B) = 9/36 = 1/4 = (18/36) \times (18/36) = \mathbb{P}(A)\mathbb{P}(B)$$

This confirms that A and B are independent.

To state the next result, we need the concept of a **partition** of Ω, by which we mean a countable set of events $\{B_m\}_{m \geqslant 1}$ with the property that distinct pairs are disjoint and $\cup_{m \geqslant 1} B_m = \Omega$.

Example 4.1.9 Let $\Omega = (0, \infty)$ and $B_m = (m-1, m]$ for all $m \in \mathbb{N}$. The events $\{B_m\}_{m \geqslant 1}$ form a partition of Ω.

The following fact is known as the **law of total probability**.

Fact 4.1.3 Let $\{B_m\}_{m \geqslant 1}$ be a partition of Ω and let A be any event. If $\mathbb{P}(B_m) > 0$ for all m, then

$$\mathbb{P}(A) = \sum_{m \geqslant 1} \mathbb{P}(A \,|\, B_m) \cdot \mathbb{P}(B_m)$$

The proof is as follows: It is a basic result from set theory that $A \cap (\cup_m B_m) = \cup_m (A \cap B_m)$. From this equality, the definition of a partition and countable additivity of $\mathbb{P}$, we get

$$\mathbb{P}(A) = \mathbb{P}[A \cap (\cup_{m \geqslant 1} B_m)] = \mathbb{P}[\cup_{m \geqslant 1}(A \cap B_m)] = \sum_{m \geqslant 1} \mathbb{P}(A \cap B_m)$$

Applying (4.4) completes the proof.

Example 4.1.10 Consider a bank that lends to two types of customers, type A and type B. Types are not observable to the bank. Type A customers have a default probability of 5%. Type B customers have a default probability of 10%. Of potential customers, 90% are of type B and 10% are of type A. Given a randomly selected customer, we wish to calculate on behalf of the bank the default probability associated with this customer.

To this end, let D be the event that the customer defaults, let A be the event that the customer is of type A, and let B be the event that the customer is of type B. Since the customer must be one of these two types, we have, by the law of total probability,

$$\mathbb{P}(D) = \mathbb{P}(D \mid A)\mathbb{P}(A) + \mathbb{P}(D \mid B)\mathbb{P}(B)$$

The right-hand side evaluates to $0.05 \times 0.1 + 0.1 \times 0.9 = 0.005 + 0.09 = 0.095$.

Another useful result concerning conditional probability is **Bayes' law**, which states that for any events A and B with positive probability,

$$\mathbb{P}(A \,|\, B) = \frac{\mathbb{P}(B \,|\, A)\mathbb{P}(A)}{\mathbb{P}(B)} \tag{4.6}$$

To prove (4.6), observe that, from the definition of conditional probability,

$$\mathbb{P}(A \,|\, B) = \frac{\mathbb{P}(A \cap B)}{\mathbb{P}(B)} \quad \text{and} \quad \mathbb{P}(B \,|\, A) = \frac{\mathbb{P}(A \cap B)}{\mathbb{P}(A)}$$

Hence $\mathbb{P}(A \cap B) = \mathbb{P}(A \,|\, B)\, \mathbb{P}(B) = \mathbb{P}(B \,|\, A)\, \mathbb{P}(A)$. Rearranging yields (4.6).

Example 4.1.11 Banks use automated systems to detect fraudulent or illegal transactions. Consider a test that responds to each transaction with P or N, where P means "positive" (transaction flagged as fraudulent) and N means "negative" (transaction flagged as normal). Letting F mean fraudulent, suppose that

- $\mathbb{P}(P \mid F) = 0.99$ (the test flags 99% of fraudulent transactions),
- $\mathbb{P}(P \mid F^c) = 0.01$ (rate of false positives), and
- $\mathbb{P}(F) = 0.001$ (prevalence of fraud).

We want to know the probability of fraud given a positive test. To answer this question, we use Bayes' law

$$\mathbb{P}(F \mid P) = \frac{\mathbb{P}(P \mid F)\mathbb{P}(F)}{\mathbb{P}(P)}$$

and the law of total probability $\mathbb{P}(P) = \mathbb{P}(P \mid F)\mathbb{P}(F) + \mathbb{P}(P \mid F^c)\mathbb{P}(F^c)$ to get

$$\mathbb{P}(F \mid P) = \frac{0.99 \times 0.001}{0.99 \times 0.001 + 0.01 \times 0.999} = \frac{11}{122} \approx \frac{1}{11}$$

Less than one in ten positives are actually fraudulent.

4.1.3 Random Variables

In some probability courses, a random variable is defined as a "value that changes randomly," or something to that effect. This is a fairly useless definition. A better definition of a random variable is a function x from a sample space Ω into $\mathbb{R}$. Think of it this way:

(i) "Nature" picks out an element ω in Ω according to some probability.

(ii) The random variable x sends this ω into numerical value $x(\omega)$.

Thus a random variable is a map x that converts outcomes in sample space—which can be any kind of object—*into numerical outcomes*. This is valuable because numerical outcomes are easy to order, add, subtract and so forth. In other words, random variables "report" the outcome of an experiment in a format amenable to further analysis.

Example 4.1.12 Consider an experiment where we flip a coin until we get heads. Let 0 represent tails and 1 represent heads. As our sample space we take the set of infinite binary sequences

$$\Omega := \{(b_1, b_2, \ldots) : b_n \in \{0, 1\} \text{ for each } n\}$$

Here's a random variable giving the number of flips until the first heads:

$$x(\omega) = x(b_1, b_2, \ldots) = \min\{n \in \mathbb{N} : b_n = 1\}$$

Suppose that we also wish to know whether any heads occur in the first 10 flips. If so we can introduce a new random variable

$$y(\omega) = y(b_1, b_2, \ldots) := \min\left\{\sum_{n=1}^{10} b_n, 1\right\} \tag{4.7}$$

that returns a 1 when this event occurs and zero otherwise. As per the definition, x and y are functions from Ω into $\mathbb{R}$.[2]

The random variable y in (4.7) is an example of a **binary** (or **Bernoulli**) random variable, which is a random variable taking values in the set $\{0, 1\}$. There is a generic way to create binary random variables that often comes in handy, using **indicator functions**. If Q is a statement, such as "on the planet Uranus, there exists a tribe of three-headed monkeys," then $\mathbb{1}\{Q\}$ is considered as equal to 1 when the statement Q is true, and zero when the statement Q is false. Another common variation on the notation is, for arbitrary $A \in \mathscr{F}$,

$$\mathbb{1}_A(\omega) := \mathbb{1}\{\omega \in A\} := \begin{cases} 1 & \text{if } \omega \in A \\ 0 & \text{otherwise} \end{cases}$$

So defined, $\mathbb{1}_A$ is a binary random variable. In fact any binary random variable x can be expressed as $\mathbb{1}_A$ by setting $A := \{\omega \in \Omega : x(\omega) = 1\}$.

Fact 4.1.4 If $A_1, \ldots, A_N$ are subsets of Ω, then

(i) $\mathbb{1}_{\cap_{n=1}^N A_n} = \prod_{n=1}^N \mathbb{1}_{A_n}$ and

(ii) $\mathbb{1}_{\cup_{n=1}^N A_n} = \sum_{n=1}^N \mathbb{1}_{A_n}$ whenever the sets are disjoint.

Here equality means when evaluated at any $\omega \in \Omega$. See exercise 4.4.5.

4.1.3.1 Notational Conventions

Given random variable x, you will often see notation such as

$$\{x \text{ has some property}\}$$

2. Is this true? If $\omega = \omega_0$ is an infinite sequence containing only zeros, then $\{n \in \mathbb{N} : b_n = 1\} = \emptyset$. What is $x(\omega_0)$ in this case? The convention is $\min \emptyset = \infty$, which is reasonable, but now x can take the value ∞. However, in most applications this event has probability zero. We could set $x(\omega_0) = 0$ without changing anything significant. Now we're back to a well-defined function from Ω to $\mathbb{R}$.

This is a shorthand for the *event*

$$\{\omega \in \Omega : x(\omega) \text{ has some property}\}$$

Example 4.1.13 Consider the claim that, for any random variable x,

$$\mathbb{P}\{x \leqslant a\} \leqslant \mathbb{P}\{x \leqslant b\} \quad \text{whenever} \quad a \leqslant b \tag{4.8}$$

The proof goes as follows: Pick any $a, b \in \mathbb{R}$ with $a \leqslant b$. The symbol $\{x \leqslant a\}$ is shorthand for the event $\{\omega \in \Omega : x(\omega) \leqslant a\}$. Likewise, $\{x \leqslant b\}$ is shorthand for $\{\omega \in \Omega : x(\omega) \leqslant b\}$. Since $a \leqslant b$, we have

$$\{\omega \in \Omega : x(\omega) \leqslant a\} \subset \{\omega \in \Omega : x(\omega) \leqslant b\}$$

(Any ω giving $x(\omega) \leqslant a$ must also give $x(\omega) \leqslant b$.) The result in (4.8) now follows from monotonicity of $\mathbb{P}$ (fact 4.1.1 on page 86).

Example 4.1.14 Recall example 4.1.6, with sample space $\Omega := \{0,1\}^N$, events $\mathscr{F} :=$ all subsets of Ω and $\mathbb{P}(A) := 2^{-N}|A|$. Consider a random variable x on Ω that returns the first element of any given sequence. That is, $x(\omega) = x(b_1, \ldots, b_N) = b_1$. The probability that $x = 1$ is $1/2$. Indeed

$$\mathbb{P}\{x = 1\} := \mathbb{P}\{\omega \in \Omega : x(\omega) = 1\} = \mathbb{P}\{(b_1, \ldots, b_N) \in \Omega : b_1 = 1\}$$

Because the number of length N binary sequences with $b_1 = 1$ is 2^{N-1}, we have $\mathbb{P}\{x = 1\} = 2^{-N}2^{N-1} = 1/2$.

Another notational convention you should be aware of is that, for random variables, equalities, inequalities and arithmetic operations should be interpreted *pointwise*. For example,

- $x \leqslant y \iff x(\omega) \leqslant y(\omega)$ for all $\omega \in \Omega$,
- $x = y \iff x(\omega) = y(\omega)$ for all $\omega \in \Omega$, and
- $z = \alpha x + \beta y \iff z(\omega) = \alpha x(\omega) + \beta y(\omega)$ for all $\omega \in \Omega$.

4.1.3.2 Random Variables Are Measurable Functions

We've omitted a technical detail in our construction of random variables. It arises because we cannot always take the set of events $\mathscr{F}$ to be the set of all subsets of Ω (since assigning probabilities to arbitrarily complex sets causes problems—see the discussion in §4.1.1).

To explain, let $(\Omega, \mathscr{F}, \mathbb{P})$ be any probability space. Let B be any subset of $\mathbb{R}$ and consider evaluating the probability

$$\mathbb{P}\{x \in B\} := \mathbb{P}\{\omega \in \Omega : x(\omega) \in B\}$$

Here x is some function from Ω to $\mathbb{R}$. Now observe that if we put no restrictions on x, we might end up in a mess. The reason is that we have no way of being sure that the set $\{\omega \in \Omega : x(\omega) \in B\}$ is in fact an element of $\mathscr{F}$. Since $\mathbb{P}$ is only defined over elements of $\mathscr{F}$ (i.e., for *bona fide* events), it is possible that $\mathbb{P}\{x \in B\}$ is undefined.

To prevent such embarrassment, it's standard to put some restrictions both on x and B that ensure $\{x \in B\} \in \mathscr{F}$. For B, we naturally restrict attention to $\mathscr{B}(\mathbb{R})$, the Borel subsets of $\mathbb{R}$, since we know these sets to be both relatively well behaved and common enough to satisfy our purposes (see §4.1.1). For x, we simply require that $\{x \in B\} \in \mathscr{F}$ whenever B is a Borel set. Thus, our formal definition is that a **random variable** on $(\Omega, \mathscr{F})$ is a function $x \colon \Omega \to \mathbb{R}$ satisfying

$$\{\omega \in \Omega : x(\omega) \in B\} \in \mathscr{F} \quad \text{for all } B \in \mathscr{B}(\mathbb{R}) \tag{4.9}$$

These kinds of functions are also sometimes called $\mathscr{F}$-measurable functions. In other texts you will see (4.9) expressed using preimage notation. In the preimage notation, $x^{-1}(B)$ is all $\omega \in \Omega$ such that $x(\omega) \in B$. This is just the left-hand side of (4.9), so we can rewrite (4.9) as

$$x^{-1}(B) \in \mathscr{F} \quad \text{for all } B \in \mathscr{B}(\mathbb{R})$$

Thus x "pulls back" Borel sets to events.

4.1.3.3 Measurable Transformations

So far so good. If x is a random variable, then $\{x \in B\}$ is a well-defined event for every $B \in \mathscr{B}(\mathbb{R})$. But suppose now that we want to discuss some transformation of x. For example, we might be interested in the properties of $y := e^x$. Is y also a random variable? That is, is $\{y \in B\}$ always a well-defined event?

The answer to this question is affirmative provided that our transformation satisfies a regularity condition called Borel measurability. Formally, $f \colon \mathbb{R} \to \mathbb{R}$ is called **Borel measurable**, or **$\mathscr{B}$-measurable**, if

$$f^{-1}(B) \in \mathscr{B}(\mathbb{R}) \quad \text{for all } B \in \mathscr{B}(\mathbb{R}) \tag{4.10}$$

Thus f "pulls back" Borel sets to Borel sets. Although we omit the details, the class of $\mathscr{B}$-measurable functions is vast (any continuous function, any increasing function, etc., etc.), and all transformations we work with below are $\mathscr{B}$-measurable.

So why is $\mathscr{B}$-measurability of f the key to ensuring that $y = f(x)$ is a random variable? Suppose that f is $\mathscr{B}$-measurable and that x is a random variable. We claim that $\{y \in B\} \in \mathscr{F}$ for all $B \in \mathscr{B}(\mathbb{R})$. This holds because

$$\{y \in B\} = \{f(x) \in B\} = \{x \in f^{-1}(B)\} \tag{4.11}$$

for all $B \in \mathscr{B}(\mathbb{R})$. By (4.10) we know that $f^{-1}(B)$ is a Borel set. Since x is a random variable, it follows that $\{x \in f^{-1}(B)\}$ is an element of $\mathscr{F}$.

4.1.4 Expectations

Our next task is to define expectations of random variables and state their basic properties. Elementary probability courses define expectations by summing or integrating functions over densities. The view of a random variable as a function on a sample space plays no part in these definitions. However, when we move to more sophisticated arguments, particularly those involving a large number of random variables, we need a better definition. This section outlines the modern treatment of expectations found in probability and statistics. As we'll see later, the definition in this section is a generalization of the elementary definition. The two agree whenever the latter is well defined.

For finite random variables (i.e., random variables with finite range) the expectation is just the sum of all possible values of the variable, weighted by the corresponding probabilities. More formally, given probability space $(\Omega, \mathscr{F}, \mathbb{P})$ and random variable x taking only finitely many distinct values $s_1, \ldots, s_J$, the **expectation** of x is defined as

$$\mathbb{E}x = \sum_{j=1}^{J} s_j \, \mathbb{P}\{x = s_j\} \tag{4.12}$$

Example 4.1.15 Let's apply this definition to the simplest possible case, which is a random variable x satisfying $x(\omega) = \alpha$ for all $\omega \in \Omega$, where α is some constant scalar value. In this case the sum in (4.12) has only one term, and

$$\mathbb{E}x = \alpha\mathbb{P}\{x = \alpha\} = \alpha\mathbb{P}\{\omega \in \Omega : x(\omega) = \alpha\} = \alpha\mathbb{P}(\Omega) = \alpha$$

Example 4.1.16 To evaluate the expectation of a binary random variable x, we apply (4.12) to obtain

$$\mathbb{E}x = 1 \times \mathbb{P}\{x = 1\} + 0 \times \mathbb{P}\{x = 0\} = \mathbb{P}\{x = 1\} \tag{4.13}$$

Example 4.1.17 Recall example 4.1.14, which models N flips of a fair coin. The sample space is $\Omega := \{0,1\}^N$, the events are $\mathscr{F} :=$ all subsets of Ω, and $\mathbb{P}(A) := 2^{-N}|A|$ for all $A \in \mathscr{F}$. Let $x(\omega) = x(b_1, \ldots, b_N) = \sum_{n=1}^{N} b_n$. This value corresponds to the number of "heads" observed in one possible outcome $(b_1, \ldots, b_N)$. The probability $\mathbb{P}$ we've assigned makes all draws equally likely. Hence a good guess is that half the flips will come up heads, or $\mathbb{E}x = N/2$. Let's try to obtain this from (4.12).

Observe first that $0 \leqslant x \leqslant N$. Also, by the definition of $\mathbb{P}$, for any k we have $\mathbb{P}\{x = k\} = 2^{-N}|A_k|$, where

$$A_k := \{x = k\} = \left\{(b_1, \ldots, b_N) \in \Omega \,:\, \sum_{n=1}^{N} b_n = k\right\}$$

It is a standard result from combinatorics that $|A_k| = \binom{N}{k}$, where the right-hand side is the so-called **binomial coefficient** for N, k. One identity it satisfies is $\sum_{k=0}^{N} k\binom{N}{k} = N2^{N-1}$ for all N. Combining this identity with (4.12), the expectation of x is

$$\mathbb{E}x = \sum_{k=0}^{N} k 2^{-N}|A_k| = 2^{-N} \sum_{k=0}^{N} k \binom{N}{k} = \frac{N}{2}$$

4.1.4.1 Expectations for Arbitrary Random Variables

Definition (4.12) only applies for random variables with finite range. We still need to define expectation for general x. This is done by bootstrapping up from the finite case. The procedure is based on approximating arbitrary random variables with finite random variables. One finite approximation x_n to an arbitrary random variable x is shown in figure 4.3. The approximation can be improved without limit if we allow x_n to take a larger and larger number of distinct values. This process yields a sequence of finite random variables x_n converging to x (e.g., see Çinlar (2011), lemma 2.16). The expectation of x is then defined as

$$\mathbb{E}x := \lim_{n \to \infty} \mathbb{E}x_n \tag{4.14}$$

The value $\mathbb{E}x$ is also referred to as the **Lebesgue integral** of x with respect to $\mathbb{P}$, with the alternative notation $\mathbb{E}x = \int x(\omega)\mathbb{P}(d\omega)$.

Can we be sure that the limit in (4.14) makes sense? Suppose first that x is nonnegative (i.e., $x(\omega) \geqslant 0$ for all $\omega \in \Omega$). It can be shown that the sequence $\{x_n\}$ approximating x can then be chosen so that $\mathbb{E}x_n$ is monotone increasing and hence convergent, and that the limiting value does not depend on the particular approximating sequence $\{x_n\}$. See, for example, Dudley (2002), proposition 4.1.5. Hence $\mathbb{E}x$ is well defined, although we cannot rule out divergence of the sequence, which gives $\mathbb{E}x = \infty$.

We've assumed that x is nonnegative. If we drop this assumption, we can still treat x with similar methods by writing it as the difference between two nonnegative ran-

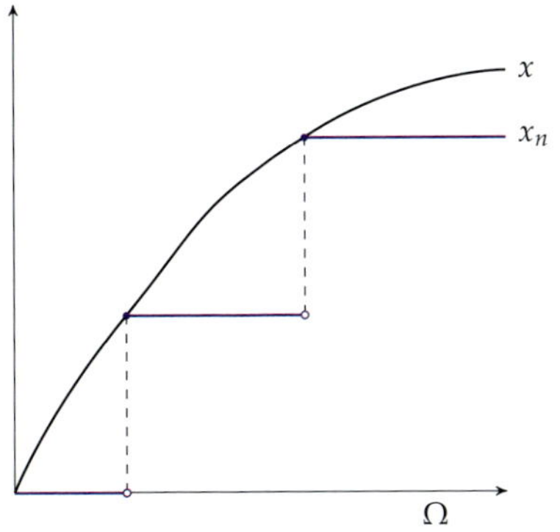

Figure 4.3 Finite approximation to a general random variable

dom variables. Typically this is done by writing $x = x^+ - x^-$, where $x^+ := \max\{x, 0\}$ and $x^- := -\min\{x, 0\}$. Both x^+ and x^- are nonnegative random variables. The expectation can then be defined as

$$\mathbb{E}x := \mathbb{E}x^+ - \mathbb{E}x^- \tag{4.15}$$

This is fine except that (4.15) might have the form $\infty - \infty$, which isn't well-defined. For this reason we often restrict attention to **integrable** random variables, which are all random variables x such that $\mathbb{E}|x| < \infty$. Since $x^+ \leqslant |x|$ and $x^- \leqslant |x|$, this is enough to ensure that (4.15) is well-defined.

The definition of $\mathbb{E}$ given in this section doesn't really tell us how to calculate $\mathbb{E}x$ in specific instances, but we'll see how to do so in §4.2.5.

4.1.4.2 Properties of Expectation

Let's summarize the main results concerning expectations and list some properties of this operation.

Fact 4.1.5 Given any probability space $(\Omega, \mathscr{F}, \mathbb{P})$, there exists a uniquely defined function $\mathbb{E}$ that maps each integrable random variable x on $(\Omega, \mathscr{F}, \mathbb{P})$ into a value

$$\mathbb{E}x = \int x(\omega)\mathbb{P}(\mathrm{d}\omega) \tag{4.16}$$

in $\mathbb{R}$, called the **expectation of x** under $\mathbb{P}$. The function has the following properties:

(i) $\mathbb{E}\alpha = \alpha$ for all $\alpha \in \mathbb{R}$.

(ii) $\mathbb{E}\mathbb{1}_A = \mathbb{P}(A)$ for all $A \in \mathscr{F}$.

(iii) $x \leqslant y \implies \mathbb{E}x \leqslant \mathbb{E}y$.

(iv) $\mathbb{E}[\alpha x + \beta y] = \alpha\mathbb{E}x + \beta\mathbb{E}y$ for all integrable x, y and constants α, β.

If we need to remind ourselves of the underlying probability measure $\mathbb{P}$ we will write $\mathbb{E}_{\mathbb{P}}x$ instead of $\mathbb{E}x$.

Since we only know how to take expectations of random variables, the expression $\mathbb{E}\alpha$ in part (i) should be understood as the expectation of a constant random variable everywhere equal to α. (We could write this object more precisely as $\alpha\mathbb{1}_\Omega$.) That the expectation equals α was already established in example 4.1.15. It also follows from (ii) and (iv), by taking $x = \mathbb{1}_\Omega$ and $\beta = 0$.

Part (ii) follows from example 4.1.16. It is restated here to emphasize this fundamental link between probabilities and expectations. Part (iii) is called **monotonicity of expectations**. The statement $x \leqslant y$ means that $x(\omega) \leqslant y(\omega)$ for all $\omega \in \Omega$. Exercise 4.4.23 asks you to prove this monotonicity in a special case. For a general proof see lemma 4.1.9 of Dudley (2002). Part (iv) is called **linearity of expectations**. Here $\alpha x + \beta y$ should be understood as the random variable $(\alpha x + \beta y)(\omega) := \alpha x(\omega) + \beta y(\omega)$. Exercises 4.4.13 and 4.4.14 ask you to check linearity in some special cases. For the general case see theorem 4.1.10 of Dudley (2002).

As an exercise, let's use these results to prove that if x is a finite random variable with range $\{s_j\}_{j=1}^J$ and h is any $\mathscr{B}$-measurable function, then $h(x)$ has expectation

$$\mathbb{E}h(x) = \sum_{j=1}^J h(s_j)\mathbb{P}\{x = s_j\} \tag{4.17}$$

First observe that $\sum_{j=1}^J \mathbb{1}\{x = s_j\} = 1$, and hence we can write $h(x)$ as

$$h(x) = h(x)\sum_{j=1}^J \mathbb{1}\{x = s_j\} = \sum_{j=1}^J h(s_j)\mathbb{1}\{x = s_j\}$$

Using linearity of expectations gives $\mathbb{E}h(x) = \sum_{j=1}^J h(s_j)\mathbb{E}\mathbb{1}\{x = s_j\}$. Applying part (ii) of fact 4.1.5 leads to (4.17).

The next result is another useful link between probabilities and expectations, typically called **Chebyshev's inequality**.

Fact 4.1.6 For any nonnegative random variable x and any $\delta > 0$, we have

$$\mathbb{P}\{x \geqslant \delta\} \leqslant \frac{\mathbb{E}x}{\delta} \tag{4.18}$$

A common variation of Chebyshev's inequality is the bound

$$\mathbb{P}\{|x| \geqslant \delta\} \leqslant \frac{\mathbb{E}\, x^2}{\delta^2} \tag{4.19}$$

Exercise 4.4.29 asks you to check both (4.18) and (4.19).

4.1.5 Moments and Co-Moments

Let x be a random variable and let $k \in \mathbb{N}$. If x^k is integrable, then

- $\mathbb{E}\,[x^k]$ is called the **kth moment** of x.
- $\mathbb{E}\,[(x - \mathbb{E}\, x)^k]$ is called the **kth central moment** of x.

If $\mathbb{E}\,[|x|^k] = \infty$, then the kth moment is said not to exist. For some random variables even the first moment does not exist. For others every moment exists.

Fact 4.1.7 If the kth moment of x exists, then so does the jth for all $j \leqslant k$.

Exercise 4.4.24 asks you to confirm this. The next fact is called the **Cauchy–Schwarz inequality for random variables**. Its proof will be given later, once we've covered orthogonal projection (ex. 5.4.15).

Fact 4.1.8 If x and y are random variables with finite second moment, then

$$|\, \mathbb{E}\,[xy]\,| \leqslant \sqrt{\mathbb{E}\,[x^2]\mathbb{E}\,[y^2]} \tag{4.20}$$

The second central moment of x is called the **variance** of x:

$$\operatorname{var} x := \mathbb{E}\,[(x - \mathbb{E}\, x)^2]$$

This gives a measure of the dispersion of x. The **standard deviation** of x is

$$\sigma_x := \sqrt{\operatorname{var} x}$$

The **covariance** of random variables x and y is defined as

$$\operatorname{cov}[x, y] := \mathbb{E}\,[(x - \mathbb{E}\, x)(y - \mathbb{E}\, y)]$$

Fact 4.1.9 If x and y have finite second moments, then

(i) $\operatorname{var} x$ and $\operatorname{cov}[x, y]$ are finite,

(ii) $\operatorname{var} x = \mathbb{E}\,[x^2] - [\mathbb{E}\, x]^2$, and

(iii) $\operatorname{cov}[x, y] = \mathbb{E}\,[xy] - \mathbb{E}\,[x]\mathbb{E}\,[y]$.

Part (i) follows from (ii)–(iii), the Cauchy–Schwarz inequality and fact 4.1.7. Parts (ii)–(iii) follow from linearity of $\mathbb{E}$ and some simple manipulations.

Fact 4.1.10 If $x_1, \ldots, x_N$ are random variables and $\alpha_0, \alpha_1, \ldots, \alpha_N$ are constant scalars, then

$$\operatorname{var}\left[\alpha_0 + \sum_{n=1}^{N} \alpha_n x_n\right] = \sum_{n=1}^{N} \alpha_n^2 \operatorname{var}[x_n] + 2 \sum_{n<m} \alpha_n \alpha_m \operatorname{cov}[x_n, x_m]$$

Some simple implications of this fact are that

(i) $\operatorname{var}[\alpha + \beta x] = \beta^2 \operatorname{var}[x]$ and

(ii) $\operatorname{var}[\alpha x + \beta y] = \alpha^2 \operatorname{var}[x] + \beta^2 \operatorname{var}[y] + 2\alpha\beta \operatorname{cov}[x, y]$.

The **correlation** of x and y is defined as

$$\operatorname{corr}[x, y] := \frac{\operatorname{cov}[x, y]}{\sigma_x \, \sigma_y}$$

If $\operatorname{corr}[x, y] = 0$, we say that x and y are **uncorrelated**. Positive correlation means that $\operatorname{corr}[x, y]$ is positive and negative correlation means that $\operatorname{corr}[x, y]$ is negative. The first part of the next fact follows immediately from fact 4.1.8; the second is just algebra.

Fact 4.1.11 Given any two random variables x, y and positive constants α, β, we have

$$-1 \leqslant \operatorname{corr}[x, y] \leqslant 1 \quad \text{and} \quad \operatorname{corr}[\alpha x, \beta y] = \operatorname{corr}[x, y]$$

4.1.5.1 Best Linear Predictors

As an application of covariance and a prelude to our discussion of prediction, let's consider the problem of predicting the value of a random variable y given knowledge of the value of a second random variable x (and also knowledge of the underlying probability distributions, which makes this a problem in probability rather than statistics). Thus we seek a function f such that $f(x)$ is close to y on average. To measure the latter, we will use **mean squared error**, which amounts in this case to

$$\mathbb{E}\left[(y - f(x))^2\right]$$

As we'll see in §5.2.5, the minimizer of the mean squared deviation over all functions of x is obtained by choosing $f(x) = \mathbb{E}[y \mid x]$, where the right-hand side is the conditional expectation of y given x. Here we'll consider the simpler problem of finding a good predictor of y within the class of "linear" functions

$$\mathcal{H}_\ell := \{ \text{all functions of the form } \ell(x) = \alpha + \beta x \}$$

(We defer to common usage and call such functions linear in this context, despite the fact that they are, in general, affine; see example 2.1.23.) Thus we consider the problem

$$\min_{\ell \in \mathcal{H}_\ell} \mathbb{E}\left[(y - \ell(x))^2\right] = \min_{\alpha,\beta \in \mathbb{R}} \mathbb{E}\left[(y - \alpha - \beta x)^2\right] \tag{4.21}$$

If α and β solve (4.21), then the function

$$\ell^*(x) := \alpha^* + \beta^* x \tag{4.22}$$

is called the **best linear predictor** of y given x.

Example 4.1.18 In finance, the relationship between returns on a given asset R_a and returns on a market benchmark R_m is called the **beta** of the asset. It measures exposure to systemic risk, as opposed to idiosyncratic risk specific to the asset. The beta of R_a is often defined as the coefficient β^* in the best linear prediction (4.22) when x is returns on the market benchmark and $y = R_a$.

To solve (4.21) we expand the square on the right-hand side and use linearity of $\mathbb{E}$ to write the objective function as

$$\psi(\alpha, \beta) := \mathbb{E}\left[y^2\right] - 2\alpha\mathbb{E}\left[y\right] - 2\beta\mathbb{E}\left[xy\right] + 2\alpha\beta\mathbb{E}\left[x\right] + \alpha^2 + \beta^2\mathbb{E}\left[x^2\right]$$

Computing the derivatives and solving the first-order conditions yields (ex. 4.4.27) the minimizers

$$\beta^* := \frac{\operatorname{cov}[x, y]}{\operatorname{var}[x]} \quad \text{and} \quad \alpha^* := \mathbb{E}\left[y\right] - \beta^*\mathbb{E}\left[x\right] \tag{4.23}$$

If you've studied simple linear least squares regression before, you might realize that α^* and β^* are the "population" counterparts of coefficient estimates in an empirical setting. In example 4.1.18, this allows us to take the coefficient β^* as the definition of an asset's beta, independent of any particular data set. If we wish to evaluate β^*, however, we need to use data, since the underlying probabilities, and hence the expectation operator $\mathbb{E}$, are not observable. It is at this stage that the population regression is replaced by simple linear least squares using data. More on this below.

4.2 Distributions

Any random variable x on a given probability space $(\Omega, \mathscr{F}, \mathbb{P})$ assigns to each Borel set $B \subset \mathbb{R}$ a number $\mathbb{P}\{x \in B\}$ indicating the probability that x lies in B. While this is an important construction, as a means of specifying probabilities for outcomes in $\mathbb{R}$, it is somewhat indirect. When building statistical models, it's often more convenient to assign probabilities to subsets of $\mathbb{R}$ directly. This is typically done by specifying a *distribution* over $\mathbb{R}$. In this section we look at how one might go about specifying such distributions.

4.2.1 Defining Distributions on $\mathbb{R}$

How can we specify probabilities over subsets of $\mathbb{R}$? In §4.1.1.2–§4.1.2 we learned how to construct a set of events $\mathscr{F}$ on an arbitrary sample space Ω and define a probability measure $\mathbb{P}$ on $\mathscr{F}$. If we want to describe probabilities over $\mathbb{R}$, then the natural thing to do is to repeat the process with Ω specialized to $\mathbb{R}$. For the set of events over $\mathbb{R}$ we take the Borel sets $\mathscr{B}(\mathbb{R})$, as discussed in §4.1.1.2. A probability measure defined over $\mathscr{B}(\mathbb{R})$ is called a **law** or **distribution**.

Distributions will be represented by symbols such as P and Q. Referring back to the definition on page 83, a distribution P is a map from $\mathscr{B}(\mathbb{R})$ to $[0,1]$ such that

(i) $P(\mathbb{R}) = 1$ and

(ii) $P(\cup_{n=1}^{\infty} B_n) = \sum_{n=1}^{\infty} P(B_n)$ for any disjoint sequence $\{B_n\}$.

Being a probability measure, P satisfies all the properties in fact 4.1.1 on page 86. If there exists a Borel set S with $P(S) = 1$, then we say that P is **supported** on S.

Probability measures are both general and comprehensive. Each one pins down probabilistic information for every event in $\mathbb{R}$ that we might care about in econometrics or statistics. At the same time, this kind of generality can also be a hindrance. For example, it's not a trivial task to assign a specific value $P(B)$ to every single Borel set.

Fortunately, we can characterize distributions more succinctly. To begin, we recall the notion of a **cumulative distributed function**, or CDF, which is any function $F\colon \mathbb{R} \to [0,1]$ satisfying

(i) monotonicity: $s \leqslant s'$ implies $F(s) \leqslant F(s')$,

(ii) right-continuity: $F(s_n) \downarrow F(s)$ whenever $s_n \downarrow s$, and

(iii) $\lim_{s \to -\infty} F(s) = 0$ and $\lim_{s \to \infty} F(s) = 1$.

CDFs and distributions on $\mathbb{R}$ can be put in one-to-one correspondence as follows: First, it's true by definition that any two distributions Q and P satisfying $Q(B) = P(B)$ for all $B \in \mathscr{B}(\mathbb{R})$ are the same distribution, but it's also true that if $Q(B) = P(B)$ for all sets B of the form $(-\infty, s]$, then Q and P are again the same distribution. In other words, a distribution P is entirely characterized by the values of the function

$$F(s) := P((-\infty, s]) \qquad (s \in \mathbb{R}) \tag{4.24}$$

Moreover this function turns out to have properties (i)–(iii) above. The next fact summarizes the relationship between F and P.

Fact 4.2.1 The following statements are true:

(i) If P is any distribution on $\mathbb{R}$, then the function F in (4.24) is a CDF.

(ii) Given any CDF F on $\mathbb{R}$, there exists exactly one distribution P satisfying (4.24).

For a full proof, see Williams (1991), lemma 1.6, or Dudley (2002), theorem 9.1.1. Here let's restrict ourselves to showing that the function F in (4.24) satisfies part (i) of the definition of a CDF. To see why (i) holds for this F, observe that $s \leqslant s'$ implies $(-\infty, s] \subset (-\infty, s']$. Part (ii) of fact 4.1.1 on page 86 then gives $P((-\infty, s]) \leqslant P((-\infty, s'])$. Hence $F(s) \leqslant F(s')$ as claimed.

CDFs are relatively easy to specify and work with. Here are some examples.

Example 4.2.1 The **univariate normal distributions** or **Gaussian distributions** refer to the class of distributions identified by CDFs of the form

$$F(s) = \frac{1}{\sqrt{2\pi}\sigma} \int_{-\infty}^{s} \exp\left\{-\frac{(t-\mu)^2}{2\sigma^2}\right\} dt \qquad (s \in \mathbb{R})$$

where $\mu \in \mathbb{R}$ and $\sigma > 0$. We represent the distribution associated with (μ, σ) by $\mathrm{N}(\mu, \sigma^2)$. The distribution $\mathrm{N}(0, 1)$ is called the **standard normal distribution**. We use the symbol Φ for its CDF. Examples of normal CDFs are shown in figure 4.4.

Example 4.2.2 The **Pareto distributions** are the univariate distributions with CDFs of the form

$$F(s) = \begin{cases} 0 & \text{if } s < s_0 \\ 1 - \left(\frac{s_0}{s}\right)^{\alpha} & \text{if } s_0 \leqslant s \end{cases} \qquad (s \in \mathbb{R},\ s_0,\ \alpha > 0)$$

Pareto distributions are often used to model phenomena with heavy right-hand tails, such as the distribution of wealth or income.

Example 4.2.3 The class of **beta CDFs** is given by

$$F(s) = \begin{cases} 0 & \text{if } s \leqslant 0 \\ \frac{1}{B(\alpha,\beta)} \int_0^s u^{\alpha-1}(1-u)^{\beta-1}\, du & \text{if } 0 < s < 1 \\ 1 & \text{if } 1 \leqslant s \end{cases}$$

where $\alpha, \beta > 0$. See figure 4.5. In this example $B(\alpha, \beta)$ is the **beta function**

$$B(\alpha, \beta) := \frac{\Gamma(\alpha)\Gamma(\beta)}{\Gamma(\alpha+\beta)} \qquad \text{where} \qquad \Gamma(a) := \int_0^{\infty} u^{a-1} e^{-u}\, du$$

The function Γ is called the **gamma function**.

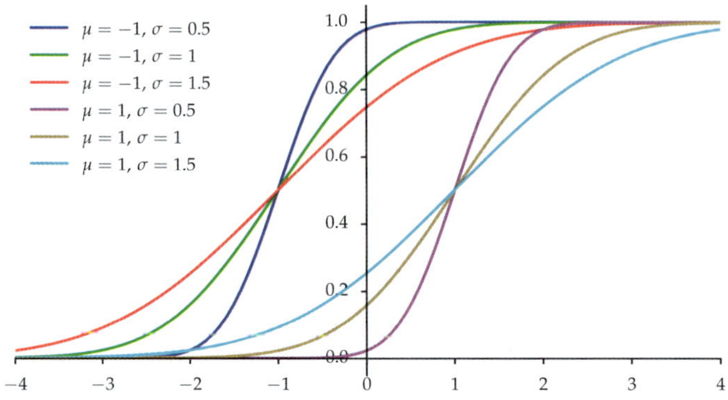

Figure 4.4 Normal CDFs

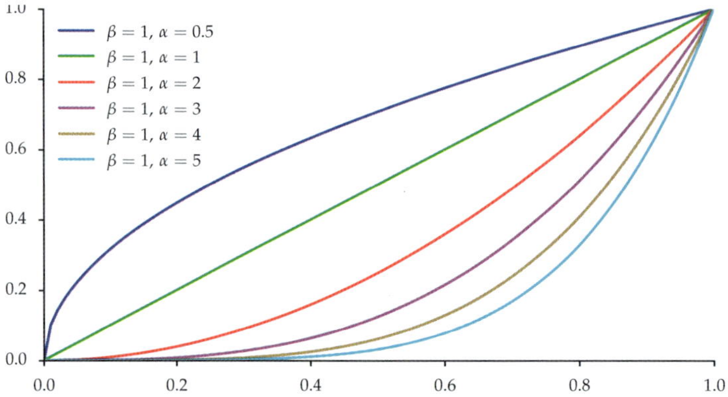

Figure 4.5 Beta CDFs

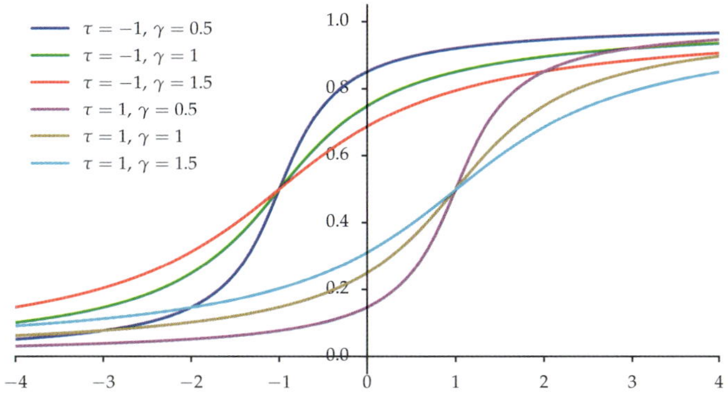

Figure 4.6 Cauchy CDFs

Example 4.2.4 The class of **Cauchy CDFs** is given by

$$F(s) = \frac{1}{\pi} \arctan\left(\frac{s-\tau}{\gamma}\right) + \frac{1}{2} \qquad (s \in \mathbb{R})$$

The parameters $\tau \in \mathbb{R}$ and $\gamma > 0$ are the location and scale parameters respectively. If $\tau = 0$ and $\gamma = 1$, then F is called **standard Cauchy**. See figure 4.6.

Example 4.2.5 Given $a < b$, the **uniform CDF** on $[a, b]$ is the CDF

$$F(s) = \begin{cases} 0 & \text{if } s \leqslant a \\ \frac{s-a}{b-a} & \text{if } a < s < b \\ 1 & \text{if } b \leqslant s \end{cases}$$

We represent this distribution symbolically by $U[a, b]$.

4.2.2 Densities and PMFs

There are two important sub-cases for distributions: the discrete case and the absolutely continuous case. As we'll see, in these two sub-cases distributions have nice visual representations and expectations are easy to compute. Almost all "named" distributions fall into one of these two categories.

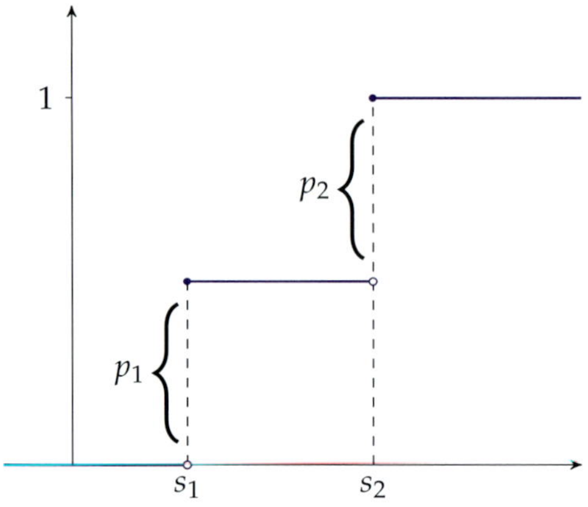

Figure 4.7 Discrete CDF

4.2.2.1 The Discrete Case

A distribution P is called **discrete** if it is supported on a countable set; that is, if there exists a countable set $\{s_j\}_{j\geqslant 1}$ with $P(\{s_j\}_{j\geqslant 1}) = 1$. For such a P let

$$p_j := P\{s_j\} := P(\{s_j\}) = \text{probability mass on the single point } s_j$$

Property (ii) of P on page 100 and $P(\{s_j\}_{j\geqslant 1}) = 1$ imply that $\sum_{j\geqslant 1} p_j = 1$ (ex. 4.4.15). Hence $\{p_j\}_{j\geqslant 1}$ is an example of a **probability mass function**, or PMF, which is any nonnegative sequence (finite or infinite) that sums to unity.

Together, $\{s_j\}_{j\geqslant 1}$ and $\{p_j\}_{j\geqslant 1}$ characterize the underlying distribution. For example, we can express the CDF corresponding to P via (4.24) as

$$F(s) = \sum_{j\geqslant 1} \mathbb{1}\{s_j \leqslant s\} p_j \tag{4.25}$$

This is intuitive: $F(s)$ represents the probability of an outcome in $(-\infty, s]$ under P. Since P puts all its probability mass on $\{s_j\}_{j\geqslant 1}$, this should equal the sum of the probabilities of hitting s_j over all $s_j \leqslant s$.

Figure 4.7 gives a visualization when $\{s_j\}_{j\geqslant 1} = \{s_1, s_2\}$. F is a step function, with a jump up of size p_j at point s_j. The CDF is right-continuous but not continuous.

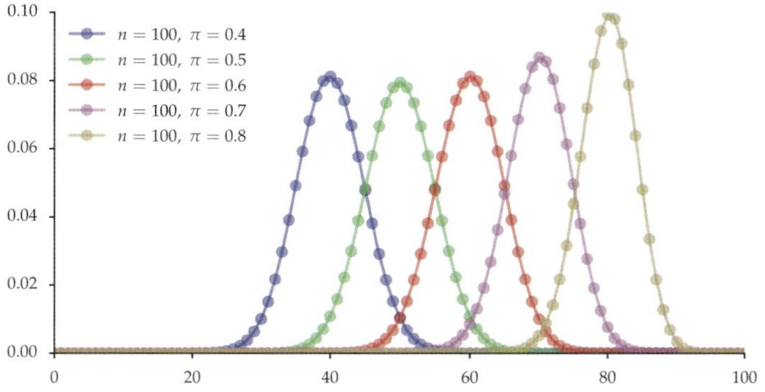

Figure 4.8 Binomial PMFs

Example 4.2.6 Given $N \in \mathbb{N}$ and $\pi \in (0,1)$, the sequence $\{p_0, \ldots, p_N\}$ defined by

$$p_j = \binom{N}{j} \pi^j (1-\pi)^{N-j}$$

is called the **binomial** PMF. The value p_j represents the probability of j successes in N independent trials, each having success probability π.

4.2.2.2 The Absolutely Continuous Case

Another case of interest is what elementary books on probability call the "continuous" case, where distributions can be described by densities. A **density** is a nonnegative function p on $\mathbb{R}$ that integrates to 1. We say that distribution P is **represented by density** p (or **has density** p) if p is a density and

$$P(B) = \int_B p(s)\, \mathrm{d}s \qquad \text{for all } B \in \mathscr{B}(\mathbb{R}) \tag{4.26}$$

Here the integral over B can be understood as

$$\int_B p(s)\, \mathrm{d}s := \int_{-\infty}^{\infty} \mathbb{1}_B(s) p(s)\, \mathrm{d}s$$

Recall from our discussion in §4.2.1 that distributions are characterized by their values on simple sets, like half lines of the form $(-\infty, s]$. Thus, if p is a density and

$$P((-\infty, s]) = \int_{-\infty}^{s} p(t)\,dt \qquad \text{for all } s \in \mathbb{R} \tag{4.27}$$

then (4.26) also holds.

Not every distribution has a density representation. An exact necessary and sufficient condition for existence is absolute continuity. A distribution P on the Borel subsets of $\mathbb{R}$ is called **absolutely continuous** if $P(B) = 0$ whenever B has Lebesgue measure zero. A definition of the latter property is given in §15.3.1, although for us it is enough to know that any countable subset of $\mathbb{R}$ has Lebesgue measure zero. This leads to the following fact:

Fact 4.2.2 If P is absolutely continuous, then $P(C) = 0$ whenever C is countable.

Compare with the discrete distributions, which put all mass on a countable set. One important implication of fact 4.2.2 is that individual points receive no probability mass under absolute continuity, and the corresponding CDF contains no jumps. In fact, when (4.27) holds, the fundamental theorem of calculus tells us that $F(s) = P((-\infty, s])$ is differentiable at all continuity points of p, and, in particular,

$$F'(s) = p(s) \qquad \text{for all } s \in \mathbb{R} \text{ such that } p \text{ is continuous at } s$$

Example 4.2.7 The normal CDFs from example 4.2.1 are differentiable for all μ, σ, with density

$$p(s) = F'(s) = \frac{1}{\sqrt{2\pi}\sigma} \exp\left\{ -\frac{(s-\mu)^2}{2\sigma^2} \right\}$$

See figure 4.9. We reserve the symbol ϕ for the standard normal density.

Example 4.2.8 The Cauchy CDF from example 4.2.4 has density

$$p(s) = \frac{1}{\pi\gamma} \left[1 + \left(\frac{s-\tau}{\gamma} \right)^2 \right]^{-1} \qquad (s \in \mathbb{R},\ \gamma > 0,\ \tau \in \mathbb{R})$$

The Cauchy densities are more peaked around their modes and have greater mass in their tails than normal densities. See figure 4.10.

Example 4.2.9 The beta CDFs from example 4.2.3 have densities given by

$$p(s) = \frac{s^{\alpha-1}(1-s)^{\beta-1}}{B(\alpha, \beta)} \qquad (\alpha, \beta > 0)$$

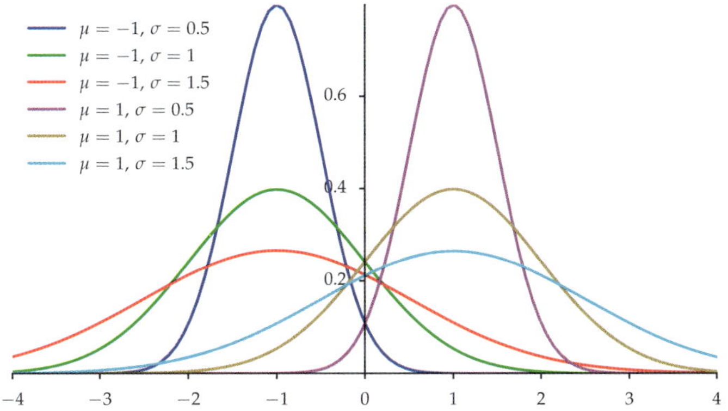

Figure 4.9 Normal densities

when $0 < s < 1$ and zero elsewhere.

Example 4.2.10 The $U[a, b]$ distribution (see page 103) is represented by the density

$$p(s) = \frac{1}{b-a} \mathbb{1}\{a \leqslant s \leqslant b\} \qquad (s \in \mathbb{R},\ a,\ b \in \mathbb{R},\ a < b)$$

Example 4.2.11 The **gamma distribution** with shape parameter α and scale parameter β is the distribution with density

$$p(s) = \frac{s^{\alpha-1} e^{-s/\beta}}{\beta^\alpha \Gamma(\alpha)} \qquad (\alpha, \beta > 0)$$

when $0 < s < 1$ and zero elsewhere.

Example 4.2.12 The **chi-squared distribution with k degrees of freedom** is the distribution with density

$$p(s) := \frac{1}{2^{k/2}\Gamma(k/2)} s^{k/2-1} e^{-s/2} \qquad (s > 0,\ k \in \mathbb{N})$$

This distribution is represented by the symbol $\chi^2(k)$. Figure 4.11 illustrates.

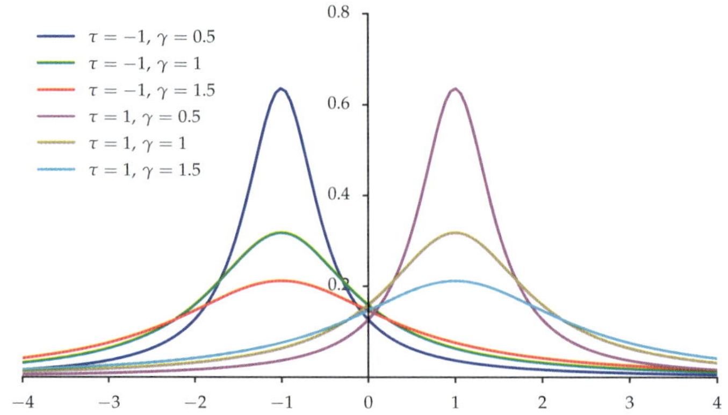

Figure 4.10 Cauchy densities

Example 4.2.13 **Student's t-distribution with k degrees of freedom**, or, more simply, the t-distribution with k degrees of freedom, is the distribution on $\mathbb{R}$ with density

$$p(s) := \frac{\Gamma(\frac{k+1}{2})}{(k\pi)^{1/2}\Gamma(\frac{k}{2})}\left(1 + \frac{s^2}{k}\right)^{-(k+1)/2} \qquad (s \in \mathbb{R},\ k > 0)$$

Example 4.2.14 The **F-distribution** with parameters k_1, k_2 is the distribution with the unlikely looking density

$$p(s) := \frac{\sqrt{(k_1 s)^{k_1} k_2^{k_2} / [k_1 s + k_2]^{k_1+k_2}}}{sB(k_1/2, k_2/2)} \qquad (s \geqslant 0,\ k_1, k_2 > 0)$$

The F-distribution arises in a number of hypothesis tests, as discussed below.

4.2.3 Integrating with Distributions

We all understand what it means to take the ordinary integral $\int_a^b h(s)\,ds$ of a well-behaved function h on some interval $[a, b]$. Sometimes we want to weight this integral, assigning more mass to different regions of $[a, b]$. This leads to integrals such as $\int_a^b h(s)p(s)\,ds$. For example, h could be a welfare function and p might record the density of agents of a certain type. In a probabilistic context, p might be a density indicating probabilities of outcomes, h might be a payoff function and $\int_a^b h(s)p(s)\,ds$ would be expected payoff.

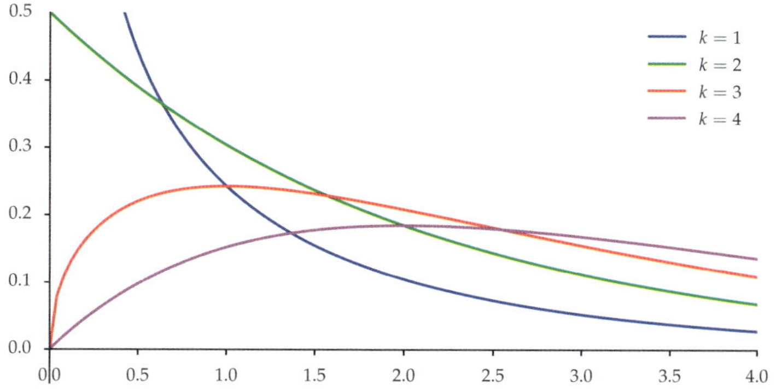

Figure 4.11 Chi-squared densities

We now wish to give meaning to expressions of the form $\int h(s)P(\mathrm{d}s)$ that can be viewed as generalizations of these integrals. The nature of the generalization is that the probability P might not have a density, and yet we still want to compute a weighted integral using P. As motivation we'll continue with the previous example, where $h(s)$ is the payoff from outcome $s \in \mathbb{R}$, and the likelihood of outcomes is determined by probability measure P. To provide some basic regularity, we assume that h is a $\mathscr{B}$-measurable function $\mathbb{R}$.

Actually our task is straightforward given the foundations already laid. In particular, we already have a general notion of integration suitable for understanding the expression $\int h(s)P(\mathrm{d}s)$. In §4.1.4 we saw how to take an arbitrary probability space $(\Omega, \mathscr{F}, \mathbb{P})$ and construct an expectation operator $\mathbb{E}$ that assigns to any integrable random variable a notion of expectation. Expectations can be thought of as integrals, as suggested by the alternative notation $\int x(\omega)\mathbb{P}(\mathrm{d}\omega)$ for $\mathbb{E}x$ used in (4.16) on page 95.

So now take our distribution P on $\mathbb{R}$ and consider $(\mathbb{R}, \mathscr{B}(\mathbb{R}), P)$ as a probability space. This new probability space has its own expectation operator $\mathbb{E}_P$. (See fact 4.1.5 if you wish to refresh your memory on this point.) Moreover we can use it to take the expectation of the payoff function h, which, being a $\mathscr{B}$-measurable function on $\mathbb{R}$, is by definition a random variable on $(\mathbb{R}, \mathscr{B}(\mathbb{R}), P)$. This gives us a value $\mathbb{E}_P h$, which is exactly the integral we're after:

$$\mathbb{E}_P h =: \int h(s)P(\mathrm{d}s) := \text{the expectation of } h \text{ under } P$$

While the preceding discussion gives a neat definition of $\int h(s)P(\mathrm{d}s)$, it would be disappointing if this definition didn't lead us back to familiar expressions like $\int h(s)p(s)\,\mathrm{d}s$ when P has a density. Fortunately, it does:

Fact 4.2.3 Let $h\colon \mathbb{R} \to \mathbb{R}$ be $\mathscr{B}$-measurable and let P be a distribution on $\mathbb{R}$. If P is discrete, with PMF $\{p_j\}_{j\geqslant 1}$ and support $\{s_j\}_{j\geqslant 1}$, then

$$\int h(s)P(\mathrm{d}s) = \sum_{j\geqslant 1} h(s_j)p_j \tag{4.28}$$

If P is absolutely continuous with density p, then

$$\int h(s)P(\mathrm{d}s) = \int_{-\infty}^{\infty} h(s)p(s)\,\mathrm{d}s \tag{4.29}$$

For a proof of fact 4.2.3, see §6.12 of Williams (1991).

4.2.4 Distributions of Random Variables

In §4.1.3 we defined random variables. Over the last few sections we've defined and discussed distributions over the Borel subsets of $\mathbb{R}$. Our next job is to connect them. We'll see that the connection runs in both directions: Every random variable defines a distribution on $\mathbb{R}$. Conversely, given any distribution, we can reverse engineer a random variable having that distribution.

To begin, let x be a random variable on some probability space $(\Omega, \mathscr{F}, \mathbb{P})$. By construction, the probability $\mathbb{P}\{x \in B\}$ is well-defined for every $B \in \mathscr{B}(\mathbb{R})$ (see (4.9)). The values obtained from this expression when x is held fixed and B is varied is called the **distribution of** x. In particular, the set function P defined by

$$P(B) = \mathbb{P}\{x \in B\} \qquad (B \in \mathscr{B}(\mathbb{R})) \tag{4.30}$$

is both the distribution of x and also a distribution in the sense of §4.1.3 (i.e., a probability measure over the Borel sets). It records the probabilities of all outcomes of interest for the variable x when regarded as a single entity.[3] In what follows we write $\mathcal{L}(x)$ for the distribution (or "law") of x. The relationship in (4.30) is summarized by writing $\mathcal{L}(x) = P$.

By (4.24), the CDF corresponding to the distribution P of x satisfies

$$F(s) = \mathbb{P}\{x \leqslant s\} \qquad (s \in \mathbb{R}) \tag{4.31}$$

Sometimes F is called the **distribution function** or just distribution of x. Since F characterizes P, we also write $\mathcal{L}(x) = F$ to indicate that F represents the distribution of x.

3. When we want to combine x with other random variables we'll need their joint distribution. See §5.1.3.

Fact 4.2.4 If $\mathcal{L}(x) = F$, then $\mathbb{P}\{a < x \leqslant b\} = F(b) - F(a)$ for any $a \leqslant b$.

Indeed, if $a \leqslant b$, then $\{a < x \leqslant b\} = \{x \leqslant b\} \setminus \{x \leqslant a\}$ and $\{x \leqslant a\} \subset \{x \leqslant b\}$. Applying fact 4.1.1 on page 86 gives

$$\mathbb{P}\{a < x \leqslant b\} = \mathbb{P}\{x \leqslant b\} - \mathbb{P}\{x \leqslant a\} = F(b) - F(a)$$

From (4.31) we get for each random variable a uniquely defined CDF. It's also true that for every CDF F, there exists a probability space $(\Omega, \mathscr{F}, \mathbb{P})$ and a random variable $x \colon \Omega \to \mathbb{R}$ such that $\mathcal{L}(x) = F$; §7.4.1 outlines one construction.

In what follows, if $\mathcal{L}(x) = P$ and P has density p, we'll say that x **has density** p. If the distribution of x is discrete, we'll call x a **discrete random variable**. In the former case, where the distribution of x is absolutely continuous, no probability mass is placed on finite sets, leading to the next fact.

Fact 4.2.5 If x has a density, then $\mathbb{P}\{x = s\} = 0$ for all $s \in \mathbb{R}$, and for any $a < b$,

$$\mathbb{P}\{a < x < b\} = \mathbb{P}\{a < x \leqslant b\} = \mathbb{P}\{a \leqslant x < b\} = \mathbb{P}\{a \leqslant x \leqslant b\}$$

4.2.4.1 Distributions of Transformations

One often needs to obtain the distribution of the transform of a random variable. This is easy in the monotone case.

Fact 4.2.6 If $\mathcal{L}(x) = F$ and $y := \psi(x)$, where $\psi \colon \mathbb{R} \to \mathbb{R}$ is strictly increasing, then $\mathcal{L}(y) = G$ where $G(s) := F(\psi^{-1}(s))$.

To see why, observe that under these hypotheses ψ^{-1} exists and is (weakly) increasing. Hence

$$\mathbb{P}\{y \leqslant s\} = \mathbb{P}\{\psi(x) \leqslant s\} = \mathbb{P}\{x \leqslant \psi^{-1}(s)\} = F(\psi^{-1}(s))$$

Note how monotonicity is used in the second equality. (A related result can be derived for the strictly decreasing case, where the direction of the inequality flips.)

Example 4.2.15 If $\mathcal{L}(x) = F$ and $y := \exp(x)$, then the CDF of y is $G(s) := F(\ln(s))$.

An important related question is to determine when $y = \psi(x)$ has a density, and what the form of this density is.

Fact 4.2.7 If x has density p on $\mathbb{R}$ and $y := \psi(x)$ where ψ is a diffeomorphism on $\mathbb{R}$, then the distribution of y is absolutely continuous, with density

$$q(s) = p(\psi^{-1}(s)) \left| \frac{\mathrm{d}\psi^{-1}(s)}{\mathrm{d}s} \right| \qquad (s \in \mathbb{R}) \tag{4.32}$$

Exercise 5.4.1 asks you to confirm (4.32). The term **diffeomorphism** just means that ψ is a bijection on $\mathbb{R}$ and both ψ and its inverse are differentiable.

Example 4.2.16 If x has density p on $\mathbb{R}$ and μ and σ are constants with $\sigma > 0$, then the density of $y := \mu + \sigma x$ is

$$q(s) = p\left(\frac{s-\mu}{\sigma}\right)\frac{1}{\sigma} \qquad (s \in \mathbb{R})$$

When x is standard normal, this implies that $y = \mu + \sigma x$ is $\mathrm{N}(\mu, \sigma^2)$, as can be seen by taking p to be the standard normal density ϕ and comparing with the expression for the $\mathrm{N}(\mu, \sigma^2)$ density on page 106.

Fact 4.2.7 can be generalized. See, for example, theorem 15.5 of Schilling (2005).

4.2.5 Expectations from Distributions

Let x be a random variable on probability space $(\Omega, \mathscr{F}, \mathbb{P})$. The distribution of x encodes all the information necessary to calculate expectations of x or of any $\mathscr{B}$-measurable transformation $h(x)$. This is clearest when x is finite. For example, suppose that $\mathcal{L}(x) = P$, that $h\colon \mathbb{R} \to \mathbb{R}$ is any $\mathscr{B}$-measurable function, and that P puts all mass on finite set $\{s_j\}_{j=1}^J$. Let $\{p_j\}$ be the PMF of P, so that $p_j = P\{s_j\}$. Applying the definition of expectations (see in particular (4.17) on page 96) and using $\mathbb{P}\{x = s_j\} = P\{s_j\}$ gives

$$\mathbb{E}h(x) = \sum_{j=1}^J h(s_j)\mathbb{P}\{x = s_j\} = \sum_{j=1}^J h(s_j)P\{s_j\} = \sum_{j=1}^J h(s_j)p_j \tag{4.33}$$

Comparing this with (4.28) on page 110, we can also write $\mathbb{E}h(x) = \int h(s)P(\mathrm{d}s)$. Put differently, the expectation of $h(x)$ on $(\Omega, \mathscr{F}, \mathbb{P})$ is equal to the expectation of h on $(\mathbb{R}, \mathscr{B}(\mathbb{R}), P)$. This is also true in the infinite case (see, e.g., theorem 5.2 of Çinlar (2011)), as stated in the next fact.

Fact 4.2.8 Let x be a random variable on some probability space $(\Omega, \mathscr{F}, \mathbb{P})$, let $\mathcal{L}(x) = P$ and let h be a $\mathscr{B}$-measurable function such that $h(x)$ is integrable. The expectation $\mathbb{E}h(x)$ is entirely determined by h and P. In particular,

$$\mathbb{E}h(x) = \int h(s)P(\mathrm{d}s)$$

where $\int h(s)P(\mathrm{d}s)$ is the expectation of h on $(\mathbb{R}, \mathscr{B}(\mathbb{R}), P)$.

Example 4.2.17 Let x be a random variable whose distribution P is the uniform distribution on $[a, b]$. Applying the definition of the uniform density in example 4.2.10, we obtain

$$\mathbb{E} x = \int s P(\mathrm{d}s) = \int s p(s) \,\mathrm{d}s = \int_{-\infty}^{\infty} \frac{s}{b-a} \mathbb{1}\{a \leqslant s \leqslant b\} \,\mathrm{d}s$$

Solving the integral gives $\mathbb{E} x = \mu := (a+b)/2$. The variance is

$$\operatorname{var}[x] = \int (s-\mu)^2 P(\mathrm{d}s) = \int_a^b \left(s - \frac{a+b}{2}\right)^2 \frac{1}{b-a} \,\mathrm{d}s = \frac{1}{12}(b-a)^2$$

Example 4.2.18 Suppose that $\mathcal{L}(x) = \mathrm{N}(\mu, \sigma)$. In the case where $\sigma > 0$, the mean can be computed via

$$\mathbb{E} x = \int_{-\infty}^{\infty} s \frac{1}{\sqrt{2\pi}\sigma} \exp\left\{-\frac{(s-\mu)^2}{2\sigma^2}\right\} \mathrm{d}s = \mu$$

The variance is given by

$$\operatorname{var}[x] = \int_{-\infty}^{\infty} (s-\mu)^2 \frac{1}{\sqrt{2\pi}\sigma} \exp\left\{-\frac{(s-\mu)^2}{2\sigma^2}\right\} \mathrm{d}s = \sigma^2$$

For a discussion of how these integrals are solved, see §9.4 of Dudley (2002).

4.2.5.1 Moments from Distributions

In §4.1.5 we defined moments of random variables. For example, $\mathbb{E} x^k$ is the kth moment of x, assuming it exists. It is clear from fact 4.2.8 that any two random variables with the same distribution share the same moments. Hence moments are best thought of as a property of the distribution, not the random variable. Thus we define

- the **mean** of P as $\mu = \int s P(\mathrm{d}s)$,
- the **kth moment** of P as $\int s^k P(\mathrm{d}s)$,
- the **variance** of P as $\int (s-\mu)^2 P(\mathrm{d}s)$,

and so on.

4.2.6 Quantile Functions

In this section it will be convenient to describe distributions in terms of CDFs. So let F be a CDF on $\mathbb{R}$, which, for the moment, we assume to be strictly increasing. Given $\tau \in (0,1)$, the **τth quantile** of F is the $\xi \in \mathbb{R}$ that solves $F(\xi) = \tau$. Under our

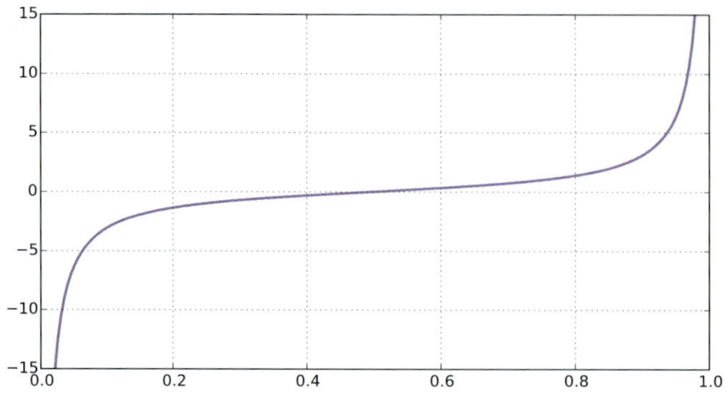

Figure 4.12 Cauchy quantile function

assumptions on F, such a ξ exists and is uniquely defined. The 0.5th quantile is called the **median** of F. It provides a measure of central tendency for the distribution.

We can of course express the τth quantile of F using the inverse function:

$$F^{-1}(\tau) := \text{ the unique } \xi \text{ such that } F(\xi) = \tau \qquad (0 < \tau < 1) \tag{4.34}$$

Not surprisingly, the inverse of F is also called the **quantile function**.

Example 4.2.19 The quantile function associated with the standard Cauchy distribution (see page 103) is $F^{-1}(\tau) = \tan[\pi(\tau - 1/2)]$. Figure 4.12 illustrates. The horizontal axis is $\tau \in (0, 1)$.

If F is not strictly increasing, then there exist at least two distinct points s, s' such that $F(s) = F(s')$, and hence F^{-1} in (4.34) is not well-defined. This problem is negotiated by setting

$$F^{-1}(\tau) := \inf\{s \in \mathbb{R} : F(s) \geqslant \tau\} \qquad (0 < \tau < 1) \tag{4.35}$$

(See §15.4.1 for a definition of inf.) In the case where F is strictly increasing, (4.35) reduces to (4.34).

The quantile function is used in hypothesis testing to determine critical values. Let's outline a common scenario.

Fact 4.2.9 Let x be a random variable with density p. If p is symmetric, then the CDF

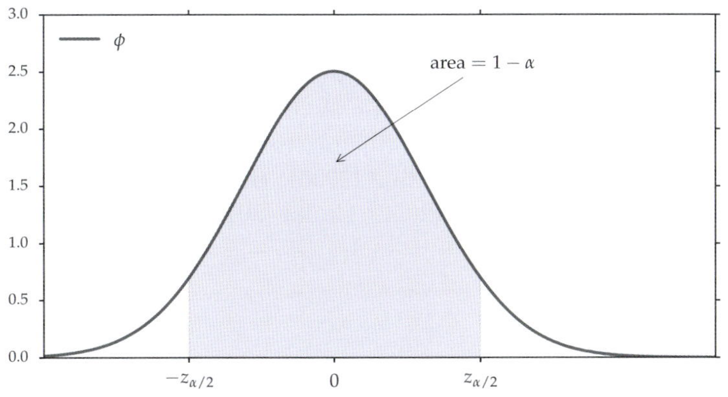

Figure 4.13 Critical values for the standard normal density

G of $y := |x|$ is given by

$$G(s) := \mathbb{P}\{y \leqslant s\} = \begin{cases} 2F(s) - 1 & \text{if } s \geqslant 0 \\ 0 & \text{otherwise} \end{cases}$$

Here **symmetry** of p means that $p(s) = p(-s)$ for all $s \in \mathbb{R}$. This is equivalent to $F(s) = 1 - F(-s)$, as can be seen by differentiating or integrating. Exercise 4.4.18 asks you to prove fact 4.2.9.

Now take a random variable x with $\mathcal{L}(x) = F$ and constant $\alpha \in (0, 1)$ as given, and consider the c that solves $\mathbb{P}\{-c \leqslant x \leqslant c\} = 1 - \alpha$.

Fact 4.2.10 If $\mathcal{L}(x) = F$, x has a symmetric density and F is strictly increasing, then

$$c = F^{-1}(1 - \alpha/2) \quad \Longrightarrow \quad \mathbb{P}\{-c \leqslant x \leqslant c\} = 1 - \alpha \tag{4.36}$$

To see this, fix $\alpha \in (0, 1)$ and let c be as in (4.36). From fact 4.2.9, we have

$$\mathbb{P}\{|x| \leqslant c\} = 2F(c) - 1 = 2F[F^{-1}(1 - \alpha/2)] - 1 = 1 - \alpha$$

In the case where F is the standard normal CDF Φ, this value c is usually denoted by $z_{\alpha/2}$. We will adopt the same notation:

$$z_{\alpha/2} := \Phi^{-1}(1 - \alpha/2) \tag{4.37}$$

See figure 4.13.

4.3 Further Reading

The modern axiomatic treatment of probability based on measure theory was formulated in the 1930s by Andrei N. Kolmogorov. A discussion of his life and work can be found in Kendall et al. (1990). Nice introductory texts on measure-theoretic probability include Williams (1991) and Rosenthal (2006). Beautiful expositions at a slightly higher level can be found in Dudley (2002), Çinlar (2011), and Pollard (2002).

4.4 Exercises

Ex. 4.4.1 Show that if $\mathscr{F}$ is a σ-algebra and $A, B \in \mathscr{F}$, then $A \cap B \in \mathscr{F}$ also holds.[4]

Ex. 4.4.2 Prove fact 4.1.2: $\mathbb{P}(A \cup B) = \mathbb{P}(A) + \mathbb{P}(B) - \mathbb{P}(A \cap B)$ for any A, B.[5]

Ex. 4.4.3 Given sample space $\Omega := \{1, 2, 3\}$, let $A := \{1\}$, $B := \{2\}$, and $C := \{3\}$. Let $\mathbb{P}(A) = \mathbb{P}(B) = 1/3$. Compute $\mathbb{P}(C)$, $\mathbb{P}(A \cup B)$, $\mathbb{P}(A \cap B)$, $\mathbb{P}(A^c)$, $\mathbb{P}(A^c \cup B^c)$, and $\mathbb{P}(A \mid B)$. Are A and C independent?

Ex. 4.4.4 A die is designed so that the probability of getting face m is qm, where $m \in \{1, \ldots, 6\}$ and q is a constant. Compute q.

Ex. 4.4.5 Prove the claims in fact 4.1.4 on page 90.

Ex. 4.4.6 Let Ω be a nonempty finite set, and let ω_0 be a fixed element of Ω. For each $A \subset \Omega$, define $\mathbb{P}(A) := \mathbb{1}\{\omega_0 \in A\}$. Is $\mathbb{P}$ a probability on Ω? Why or why not?

Ex. 4.4.7 Let Ω be any sample space, and let $\mathbb{P}$ be a probability on the subsets $\mathscr{F}$. Let $A \in \mathscr{F}$. Show that if $\mathbb{P}(A) = 0$ or $\mathbb{P}(A) = 1$, then A is independent of every other event in $\mathscr{F}$. Show that if A is independent of itself, then either $\mathbb{P}(A) = 0$ or $\mathbb{P}(A) = 1$. Show that if A and B are independent, then A^c and B^c are also independent.

Ex. 4.4.8 Let $\mathbb{P}$ and Ω be defined as in example 4.1.6. Show that $\mathbb{P}$ is additive, in the sense that if A and B are disjoint events, then $\mathbb{P}(A \cup B) = \mathbb{P}(A) + \mathbb{P}(B)$.

Ex. 4.4.9 Let $\mathbb{P}$ and Ω be defined as in example 4.1.6. Let A be the event that the first flip is heads, and let B be the event that the second flip is heads. Show that A and B are independent under $\mathbb{P}$.

Ex. 4.4.10 Show that when Ω is finite, each random variable on Ω is finite.[6]

---

4. Hint: See the rules concerning set-theoretic operations in fact 15.1.1 on page 407.

5. Hint: Sketching the Venn diagram, convince yourself that $A = [(A \cup B) \setminus B] \cup (A \cap B)$. Finish the proof using the definition of a probability and fact 4.1.1 (page 86).

6. Hint: Review the definition of a function in §15.2.

Ex. 4.4.11 Show that any finite random variable can be expressed as

$$x = \sum_{j=1}^{J} s_j \mathbb{1}_{A_j} \tag{4.38}$$

where the scalars $\{s_j\}$ are distinct and the sets $\{A_j\}$ are events that partition Ω.

Ex. 4.4.12 For the generic finite random variable x defined in exercise 4.4.11, show that $\mathbb{E}\, x := \sum_{j=1}^{J} s_j \mathbb{P}(A_j)$.

Ex. 4.4.13 Fact 4.1.5 on page 95 states, among other things, that if x is a random variable and α is a constant, then $\mathbb{E}[\alpha x] = \alpha \mathbb{E}[x]$. Prove this for the case where x is a finite random variable using the definition (4.12).

Ex. 4.4.14 Fact 4.1.5 on page 95 states that, among other things, if x and y are two random variables, then $\mathbb{E}[x+y] = \mathbb{E}[x] + \mathbb{E}[y]$. Prove this for the binary random variables

$$x(\omega) = \mathbb{1}_A(\omega) \quad \text{and} \quad y(\omega) = \mathbb{1}_B(\omega) \tag{4.39}$$

using the definition (4.12).

Ex. 4.4.15 Let P be a discrete distribution with $P(\{s_j\}_{j \geqslant 1}) = 1$, and let $p_j := P\{s_j\}$. Show that $\sum_{j \geqslant 1} p_j = 1$.

Ex. 4.4.16 Let P, s_j and p_j be as in exercise 4.4.15. Show that if F is the CDF of P, then $F(s) = \sum_{j \geqslant 1} \mathbb{1}\{s_j \leqslant s\} p_j$ for all $s \in \mathbb{R}$.

Ex. 4.4.17 Let P, s_j and p_j be as in exercise 4.4.15. Show that $\lim_{s \to \infty} F(s) = 1$.

Ex. 4.4.18 Prove the claim in fact 4.2.9 on page 114.

Ex. 4.4.19 Let x be a discrete random variable taking values $s_1, \ldots, s_J$, and let $p_j := \mathbb{P}\{x = s_j\}$. Show that $0 \leqslant p_j \leqslant 1$ for each j, and $\sum_{j=1}^{J} p_j = 1$.

Ex. 4.4.20 Let $\mathcal{L}(x) = F$ where F is the uniform CDF on $[0, 1]$. Give an expression for the CDF G of the random variable $y = x^2$.

Ex. 4.4.21 Let F be the CDF on $\mathbb{R}$ defined by $F(s) = e^s / (1 + e^s)$ for $s \in \mathbb{R}$.

(i) Obtain the quantile function corresponding to F.

(ii) Let $\mathcal{L}(x) = F$ and compute $\mathbb{P}\{0 \leqslant x \leqslant \ln 2\}$.

Ex. 4.4.22 Let $\mathcal{L}(y) = F$, where F is a CDF. Show that $F(s) = \mathbb{E}\, \mathbb{1}\{y \leqslant s\}$ for any s.

Ex. 4.4.23 Confirm monotonicity of expectations (see fact 4.1.5 on page 95) for the special case where x and y are the random variables in (4.39).

Ex. 4.4.24 Prove fact 4.1.7 (existence of kth moment implies existence of jth moment for all $j \leqslant k$).

Ex. 4.4.25 Confirm the expression for variance of linear combinations in fact 4.1.10.

Ex. 4.4.26 Let x and y be scalar random variables. With reference to fact 4.1.11 on page 98, is it true that $\mathrm{corr}[\alpha x, \beta y] = \mathrm{corr}[x, y]$ for *any* constant scalars α and β? Why or why not?

Ex. 4.4.27 Confirm the solutions in (4.23).

Ex. 4.4.28 Consider the setting of §4.1.5. Let α^*, β^* and ℓ^* be as defined there. Let the prediction error u be defined as $u := y - \ell^*(x)$. Show that

(i) $\mathbb{E}\,\ell^*(x) = \mathbb{E}\,y$

(ii) $\mathrm{var}[\ell^*(x)] = \mathrm{corr}[x, y]^2 \,\mathrm{var}[y]$

(iii) $\mathrm{cov}[\ell^*(x), u] = 0$

(iv) $\mathrm{var}[u] = (1 - \mathrm{corr}[x, y]^2)\,\mathrm{var}[y]$

Ex. 4.4.29 Prove the Chebyshev inequalities (4.18) and (4.19).

4.4.1 Solutions to Selected Exercises

Solution to Ex. 4.4.1. Let $\mathscr{F}$ be a σ-algebra and let $A, B \in \mathscr{F}$. The claim is that $A \cap B \in \mathscr{F}$. To see this, note that by the definition of a σ-algebra we must have $A^c \in \mathscr{F}$ and $B^c \in \mathscr{F}$. Since $\mathscr{F}$ is closed under the taking of unions, this means that $A^c \cup B^c \in \mathscr{F}$. Applying fact 15.1.1 on page 407 gives $(A \cap B)^c \in \mathscr{F}$. But then $A \cap B \in \mathscr{F}$, as was to be shown. □

Solution to Ex. 4.4.2. Pick any sets $A, B \in \mathscr{F}$. To show that

$$\mathbb{P}(A \cup B) = \mathbb{P}(A) + \mathbb{P}(B) - \mathbb{P}(A \cap B)$$

we start by decomposing A into the union of two disjoint sets: $A = [(A \cup B) \setminus B] \cup (A \cap B)$. Using additivity of $\mathbb{P}$, we then have

$$\mathbb{P}(A) = \mathbb{P}[(A \cup B) \setminus B] + \mathbb{P}(A \cap B)$$

Since $B \subset (A \cup B)$, we can apply part 1 of fact 4.1.1 (page 86) to obtain

$$\mathbb{P}(A) = \mathbb{P}(A \cup B) - \mathbb{P}(B) + \mathbb{P}(A \cap B)$$

Rearranging this expression gives the result that we are seeking. □

Solution to Ex. 4.4.3. First $\mathbb{P}(C) = 1/3$ as $1 = \mathbb{P}(\Omega) = \mathbb{P}(A \cup B \cup C) = \mathbb{P}(A) + \mathbb{P}(B) + \mathbb{P}(C) = 1/3 + 1/3 + \mathbb{P}(C)$, and hence $\mathbb{P}(C) = 1/3$. In addition $\mathbb{P}(A \cup B) = 2/3$, $\mathbb{P}(A \cap B) = 0$, $\mathbb{P}(A^c) = 2/3$, $\mathbb{P}(A^c \cup B^c) = \mathbb{P}((A \cap B)^c) = \mathbb{P}(\Omega) = 1$, and $\mathbb{P}(A \cap C) = 0 \neq 1/9 = \mathbb{P}(A)\mathbb{P}(C)$. Therefore A is not independent of C. □

Solution to Ex. 4.4.4. When the die is rolled one face must come up, so the sum of the probabilities is one. More formally, letting $\Omega = \{1, \dots, 6\}$ be the sample space, we have

$$\mathbb{P}\{1, \dots, 6\} = \mathbb{P} \cup_{m=1}^{6} \{m\} = \sum_{m=1}^{6} \mathbb{P}\{m\} = \sum_{m=1}^{6} qm = 1$$

Solving the last equality for q, we get $q = 1/21$. □

Solution to Ex. 4.4.5. Let $A_1, \dots, A_N$ be subsets of Ω. Pick any $\omega \in \Omega$. Regarding part (i), suppose first that $\mathbb{1}_{\cap_{n=1}^N A_n}(\omega) = 1$. Then $\omega \in \cap_{n=1}^N A_n$, and hence $\omega \in A_n$ for all n. But then $\prod_{n=1}^N \mathbb{1}_{A_n}(\omega) = 1$. Conversely, if $\mathbb{1}_{\cap_{n=1}^N A_n}(\omega) = 0$, then ω is not in at least one A_n, so $\prod_{n=1}^N \mathbb{1}_{A_n}(\omega) = 0$. This verifies part (i) of fact 4.1.4. The proof of (ii) is similar. □

Solution to Ex. 4.4.6. To show that $\mathbb{P}$ is a probability on Ω, we need to check that

(i) $\mathbb{1}\{\omega_0 \in A\} \in [0, 1]$ for every $A \subset \Omega$.

(ii) $\mathbb{1}\{\omega_0 \in \Omega\} = 1$.

(iii) If $A \cap B = \emptyset$, then $\mathbb{1}\{\omega_0 \in A \cup B\} = \mathbb{1}\{\omega_0 \in A\} + \mathbb{1}\{\omega_0 \in B\}$.

Part (i) is immediate from the definition of an indicator function. Part (ii) holds because $\omega_0 \in \Omega$. Regarding (iii), pick any disjoint A and B. If $\omega_0 \in A$, then $\omega_0 \notin B$, and we have

$$\mathbb{1}\{\omega_0 \in A \cup B\} = 1 = \mathbb{1}\{\omega_0 \in A\} + \mathbb{1}\{\omega_0 \in B\}$$

If $\omega_0 \in B$, then $\omega_0 \notin A$, and once again we have

$$\mathbb{1}\{\omega_0 \in A \cup B\} = 1 = \mathbb{1}\{\omega_0 \in A\} + \mathbb{1}\{\omega_0 \in B\}$$

Finally, if ω_0 is in neither A nor B, then

$$\mathbb{1}\{\omega_0 \in A \cup B\} = 0 = \mathbb{1}\{\omega_0 \in A\} + \mathbb{1}\{\omega_0 \in B\}$$

We have shown that (i)–(iii) hold, and hence $\mathbb{P}$ is a probability on Ω. □

Solution to Ex. 4.4.7. Suppose that $\mathbb{P}(A) = 0$ and that $B \in \mathscr{F}$. We claim that $\mathbb{P}(A \cap B) = \mathbb{P}(A)\mathbb{P}(B)$, or, in this case, $\mathbb{P}(A \cap B) = 0$. Using nonnegativity and monotonicity of $\mathbb{P}$ (fact 4.1.1), we obtain

$$0 \leqslant \mathbb{P}(A \cap B) \leqslant P(A) = 0$$

Therefore $\mathbb{P}(A \cap B) = 0$ as claimed.

Now suppose that $\mathbb{P}(A) = 1$. We claim that $\mathbb{P}(A \cap B) = \mathbb{P}(A)\mathbb{P}(B)$, or, in this case, $\mathbb{P}(A \cap B) = \mathbb{P}(B)$. In view of fact 4.1.2 on page 86, we have

$$\mathbb{P}(A \cap B) = \mathbb{P}(A) + \mathbb{P}(B) - \mathbb{P}(A \cup B)$$

Since $\mathbb{P}(A) = 1$, it suffices to show that $\mathbb{P}(A \cup B) = 1$. This last equality is implied by monotonicity of $\mathbb{P}$, because $1 = \mathbb{P}(A) \leqslant \mathbb{P}(A \cup B) \leqslant 1$.

Next, suppose that A is independent of itself. In that case we have $\mathbb{P}(A) = \mathbb{P}(A \cap A) = \mathbb{P}(A)\mathbb{P}(A) = \mathbb{P}(A)^2$. If $a = a^2$, then either $a = 0$ or $a = 1$.

Finally, let A and B be independent. We have

$$\mathbb{P}(A^c \cap B^c) = \mathbb{P}((A \cup B)^c) = 1 - \mathbb{P}(A \cup B)$$

Applying fact 4.1.2 and independence, we can transform the right-hand side to obtain

$$\mathbb{P}(A^c \cap B^c) = (1 - \mathbb{P}(A))(1 - \mathbb{P}(B)) = \mathbb{P}(A^c)\mathbb{P}(B^c)$$

In other words, A^c and B^c are independent. □

Solution to Ex. 4.4.8. The proof is almost identical to the proof of additivity in example 4.1.5 (page 85). □

Solution to Ex. 4.4.9. The proof of independence is essentially the same as the proof of independence of A and B in example 4.1.8 (page 87). □

Solution to Ex. 4.4.11. Let x be finite-valued, with range $\{s_1, \ldots, s_J\}$. Let $A_j := \{x = s_j\}$. By the definition of a function (see §15.2), each $\omega \in \Omega$ lies in exactly one A_j. Hence $A_1, \ldots, A_J$ is a partition of Ω, and $x = \sum_{j=1}^J s_j \mathbb{1}_{A_j}$. □

Solution to Ex. 4.4.12. Clearly x is finite-valued, so, by (4.12), the expectation is given by $\mathbb{E}x = \sum_{j=1}^J s_j \mathbb{P}\{x = s_j\}$. Hence, to confirm $\mathbb{E}x := \sum_{j=1}^J s_j \mathbb{P}(A_j)$, we need only show that $\{x = s_j\} = A_j$. That the last statement is true follows from (4.38) and the fact that $A_1, \ldots, A_J$ is a partition of Ω. □

Solution to Ex. 4.4.13. Let x be finite with range $\{s_1, \ldots, s_J\}$ and let α be any constant. We claim that $\mathbb{E}[\alpha x] = \alpha\mathbb{E}[x]$. If $\alpha = 0$ the result is trivial, as both sides are clearly zero. If not then $\alpha x = \alpha s_j$ if and only if $x = s_j$. Hence, applying (4.12),

$$\mathbb{E}[\alpha x] = \sum_{j=1}^{J} \alpha s_j \mathbb{P}\{x = s_j\} = \alpha \left[\sum_{j=1}^{J} s_j \mathbb{P}\{x = s_j\} \right] = \alpha \mathbb{E}[x] \qquad \square$$

Solution to Ex. 4.4.14. Consider the sum $x + y$. By this, we mean the random variable $(x + y)(\omega) := x(\omega) + y(\omega)$. We claim that $\mathbb{E}[x + y] = \mathbb{E}[x] + \mathbb{E}[y]$. To see this, note first that

$$(x + y)(\omega) = \mathbb{1}_{A \setminus B}(\omega) + \mathbb{1}_{B \setminus A}(\omega) + 2\mathbb{1}_{A \cap B}(\omega)$$

(To check this, just go through the different cases for ω, and verify that the right-hand side of this expression agrees with $x(\omega) + y(\omega)$. Sketching a Venn diagram will help.) Therefore, by the definition of expectation,

$$\mathbb{E}[x + y] = \mathbb{P}(A \setminus B) + \mathbb{P}(B \setminus A) + 2\mathbb{P}(A \cap B) \tag{4.40}$$

Now observe that $A = (A \setminus B) \cup (A \cap B)$, and hence, by disjointness,

$$\mathbb{E}[x] := \mathbb{P}(A) = \mathbb{P}(A \setminus B) + \mathbb{P}(A \cap B)$$

Performing a similar calculation with y produces

$$\mathbb{E}[y] := \mathbb{P}(B) = \mathbb{P}(B \setminus A) + \mathbb{P}(A \cap B)$$

Summing these equations produces the value on the right-hand side of (4.40), thereby confirming $\mathbb{E}[x + y] = \mathbb{E}[x] + \mathbb{E}[y]$. $\square$

Solution to Ex. 4.4.15. Let $P(\{s_j\}_{j \geqslant 1}) = 1$ and $p_j := P\{s_j\}$ as stated in the exercise. The set $\{s_j\}_{j \geqslant 1}$ can be written as $\cup_{j=1}^{\infty} \{s_j\}$. Since P is a distribution it is countably additive (see page 100) and hence $1 = P(\cup_{j=1}^{\infty} \{s_j\}) = \sum_{j=1}^{\infty} P\{s_j\} = \sum_{j=1}^{\infty} p_j$. $\square$

Solution to Ex. 4.4.16. Using additivity and the fact that $P\{s_j\}_{j \geqslant 1} = 1$, we have

$$F(s) = P(-\infty, s] = P\left(\bigcup_{j \text{ s.t. } s_j \leqslant s} \{s_j\} \right) = \sum_{j \text{ s.t. } s_j \leqslant s} P\{s_j\} = \sum_{j=1}^{J} \mathbb{1}\{s_j \leqslant s\} p_j \qquad \square$$

Solution to Ex. 4.4.17. We are assuming that x has finite range, and hence takes only finitely many different values. Let m be the largest such value. For this m, we have

$$\lim_{s \to \infty} F_x(s) \geqslant F_x(m) = \mathbb{P}\{\omega \in \Omega : x(\omega) \leqslant m\} = \mathbb{P}(\Omega) = 1$$

(The inequality is due to the fact that F_x is increasing.) On the other hand,

$$\lim_{s\to\infty} F_x(s) = \lim_{s\to\infty} \mathbb{P}\{x \leqslant s\} \leqslant \lim_{s\to\infty} \mathbb{P}(\Omega) = 1$$

From these two inequalities we get $1 \leqslant \lim_{s\to\infty} F_x(s) \leqslant 1$, which is equivalent to $\lim_{s\to\infty} F_x(s) = 1$. □

Solution to Ex. 4.4.18. Fix $s \geqslant 0$. Using additivity over disjoint sets, we have

$$F_{|x|}(s) := \mathbb{P}\{|x| \leqslant s\} = \mathbb{P}\{-s \leqslant x \leqslant s\} = \mathbb{P}\{x = -s\} + \mathbb{P}\{-s < x \leqslant s\}$$

By assumption, $\mathbb{P}\{x = -s\} = 0$. Applying fact 4.2.4 on page 111 then yields

$$F_{|x|}(s) = \mathbb{P}\{-s < x \leqslant s\} = F(s) - F(-s)$$

As discussed after fact 4.2.9, symmetry is equivalent to $F(-s) = 1 - F(s)$. Plugging this in to the right-hand side of the previous expression gives $F_{|x|}(s) = 2F(s) - 1$. □

Solution to Ex. 4.4.19. That $0 \leqslant p_j \leqslant 1$ for each j follows immediately from the definition of $\mathbb{P}$. In addition, using additivity of $\mathbb{P}$, we have

$$\sum_{j=1}^{J} p_j = \sum_{j=1}^{J} \mathbb{P}\{x = s_j\} = \mathbb{P} \cup_{j=1}^{J} \{x = s_j\} = \mathbb{P}(\Omega) = 1 \tag{4.41}$$

(We are using the fact that the sets $\{x = s_j\}$ are disjoint. Why is this always true? Look at the definition of a function given in §15.2.) □

Solution to Ex. 4.4.20. Evidently $G(s) = 0$ when $s < 0$. For $s \geqslant 0$ we have

$$\mathbb{P}\{x^2 \leqslant s\} = \mathbb{P}\{|x| \leqslant \sqrt{s}\} = \mathbb{P}\{x \leqslant \sqrt{s}\} = F(\sqrt{s})$$

Thus, $G(s) = F(\sqrt{s})\mathbb{1}\{s \geqslant 0\}$. □

Solution to Ex. 4.4.23. If $x(\omega) := \mathbb{1}\{\omega \in A\} \leqslant \mathbb{1}\{\omega \in B\} =: y(\omega)$ for any $\omega \in \Omega$, then $A \subset B$. (If $\omega \in A$, then $x(\omega) = 1$. Since $x(\omega) \leqslant y(\omega) \leqslant 1$, we have $y(\omega) = 1$, and hence $\omega \in B$.) Using fact 4.1.5 and monotonicity of $\mathbb{P}$, we then have

$$\mathbb{E}x = \mathbb{E}\mathbb{1}\{\omega \in A\} = \mathbb{P}(A) \leqslant \mathbb{P}(B) = \mathbb{E}\mathbb{1}\{\omega \in B\} = \mathbb{E}y$$ □

Solution to Ex. 4.4.24. Let a be any nonnegative number, and let $j \leqslant k$. If $a \geqslant 1$, then $a^j \leqslant a^k$. If $a < 1$, then $a^j \leqslant 1$. Thus, for any $a \geqslant 0$, we have $a^j \leqslant a^k + 1$, and for any random variable x we have $|x|^j \leqslant |x|^k + 1$. Using linearity and monotonicity of expectations and $\mathbb{E}1 = 1$, we then have $\mathbb{E}|x|^j \leqslant \mathbb{E}|x^k| + 1$. Hence the jth moment exists whenever the kth moment exists. □

Solution to Ex. 4.4.25. We have

$$\begin{aligned}
\operatorname{var}\left[\sum_{n=1}^{N} \alpha_n x_n\right] &= \mathbb{E}\left[\left(\sum_{n=1}^{N} \alpha_n x_n - \mathbb{E}\left[\sum_{n=1}^{N} \alpha_n x_n\right]\right)^2\right] \\
&= \mathbb{E}\left[\left(\sum_{n=1}^{N} \alpha_n (x_n - \mathbb{E}[x_n])\right)^2\right] \\
&= \mathbb{E}\left[\sum_{n=1}^{N} \alpha_n^2 (x_n - \mathbb{E}[x_n])^2 + 2\sum_{n<m} \alpha_n \alpha_m (x_n - \mathbb{E}[x_n])(x_m - \mathbb{E}[x_m])\right] \\
&= \sum_{n=1}^{N} \alpha_n^2 \operatorname{var}[x_n] + \sum_{n<m} \alpha_n \alpha_m \operatorname{cov}[x_n, x_m]
\end{aligned}$$

as required. □

Solution to Ex. 4.4.29. Pick any nonnegative random variable x and $\delta > 0$. By considering what happens at an arbitrary $\omega \in \Omega$, you should be able to convince yourself that

$$x = \mathbb{1}\{x \geqslant \delta\}x + \mathbb{1}\{x < \delta\}x \geqslant \mathbb{1}\{x \geqslant \delta\}\delta$$

Using the results in fact 4.1.5 (page 95) and rearranging gives (4.18). Regarding (4.19), observe that

$$x^2 = \mathbb{1}\{|x| \geqslant \delta\}x^2 + \mathbb{1}\{|x| < \delta\}x^2 \geqslant \mathbb{1}\{|x| \geqslant \delta\}\delta^2$$

Proceeding as before leads to (4.19). □

Chapter 5

Modeling Dependence

To study relationships between random variables we need to add more concepts to our toolkit. In this chapter we review multivariate distributions and give a rigorous construction of conditional expectation.

5.1 Random Vectors and Matrices

Let's begin with random vectors and matrices.

5.1.1 Random Vectors

In §4.1.3 we defined a random variable to be a function $x \colon \Omega \to \mathbb{R}$ with the property that $\{x \in B\}$ is an event for any Borel set $B \in \mathscr{B}(\mathbb{R})$. The definition of a random vector is analogous. A **random vector** $\mathbf{x}$ in $\mathbb{R}^N$ is a function from Ω to $\mathbb{R}^N$ with the property that

$$\{\omega \in \Omega : \mathbf{x}(\omega) \in B\} \in \mathscr{F} \quad \text{for all } B \in \mathscr{B}(\mathbb{R}^N) \tag{5.1}$$

This is just (4.9) on page 92 with $\mathscr{B}(\mathbb{R}^N)$ replacing $\mathscr{B}(\mathbb{R})$. In statistical applications we can almost always cook up a sample space Ω and a set of events $\mathscr{F}$ on Ω such that all random vectors we care about satisfy (5.1).[1]

It's also possible to define a **random vector** $\mathbf{x}$ in $\mathbb{R}^N$ as a tuple of N random variables $(x_1, \ldots, x_N)$. The two definitions are equivalent. As with ordinary vectors, random vectors have no intrinsic shape, and we'll write them in rows or columns according to convenience. However, in expressions involving matrix multiplication, random vectors will default to column vectors unless otherwise stated.

1. For technical details on these constructions see, for example, chapter 4 of Çinlar (2011).

Example 5.1.1 Recall the blindfolded monkey experiment from page 80. The sample space is the unit disk $\Omega := \{(h, v) \in \mathbb{R}^2 : \|(h, v)\| \leqslant 1\}$ and the event space is the Borel sets in Ω. If $\mathbf{x}$ is the identity on Ω, then it simply reports the outcome (h, v). This is one instance of a random vector.

Example 5.1.2 Consider a random sample listing the income y_n of $n = 1, \ldots, N$ individuals from a given population. The vector $(y_1, \ldots, y_N)$ that reports the outcome of this sampling can be regarded as a random vector in $\mathbb{R}^N$.

The definition of a random vector ensures that $\{\mathbf{x} \in B\}$ is a well-defined event for every $B \in \mathscr{B}(\mathbb{R}^N)$. If we want to ensure that some transformation $\mathbf{y} = f(\mathbf{x})$ is likewise a random vector, we need a restriction on f so that $\{\mathbf{y} \in B\}$ is also a well-defined event. The appropriate restriction is $\mathscr{B}$-measurability, which, analogous to the scalar case (see page 92), means that $f \colon \mathbb{R}^N \to \mathbb{R}^M$ satisfies $f^{-1}(B) \in \mathscr{B}(\mathbb{R}^N)$ for all $B \in \mathscr{B}(\mathbb{R}^M)$. As in the scalar case, every kind of transformation we use in this text is $\mathscr{B}$-measurable, so the restriction is never binding.

Expectations of random vectors are defined element-by-element. In particular, if $\mathbf{x} = (x_1, \ldots, x_N)$ is a random vector in $\mathbb{R}^N$, then its **expectation** $\mathbb{E}\,\mathbf{x}$ is defined as the vector of expectations

$$\mathbb{E}\,\mathbf{x} = \mathbb{E} \begin{pmatrix} x_1 \\ x_2 \\ \vdots \\ x_N \end{pmatrix} := \begin{pmatrix} \mathbb{E}\,x_1 \\ \mathbb{E}\,x_2 \\ \vdots \\ \mathbb{E}\,x_N \end{pmatrix}$$

An $M \times N$ **random matrix** $\mathbf{X}$ is an $M \times N$ array of random variables. Its expectation is defined as

$$\mathbb{E}\,\mathbf{X} := \begin{pmatrix} \mathbb{E}\,x_{11} & \cdots & \mathbb{E}\,x_{1N} \\ \vdots & & \vdots \\ \mathbb{E}\,x_{M1} & \cdots & \mathbb{E}\,x_{MN} \end{pmatrix}$$

Fact 5.1.1 If $\mathbf{X}$ and $\mathbf{Y}$ are random matrices or vectors and $\mathbf{A}$ and $\mathbf{B}$ are constant and conformable, then

$$\mathbb{E}\,[\mathbf{A}\mathbf{X} + \mathbf{B}\mathbf{Y}] = \mathbf{A}\,\mathbb{E}\,[\mathbf{X}] + \mathbf{B}\,\mathbb{E}\,[\mathbf{Y}]$$

Fact 5.1.1 is obtained by repeated application of the linearity of scalar expectations stated in fact 4.1.5.

The **variance–covariance matrix** of a random vector $\mathbf{x}$ in $\mathbb{R}^N$ with $\boldsymbol{\mu} := \mathbb{E}\,\mathbf{x}$ is the $N \times N$ matrix

$$\operatorname{var}[\mathbf{x}] := \mathbb{E}\,[(\mathbf{x} - \boldsymbol{\mu})(\mathbf{x} - \boldsymbol{\mu})^\top] \tag{5.2}$$

Expanding this out gives

$$\operatorname{var}[\mathbf{x}] = \begin{pmatrix} \mathbb{E}[(x_1-\mu_1)(x_1-\mu_1)] & \cdots & \mathbb{E}[(x_1-\mu_1)(x_N-\mu_N)] \\ \vdots & & \vdots \\ \mathbb{E}[(x_N-\mu_N)(x_1-\mu_1)] & \cdots & \mathbb{E}[(x_N-\mu_N)(x_N-\mu_N)] \end{pmatrix}$$

The j,kth term is the scalar covariance between x_j and x_k and the principal diagonal contains the variance of each x_n.

Fact 5.1.2 For any random vector $\mathbf{x}$ with $\mathbb{E}[\mathbf{x}^\top \mathbf{x}] < \infty$,

(i) $\operatorname{var}[\mathbf{x}]$ exists and is nonnegative definite,

(ii) $\operatorname{var}[\mathbf{x}] = \mathbb{E}[\mathbf{x}\mathbf{x}^\top] - \mu\mu^\top$, and

(iii) $\operatorname{var}[\mathbf{A}\mathbf{x} + \mathbf{b}] = \mathbf{A}\operatorname{var}[\mathbf{x}]\mathbf{A}^\top$ (any $\mathbf{A}, \mathbf{b}$ constant and conformable).

The **cross-covariance** between random vectors $\mathbf{x}$ and $\mathbf{y}$ is defined as

$$\operatorname{cov}[\mathbf{x}, \mathbf{y}] := \mathbb{E}[(\mathbf{x} - \mathbb{E}[\mathbf{x}])(\mathbf{y} - \mathbb{E}[\mathbf{y}])^\top]$$

Evidently $\operatorname{var}[\mathbf{x}] = \operatorname{cov}[\mathbf{x}, \mathbf{x}]$.

Here's a useful fact concerning expectations of quadratic forms. The proof is a solved exercise (see ex. 5.4.7).

Fact 5.1.3 If $\mathbf{z}$ is a random vector in $\mathbb{R}^N$ satisfying $\mathbb{E}[\mathbf{z}\mathbf{z}^\top] = \mathbf{I}$ and $\mathbf{A}$ is any constant $N \times N$ matrix, then

$$\mathbb{E}[\mathbf{z}^\top \mathbf{A}\mathbf{z}] = \operatorname{trace} \mathbf{A}$$

5.1.2 Multivariate Distributions

The definition of a distribution over $\mathbb{R}^N$ generalizes that of a distribution over $\mathbb{R}$ given in 4.2.1. In particular, a **distribution** or **law** P on $\mathbb{R}^N$ is a probability measure over the Borel sets $\mathscr{B}(\mathbb{R}^N)$. By definition, it satisfies $P(\mathbb{R}^N) = 1$ and $P(\cup_{n=1}^{\infty} B_n) = \sum_{n=1}^{\infty} P(B_n)$ for any disjoint sequence $\{B_n\}$ in $\mathscr{B}(\mathbb{R}^N)$. See also the properties of probability measures listed in fact 4.1.1 on page 86.

Figure 5.1 shows a visualization of a distribution P on $\mathbb{R}^2$, with hot colors indicating regions of high probability. (The distribution is multivariate Gaussian, to be defined below.) The sets A and B are typical Borel sets. In the figure, B has the same area as A but is assigned greater probability by P. By additivity, we know that $P(A \cup B) = P(A) + P(B)$ must hold.

As was the case for $\mathbb{R}$, distributions on $\mathbb{R}^N$ are fully characterized by their values on certain more elementary families of subsets of $\mathbb{R}^N$. For example, for any two

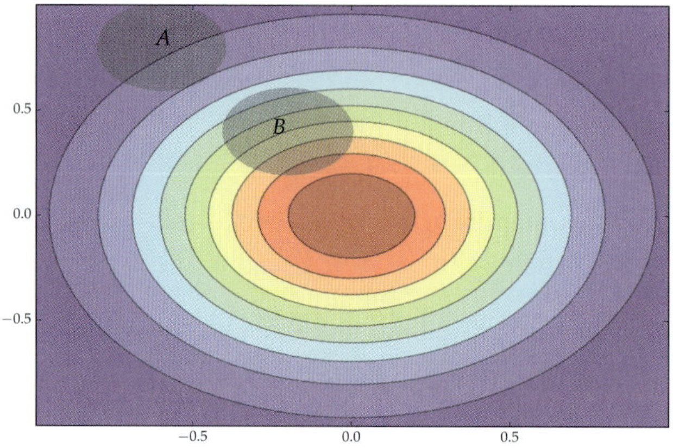

Figure 5.1 Example distribution and events A and B

distributions Q, P on $\mathbb{R}^N$,

$$P(I) = Q(I) \text{ for all } I \in \mathscr{R} \quad \Longrightarrow \quad P(B) = Q(B) \text{ for all } B \in \mathscr{B}(\mathbb{R}^N)$$

where $\mathscr{R}$ denotes the family of all **cylinder sets**

$$C = B_1 \times \cdots \times B_N, \qquad B_n \in \mathscr{B}(\mathbb{R}),\ n = 1, \ldots, N$$

or, specializing further, the family of all rectangles[2]

$$I = (-\infty, s_1] \times \cdots \times (-\infty, s_N], \qquad s_n \in \mathbb{R},\ n = 1, \ldots, N$$

(See prop 3.7 of Çinlar 2011.) Figure 5.2 shows an example set $I = (-\infty, s_1] \times (-\infty, s_2]$ in the case of $\mathbb{R}^2$.

Thus, analogous to (4.24), any distribution P on $\mathbb{R}^N$ is characterized by the function

$$F(\mathbf{s}) := F(s_1, \ldots, s_N) := P\left(\times_{n=1}^N (-\infty, s_n]\right) \qquad (\mathbf{s} \in \mathbb{R}^N) \tag{5.3}$$

This is an example of a **multivariate cumulative distribution function**, which is a function $F\colon \mathbb{R}^N \to [0,1]$ that is

(i) right-continuous in each of its arguments,

2. See page 408 for more discussion of rectangles.

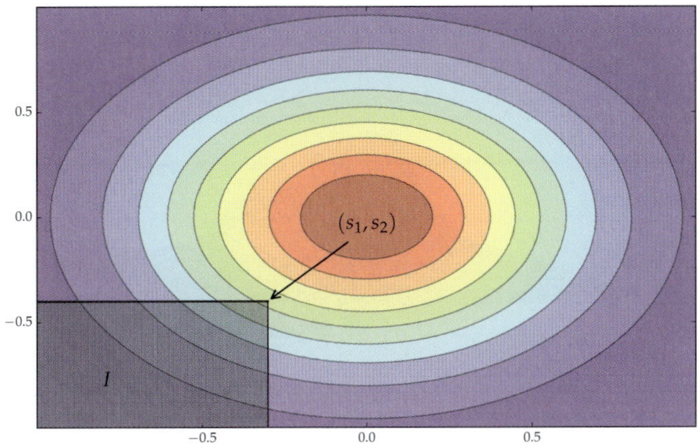

Figure 5.2 Distributions are characterized by their values on elements of $\mathscr{R}$

(ii) increasing in each of its arguments, and

(iii) satisfies

$$F(\mathbf{s}_j) \to 1 \text{ as } \mathbf{s}_j \to \infty \quad \text{and} \quad F(s_1, \dots, s_{nj}, \dots, s_N) \to 0 \text{ as } s_{nj} \to -\infty$$

As in the one-dimensional case, we will call a distribution P on $\mathbb{R}^N$ **discrete** if P is supported on a countable subset of $\mathbb{R}^N$, and **absolutely continuous** if $P(B) = 0$ whenever B has zero Lebesgue measure. The latter condition is again necessary and sufficient for existence of a density representation, by which we mean existence of a density p on $\mathbb{R}^N$ such that

$$P(B) = \int_B p(\mathbf{s})\, \mathrm{d}\mathbf{s} \qquad \text{for all } B \in \mathscr{B}(\mathbb{R}^N) \tag{5.4}$$

The right-hand side of (5.4) is a multivariate integral that we can write out more explicitly as

$$\int_{-\infty}^{\infty} \cdots \int_{-\infty}^{\infty} \mathbb{1}_B(s_1, \dots, s_N) p(s_1, \dots, s_N)\, \mathrm{d}s_1 \cdots \mathrm{d}s_N \tag{5.5}$$

Conversely, if p is any density on $\mathbb{R}^N$, then (5.4) defines a distribution.

Example 5.1.3 The **multivariate normal density** or **multivariate Gaussian density** on

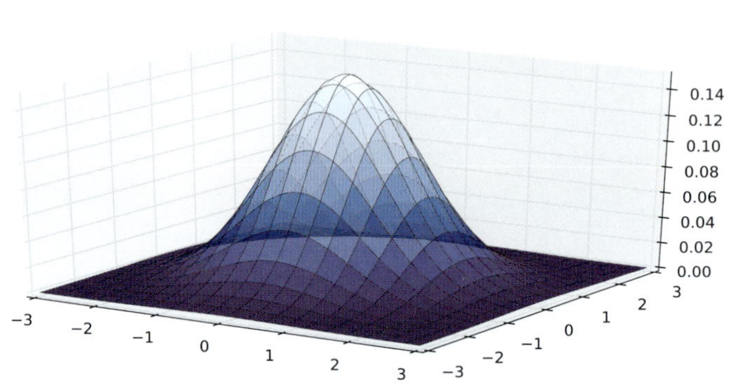

Figure 5.3 Bivariate standard normal density

$\mathbb{R}^N$ is a function p of the form

$$p(\mathbf{s}) = (2\pi)^{-N/2} \det(\mathbf{\Sigma})^{-1/2} \exp\left\{-\frac{1}{2}(\mathbf{s}-\boldsymbol{\mu})^\top \mathbf{\Sigma}^{-1}(\mathbf{s}-\boldsymbol{\mu})\right\} \tag{5.6}$$

where $\boldsymbol{\mu}$ is any $N \times 1$ vector and $\mathbf{\Sigma}$ is a positive definite $N \times N$ matrix. In symbols, we represent this distribution by $\mathrm{N}(\boldsymbol{\mu}, \mathbf{\Sigma})$. The case $\mathrm{N}(\mathbf{0}, \mathbf{I})$ is called the **multivariate standard normal distribution**. Figure 5.3 shows the standard normal density when $N = 2$.

Let's describe one important way to construct multivariate distributions.

Fact 5.1.4 Given distributions $P_1, \ldots, P_N$ on $\mathbb{R}$, there exists a unique and well-defined distribution $\mathring{P}$ on $\mathbb{R}^N$ such that

$$\mathring{P}(B_1 \times \cdots \times B_N) = \prod_{n=1}^{N} P_n(B_n) \qquad \text{for all } B_n \in \mathscr{B}(\mathbb{R}),\ n = 1, \ldots, N$$

This distribution is called the **product distribution** of $P_1, \ldots, P_N$. If $P_n = P$ for all n, then we'll call $\mathring{P}$ the **Nth product of P**. The uniqueness part of fact 5.1.4 follows from the claim above that distributions on $\mathbb{R}^N$ are uniquely pinned down by their values on cylinder subsets of $\mathbb{R}^N$. As we'll see, product distributions correspond to joint distributions of independent random variables.

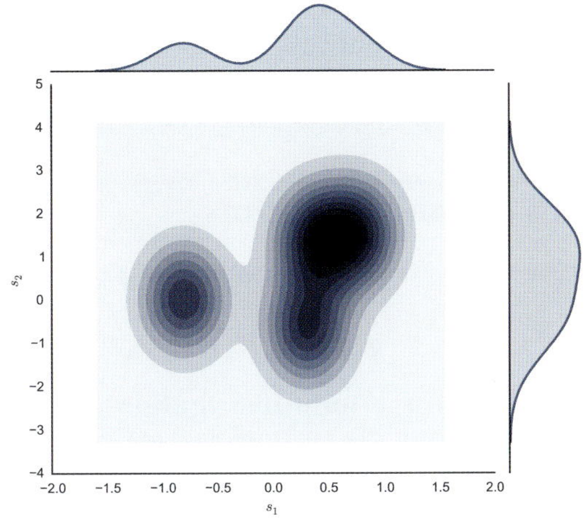

Figure 5.4 Bivariate joint density and its two marginals

5.1.2.1 Marginals of Multivariate Distributions

Given any distribution P on $\mathbb{R}^N$, the nth **marginal distribution** of P is the distribution on $\mathbb{R}$ defined by

$$P_n(B) = P(\mathbb{R} \times \cdots \times \mathbb{R} \times B \times \mathbb{R} \times \cdots \times \mathbb{R})$$

Here B is the nth element of the Cartesian product. We can also write this as

$$P_n(B) = P\{\mathbf{s} \in \mathbb{R}^N : \mathbf{s}^\top \mathbf{e}_n \in B\}$$

The nth marginal tells us the probabilistic implications of P when we only concern ourselves with the outcomes for the nth coordinate. From P_n we can also extract the **marginal** CDF F_n via (4.24) on page 100.

If P_n is absolutely continuous, it has density p_n. When the joint distribution P has a density p, the marginal distribution P_n has a density, and p_n can be obtained directly from p by integrating out the other variables. For example, in the bivariate case,

$$p_1(s_1) = \int_{-\infty}^{\infty} p(s_1, s_2) \, \mathrm{d}s_2$$

Figure 5.4 shows a bivariate density represented by contours and the two marginals obtained from projecting onto each axis.

In general, the joint distribution cannot be determined from the marginals alone, since the marginals do not tell us about the interactions across coordinates. The exception is when there is no interaction. This is the case for product distributions, as described in fact 5.1.4 and further discussed in §5.1.4.

5.1.3 Distributions of Random Vectors

Let $\mathbf{x}$ be a random vector in $\mathbb{R}^N$. The **distribution** of $\mathbf{x}$ is the probability measure P on $\mathscr{B}(\mathbb{R}^N)$ defined by

$$P(B) = \mathbb{P}\{\mathbf{x} \in B\} \qquad (B \in \mathscr{B}(\mathbb{R}^N)) \tag{5.7}$$

In this context, P is also called the **joint distribution** of $x_1, \ldots, x_N$, and we write $\mathcal{L}(\mathbf{x}) = P$. The joint distribution can also be represented by the multivariate CDF $F \colon \mathbb{R}^N \to [0,1]$ defined by (5.3), which in this case can be written as $F(s_1, \ldots, s_N) = \mathbb{P}\{x_1 \leqslant s_1, \ldots, x_N \leqslant s_N\}$, or, in vector notation,

$$F(\mathbf{s}) = \mathbb{P}\{\mathbf{x} \leqslant \mathbf{s}\} \qquad (\mathbf{s} \in \mathbb{R}^N)$$

It follows from (5.4) that when the distribution P of $\mathbf{x}$ is absolutely continuous, there exists a nonnegative function p on $\mathbb{R}^N$ satisfying

$$\int_B p(\mathbf{s})\, \mathrm{d}\mathbf{s} = \mathbb{P}\{\mathbf{x} \in B\} \qquad (B \in \mathscr{B}(\mathbb{R}^N)) \tag{5.8}$$

Here $\int_B$ is a multivariate integral over the region B. The function p is called either the density or **joint density** of $\mathbf{x}$. For (5.8) to hold, it suffices that

$$\int_{-\infty}^{s_N} \cdots \int_{-\infty}^{s_1} p(t_1, \ldots, t_N)\, \mathrm{d}t_1 \cdots \mathrm{d}t_N = F(s_1, \ldots, s_N) \tag{5.9}$$

for all $s_n \in \mathbb{R}$, $n = 1, \ldots, N$.

5.1.3.1 Joint versus Marginal

If $\mathbf{x} = (x_1, \ldots, x_N)$ is a random vector in $\mathbb{R}^N$, then each x_n is a random variable on $\mathbb{R}$. Let $P_n = \mathcal{L}(x_n)$, so that

$$P_n(B) = \mathbb{P}\{x_n \in B\} \qquad (B \in \mathscr{B}(\mathbb{R}),\ n = 1, \ldots, N) \tag{5.10}$$

This is of course the marginal distribution relative to the joint distribution of $\mathbf{x}$, as introduced in §5.1.2.1. In this context it is called the **marginal distribution of x_n** in order to distinguish it from the (joint) distribution of $\mathbf{x}$. From a mathematical perspective, the marginal distribution of x_n and the distribution of x_n are identical.

If $P_1 = P_2 = \cdots = P_N$, then we say that $x_1, \ldots, x_N$ are **identically distributed**.

5.1.3.2 Gaussian Random Vectors

Let z be standard normal on $\mathbb{R}$. A random variable x is said to be **normally distributed** if $x = \mu + \sigma z$ for some $\sigma \geqslant 0$, and we write $\mathcal{L}(x) = \mathrm{N}(\mu, \sigma)$. Here we explicitly allow the possibility that $\sigma = 0$, in which case $\mathrm{var}[x] = 0$ and $\mathbb{P}\{x = \mu\} = 1$.

A random vector $\mathbf{x}$ in $\mathbb{R}^N$ is called **multivariate normal** or **multivariate Gaussian** if there exists a $K \times 1$ standard normal random vector $\mathbf{z}$, an $N \times K$ matrix $\mathbf{C}$ and an $N \times 1$ vector $\boldsymbol{\mu}$ such that

$$\mathbf{x} = \boldsymbol{\mu} + \mathbf{C}\mathbf{z} \tag{5.11}$$

Once again we explicitly allow degenerate cases, since they occur frequently in statistics. If $\mathbf{x}$ is multivariate normal, then we write $\mathcal{L}(\mathbf{x}) = \mathrm{N}(\boldsymbol{\mu}, \boldsymbol{\Sigma})$, where

$$\boldsymbol{\mu} := \mathbb{E}\,\mathbf{x} \quad \text{and} \quad \boldsymbol{\Sigma} := \mathrm{var}\,\mathbf{x}$$

In the case of (5.11) we have $\boldsymbol{\Sigma} = \mathbf{C}\mathbf{C}^\top$. See fact 5.1.2 on page 127.

Be aware that $\mathcal{L}(\mathbf{x}) = \mathrm{N}(\boldsymbol{\mu}, \boldsymbol{\Sigma})$ does not imply that $\mathbf{x}$ has the multivariate normal density in (5.6). The reason is that the distribution of $\mathbf{x}$ can fail to be absolutely continuous. For example, if $\mathbf{C} = \mathbf{0}$ in (5.11), then $\mathbf{x}$ puts all mass on a single point in $\mathbb{R}^N$. Without absolute continuity, no density representation can exist.

Absolute continuity of the distribution of $\mathbf{x}$ coincides with the setting where $\boldsymbol{\Sigma} := \mathrm{var}\,\mathbf{x}$ is nonsingular. (Perhaps because of this, the scenario where a random vector has a density is sometimes called the "nonsingular case" by econometricians.) For $\mathbf{x}$ defined in (5.11), nonsingularity of $\boldsymbol{\Sigma}$ will be true if and only if $\mathbf{C}^\top$ has full column rank (see ex. 3.5.28 on page 72).

Fact 5.1.5 Let $\mathbf{x}$ be a random vector in $\mathbb{R}^N$. The following statements are true:

(i) The vector $\mathbf{x}$ is multivariate normal if and only if $\mathbf{a}^\top\mathbf{x}$ is normally distributed in $\mathbb{R}$ for every constant $N \times 1$ vector $\mathbf{a}$.

(ii) If $\mathcal{L}(\mathbf{x}) = \mathrm{N}(\boldsymbol{\mu}, \boldsymbol{\Sigma})$, then

$$\mathcal{L}(\mathbf{A}\mathbf{x} + \mathbf{b}) = \mathrm{N}(\mathbf{A}\boldsymbol{\mu} + \mathbf{b}, \mathbf{A}\boldsymbol{\Sigma}\mathbf{A}^\top)$$

for all constant conformable $\mathbf{A}, \mathbf{b}$.

One corollary of fact 5.1.5 is that if $\mathbf{x} = (x_1, \ldots, x_N)$ is multivariate normal, then the marginal distribution of x_n is univariate normal. This can be seen by taking $\mathbf{a} = \mathbf{e}_n$ in part (i). In fact the rule in part (ii) implies that

$$\mathcal{L}(x_n) = \mathcal{L}(\mathbf{e}_n^\top\mathbf{x}) = \mathrm{N}(\mathbf{e}_n^\top\boldsymbol{\mu}, \mathbf{e}_n^\top\boldsymbol{\Sigma}\mathbf{e}_n) = \mathrm{N}(\mu_n, \sigma_n^2) \tag{5.12}$$

where σ_n^2 is the n, nth element of $\boldsymbol{\Sigma}$.

Here's a common exam question: Is it true that the joint distribution of N univariate normal random variables is always multivariate normal? The answer is no. A counterexample is given in §5.1.5. See also fact 5.1.14 below.

5.1.3.3 Expectations from Distributions

Let $h \colon \mathbb{R}^N \to \mathbb{R}$ be any $\mathscr{B}$-measurable function and let P be a distribution on $\mathbb{R}^N$. In §4.2.3 we saw that one can assign meaning to the expression $\int h(s)P(ds)$ by treating h as a random variable on $(\mathbb{R}, \mathscr{B}(\mathbb{R}), P)$ and taking its expectation. We can do exactly the same thing in $\mathbb{R}^N$, with h now regarded as a random variable on $(\mathbb{R}^N, \mathscr{B}(\mathbb{R}^N), P)$. Its expectation will be written as

$$\mathbb{E}_P h :=: \int h(\mathbf{s})P(d\mathbf{s}) \tag{5.13}$$

Here's a multivariate version of fact 4.2.3 on page 110:

Fact 5.1.6 Let $h \colon \mathbb{R}^N \to \mathbb{R}$ be $\mathscr{B}$-measurable and let P be a distribution on $\mathbb{R}^N$. If P is discrete, with PMF $\{p_j\}_{j \geqslant 1}$ and support $\{\mathbf{s}_j\}_{j \geqslant 1}$, then

$$\int h(\mathbf{s})P(d\mathbf{s}) = \sum_{j \geqslant 1} h(\mathbf{s}_j) p_j \tag{5.14}$$

If P is absolutely continuous with density p, then

$$\int h(\mathbf{s})P(d\mathbf{s}) = \int h(\mathbf{s})p(\mathbf{s})\, d\mathbf{s} \tag{5.15}$$

The right-hand side of (5.15) should be understood as

$$\int_{-\infty}^{\infty} \cdots \int_{-\infty}^{\infty} h(s_1, \dots, s_N)\, p(s_1, \dots, s_N)\, ds_1 \cdots ds_N$$

In §4.2.5 we saw that expectations of functions of random variables can be computed from their distributions. The same is true for functions of random vectors. In particular, suppose that we want to compute $\mathbb{E} h(\mathbf{x})$, where $h \colon \mathbb{R}^N \to \mathbb{R}$ is $\mathscr{B}$-measurable. We can do this either by evaluating the expectation of $h(\mathbf{x})$ on the original probability space $(\Omega, \mathscr{F}, \mathbb{P})$, or we can take the distribution P of $\mathbf{x}$ and compute the expectation of h on $(\mathbb{R}^N, \mathscr{B}(\mathbb{R}^N), P)$. This is formalized in the following extension to fact 4.2.8 on page 112.

Fact 5.1.7 If $\mathcal{L}(\mathbf{x}) = P$ and $h\colon \mathbb{R}^N \to \mathbb{R}$ is a $\mathscr{B}$-measurable function such that $h(\mathbf{x})$ is integrable, then

$$\mathbb{E}h(\mathbf{x}) = \int h(\mathbf{s})P(d\mathbf{s})$$

where $\int h(\mathbf{s})P(d\mathbf{s})$ is the expectation of h on $(\mathbb{R}^N, \mathscr{B}(\mathbb{R}^N), P)$.

As in the univariate case, this means that objects like moments are properties of the distribution. For example, let $\mathbf{x}$ be a random vector in $\mathbb{R}^K$ with $\mathcal{L}(\mathbf{x}) = P$. The variance–covariance matrix var$[\mathbf{x}]$ of $\mathbf{x}$ has i,jth element $\mathbb{E}[x_i x_j] - \mathbb{E}[x_i]\mathbb{E}[x_j]$. We can write this in terms of P. In particular, if

$$\boldsymbol{\Sigma}_P = (\sigma_{ij}) \quad \text{where} \quad \sigma_{ij} := \int (s_i s_j)P(d\mathbf{s}) - \int s_i P(d\mathbf{s}) \cdot \int s_j P(d\mathbf{s}) \tag{5.16}$$

then $\boldsymbol{\Sigma}_P = \text{var}[\mathbf{x}]$.

5.1.4 Independence

A collection of N random variables $x_1, \ldots, x_N$ is said to be **independent** if

$$\mathbb{P} \bigcap_{n=1}^{N} \{x_n \in B_n\} = \prod_{n=1}^{N} \mathbb{P}\{x_n \in B_n\} \tag{5.17}$$

for any $B_1, \ldots, B_N$, where each B_n is a Borel subset of $\mathbb{R}$. In view of the definition of independence of events on page 87, the random variables $x_1, \ldots, x_N$ are independent precisely when sets of the form $\{x_1 \in B_1\}, \ldots, \{x_N \in B_N\}$ are independent events.

An infinite set of random variables $\{x_n\}_{n=1}^{\infty}$ is called independent if any finite subset of $\{x_n\}_{n=1}^{\infty}$ is independent in the sense of the preceding definition. We use the abbreviation IID for collections of random variables that are both independent and identically distributed. If we state that $\{x_n\}_{n=1}^{\infty}$ are IID **copies of** x, we mean that the random variables $\{x_n\}_{n=1}^{\infty}$ are IID with the same distribution as x.

There are a number of equivalent ways that we can rephrase the definition of independence. Since $\cap_{n=1}^{N}\{x_n \in B_n\} = \{(x_1, \ldots, x_N) \in B_1 \times \cdots \times B_N\}$, a direct translation of (5.17) using (5.7) and (5.10) gives

$$P(B_1 \times \cdots \times B_N) = \prod_{n=1}^{N} P_n(B_n) \tag{5.18}$$

Here P is the joint distribution of $\mathbf{x} = (x_1, \ldots, x_N)$ and P_n is its nth marginal. Thus, the elements of a random vector are independent if and only if their joint distribution equals the product distribution formed from their marginals (see fact 5.1.4).

The left- and right-hand sides of (5.18) agree for all $B_1, \ldots, B_N$ if they agree on certain families of sets, like the rectangles discussed in §5.1.2. For this reason a necessary and sufficient condition for independence of $x_1, \ldots, x_N$ is

$$F(s_1, \ldots, s_N) = \prod_{n=1}^{N} F_n(s_n) \tag{5.19}$$

for all $(s_1, \ldots, s_N) \in \mathbb{R}^N$, where F is the CDF of $\mathbf{x}$ and $F_1, \ldots, F_N$ are the marginal CDFs . If the distribution of $\mathbf{x}$ is absolutely continuous we can also test independence via its density:

Fact 5.1.8 If $\mathbf{x} = (x_1, \ldots, x_N)$ has joint density p and marginals $p_1, \ldots, p_N$, then $x_1, \ldots, x_N$ are independent if and only if

$$p(s_1, \ldots, s_N) = \prod_{n=1}^{N} p_n(s_n) \qquad \text{for all} \quad (s_1, \ldots, s_N) \in \mathbb{R}^N$$

Example 5.1.4 Let $\mathcal{L}(\mathbf{x}) = \mathcal{L}(x_1, \ldots, x_N) = N(\boldsymbol{\mu}, \boldsymbol{\Sigma})$. Suppose in addition that $\boldsymbol{\Sigma}$ is diagonal, with nth diagonal component $\sigma_n > 0$. Then $x_1, \ldots, x_N$ are independent. To see this observe that for any $\mathbf{s} = (s_1, \ldots, s_N) \in \mathbb{R}^N$ we have

$$\begin{aligned} p(\mathbf{s}) &= (2\pi)^{-N/2} \det(\boldsymbol{\Sigma})^{-1/2} \exp\left\{-\frac{1}{2}(\mathbf{s}-\boldsymbol{\mu})^\top \boldsymbol{\Sigma}^{-1}(\mathbf{s}-\boldsymbol{\mu})\right\} \\ &= \frac{1}{(2\pi)^{N/2}\prod_{n=1}^{N}\sigma_n} \exp\left\{-\frac{1}{2}\sum_{n=1}^{N}(s_n-\mu_n)^2\sigma_n^{-2}\right\} \end{aligned}$$

where the computation of the determinant and inverse of $\boldsymbol{\Sigma}$ used facts 3.2.1 and 3.2.2 (see page 53). The last expression can be factored further, leading to

$$p(\mathbf{s}) = \prod_{n=1}^{N} \frac{1}{(2\pi)^{1/2}\sigma_n} \exp\left\{\frac{-(s_n-\mu_n)^2}{2\sigma_n^2}\right\} = \prod_{n=1}^{N} p_n(s_n)$$

where p_n is the density of $\mathrm{N}(\mu_n, \sigma_n^2)$. Independence now follows from fact 5.1.8.

The next fact is true in general but most easily verified in the density case, where you can apply (5.15) and fact 5.1.8.

Fact 5.1.9 If $x_1, \ldots, x_N$ are independent and each x_n is integrable, then

$$\mathbb{E}\left[\prod_{n=1}^{N} x_n\right] = \prod_{n=1}^{N} \mathbb{E}[x_n]$$

The definition of independence of random vectors is almost identical to the scalar case. Random vectors $\mathbf{x}_1, \ldots, \mathbf{x}_N$ in $\mathbb{R}^K$ are called **independent** if

$$\mathbb{P} \bigcap_{n=1}^{N} \{\mathbf{x}_n \in B_n\} = \prod_{n=1}^{N} \mathbb{P}\{\mathbf{x}_n \in B_n\} \tag{5.20}$$

for any $B_1, \ldots, B_N$, where each B_n is a Borel subset of $\mathbb{R}^K$.

Fact 5.1.10 If $\mathbf{x}_1, \ldots, \mathbf{x}_N$ are independent random vectors in $\mathbb{R}^K$ and $f_1, \ldots, f_N$ are any $\mathscr{B}$-measurable functions, then $f_1(\mathbf{x}_1), \ldots, f_N(\mathbf{x}_N)$ are also independent.

To see why, observe that $f_n(\mathbf{x}_n) \in B_n$ if and only if $\mathbf{x}_n \in f^{-1}(B_n)$, as follows from the definition of preimage of a set (see 15.2). This leads to

$$\bigcap_{n=1}^{N} \{f_n(\mathbf{x}_n) \in B_n\} = \bigcap_{n=1}^{N} \{\mathbf{x}_n \in f^{-1}(B_n)\}$$

Applying independence of $\mathbf{x}_1, \ldots, \mathbf{x}_N$ now gives

$$\mathbb{P} \bigcap_{n=1}^{N} \{f_n(\mathbf{x}_n) \in B_n\} = \prod_{n=1}^{N} \mathbb{P}\{\mathbf{x}_n \in f^{-1}(B_n)\} = \prod_{n=1}^{N} \mathbb{P}\{f_n(\mathbf{x}_n) \in B_n\}$$

This completes the proof of fact 5.1.10.

Fact 5.1.11 If $\mathbf{x}$ and $\mathbf{y}$ are independent, then $\text{cov}(\mathbf{x}, \mathbf{y}) = 0$.

Note that the converse is not true: one can construct examples of dependent random variables with zero covariance. However,

Fact 5.1.12 If $\mathbf{x}$ is multivariate Gaussian and $\mathbf{A}$ and $\mathbf{B}$ are conformable constant matrices, then $\mathbf{Ax}$ and $\mathbf{Bx}$ are independent if and only if $\text{cov}(\mathbf{Ax}, \mathbf{Bx}) = \mathbf{0}$.

We already proved a simple version of this in example 5.1.4. A full proof can be put together using the theory of characteristic functions (see, e.g., ch. 5 of Gut 2009). Below are two useful related results. The first one links orthogonal projection and multivariate Gaussians (ex. 5.4.11 requests a proof).

Fact 5.1.13 Let S be any linear subspace of $\mathbb{R}^N$, let $\mathbf{P} := \text{proj}\, S$ and let $\mathbf{M}$ be the residual projection. If $\mathcal{L}(\mathbf{z}) = \text{N}(\mathbf{0}, \sigma^2 \mathbf{I})$ in $\mathbb{R}^N$ for some $\sigma^2 > 0$, then $\mathbf{Pz}$ and $\mathbf{Mz}$ are independent.

Fact 5.1.14 If $w_1, \ldots, w_N$ are independent with $\mathcal{L}(w_n) = \text{N}(\mu_n, \sigma_n^2)$ for all n, then

$$\mathcal{L}\left[\alpha_0 + \sum_{n=1}^{N} \alpha_n w_n\right] = \text{N}\left(\alpha_0 + \sum_{n=1}^{N} \alpha_n \mu_n, \; \sum_{n=1}^{N} \alpha_n^2 \sigma_n^2\right)$$

This last fact is important because sums of arbitrary normals are not always normal. What is required is a multivariate normal distribution. Fact 5.1.14 works because independence pins down the joint distribution as multivariate normal. In particular, $\mathcal{L}(w_1, \ldots, w_N) = \mathrm{N}(\boldsymbol{\mu}, \boldsymbol{\Sigma})$ where $\mathbf{e}_n^\top \boldsymbol{\mu} = \mu_n$ and $\boldsymbol{\Sigma} = \mathrm{diag}(\sigma_1^2, \ldots, \sigma_N^2)$. The expression for the variance in fact 5.1.14 follows from fact 4.1.10 on page 98.

5.1.5 Copulas

A **copula** C on $\mathbb{R}^N$ is a multivariate CDF (see page 128) supported on the unit hypercube $[0,1]^N$ with the property that all its marginals are uniform on $[0,1]$. In other words, C is a function of the form

$$C(s_1, \ldots, s_N) = \mathbb{P}\{u_1 \leqslant s_1, \ldots, u_N \leqslant s_N\} \tag{5.21}$$

where $0 \leqslant s_n \leqslant 1$ and $\mathcal{L}(u_n) = U[0,1]$ for all n. There are many possible copulas because, while each u_n has its marginal distribution pinned down, there are infinitely many ways to specify the joint distribution.

Example 5.1.5 The function $C(s_1, s_2) = s_1 s_2$ on $[0,1]^2$ is called the **independence copula**. The marginal distributions are $C(s_1, 1) = s_1$ and $C(1, s_2) = s_2$ as required. (These are CDFs for the $U[0,1]$ distribution.)

Example 5.1.6 The **Gumbel copulas** are the class of functions on $[0,1]^2$ defined by

$$C(s_1, s_2) = \exp\left\{ - \left[(-\ln s_1)^\theta + (-\ln s_2)^\theta \right]^{1/\theta} \right\} \qquad (\theta \geqslant 1)$$

The **Clayton copulas** are given by

$$C(s_1, s_2) = \left\{ \max\left[s_1^{-\theta} + s_2^{-\theta} - 1, \, 0 \right] \right\}^{-1/\theta} \qquad (\theta \geqslant -1, \, \theta \neq 0)$$

Both of these belong to a general class called the **Archimedean copulas**.

One reason that copulas are useful is that we can take univariate CDFs $F_1, \ldots, F_N$ and a copula C and create a multivariate CDF on $\mathbb{R}^N$ via

$$F(s_1, \ldots, s_N) = C(F_1(s_1), \ldots, F_N(s_N)) \qquad (s_n \in \mathbb{R}, \, n = 1, \ldots, N) \tag{5.22}$$

The benefit of creating a multivariate CDF using this two step procedure is that in specifying a multivariate distribution we can separate out specification of the marginals, which give probabilities for isolated coordinates, and specification of the joint distribution, which defines the interactions.

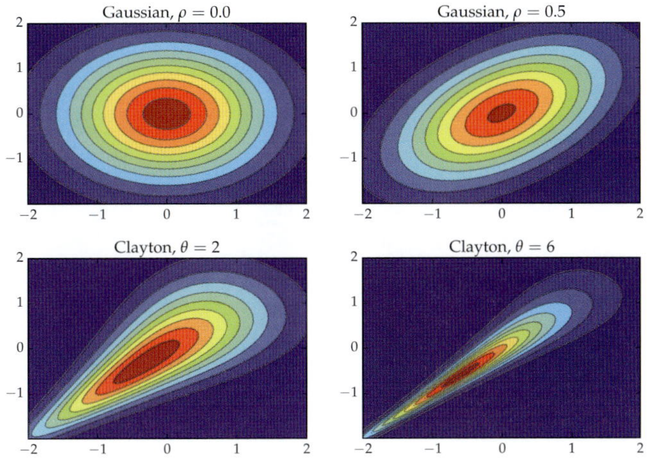

Figure 5.5 Bivariate Gaussian (top) and non-Gaussian (bottom)

Example 5.1.7 Bonhomme and Robin (2009) use copulas to model one component of earnings dynamics in a study based on three-year panels from the French Labor Force Survey. The cross sections are relatively large (around 30,000), allowing for flexible modeling of the marginal distributions via a mixture of normals. However, the time series dimension is short, so a one-parameter family of copulas is used to bind the marginals across time in a parsimonious way.

How rich is the set of multivariate CDFs we can create via (5.22)? It is universal. This is one part of a well-known theorem due to Sklar (1959):

Theorem 5.1.1 *If F is any* CDF *on $\mathbb{R}^N$ with marginals $F_1, \ldots, F_N$, then there exists a copula C such that* (5.22) *holds. If each F_n is continuous, then this representation is unique.*

Copulas can be used to clarify a point raised in §5.1.3.2: normal marginals are not sufficient for the multivariate normal property. If $F_1, \ldots, F_N$ are univariate normal, then $C(F_1(s_1), \ldots, F_N(s_N))$ will equal the multivariate normal CDF for one choice of copula, called the Gaussian copula. Other choices lead to different distributions. Figure 5.5 gives an illustration where the top two distributions are multivariate normal and the bottom two are created by pairing the Clayton copula with univariate normal marginals. The distributions are represented as densities.

A related point is that while linear combinations of normal random variables are often thought to be normal, this isn't true unless the original random variables are multivariate normal (cf., fact 5.1.5 on page 133) or independent (which is a special case of multivariate normal). As an example, figure 5.6 shows a histogram of draws from

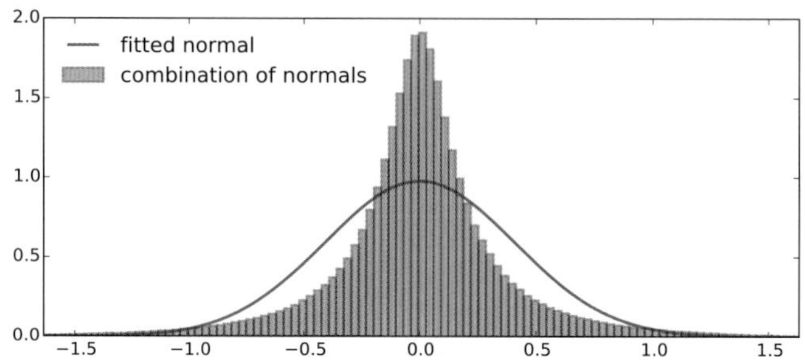

Figure 5.6 Normality is not necessarily preserved under linear transformations

$w = x - y$ when (x, y) is distributed according to the density in the lower right panel of figure 5.5. For comparison, a normal density with the same mean and standard deviation is plotted.

5.1.6 Properties of Named Distributions

Here are some useful facts relating independence and certain common distributions.

Fact 5.1.15 If $x_1, \ldots, x_N$ are independent and $\mathcal{L}(x_n) = \chi^2(k_n)$, then $\mathcal{L}(\sum_n x_n) = \chi^2(\sum_n k_n)$.

Fact 5.1.16 If z and x are independent with $\mathcal{L}(z) = \mathrm{N}(0, 1)$ and $\mathcal{L}(x) = \chi^2(k)$, then

$$z\sqrt{\frac{k}{x}} \quad \text{is } t \text{ distributed with } k \text{ degrees of freedom}$$

Fact 5.1.17 If x_1 and x_2 are independent with $\mathcal{L}(x_i) = \chi^2(k_i)$ for $i = 1, 2$, then

$$\frac{x_1/k_1}{x_2/k_2} \quad \text{is } F \text{ distributed with parameters } k_1, k_2$$

Let's note some facts connecting chi-squared and normal random variables. First, if $\mathcal{L}(x) = \mathrm{N}(0, 1)$, then $\mathcal{L}(x^2) = \chi^2(1)$. Exercise 5.4.4 asks you to prove this. Second, if a collection of standard normals are independent, then so are their squares (fact 5.1.10). Combining this result with fact 5.1.15 gives

Fact 5.1.18 If $\mathcal{L}(z_1, \ldots, z_N) = \mathrm{N}(\mathbf{0}, \mathbf{I})$, then $\mathcal{L}(\sum_{n=1}^N z_n^2) = \chi^2(N)$.

The next result generalizes fact 5.1.18 and crops up frequently in statistics.

Fact 5.1.19 If $\mathcal{L}(\mathbf{z}) = \mathrm{N}(\mathbf{0}, \mathbf{I})$ and $\mathbf{A}$ is symmetric and idempotent, then

$$\mathcal{L}\left(\mathbf{z}^\top \mathbf{A} \mathbf{z}\right) = \chi^2(K) \quad \text{where} \quad K := \text{trace}\, \mathbf{A}$$

We can obtain fact 5.1.19 from fact 5.1.18 as follows. Since $\mathbf{A}$ is symmetric, we use the spectral decomposition theorem (page 66) to write it as $\mathbf{A} = \mathbf{Q}\mathbf{\Lambda}\mathbf{Q}^\top$, where $\mathbf{Q}$ is an orthogonal matrix and $\mathbf{\Lambda} = \text{diag}(\lambda_1, \ldots, \lambda_N)$ with $\lambda_n :=$ the nth eigenvalue of $\mathbf{A}$. Setting $\mathbf{y} := \mathbf{Q}^\top \mathbf{z}$, we have

$$\mathbf{z}^\top \mathbf{A} \mathbf{z} = \mathbf{z}^\top \mathbf{Q}\mathbf{\Lambda}\mathbf{Q}^\top \mathbf{z} = \mathbf{y}^\top \mathbf{\Lambda} \mathbf{y} = \sum_{n=1}^{N} \lambda_n y_n^2$$

By exercise 3.5.35, idempotence of $\mathbf{A}$ implies all eigenvalues lie in $\{0, 1\}$. By fact 3.2.7 on page 57, the number of nonzero eigenvalues is equal to trace $\mathbf{A}$. It follows that $\mathbf{z}^\top \mathbf{A} \mathbf{z}$ is the sum of y_n^2 over $K :=$ trace $\mathbf{A}$ nonzero terms. By fact 5.1.18, a random variable with this property is $\chi^2(K)$ whenever $\mathbf{y}$ is standard normal. Combining $\mathcal{L}(\mathbf{z}) = \mathrm{N}(\mathbf{0}, \mathbf{I})$ and fact 5.1.5 on page 133, we have $\mathcal{L}(\mathbf{y}) = \mathrm{N}(\mathbf{0}, \mathbf{Q}^\top \mathbf{Q})$. But $\mathbf{Q}$ is an orthogonal matrix, so $\mathbf{Q}^\top \mathbf{Q} = \mathbf{I}$.

5.2 Conditioning and Expectation

Conditional expectation is one of the most important concepts in both economic theory and econometrics. This section gives a construction of expectation based around projection, which, in my view, is more intuitive and rewarding than both the elementary treatments using conditional distributions and the advanced treatments using Radon–Nykodym derivatives. The construction begins by formalizing the concepts of information and conditioning. We then build on our knowledge of orthogonal projection from §3.3 to frame conditional expectation as optimal prediction given limited information.

5.2.1 Conditional Distributions

Let's briefly discuss conditional distributions, focusing on the density case. Let x_1 and x_2 be random variables. The **conditional density** of x_2 given $x_1 = s_1$ is defined as

$$p(s_2 \,|\, s_1) := \frac{p(s_1, s_2)}{p(s_2)} \tag{5.23}$$

whenever the denominator is nonzero. Here p stands in for either joint, marginal, or conditional density, with the type determined by the argument. (For example, $p(s_i)$ is the marginal density of x_i evaluated at s_i.)

The law of total probability (see page 88) extends to the density case as follows: If (x_1, x_2) is a random vector on $\mathbb{R}^2$, then

$$p(s_2) = \int_{-\infty}^{\infty} p(s_2 \mid s_1) p(s_1) \, ds_1 \qquad (s_2 \in \mathbb{R}) \tag{5.24}$$

To see this, fix $s_2 \in \mathbb{R}$ and integrate the joint density to get the marginal, giving

$$p(s_2) = \int_{-\infty}^{\infty} p(s_1, s_2) \, ds_1$$

Combining this result with $p(s_2 \mid s_1) = p(s_1, s_2)/p(s_1)$ yields (5.24). Bayes' law (see page 88) also extends to the density case, giving

$$p(s_2 \mid s_1) = \frac{p(s_1 \mid s_2) p(s_2)}{p(s_1)} \tag{5.25}$$

The same ideas extend to additional arguments in a natural way. For example, the conditional density of $x_{k+1}, \ldots, x_N$ given $x_1 = s_1, \ldots, x_k = s_k$ is defined by

$$p(s_{k+1}, \ldots, s_N \mid s_1, \ldots, s_k) = \frac{p(s_1, \ldots, s_N)}{p(s_1, \ldots, s_k)} \tag{5.26}$$

Rearranging this expression, we obtain a useful decomposition of the joint density:

$$p(s_1, \ldots, s_N) = p(s_{k+1}, \ldots, s_N \mid s_1, \ldots, s_k) p(s_1, \ldots, s_k) \tag{5.27}$$

5.2.2 The Space L_2

Suppose we want to predict random variable y using another variable x. In this case we should choose x such that x and y are expected to be close under most realizations of uncertainty. But what does "expected to be close" mean?

Perhaps the most common measure of distance between random variables is **mean squared error** (MSE), which is defined in this case as $\mathbb{E}[(x-y)^2]$. We met this concept previously in the linear prediction problem of §4.1.5. A common variation on MSE is **root mean squared error**, which, as the name suggests, is defined as

$$\|x - y\| := \sqrt{\mathbb{E}[(x-y)^2]} \tag{5.28}$$

On the right-hand side of (5.28) we have a measure of distance between random variables. On the left-hand side we have used the same symbol as we used for Euclidean norm distance between two vectors. This is both deliberate and conventional, as there are many parallels between ordinary vector space with the Euclidean norm and the set of random variables combined with the "norm" defined in (5.28). Let's now clarify and formalize these ideas.

The first geometric concept we defined for vectors was inner product. Analogously, we define here the **inner product between two random variables** x and y as

$$\langle x, y \rangle := \mathbb{E}[xy] \tag{5.29}$$

Of course we want this definition to make sense, and the Cauchy–Schwarz inequality for random variables (page 97) tells us that $\mathbb{E}[xy]$ will be finite and well-defined whenever x and y both have finite second moments. Hence we restrict attention to this set, which is commonly denoted L_2. That is,

$$L_2 := \{ \text{ all random variables } x \text{ on } (\Omega, \mathscr{F}, \mathbb{P}) \text{ with } \mathbb{E}[x^2] < \infty \}$$

Here's a list of some of the ways that L_2 inner product is similar to the Euclidean inner product on $\mathbb{R}^N$.

Fact 5.2.1 For any $\alpha, \beta \in \mathbb{R}$ and any $x, y, z \in L_2$, the following statements are true:

(i) $\langle x, y \rangle = \langle y, x \rangle$.

(ii) $\langle \alpha x, \beta y \rangle = \alpha\beta \langle x, y \rangle$.

(iii) $\langle x, \alpha y + \beta z \rangle = \alpha \langle x, y \rangle + \beta \langle x, z \rangle$.

If you compare fact 5.2.1 with fact 2.1.1 on page 13 you'll see that the correspondence is essentially one-to-one. The properties in fact 5.2.1 follow from the definition of the inner product and linearity of $\mathbb{E}$ (see fact 4.1.5 on page 95).

Analogous to the Euclidean vector norm, we define the **L_2 norm** by

$$\|x\| := \sqrt{\langle x, x \rangle} := \sqrt{\mathbb{E}[x^2]} \qquad (x \in L_2) \tag{5.30}$$

From this norm we get a notion of distance $\|x - y\|$ between random variables that agrees with the notion of root MSE in (5.28). As with inner product, the properties of the L_2 norm and vector norm are largely identical. (Compare the following with fact 2.1.2 on page 13.)

Fact 5.2.2 For any $\alpha \in \mathbb{R}$ and any $x, y \in L_2$, the following statements are true:

(i) $\|x\| \geqslant 0$ and $\|x\| = 0$ if and only if $x = 0$

(ii) $\|\alpha x\| = |\alpha| \|x\|$

(iii) $\|x + y\| \leqslant \|x\| + \|y\|$

(iv) $|\langle x, y\rangle| \leqslant \|x\|\|y\|$

Point (i) requires a clarification, which is given below. Property (ii) is immediate from (5.30) and the linearity of $\mathbb{E}$. Property (iii) is called the **triangle inequality**, as in the vector case. Property (iv) is just the **Cauchy–Schwarz inequality** from page 97, restated in new notation. As in the vector case, the triangle inequality can be proved from the Cauchy–Schwarz inequality (see page 13). For a proof, see exercise 5.4.15.

Returning to (i), it isn't true that $\|x\| = 0$ implies $x(\omega) = 0$ for all $\omega \in \Omega$. What we can say is that if $\|x\| = 0$ then $\mathbb{P}\{x = 0\} = 1$ (see, e.g., Williams 1991, §5.2). If we agree not to distinguish between random variables that only differ with zero probability, then (i) is valid. This is the standard convention when dealing with L_2.

5.2.2.1 Linear Subspaces in L_2

From (ii) and (iii) of fact 5.2.2, we see that if $\alpha, \beta \in \mathbb{R}$ and $x, y \in L_2$, then $\alpha x + \beta y$ also has finite norm, and is therefore in L_2. More generally, any **linear combination**

$$\alpha_1 x_1 + \cdots \alpha_K x_K, \qquad \alpha_k \in \mathbb{R},\ x_k \in L_2$$

is again in L_2. As in the vector case (see §2.1.2), when X is a subset of L_2, the set of finite linear combinations that can be formed from elements of X is called the **span** of X, and denoted by span X.

Example 5.2.1 If $x \in L_2$ and $\mathbb{1} := \mathbb{1}_\Omega$ is the constant random variable always equal to 1, then span$\{\mathbb{1}, x\}$ is the set of random variables

$$\alpha + \beta x := \alpha \mathbb{1} + \beta x \quad \text{for scalars} \quad \alpha, \beta \tag{5.31}$$

This is the set $\mathcal{L}$ introduced on page 98 when we discussed best linear predictors.

A subset S of L_2 is called a **linear subspace** of L_2 if it is closed under addition and scalar multiplication. That is, for each $x, y \in S$ and $\alpha, \beta \in \mathbb{R}$, we have $\alpha x + \beta y \in S$.

Example 5.2.2 The span of any set of elements of L_2 is a linear subspace in L_2. (Compare with example 2.1.9 on page 20.)

Example 5.2.3 The set $Z := \{x \in L_2 : \mathbb{E}x = 0\}$ is a linear subspace of L_2 because

$$x, y \in Z \text{ and } \alpha, \beta \in \mathbb{R} \quad \Longrightarrow \quad \mathbb{E}[\alpha x + \beta y] = \alpha \mathbb{E}[x] + \beta \mathbb{E}[y] = 0$$

As in $\mathbb{R}^N$, an **orthonormal basis** of a linear subspace S of L_2 is a set $\{u_1, \ldots, u_K\} \subset S$ with the property that

$$\langle u_j, u_k \rangle = \mathbb{1}\{j = k\} \quad \text{and} \quad \text{span}\{u_1, \ldots, u_K\} = S$$

Example 5.2.4 Let $x \in L_2$ so that $S := \text{span}\{\mathbb{1}, x\}$ is as in (5.31). If we define

$$u_1 := \mathbb{1} \quad \text{and} \quad u_2 := \frac{x - \mu}{\sigma_x}$$

Then

$$\langle u_1, u_2 \rangle = \mathbb{E}[u_1 u_2] = \mathbb{E}\left[\frac{x - \mu}{\sigma_x}\right] = 0$$

Clearly, $\|u_1\| = \|u_2\| = 1$, so this pair is orthonormal. It's also straightforward to show that $\text{span}\{u_1, u_2\} = \text{span}\{\mathbb{1}, x\}$, so $\{u_1, u_2\}$ is an orthonormal basis for S.

5.2.3 Projections in L_2

Given that inner products and norms in L_2 share so many properties with their Euclidean cousins, it's not surprising that many results about $\mathbb{R}^N$ carry over to L_2. Often we can just lift the proofs across with barely a change to notation. We know a great deal about vectors and Euclidean space, so this process yields many insights about random variables. Let's illustrate this in the context of orthogonal projection.

As in the Euclidean case, if $\langle x, y \rangle = 0$, then we say that x and y are **orthogonal**, and write $x \perp y$. This terminology is used frequently in econometrics. Its importance stems partly from the next fact, the proof of which is a short exercise.

Fact 5.2.3 If $x, y \in L_2$ and $\mathbb{E}x = 0$ or $\mathbb{E}y = 0$ then $x \perp y \iff \text{cov}[x, y] = 0$.

Now consider the following problem. Given $y \in L_2$ and linear subspace $S \subset L_2$, we seek the closest element $\hat{y}$ of S to y. Closeness is in terms of L_2 norm, so $\hat{y}$ is the minimizer of $\|y - z\|$ over all $z \in S$. That is, we seek

$$\hat{y} = \operatorname*{argmin}_{z \in S} \|y - z\| = \operatorname*{argmin}_{z \in S} \sqrt{\mathbb{E}[(y - z)^2]} \tag{5.32}$$

The next theorem mimics theorem 2.2.1 on page 29. A nice treatment that covers the current setting can be found in chapter 2 of Cheney (2001).

Theorem 5.2.1 (Orthogonal Projection Theorem IV) *Let $y \in L_2$ and let S be any nonempty closed linear subspace of L_2. The following statements are true:*

(i) The optimization problem (5.32) *has exactly one solution.*

(ii) $\hat{y} \in L_2$ is the unique solution[3] *to* (5.32) *if and only if $\hat{y} \in S$ and $y - \hat{y} \perp S$.*

---

3. Uniqueness is a probability one statement: Any two solutions $\hat{y}_1$ and $\hat{y}_2$ satisfy $\mathbb{P}\{\hat{y}_1 = \hat{y}_2\} = 1$. We've already agreed not to distinguish between such elements. See the discussion after fact 5.2.2.

The statement that S is closed means that $\{x_n\} \subset S$ and $x \in L_2$ with $\|x_n - x\| \to 0$ implies $x \in S$. This condition is true for all the linear subspaces we want to work with.

Analogous with the case of $\mathbb{R}^N$, the random variable $\hat{y}$ in theorem 5.2.1 is called the **orthogonal projection of y onto S**. Holding S fixed, we can think of the operation

$$y \mapsto \text{the orthogonal projection of } y \text{ onto } S$$

as a function from L_2 to L_2. The function will be denoted by $\mathbf{P}$, so that, for each $y \in L_2$, the symbol $\mathbf{P}y$ represents the image of y under $\mathbf{P}$, which is the orthogonal projection $\hat{y}$. As before, $\mathbf{P}$ is called the **orthogonal projection onto S**, and we write $\mathbf{P} = \operatorname{proj} S$. Since $\mathbf{P}y$ solves (5.32), we can and do interpret $\mathbf{P}y$ as the *best predictor of y from within the collection of random variables contained in S.*

Fact 5.2.4 Let S be any linear subspace of L_2, and let $\mathbf{P} = \operatorname{proj} S$. The following statements are true:

(i) $\mathbf{P}$ is a linear function.

Moreover, for any $y \in L_2$, we have

(ii) $\mathbf{P}y \in S$,

(iii) $y - \mathbf{P}y \perp S$,

(iv) $\|y\|^2 = \|\mathbf{P}y\|^2 + \|y - \mathbf{P}y\|^2$,

(v) $\|\mathbf{P}y\| \leqslant \|y\|$, and

(vi) $\mathbf{P}y = y$ if and only if $y \in S$.

Compare with theorem 2.2.2 on page 31. In (i), the statement that $\mathbf{P}$ is linear means that $\mathbf{P}(\alpha x + \beta y) = \alpha \mathbf{P}x + \beta \mathbf{P}y$ for all $x, y \in L_2$ and $\alpha, \beta \in \mathbb{R}$.

The next two results are L_2 versions of fact 2.2.7 on page 32 and fact 2.2.6 on page 32 respectively. The proofs are essentially the same.

Fact 5.2.5 Let S_i be a linear subspace of L_2 for $i = 1, 2$ and let $\mathbf{P}_i = \operatorname{proj} S_i$. If $S_1 \subset S_2$, then $\mathbf{P}_1 \mathbf{P}_2 y = \mathbf{P}_1 y$ for all $y \in L_2$.

Fact 5.2.6 If $\{u_1, \ldots, u_K\}$ is an orthonormal basis of S, then, for all $y \in L_2$,

$$\mathbf{P}y = \sum_{k=1}^{K} \langle y, u_k \rangle \, u_k \tag{5.33}$$

Example 5.2.5 The mean of a random variable x can be thought of as the "best predictor of x within the set of constants." To see this from a new perspective, let $S := \operatorname{span}\{\mathbb{1}\}$, where $\mathbb{1} := \mathbb{1}_\Omega$, and let $\mathbf{P} := \operatorname{proj} S$. The object $\mathbf{P}x$ is precisely the best predictor of x within the class of constant random variables. Not surprisingly, $\mathbf{P}x = \mu\mathbb{1}$, where $\mu := \mathbb{E}\, x$. The easiest way to check this is to observe that $\{\mathbb{1}\}$ is an orthonormal set spanning S, and hence, by (5.33),

$$\mathbf{P}x = \langle x, \mathbb{1} \rangle \, \mathbb{1} = \mathbb{E}\,[x\mathbb{1}]\mathbb{1} = \mathbb{E}\,[x]\mathbb{1} = \mu\, \mathbb{1}$$

You can also check the claim that $\mu\mathbb{1}$ is the projection of x onto S by verifying the conditions in (ii) of theorem 5.2.1.

Example 5.2.6 Let's revisit the problem of best linear predictors from §4.1.5, establishing the same result in a different way. Fix $x, y \in L_2$ and consider projecting y onto $S := \operatorname{span}\{\mathbb{1}, x\}$. The set S is as given in (5.31). The problem of projecting y onto S is equivalent to the best linear prediction problem in (4.21) on page 99. To implement the projection recall from example 5.2.4 that

$$u_1 := \mathbb{1} \quad \text{and} \quad u_2 := \frac{x - \mu}{\sigma_x}$$

form an orthonormal basis for S. Hence, letting $\mathbf{P} = \operatorname{proj} S$ and applying (5.33),

$$\mathbf{P}y = \langle y, u_1 \rangle u_1 + \langle y, u_2 \rangle u_2 = \mathbb{E}\,[y] + \frac{\operatorname{cov}[x, y]}{\operatorname{var}[x]}(x - \mathbb{E}\,[x])$$

Alternatively, we can write

$$\mathbf{P}y = \alpha^* + \beta^* x \quad \text{where} \quad \beta^* := \frac{\operatorname{cov}[x, y]}{\operatorname{var}[x]} \quad \text{and} \quad \alpha^* := \mathbb{E}\,[y] - \beta^* \mathbb{E}\,[x]$$

These are the same solutions we obtained using calculus in §4.1.5.

5.2.3.1 Population Regression

Let's consider an extension of the best linear prediction problem of example 5.2.6 to a more general setting, where the information for predicting y is a random vector $\mathbf{x}$ in $\mathbb{R}^K$. As before, prediction will be linear, with the aim of minimizing squared error. Hence the object we seek is the L_2 orthogonal projection of y onto the linear subspace

$$\operatorname{span}\{\mathbf{x}\} := \text{ all random variables of the form } \mathbf{x}^\top \mathbf{b} \text{ for some } \mathbf{b} \in \mathbb{R}^K$$

To make sure that $\operatorname{span}\{\mathbf{x}\} \subset L_2$, we will assume that $\mathbb{E}\,[\mathbf{x}^\top \mathbf{x}] < \infty$.

Fact 5.2.7 If $\mathbb{E}\,[\mathbf{x}\mathbf{x}^\top]$ is positive definite, then the projection $\mathbf{P}y$ of any $y \in L_2$ onto $\operatorname{span}\{\mathbf{x}\}$ is given by

$$\hat{y} = \mathbf{x}^\top \mathbf{b}^* \quad \text{where} \quad \mathbf{b}^* := \mathbb{E}\,[\mathbf{x}\mathbf{x}^\top]^{-1}\mathbb{E}\,[\mathbf{x}y] \tag{5.34}$$

Exercise 5.4.16 asks you to prove this. Positive definiteness of $\mathbb{E}[\mathbf{x}\mathbf{x}^\top]$ ensures invertibility, without which the vector $\mathbf{b}^*$ is not uniquely defined (see ex. 3.5.34). Note that, by the definition of orthogonal projections, $\mathbf{b}^*$ necessarily satisfies

$$\mathbf{b}^* = \underset{\mathbf{a} \in \mathbb{R}^K}{\operatorname{argmin}} \, \mathbb{E}[(y - \mathbf{x}^\top \mathbf{a})^2]$$

The linear prediction problem considered here is also called **population linear regression**. The "population" qualifier is because we are using the true joint distribution of $(\mathbf{x}, y)$ when we compute expectations. Population regression has a sample counterpart called multivariate linear regression, based on observations of $(\mathbf{x}, y)$. We will discuss it at length in chapter 11.

5.2.4 Measurability

While the use of projections to obtain best linear predictors in example 5.2.6 and fact 5.2.7 is elegant and useful, we don't always want to constrain ourselves to linear predictions. To drop the linearity requirement, we change the linear subspaces used for projection from the set of linear functions of $\mathbf{x}$ to the set of arbitrary functions of $\mathbf{x}$. As we now show, the best predictor that results is exactly the conditional expectation with respect to $\mathbf{x}$.

The key to this process is defining the subspace to project onto. In the language of probability, the subspace of arbitrary real-valued functions of $\mathbf{x}$ is called the $\mathbf{x}$-measurable functions. Let's take these ideas one step at a time, starting with the notion of measurability with respect to information sets.

Let $\mathcal{G} := \{x_1, \ldots, x_D\}$ be any set of random variables and let z be any other random variable. The variable z is said to be **$\mathcal{G}$-measurable** if there exists a $\mathscr{B}$-measurable function $g \colon \mathbb{R}^D \to \mathbb{R}$ such that

$$z = g(x_1, \ldots, x_D) \tag{5.35}$$

As usual, this equality between random variables should be interpreted pointwise, so the more explicit version is

$$z(\omega) = g(x_1(\omega), \ldots, x_D(\omega)) \qquad \text{for all } \omega \in \Omega \tag{5.36}$$

In this context, $\mathcal{G}$ is sometimes referred to as the **information set**. When convenient we'll also write $\mathbf{x} = (x_1, \ldots, x_D)$ and say that z is $\mathbf{x}$-measurable. Similar terminology will be used for scalars and matrices. For example, if $\mathbf{X}$ is a random matrix, then $\mathbf{X}$-measurability means $\mathcal{G}$-measurability when $\mathcal{G}$ lists all elements of $\mathbf{X}$.

The intuitive meaning of $\mathcal{G}$-measurability of z is that z is completely determined by the elements in $\mathcal{G}$. Imagine it like this: When uncertainty is realized, some ω is selected from Ω. We don't get to view ω itself, but we do get to observe the realized values $x_1(\omega), \ldots, x_D(\omega)$ on the right-hand side of (5.36). If z is $\mathcal{G}$-measurable, we can now calculate the realized value $z(\omega)$ of z, even without knowing ω.

Example 5.2.7 Let x, y and z be random variables and let α and β be scalars. If $z = \alpha x + \beta y$, then z is $\{x, y\}$-measurable (take $g(s, t) := \alpha s + \beta t$).

Example 5.2.8 If $x_1, \ldots, x_N$ are random variables and $\mathcal{G} := \{x_1, \ldots, x_N\}$, then the sample mean $\bar{x}_N := \frac{1}{N} \sum_{n=1}^N x_n$ is $\mathcal{G}$-measurable.

Example 5.2.9 Let $\mathbf{x}$ and y be independent and nondegenerate. Then y is not $\mathbf{x}$-measurable, for if it were, then we would have $y = g(\mathbf{x})$ for some function g, contradicting independence of $\mathbf{x}$ and y.[4]

Example 5.2.10 Let y be a noisy signal of x, in the sense that $y = x + u$ where x and u are independent and u is nondegenerate. Then y is not x-measurable. Intuitively, even if we know the value of x, the realization of y cannot be computed until we know the value of the disturbance term u. More formally, if y is x-measurable, then $y = g(x)$ for some g, in which case $u = g(x) - x$. But then u is x-measurable, contradicting independence.

Example 5.2.11 Let $y = \alpha$, where α is a constant. This degenerate random variable is $\mathcal{G}$-measurable for any information set $\mathcal{G}$, because y is already deterministic. For example, if $\mathcal{G} = \{x_1, \ldots, x_p\}$, then we can take $y = g(x_1, \ldots, x_p) = \alpha + \sum_{i=1}^p 0 x_i$.

If x and y are known given the information in $\mathcal{G}$, then a third random variable that depends only on x and y is likewise known given $\mathcal{G}$. Hence $\mathcal{G}$-measurability is preserved under the taking of sums, products, and so on. In particular,

Fact 5.2.8 Let α, β be any scalars, and let x and y be random variables. If x and y are both $\mathcal{G}$-measurable, then $u := xy$ and $v := \alpha x + \beta y$ are also $\mathcal{G}$-measurable.

Suppose now that $\mathcal{G} \subset L_2$, which just means that all the random variables in $\mathcal{G}$ have finite second moment. Consider the set

$$L_2(\mathcal{G}) := \{\text{all } \mathcal{G}\text{-measurable random variables in } L_2\}$$

In view of fact 5.2.8, we have the following result:

Fact 5.2.9 For any $\mathcal{G} \subset L_2$, the set $L_2(\mathcal{G})$ is a linear subspace of L_2.

4. A tighter proof can be given using the language of σ-algebras, although the intuition is less immediate.

This furnishes us with a subspace to project onto, allowing us to define conditional expectations. But before we do so let's cover ordering of information sets by set inclusion.

Fact 5.2.10 If $\mathcal{G} \subset \mathcal{H}$ and z is $\mathcal{G}$-measurable, then z is $\mathcal{H}$-measurable.

This is intuitive: If z is known once the variables in $\mathcal{G}$ are known, then it is certainly known when the extra information provided by $\mathcal{H}$ is available.

Example 5.2.12 Let x_1, x_2 and y be random variables and let

$$\mathcal{G} := \{x_1\} \subset \{x_1, x_2\} =: \mathcal{H}$$

If y is $\mathcal{G}$-measurable, then $y = g(x_1)$ for some $\mathscr{B}$-measurable g. But then y will also be $\mathcal{H}$-measurable. For example, we can write $y = h(x_1, x_2)$ where $h(x_1, x_2) = g(x_1) + 0x_2$.

The next result is immediate from fact 5.2.10.

Fact 5.2.11 If $\mathcal{G} \subset \mathcal{H}$, then $L_2(\mathcal{G}) \subset L_2(\mathcal{H})$.

Incidentally, most advanced probability texts give a definition of $\mathcal{G}$-measurability framed in terms of σ-algebras. This is necessary if you wish to work through all related proofs. But the definition given here is equivalent and intuitive. See theorem 4.4 of Çinlar (2011) if you wish to learn more.

5.2.5 Conditional Expectation

Now it's time to define conditional expectations. Let $\mathcal{G} \subset L_2$ and y be some random variable in L_2. The **conditional expectation** of y given $\mathcal{G}$ is written as $\mathbb{E}[y \mid \mathcal{G}]$ or $\mathbb{E}^{\mathcal{G}}[y]$, and defined as the closest $\mathcal{G}$-measurable random variable to y. More formally,

$$\mathbb{E}[y \mid \mathcal{G}] := \operatorname*{argmin}_{z \in L_2(\mathcal{G})} \|y - z\| \tag{5.37}$$

This definition makes sense. Our understanding of the conditional expectation $\mathbb{E}[y \mid \mathcal{G}]$ is that it is the best predictor of y given the information contained in $\mathcal{G}$. The definition in (5.37) says the same thing. It simultaneously restricts $\mathbb{E}[y \mid \mathcal{G}]$ to be $\mathcal{G}$-measurable, so we can actually compute it once the variables in $\mathcal{G}$ are realized, and selects $\mathbb{E}[y \mid \mathcal{G}]$ as the closest such variable to y in terms of RMSE.

But does the minimizer generally exist? And is it unique? The answer to both questions is yes. Comparing (5.37) and (5.32), we see that

$$\mathbb{E}[y \mid \mathcal{G}] = \mathbf{P}y \quad \text{when } \mathbf{P} := \operatorname{proj} L_2(\mathcal{G})$$

By theorem 5.2.1, the projection exists and is unique. Theorem 5.2.1 also characterizes $\mathbb{E}[y \mid \mathcal{G}]$ as the unique point $\hat{y}$ in L_2 such that

$$\hat{y} \in L_2(\mathcal{G}) \quad \text{and} \quad y - \hat{y} \perp z \ \text{ for all } z \in L_2(\mathcal{G})$$

Rewriting these conditions in a slightly different way, we can give an alternative (and equivalent) definition of conditional expectation: $\hat{y} \in L_2$ is the **conditional expectation** of y given $\mathcal{G}$ if

(i) $\hat{y}$ is $\mathcal{G}$-measurable and

(ii) $\mathbb{E}[\hat{y}\, z] = \mathbb{E}[yz]$ for all $\mathcal{G}$-measurable $z \in L_2$.

When convenient we'll also use symbols like $\mathbb{E}[y \mid x_1, \ldots, x_D]$ or $\mathbb{E}[y \mid \mathbf{x}]$. These are the same as $\mathbb{E}[y \mid \mathcal{G}]$ when $\mathcal{G}$ is defined as the information set containing the variables we condition on.

Example 5.2.13 If x and u are independent, $\mathbb{E}\, u = 0$ and $y = x + u$, then $\mathbb{E}[y \mid x] = x$. To prove this we need to show that x satisfies (i)–(ii) above. Clearly, x is x-measurable. For (ii) we need to show that $\mathbb{E}[x\, z] = \mathbb{E}[y\, z]$ for all x-measurable z. This translates to the claim that

$$\mathbb{E}[xg(x)] = \mathbb{E}[(x + u)g(x)]$$

for any $\mathscr{B}$-measurable g, which is true from independence and $\mathbb{E}\, u = 0$.

Fact 5.2.12 Given $\mathbf{x} \in \mathbb{R}^D$ and y in L_2, there exists a $\mathscr{B}$-measurable function $f^* \colon \mathbb{R}^D \to \mathbb{R}$ such that $\mathbb{E}[y \mid \mathbf{x}] = f^*(\mathbf{x})$.

This is obvious because $\mathbb{E}[y \mid \mathbf{x}]$ is by definition $\mathbf{x}$-measurable. A prediction of y given $\mathbf{x}$ has to be a deterministic function of $\mathbf{x}$. The particular function f^* satisfying $f^*(\mathbf{x}) = \mathbb{E}[y \mid \mathbf{x}]$ is called the **regression function** of y given $\mathbf{x}$. It is, by construction, the best predictor of y given $\mathbf{x}$ in terms of mean squared error.

The next example shows that when x and y are linked by a conditional density, then our definition of conditional expectation reduces to the one seen in elementary probability texts. The proof of the claim in the example is the topic of exercise 5.4.23.

Example 5.2.14 If x and y are random variables and $p(y \mid x)$ is the conditional density of y given x, then

$$\mathbb{E}[y \mid x] = \int tp(t \mid x)\, \mathrm{d}t$$

Here are some goodies we can harvest using the fact that $\mathbb{E}[\cdot \mid \mathcal{G}] = \operatorname{proj} L_2(\mathcal{G})$.

Fact 5.2.13 Let x and y be random variables in L_2, let α and β be scalars, and let $\mathcal{G}$ and $\mathcal{H}$ be subsets of L_2. The following properties hold:

(i) Linearity: $\mathbb{E}[\alpha x + \beta y \mid \mathcal{G}] = \alpha\mathbb{E}[x \mid \mathcal{G}] + \beta\mathbb{E}[y \mid \mathcal{G}]$.

(ii) If $\mathcal{G} \subset \mathcal{H}$, then $\mathbb{E}[\mathbb{E}[y \mid \mathcal{H}] \mid \mathcal{G}] = \mathbb{E}[y \mid \mathcal{G}]$ and $\mathbb{E}[\mathbb{E}[y \mid \mathcal{G}]] = \mathbb{E}[y]$.

(iii) If y is independent of the variables in $\mathcal{G}$, then $\mathbb{E}[y \mid \mathcal{G}] = \mathbb{E}[y]$.

(iv) If y is $\mathcal{G}$-measurable, then $\mathbb{E}[y \mid \mathcal{G}] = y$.

(v) If x is $\mathcal{G}$-measurable, then $\mathbb{E}[xy \mid \mathcal{G}] = x\mathbb{E}[y \mid \mathcal{G}]$.

Some of these claims are given as solved exercises. Others follow directly from the definition and from the properties of projections. For example, in (iv) we are saying that if $y \in L_2(\mathcal{G})$, then y is projected into itself. This is immediate from (vi) in fact 5.2.4 on page 146.

Part (ii) is called the **the law of iterated expectations**. The law follows from the property of orthogonal projections given in fact 2.2.7 on page 32: Projecting onto the bigger subspace $L_2(\mathcal{H})$ and from there onto $L_2(\mathcal{G})$ is the same as projecting directly onto the smaller subspace $L_2(\mathcal{G})$.

Part (v) is called **conditional determinism**. It says that if x is known given $\mathcal{G}$ then we can treat it as a constant in the conditional expectation.

5.2.5.1 Conditional Expectations and Prediction

To recap, given $y \in L_2$ and random vector $\mathbf{x}$ in $\mathbb{R}^D$, the conditional expectation $\mathbb{E}[y \mid \mathbf{x}]$ is a function f^* of $\mathbf{x}$, called the regression function of y given $\mathbf{x}$, such that $f^*(\mathbf{x})$ is the best predictor of y in terms of MSE. In other words,

$$f^* = \operatorname*{argmin}_{g \in G} \mathbb{E}[(y - g(\mathbf{x}))^2] \tag{5.38}$$

where G is the functions from $\mathbb{R}^D$ to $\mathbb{R}$ with $g(\mathbf{x}) \in L_2$. In fact a more explicit result can be obtained: For any $g \in G$, we have

$$\mathbb{E}[(y - g(\mathbf{x}))^2] = \mathbb{E}[(y - f^*(\mathbf{x}))^2] + \mathbb{E}[(f^*(\mathbf{x}) - g(\mathbf{x}))^2] \tag{5.39}$$

This implies (5.38) because $(f^*(\mathbf{x}) - g(\mathbf{x}))^2 \geqslant 0$.

To prove (5.39), let f^* be the regression function, pick any $g \in G$ and observe that

$$\begin{aligned}(y - g(\mathbf{x}))^2 &= (y - f^*(\mathbf{x}) + f^*(\mathbf{x}) - g(\mathbf{x}))^2 \\ &= (y - f^*(\mathbf{x}))^2 + 2(y - f^*(\mathbf{x}))(f^*(\mathbf{x}) - g(\mathbf{x})) + (f^*(\mathbf{x}) - g(\mathbf{x}))^2\end{aligned}$$

Consider the expectation of the cross-product term. From the law of iterated expectations,

$$\mathbb{E}\{(y - f^*(\mathbf{x}))(f^*(\mathbf{x}) - g(\mathbf{x}))\} = \mathbb{E}\{\,\mathbb{E}[(y - f^*(\mathbf{x}))(f^*(\mathbf{x}) - g(\mathbf{x})) \mid \mathbf{x}]\,\} \tag{5.40}$$

Using conditional determinism we can rewrite the term inside the curly brackets on the right-hand side of (5.40) as $(f^*(\mathbf{x}) - g(\mathbf{x}))\mathbb{E}[(y - f^*(\mathbf{x})) \,|\, \mathbf{x}]$. For the second term in this product we have

$$\mathbb{E}[y - f^*(\mathbf{x}) \,|\, \mathbf{x}] = \mathbb{E}[y \,|\, \mathbf{x}] - \mathbb{E}[f^*(\mathbf{x}) \,|\, \mathbf{x}] = \mathbb{E}[y \,|\, \mathbf{x}] - f^*(\mathbf{x}) = 0$$

Hence the expectation in (5.40) is zero. Equation (5.39) now follows.

5.2.6 The Vector Case

Conditional expectations of random matrices are defined using the notion of conditional expectations for scalar random variables. For example, given random matrices $\mathbf{X}$ and $\mathbf{Y}$, we set

$$\mathbb{E}[\mathbf{Y} \,|\, \mathbf{X}] := \begin{pmatrix} \mathbb{E}[y_{11} \,|\, \mathbf{X}] & \cdots & \mathbb{E}[y_{1K} \,|\, \mathbf{X}] \\ \vdots & & \vdots \\ \mathbb{E}[y_{N1} \,|\, \mathbf{X}] & \cdots & \mathbb{E}[y_{NK} \,|\, \mathbf{X}] \end{pmatrix}$$

We also define

(i) $\operatorname{cov}[\mathbf{x}, \mathbf{y} \,|\, \mathbf{Z}] := \mathbb{E}[\mathbf{x}\mathbf{y}^\top \,|\, \mathbf{Z}] - \mathbb{E}[\mathbf{x} \,|\, \mathbf{Z}]\mathbb{E}[\mathbf{y} \,|\, \mathbf{Z}]^\top$

(ii) $\operatorname{var}[\mathbf{x} \,|\, \mathbf{Z}] := \mathbb{E}[\mathbf{x}\mathbf{x}^\top \,|\, \mathbf{Z}] - \mathbb{E}[\mathbf{x} \,|\, \mathbf{Z}]\mathbb{E}[\mathbf{x} \,|\, \mathbf{Z}]^\top$

Using the definitions, one can show that the properties of scalar conditional expectations in fact 5.2.13 carry over to the matrix setting. Here's a partial list:

Fact 5.2.14 If $\mathbf{X}$, $\mathbf{Y}$ and $\mathbf{Z}$ are random matrices and $\mathbf{A}$ and $\mathbf{B}$ are constant and conformable, then

(i) $\mathbb{E}[\mathbf{Y} \,|\, \mathbf{Z}]^\top = \mathbb{E}[\mathbf{Y}^\top \,|\, \mathbf{Z}]$.

(ii) $\mathbb{E}[\mathbf{A}\mathbf{X} + \mathbf{B}\mathbf{Y} \,|\, \mathbf{Z}] = \mathbf{A}\mathbb{E}[\mathbf{X} \,|\, \mathbf{Z}] + \mathbf{B}\mathbb{E}[\mathbf{Y} \,|\, \mathbf{Z}]$.

(iii) $\mathbb{E}[\mathbb{E}[\mathbf{Y} \,|\, \mathbf{X}]] = \mathbb{E}[\mathbf{Y}]$ and $\mathbb{E}[\mathbb{E}[\mathbf{Y} \,|\, \mathbf{X}, \mathbf{Z}] \,|\, \mathbf{X}] = \mathbb{E}[\mathbf{Y} \,|\, \mathbf{X}]$.

(iv) If $\mathbf{X}$ and $\mathbf{Y}$ are independent, then $\mathbb{E}[\mathbf{Y} \,|\, \mathbf{X}] = \mathbb{E}[\mathbf{Y}]$.

(v) If $g(\mathbf{X})$ is a matrix depending only on $\mathbf{X}$, then

  (a) $\mathbb{E}[g(\mathbf{X}) \,|\, \mathbf{X}] = g(\mathbf{X})$

  (b) $\mathbb{E}[g(\mathbf{X})\,\mathbf{Y} \,|\, \mathbf{X}] = g(\mathbf{X})\mathbb{E}[\mathbf{Y} \,|\, \mathbf{X}]$ and $\mathbb{E}[\mathbf{Y}\,g(\mathbf{X}) \,|\, \mathbf{X}] = \mathbb{E}[\mathbf{Y} \,|\, \mathbf{X}]\,g(\mathbf{X})$

Part (v) shows examples of conditional determinism in the matrix case.

5.3 Further Reading

Comprehensive treatments of multivariate distributions can be found in monographs such as Izenman (2008) and Joe (1997). Beautiful treatments of conditional expectation via orthogonal projection in L_2 can be found in Williams (1991), Taylor (1997), Schilling (2005), and Çinlar (2011).

5.4 Exercises

Ex. 5.4.1 Confirm the expression for the density q of $y = \psi(x)$ in (4.32) in the case where ψ is strictly increasing.[5]

Ex. 5.4.2 Let x_1 and x_2 be random variables with joint density p and marginals p_1 and p_2. Show that x_1 and x_2 are independent in the sense that (5.19) holds whenever $p(s_1, s_2) = p_1(s_1)p_2(s_2)$ for every $(s_1, s_2) \in \mathbb{R}^2$.[6]

Ex. 5.4.3 Let $p\colon \mathbb{R}^2 \to \mathbb{R}$ be defined by

$$p(s_1, s_2) = \begin{cases} \exp(s_1 + s_2) & \text{if } s_1 \leqslant 0 \text{ and } s_2 \leqslant 0 \\ 0 & \text{otherwise} \end{cases}$$

Let x_1, x_2 have joint density p. Show that x_1 and x_2 are independent.

Ex. 5.4.4 Show that if $\mathcal{L}(x) = \mathrm{N}(0,1)$, then $\mathcal{L}(x^2) = \chi^2(1)$.[7]

Ex. 5.4.5 Confirm fact 5.1.11: If $\mathbf{x}$ and $\mathbf{y}$ are independent, then $\mathrm{cov}[\mathbf{x}, \mathbf{y}] = 0$.

Ex. 5.4.6 Let x and y be independent uniform random variables on $[0,1]$. Let $z := \max\{x, y\}$. Compute the CDF, density and mean of z.[8] In addition, compute the CDF of $w := \min\{x, y\}$.

Ex. 5.4.7 Confirm fact 5.1.3 on page 127.

Ex. 5.4.8 Let $\mathbf{x}$ be a random vector. Confirm the claim in fact 5.1.2 that $\mathrm{var}[\mathbf{x}]$ is nonnegative definite.

Ex. 5.4.9 Let $\mathcal{L}(\mathbf{x}) = \mathcal{L}(x_1, \ldots, x_N) = \mathrm{N}(\mathbf{0}, \mathbf{I})$.

---

5. Hint: Use fact 4.2.6 on page 111.
6. Hint: Apply (5.9) on page 132.
7. Hints: You need to match the density in example 4.2.12 when $k = 1$. Use the fact that $\Gamma(1/2) = \sqrt{\pi}$. Try to find the CDF of z^2 and differentiate it. In finding the CDF, the solution to exercise 4.4.18 on page 117 might be helpful.
8. Hint: Fix $s \in \mathbb{R}$ and compare the sets $\{z \leqslant s\}$ and $\{x \leqslant s\} \cap \{y \leqslant s\}$. What is the relationship between these two sets?

(i) What is the distribution of x_1^2/x_2^2?

(ii) What is the distribution of $x_1[2/(x_2^2 + x_3^2)]^{1/2}$?

(iii) What is the distribution of $\|\mathbf{x}\|^2$?

(iv) If $\mathbf{a}$ is an $N \times 1$ constant vector, what is the distribution of $\mathbf{a}^\top \mathbf{x}$?

Ex. 5.4.10 Let x and y be independent random variables taking values in $\{0\} \cup \mathbb{N}$ with PMFs $p = \{p(j)\}$ and $q = \{q(j)\}$ respectively. (I'm using function rather than subscript style notation for this exercise to make the arguments a bit easier to follow.) The **convolution** of p and q is the PMF $p \star q$ defined by

$$(p \star q)(j) = \sum_{k \geqslant 0} p(j-k)q(k) \tag{5.41}$$

Show that $p \star q$ is the PMF of $z := x + y$ when x and y are independent with $\mathcal{L}(x) = p$ and $\mathcal{L}(y) = q$.

Ex. 5.4.11 Prove fact 5.1.13 on page 137.

Ex. 5.4.12 Fix $z \in L_2$ with $\mathbb{E} z = 0$ and let $S := \{x \in L_2 : \operatorname{cov}[x, z] = 0\}$. Show that S is a linear subspace of L_2.

Ex. 5.4.13 Let $x \in L_2$ with $\mathbb{E} x = \mu$ and $\operatorname{var}[x] = \sigma^2$. Let $S := \operatorname{span}\{\mathbb{1}\}$, as in example 5.2.5 on page 146. Let $\mathbf{P} := \operatorname{proj} S$ and let $\mathbf{M}$ be the residual projection (see page 32) defined by $\mathbf{M}x = x - \mathbf{P}x$. Show that $\|\mathbf{M}x\| = \sigma$.

Ex. 5.4.14 Let $x, y \in L_2$, let $S := \operatorname{span}\{x\}$, and let $\mathbf{P} := \operatorname{proj} S$. Show that

$$\mathbf{P}y = \mathbb{E}[x^2]^{-1} \mathbb{E}[xy]\, x \tag{5.42}$$

Ex. 5.4.15 Prove the Cauchy–Schwarz inequality for random variables, which was first stated as fact 4.1.8 on page 97 as $|\mathbb{E}[xy]| \leqslant (\mathbb{E}[x^2]\mathbb{E}[y^2])^{1/2}$ and repeated as part (iv) of fact 5.2.2. Use the results on orthogonal projections in L_2 as found in §5.2.3.[9]

Ex. 5.4.16 Prove that $\hat{y}$ in (5.34) is the orthogonal projection of y onto $\operatorname{span}\{\mathbf{x}\}$ under the conditions stated in fact 5.2.7.

Ex. 5.4.17 Let $\mathbf{x} \in \mathbb{R}^K$ be a random vector and let $\|\cdot\|$ be the ordinary vector norm. Show that if $\|\mathbf{x}\|$ is in L_2, then the random variable $z = \ell(\mathbf{x})$ is in L_2 whenever $\ell \colon \mathbb{R}^K \to \mathbb{R}$ is linear.

---

9. Hint: Use (5.42) and review the solution to exercise 3.5.33.

Ex. 5.4.18 Consider the setting of the population regression discussion in §5.2.3.1. In particular, let y be an element of L_2, let $\mathbf{b}^*$ be the coefficients of the best linear predictor, as defined in (5.34), let $S = \operatorname{span}\{\mathbf{x}\}$, and let $f^*(\mathbf{x}) = \mathbb{E}[y \mid \mathbf{x}]$. Show that $\ell^*(\mathbf{x}) := \mathbf{x}^\mathsf{T}\mathbf{b}^*$ is the orthogonal projection of $f^*(\mathbf{x})$ onto S.

Ex. 5.4.19 Prove part (iii) of fact 5.2.13 when $\mathcal{G} = \{\mathbf{x}\}$.

Ex. 5.4.20 Prove part (v) of fact 5.2.13.

Ex. 5.4.21 Let $\operatorname{var}[y \mid x] := \mathbb{E}[y^2 \mid x] - (\mathbb{E}[y \mid x])^2$. Show that

$$\operatorname{var} y = \mathbb{E}[\operatorname{var}[y \mid x]] + \operatorname{var}[\mathbb{E}[y \mid x]]$$

Ex. 5.4.22 Show that the conditional expectation of a constant α is α. In particular, using the results in fact 5.2.13 (page 151) as appropriate, show that if α is a constant and $\mathcal{G}$ is any information set, then $\mathbb{E}[\alpha \mid \mathcal{G}] = \alpha$.

Ex. 5.4.23 Prove the claim in example 5.2.14.

5.4.1 Solutions to Selected Exercises

Solution to Ex. 5.4.1. Let x, p and $y = \psi(x)$ be as stated in fact 4.2.7 on page 111. Assume in addition that ψ is strictly increasing. Let F be the CDF of x and let G be the CDF of y. By fact 4.2.6 on page 111 we have $G(s) = F(\psi^{-1}(s))$. Differentiating gives

$$q(s) = G'(s) = p(\psi^{-1}(s)) \, \frac{\mathrm{d}\psi^{-1}(s)}{\mathrm{d}s}$$

Since ψ^{-1} is increasing, this agrees with (4.32). □

Solution to Ex. 5.4.3. Let p_1 be the marginal density of x_1 and p_2 be the marginal density of x_2. It suffices to show that

$$p(s_1, s_2) = p_1(s_1) p_2(s_2) \quad \text{for all } (s_1, s_2) \in \mathbb{R}^2 \tag{5.43}$$

To see that this is the case, first we obtain the marginal distributions by integrating out the other variable. To start, let $s_1 \leqslant 0$ and observe that

$$p_1(s_1) = \int_{-\infty}^{0} p(s_1, s_2) \, \mathrm{d}s_2 = \int_{-\infty}^{0} e^{s_1} e^{s_2} \, \mathrm{d}s_2 = e^{s_1} \int_{-\infty}^{0} e^{s_2} \, \mathrm{d}s_2 = e^{s_1}$$

Conversely, if $s_1 > 0$, then $p(s_1, s_2) = 0$ for any s_2, and hence

$$p_1(s_1) = \int_{-\infty}^{0} p(s_1, s_2) \, \mathrm{d}s_2 = 0$$

From this and a symmetric argument in the case of p_2, we get

$$p_1(s_1) = \begin{cases} e^{s_1} & \text{if } s_1 \leqslant 0 \\ 0 & \text{otherwise} \end{cases} \quad \text{and} \quad p_2(s_2) = \begin{cases} e^{s_2} & \text{if } s_2 \leqslant 0 \\ 0 & \text{otherwise} \end{cases}$$

It follows that (5.43) is valid. □

Solution to Ex. 5.4.4. Let $F(s)$ be the CDF of x^2 and let f be the density. Let Φ and ϕ be the $\mathrm{N}(0,1)$ cdf and density respectively. Following arguments similar to the solution to exercise 4.4.18 we have

$$F(s) = \mathbb{P}\{x^2 \leqslant s\} = \mathbb{P}\{-\sqrt{s} \leqslant x \leqslant \sqrt{s}\} = 2\Phi(\sqrt{s}) - 1$$

Differentiating with respect to s gives $f(s) = \phi(\sqrt{s})s^{-1/2}$. Plugging in the definition of the $\mathrm{N}(0,1)$ density and using $\Gamma(1/2) = \sqrt{\pi}$ gives the density in example 4.2.12 when $k = 1$. □

Solution to Ex. 5.4.6. As in the statement of the exercise, x and y are independent uniform random variables on $[0,1]$, $z := \max\{x,y\}$ and $w := \min\{x,y\}$. As a first step to the proofs, note that if a, b and c are three numbers, then

- $\max\{a,b\} \leqslant c$ if and only if $a \leqslant c$ and $b \leqslant c$.
- $\min\{a,b\} \leqslant c$ if and only if $a \leqslant c$ or $b \leqslant c$.

From these facts we can see that, for any $s \in \mathbb{R}$,

$$\{z \leqslant s\} = \{x \leqslant s\} \cap \{y \leqslant s\} \quad \text{and} \quad \{w \leqslant s\} = \{x \leqslant s\} \cup \{y \leqslant s\}$$

Now, for $s \in [0,1]$, we have

$$\mathbb{P}\{z \leqslant s\} = \mathbb{P}[\{x \leqslant s\} \cap \{y \leqslant s\}] = \mathbb{P}\{x \leqslant s\}\mathbb{P}\{y \leqslant s\} = s^2$$

By differentiating, we get the density $p(s) = 2s$, and by integrating $\int_0^1 sp(s)\,ds$, we get $\mathbb{E}[z] = 2/3$. Finally, regarding the CDF of w, for $s \in [0,1]$, we have

$$\begin{aligned}\mathbb{P}\{w \leqslant s\} &= \mathbb{P}[\{x \leqslant s\} \cup \{y \leqslant s\}] \\ &= \mathbb{P}\{x \leqslant s\} + \mathbb{P}\{y \leqslant s\} - \mathbb{P}[\{x \leqslant s\} \cap \{y \leqslant s\}]\end{aligned}$$

Hence $\mathbb{P}\{w \leqslant s\} = 2s - s^2$. □

Solution to Ex. 5.4.7. Since $\mathbf{z}^\top \mathbf{A}\mathbf{z}$ has the form $\sum_{i=1}^N \sum_{j=1}^N a_{ij} z_i z_j$, under the stated assumptions we have

$$\mathbb{E}[\mathbf{z}^\top \mathbf{A}\mathbf{z}] = \sum_{i=1}^{N}\sum_{j=1}^{N} a_{ij}\mathbb{E}[z_i z_j] = \operatorname{trace}\mathbf{A} \qquad \square$$

Solution to Ex. 5.4.9. The respective solutions are as follows:

(i) $\mathcal{L}(x_1^2/x_2^2) = F(1,1)$ by fact 5.1.17.

(ii) $\mathcal{L}[x_1[2/(x_2^2+x_3^2)]^{1/2}] = t(2)$ by fact 5.1.16.

(iii) $\mathcal{L}(\|\mathbf{x}\|^2) = \chi^2(N)$ by fact 5.1.18.

(iv) $\mathcal{L}(\mathbf{a}^\top \mathbf{x}) = \mathrm{N}(0, \|\mathbf{a}\|^2)$ by fact 5.1.5.

$\square$

Solution to Ex. 5.4.10. Let $p \star q$ be as defined in (5.41), let $z := x + y$ where x and y are independent, and let $\mathcal{L}(x) = p$ and $\mathcal{L}(y) = q$. The claim is that $(p \star q)(j) = \mathbb{P}\{z = j\}$ for any $j \geqslant 0$. To see this, fix any such j and apply the law of total probability (page 88) to get

$$\mathbb{P}\{z = j\} = \sum_{k \geqslant 0} \mathbb{P}\{z = j \,|\, y = k\}\mathbb{P}\{y = k\} = \sum_{k \geqslant 0} \mathbb{P}\{x + k = j\} q(k)$$

Using $\mathbb{P}\{x + k = j\} = \mathbb{P}\{x = j - k\} = p(j - k)$ completes the proof. $\square$

Solution to Ex. 5.4.11. Let S, $\mathbf{P}$, $\mathbf{M}$, and $\mathbf{z}$ be as in the statement of the question. In view of fact 5.1.12, to prove independence of $\mathbf{Pz}$ and $\mathbf{Mz}$ it suffices to show that $\operatorname{cov}[\mathbf{Pz}, \mathbf{Mz}] = \mathbf{0}$. Since these vectors are zero-mean and $\mathbf{M}$ is symmetric (see page 61), the covariance is equal to

$$\mathbb{E}[(\mathbf{Pz})(\mathbf{Mz})^\top] = \mathbb{E}[\mathbf{P}\mathbf{z}\mathbf{z}^\top\mathbf{M}] = \mathbf{P}\mathbb{E}[\mathbf{z}\mathbf{z}^\top]\mathbf{M} = \sigma^2\mathbf{PM} = \mathbf{0}$$

The final equality follows from fact 2.2.8 on page 33. $\square$

Solution to Ex. 5.4.12. Let z and S be as described in the question. S is a linear subspace of L_2 because if $x, y \in S$ and $\alpha, \beta \in \mathbb{R}$, then

$$\operatorname{cov}[\alpha x + \beta y, z] = \alpha\mathbb{E}[xz] + \beta\mathbb{E}[yz] = \alpha\operatorname{cov}[x, z] + \beta\operatorname{cov}[y, z] = 0 \qquad \square$$

Solution to Ex. 5.4.13. We saw in example 5.2.5 that $\mathbf{P}x = \mu\mathbb{1}$, so $\mathbf{M}x = x - \mu\mathbb{1}$, or, written more conventionally, $\mathbf{M}x = x - \mu$. The norm of $\mathbf{M}x$ is $\|\mathbf{M}x\| = \sqrt{\mathbb{E}[(x-\mu)^2]} = \sigma$, as was to be shown. $\square$

Solution to Ex. 5.4.14. Let x, y, S, and $\mathbf{P}$ be as in the statement of the exercise, and let $\mathbf{P}y$ be as defined in (5.42). As a scalar multiple of x it's clear that $\mathbf{P}y \in S$, so we need only show that $y - \mathbf{P}y \perp x$, or, equivalently, $\mathbb{E}[xy - x\mathbf{P}y] = 0$. Substituting in the expression for $\mathbf{P}y$ in (5.42) and using linearity of $\mathbb{E}$ confirms this equality. □

Solution to Ex. 5.4.16. Assume the conditions of fact 5.2.7 and adopt the notation stated there. Let y be any element of L_2. In view of theorem 5.2.1, to show that $\hat{y} = \mathbf{P}y$, we need to show that $\hat{y} \in S := \text{span}\{\mathbf{x}\}$ and that $y - \hat{y} \perp S$. The first part is trivial, since $\hat{y} = \mathbf{x}^\top \mathbf{b}^*$ where $\mathbf{b}^*$ is the vector $\mathbb{E}[\mathbf{x}\mathbf{x}^\top]^{-1}\mathbb{E}[\mathbf{x}y]$. To prove the second part, it suffices to show that

$$\mathbb{E}[\mathbf{a}^\top \mathbf{x} y] = \mathbb{E}[\mathbf{a}^\top \mathbf{x}\mathbf{x}^\top \mathbf{b}^*]$$

Substituting in the definition of $\mathbf{b}^*$ and some easy manipulations confirm that this equality holds. □

Solution to Ex. 5.4.17. Let $z = \ell(\mathbf{x})$ where ℓ is a linear function. The claim is that z is square integrable. By theorem 3.1.1 on page 48, we can write z as $z = \mathbf{x}^\top \mathbf{a}$ for some $\mathbf{a} \in \mathbb{R}^K$. Applying the Cauchy–Schwarz inequality for vectors, we have $z^2 \leqslant \|\mathbf{x}\|^2 \|\mathbf{a}\|^2$. Since $\|\mathbf{x}\|$ is in L_2, it follows that $\mathbb{E}[z^2] < \infty$. □

Solution to Ex. 5.4.18. Adopt the setting and notation of exercise 5.4.18. Let $\mathcal{G}$ be the set of all $\mathbf{x}$-measurable functions in L_2. Let $S = \text{span}\{\mathbf{x}\}$ = the linear $\mathbf{x}$-measurable functions in L_2. (As in §5.2.3.1, we are assuming that $\|\mathbf{x}\|$ is in L_2, which assures us that elements of S are in fact in L_2. See ex. 5.4.17.) Clearly $S \subset \mathcal{G}$. The result now follows from fact 5.2.5 on page 146. □

Solution to Ex. 5.4.19. Let y be independent of $\mathbf{x}$. From the definition of conditional expectation, to show that $\mathbb{E}[y \mid \mathbf{x}] = \mathbb{E}[y]$ we need to show that

(i) $\mathbb{E}[y]$ is $\mathcal{G}$-measurable, and

(ii) $\mathbb{E}[\mathbb{E}[y]g(\mathbf{x})] = \mathbb{E}[yg(\mathbf{x})]$ for any $\mathscr{B}$-measurable g.

Part (i) is trivial because $\mathbb{E}[y]$ is constant (see example 5.2.11 on page 149). Regarding (ii), if g is any such function, then by facts 5.1.9 and 5.1.10 (see page 136) we have $\mathbb{E}[yg(\mathbf{x})] = \mathbb{E}[y]\mathbb{E}[g(\mathbf{x})]$. The result follows. □

Solution to Ex. 5.4.20. We need to show that if x is $\mathcal{G}$-measurable, then $\mathbb{E}[xy \mid \mathcal{G}] = x\mathbb{E}[y \mid \mathcal{G}]$. To confirm this, we must show that

(i) $x\mathbb{E}[y \mid \mathcal{G}]$ is $\mathcal{G}$-measurable, and

(ii) $\mathbb{E}[x\mathbb{E}[y \mid \mathcal{G}]z] = \mathbb{E}[xyz]$ for any $z \in L_2(\mathcal{G})$.

Regarding (i), $\mathbb{E}[y \mid \mathcal{G}]$ is $\mathcal{G}$-measurable by definition, and x is $\mathcal{G}$-measurable by assumption, so $x\mathbb{E}[y \mid \mathcal{G}]$ is $\mathcal{G}$-measurable by fact 5.2.8 on page 149. Regarding (ii), fix $z \in L_2(\mathcal{G})$, and let $u := xz$. Since $x \in L_2(\mathcal{G})$, we have $u \in L_2(\mathcal{G})$. We need to show that

$$\mathbb{E}[\mathbb{E}[y \mid \mathcal{G}]u] = \mathbb{E}[yu]$$

Since $u \in L_2(\mathcal{G})$, this is immediate from the definition of $\mathbb{E}[y \mid \mathcal{G}]$. □

Solution to Ex. 5.4.22. By fact 5.2.13 (page 151), we know that if α is $\mathcal{G}$-measurable, then $\mathbb{E}[\alpha \mid \mathcal{G}] = \alpha$. Example 5.2.11 on page 149 tells us that α is indeed $\mathcal{G}$-measurable. □

Solution to Ex. 5.4.23. As in example 5.2.14, let x and y be random variables where $p(y \mid x)$ is the conditional density of y given x. Let $g(x) := \int tp(t \mid x)\,dt$. The claim is that $\mathbb{E}[y \mid x] = g(x)$. To prove this, we need to show that $g(x)$ is x-measurable, and that

$$\mathbb{E}[g(x)h(x)] = \mathbb{E}[yh(x)] \quad \text{for any } \mathscr{B}\text{-measurable } h \tag{5.44}$$

The first claim is obvious. Regarding (5.44), let h be any such function. Using the notation in (5.26) on page 142, we can write

$$\begin{aligned}
\mathbb{E}[g(x)h(x)] &= \mathbb{E}\left[\int tp(t \mid x)\,dt\; h(x)\right] \\
&= \int \int tp(t \mid s)\,dt\; h(s)p(s)\,ds \\
&= \int \int t\frac{p(s,t)}{p(s)}\,dt\; h(s)p(s)\,ds = \int \int t\,h(s)p(s,t)\,dt\,ds
\end{aligned}$$

This is equal to the right-hand side of (5.44), and the proof is done. □

Chapter 6

Asymptotics

In this chapter we cover some fundamental results from probability theory concerning asymptotics of random sequences.

6.1 LLN and CLT

The law of large numbers and central limit theorem are two of the pillars of econometrics and statistics. Below we review both theorems, starting with the necessary concepts of convergence in probability and distribution.

6.1.1 Convergence of Random Vectors

A sequence of random vectors $\{\mathbf{x}_n\}$ is said to **converge in probability** to a random vector $\mathbf{x}$ if,

$$\text{for all } \delta > 0, \quad \mathbb{P}\{\|\mathbf{x}_n - \mathbf{x}\| > \delta\} \to 0 \quad \text{as} \quad n \to \infty \tag{6.1}$$

In symbols, we write $\mathbf{x}_n \stackrel{p}{\to} \mathbf{x}$. In the scalar case $\|\mathbf{x}_n - \mathbf{x}\|$ reduces to $|x_n - x|$.

Example 6.1.1 If $\mathcal{L}(\mathbf{x}_n) = \mathrm{N}(\mathbf{0}, \sigma_n \mathbf{I})$ and $\sigma_n \to 0$, then $\mathbf{x}_n \stackrel{p}{\to} \mathbf{0}$ as $n \to \infty$. Figure 6.1 illustrates this visually for the scalar case. The variance is $\sigma_n = 1/n$. With fixed $\delta > 0$, the probability $\mathbb{P}\{|x_n| > \delta\}$ is shown for different values of n. This probability collapses to zero as $n \to \infty$. If we now fix δ at a smaller positive value, $\mathbb{P}\{|x_n| > \delta\}$ can again be made arbitrarily small by increasing n. In other words, (6.1) holds.

Fact 6.1.1 The following statements are true:

(i) $\mathbf{x}_n \stackrel{p}{\to} \mathbf{x} \iff \|\mathbf{x}_n - \mathbf{x}\| \stackrel{p}{\to} 0$.

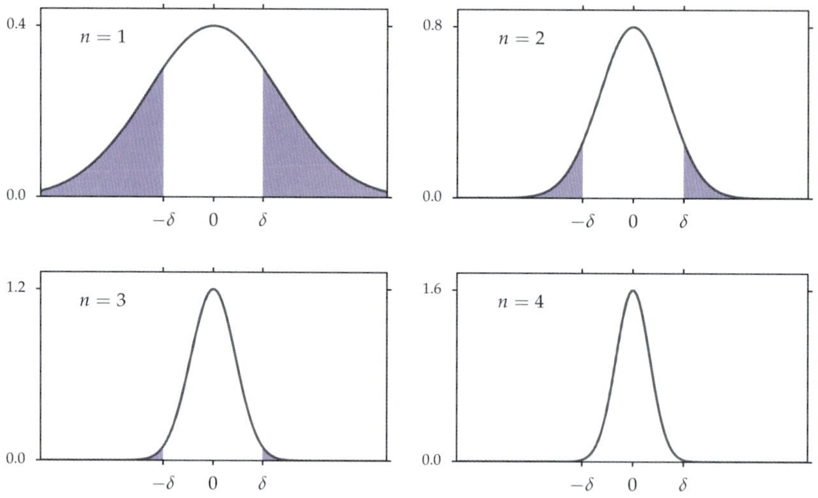

Figure 6.1 $\mathbb{P}\{|x_n| > \delta\} \to 0$ when $\mathcal{L}(x_n) = \text{N}(0, 1/n)$

(ii) $\mathbf{x}_n \xrightarrow{p} \mathbf{x} \implies g(\mathbf{x}_n) \xrightarrow{p} g(\mathbf{x})$ whenever g is continuous at $\mathbf{x}$.

(iii) $\mathbf{x}_n \xrightarrow{p} \mathbf{x}$ and $\mathbf{y}_n \xrightarrow{p} \mathbf{y} \implies \mathbf{x}_n + \mathbf{y}_n \xrightarrow{p} \mathbf{x} + \mathbf{y}$ and $\mathbf{x}_n^\top \mathbf{y}_n \xrightarrow{p} \mathbf{x}^\top \mathbf{y}$.

(iv) $\mathbf{x}_n \xrightarrow{p} \mathbf{x}$ and $\mathbf{a}_n \to \mathbf{a} \implies \mathbf{x}_n + \mathbf{a}_n \xrightarrow{p} \mathbf{x} + \mathbf{a}$ and $\mathbf{x}_n^\top \mathbf{a}_n \xrightarrow{p} \mathbf{x}^\top \mathbf{a}$.

(v) $\mathbf{x}_n \xrightarrow{p} \mathbf{x} \iff \mathbf{a}^\top \mathbf{x}_n \xrightarrow{p} \mathbf{a}^\top \mathbf{x}$ for any $\mathbf{a} \in \mathbb{R}^K$.

Part (i) is an immediate consequence of the definition. Other proofs are touched on in the exercises. For more details, see, for example, Çinlar (2011).

The scalar sequence $\{x_n\}$ is said to converge to x **in mean square** if

$$\mathbb{E}(x_n - x)^2 \to 0 \quad \text{as} \quad n \to \infty \tag{6.2}$$

and we write $x_n \xrightarrow{ms} x$. Unlike convergence in probability, for convergence in mean square to be defined we require that our variables have finite second moments.

Fact 6.1.2 Let $\{x_n\}$ and x have finite second moments and let α be any constant. The following statements are true:

(i) $x_n \xrightarrow{ms} x \implies x_n \xrightarrow{p} x$.

(ii) $x_n \xrightarrow{ms} \alpha \iff \mathbb{E} x_n \to \alpha$ and $\text{var}[x_n] \to 0$.

Part (i) follows from Chebyshev's inequality (page 97). In particular, from monotonicity of $\mathbb{P}$ and (4.19) we get

$$\mathbb{P}\{|x_n - x| > \delta\} \leqslant \mathbb{P}\{|x_n - x| \geqslant \delta\} \leqslant \frac{\mathbb{E}\,(x_n - x)^2}{\delta^2}$$

Part (ii) is implied by the next fact.

Fact 6.1.3 For any $x \in L_2$ and any constant α we have

$$\mathbb{E}\,[(x - \alpha)^2] = \mathrm{var}[x] + (\mathbb{E}\,[x] - \alpha)^2 \tag{6.3}$$

As we'll see later, (6.3) plays an important role in statistics. Its verification is an exercise. (The proof is straightforward. If you want more of a challenge, try to obtain it as a consequence of (iv) of fact 5.2.4 on page 146.)

Example 6.1.2 In figure 6.1 we showed visually how $\mathcal{L}(x_n) = \mathrm{N}(0, 1/n)$ implies $x_n \xrightarrow{p} 0$. This also follows from (i)–(ii) of fact 6.1.2, since $\mathbb{E}\,x_n = 0$ and $\mathrm{var}[x_n] = 1/n \to 0$.

6.1.2 The Law of Large Numbers

The law of large numbers (LLN) is one of the most fundamental theorems of both probability and statistics. As a prelude to the LLN, let's consider the effects of averaging over independent random quantities. We'll take the perspective of investors, who often diversify their portfolios in order to decrease risk. To formalize this idea let

- x_n be the payoff from holding one dollar of asset n,
- $\mathbb{E}\,x_n = \mu$ and $\mathrm{var}[x_n] = \sigma^2$ for all n, and
- $\mathrm{cov}[x_j, x_k] = 0$ when $j \neq k$.

If we hold just asset 1, then the payoff is x_1, the expected payoff is μ and the variance is σ^2. If we diversify by spreading one dollar evenly over N of these assets, our payoff is

$$\bar{x}_N := \frac{1}{N} \sum_{n=1}^{N} x_n$$

The expected payoff is unchanged at

$$\mathbb{E}\,\bar{x}_N = \mathbb{E}\left[\frac{1}{N} \sum_{n=1}^{N} x_n\right] = \frac{1}{N} \sum_{n=1}^{N} \mathbb{E}\,x_n = \mu \tag{6.4}$$

But the variance declines at rate $\frac{1}{N}$ because

$$\mathbb{E}\,[(\bar{x}_N - \mu)^2] = \mathbb{E}\left\{\left[\frac{1}{N}\sum_{i=1}^{N}(x_i - \mu)\right]^2\right\}$$
$$= \frac{1}{N^2}\sum_{i=1}^{N}\sum_{j=1}^{N}\mathbb{E}\,(x_i - \mu)(x_j - \mu) = \frac{1}{N^2}\sum_{i=1}^{N}\mathbb{E}\,(x_i - \mu)^2 = \frac{\sigma^2}{N}$$

The important equality here is the third one, which holds because of the zero covariance between assets. In this step N^2 terms become N terms. To summarize,

$$\mathbb{E}\,\bar{x}_N = \mu \quad \text{and} \quad \operatorname{var}[\bar{x}_N] = \frac{\sigma^2}{N} \quad \text{for all } N \tag{6.5}$$

Now imagine someone is kind enough to sell us an unlimited quantity of such assets, so we can diversify without limit. By taking $N \to \infty$ and combining (6.5) with fact 6.1.2 on page 162 we obtain a proof of the **law of large numbers**:

Theorem 6.1.1 *Let $\{x_n\}$ be* IID *copies of x. If x is integrable, then*

$$\frac{1}{N}\sum_{n=1}^{N} x_n \xrightarrow{p} \mathbb{E}\,x \quad \textit{as} \quad N \to \infty \tag{6.6}$$

Actually we haven't fully proved the LLN because we assumed existence of second moments above, while theorem 6.1.1 assumes only existence of the first moment. However, the proof above captures the spirit of the LLN most cleanly. (See theorem 8.3.5 of Dudley 2002 for the general case.)

At first glance, the law of large numbers (6.6) appears to only be a statement about the sample mean but in fact it's self-improving: We can go from (6.6) to arbitrary functions of random variables, or even random vectors. In particular, if $\mathbf{x}$ is any random vector, $\{\mathbf{x}_n\}$ are IID copies and $h \colon \mathbb{R}^N \to \mathbb{R}$ is any $\mathscr{B}$-measurable function such that $h(\mathbf{x})$ is integrable, then

$$\frac{1}{N}\sum_{n=1}^{N} h(\mathbf{x}_n) \xrightarrow{p} \mathbb{E}\,h(\mathbf{x}) \quad \text{as} \quad N \to \infty \tag{6.7}$$

This can be confirmed by letting $y_n := h(\mathbf{x}_n)$ and then applying theorem 6.1.1. The independence of $\{y_n\}$ is confirmed by fact 5.1.10 on page 137. That each y_n has the same distribution as $y := h(\mathbf{x})$ follows from

$$\mathbb{P}\{y_n \in B\} = \mathbb{P}\{h(\mathbf{x}_n) \in B\} = \mathbb{P}\{\mathbf{x}_n \in h^{-1}(B)\} = \mathbb{P}\{\mathbf{x} \in h^{-1}(B)\}$$

The law of large numbers applies to probabilities as well as expectations. To see this, fix $B \subset \mathscr{B}(\mathbb{R}^N)$, and consider the probability $\mathbb{P}\{\mathbf{x} \in B\}$. Letting h be the indicator function $h(\mathbf{s}) = \mathbb{1}_B(\mathbf{s}) = \mathbb{1}\{\mathbf{s} \in B\}$ and using the principle that expectations of indicators equal probabilities of events (page 95), we have

$$\mathbb{E} h(\mathbf{x}) = \mathbb{E}\, \mathbb{1}\{\mathbf{x} \in B\} = \mathbb{P}\{\mathbf{x} \in B\}$$

Combining this equality with (6.7), we see that if $\{\mathbf{x}_n\}$ is IID with distribution P, then

$$\frac{1}{N} \sum_{n=1}^{N} \mathbb{1}\{\mathbf{x}_n \in B\} \xrightarrow{p} P(B) \tag{6.8}$$

In words, the fraction of the sample that falls in B converges to the probability that the distribution assigns to B.

6.1.2.1 An Illustration

To illustrate the law of large numbers, consider flipping a coin until 10 heads have occurred. The coin is not fair: The probability of heads is 0.4. Let x be the number of tails observed in the process. This random variable is known to have the **negative binomial distribution**, with $\mathbb{E} x = 15$. The LLN predicts that if we simulate a large number of observations of x and take the average, we get a value close to 15. Running the Julia code in listing 1 gives outcomes consistent with this claim.[1]

Figure 6.2 shows what can happen when the finite first moment condition in the LLN is not enforced. The draws are from the standard Cauchy distribution, which fails to have a finite first moment. The top panel shows observations and the bottom shows a running sample mean of observations $\bar{x}_N$, with N on the horizontal axis. A few extreme observations dominate the average and the sample mean does not converge.[2]

6.1.3 Convergence in Distribution

As a prelude to the central limit theorem we need to review convergence in distribution. This is conceptually quite different to convergence of random variables, whether in probability or mean square. For example, the distributions $\mathrm{N}(0, 1)$ and $\mathrm{N}(10^{-10}, 1)$ are very close, but independent draws from these respective distributions need not be.

1. See `johnstachurski.net/emet.html` for code. A routine to draw from the negative binomial distribution is available from the *Distributions* package, but we've rolled our own for extra transparency.
2. In fact it can be shown that the sample mean is itself standard Cauchy for all N.

Listing 1 Illustrates the LLN (Julia)

```
num_reps = 10^6
outcomes = Array(Float64, num_reps)

for i in 1:num_reps
    num_tails = num_heads = 0
    while num_heads < 10
        b = rand()
        num_heads = num_heads + (b < 0.4)   # +1 with prob 0.4
        num_tails = num_tails + (b >= 0.4)  # +1 with prob 0.6
    end
    outcomes[i] = num_tails
end

println(mean(outcomes))
```

Let $\{P_n\}$ and P be distributions on $\mathbb{R}^K$ in the sense of §5.1.2. To represent the notion that P_n converges to P we could require that $P_n(B) \to P(B)$ for all $B \in \mathscr{B}(\mathbb{R}^K)$. However, this turns out to be rather strict and also indifferent to closeness in the sense of Euclidean norm. For example, suppose that P_n is a distribution on $\mathbb{R}$ that puts all mass on $\frac{1}{n}$, while P puts all mass on 0. Intuition suggests that $P_n \to P$, but if we take $B = (0, \infty)$, we have $P_n(B) = 1$ for all n, while $P(B) = 0$.

For this reason the common notion of convergence of distributions, which is called weak convergence, requires only that $P_n(B) \to P(B)$ for all "continuity sets" in $\mathbb{R}^K$. There's an equivalent way to phrase this that's easier to work with in applications: We say that $\{P_n\}$ **converges weakly** to P if

$$\int h(\mathbf{s}) P_n(d\mathbf{s}) \to \int h(\mathbf{s}) P(d\mathbf{s}) \quad \text{for all continuous bounded } h \colon \mathbb{R}^K \to \mathbb{R}$$

and write $P_n \xrightarrow{w} P$. For the definition of these integrals see §5.1.3.3. Continuity of h enforces respect for the topology on $\mathbb{R}^K$, while boundedness is imposed only to ensure that the integrals are finite.

Fact 6.1.4 Let F_n be the CDF of P_n and let F be the CDF of P. In the univariate case ($K = 1$) we have

$$P_n \xrightarrow{w} P \quad \iff \quad F_n(s) \to F(s) \text{ for all } s \text{ at which } F \text{ is continuous}$$

Example 6.1.3 It can be shown that the t-distribution with k degrees of freedom con-

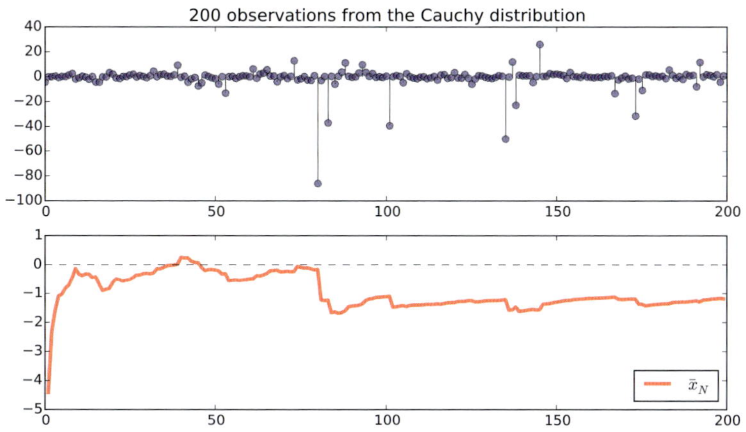

Figure 6.2 Samples from the Cauchy distribution and sample mean

verges weakly to the standard normal distribution as $k \to \infty$; see figure 6.3.

Sometimes densities are easier to work with than CDFs. In this connection, the following sufficient condition can be useful.

Fact 6.1.5 Let $\{P_n\}$ and P be absolutely continuous probability measures on $\mathbb{R}^K$, with densities p_n and p. If $p_n(\mathbf{s}) \to p(\mathbf{s})$ for all $\mathbf{s} \in \mathbb{R}^K$, then $P_n \stackrel{w}{\to} P$.

Let $\{\mathbf{x}_n\}$ and $\mathbf{x}$ be random vectors. We say that $\mathbf{x}_n \to \mathbf{x}$ **in distribution** if their respective distributions converge weakly. This convergence is symbolized by $\mathbf{x}_n \stackrel{d}{\to} \mathbf{x}$. Thus

$$\mathbf{x}_n \stackrel{d}{\to} \mathbf{x} \iff \mathcal{L}(\mathbf{x}_n) \stackrel{w}{\to} \mathcal{L}(\mathbf{x})$$

In view of fact 5.1.7 on page 134, this is equivalent to

$$\mathbb{E}\,[h(\mathbf{x}_n)] \to \mathbb{E}\,[h(\mathbf{x})] \quad \text{for all continuous bounded } h\colon \mathbb{R}^K \to \mathbb{R}$$

Fact 6.1.6 The following statements are true:

(i) If $g\colon \mathbb{R}^K \to \mathbb{R}^J$ is continuous and $\mathbf{x}_n \stackrel{d}{\to} \mathbf{x}$, then $g(\mathbf{x}_n) \stackrel{d}{\to} g(\mathbf{x})$.

(ii) If $\mathbf{a}^\top \mathbf{x}_n \stackrel{d}{\to} \mathbf{a}^\top \mathbf{x}$ for any $\mathbf{a} \in \mathbb{R}^K$, then $\mathbf{x}_n \stackrel{d}{\to} \mathbf{x}$.

(iii) $\mathbf{x}_n \stackrel{p}{\to} \mathbf{x} \implies \mathbf{x}_n \stackrel{d}{\to} \mathbf{x}$.

(iv) If $\mathbf{a}$ is a constant vector and $\mathbf{x}_n \stackrel{d}{\to} \mathbf{a}$, then $\mathbf{x}_n \stackrel{p}{\to} \mathbf{a}$.

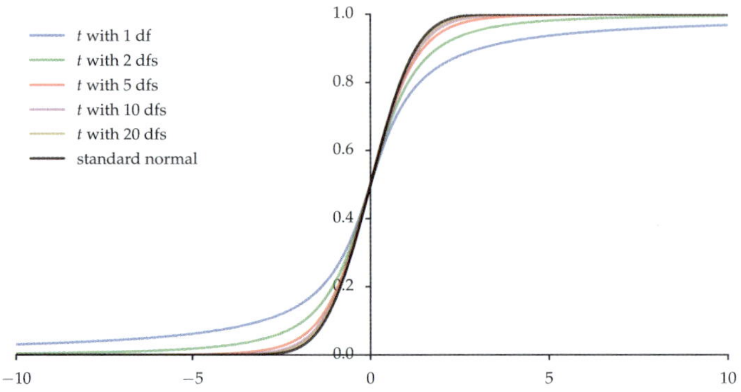

Figure 6.3 t-Distribution with k df converges to $\mathrm{N}(0, 1)$ as $k \to \infty$

Part (i) of fact 6.1.6 is called the **continuous mapping theorem**. Part (ii) is called the Cramér–Wold theorem, or the **Cramér–Wold device**. The next result is sometimes known as **Slutsky's theorem**.

Fact 6.1.7 If α is constant, $x_n \xrightarrow{p} \alpha$ and $y_n \xrightarrow{d} y$, then $x_n + y_n \xrightarrow{d} \alpha + y$ and $x_n y_n \xrightarrow{d} \alpha y$.

An immediate but useful consequence is that

Fact 6.1.8 $x_n \xrightarrow{p} 0$ and $y_n \xrightarrow{d} y \implies x_n y_n \xrightarrow{p} 0$.

6.1.4 The Central Limit Theorem

The **central limit theorem** is among the most striking and important results in all of mathematics. Relative to the LLN, it requires an additional second moment condition. Here's a statement of the theorem in the scalar IID case.

Theorem 6.1.2 *Let x have finite second moment and let $\{x_n\}$ be* IID *copies of x. If $\mu := \mathbb{E}\, x$ and $\sigma^2 :=$ var x, then*

$$\sqrt{N}(\bar{x}_N - \mu) \xrightarrow{d} \mathrm{N}(0, \sigma^2) \quad \textit{as} \quad N \to \infty \tag{6.9}$$

The meaning of $\xrightarrow{d}$ here is that the distribution of the left-hand side $\xrightarrow{w} \mathrm{N}(0, \sigma^2)$. We can interpret (6.9) as follows: On one hand, $(\bar{x}_N - \mu) \xrightarrow{p} 0$ by the LLN; on the other, $\sqrt{N} \to \infty$. If we take the product, these two competing terms just balance.

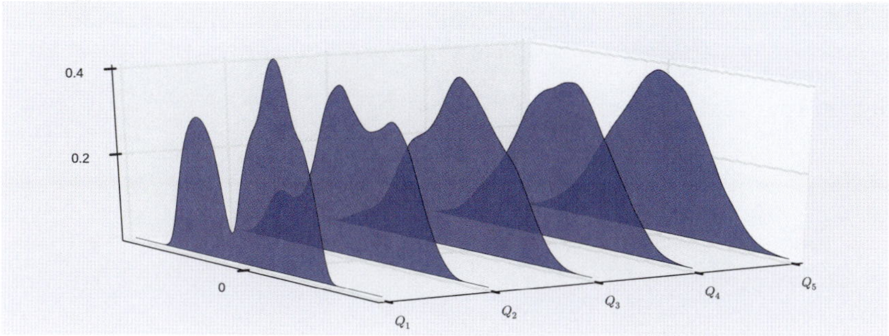

Figure 6.4 CLT in action, starting from a beta mixture

Remarkably, the distribution of the product approaches a zero-mean Gaussian as $N \to \infty$, regardless of the distribution of x.

We'll skip the proof of the CLT (which provides little intuition) and turn to simulation. For starters, see figure 6.4, where $Q_N :=$ the distribution of the left-hand side of (6.9) for $N = 1, \ldots, 5$. The initial distribution $Q = Q_1$ is multi-modal, and was constructed as a convex combination of three beta distributions. The CLT predicts that $Q_N \stackrel{w}{\to} \mathrm{N}(0, \sigma^2)$, where $\sigma^2 = \int s^2 Q_1(ds)$. Note how quickly the bell shape emerges, despite the irregularity of the initial distribution.

Another common statement of the central limit theorem is as follows: If all the conditions of theorem 6.1.2 are satisfied, then

$$z_N := \sqrt{N} \left\{ \frac{\bar{x}_N - \mu}{\sigma} \right\} \stackrel{d}{\to} \mathrm{N}(0, 1) \quad \text{as} \quad N \to \infty \tag{6.10}$$

Exercise 6.4.6 asks you to confirm this.

The convergence in (6.10) is illustrated by listing 2, the output of which is given in figure 6.5. The listing generates 5,000 observations of the random variable z_N defined in (6.10), where each x_n is $\chi^2(5)$. (The mean of this distribution is 5, and the variance is $2 \times 5 = 10$.) The observations of z_N are stored in the vector `outcomes`. The figure histograms this vector and then superimposes the density of the $\mathrm{N}(0, 1)$ distribution.

6.2 Extensions

In this section we cover some extensions to the classical LLN and CLT.

Listing 2 Illustrates the CLT (Python)

```
import numpy as np
import scipy.stats as st

num_reps = 5000
outcomes = np.empty(num_reps)
N, k = 1000, 5      # k = degrees of freedom
chi = st.chi2(k)

for i in range(num_reps):
    xvec = chi.rvs(N)
    outcomes[i] = np.sqrt(N / (2 * k)) * (xvec.mean() - k)

# code to histogram outcomes and plot st.norm.pdf
# see johnstachurski.net/emet.html
```

6.2.1 Convergence of Random Matrices

The notion of convergence in probability discussed in §6.1.1 extends naturally to matrices. Let $\{\mathbf{X}_n\}_{n=1}^{\infty}$ be a sequence of random $N \times K$ matrices. We say that $\mathbf{X}_n$ converges to a random $N \times K$ matrix $\mathbf{X}$ **in probability** and write $\mathbf{X}_n \stackrel{p}{\to} \mathbf{X}$ if

$$\|\mathbf{X}_n - \mathbf{X}\| \stackrel{p}{\to} 0 \quad \text{as} \quad n \to \infty$$

where $\|\cdot\|$ is the matrix norm defined in §3.3.5.

Fact 6.2.1 Assuming conformability, the following statements are true:

(i) If $\mathbf{X}_n \stackrel{p}{\to} \mathbf{X}$ and $\mathbf{X}_n$ and $\mathbf{X}$ are nonsingular, then $\mathbf{X}_n^{-1} \stackrel{p}{\to} \mathbf{X}^{-1}$.

(ii) If $\mathbf{X}_n \stackrel{p}{\to} \mathbf{X}$ and $\mathbf{Y}_n \stackrel{p}{\to} \mathbf{Y}$, then

$$\mathbf{X}_n + \mathbf{Y}_n \stackrel{p}{\to} \mathbf{X} + \mathbf{Y}, \quad \mathbf{X}_n\mathbf{Y}_n \stackrel{p}{\to} \mathbf{XY}, \quad \text{and} \quad \mathbf{Y}_n\mathbf{X}_n \stackrel{p}{\to} \mathbf{YX}$$

(iii) If $\mathbf{X}_n \stackrel{p}{\to} \mathbf{X}$ and $\mathbf{A}_n \to \mathbf{A}$, then

$$\mathbf{X}_n + \mathbf{A}_n \stackrel{p}{\to} \mathbf{X} + \mathbf{A}, \quad \mathbf{X}_n\mathbf{A}_n \stackrel{p}{\to} \mathbf{XA}, \quad \text{and} \quad \mathbf{A}_n\mathbf{X}_n \stackrel{p}{\to} \mathbf{AX}$$

(iv) $\mathbf{X}_n \stackrel{p}{\to} \mathbf{X}$ if and only if $\mathbf{X}_n\mathbf{a} \stackrel{p}{\to} \mathbf{Xa}$ for any conformable vector $\mathbf{a}$.

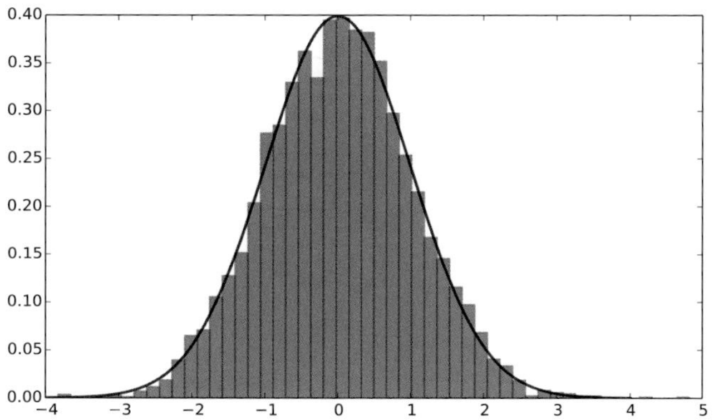

Figure 6.5 Observations of z_N in (6.10) when the underlying distribution is $\chi^2(5)$

(v) $\mathbf{a}^\top \mathbf{X}_n \mathbf{a} \xrightarrow{p} \mathbf{a}^\top \mathbf{X} \mathbf{a}$ whenever $\mathbf{a}$ is a conformable constant vector and $\mathbf{X}_n \xrightarrow{p} \mathbf{X}$.

In part (iii) of fact 6.2.1, the matrices $\mathbf{A}_n$ and $\mathbf{A}$ are nonrandom and convergence is in matrix norm. Note that part (v) can be obtained from two applications of part (iii).

In econometrics we often use the vector version of Slutsky's theorem:

Fact 6.2.2 Let $\mathbf{x}_n$ and $\mathbf{x}$ be random vectors in $\mathbb{R}^K$, let $\mathbf{Y}_n$ be random matrices, and let $\mathbf{C}$ be a constant matrix. Assuming conformability, we have

$$\mathbf{Y}_n \xrightarrow{p} \mathbf{C} \text{ and } \mathbf{x}_n \xrightarrow{d} \mathbf{x} \quad \implies \quad \mathbf{Y}_n \mathbf{x}_n \xrightarrow{d} \mathbf{C}\mathbf{x} \quad \text{and} \quad \mathbf{Y}_n + \mathbf{x}_n \xrightarrow{d} \mathbf{C} + \mathbf{x}$$

6.2.2 Vector-Valued LLNs and CLTs

The scalar LLN and CLT that we discussed above extend to the vector case in a natural way. For example,

Theorem 6.2.1 *Let $\mathbf{x}$ be a random vector in $\mathbb{R}^K$ and let $\{\mathbf{x}_n\}$ be* IID *copies of $\mathbf{x}$. If $\boldsymbol{\mu} := \mathbb{E}\,\mathbf{x}$ is finite, then*

$$\bar{\mathbf{x}}_N := \frac{1}{N} \sum_{n=1}^{N} \mathbf{x}_n \xrightarrow{p} \boldsymbol{\mu} \quad \textit{as} \quad N \to \infty \tag{6.11}$$

If, in addition, $\mathbb{E}\,\|\mathbf{x}\|^2 < \infty$, then

$$\sqrt{N}\,(\bar{\mathbf{x}}_N - \boldsymbol{\mu}) \xrightarrow{d} \mathrm{N}(\mathbf{0}, \Sigma) \quad \textit{where} \quad \Sigma := \operatorname{var} \mathbf{x} \tag{6.12}$$

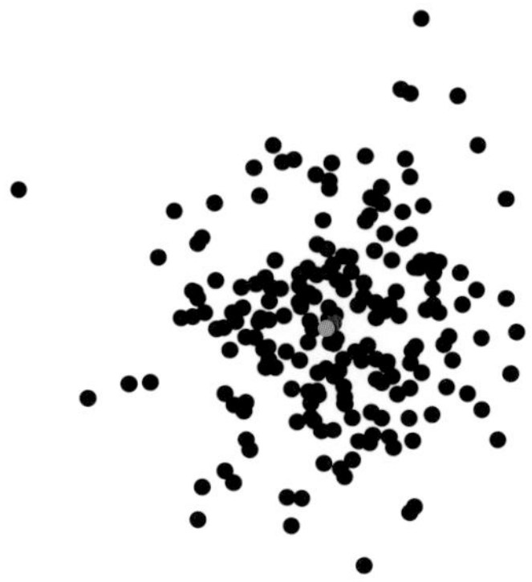

Figure 6.6 LLN, vector case

Here $\frac{1}{N}\sum_{n=1}^{N}\mathbf{x}_n$ should be understood in terms of vector addition and scalar multiplication. Thus $\bar{\mathbf{x}}_N$ is a convex combination of the sample points in $\mathbb{R}^K$. Figure 6.6 illustrates this in two dimensions. The green dot is $\boldsymbol{\mu}$. The black dots are realizations of $\mathbf{x}_1, \ldots, \mathbf{x}_N$. The red dot is the sample mean $\frac{1}{N}\sum_{n=1}^{N}\mathbf{x}_n$. By (6.11), the red dot converges to the green dot.

The vector LLN in theorem 6.2.1 follows from the scalar LLN. To see this, let $\mathbf{x}_n$ be as in theorem 6.2.1, let $\mathbf{a}$ be any constant vector in $\mathbb{R}^K$, let $y_n := \mathbf{a}^\mathsf{T}\mathbf{x}_n$ and let $y := \mathbf{a}^\mathsf{T}\mathbf{x}$. The sequence $\{y_n\}$ is IID (see fact 5.1.10 on page 137) with the same distribution as y. By the scalar LLN (theorem 6.1.1), we have

$$\frac{1}{N}\sum_{n=1}^{N} y_n \stackrel{p}{\to} \mathbb{E}\,y = \mathbb{E}\left[\mathbf{a}^\mathsf{T}\mathbf{x}\right] = \mathbf{a}^\mathsf{T}\mathbb{E}\left[\mathbf{x}\right] = \mathbf{a}^\mathsf{T}\boldsymbol{\mu}$$

At the same time,

$$\frac{1}{N}\sum_{n=1}^{N} y_n = \frac{1}{N}\sum_{n=1}^{N}\mathbf{a}^\mathsf{T}\mathbf{x}_n = \mathbf{a}^\mathsf{T}\left[\frac{1}{N}\sum_{n=1}^{N}\mathbf{x}_n\right] = \mathbf{a}^\mathsf{T}\bar{\mathbf{x}}_N$$

We have shown that

$$\mathbf{a}^\mathsf{T}\bar{\mathbf{x}}_N \stackrel{p}{\to} \mathbf{a}^\mathsf{T}\boldsymbol{\mu} \;\text{ for any }\; \mathbf{a} \in \mathbb{R}^K$$

The claim $\bar{\mathbf{x}}_N \stackrel{p}{\to} \boldsymbol{\mu}$ now follows from fact 6.1.1.

The vector CLT in theorem 6.2.1 also follows from the scalar case and the proof is quite similar. See exercise 6.4.10.

These results can be further extended to random matrices. In fact we will need a matrix LLN in our investigation of linear regression. Here's a suitable result:

Fact 6.2.3 Let $\mathbf{X}$ be a random matrix and let $\{\mathbf{X}_n\}$ be IID copies of $\mathbf{X}$. If $\mathbb{E}\,\|\mathbf{X}\| < \infty$, then

$$\frac{1}{N}\sum_{n=1}^{N} \mathbf{X}_n \stackrel{p}{\to} \mathbb{E}\,\mathbf{X} \quad \text{as} \quad N \to \infty \tag{6.13}$$

The proof is straightforward: By fact 6.2.1, to prove (6.13), it suffices to show that $\frac{1}{N}\sum_{n=1}^{N} \mathbf{X}_n \mathbf{a} \stackrel{p}{\to} \mathbb{E}\,[\mathbf{X}]\mathbf{a}$ for any conformable vector $\mathbf{a}$. Since $\mathbf{X}_n\mathbf{a}$ is a vector with expectation $\mathbb{E}\,[\mathbf{X}]\mathbf{a}$, this is immediate from the vector LLN in theorem 6.2.1.

6.2.3 The Delta Method

The asymptotic normality result in the central limit theorem is preserved under linear transformations, as follows from fact 6.2.2. It turns out that the same thing is true even for functions that are only locally almost linear—that is, for differentiable functions. This greatly extends the power and reach of the central limit theorem.

Theorem 6.2.2 *Let $g \colon \mathbb{R}^K \to \mathbb{R}$, let $\boldsymbol{\theta}$ be a point in the domain of g, and let $\{\mathbf{t}_n\}$ be a sequence of random vectors in $\mathbb{R}^K$. If*

(i) $\sqrt{n}(\mathbf{t}_n - \boldsymbol{\theta}) \stackrel{d}{\to} \mathrm{N}(0, \boldsymbol{\Sigma})$ *for some positive definite* $\boldsymbol{\Sigma}$ *and*

(ii) $\nabla g(\boldsymbol{\theta})$ *exists, is continuous, and each element is nonzero,*

then

$$\sqrt{n}\{g(\mathbf{t}_n) - g(\boldsymbol{\theta})\} \stackrel{d}{\to} \mathrm{N}(0, \nabla g(\boldsymbol{\theta})^\top \boldsymbol{\Sigma} \nabla g(\boldsymbol{\theta})) \quad \textit{as} \quad n \to \infty \tag{6.14}$$

Here $\nabla g(\boldsymbol{\theta})$ is the **gradient vector** of g at $\boldsymbol{\theta}$, which is defined as

$$\nabla g(\boldsymbol{\theta}) := \begin{pmatrix} g_1'(\boldsymbol{\theta}) \\ \vdots \\ g_K'(\boldsymbol{\theta}) \end{pmatrix} \quad \text{where} \quad g_k'(\boldsymbol{\theta}) := \frac{\partial g(\boldsymbol{\theta})}{\partial \theta_k}$$

In the scalar case, (6.14) translates to

$$\sqrt{n}\{g(t_n) - g(\theta)\} \stackrel{d}{\to} \mathrm{N}(0, g'(\theta)^2\sigma^2) \quad \text{as} \quad n \to \infty \tag{6.15}$$

In statistical settings, the technique of obtaining asymptotic distributions by appealing to theorem 6.2.2 is called the **delta method**. We will see its importance later on. The proof of theorem 6.2.2 is based on a Taylor expansion of g around the point θ. See theorem 3.1 of Van der Vaart (2000). Exercise 6.4.9 walks you through some of the key ideas.

6.3 Further Reading

For high quality treatments of the law of large numbers and the central limit theorem see, for example, Dudley (2002), Taylor (1997), Durrett (2010), Pollard (2002), DasGupta (2008), or Çinlar (2011). An advanced but thorough treatment of the delta method can be found in Van der Vaart (2000).

6.4 Exercises

Ex. 6.4.1 Let $\{x_n\}$ be a sequence of random variables satisfying $x_n = y$ for all n, where y is a single random variable. Show that if $\mathbb{P}\{y = -1\} = \mathbb{P}\{y = 1\} = 0.5$, then $x_n \stackrel{p}{\to} 0$ fails. Show that if $\mathbb{P}\{y = 0\} = 1$, then $x_n \stackrel{p}{\to} 0$ holds.

Ex. 6.4.2 Prove the following part of fact 6.1.1: $\mathbf{x}_n \stackrel{p}{\to} \mathbf{x}$ and $\mathbf{y}_n \stackrel{p}{\to} \mathbf{y} \implies \mathbf{x}_n + \mathbf{y}_n \stackrel{p}{\to} \mathbf{x} + \mathbf{y}$. (The proof is nontrivial if you are still getting used to these kinds of arguments.)

Ex. 6.4.3 Show that $\mathbf{x}_n \stackrel{p}{\to} \mathbf{x}$ implies $\mathbf{a}^\top \mathbf{x}_n \stackrel{p}{\to} \mathbf{a}^\top \mathbf{x}$ for every $\mathbf{a} \in \mathbb{R}^K$.

Ex. 6.4.4 We saw in fact 6.1.6 that if $x_n \stackrel{p}{\to} x$, then $x_n \stackrel{d}{\to} x$. Show that the converse is not in general true.

Ex. 6.4.5 Show that $\mathbf{X}_n \stackrel{p}{\to} \mathbf{X}$ if and only if every element of $\mathbf{X}_n$ converges in probability to the corresponding element of $\mathbf{X}$.[3]

Ex. 6.4.6 Confirm (6.10).[4]

Ex. 6.4.7 Let $\mathcal{L}(u) = U[0,1]$ and $x_n := n\mathbb{1}\{0 \leqslant u \leqslant 1/n\}$ for $n \in \mathbb{N}$.

(i) Calculate the expectation of x_n^2.

(ii) Show that $x_n \stackrel{p}{\to} 0$ as $n \to \infty$.

Conclude that $x_n \stackrel{p}{\to} x$ does not imply $x_n \stackrel{ms}{\to} x$.

Ex. 6.4.8 Let x be any random variable with $\mathbb{E}\, x = \mu$ and $\operatorname{var} x = \sigma^2 < \infty$. Show that $x_n := x/n$ converges to zero in probability as $n \to \infty$.

Ex. 6.4.9 Suppose that $\{t_n\}$ is a sequence of random variables, θ is a constant, and

$$\sqrt{n}(t_n - \theta) \stackrel{d}{\to} \mathrm{N}(0, \sigma^2) \quad \text{as} \quad n \to \infty$$

3. Hint: To prove the "if" part use fact 3.3.13 on page 68.
4. Hint: Combine theorem 6.1.2 and fact 6.1.6.

Let $g \colon \mathbb{R} \to \mathbb{R}$ be differentiable at θ with $g'(\theta) \neq 0$. Taking a first-order Taylor expansion of g around θ, we can write $g(t_n) = g(\theta) + g'(\theta)(t_n - \theta) + R(t_n - \theta)$, where $R(t_n - \theta)$ is a remainder term. As shown in theorem 3.1 of Van der Vaart (2000), under these conditions we have $\sqrt{n}R(t_n - \theta) \stackrel{p}{\to} 0$. Using this fact, prove that $\sqrt{n}\{g(t_n) - g(\theta)\} \stackrel{d}{\to} \mathrm{N}(0, g'(\theta)^2\sigma^2)$.

Ex. 6.4.10 Confirm the claim $\sqrt{N}\,(\bar{\mathbf{x}}_N - \boldsymbol{\mu}) \stackrel{d}{\to} \mathrm{N}(\mathbf{0}, \Sigma)$ in theorem 6.2.1.

Ex. 6.4.11 Let $\{\mathbf{x}_n\}$ be an IID sequence of random vectors in $\mathbb{R}^K$ with $\mathbb{E}\,\mathbf{x}_n = \mathbf{0}$ and $\operatorname{var} \mathbf{x}_n = \mathbf{I}$. Let

$$\bar{\mathbf{x}}_N := \frac{1}{N} \sum_{n=1}^{N} \mathbf{x}_n \quad \text{and} \quad y_N := N \cdot \|\bar{\mathbf{x}}_N\|^2$$

What is the asymptotic distribution of $\{y_N\}$?

6.4.1 Solutions to Selected Exercises

Solution to Ex. 6.4.1. From the definition, $x_n \stackrel{p}{\to} 0$ means that, given any $\delta > 0$, we have $\mathbb{P}\{|x_n| > \delta\} \to 0$. If $x_n = y$ for all n and $\mathbb{P}\{y = -1\} = \mathbb{P}\{y = 1\} = 0.5$, then this fails for $\delta := 1/2$, say, since $\mathbb{P}\{|x_n| > 1/2\} = 1$ for all n.

However, if $\mathbb{P}\{y = 0\} = 1$, then for any $\delta > 0$ we have $\mathbb{P}\{|x_n| > \delta\} = \mathbb{P}\{|y| > \delta\} = 0$. This sequence is constant at zero and hence $x_n \stackrel{p}{\to} 0$ holds. □

Solution to Ex. 6.4.2. Let $\mathbf{x}_n \stackrel{p}{\to} \mathbf{x}$ and $\mathbf{y}_n \stackrel{p}{\to} \mathbf{y}$. Fix $\delta > 0$. Using the triangle inequality and elementary reasoning we can establish the following ordering of events:

$$\begin{aligned}\{\|\mathbf{x}_n + \mathbf{y}_n - (\mathbf{x} + \mathbf{y})\| > \delta\} &\subset \{\|\mathbf{x}_n - \mathbf{x}\| + \|\mathbf{y}_n - \mathbf{y}\| > \delta\} \\ &\subset \{\|\mathbf{x}_n - \mathbf{x}\| > \delta/2\} \cup \{\|\mathbf{y}_n - \mathbf{y}\| > \delta/2\}\end{aligned}$$

By monotonicity and subadditivity of $\mathbb{P}$ (see page 86), we then have

$$\mathbb{P}\{\|\mathbf{x}_n + \mathbf{y}_n - (\mathbf{x} + \mathbf{y})\| > \delta\} \leqslant \mathbb{P}\{\|\mathbf{x}_n - \mathbf{x}\| > \delta/2\} + \mathbb{P}\{\|\mathbf{y}_n - \mathbf{y}\| > \delta/2\}$$

By hypothesis, both terms on the right-hand side converge to zero in n. Hence $\mathbf{x}_n + \mathbf{y}_n \stackrel{p}{\to} \mathbf{x} + \mathbf{y}$ as claimed. □

Solution to Ex. 6.4.3. Let $\mathbf{x}_n \stackrel{p}{\to} \mathbf{x}$ in $\mathbb{R}^K$ and fix any $\mathbf{a} \in \mathbb{R}^K$. If $\mathbf{a} = \mathbf{0}$ the claim is trivial, so suppose instead that $\mathbf{a}$ is nonzero. Let $\delta > 0$. By the Cauchy–Schwarz inequality,

$$\{|\mathbf{a}^\top \mathbf{x}_n - \mathbf{a}^\top \mathbf{x}| > \delta\} \subset \{\|\mathbf{a}\|\,\|\mathbf{x}_n - \mathbf{x}\| > \delta\}$$

Using monotonicity of $\mathbb{P}$ now gives

$$\mathbb{P}\{|\mathbf{a}^\top \mathbf{x}_n - \mathbf{a}^\top \mathbf{x}| > \delta\} \leqslant \mathbb{P}\{\|\mathbf{x}_n - \mathbf{x}\| > \delta / \|\mathbf{a}\|\}$$

Since $\mathbf{x}_n \xrightarrow{p} \mathbf{x}$, the right-hand side converges to zero. □

Solution to Ex. 6.4.4. On one hand, if $\{x_n\}$ and x are IID and $\text{N}(0,1)$, then $\mathcal{L}(x_n) = \mathcal{L}(x)$ for all n, and hence $x_n \xrightarrow{d} x$. On the other hand, $\mathcal{L}(x_n - x) = \text{N}(0,2)$ for all n. Hence $\mathbb{P}\{|x_n - x| \geqslant \delta\}$ is a positive constant for any $\delta > 0$, and $x_n \xrightarrow{p} x$ fails. □

Solution to Ex. 6.4.10. Define

$$\mathbf{z}_N := \sqrt{N}\,(\bar{\mathbf{x}}_N - \boldsymbol{\mu}) \quad \text{and} \quad \mathcal{L}(\mathbf{z}) = \text{N}(\mathbf{0}, \Sigma)$$

We need to show that $\mathbf{z}_N \xrightarrow{d} \mathbf{z}$. To do this, we apply the Cramér–Wold device (fact 6.1.6, page 167) and the scalar CLT (theorem 6.1.2, page 168). To begin, fix $\mathbf{a} \in \mathbb{R}^K$. Observe that

$$\mathbf{a}^\top \mathbf{z}_n := \sqrt{N}\,(\bar{y}_n - \mathbb{E}[y_n])$$

where $y_n := \mathbf{a}^\top \mathbf{x}_n$. Since y_n is IID and

$$\operatorname{var} y_n = \operatorname{var}[\mathbf{a}^\top \mathbf{x}_n] = \mathbf{a}^\top \operatorname{var}[\mathbf{x}_n]\mathbf{a} = \mathbf{a}^\top \Sigma \mathbf{a}$$

the scalar CLT yields

$$\mathbf{a}^\top \mathbf{z}_N \xrightarrow{d} \text{N}(0, \mathbf{a}^\top \Sigma \mathbf{a})$$

Since $\mathcal{L}(\mathbf{a}^\top \mathbf{z}) = \text{N}(0, \mathbf{a}^\top \Sigma \mathbf{a})$, we have shown that $\mathbf{a}^\top \mathbf{z}_N \xrightarrow{d} \mathbf{a}^\top \mathbf{z}$. Since $\mathbf{a}$ was arbitrary, the Cramér–Wold device tells us that $\mathbf{z}_N$ converges in distribution to $\mathbf{z}$. □

Solution to Ex. 6.4.11. By assumption, $\{\mathbf{x}_n\}$ is an IID sequence in $\mathbb{R}^K$ with $\mathbb{E}\mathbf{x}_n = \mathbf{0}$ and $\operatorname{var} \mathbf{x}_n = \mathbf{I}$. It follows from the vector central limit theorem that

$$\sqrt{N}\bar{\mathbf{x}}_N \xrightarrow{d} \mathbf{z} \quad \text{where} \quad \mathcal{L}(\mathbf{z}) = \text{N}(\mathbf{0}, \mathbf{I})$$

Letting $g(\mathbf{s}) := \|\mathbf{s}\|^2$ and applying the continuous mapping theorem (fact 6.1.6 on page 167), we obtain

$$y_N = \|\sqrt{N}\bar{\mathbf{x}}_N\|^2 \xrightarrow{d} \|\mathbf{z}\|^2 = \sum_{k=1}^{K} z_k^2$$

From fact 5.1.18 on page 140, we conclude that $y_N \xrightarrow{d} \chi^2(K)$. □

Chapter 7

Further Topics in Probability

There are two important topics in probability that we haven't yet managed to cover. One is stochastic process theory and the other is simulation. Let's go over some of the key results.

7.1 Stochastic Processes

A **stochastic process** on $\mathbb{R}^K$ is a sequence of random vectors $\{\mathbf{x}_t\}_{t \geqslant 0}$ defined on a common probability space $(\Omega, \mathscr{F}, \mathbb{P})$. The definition has relatively little content, but the fact that all these random vectors live on the same probability space should not be overlooked. It means that probabilities such as $\mathbb{P}\{\mathbf{x}_t \geqslant 0 \text{ for all } t\}$ or $\mathbb{P}\{\mathbf{x}_t \leqslant -10 \text{ for some } t\}$ are well defined. Putting the elements of the process on a common probability space pins down the joint distribution across t.

To do any kind of analysis with stochastic processes, we need to put some structure on the joint distribution, or, equivalently, on the random elements. In practice, this is almost always done recursively. Examples are given below. For the moment, however, let's look at stochastic processes in an abstract setting and state some definitions.

One kind of stochastic process is an IID sequence. Such sequences are ideal to work with in a statistical setting. For example, the law of large numbers tells us that in an IID environment, finite expectations can always be approximated with sample averages. If we want to know how good the approximation is, we can look to the central limit theorem.

Once we move out of the IID world, however, these helpful properties can break down. Without restrictions on our stochastic process, we can say very little about estimation. The first task, then is to describe some properties that make our stochastic process resemble an IID process in *some* way.

7.1.1 Stationarity and Ergodicity

As a first step, let's define a type of process that preserves one of the properties of IID processes (the "ID" part). A stochastic process $\{\mathbf{x}_t\}_{t \geqslant 0}$ is called **stationary** if it has the property that the distribution of any subset of these random vectors is unaffected by shifting them forward in time. That is,

$$\mathcal{L}(\mathbf{x}_{t_1}, \ldots, \mathbf{x}_{t_k}) = \mathcal{L}(\mathbf{x}_{t_1+m}, \ldots, \mathbf{x}_{t_k+m}) \tag{7.1}$$

for any $m \in \mathbb{N}$ and any sequence of integers $t_1, \ldots, t_k$.

Clearly, any stationary sequence is identically distributed. In other words, for any stationary sequence, the sequence of marginals $\{\mathcal{L}(\mathbf{x}_t)\}$ is a constant sequence.

Example 7.1.1 An IID process $\{\mathbf{x}_t\}$ is stationary, since independence implies that the laws on both sides of (7.1) are just k products of the marginal $\mathcal{L}(\mathbf{x}_1)$.

Example 7.1.2 For a simple example of a stationary process, let x_1 be a draw from some arbitrary law P on $\mathbb{R}$ and let $x_{t+1} = x_t$ for all t. For any collection of integers $t_1, \ldots, t_k$ and any Borel sets $B_1, \ldots, B_k$, we have

$$\mathbb{P}\{x_{t_1} \in B_1, \ldots, x_{t_k} \in B_k\} = \mathbb{P}\{x_1 \in \cap_{i=1}^k B_k\} = P(\cap_{i=1}^k B_k)$$

If we replace each x_{t_i} with x_{t_i+m}, we get the same number. Hence $\{x_t\}$ is stationary.

Example 7.1.3 A **random walk** on $\mathbb{R}$ is a stochastic process $\{x_t\}$ where $x_t = \sum_{j=1}^t w_j$ for some IID zero-mean process $\{w_j\}$. Let $\sigma^2 := \operatorname{var} w_t$. If $\sigma > 0$, then $\{x_t\}$ is not stationary, since $\operatorname{var} x_t = t\sigma^2$. In particular, $\mathcal{L}(x_t)$ depends on t.

Stationarity alone isn't strong enough to give us properties like the LLN and CLT.

Example 7.1.4 For the process $\{x_t\}$ in example 7.1.2, the LLN fails whenever P is nondegenerate. Indeed $\bar{x}_T := \frac{1}{T}\sum_{t=1}^T x_t = x_1$, and hence $\mathcal{L}(\bar{x}_T) = \mathcal{L}(x_1) = P$ for all t. In particular, $\bar{x}_T$ does not converge in probability to any constant.

The problem with the process in example 7.1.4 is excessive dependence. New realizations provide insufficient (in fact no) new information. On the flip side, dependent processes can satisfy versions of the LLN if dependence is not too excessive (e.g., if x_t and x_{t+k} are "almost independent" for k sufficiently large.) These are the so-called ergodic processes.

The formal definition of ergodicity varies across different literatures. Here we define a stationary stochastic process $\{\mathbf{x}_t\}$ on $\mathbb{R}^K$ to be **ergodic** if the LLN holds; that is, if

$$\frac{1}{T}\sum_{t=1}^{T} h(\mathbf{x}_t) \xrightarrow{p} \mu_h := \mathbb{E}\, h(\mathbf{x}_t) \quad \text{as} \quad T \to \infty \tag{7.2}$$

for any $\mathscr{B}$-measurable $h: \mathbb{R}^N \to \mathbb{R}$ such that $\mathbb{E}|h(\mathbf{x}_t)| < \infty$. (Since $\{\mathbf{x}_t\}$ is stationary, this expectation does not depend on t.) One of the main tasks of this chapter will be deriving sufficient conditions for ergodicity in the kinds of processes economists often work with.

Incidentally, a casual definition of ergodicity one often hears is that "cross sectional and time series averages coincide." What does that mean in the present context?

To answer the question, imagine that $\mathbf{x}_t = x_t$ is a binary variable with $x_1 = 1$ if a given individual is currently employed and zero otherwise. In this case, $\frac{1}{T}\sum_{t=1}^T x_t$ is the fraction of time spent employed over the period $1, \ldots, T$. With $h(x) = x$, the right-hand side of (7.2) is $\mathbb{E}\, x_t = \mathbb{P}\{x_t = 1\}$, or the stationary probability of employment. If we observe time t employment outcomes $x_t^1, \ldots, x_t^N$ of individuals $1, \ldots, N$ and, moreover, the individuals all follow the same model and are sufficient independent, the cross sectional average $\frac{1}{N}\sum_{n=1}^N x_t^n$ will also be close to $\mathbb{P}\{x_t = 1\}$. Hence, with ergodicity and large samples, cross-sectional and time series averages (almost) coincide.

7.1.2 Stochastic Recursive Sequences

In this section let's turn to a more concrete view of stochastic processes. Afterward we'll circle back and consider issues like ergodicity again.

Figure 7.1 shows the evolution of US GDP per capita since the early postwar era. The top panel is per capita GDP itself, while the second panel is the growth rate. How could we go about modeling such time series in a parsimonious way?

No reasonable model can be deterministic, since shocks play an important role in year-on-year change in GDP, and an IID process is too simple. We can, however, get close to both of these time series with one of the most common nontrivial stochastic processes: the scalar Gaussian AR(1) model

$$x_{t+1} = b + a x_t + c w_{t+1} \quad \text{with } \{w_t\} \overset{\text{IID}}{\sim} \text{N}(0,1) \text{ and } x_0 \text{ given} \tag{7.3}$$

Here a, b, and c are parameters, while x_t is called the **state variable**. Equation (7.3) is an example of a **stochastic difference equation**. The process $\{x_t\}$ it defines is called a stochastic process or **stochastic recursive sequence**. A realization of the process is called a **time series**.

The dynamics of $\{x_t\}$ depends on the parameters. We can get some sense of this from simulation. Six individual time series $\{x_t\}$ are shown in figure 7.2, each generated using a different value of a. The values of b and c are both held fixed at 1, while $x_0 = 0$. `R` code for generating the figure is given in listing 3.

As suggested by the figure, the simulated time paths are sensitive to the value of a. If a is outside the interval $(-1, 1)$, the series tend to diverge. If $|a| < 1$, then the

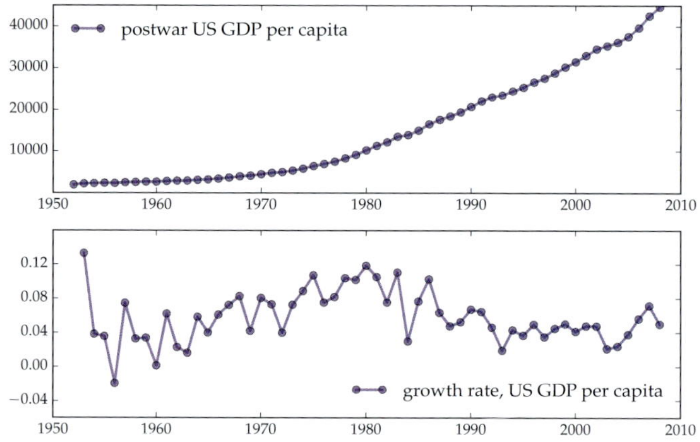

Figure 7.1 Postwar US GDP per capita. Source: Penn World Tables

opposite is true. For example, if you look at the time series for $a = 0.9$ in figure 7.2, you will see that, after an initial burn in period where the series is affected by the initial condition x_0, the process settles down to random motion within a band (between about 5 and 15 in this case).

If the scalar Gaussian AR(1) model in (7.3) is unable to capture important aspects of a time series that we wish to model, we can generalize it in several different directions. For example, we can remove the assumption that the shocks are normally distributed, in which case it is simply called the scalar AR(1) model. This might be desirable, if, say, the state process has heavy tails.

We can also generalize the scalar AR(1) model to $\mathbb{R}^K$, yielding the vector AR(1) model, or VAR(1) model

$$\mathbf{x}_{t+1} = \mathbf{b} + \mathbf{A}\mathbf{x}_t + \mathbf{C}\mathbf{w}_{t+1} \tag{7.4}$$

Here $\{\mathbf{w}_t\}$ is assumed to be IID and to satisfy $\mathbb{E}\,\mathbf{w}_t = \mathbf{0}$ and $\mathbb{E}\,[\mathbf{w}_t\mathbf{w}_t'] = \mathbf{I}$. If $\mathbf{w}_t$ is multivariate normal, then (7.4) is called the Gaussian VAR(1). The vector $\mathbf{x}_t$ is called the **state vector**. A huge variety of models can be represented as a VAR(1) process or contain VAR processes as subcomponents (e.g., linear state space models).

An alternative generalization of the scalar AR(1) model is the scalar AR(p) model, where the next state x_{t+1} is a linear function not just of the current state x_t, but of the last p previous states. For example, the AR(2) process has dynamics

$$x_{t+1} = b + ax_t + \gamma x_{t-1} + w_{t+1}$$

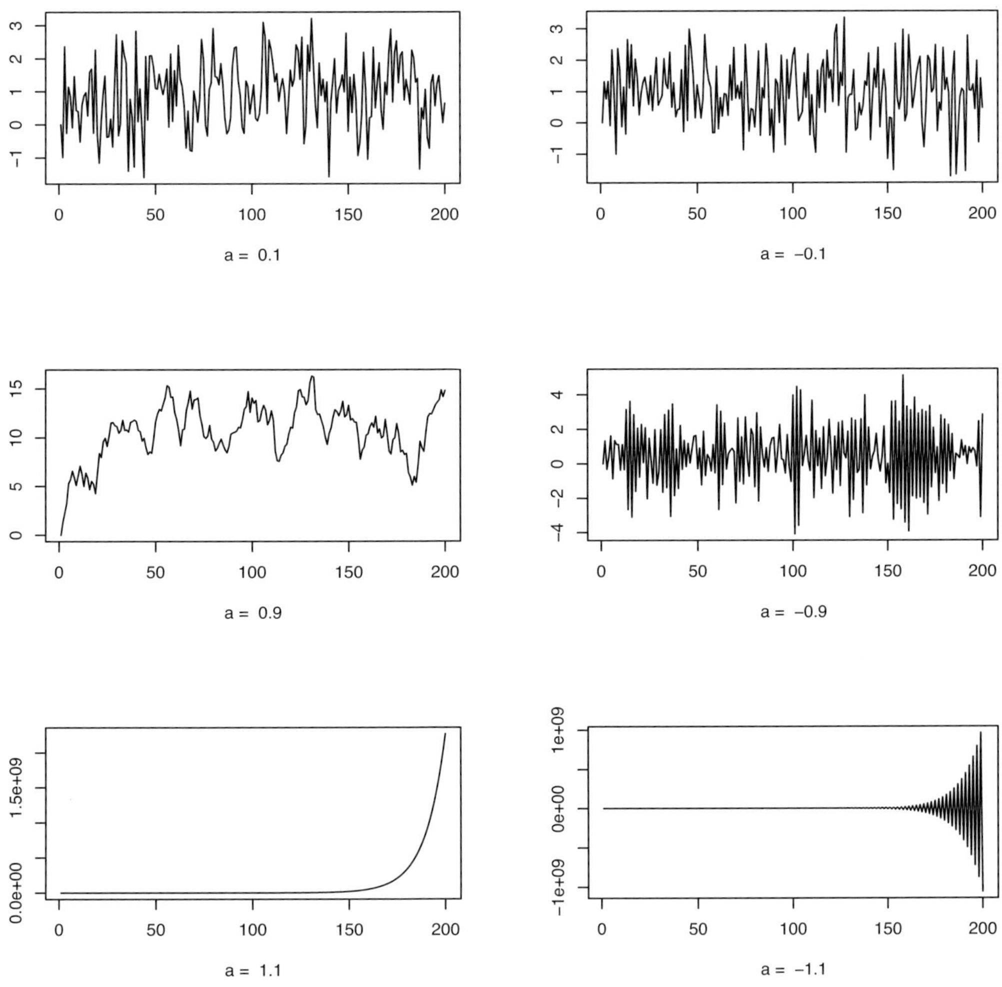

Figure 7.2 Dynamics of the linear AR(1) model

Listing 3 Code for figure 7.2 (R)

```
# Generates an AR(1) time series starting from x = init
ar1ts <- function(init, n, b, a) {
    x <- numeric(n)
    x[1] <- init
    w <- rnorm(n-1)
    for (t in 1:(n-1)) {
        x[t+1] <- b + a * x[t] + w[t]
    }
    return(x)
}

avec <- c(0.1, -0.1, 0.9, -0.9, 1.1, -1.1)
N <- 200
par(mfrow=c(3,2))  # Arrangement of figures
for (a in avec) {
    plot(ar1ts(0, N, 1, a), type="l", xlab=paste("a = ", a), ylab="")
}
```

Although x_{t+1} is a function of two lagged states, x_t and x_{t-1}, we can reformulate it as a first-order model. To begin, we define an additional state variable y_t via $y_t = x_{t-1}$. The dynamics can then be expressed as

$$\begin{aligned} x_{t+1} &= b + ax_t + \gamma y_t + w_{t+1} \\ y_{t+1} &= x_t \end{aligned}$$

We can write this in matrix form as

$$\begin{pmatrix} x_{t+1} \\ y_{t+1} \end{pmatrix} = b \begin{pmatrix} 1 \\ 0 \end{pmatrix} + \begin{pmatrix} a & \gamma \\ 1 & 0 \end{pmatrix} \begin{pmatrix} x_t \\ y_t \end{pmatrix} + \begin{pmatrix} 1 \\ 0 \end{pmatrix} w_{t+1}$$

This is a special case of the VAR(1) model in (7.4). This example shows how higher order processes can be reduced to first-order processes by increasing the number of state variables. For this reason most theoretical discussion below takes place in the context of first-order models.

7.1.2.1 Nonlinear Models

Linear models are simple but that isn't always an advantage. Sometimes they are unable to capture the kinds of dynamics we observe in data. For example, the bursts

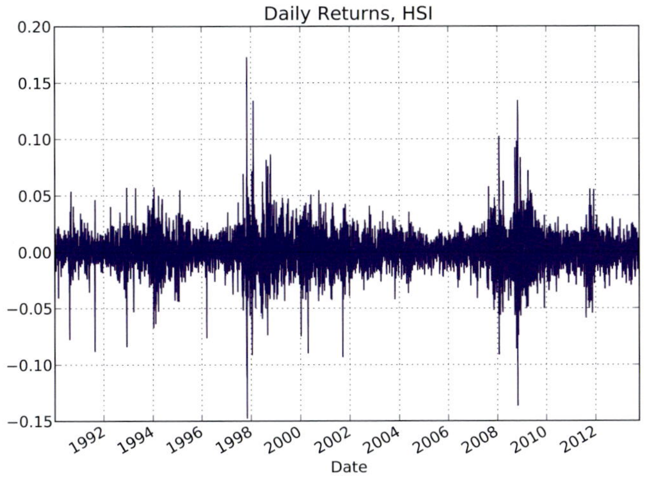

Figure 7.3 Daily returns on the Hang Seng Index. Source: Yahoo! Finance

of volatility in the graph of daily returns on the Hang Seng Index from 1990 to 2014 shown in figure 7.3 are difficult to replicate without introducing nonlinearities into our model. It's also true that many theoretical modeling exercises produce models that are nonlinear.

One well-known nonlinear model is the pth order autoregressive conditional heteroskedasticity model (ARCH(p) model). The model arose from the need to attach a time varying volatility component σ_t to asset return models. Suppose, for example, that $x_t = \sigma_t w_t$ where $\sigma_{t+1}^2 = \alpha_0 + \alpha_1 x_t^2$. Combining these equations gives the ARCH(1) model

$$x_{t+1} = (\alpha_0 + \alpha_1 x_t^2)^{1/2} w_{t+1} \quad \text{with} \quad \{w_t\} \overset{\text{IID}}{\sim} \text{N}(0,1) \tag{7.5}$$

and $\alpha_0 > 0$, $\alpha_1 \geqslant 0$. Still better fits to asset returns data can be obtained via Generalized ARCH models, the simplest of which is the GARCH(1,1) process

$$x_t = \sigma_t w_t$$
$$\sigma_{t+1}^2 = \alpha_0 + \alpha_1 x_t^2 + \alpha_2 \sigma_t^2$$

Now next period volatility depends on its own lagged state as well as x_t.

Another popular nonlinear model is the **smooth transition autoregression** (STAR) model

$$x_{t+1} = g(x_t) + w_{t+1} \tag{7.6}$$

where g is of the form

$$g(s) := (b_0 + a_0 s)(1 - \tau(s)) + (b_1 + a_1 s)\tau(s)$$

Here $\tau\colon \mathbb{R} \to [0,1]$ is increasing and satisfies $\lim_{s\to-\infty} \tau(s) = 0$ and $\lim_{s\to\infty} \tau(s) = 1$. For s near $-\infty$, $g(s)$ is similar to $b_0 + a_0 s$. For s near $+\infty$, $g(s)$ is close to $b_1 + a_1 s$. Thus the dynamics transition between two different linear models, with the smoothness of the transition depending on the shape of τ.

7.2 Markov Processes

All of the examples in §7.1.2 are special cases of a general class of process called Markov processes. Markov processes are very rewarding to study because the concepts are broad enough to include a vast array of different stochastic processes, while at the same time having enough structure to support elegant and powerful theory. Here we cover the foundations, from definitions and basic properties to stability and asymptotics.

7.2.1 The Markov Assumption

Let S be a subset of $\mathbb{R}^K$ and let $\mathscr{B}(S)$ be the Borel subsets of S. The fundamental primitive of a discrete time Markov process on S is a **stochastic kernel** or **transition probability function**, which is a function $Q\colon S \times \mathscr{B}(S) \to [0,1]$ such that

(i) $Q(\mathbf{s}, \cdot)$ is a probability measure over $\mathscr{B}(S)$ for all $\mathbf{s} \in S$ and

(ii) $g(\mathbf{s}) := Q(\mathbf{s}, B)$ is $\mathscr{B}$-measurable for each $B \in \mathscr{B}(S)$.

S is called the **state space** of the model. Part (ii) is a mild regularity condition that ensures certain integrals are well defined. Part (i) is the major defining characteristic, yielding a distribution supported on S for every point $\mathbf{s}$ in S. We think of Q and some initial distribution P_0 as generating a corresponding Markov process $\{\mathbf{x}_t\}$ taking values in S via

draw $\mathbf{x}_0$ from P_0
for t in $0, 1, 2, \ldots$ **do**
    draw $\mathbf{x}_{t+1}$ from the distribution $Q(\mathbf{x}_t, \cdot)$
end for

The value $Q(\mathbf{s}, B)$ is then the probability that $\mathbf{x}_{t+1}$ lands in B given $\mathbf{x}_t = \mathbf{s}$. The sequence $\{\mathbf{x}_t\}$ so generated is also called a **sample path** for Q.

There is a measure-theoretic procedure for building this process $\{\mathbf{x}_t\}$ more formally but the construction is usually unnecessary because most Markov processes are introduced via a stochastic difference equation, which specifies both the process $\{\mathbf{x}_t\}$ and, implicitly, the associated stochastic kernel Q. The canonical stochastic difference equation for a **first-order Markov process** takes the form

$$\mathbf{x}_{t+1} = G(\mathbf{x}_t, \mathbf{w}_{t+1}) \quad \text{with} \quad \mathcal{L}(\mathbf{x}_0) = P_0 \tag{7.7}$$

Here $\{\mathbf{w}_t\}_{t \geqslant 1}$ is an IID sequence of $\mathbb{R}^M$-valued shocks with common distribution Ψ and G is a given $\mathscr{B}$-measurable function mapping the current state $\mathbf{x}_t \in S$ and shock $\mathbf{w}_{t+1} \in \mathbb{R}^M$ into the new state $\mathbf{x}_{t+1} \in S$. The initial condition $\mathbf{x}_0$ and the shocks $\{\mathbf{w}_t\}_{t \geqslant 1}$ are also assumed to be independent of each other. The corresponding stochastic kernel is

$$Q(\mathbf{s}, B) = \mathbb{P}\{G(\mathbf{s}, \mathbf{w}_{t+1}) \in B\} \qquad (\mathbf{s} \in S,\ B \in \mathscr{B}(S))$$

The choice of date $t+1$ is irrelevant here because of the IID assumption, and is used only to tie in with (7.7). Recalling that Ψ is the distribution of $\mathbf{w}_{t+1}$, the stochastic kernel can also be written as

$$Q(\mathbf{s}, B) = \Psi\left\{\mathbf{w} \in \mathbb{R}^M \ : \ G(\mathbf{s}, \mathbf{w}) \in B\right\}$$

This expression makes it clear that Q is defined by the two primitives G and Ψ.

Example 7.2.1 For the ARCH(1) model of (7.5), the stochastic kernel is

$$Q(s, B) = \mathbb{P}\{(\alpha_0 + \alpha_1 s^2)^{1/2} w_{t+1} \in B\}$$

when w_{t+1} is standard normal.

Returning to the general process (7.7), repeated substitution gives

$$\begin{aligned}
\mathbf{x}_1 &= G(\mathbf{x}_0, \mathbf{w}_1) \\
\mathbf{x}_2 &= G(G(\mathbf{x}_0, \mathbf{w}_1), \mathbf{w}_2) \\
\mathbf{x}_3 &= G(G(G(\mathbf{x}_0, \mathbf{w}_1), \mathbf{w}_2), \mathbf{w}_3)
\end{aligned}$$

and so on. Continuing in this fashion, we see that the state vector $\mathbf{x}_t$ can be written as a function of $\mathbf{x}_0$ and the shocks $\mathbf{w}_1, \ldots, \mathbf{w}_t$ for any t. In other words, for each t, there exists a function H_t such that

$$\mathbf{x}_t = H_t(\mathbf{x}_0, \mathbf{w}_1, \mathbf{w}_2, \ldots, \mathbf{w}_t) \tag{7.8}$$

Example 7.2.2 For the scalar linear AR(1) process (7.3) we can write the right-hand side of (7.8) explicitly as

$$x_t = b \sum_{k=0}^{t-1} a^k + \sum_{k=0}^{t-1} a^k c w_{t-k} + a^t x_0 \tag{7.9}$$

This is called the **moving average representation** of x_t. The proof is an exercise.

Often there is no neat expression for the function H_t. Nonetheless, (7.8) clarifies the fact that (7.7) pins down each $\mathbf{x}_t$ as a well-defined random vector, depending on the initial condition and the shocks up until date t. Since $\mathbf{x}_t$ is a function of $\mathbf{x}_0, \mathbf{w}_1, \mathbf{w}_2, \ldots, \mathbf{w}_t$, and these random vectors are all, by the IID assumption, independent of $\mathbf{w}_{t+k}$ for any $k \geqslant 1$, fact 5.1.10 on page 137 tells us that the current state $\mathbf{x}_t$ and future shocks are independent. Let's record this:

Fact 7.2.1 For the process (7.7), the pair $\mathbf{x}_t$ and $\mathbf{w}_{t+k}$ are independent for all $k \geqslant 1$.

Although it's rarely made explicit, behind all the random vectors $\{\mathbf{x}_t\}$ lies a single probability space $(\Omega, \mathscr{F}, \mathbb{P})$. The idea is that an element ω of Ω is selected by "nature" at the start of time. This determines the initial condition $\mathbf{x}_0$ and the shocks $\mathbf{w}_t$ as

$$\mathbf{x}_0(\omega), \mathbf{w}_1(\omega), \mathbf{w}_2(\omega), \mathbf{w}_3(\omega), \ldots$$

From these, each state vector $\mathbf{x}_t$ is determined via

$$\mathbf{x}_t(\omega) = H_t(\mathbf{x}_0(\omega), \mathbf{w}_1(\omega), \mathbf{w}_2(\omega), \ldots, \mathbf{w}_t(\omega))$$

where H_t is the function in (7.8).

7.2.1.1 The Density Case

If $Q(\mathbf{s}, \cdot)$ is absolutely continuous for all $\mathbf{s}$, then we can define the corresponding **stochastic density kernel** or the **transition density** via

$$q(\mathbf{s}, \cdot) := \text{ the density of } Q(\mathbf{s}, \cdot) \text{ for all } \mathbf{s} \in S \tag{7.10}$$

In other words, $q(\mathbf{s}, \cdot)$ is the conditional density of $\mathbf{x}_{t+1}$ given $\mathbf{x}_t = \mathbf{s}$. Heuristically, $q(\mathbf{s}, \mathbf{s}')\, \mathrm{d}\mathbf{s}'$ is the probability of transitioning from $\mathbf{s}$ to $\mathbf{s}'$ in one step.

Example 7.2.3 Recall the ARCH(1) process, with stochastic kernel Q as given in example 7.2.1. The transition density $q(s, \cdot)$ is the density of $y = (\alpha_0 + \alpha_1 s^2)^{1/2} w_{t+1}$ when $\mathcal{L}(w_{t+1}) = \mathrm{N}(0, 1)$. Hence

$$q(s, s') = \frac{1}{\sqrt{2\pi\sigma_s^2}} \exp\left\{-\frac{(s')^2}{2\sigma_s^2}\right\} \quad \text{where} \quad \sigma_s^2 := \alpha_0 + \alpha_1 s^2 \tag{7.11}$$

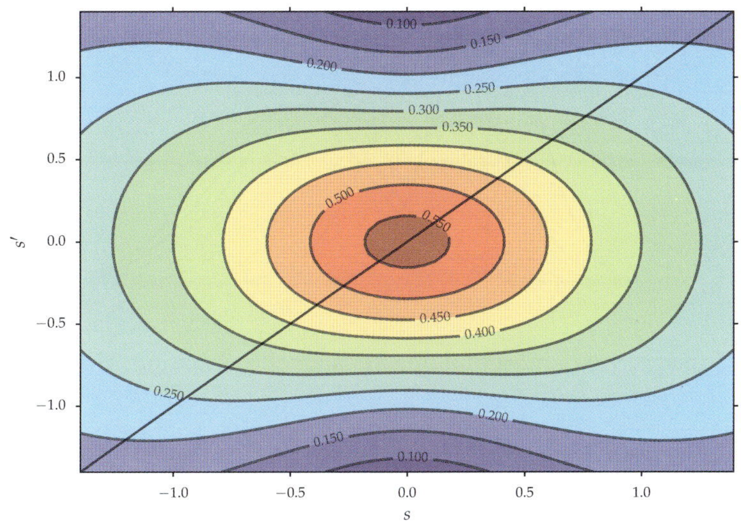

Figure 7.4 Transition density $q(s, s')$ for the ARCH kernel (7.11)

A visualization of the ARCH kernel (7.11) is given in figure 7.4 when $\alpha_0 = 0.5$ and $\alpha_1 = 0.8$. The diagonal line is the 45 degree line. Each vertical fiber of the graph corresponds to one density $s' \mapsto q(s, s')$. For large s (to the right on the horizontal axis), the corresponding density puts most mass below the 45 degree line, indicating a tendency to decrease. Conversely, when $-s$ is large, the process tends to increase.

Example 7.2.4 Consider a general model with additive shock, so that

$$\mathbf{x}_{t+1} = G(\mathbf{x}_t, \mathbf{w}_{t+1}) = g(\mathbf{x}_t) + \mathbf{w}_{t+1} \quad \text{with} \quad \{\mathbf{w}_t\} \overset{\text{IID}}{\sim} \psi \tag{7.12}$$

for some function g and density ψ. In this case the transition density has the form

$$q(\mathbf{s}, \mathbf{s}') = \psi(\mathbf{s}' - g(\mathbf{s})) \tag{7.13}$$

In the scalar case, (7.13) follows from example 4.2.16 on page 112, since $q(s, \cdot)$ is the density of $y = g(s) + w_{t+1}$ with $\mathcal{L}(w_{t+1}) = \psi$. This gives $q(s, s') = \psi(s' - g(s))$. The multivariate proof uses a similar argument.

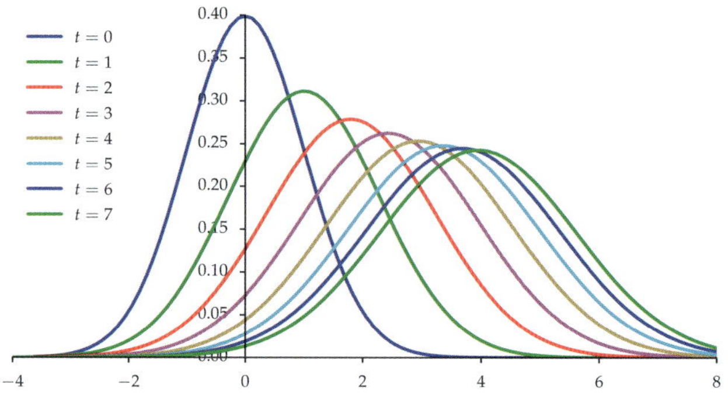

Figure 7.5 Sequence of marginal densities for the Gaussian AR(1) process

7.2.2 Marginal and Joint Distributions

Let's note some features of the marginal and joint distributions of a Markov process. Consider our generic process $\mathbf{x}_{t+1} = G(\mathbf{x}_t, \mathbf{w}_{t+1})$ from (7.7), where $\mathcal{L}(\mathbf{x}_0) = P_0$ and $\{\mathbf{w}_t\}$ is IID on $\mathbb{R}^M$ with common distribution Ψ. The **marginal distribution of the state vector** is just $\mathcal{L}(\mathbf{x}_t)$. Since $\mathbf{x}_t$ is a well-defined random vector (see in particular (7.8)), $\mathcal{L}(\mathbf{x}_t)$ also well-defined, and we denote it in what follows by P_t. That is,

$$P_t(B) = \mathbb{P}\{\mathbf{x}_t \in B\} \qquad (B \in \mathscr{B}(S))$$

Example 7.2.5 Consider the Gaussian AR(1) process in (7.3). Suppose that $\mathcal{L}(x_0) = \mathrm{N}(\mu_0, \sigma_0^2)$, where μ_0 and σ_0 are given constants, and that x_0 is independent of the shock process $\{w_t\}$. Combining the moving average representation of x_t in (7.9) with fact 5.1.14 on page 137, we have

$$P_t = \mathrm{N}\left(\mu_t, \sigma_t^2\right) \quad \text{where} \quad \mu_t := b\sum_{k=0}^{t-1} a^k + a^t\mu_0 \text{ and } \sigma_t^2 := \sum_{k=0}^{t-1} a^{2k}c^2 + a^{2t}\sigma_0^2$$

Figure 7.5 shows a visualization of this sequence when $\mu_0 = 0, \sigma_0 = b = c = 1$ and $a = 0.8$. In fact we don't actually need to recompute the sums in the definition of μ_t and σ_t^2 at each step because these sequences satisfy the recursions

$$\mu_{t+1} = b + a\mu_t \quad \text{and} \quad \sigma_{t+1}^2 = a^2\sigma_t^2 + c^2 \tag{7.14}$$

You can verify this by taking expectations and variances on both side of (7.3). For code replicating the figure, see `johnstachurski.net/emet.html`.

For a general Markov process, tracking evolution of the first two moments is usually more complicated, and even then fails to provide full information on the distributions. We do, however, have the following general result:

Fact 7.2.2 The marginal distributions of a Markov process with stochastic kernel Q obey the recursion

$$P_{t+1}(B) = \int Q(\mathbf{s}, B) P_t(d\mathbf{s}) \qquad (B \in \mathscr{B}(S),\ t \geqslant 0) \tag{7.15}$$

Exercise 7.6.4 asks you to prove this. Fact 7.2.2 is a version of the law of total probability (see page 142). To calculate the probability of reaching B next period, we sum the probability of that event given outcome $\mathbf{s}$ today, weighted by the probability that $\mathbf{s}$ occurs today. Here's a parallel result for the density case.

Fact 7.2.3 If $Q(\mathbf{s}, \cdot)$ is absolutely continuous for all $\mathbf{s} \in S$, then P_t is absolutely continuous for all $t \geqslant 1$. Letting p_t be the corresponding density, the sequence $\{p_t\}$ satisfies

$$p_{t+1}(\mathbf{s}') = \int q(\mathbf{s}, \mathbf{s}') p_t(\mathbf{s})\, d\mathbf{s} \qquad (B \in \mathscr{B}(S),\ t \geqslant 1) \tag{7.16}$$

where q is the transition density corresponding to Q.

Let's now look at joint distributions. We'll cover these only in the density case, which is the most important case in econometrics.

Fact 7.2.4 Let $\{\mathbf{x}_t\}$ be a Markov process with transition density q and initial density p_0. Under the conditions of fact 7.2.3, the joint density p_T of $\mathbf{x}_0, \ldots, \mathbf{x}_T$ is

$$p_T(\mathbf{s}_0, \ldots, \mathbf{s}_T) = p_0(\mathbf{s}_0) \prod_{t=0}^{T-1} q(\mathbf{s}_t, \mathbf{s}_{t+1}) \tag{7.17}$$

This result can be obtained in a few different ways. One is to repeatedly apply (5.27) on page 142 to factor the joint density into

$$p_T(\mathbf{s}_0, \ldots, \mathbf{s}_T) = p_0(\mathbf{s}_0) \prod_{t=0}^{T-1} p(\mathbf{s}_{t+1} \,|\, \mathbf{s}_t, \ldots, \mathbf{s}_0)$$

This is the expression for the joint density of a general stochastic process, where the current state depends on lagged states of all orders. With the first-order Markov property, an expression like $p(\mathbf{s}_{t+1} \,|\, \mathbf{s}_t, \ldots, \mathbf{s}_0)$ reduces to $p(\mathbf{s}_{t+1} \,|\, \mathbf{s}_t)$, which is just $q(\mathbf{s}_t, \mathbf{s}_{t+1})$.

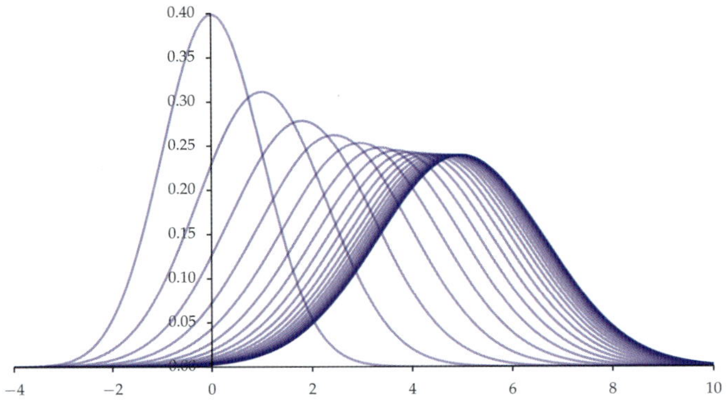

Figure 7.6 Convergence of marginal densities, Gaussian AR(1) case

7.2.3 Stationarity of Markov Processes

Consider the notion of stationarity introduced in §7.1.1. Not every Markov process is stationary. As stated above, a necessary condition is that the marginals are constant, and in figure 7.5 we saw an example of how the marginals $\{P_t\}$ can change over time. Figure 7.6 shows the same sequence but now longer, with identical parameters. Probability mass moves from left to right.

While $\{P_t\}$ is not typically constant, for the particular sequence shown in figure 7.6, the difference between successive distributions is diminishing over time. We can see this analytically as well by recalling that $P_t = \mathrm{N}(\mu_t, \sigma_t^2)$, where μ_t and σ_t^2 are as given in (7.14). Provided that $|a| < 1$, these sequences converge, with

$$\mu_t \to \mu_\infty := \frac{b}{1-a} \quad \text{and} \quad \sigma_t^2 \to \sigma_\infty^2 := \frac{c^2}{1-a^2}$$

Let P_∞ denote the distribution associated with these limits. That is,

$$P_\infty = \mathrm{N}(\mu_\infty, \sigma_\infty^2) = \mathrm{N}\left[\frac{b}{1-a}, \frac{c^2}{1-a^2}\right] \tag{7.18}$$

What happens if we actually attain this limiting distribution, or if we take our initial draw x_0 from this distribution? On an intuitive level, it seems that the distribution sequence will be constant, remaining at P_∞ over time. Indeed this is the case, as exercise 7.6.1 asks you to confirm.

The limiting distribution is an example of what is called a stationary distribution. More generally, a **stationary distribution** for a Markov process on S with stochastic kernel Q is any distribution P_∞ on S satisfying

$$P_\infty(B) = \int Q(\mathbf{s}, B) P_\infty(d\mathbf{s}) \qquad \text{for all } B \in \mathscr{B}(S)$$

Comparing with the recursion $P_{t+1}(B) = \int Q(\mathbf{s}, B) P_t(d\mathbf{s})$ from fact 7.2.2, we see that the definition of stationarity of P_∞ means precisely that

$$\mathcal{L}(\mathbf{x}_t) = P_\infty \implies \mathcal{L}(\mathbf{x}_{t+1}) = P_\infty$$

From this we see that any process starting at P_∞ will be identically distributed. In fact it is stationary, in the sense that (7.1) holds. Let's record this:

Fact 7.2.5 Let $\{\mathbf{x}_t\}$ be a Markov process with stationary distribution P_∞. If $\mathcal{L}(\mathbf{x}_0) = P_\infty$, then $\{\mathbf{x}_t\}$ is a stationary stochastic process, with $\mathcal{L}(\mathbf{x}_t) = P_\infty$ for all t.

Example 7.2.6 Consider the scalar Gaussian linear AR(1) process from (7.3). If $|a| < 1$ and $\mathcal{L}(x_0) = P_\infty$, where P_∞ is as in (7.18), then $\{x_t\}$ is stationary.

Moments of the stationary distribution are called the **stationary moments** of the Markov process. Other names for the stationary distribution include the "invariant" or "unconditional" distribution, and the moments are then called the invariant or unconditional moments.

Fact 7.2.6 If $Q(\mathbf{s}, \cdot)$ is absolutely continuous for all $\mathbf{s} \in S$ with transition density $q(\mathbf{s}, \cdot)$, then every stationary distribution P_∞ is absolutely continuous, and its density p_∞ satisfies

$$p_\infty(\mathbf{s}') = \int q(\mathbf{s}, \mathbf{s}') p_\infty(\mathbf{s}) \, d\mathbf{s} \quad \text{for all } \mathbf{s}' \in S \tag{7.19}$$

Such a density is called a **stationary density**.

7.2.3.1 Existence

Not every Markov process has a stationary distribution. For example, in the linear scalar AR(1) model $x_{t+1} = b + ax_t + cw_{t+1}$, we know that the marginal variance evolves according to $\sigma_{t+1}^2 = a^2\sigma_t^2 + c^2$. If $|a| \geqslant 1$, then this sequence diverges. Because the variance is not constant, the distribution sequence cannot be constant either.

Let's state one sufficient condition for existence. The condition we give slightly specializes a famous result known as the Krylov–Bogolyubov theorem. It uses the notion of a **coercive** function, which is any nonnegative function V on the state space S such that

$$C_\gamma := \{\mathbf{s} \in S : V(\mathbf{s}) \leqslant \gamma\}$$

is a compact subset of S for all $\gamma \in \mathbb{R}$. Intuitively, coercive functions are functions that go to $+\infty$ as we move "away from the center" of the state space.

Example 7.2.7 If $S = \mathbb{R}^K$ and $V(\mathbf{s}) = \|\mathbf{s}\|$, then V is coercive on S. Indeed, for this function, each C_γ is a closed sphere centered on the origin. Closed and bounded subsets of $\mathbb{R}^K$ are compact.

Example 7.2.8 If $S = \mathbb{R}$ and $V(s) = s^2$, then V is coercive on S. To see this, just observe that $C_\gamma = [-\sqrt{\gamma}, \sqrt{\gamma}]$. This is a closed, bounded subset of S.

Now we can state the following:

Theorem 7.2.1 *Let $\mathbf{x}_{t+1} = G(\mathbf{x}_t, \mathbf{w}_{t+1})$ be the process on S defined in (7.7). If*

(i) $\mathbf{s} \mapsto G(\mathbf{s}, \mathbf{w})$ is continuous for each fixed $\mathbf{w} \in \mathbb{R}^M$, and

(ii) there exists a coercive function V on S and constants λ and L such that $0 \leqslant \lambda < 1$ and

$$\mathbb{E}\, V[G(\mathbf{s}, \mathbf{w}_{t+1})] \leqslant \lambda V(\mathbf{s}) + L \qquad (\mathbf{s} \in S) \tag{7.20}$$

then the Markov process has at least one stationary distribution.

See §11.2 of Stachurski (2009) for proofs and references. Condition (7.20) is an example of a **drift condition**. One way to understand it is to write it as

$$\frac{\mathbb{E}\, V[G(\mathbf{s}, \mathbf{w}_{t+1})]}{V(\mathbf{s})} \leqslant \lambda + \frac{L}{V(\mathbf{s})}$$

As we move "away from the center" of the state space, $V(\mathbf{s})$ becomes large, and the term on the right is eventually < 1. Looking at the left hand side, this tells us that the value attached to the state by V is expected to decrease, which in turn suggests movement away from the "edges" of the state space and back towards the center.

Example 7.2.9 Consider again the ARCH(1) process $x_{t+1} = (\alpha_0 + \alpha_1 x_t^2)^{1/2} w_{t+1}$ from (7.5), where, as usual $\alpha_0 > 0$ and $\alpha_1 \geqslant 0$. Let $S = \mathbb{R}$. If $\alpha_1 < 1$, then this process has a stationary distribution on S. To see this, observe that

$$G(s, w) = (\alpha_0 + \alpha_1 s^2)^{1/2} w \qquad (s, w \in \mathbb{R})$$

is continuous in s for each fixed w. Moreover $V(s) = s^2$ is coercive on S by example 7.2.8, and

$$\mathbb{E}\, G(s, w_{t+1})^2 = (\alpha_0 + \alpha_1 s^2) \mathbb{E}\, w_{t+1}^2 = \alpha_0 + \alpha_1 s^2 \tag{7.21}$$

Hence (7.20) holds with equality when $V(s) := s^2$, $\lambda := \alpha_1$ and $L := \alpha_0$.

7.2.4 Asymptotics of Markov Processes

When do Markov processes exhibit nice properties such as ergodicity? To gain some intuition, let's first consider the process $x_{t+1} = ax_t + w_{t+1}$, where $\{w_t\}$ is IID $\mathrm{N}(0,1)$ and $|a| < 1$. We consider a stationary process, where each x_t has marginal

$$P_\infty := \mathrm{N}\left(0,\, (1-a^2)^{-1}\right) \tag{7.22}$$

A law of large numbers for this process takes the form

$$\bar{x}_T \xrightarrow{p} \int s\, P_\infty(\mathrm{d}s) = 0 \quad \text{as} \quad T \to \infty \tag{7.23}$$

Fact 6.1.2 on page 162 tells us that for (7.23) to hold it suffices that

$$\mathbb{E}\,\bar{x}_T \to 0 \quad \text{and} \quad \operatorname{var}\bar{x}_T \to 0 \quad \text{as} \quad T \to \infty \tag{7.24}$$

The first part is obvious, since $\mathbb{E}\,\bar{x}_T = \frac{1}{T}\sum_{t=1}^T \mathbb{E}\,x_t$ and $\mathbb{E}\,x_t = 0$. For the second part, since $\mathbb{E}\,\bar{x}_T = 0$,

$$\operatorname{var}\left[\frac{1}{T}\sum_{t=1}^T x_t\right] = \mathbb{E}\left[\frac{1}{T}\sum_{t=1}^T x_t\right]^2 = \frac{1}{T^2}\sum_{n=1}^T\sum_{m=1}^T \mathbb{E}\,[x_n x_m]$$

Using $\mathbb{E}\,[x_n x_m] = \mathbb{E}\,[x_m x_n]$ we obtain the bound

$$\operatorname{var}\bar{x}_T \leqslant \frac{2}{T^2}\sum_{1\leqslant n\leqslant m\leqslant T} \mathbb{E}\,[x_n x_m] = \frac{2}{T^2}\sum_{j=0}^{T-1}\sum_{t=1}^{T-j} \mathbb{E}\,[x_{t+j}x_t] \tag{7.25}$$

Thus, to obtain $\operatorname{var}\bar{x}_T \to 0$ as $T \to \infty$, we require the covariance terms $\mathbb{E}\,[x_{t+j}x_t]$ to converge to zero in j sufficiently quickly. That they do in this particular instance is the subject of exercise 7.6.3.

To summarize, if correlations die out sufficiently quickly, then we can regain the LLN. The same is true for the CLT when second moment conditions hold. We now state a much more general result for sample paths of Markov processes. The proofs are omitted but the essential ideas are the same.

Theorem 7.2.2 *Let $\{\mathbf{x}_t\}$ be a Markov process on S with stochastic kernel Q. Suppose that $Q(\mathbf{s},\cdot)$ is absolutely continuous for all $\mathbf{s} \in S$ and let $q(\mathbf{s},\cdot)$ be the corresponding transition density. If*

(a) q is strictly positive and continuous on $S \times S$, and

(b) *there exists a coercive function V on S and constants λ and L such that $0 \leqslant \lambda < 1$ and*

$$\int V(\mathbf{s}')q(\mathbf{s},\mathbf{s}')\,d\mathbf{s}' \leqslant \lambda V(\mathbf{s}) + L \qquad (\mathbf{s} \in S)$$

then the following statements are true:

(i) *Q has a unique stationary distribution P_∞ with density p_∞.*

(ii) *$P_t \stackrel{w}{\to} P_\infty$ as $t \to \infty$ for all initial P_0.*

(iii) *If $h\colon S \to \mathbb{R}$ is $\mathscr{B}$-measurable and $\int |h(\mathbf{s})| p_\infty(\mathbf{s})\,d\mathbf{s} < \infty$, then*

$$\frac{1}{T}\sum_{t=1}^{T} h(\mathbf{x}_t) \stackrel{p}{\to} \int h(\mathbf{s})p_\infty(\mathbf{s})\,d\mathbf{s} \quad \text{as} \quad T \to \infty \tag{7.26}$$

(iv) *If, in addition, $h^2 \leqslant V$, then there exists a $\sigma_h^2 \geqslant 0$ such that*

$$\sqrt{T}\left\{\frac{1}{T}\sum_{t=1}^{T} h(\mathbf{x}_t) - \int h(\mathbf{s})p_\infty(\mathbf{s})\,d\mathbf{s}\right\} \stackrel{d}{\to} \mathrm{N}(0,\sigma_h^2) \quad \text{as} \quad T \to \infty \tag{7.27}$$

Conditions (a) and (b) are not dissimilar to the conditions for existence in theorem 7.2.1. Condition (b) is the drift condition in (7.20) specialized to the density setting. The major difference is that q is required to be strictly positive. This gives enough mixing to generate uniqueness and the sample path properties. Theorem 7.2.2 can be proved from results in Meyn and Tweedie (2009).[1]

Theorem 7.2.2 is but one of a vast range of results on asymptotic properties of Markov processes. Discussion of alternatives is given in §7.5. In fact the conditions are rather strict and can certainly be weakened at the expense of a more complex theorem statement. Nonetheless, they suffice for many applications of interest.

The constant σ_h^2 in (7.27) is given by the expression

$$\sigma_h^2 := \operatorname{var} h(\mathbf{x}_0) + 2\sum_{t=1}^{\infty} \operatorname{cov}[h(\mathbf{x}_0), h(\mathbf{x}_t)] \tag{7.28}$$

with the understanding that $\{\mathbf{x}_t\}$ is a stationary process. If $\sigma_h^2 = 0$, then the limiting distribution is degenerate.

---

1. The stated results are a consequence of theorem 17.0.1 in Meyn and Tweedie (2009), which in turn requires that the process is V-uniformly ergodic. In our case, the latter property follows from aperiodicity and irreducibility, which are immediate consequences of strict positivity of q on $S \times S$, and from the drift condition (b). In the language of Meyn and Tweedie (2009), the function V is "unbounded off petite sets." This holds for any coercive function V when q is positive and continuous, since compact sets are then petite.

Fact 7.2.7 Let $\mathbf{x}_{t+1} = g(\mathbf{x}_t) + \mathbf{w}_{t+1}$ be the additive shock process on $\mathbb{R}^K$ from (7.12). If $\mathbb{E}\,\|\mathbf{w}_t\|$ is finite, g is continuous, the density ψ of $\mathbf{w}_t$ is continuous and positive everywhere on $\mathbb{R}^K$, and there exist constants λ and L such that $0 \leqslant \lambda < 1$ and

$$\|g(\mathbf{s})\| \leqslant \lambda\|\mathbf{s}\| + L \quad \text{for all } \mathbf{s} \in \mathbb{R}^K \tag{7.29}$$

then the conditions of theorem 7.2.2 are satisfied.

To see why, recall from (7.13) that the transition density satisfies $q(\mathbf{s}, \mathbf{s}') = \psi(\mathbf{s}' - g(\mathbf{s}))$. Since ψ is assumed continuous and positive on $\mathbb{R}^K$, the transition density has these properties on $\mathbb{R}^K \times \mathbb{R}^K$. Hence condition (a) in theorem 7.2.2 is satisfied. Condition (b) is also satisfied because, taking λ and L as in (7.29), we have

$$\int \|\mathbf{s}'\| q(\mathbf{s}, \mathbf{s}') \, d\mathbf{s}' = \mathbb{E}\,\|g(\mathbf{s}) + \mathbf{w}_{t+1}\| \leqslant \lambda\|\mathbf{s}\| + L + \int \|\mathbf{w}\|\psi(\mathbf{w}) \, d\mathbf{w}$$

Example 7.2.10 Let $\{x_t\}$ be a scalar AR(1) process $x_{t+1} = ax_t + b + cw_{t+1}$, where $\{w_t\}$ is IID and standard normal. If $|a| < 1$ and $c > 0$, then the conditions of fact 7.2.7 are satisfied. The density of cw_t is $\text{N}(0, c^2)$, which is continuous and strictly positive on $\mathbb{R}$. To see that (7.29) holds, rewrite the model as $x_{t+1} = g(x_t) + cw_{t+1}$, where $g(s) := as + b$. By the triangle inequality, $|g(s)| \leqslant \lambda|s| + L$, where $\lambda := |a|$ and $L := |b|$.

Example 7.2.11 Here's a variation on the scalar "threshold autoregressive" model:

$$x_{t+1} = a|x_t| + (1 - a^2)^{1/2} w_{t+1} \quad \text{with} \quad |a| < 1 \quad \text{and} \quad \{w_t\} \overset{\text{IID}}{\sim} \text{N}(0, 1)$$

The conditions of fact 7.2.7 are satisfied. To see this, we can rewrite the model as

$$x_{t+1} = g(x_t) + v_{t+1}, \quad g(s) = a|s| \quad \text{and} \quad \{v_t\} \overset{\text{IID}}{\sim} \text{N}(0, 1 - a^2)$$

Clearly (7.29) is satisfied with $\lambda = |a|$ and $L = 0$. Moreover $\mathcal{L}(v_t) = \text{N}(0, 1 - a^2)$, which has finite mean and a bounded density everywhere positive on $\mathbb{R}$.

For most Markov processes the stationary density has no known closed-form. However, in the case of example 7.2.11, the stationary density is known to have the form $p_\infty(s) = 2\phi(s)\Phi(qs)$, where $q := a(1 - a^2)^{-1/2}$, ϕ is the standard normal density and Φ is the standard normal CDF.

Example 7.2.12 Consider the STAR model from (7.6), where the function g is given by $g(s) := (b_0 + a_0 s)(1 - \tau(s)) + (b_1 + a_1 s)\tau(s)$ for some $\tau \colon \mathbb{R} \to [0, 1]$. Applying the triangle inequality and using $0 \leqslant \tau(s) \leqslant 1$, we have

$$|g(s)| \leqslant |b_0| + |b_1| + \max\{|a_0|, |a_1|\}|s|$$

Letting $L := |b_0| + |b_1|$ and $\lambda := \max\{|a_0|, |a_1|\}$, we then have $|g(s)| \leqslant \lambda|s| + L$. If both $|a_0|$ and $|a_1|$ are strictly less than one, then condition (7.29) is satisfied.

Example 7.2.13 Recall the ARCH process $x_{t+1} = (\alpha_0 + \alpha_1 x_t^2)^{1/2} w_{t+1}$ from (7.5), where $\{w_t\}$ is IID and standard normal. In example 7.2.9 we saw that this model has a stationary distribution on $S = \mathbb{R}$ whenever $\alpha_0 > 0$ and $0 \leqslant \alpha_1 < 1$. In particular, we showed in (7.21) that it satisfies drift with respect to the coercive function $V(s) = s^2$. This gives condition (b) of theorem 7.2.2. Condition (a) also holds because the transition density is continuous and everywhere positive (see page 186).

7.2.5 The Linear Case

Recall the VAR process in (7.4), which, to repeat, takes the form

$$\mathbf{x}_{t+1} = \mathbf{b} + \mathbf{A}\mathbf{x}_t + \mathbf{C}\mathbf{w}_{t+1} \tag{7.30}$$

where $\{\mathbf{w}_t\}$ is assumed to be IID and to satisfy $\mathbb{E}\,\mathbf{w}_t = \mathbf{0}$ and $\mathbb{E}[\mathbf{w}_t \mathbf{w}_t'] = \mathbf{I}$. Regarding the asymptotics of this process, if the shock vector has a continuous and positive density, then we can apply fact 7.2.7 on page 195 to obtain asymptotic stability and LLN and CLT results whenever the matrix norm of $\mathbf{A}$ satisfies $\|\mathbf{A}\| < 1$. To see this, let $g(\mathbf{s}) = \mathbf{b} + \mathbf{A}\mathbf{s}$. By the norm triangle inequality and the definition of the matrix norm, we have

$$\|g(\mathbf{s})\| = \|\mathbf{b} + \mathbf{A}\mathbf{s}\| \leqslant \|\mathbf{b}\| + \|\mathbf{A}\mathbf{s}\| \leqslant \|\mathbf{b}\| + \|\mathbf{A}\|\|\mathbf{s}\|$$

Hence (7.29) holds.

As mentioned above, the stability and sample path conditions considered above are relatively strict. In the linear case, we can certainly do better. Here's one such result:

Fact 7.2.8 For the VAR process (7.30), the conclusions of theorem 7.2.2 hold with $V = \|\cdot\|$ whenever $\varrho(\mathbf{A}) < 1$.

Here $\varrho(\mathbf{A})$ is the spectral radius of $\mathbf{A}$, as defined on page 69. Under this condition, a unique stationary distribution exists. Taking expectations across (7.30), we see that its mean μ_∞ must satisfy $\mu_\infty = \mathbf{b} + \mathbf{A}\mu_\infty$. Applying the Neumann series lemma (page 69), this equation has the unique solution

$$\mu_\infty = (\mathbf{I} - \mathbf{A})^{-1}\mathbf{b} = \sum_{i=0}^{\infty} \mathbf{A}^i \mathbf{b}$$

Let $\mathbf{\Sigma}_\infty$ be the asymptotic variance (i.e., the variance–covariance matrix of the stationary distribution). From (7.30) it must satisfy

$$\mathbf{\Sigma}_\infty = \mathbf{A}\mathbf{\Sigma}_\infty\mathbf{A}^\top + \mathbf{C}\mathbf{C}^\top$$

This is an example of a **discrete time Lyapunov equation**. Under the condition $\varrho(\mathbf{A}) < 1$ it can be solved by iteration or by using existing numerical solvers. Here's an example in Julia that uses a solver from the QuantEcon package:

```
using QuantEcon

A = [0.8 -0.2;
    -0.1 0.7]
C = [0.5 0.4;
     0.4 0.6]

solve_discrete_lyapunov(A, C * C')
```

7.3 Martingales

Martingales generalize the notion of a random walk, where increments to the current state are draws from a white noise process. The concept of martingales has been central to many advances in probability since the mid twentieth century. Econometricians also like martingales because they neatly capture the idea of "unpredictable" change.

7.3.1 Definitions

To define martingales, we need the notion of a filtration, which is an increasing sequence of information sets. Recall from §5.2.4 that an information set is just a set of random variables. Let $\{\mathscr{F}_t\}$ be a sequence of information sets. That is, $\mathscr{F}_t$ is an information set for each t. The sequence $\{\mathscr{F}_t\}$ is called a **filtration** if, in addition, $\mathscr{F}_t \subset \mathscr{F}_{t+1}$ for all t. Intuitively, expanding information sets reflect the idea that more information is revealed over time.

Example 7.3.1 Let $\{\mathbf{x}_t\}$ be a sequence of random vectors, and let

$$\mathscr{F}_0 := \varnothing \quad \text{and} \quad \mathscr{F}_t := \{\mathbf{x}_1, \ldots, \mathbf{x}_t\} \quad \text{for all } t \geqslant 1 \tag{7.31}$$

The sequence $\{\mathscr{F}_t\}$ is a filtration. It is called the **filtration generated by** $\{\mathbf{x}_t\}$.

Now let $\{m_t\}$ be a scalar stochastic process and let $\{\mathscr{F}_t\}$ be a filtration. We say that $\{m_t\}$ is **adapted** to $\{\mathscr{F}_t\}$ if m_t is $\mathscr{F}_t$-measurable for every t. (For the definition of measurability, see §5.2.4.)

The intuitive meaning is this: $\mathscr{F}_t$ represents the variables we know as of time t. If $\{m_t\}$ is adapted to $\mathscr{F}_t$, then we can compute m_t at time t as well.

Example 7.3.2 Let $\{x_t\}$ be any stochastic process, let $\{\mathscr{F}_t\}$ be the filtration generated by $\{x_t\}$ and let $\bar{x}_t := \frac{1}{t}\sum_{j=1}^t x_j$ be the sample mean up until date t. Then $\{\bar{x}_t\}$ is adapted to $\{\mathscr{F}_t\}$.

Example 7.3.3 Let $\{w_t\}$ be IID standard normal, let $\{\mathscr{F}_t\}$ be the filtration generated by $\{w_t\}$ and let $x_t := \sup_{j \geqslant t} w_j$. This process is not adapted to $\{\mathscr{F}_t\}$ because the value x_t cannot be determined from $\{w_1, \ldots, w_t\}$.

Fact 7.3.1 If $\{m_t\}$ is adapted to $\{\mathscr{F}_t\}$, then $\mathbb{E}[m_t \,|\, \mathscr{F}_{t+j}] = m_t$ for any $j \geqslant 0$.

The proof goes like this: By adaptedness, m_t is $\mathscr{F}_t$-measurable. From the definition of a filtration we have $\mathscr{F}_t \subset \mathscr{F}_{t+j}$. Applying fact 5.2.10 on page 150, it follows that m_t is $\mathscr{F}_{t+j}$-measurable. Fact 7.3.1 now follows from fact 5.2.13 on page 151.

A sequence of integrable random variables $\{m_t\}$ adapted to a filtration $\{\mathscr{F}_t\}$ is called a **martingale** with respect to $\{\mathscr{F}_t\}$ if

$$\mathbb{E}[m_{t+1} \,|\, \mathscr{F}_t] = m_t \quad \text{for all} \quad t$$

The expression $\mathbb{E}[m_{t+1} \,|\, \mathscr{F}_t]$ is sometimes simplified to $\mathbb{E}_t[m_{t+1}]$ when the filtration is understood.

Example 7.3.4 (Random Walk) Let $\{\eta_t\}$ be an IID sequence of zero-mean random variables and let $m_t := \sum_{j=1}^t \eta_j$. For example, η_t might be the payoff on the tth round of a fair game and m_t is the wealth of a gambler after the tth round.[2] We can also express $\{m_t\}$ recursively via $m_{t+1} = m_t + \eta_{t+1}$ with $m_0 = 0$. The process $\{m_t\}$ is a martingale with respect to the filtration $\{\mathscr{F}_t\}$ generated by $\{\eta_t\}$. That $\{m_t\}$ is adapted to $\{\mathscr{F}_t\}$ follows immediately from the definitions. Moreover

$$\mathbb{E}[m_{t+1} \,|\, \mathscr{F}_t] = \mathbb{E}[m_t + \eta_{t+1} \,|\, \mathscr{F}_t] = m_t + \mathbb{E}[\eta_{t+1} \,|\, \mathscr{F}_t]$$

where the last equality follows from linearity and fact 7.3.1. Since $\{\eta_t\}$ is IID, we know that η_{t+1} is independent of the variables in $\mathscr{F}_t$, and hence $\mathbb{E}[\eta_{t+1} \,|\, \mathscr{F}_t] = \mathbb{E}[\eta_{t+1}] = 0$. Therefore $\{m_t\}$ is a martingale with respect to $\{\mathscr{F}_t\}$ as claimed.

Example 7.3.5 A well-known example of a martingale from economic theory is the consumption process in Hall (1978). To understand the idea, consider the Euler equation

$$u'(c_t) = \mathbb{E}_t \left[\frac{1 + r_{t+1}}{1 + \varrho} u'(c_{t+1}) \right]$$

2. We are assuming that wealth starts at zero and may take arbitrarily large negative values without the gambler getting knee-capped by the mafia.

where u' is the derivative of a utility function u, r_t is an interest rate and ϱ is a discount factor. The expectation $\mathbb{E}_t[\cdot]$ can be thought of as $\mathbb{E}[\cdot \mid \mathscr{F}_t]$, where $\mathscr{F}_t$ contains all variables observable at time t. Specializing to the case $r_{t+1} = \varrho$ and $u(c) = c - ac^2/2$, the Euler equation reduces to

$$c_t = \mathbb{E}_t[c_{t+1}] =: \mathbb{E}[c_{t+1} \mid \mathscr{F}_t]$$

Thus consumption is a martingale with respect to $\{\mathscr{F}_t\}$.

7.3.1.1 Martingale Difference Sequences

A stochastic process $\{d_t\}$ is called a **martingale difference sequence** (or MDS) with respect to some filtration $\{\mathscr{F}_t\}$ if

$$\mathbb{E}[d_{t+1} \mid \mathscr{F}_t] = 0 \quad \text{for all} \quad t$$

An MDS is so named because if $\{m_t\}$ is a martingale with respect to $\{\mathscr{F}_t\}$, then $d_t = m_t - m_{t-1}$ is an MDS with respect to $\{\mathscr{F}_t\}$. See exercise 7.6.7.

Fact 7.3.2 If $\{d_t\}$ is an MDS, then $\mathbb{E} d_t = 0$ for all t.

Indeed, by the law of iterated expectations, $\mathbb{E} d_t = \mathbb{E}[\mathbb{E}[d_t \mid \mathscr{F}_{t-1}]] = \mathbb{E} 0 = 0$.

7.3.2 Martingale Difference LLN and CLT

Next we consider asymptotics for martingale difference sequences. Such sequences are good candidates for the LLN and CLT. To see this, recall that integrable IID sequences always satisfy the LLN. With finite second moment they also satisfy the CLT. Suppose now that $\{m_t\}$ is a stationary MDS with respect to some filtration $\{\mathscr{F}_t\}$. We don't have independence in this case but we do have the following:

Fact 7.3.3 If $\{m_t\}$ is an MDS, then $\text{cov}[m_{t+j}, m_t] = 0$ for all $j \geqslant 1$.

To see this, fix $t \geqslant 0$ and $j \geqslant 1$. We have

$$\text{cov}[m_{t+j}, m_t] = \mathbb{E}[m_{t+j} m_t] = \mathbb{E}[\mathbb{E}[m_{t+j} m_t \mid \mathscr{F}_{t+j-1}]]$$

Since $t + j - 1 \geqslant t$ and $\{\mathscr{F}_t\}$ is a filtration, we know that m_t is $\mathscr{F}_{t+j-1}$-measurable. Hence

$$\mathbb{E}[\mathbb{E}[m_{t+j} m_t \mid \mathscr{F}_{t+j-1}]] = \mathbb{E}[m_t \mathbb{E}[m_{t+j} \mid \mathscr{F}_{t+j-1}]] = \mathbb{E}[m_t \cdot 0] = 0$$

The lack of correlation in fact 7.3.3 is a key part of the next result.

Theorem 7.3.1 *If $\{m_t\}$ is a stationary* MDS *with respect to some filtration $\{\mathscr{F}_t\}$, then*

$$\frac{1}{T}\sum_{t=1}^{T} m_t \xrightarrow{p} 0 \quad as \quad T \to \infty \tag{7.32}$$

If, in addition, $\gamma^2 := \mathbb{E}[m_t^2] < \infty$ and $\frac{1}{T}\sum_{t=1}^{T}\mathbb{E}[m_t^2 \mid \mathscr{F}_{t-1}] \xrightarrow{p} \gamma^2$ as $T \to \infty$, then

$$T^{-1/2}\sum_{t=1}^{T} m_t \xrightarrow{d} \mathrm{N}(0, \gamma^2) \quad as \quad T \to \infty \tag{7.33}$$

The proof of (7.32) is identical to that of the classical LLN in theorem 6.1.1. Theorem 7.3.1 can be established from a martingale CLT proved in Durrett (2010).

7.4 Simulation

Simulation is invaluable as a tool for exploring statistical concepts and solving applied problems. For example, the current popularity of Bayesian methods for econometrics and machine learning has been driven to a large extent by clever simulation algorithms that have proved successful at solving hard estimation problems.

Modern scientific programming environments all have good routines for simulating independent observations from a range of common named distributions. We've seen examples of this in the displayed computer code. But it's easy to run into situations where the distribution we are working with is nonstandard, or has no closed-form solution. We then need to roll our own routines for producing random variates. Let's review two of the most important algorithms.

7.4.1 Inverse Transforms

Suppose that we wish to draw from a distribution on $\mathbb{R}$ with CDF F. Assuming that we can generate uniform random variables, we can do so via the **inverse transform** method:

1: draw u from the uniform distribution on $[0, 1]$
2: return $F^{-1}(u)$, where F^{-1} is the quantile function of F (see (4.35))

We wish to show that this technique is valid, or, equivalently, that

$$\mathcal{L}(u) = U[0, 1] \quad \Longrightarrow \quad \mathcal{L}[F^{-1}(u)] = F \tag{7.34}$$

In the proof we'll assume that F is strictly increasing. (This isn't necessary, but the proof of the general case provides no additional intuition.) Let $\mathcal{L}(u) = U[0, 1]$ and let

$z := F^{-1}(u)$. To see that $\mathcal{L}(z) = F$, observe that, by strict monotonicity, $F(a) \leqslant F(b)$ if and only if $a \leqslant b$. As a result, for any $s \in \mathbb{R}$,

$$\mathbb{P}\{z \leqslant s\} = \mathbb{P}\{F^{-1}(u) \leqslant s\} = \mathbb{P}\{u \leqslant F(s)\}$$

The defining property of a $U[0,1]$ random variable u is that $\mathbb{P}\{u \leqslant t\} = t$ whenever $0 \leqslant t \leqslant 1$. Using this fact in the preceding calculation gives $\mathbb{P}\{z \leqslant s\} = F(s)$, proving (7.34).

Here's one extension for the basic inverse transform method. Suppose that we want to simulate from a joint distribution on $\mathbb{R}^N$ that is defined in terms of a copula (see §5.1.5). In particular, suppose that F_n is a continuous CDF on $\mathbb{R}$ for $n = 1, \ldots, N$, that C is a copula on $\mathbb{R}^N$ and that the joint distribution of interest is

$$F(s_1, \ldots, s_N) = C(F_1(s_1), \ldots, F_N(s_N))$$

(This is just (5.22) from page 138.) If we can simulate from C, then we can simulate from F. The method is

1: draw $u_1, \ldots, u_N$ from C
2: return $(x_1, \ldots, x_N) := (F_1^{-1}(u_1), \ldots, F_N^{-1}(u_N))$

Exercise 7.6.13 asks you to prove that $(x_1, \ldots, x_N)$ is a draw from F.

7.4.2 Markov Chain Monte Carlo

Markov chain Monte Carlo (MCMC) is a way of simulating from a given density π on $S \subset \mathbb{R}^K$. The idea is to construct a stochastic kernel P on S such that

(i) π is a stationary distribution for P, and

(ii) P is sufficiently ergodic that its sample path averages converge to expectations under π

See (7.26) on page 194 for a clearer statement of (ii). If we specialize to indicator functions we can approximate probabilities under π too.

There are two major strands of MCMC algorithms: Metropolis–Hastings and the Gibbs sampler. Here we'll cover the former. While boldface symbols are omitted in what follows, the ideas are valid in any dimension. In the section on Bayesian estimation in §8.3.4, I will explain why Metropolis–Hastings fits so beautifully with Bayesian updating.

The **Metropolis–Hastings algorithm** starts with a Markov process in the form of a stochastic density kernel $q = q(s, s')$ called the **proposal density**. Draws from the proposal density are called **proposals**. Each time we draw a proposal, we either (i) accept it and move to that new state, or (ii) reject it and stay put. The probability of accepting is structured so that the chain tends to stay in regions where π puts most probability mass. As a consequence, for a sequence $\{x_t\}$ generated by this process, we get

$$\text{fraction of time spent in } B = \frac{1}{T}\sum_{t=1}^{T} \mathbb{1}\{x_t \in B\} \approx \pi(B) \quad \text{for large } T$$

This is a version of (7.26) with $h = \mathbb{1}_B$.

The ideas are subtle, so let's build up in steps. Consider first a general accept-reject style process of the kind discussed above, where the probability of acceptance is determined by an arbitrary function $\alpha = \alpha(x_t, y)$ of the current state x_t and proposal y. The function takes values in $[0,1]$. The algorithm for generating x_{t+1} from x_t given α and proposal density q is given in algorithm 1.

Algorithm 1 A Markov process with proposal density q and acceptance function α

draw y from $q(x_t, \cdot)$
draw u independently from the uniform $[0,1]$ distribution
if $u \leqslant \alpha(x_t, y)$ **then** ▷ with probability $\alpha(x_t, y)$
    set $x_{t+1} = y$
else ▷ with probability $1 - \alpha(x_t, y)$
    set $x_{t+1} = x_t$
end if

The stochastic kernel P associated with $\{x_t\}$ in algorithm 1 has the form

$$P(s, B) = \int_B p(s, s')\, ds' + (1 - \lambda(s))\mathbb{1}\{s \in B\} \tag{7.35}$$

for all $s \in S$ and $B \in \mathscr{B}(S)$, where

$$p(s, s') := q(s, s')\alpha(s, s') \quad \text{and} \quad \lambda(s) := \int p(s, s')\, ds'$$

To show this, we can break the probabilities up as follows. Fix any Borel set B and let x_t be given at s. Let x_{t+1} be drawn according to algorithm 1 when $x_t = s$. By additivity of $\mathbb{P}$ we can write $\mathbb{P}\{x_{t+1} \in B\}$ as

$$\mathbb{P}\{x_{t+1} \in B\} \cap \{u \leqslant \alpha(s, y)\} + \mathbb{P}\{x_{t+1} \in B\} \cap \{u > \alpha(s, y)\} \tag{7.36}$$

Our aim is to show that the two terms in (7.36) match the two terms on the right-hand side of (7.35).

Using the fact that intersections become products when we switch to indicators (fact 4.1.4, page 90), we can applying the law of iterated expectations to obtain

$$\begin{aligned}\mathbb{P}\{x_{t+1} \in B\} \cap \{u \leqslant \alpha(s,y)\} &= \mathbb{P}\{y \in B\} \cap \{u \leqslant \alpha(s,y)\} \\ &= \mathbb{E}\left[\mathbb{1}\{y \in B\}\mathbb{1}\{u \leqslant \alpha(s,y)\}\right] \\ &= \mathbb{E}\left\{\mathbb{E}\left[\mathbb{1}\{y \in B\}\mathbb{1}\{u \leqslant \alpha(s,y)\} \,|\, y\right]\right\} \\ &= \mathbb{E}\left\{\mathbb{1}\{y \in B\}\mathbb{E}\left[\mathbb{1}\{u \leqslant \alpha(s,y)\} \,|\, y\right]\right\}\end{aligned}$$

The term $\mathbb{E}\left[\mathbb{1}\{u \leqslant \alpha(s,y)\} \,|\, y\right]$ is just $\mathbb{P}\{u \leqslant \alpha(s,y)\}$ with y given, which, since u is uniform, evaluates to $\alpha(s,y)$. Hence the final expression in the last display evaluates to

$$\int \mathbb{1}\{s' \in B\}\alpha(s,s')q(s,s')\,\mathrm{d}s' = \int_B \alpha(s,s')q(s,s')\,\mathrm{d}s'$$

$$\therefore \quad \mathbb{P}\{x_{t+1} \in B\} \cap \{u \leqslant \alpha(s,y)\} = \int_B p(s,s')\,\mathrm{d}s' \tag{7.37}$$

Equation (7.37) says that the first term in (7.36) is equal to the first term on the right-hand side of (7.35). For the second terms, note that $x_{t+1} = x_t = s$ when $u > \alpha(s,y)$, so

$$\begin{aligned}\mathbb{P}\{x_{t+1} \in B\} \cap \{u > \alpha(s,y)\} &= \mathbb{E}\left[\mathbb{1}\{s \in B\}\mathbb{1}\{u > \alpha(s,y)\}\right] \\ &= \mathbb{1}\{s \in B\}\mathbb{E}[\mathbb{1}\{u > \alpha(s,y)\}] \\ &= \mathbb{1}\{s \in B\}[1 - \mathbb{P}\{u \leqslant \alpha(s,y)\}]\end{aligned}$$

To match this expression with the second term in (7.35), we just need to show that $\mathbb{P}\{u \leqslant \alpha(s,y)\} = \int p(s,s')\,\mathrm{d}s'$. But this is immediate from (7.37) if we take $B = S$.

So far we have verified that the kernel P in (7.35) is the stochastic kernel corresponding to algorithm 1. Now let's double back and design the selection function α so that the stationary distribution of P is the target density π. In the Metropolis–Hastings algorithm, this is done by setting

$$\alpha(s,s') := \min\left\{\frac{\pi(s')q(s',s)}{\pi(s)q(s,s')}, 1\right\} \tag{7.38}$$

If $\pi(s)q(s,s') = 0$, then $\alpha(s,s') := 1$. The min is in place so $\alpha(s,s')$ can be interpreted as a probability. We don't actually need to impose it in algorithm 1, since for $u \in [0,1]$ we have $u \leqslant \min\{a,1\}$ iff $u \leqslant a$. The important element is the ratio inside the min, which is large when the new proposal s' has high probability under π relative to the current location s and small when the reverse is true. This keeps the chain in regions where π has high mass, and leads to our next result.

Theorem 7.4.1 *Let P be the stochastic kernel in* (7.35). *If α is as defined* (7.38), *then π is a* *stationary distribution for P.*

Proof. The proof turns on the fact that for this choice of α we have $p(s,s')\pi(s) = p(s',s)\pi(s')$ for all s, s' (see ex. 7.6.14). From that observation and the definition of P we obtain

$$\begin{aligned}
\int P(s,B)\pi(s)\,\mathrm{d}s &= \int \left\{ \int_B p(s,s')\,\mathrm{d}s' \right\} \pi(s)\,\mathrm{d}s + \int (1-\lambda(s))\mathbb{1}\{s \in B\}\pi(s)\,\mathrm{d}s \\
&= \int_B \left\{ \int p(s,s')\pi(s)\,\mathrm{d}s \right\} \mathrm{d}s' + \int_B (1-\lambda(s))\pi(s)\,\mathrm{d}s \\
&= \int_B \left\{ \int p(s',s)\pi(s')\,\mathrm{d}s \right\} \mathrm{d}s' + \int_B (1-\lambda(s))\pi(s)\,\mathrm{d}s \\
&= \int_B \lambda(s')\pi(s')\,\mathrm{d}s' + \int_B (1-\lambda(s))\pi(s)\,\mathrm{d}s \\
&= \int_B \pi(s)\,\mathrm{d}s
\end{aligned}$$

Thus π is a stationary distribution of P, as was to be shown. □

It remains to establish that P has the kind of stability properties discussed in theorem 7.2.2 on page 193 (and in particular the LLN result in (7.26) of that theorem). This isn't universally true, and requires at least some conditions on the primitives q and π. One well-known result is given in corollary 3 of Tierney (1994) for the case where q and π are continuous and strictly positive on S and S itself is compact. In essence, the continuity and positivity corresponds to condition (a) of theorem 7.2.2, while the compactness of S is a strict version of the drift condition in (b) of the same theorem.[3] For further results and references, see Roberts and Rosenthal (2004).

One disadvantage of MCMC methods is that the variates they generate are not in general independent. Sample averages from dependent samples are typically less informative than IID samples. (See example 7.1.4 for the extreme case.) It is desirable, then, that dependence between x_t and x_{t+k} dies out quickly as k increases. Whether it does or not is determined by the choice of q. Extensive discussion of such issues can be found in Brooks et al. (2011).

A function implementing the Metropolis–Hastings algorithm in Julia with a random walk proposal density is given in listing 4. The proposal density takes the form $q(s,s') = \psi(s'-s)$, where ψ is a given density. This is the system (7.12)–(7.13) with g set to the identity. If ψ is symmetric, then $q(s,s') = q(s',s)$, and $\alpha(s,s')$ simplifies to $\min\{\pi(s')/\pi(s), 1\}$ if $\pi(s) > 0$ and 1 otherwise. This is the case shown in listing 4,

3. When S is compact, every constant nonnegative function on S is coercive, and if V is constant then the drift condition in (7.20) is trivial.

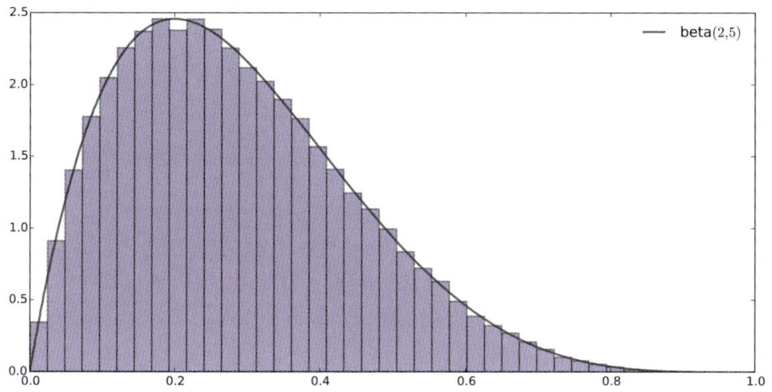

Figure 7.7 Observations from the random walk Metropolis–Hastings algorithm

with ψ set to the $N(0, \sigma^2)$ distribution. Look up Julia's ternary operator if you find it hard to follow the code.

Listing 4 The random walk Metropolis–Hastings algorithm (Julia)

```
function rw_metropolis(pi_density, T, init=0, sigma=1)
    xvec = Array(Float64, T)
    xvec[1] = init
    for t in 1:(T - 1)
        x = xvec[t]
        y = x + sigma * randn()
        alpha = pi_density(x) > 0 ? pi_density(y) / pi_density(x) : 1
        xvec[t+1] = rand() < alpha  ? y : x
    end
    return xvec
end
```

Figure 7.7 shows a histogram of 10^6 draws generated from this algorithm when π is the beta distribution with parameters $(2, 5)$. The black line is the target density. This is just a toy example, since routines for sampling from beta distributions are readily available. You can experiment with the code at `johnstachurski.net/emet.html`.

7.5 Further Reading

The modern theory of Markov processes owes much to a brilliant mathematician called Wolfgang Doeblin. His short life and shining contributions to probability theory are discussed in Bru and Yor (2002).

An excellent overview of Markov processes and their stability can be found in Meyn and Tweedie (2009). For more on Markov processes from a density perspective see Lasota and Mackey (1994) or chapter 8 of Stachurski (2009). For a nice survey of sample path properties with a focus on the central limit theorem, see Jones (2004).

Diaconis (2009) provides a fascinating overview of MCMC and its impact on different fields. Richey (2010) is a more general survey. Good references on the theoretical side include Roberts and Rosenthal (2004), Tierney (1994), and Geweke (1996). See Kroese and Chan (2014) for a more practical discussion with a focus on applications.

7.6 Exercises

Ex. 7.6.1 Show that the process in example 7.2.6 on page 191 is identically distributed.

Ex. 7.6.2 Let $x_{t+1} = ax_t + w_{t+1}$, where $\{w_t\}$ is IID standard normal and $\mathcal{L}(x_0) = \text{N}(0, 1/(1-a^2))$. Show that $\text{cov}[x_t, x_{t+j}] = a^j(1-a^2)^{-1}$ for all $j \geqslant 0$.

Ex. 7.6.3 Show that the right-hand side of (7.25) converges to zero in T.

Ex. 7.6.4 Prove fact 7.2.2 on page 189.[4]

Ex. 7.6.5 Consider the additive shock process in fact 7.2.7. Assume the conditions stated in the fact and let $\mathbb{E}\,\|\mathbf{x}_0\|$ be finite. Show that $\mathbb{E}\,\|\mathbf{x}_t\|$ is bounded in t.

Ex. 7.6.6 Consider again the scalar Markov sequence $x_{t+1} = ax_t + w_{t+1}$. Assume that $\{w_t\}$ is IID, having Student's t-distribution with 2 degrees of freedom, and that $|a| < 1$. Show that the conditions of fact 7.2.7 are satisfied.

Ex. 7.6.7 Let $\{\mathscr{F}_t\}$ be a filtration. Show that if $\{m_t\}$ is a martingale with respect to $\{\mathscr{F}_t\}$, then $d_t = m_t - m_{t-1}$ is a martingale difference sequence with respect to $\{\mathscr{F}_t\}$.

Ex. 7.6.8 Let $\{\mathscr{F}_t\}$ be a filtration, and let $\{m_t\}$ be a martingale with respect to $\{\mathscr{F}_t\}$. Let $\alpha_t := m_t + 1$, let $\kappa_t := 2m_t$, and let $\gamma_t := m_t^2$. Which of these is a martingale with respect to $\{\mathscr{F}_t\}$?

Ex. 7.6.9 Let $\{\eta_t\}$ be an IID sequence of scalar random variables with $\mathbb{E}\,\eta_1 = 0$ and $\text{var}\,\eta_1 = \sigma^2 > 0$. Let $\{\mathscr{F}_t\}$ be the filtration defined by $\mathscr{F}_t := \{\eta_1, \ldots, \eta_t\}$, and let $z_t := t \cdot \eta_t$ for each t.

4. Hint: Try converting probabilities into expectations of indicators and using the law of iterated expectations.

(i) Is $\{z_t\}$ IID? Why or why not?

(ii) Is $\{z_t\}$ a martingale difference sequence with respect to $\{\mathscr{F}_t\}$? Why or why not?

Ex. 7.6.10 Let $\{\eta_t\}$ be an IID sequence of scalar random variables with $\mathbb{P}\{\eta_1 = 1\} = \mathbb{P}\{\eta_1 = -1\} = 0.5$ and let $\{\mathscr{F}_t\}$ be the filtration defined by $\mathscr{F}_t := \{\eta_1, \ldots, \eta_t\}$. Let

$$m_t := \sum_{j=1}^{t} \eta_j \quad \text{and} \quad \kappa_t := m_t^2 - t$$

Show that $\{\kappa_t\}$ is a martingale with respect to $\{\mathscr{F}_t\}$.

Ex. 7.6.11 Consider the scalar sequence $x_{t+1} = a x_t + w_{t+1}$, where $\{w_t\} \overset{\text{IID}}{\sim} \text{N}(0,1)$ and $x_0 = 0$. Let $\mathscr{F}_t := \{w_1, \ldots, w_t\}$. Give conditions on a such that

(i) $\{x_t\}$ is a martingale with respect to $\{\mathscr{F}_t\}$ and

(ii) $\{x_t\}$ is a martingale difference sequence with respect to $\{\mathscr{F}_t\}$.

Ex. 7.6.12 Let $\{\mathscr{F}_t\}$ be a filtration. A sequence of random variables $\{\gamma_t\}$ is called **previsible** with respect to $\{\mathscr{F}_t\}$ if γ_t is $\mathscr{F}_{t-1}$-measurable for every t. Show that if $\{x_t\}$ is a martingale with respect to $\{\mathscr{F}_t\}$, and $\{\gamma_t\}$ is previsible with respect to $\{\mathscr{F}_t\}$, then the process $\{y_t\}$ defined by

$$y_t := \sum_{i=1}^{t} \gamma_i (x_i - x_{i-1})$$

is a martingale with respect to $\{\mathscr{F}_t\}$.

Ex. 7.6.13 Let $F(s_1, \ldots, s_N) = C(F_1(s_1), \ldots, F_N(s_N))$, where C is a copula and each F_n is a continuous CDF on $\mathbb{R}$. Let $\mathcal{L}(u_1, \ldots, u_N) = C$ and let

$$(x_1, \ldots, x_N) := (F_1^{-1}(u_1), \ldots, F_N^{-1}(u_N))$$

Prove that $\mathcal{L}(x_1, \ldots, x_N) = F$.

Ex. 7.6.14 Show that if $a \geqslant 0$ and b and c are any real numbers, then $a \min\{b, c\} = \min\{ab, ac\}$. Next let α be as defined in (7.38) and let $p(s, s') := q(s, s')\alpha(s, s')$. Show that $\pi(s) p(s, s') = p(s', s) \pi(s')$ for all s, s'.

7.6.1 Solutions to Selected Exercises

Solution to Ex. 7.6.1. Here's a proof for the case $b = 0$ and $c = 1$. For the induction step, suppose that $\mathcal{L}(x_t) = P_\infty$, where P_∞ is as defined in (7.18) on page 190. With

$b = 0$ and $c = 1$, this becomes $P_\infty = \mathrm{N}(0, 1/(1-a^2))$. Since $x_{t+1} = ax_t + w_{t+1}$ and linear combinations of independent normals are normal, we know that x_{t+1} is normal. Thus it remains only to show that $\mathbb{E}\, x_{t+1} = 0$ and $\operatorname{var} x_{t+1} = 1/(1-a^2)$. The first claim is true because, by linearity of expectations, $\mathbb{E}\, x_{t+1} = \mathbb{E}\,[ax_t + w_{t+1}] = a\mathbb{E}\,[x_t] + \mathbb{E}\,[w] = 0$. The second claim also holds because

$$\operatorname{var} x_{t+1} = \operatorname{var}[ax_t + w_{t+1}] = a^2 \operatorname{var}[x_t] + \operatorname{var}[w_{t+1}] + 2a \operatorname{cov}[x_t, w_{t+1}]$$

Since x_t and w_{t+1} are independent the final term is zero, and we get

$$\operatorname{var} x_{t+1} = a^2 \frac{1}{1-a^2} + 1 = \frac{1}{1-a^2} \qquad \square$$

Solution to Ex. 7.6.2. We aim to show that $\operatorname{cov}[x_t, x_{t+j}] = a^j/(1-a^2)$. Fix $j \geqslant 1$ and iterate with $x_{t+1} = ax_t + w_{t+1}$ to get $x_{t+j} = a^j x_t + \sum_{k=1}^{j} a^{j-k} w_{t+k}$. Using this expression and independence of x_t and w_{t+k} gives

$$\mathbb{E}\,[x_{t+j}x_t] = \mathbb{E}\left[a^j x_t^2 + \sum_{k=1}^{j} a^{j-k} w_{t+k} x_t\right] = a^j \mathbb{E}\,[x_t^2] + \sum_{k=1}^{j} a^{j-k} \mathbb{E}\,[w_{t+k}] \mathbb{E}\,[x_t]$$

Since $\mathbb{E}\,[w_{t+k}] = 0$, this gives $\operatorname{cov}[x_{t+j}, x_t] = \mathbb{E}\,[x_{t+j}x_t] = a^j \mathbb{E}\,[x_t^2]$. The process $\{x_t\}$ is identically distributed (fact 7.2.5) with common variance $1/(1-a^2)$. The result follows. $\square$

Solution to Ex. 7.6.3. As shown in exercise 7.6.2, we have $\mathbb{E}\,[x_t x_{t+j}] = a^j/(1-a^2)$. Hence

$$\frac{2}{T^2} \sum_{j=0}^{T-1} \sum_{t=1}^{T-j} \frac{a^j}{1-a^2} = \frac{2}{T^2} \sum_{j=0}^{T-1} (T-j) \frac{a^j}{1-a^2} \leqslant \frac{2}{T} \frac{1}{(1-a)(1-a^2)}$$

The term on the right converges to 0 as $T \to \infty$. $\square$

Solution to Ex. 7.6.4. Fix $B \in \mathscr{B}(S)$ and let P_t be the tth marginal. By the law of iterated expectations, we have

$$\mathbb{P}\{\mathbf{x}_{t+1} \in B\} = \mathbb{E}\,[\mathbb{1}\{\mathbf{x}_{t+1} \in B\}] = \mathbb{E}\,[\mathbb{E}\,[\mathbb{1}\{\mathbf{x}_{t+1} \in B\} \mid \mathbf{x}_t]] = \mathbb{E}\,[Q(\mathbf{x}_t, B)]$$

In other words, $P_{t+1}(B) = \int Q(\mathbf{s}, B) P_t(d\mathbf{s})$, as was to be shown. $\square$

Solution to Ex. 7.6.7. To prove that $\{d_t\}$ is adapted to $\{\mathscr{F}_t\}$, we need to show that d_t is a function of variables in $\mathscr{F}_t$. To see this, observe that m_t is a function of variables in $\mathscr{F}_t$ and m_{t-1} is a function of variables in $\mathscr{F}_{t-1}$. By the definition of filtrations, every variable in $\mathscr{F}_{t-1}$ is also in $\mathscr{F}_t$. Hence m_{t-1} is also a function of variables in $\mathscr{F}_t$. Since both m_t and m_{t-1} are functions of variables in $\mathscr{F}_t$, so is $d_t = m_t - m_{t-1}$.

Next we show that $\mathbb{E}[d_{t+1} \mid \mathscr{F}_t] = 0$. Since $\mathbb{E}[m_{t+1} \mid \mathscr{F}_t] = m_t$ and $\mathbb{E}[m_t \mid \mathscr{F}_t] = m_t$ (by fact 7.3.1), we have

$$\mathbb{E}[d_{t+1} \mid \mathscr{F}_t] = \mathbb{E}[m_{t+1} \mid \mathscr{F}_t] - \mathbb{E}[m_t \mid \mathscr{F}_t] = m_t - m_t = 0 \qquad \square$$

Solution to Ex. 7.6.8. First, $\{\alpha_t\}$ is a martingale with respect to $\{\mathscr{F}_t\}$. To see that $\{\alpha_t\}$ is adapted to $\{\mathscr{F}_t\}$, note that $\{m_t\}$ is adapted to $\{\mathscr{F}_t\}$ by assumption. Therefore m_t is a function of variables in $\mathscr{F}_t$ and hence $\alpha_t = m_t + 1$ is a function of variables in $\mathscr{F}_t$. Moreover, using the fact that $\{m_t\}$ is a martingale with respect to $\{\mathscr{F}_t\}$, we have

$$\mathbb{E}[\alpha_{t+1} \mid \mathscr{F}_t] = \mathbb{E}[m_{t+1} + 1 \mid \mathscr{F}_t] = \mathbb{E}[m_{t+1} \mid \mathscr{F}_t] + 1 = m_t + 1 = \alpha_t$$

Second, $\{\kappa_t\}$ is a martingale with respect to $\{\mathscr{F}_t\}$. The proof is similar and hence omitted.

Third, $\{\gamma_t\}$ is not generally a martingale with respect to $\{\mathscr{F}_t\}$. For example, let $\{m_t\}$ be the random walk martingale in example 7.3.4. The process $\{\gamma_t\}$ given by $\gamma_t = m_t^2$ is not a martingale whenever $\sigma^2 := \mathbb{E}[\eta_1^2]$ is strictly positive. To see this, observe that

$$\gamma_{t+1} = m_{t+1}^2 = \left(\sum_{j=1}^{t} \eta_j + \eta_{t+1} \right)^2 = (m_t + \eta_{t+1})^2 = m_t^2 + 2m_t\eta_{t+1} + \eta_{t+1}^2$$

$$\therefore \quad \mathbb{E}[\gamma_{t+1} \mid \mathscr{F}_t] = \mathbb{E}[m_t^2 \mid \mathscr{F}_t] + 2\mathbb{E}[m_t\eta_{t+1} \mid \mathscr{F}_t] + \mathbb{E}[\eta_{t+1}^2 \mid \mathscr{F}_t]$$

Since

$$\mathbb{E}[m_t\eta_{t+1} \mid \mathscr{F}_t] = m_t\mathbb{E}[\eta_{t+1} \mid \mathscr{F}_t] = m_t\mathbb{E}[\eta_{t+1}] = 0$$

and $\mathbb{E}[\eta_{t+1}^2 \mid \mathscr{F}_t] = \mathbb{E}[\eta_{t+1}^2] = \sigma^2$ we now have

$$\mathbb{E}[\gamma_{t+1} \mid \mathscr{F}_t] = \mathbb{E}[m_t^2 \mid \mathscr{F}_t] + \sigma^2 = m_t^2 + \sigma^2 = \gamma_t + \sigma^2 > \gamma_t$$

Hence $\{\gamma_t\}$ is not a martingale with respect to $\{\mathscr{F}_t\}$. $\square$

Solution to Ex. 7.6.11. It is clear from (7.8) on page 185 that $\{x_t\}$ is adapted to the filtration for all values of a. Regarding part (i), if $a = 1$, then $\{x_t\}$ is the random walk in example 7.3.4. Hence $\{x_t\}$ is a martingale with respect to $\{\mathscr{F}_t\}$. Regarding part (ii), if $a = 0$, then $x_t = w_t$, and

$$\mathbb{E}[x_{t+1} \mid \mathscr{F}_t] = \mathbb{E}[w_{t+1} \mid \mathscr{F}_t] = \mathbb{E}[w_{t+1}] = 0$$

Hence $\{x_t\}$ is a martingale difference sequence with respect to $\{\mathscr{F}_t\}$. □

Solution to Ex. 7.6.13. We aim to show that $\mathcal{L}(x_1, \ldots, x_N) = F$. We have

$$\mathbb{P} \cap_n \{x_n \leqslant s_n\} = \mathbb{P} \cap_n \{F_n^{-1}(u_n) \leqslant s_n\} = \mathbb{P} \cap_n \{u_n \leqslant F_n(s_n)\}$$

Since C is the CDF of $u_1, \ldots, u_N$, the right-hand side is equal to $C(F_1(s_1), \ldots, F_N(s_N))$. This is $F(s_1, \ldots, s_N)$ by the definition of F. □

Solution to Ex. 7.6.14. The first claim is immediate, since $a \geqslant 0$ implies that $f(x) = ax$ is an order preserving transform. The second claim is just algebra. You've made it this far through the book, so I guess you don't need my help with that. □

Part II

Foundations of Statistics

Chapter 8

Estimators

In probability theory we aim to deduce the likelihood of different outcomes based on known probability distributions. Statistics is the inverse problem. We want to infer unknown probability distributions from outcomes we observe. In this chapter we begin to explore these ideas.

8.1 The Estimation Problem

Let's start off by clarifying the nature of the problem we want to study.

8.1.1 Definitions

From a pedagogical point of view, it's best to start our study of statistics in a setting where successive observations are both independent and identically distributed. Later we'll extend to dependent data. In an IID setting, the fundamental problem of econometrics and statistics is this:

Problem 8.1.1 We observe independent Z-valued draws $\mathbf{z}_1, \ldots, \mathbf{z}_N$ from a common but unknown distribution $P \in \mathscr{P}$, where $\mathscr{P}$ is a class of distributions on Z. We wish to infer some features of P from this sample.

The set $\mathscr{P}$ is the universe of distributions we are willing to consider. It can be anything, including the set of all distributions on the outcome space. One of the main tasks of economic theory is to restrict $\mathscr{P}$ and thereby narrow down the set of distributions we have to search over.

Example 8.1.1 Benhabib et al. (2015) study the wealth distribution in a model with idiosyncratic capital income risk. The model predicts that the wealth distribution will have a Pareto right tail. Intuitively, this is because stochastic returns on assets are multiplicative, so positive shocks are self-reinforcing, and a sequence of positive shocks can lead to very high wealth relative to the median.

Let's set out some notation:

- Z is the **outcome space** where each **observation** $\mathbf{z}_n$ takes values.
- $\mathbf{z}_\mathcal{D}$ denotes the **sample** or **data set** $(\mathbf{z}_1, \ldots, \mathbf{z}_N)$.
- $Z_\mathcal{D} := \times_{n=1}^N Z$ is the **sample space** in which $\mathbf{z}_\mathcal{D}$ takes values.
- $P_\mathcal{D} := \mathcal{L}(\mathbf{z}_\mathcal{D})$ is the **joint distribution of the sample**.

Although calling $Z_\mathcal{D}$ the sample space follows standard nomenclature, we are overloading the terminology first used on page 79. (Unfortunately, statisticians and probabilists don't always coordinate on terminology.)

As above, $P = \mathcal{L}(\mathbf{z}_n)$ is the common distribution of the observations. For as long as we continue to focus on IID data, the joint distribution $P_\mathcal{D}$ will be the Nth product of P, as defined on page 130.

Example 8.1.2 Let $x_1, \ldots, x_N$ be observations of labor income from a given population. We model $x_1, \ldots, x_N$ as IID draws from a common univariate distribution P. In our terminology, x_n is an observation, the outcome space Z is $\mathbb{R}$, the sample space $Z_\mathcal{D}$ is $\mathbb{R}^N$, and the sample $\mathbf{z}_\mathcal{D}$ is the vector $(x_1, \ldots, x_N)$. Features of P that we might wish to learn about include

- the mean and higher moments of P,
- measures of dispersion, such as the variance, or properties of tails,
- the median and other quantiles, and
- P itself, or the density of P if it exists.

In example 8.1.2, the individual observations are scalar. In other scenarios, observations are vector-valued:

Example 8.1.3 Suppose that we wish to learn about the relationship between profitability and R&D spending within a group of firms. Let $\mathbf{z}_n = (x_n, y_n)$ be an observation of these two quantities at the nth firm. We treat the observations as IID across firms, with common marginal distribution $P = \mathcal{L}(\mathbf{z}_n)$. The outcome space is $Z = \mathbb{R}^2$, and the sample space is

$$Z_\mathcal{D} := \mathbb{R}^2 \times \cdots \times \mathbb{R}^2 = \mathbb{R}^{2 \times N}$$

Because the marginal distribution P of the observations is now multivariate, new features of the distribution come in to play, such as

- correlations across coordinates of P,
- the variance–covariance matrix associated with P, and
- parameters controlling dependence when, say, P is modeled via a copula over certain marginals.

8.1.1.1 Features

We referred above to "features" of P that we might be interested in estimating. Let's define a **feature** of P to be an object of the form

$$\gamma(P) \quad \text{for some} \quad \gamma\colon \mathscr{P} \to S \tag{8.1}$$

The set S is left arbitrary to accommodate all possible features. When P is understood, we'll write $\gamma(P)$ as γ. Here are some examples for univariate P routinely estimated in econometric studies:

- $\gamma(P) = \int s^k P(\mathrm{d}s)$, the kth moment of P.
- $\gamma(P) = \inf\{s \in \mathbb{R} : P(-\infty, s] \geqslant 1/2\}$, the median of P.
- $\gamma(P) = P$, when we want to estimate P itself.
- $\gamma(P) =$ the density of P when P is absolutely continuous.

If P is multivariate over $\mathbf{z} = (\mathbf{x}, y)$, then one feature of interest is the regression function $f^*(\mathbf{x}) := \mathbb{E}[y \mid \mathbf{x}]$. This function is uniquely determined by P (see §5.2.5).

8.1.1.2 Parametric versus Nonparametric Classes

In the statistical problems listed above, it is assumed that the unknown distribution belongs to some class $\mathscr{P}$. We call $\mathscr{P}$ a **parametric class** if it can be expressed as

$$\mathscr{P} = \{P_{\boldsymbol{\theta}}\}_{\boldsymbol{\theta} \in \Theta} =: \{P_{\boldsymbol{\theta}} : \boldsymbol{\theta} \in \Theta\} \quad \text{for some } \Theta \subset \mathbb{R}^K$$

In other words, a class of distributions is parametric if it can be indexed by finitely many parameters. A class of distributions is called **nonparametric** if it is not parametric.

Example 8.1.4 Let $\mathscr{P}$ be the set of all univariate normal distributions with positive variance. Equivalently,

$$\mathscr{P} := \left\{\text{all } p \text{ s.t. } p(s) = \frac{1}{\sqrt{2\pi}\sigma} \exp\left\{-\frac{(s-\mu)^2}{2\sigma^2}\right\} \text{ for some } \mu \in \mathbb{R},\ \sigma > 0\right\}$$

The set $\mathscr{P}$ is an example of a parametric class. The parameters are $\boldsymbol{\theta} = (\mu, \sigma)$. A particular choice of the parameters determines (parameterizes) an element of the class.

Example 8.1.5 If the outcome space Z is finite, containing J elements, then every distribution P on Z can be represented by $J-1$ parameters (the probability p_j of each outcome but the last) and hence any family $\mathscr{P}$ of distributions on Z is necessarily a parametric class.

Example 8.1.6 The set of all distributions on $\mathbb{R}$ cannot be parameterized by a finite vector of parameters because the space of distributions is infinite dimensional. Hence $\mathscr{P}$:= all distributions on $\mathbb{R}$ is a nonparametric class.

Example 8.1.7 Let $\mathscr{P}$ be the set of all absolutely continuous distributions on $\mathbb{R}$ with finite second moment:

$$\mathscr{P} := \left\{ \text{all } p\colon \mathbb{R} \to \mathbb{R} \text{ s.t. } p \geqslant 0,\ \int p(s)\,\mathrm{d}s = 1,\ \int s^2 p(s)\,\mathrm{d}s < \infty \right\}$$

This set is nonparametric.

Many traditional methods of inference are parametric in nature: The data are assumed to be generated by an unknown element $P_{\boldsymbol{\theta}}$ of a parametric class $\mathscr{P}$. The aim is to estimate $\boldsymbol{\theta}$ using the data. Once we have an estimate $\hat{\boldsymbol{\theta}}$ of $\boldsymbol{\theta}$, we can plug this estimate back into the parametric class to obtain an estimate $P_{\hat{\boldsymbol{\theta}}}$ of $P_{\boldsymbol{\theta}}$.

The concept of a feature defined in (8.1) is a generalization of the notion of a parameter or vector of parameters. In parametric settings, the feature γ that we are most interested in estimating is the parameter vector $\boldsymbol{\theta}$. If we have a good estimate $\hat{\boldsymbol{\theta}}$ of $\boldsymbol{\theta}$, we can estimate any feature $\gamma = \gamma(P_{\boldsymbol{\theta}})$ via $\hat{\gamma} = \gamma(P_{\hat{\boldsymbol{\theta}}})$.

Following common usage, we will sometimes refer to the $\boldsymbol{\theta}$ associated with the $P_{\boldsymbol{\theta}}$ that generates the data as the **true value** of the parameter vector. However, it's important to remember that this is an assumption, not a "truth." We *assume* that the data are generated by some member of a parametric class. This assumption can be completely false.

In our initial formulation of the estimation problem we considered estimation of features rather than just parameters because it is suboptimal to always restrict ourselves to parametric assumptions on $\mathscr{P}$. We'll discuss the relative merits of parametric and nonparametric estimation more in chapter 14.

8.1.2 Statistics and Estimators

A statistic is any observable function of the data. More precisely, a **statistic** is any $\mathscr{B}$-measurable function

$$T\colon Z_{\mathcal{D}} \to S$$

that can be evaluated once the data $\mathbf{z}_{\mathcal{D}}$ are observed. As in (8.1), the set S is left arbitrary to accommodate all the possible features that we might wish to estimate. Sometimes we write T as T_N to emphasize dependence on the sample size. The assumption that a statistic is $\mathscr{B}$-measurable is just a basic regularity condition.

An **estimator** is a statistic used to infer some feature $\gamma(P)$ of an unknown distribution P. Thus a statistic becomes an estimator when paired with and compared to a feature of the distribution. Note that there is nothing in the definition of an estimator that implies it will be a sensible estimator of the target feature, let alone a good one.

Example 8.1.8 If the feature γ we wish to infer is the mean of the marginal distribution P of IID data $x_1, \ldots, x_N$, then the most common estimator is the **sample mean**

$$\bar{x}_N := \frac{1}{N} \sum_{n=1}^{N} x_n$$

Formally, $\bar{x}_N$ is the mapping from $Z_{\mathcal{D}} = \mathbb{R}^N$ to $S = \mathbb{R}$ defined by

$$\mathbf{z}_{\mathcal{D}} = (x_1, \ldots, x_N) \mapsto T(x_1, \ldots, x_N) = \frac{1}{N} \sum_{n=1}^{N} x_n \in \mathbb{R}$$

This mapping is regarded as an estimator of the unknown mean $\gamma(P) = \int sP(\mathrm{d}s)$.

Example 8.1.9 The sample mean is not the only way to estimate the mean. For example, we could also use the so-called **mid-range estimator**

$$m_N := \frac{\min_n x_n + \max_n x_n}{2}$$

Another option is a **truncated sample mean**, where values x_n with $|x_n| \geqslant r$ are truncated for some specified value of r. The truncated sample mean is often used to estimate location parameters in heavy tailed distributions.

Example 8.1.10 Given sample $x_1, \ldots, x_N$, let y_n be the nth largest observation of the sample. If N is the odd number $2m + 1$, the **sample median** is defined as y_{m+1}. If $N = 2m$, the sample median is $0.5(y_m + y_{m+1})$. For example,

```
julia> median([1, 3, 5])
3.0
julia> median([2, 4, 6, 8])
5.0
```

Example 8.1.11 Following on from example 8.1.8, a common estimator of the kth moment $\int s^k P(\mathrm{d}s)$ of P is the kth **sample moment** $\frac{1}{N}\sum_{n=1}^{N} x_n^k$.

Example 8.1.12 A common estimator of the variance of P is the **sample variance**

$$s_N^2 := \frac{1}{N}\sum_{n=1}^{N}(x_n - \bar{x}_N)^2 \tag{8.2}$$

The standard deviation is usually estimated using **sample standard deviation**

$$s_N := \sqrt{s_N^2} = \left[\frac{1}{N}\sum_{n=1}^{N}(x_n - \bar{x}_N)^2\right]^{1/2} \tag{8.3}$$

In some texts the sample variance is defined as $\frac{1}{N-1}\sum_{n=1}^{N}(x_n - \bar{x}_N)^2$ rather than (8.2) in order to produce an unbiased estimator. However, (8.2) fits better with the theory in this text and is perhaps the more common definition.

Example 8.1.13 Given bivariate data $\mathbf{z}_{\mathcal{D}} = ((x_1, y_1), \ldots, (x_N, y_N))$, the **sample covariance** is the statistic

$$\frac{1}{N}\sum_{n=1}^{N}(x_n - \bar{x}_N)(y_n - \bar{y}_N) \tag{8.4}$$

The **sample correlation** is the sample covariance divided by the product of the two sample standard deviations. With some rearranging, this becomes

$$\frac{\sum_{n=1}^{N}(x_n - \bar{x}_N)(y_n - \bar{y}_N)}{\sqrt{\sum_{n=1}^{N}(x_n - \bar{x}_N)^2 \sum_{n=1}^{N}(y_n - \bar{y}_N)^2}} \tag{8.5}$$

Example 8.1.14 In the case where our observations are vectors $\mathbf{x}_1, \ldots, \mathbf{x}_N$ in $\mathbb{R}^K$, the sample mean is the random vector defined by

$$\bar{\mathbf{x}}_N := \frac{1}{N}\sum_{n=1}^{N}\mathbf{x}_n$$

The variance–covariance matrix defined in (5.16) is most often estimated with the **sample variance–covariance matrix**

$$\hat{\mathbf{\Sigma}}_N := \frac{1}{N}\sum_{n=1}^{N}[(\mathbf{x}_n - \bar{\mathbf{x}}_N)(\mathbf{x}_n - \bar{\mathbf{x}}_N)^{\top}] \tag{8.6}$$

8.1.3 Empirical Distributions

The **empirical distribution** of a given Z-valued sample $\mathbf{z}_{\mathcal{D}} = (\mathbf{z}_1, \ldots, \mathbf{z}_N)$ is the discrete distribution on Z that puts equal probability $1/N$ on each sample point $\mathbf{z}_n$. Another way to state this is that $\hat{P}_N$ assigns to each Borel set $B \subset Z$ the number

$$\hat{P}_N(B) = \frac{1}{N} \sum_{n=1}^{N} \mathbb{1}\{\mathbf{z}_n \in B\} \tag{8.7}$$

This is just the fraction of the sample that falls in B. (Refer back to figure 4.2 on page 84 if you wish to see a visual representation.) The expectation of a function h with respect to $\hat{P}_N$ is

$$\int h(\mathbf{s}) \hat{P}_N(\mathrm{d}\mathbf{s}) = \frac{1}{N} \sum_{n=1}^{N} h(\mathbf{z}_n) \tag{8.8}$$

as follows from (5.14) on page 134.

Example 8.1.15 Let $\mathbf{z}_n$ be the scalar x_n. The sample mean can be expressed in terms of the empirical distribution as

$$\bar{x}_N = \frac{1}{N} \sum_{n=1}^{N} x_n = \int s \hat{P}_N(\mathrm{d}s) \tag{8.9}$$

In other words, the sample mean is the mean of the empirical distribution.

The empirical distribution is a statistic, mapping observations $\mathbf{z}_1, \ldots, \mathbf{z}_N$ into $\hat{P}_N = \frac{1}{N} \sum_{n=1}^{N} \mathbb{1}\{\mathbf{z}_n \in \cdot\}$, a random element of the set of all distributions on Z. If we think of $\mathbf{z}_1, \ldots, \mathbf{z}_N$ as independent draws from common but unknown distribution P, then $\hat{P}_N$ becomes an estimator of P. In particular, if the feature of P we want to infer is P itself, the simplest natural estimator is the empirical distribution.[1]

With scalar data $x_1, \ldots, x_N$ we can visualize the empirical distribution by plotting its CDF. The CDF of $\hat{P}_N$ will be denoted in what follows by $\hat{F}_N$. Specializing B in (8.7) to $(-\infty, s]$, we get

$$\hat{F}_N(s) = \frac{1}{N} \sum_{n=1}^{N} \mathbb{1}\{x_n \leqslant s\} \qquad (s \in \mathbb{R})$$

The CDF $\hat{F}_N$ is called the **empirical cumulative distribution function**, or ECDF, corre-

1. Why not always try to infer P itself? Although it's true that when we know P we can in principle recover any feature $\gamma(P)$, we should also bear in mind the following general principle of inference with limited information: In solving a given problem, try to avoid first solving a more general problem as an intermediate step. Distributions are much more complicated objects than real numbers, so if we care only about the median of a distribution, say, it might be best to try to discover this single value directly rather than trying to infer the entire distribution first.

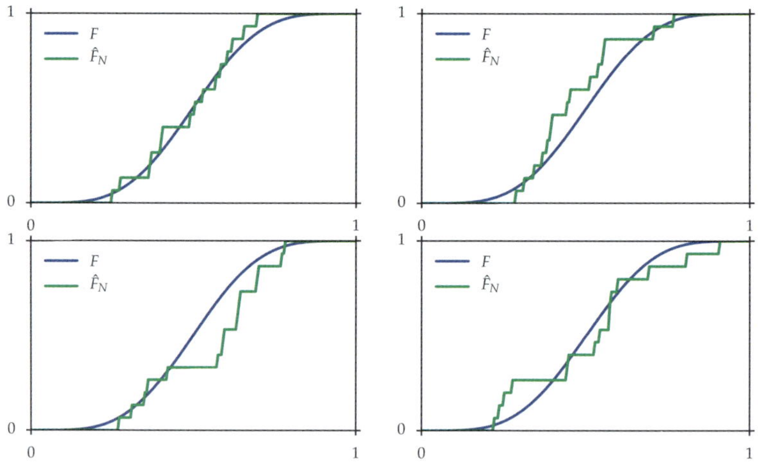

Figure 8.1 F and four observations of $\hat{F}_N$ when $N = 15$

sponding to the sample. Graphically, $\hat{F}_N$ is a step function, with an upward jump of $1/N$ at each data point. Figure 8.1 shows an example where draws are from the CDF F of the Beta$(5, 5)$ distribution. Each panel shows an observation of the ECDF, which is in turn constructed from $N = 15$ observations from F.

8.1.3.1 Convergence

The empirical distribution is asymptotically an excellent estimator of P. If $\mathbf{z}_1, \ldots, \mathbf{z}_N$ are IID with common distribution P and $\hat{P}_N$ is the empirical distribution, then, by the law of large numbers,

$$\hat{P}_N(B) = \frac{1}{N} \sum_{n=1}^{N} \mathbb{1}\{\mathbf{z}_n \in B\} \xrightarrow{p} \mathbb{P}\{\mathbf{z}_n \in B\} = P(B) \tag{8.10}$$

for any Borel set B. See, in particular, (6.8) on page 165.

Specializing to the scalar case with $B := (-\infty, s]$, we have $\hat{F}_N(s) \xrightarrow{p} F(s)$ for any $s \in \mathbb{R}$, where F is the CDF of P. In fact a much stronger statement is also true. It is sometimes called the fundamental theorem of statistics, or the **Glivenko–Cantelli theorem**:

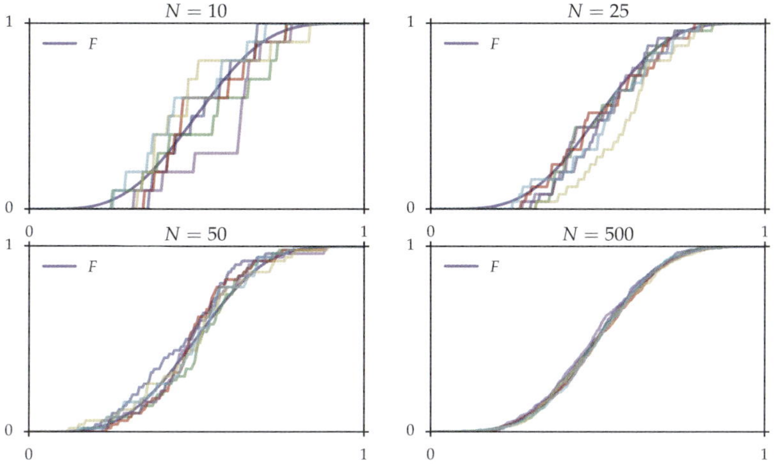

Figure 8.2 Realizations of $\hat{F}_N$ with four different sample sizes

Theorem 8.1.1 *Let $x_1, \ldots, x_N$ be* IID *draws from F. If $\hat{F}_N$ is the corresponding* ECDF, *then*

$$\|F - \hat{F}_N\|_\infty \xrightarrow{p} 0 \quad as \quad N \to \infty \tag{8.11}$$

The norm here is the supremum norm, meaning that

$$\|F - \hat{F}_N\|_\infty := \sup_{s \in \mathbb{R}} |\hat{F}_N(s) - F(s)|$$

Roughly speaking, this is the maximal deviation over the domain. (For a definition of the supremum, see §15.4.1.) In fact the convergence occurs "almost surely," which is a stronger notion than in probability. See theorem 11.4.2 of Dudley (2002).

Figure 8.2 illustrates the convergence in (8.11). Each ECDF $\hat{F}_N$ is based on a single sample $x_1, \ldots, x_N$ of independent draws from F, where F is Beta$(5,5)$. Each subplot shows 8 realizations of the ECDF at a different value of N. Across the subplots, the sample size is stepped up from 10 to 500.

Theorem 8.1.1 tells us that, at least in the IID setting, if we have an infinite amount of data, then in the limit we can learn the underlying distribution without having to impose any assumptions at all. Moreover, once we know the distribution P, we know any feature $\gamma = \gamma(P)$.

Does this offer a solution to the basic problem of estimation stated on page 213? The answer is no. In practice, we only ever have a finite amount of data. Inference is about generalization, as discussed in the introduction. There's no need to generalize if we know the full population.

Moreover, when we still have only finitely many observations, the empirical distribution puts all of its mass on these points. In other words, it treats the sample like the unknown distribution, without acknowledging the fact that we have limited information. This can be viewed as an extreme form of overfitting. We'll discuss related ideas in a number of contexts throughout the book.

8.1.3.2 Identification

A class of distributions $\mathscr{P} = \{P_{\boldsymbol{\theta}}\}$ indexed by $\boldsymbol{\theta} \in \Theta$ is called **identifiable** if the map $\boldsymbol{\theta} \mapsto P_{\boldsymbol{\theta}}$ is one-to-one (see §15.2) on Θ.

Example 8.1.16 The class of normal densities in example 8.1.4 is identifiable. In particular, it can be shown that if (μ_a, σ_a) and (μ_b, σ_b) are distinct vectors, then the distributions $\mathrm{N}(\mu_a, \sigma_a^2)$ and $\mathrm{N}(\mu_b, \sigma_b^2)$ differ at at least one point.

Identifiability means that the parameter vector associated with the unknown distribution can eventually be distinguished from the data. To see this, suppose that $\{P_{\boldsymbol{\theta}}\}$ is identified on Θ and nature generates an infinite sequence of observations $\{\mathbf{z}_n\}$ from $P = P_{\boldsymbol{\theta}}$. Let $\boldsymbol{\theta}'$ be any other vector in Θ and let $P' = P_{\boldsymbol{\theta}'}$. By identifiability, there exists at least one Borel set B with $P(B) \neq P'(B)$. Since the empirical distribution $\hat{P}_N(B)$ converges to $P(B)$, we can in the limit conclude that the data are not generated by P'.

8.2 Estimation Principles

We started off with the problem of estimating a feature $\gamma = \gamma(P)$ of the unknown distribution P from a sample. We've introduced a number of different statistics aimed at estimating various features. Where do these estimators come from and what, if anything, do they have in common?

8.2.1 The Sample Analogue Principle

Most of the estimators defined above can be derived from a simple principle. In the modern statistical literature this is often called the **plug-in method**. In econometrics it goes by a variety of names, including "analogue estimation" (see, in particular, Manski 1986). We'll call it the **sample analogue principle**. The principle is:

$$\text{to estimate } \gamma(P), \quad \text{use } \gamma(\hat{P}_N)$$

Here $\hat{P}_N$ is the empirical distribution constructed from the sample. We replace the unknown distribution P with the observable distribution $\hat{P}_N$ and then evaluate $\gamma(\hat{P}_N)$.

Example 8.2.1 Let $x_1, \ldots, x_N$ be draws from unknown distribution P. Suppose we want to estimate the mean $\gamma(P) := \int sP(\mathrm{d}s)$. The sample analogue principle tells us to replace P with $\hat{P}_N$, which gives

$$\gamma(\hat{P}_N) = \int s\hat{P}_N(\mathrm{d}s) = \bar{x}_N$$

(The last equality is just (8.9).) Thus the sample mean is the estimator of the mean produced by the sample analogue principle.

The kth sample moment applies the same principle to estimate the kth moment.

Example 8.2.2 When it exists, the variance of P can be written as

$$\sigma^2 = \gamma(P) = \int \left[t - \int sP(\mathrm{d}s)\right]^2 P(\mathrm{d}t)$$

Applying the sample analogue principle leads to the estimator

$$\int \left[t - \int s\hat{P}_N(\mathrm{d}s)\right]^2 \hat{P}_N(\mathrm{d}t) = \frac{1}{N}\sum_{n=1}^{N}(x_n - \bar{x}_N)^2$$

This is precisely the sample variance from example 8.1.12.

The estimators in these two examples are relatively straightforward, but the set of all applications of the sample analogue principle is very broad. As we'll see below, estimation methods that can be obtained as special cases include least squares regression, maximum likelihood, the method of moments, and the generalized method of moments.

8.2.1.1 Best Linear Prediction

Here's an example that illustrates the generality of the sample analogue principle. Recall the best linear prediction problem from §4.1.5.1, where α and β are chosen to minimize $\mathbb{E}\,[(y - \alpha - \beta x)^2]$. Letting P be the distribution of (x, y), we can write the problem as

$$(\alpha^*, \beta^*) = \gamma(P) := \operatorname*{argmin}_{\alpha,\beta\in\mathbb{R}} \int [(t - \alpha - \beta s)^2] P(\mathrm{d}s, \mathrm{d}t) \tag{8.12}$$

There is a corresponding statistical problem when the underlying distribution P is unknown. The problem is to produce the best linear predictor based only on a sample

$\mathbf{z}_{\mathcal{D}} = ((x_1, y_1), \ldots, (x_N, y_N))$ of observations from P. We proceed as follows: Given $\mathbf{z}_{\mathcal{D}}$, we form the empirical distribution

$$\hat{P}_N(B) = \frac{1}{N} \sum_{n=1}^{N} \mathbb{1}\{(x_n, y_n) \in B\}$$

Applying the sample analogue principle, we plug $\hat{P}_N$ into (8.12), yielding the estimator

$$(\hat{\alpha}_N, \hat{\beta}_N) = \gamma(\hat{P}_N) = \operatorname*{argmin}_{\alpha, \beta \in \mathbb{R}} \sum_{n=1}^{N} [(y_n - \alpha - \beta x_n)^2] \tag{8.13}$$

(The term $\frac{1}{N}$ has been dropped from the right-hand side of (8.13) because it doesn't affect the minimizers.) This is the simple linear bivariate least squares problem. The minimizers are

$$\hat{\beta}_N = \frac{\sum_{n=1}^{N}(x_n - \bar{x}_N)(y_n - \bar{y}_N)}{\sum_{n=1}^{N}(x_n - \bar{x}_N)^2} \quad \text{and} \quad \hat{\alpha}_N = \bar{y}_N - \hat{\beta}_N \bar{x}_N \tag{8.14}$$

(See ex. 8.5.2.) Comparing with (4.23) on page 99, we see that these estimators are themselves the sample analogues of the underlying features α^* and β^*.

8.2.1.2 Limitations

While the sample analogue principle produces sensible estimators in many situations, there are also instances where it fails completely. Let's look at one example.

Let $\mathscr{P}$ be the set of absolutely continuous distributions on $\mathbb{R}$, so that the distribution P generating the data is assumed to have a density. The density of P can be regarded as the feature

$$\gamma(P) = DP \tag{8.15}$$

Here $DP :=$ the derivative of the CDF F of P.

Let $\hat{P}_N$ be the empirical distribution from any given sample. What happens when we plug this empirical distribution into the right-hand side of (8.15)? In other words, what information do we get when we differentiate the function $\hat{F}_N$? Since $\hat{F}_N$ is a step function, the derivative is zero everywhere, except at a finite number of jump points where the derivative is undefined. Thus the density estimate produced by the sample analogue principle is useless. This statement remains true even when N is enormous.

One way to understand this outcome is that when we wish to estimate complex objects with finite samples, we need to combine the data with some kind of **regularization**. Loosely speaking, this means that we penalize complexity in our search for a solution, or impose some kind of "smoothing" a priori. This idea has a long history in the field of numerical methods, where certain inverse problems are unstable, or "ill-posed," and their solution requires regularization.

Regularization is an essential element of statistics too. It says that we should not grant the empirical distribution equal status with the unknown true distribution. That is, we should regard the empirical distribution only as partial information, and seek to combine it with some form of prior information or external theory. Regularization is one application of prior information: It applies the idea that probability mass most likely falls in places other than just the sample points observed so far. We pick up the topic of regularization again in chapter 14.

8.2.2 Empirical Risk Minimization

Let's now look at another inductive principle that combines the sample analogue principle with additional structure. The principle is called empirical risk minimization, or ERM. The terminology and main concepts come from the machine learning literature. Nonetheless, many standard estimators in econometrics are special cases of ERM, including maximum likelihood and least squares. The ideas discussed here help to frame these tools as part of a broader set of methods.

Consider a setting where we observe an input $\mathbf{x} \in \mathbb{R}^K$ to a system, followed by a scalar output y. Both are random variables and the joint distribution of $\mathbf{z} := (\mathbf{x}, y)$ is P. Our aim is to predict new output values from observed input values. We'll do this by choosing a function f such that $f(\mathbf{x})$ is our prediction of y once $\mathbf{x}$ is observed. In the machine learning literature, f is called a **prediction rule**. In economics, f is called a **strategy** or **policy function**.

Incorrect prediction incurs a loss. The size of this loss is written as $L(y, f(\mathbf{x}))$. The function L is called the **loss function**. Common choices for the loss function include

- the **quadratic loss function** $L(y, f(\mathbf{x})) = (y - f(\mathbf{x}))^2$,
- the **absolute deviation loss function** $L(y, f(\mathbf{x})) = |y - f(\mathbf{x})|$, and
- the **discrete loss function** $L(y, f(\mathbf{x})) = \mathbb{1}\{y \neq f(\mathbf{x})\}$.

Given loss function L, we consider choosing f so as to minimize the **prediction risk**, which is defined as the expected loss

$$R(f) := \mathbb{E}\, L(y, f(\mathbf{x})) \tag{8.16}$$

Sometimes $R(f)$ is also called the expected prediction error.[2] The expectation in (8.16) is computed using the joint distribution P of $(\mathbf{x}, y)$. Sometimes we'll write $\mathbb{E}_P\, L(y, f(\mathbf{x}))$ to emphasize this.

2. See, for example, §2.4 of Friedman et al. (2009).

Example 8.2.3 Let L be the quadratic loss function. As shown in §5.2.5, the minimizer of (8.16) is the regression function, defined at $\mathbf{x}$ by $f^*(\mathbf{x}) = \mathbb{E}[y \,|\, \mathbf{x}]$. In particular, from (5.39) on page 152, for any alternative policy g we have

$$R(g) = R(f^*) + \mathbb{E}[(f^*(\mathbf{x}) - g(\mathbf{x}))^2] \tag{8.17}$$

In other words, with quadratic loss, good prediction equates to choosing g to be close to the regression function, thereby minimizing the second term on the right-hand side of (8.17). In view of (8.17), the term $R(f^*)$ represents a lower bound for prediction risk.

In a statistical setting we are constrained in our ability to minimize risk by the fact that we cannot evaluate $\mathbb{E}_P$, as this requires knowledge of the joint distribution P. Suppose, however, that we have access to data $\mathbf{z}_1, \ldots, \mathbf{z}_N$, where each pair $\mathbf{z}_n = (\mathbf{x}_n, y_n)$ is an independent draw from P. To make use of the sample, we will apply the sample analogue principle, replacing P in (8.16) with the empirical distribution $\hat{P}_N$. This produces the new objective function

$$R_{\text{emp}}(f) := \mathbb{E}_{\hat{P}_N} L(y, f(\mathbf{x})) = \frac{1}{N} \sum_{n=1}^{N} L(y_n, f(\mathbf{x}_n)) \tag{8.18}$$

This function is called the **empirical risk**. The empirical risk is the prediction risk evaluated under the empirical distribution of the sample rather than the true distribution P. Minimizing the empirical risk is called **empirical risk minimization** (ERM).

There is an additional step. When we choose a decision rule the problem that we actually solve is

$$\hat{f} = \operatorname*{argmin}_{f \in \mathcal{H}} R_{\text{emp}}(f) \tag{8.19}$$

We have restricted the domain to a class of functions $\mathcal{H}$. This set of functions is called the **hypothesis space**. Choice of $\mathcal{H}$ is structure we impose on the estimation problem.

It might seem at first pass that we should set $\mathcal{H}$ to be the set of all functions $f \colon \mathbb{R}^K \to \mathbb{R}$. After all, if the risk-minimizing function $f^* := \operatorname{argmin}_f R(f)$ is not in $\mathcal{H}$, as visualized in figure 8.3, then the solution to (8.19) is not equal to f^*, and we are making a suboptimal choice.

Actually this reasoning is false. In fact we usually want to be quite restrictive in our choice of $\mathcal{H}$. This is because minimizing the empirical risk is not the same as minimizing the prediction risk. Occam's razor comes in to play here: we are solving a complex problem on the basis of limited information. It would be a serious mistake to act as if we had unlimited information. These ideas are explored further in §8.2.3.

Example 8.2.4 Specializing to scalar x and quadratic loss function $L(y, f(x)) = (y -$

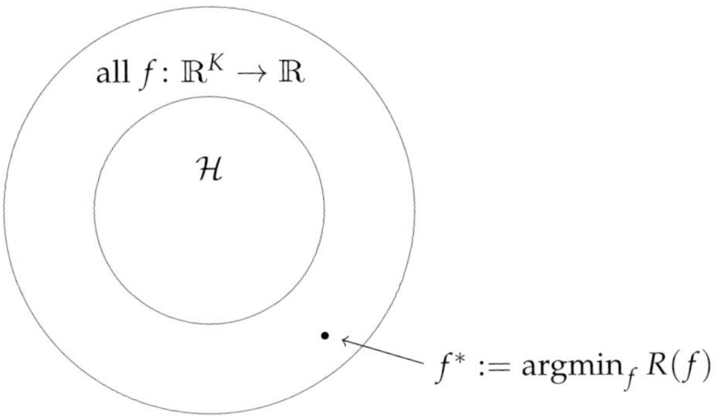

Figure 8.3 Choosing the hypothesis space

$f(x))^2$, and observing that the term $\frac{1}{N}$ makes no difference to the solution, the ERM problem becomes

$$\min_{f \in \mathcal{H}} \sum_{n=1}^{N} (y_n - f(x_n))^2 \tag{8.20}$$

For obvious reasons, this optimization problem is called the **least squares problem**. If we specialize $\mathcal{H}$ to be the set of affine functions

$$\mathcal{H}_\ell := \{ \text{ all functions of the form } \ell(x) = \alpha + \beta x\} \tag{8.21}$$

then the problem reduces to the **simple linear least squares problem**

$$\min_{\ell \in \mathcal{H}_\ell} \sum_{n=1}^{N} (y_n - \ell(x_n))^2 = \min_{\alpha, \beta} \sum_{n=1}^{N} (y_n - \alpha - \beta x_n)^2 \tag{8.22}$$

This is exactly the same minimization problem we obtained in (8.13). The solutions are given in (8.14).

While we ended up with the same minimization problem in two different ways, the reasoning here is more natural. When we first came to this problem in (8.13) it was by applying the sample analogue principle to the problem of finding best linear predictors. Here we are simply trying to find the best predictor. At the same time we have restricted ourselves to linear approximations in recognition of the fact that we are basing our estimate on limited information. Linearity implements Occam's razor by bounding the complexity of the learning algorithm.

8.2.2.1 Quantile Regression

Quantile regression is used when we want to estimate a quantile of a given distribution based on a set of predictive variables. For example, quantile regression has been used to estimate quantiles of CEO compensation as a function of the market value of their firms (Koenker and Hallock 2001). In this section we show how quantile regression can be regarded as a special case of empirical risk minimization.

To describe the idea, let F be a strictly increasing CDF on $\mathbb{R}$ and let $\tau \in (0,1)$ be given. Recall from §4.2.6 that the τth quantile of F is the ξ that solves $F(\xi) = \tau$. Although it might not be immediately obvious, the τth quantile can also be defined as the solution to the optimization problem

$$\min_{\xi \in \mathbb{R}} \mathbb{E} L_\tau(y, \xi) \tag{8.23}$$

where y is a random variable with distribution F and

$$L_\tau(y, \xi) := |(y - \xi)(\tau - \mathbb{1}\{y < \xi\})|$$

Exercise 8.5.6 asks you to confirm that the solution to (8.23) is precisely the ξ that solves $F(\xi) = \tau$.

Suppose now that we want to estimate the τth quantile of F using some input variable x (e.g., a CEO compensation quantile as a function of firm size). Motivated by (8.23), we can frame the search for a suitable function as a problem of minimizing the prediction risk

$$R(f) := \mathbb{E} L_\tau(y, f(x)) \tag{8.24}$$

where L_τ is as defined above. If we employ the principle of empirical risk minimization with data set $(x_1, y_1), \ldots, (x_N, y_N)$, we get $\min_{f \in \mathcal{H}} \sum_{n=1}^N L_\tau(y_n, f(x_n))$, where $\mathcal{H}$ is the hypothesis space. When $\mathcal{H} = \mathcal{H}_\ell$ as defined in (8.21), the ERM problem is

$$\min_{\alpha, \beta} \sum_{n=1}^N |(y_n - \alpha - \beta x_n)(\tau - \mathbb{1}\{y_n < \alpha + \beta x_n\})|$$

This is the standard expression for the quantile regression problem.

If $\tau = 0.5$, then the objective function is proportional to $\sum_{n=1}^N |y_n - \alpha - \beta x_n|$. This case is called **median regression** or **least absolute deviation regression**.

8.2.3 The Choice of Hypothesis Space

Let's return to the issue of choosing the hypothesis space. We begin with a straightforward result:

Fact 8.2.1 Let $\mathcal{H}_1$ and $\mathcal{H}_2$ be two hypothesis spaces. If $\hat{f}_i$ is the empirical risk minimizer over $\mathcal{H}_i$ as defined in (8.19), then

$$\mathcal{H}_1 \subset \mathcal{H}_2 \implies R_{\text{emp}}(\hat{f}_1) \geqslant R_{\text{emp}}(\hat{f}_2)$$

In other words, we can always decrease empirical risk by increasing the hypothesis space. The reason that fact 8.2.1 holds is that we are minimizing over a larger set.

At the same time, our actual objective is to minimize the prediction risk. The prediction risk of a given predictor f measures the **out-of-sample fit** of f, which is the expected performance of f when confronted with new data. A statistical procedure that takes a given data set and produces a predictor f with low prediction risk (relative to the benchmark f^*—see (8.17)) means that we have succeeded in meeting the goal we set at the start of the book: we have *generalized* from data.

Of course, prediction risk is unobservable. Sometimes it is tempting to use empirical risk $R_{\text{emp}}(f)$ as an estimator of $R(f)$. However, empirical risk, which measures **in-sample fit** of f, is a downward biased estimator of risk. In particular, as we vary the hypothesis space, prediction risk can rise even when empirical risk is falling.

Let's illustrate this by way of an example, where empirical risk is minimized over progressively larger hypothesis spaces. The model we will consider is one that generates input-output pairs via

$$x \sim U[-1,1] \quad \text{and then} \quad y = \cos(\pi x) + u \quad \text{where} \quad u \sim N(0,1) \tag{8.25}$$

Here $U[-1,1]$ is the uniform distribution on the interval $[-1,1]$. Our hypothesis spaces for predicting y from x will be sets of polynomial functions. To fix notation, let $\mathscr{P}_d$ be the set of all polynomials of degree d. That is,

$$\mathscr{P}_d := \{ \text{ all functions } f_d(x) = c_0 x^0 + c_1 x^1 + \cdots c_d x^d \text{ where each } c_i \in \mathbb{R}\}$$

This sequence of hypothesis spaces is increasing, in the sense that

$$\mathscr{P}_1 \subset \mathscr{P}_2 \subset \mathscr{P}_3 \subset \cdots$$

Indeed, if f is a polynomial of degree d, then f can be represented as a polynomial of degree $d+1$ just by setting the last coefficient c_{d+1} to zero. The set of linear functions $\mathcal{H}_\ell$ defined in (8.21) is equal to $\mathscr{P}_1$.

If we seek to predict y from x using quadratic loss and the set $\mathscr{P}_d$ as our candidate functions, the risk minimization problem is

$$\min_{f \in \mathscr{P}_d} R(f) \quad \text{where} \quad R(f) = \mathbb{E}[(y - f(x))^2] \tag{8.26}$$

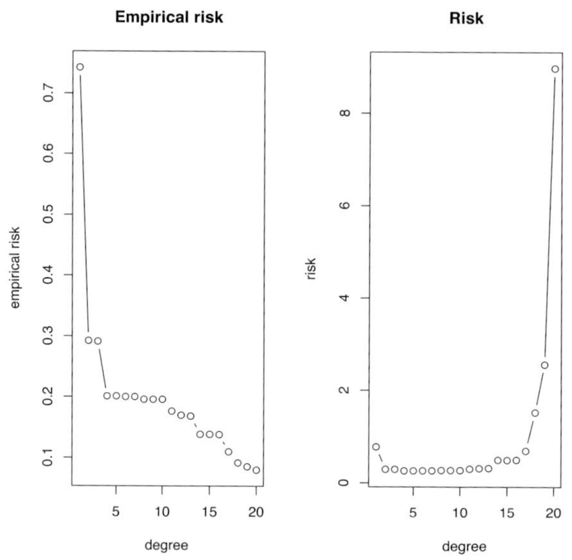

Figure 8.4 Risk and empirical risk as a function of d

while the empirical risk minimization problem is

$$\min_{f \in \mathscr{P}_d} R_{\text{emp}}(f) \quad \text{where} \quad R_{\text{emp}}(f) = \frac{1}{N} \sum_{n=1}^{N} (y_n - f(x_n))^2 \tag{8.27}$$

To illustrate the difference between risk and empirical risk, we first generate $N = 25$ data points from the model (8.25). Taking this as our data set, we then solve (8.27) repeatedly, once for each d in $1, 2, \ldots, 20$. The solution to the dth minimization problem is denoted $\hat{f}_d$, and is, by construction, a polynomial of degree d. Finally, we compare the risk $R(\hat{f}_d)$ and empirical risk $R_{\text{emp}}(\hat{f}_d)$.[3] The results are in figure 8.4.

As expected, empirical risk falls monotonically with d. But the risk decreases slightly and then increases rapidly. For large d, the minimizer $\hat{f}_d$ of the empirical risk is associated with very high risk in the sense of large expected loss.

We can get a sense for what is happening by plotting the data and the functions. In figures 8.5–8.8, the N data points are plotted alongside the function $y = \cos(\pi x)$ from the true model (8.25) in black, and fitted polynomial $\hat{f}_d$ in red. The function

3. The risk $R(\hat{f}_d)$ is evaluated by substituting $\hat{f}_d$ into the expression for R in (8.26). You can find the code at johnstachurski.net/emet.html.

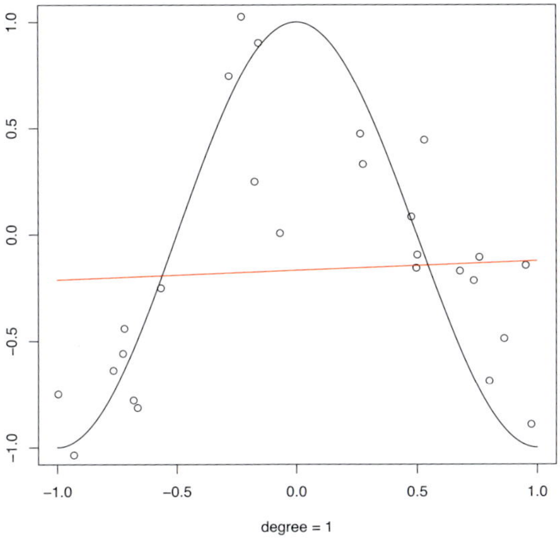

Figure 8.5 Fitted polynomial, $d = 1$

$y = \cos(\pi x)$ is the risk minimizer, and represents the ideal prediction function. In figure 8.5 we have $d = 1$, and the fitted polynomial $\hat{f}_1$ is the linear regression line. In figures 8.6, 8.7 and 8.8 we have $d = 3$, $d = 11$ and $d = 14$ respectively. The fitted polynomials are $\hat{f}_3$, $\hat{f}_{11}$ and $\hat{f}_{14}$.

On the one hand, when $d = 1$, the hypothesis space $\mathscr{P}_d = \mathscr{P}_1$ is small and no function in this class can effectively fit the underlying model. This is called **underfitting**, and is reflected in the poor fit of the red line to the black line in figure 8.5.

When $d = 3$, the class of functions $\mathscr{P}_d = \mathscr{P}_3$ is considerably larger. Given that the data are relatively noisy, and that we only have 25 observations, the fit of the function is good (figure 8.6). If we look at the risk for $d = 3$ on the right-hand side of figure 8.4, we see that it is lower than for $d = 1$.

On the other hand, if we take d larger, the fit to the underlying model becomes poor and the risk is high. Examining figures 8.7 and 8.8, which correspond to $d = 11$ and $d = 14$, we see that the fitted polynomial has been able to fit the observed data closely, passing near many of the data points. Too much emphasis has been given to this particular realization of the data. When a new input x is drawn, the prediction $\hat{f}_d(x)$ is likely to be a poor predictor of y. This situation is called **overfitting**.

To summarize, the choice of $\mathcal{H}$ is central to our ability to generalize from the data. When $\mathcal{H}$ is too small, no function in $\mathcal{H}$ provides a good fit to the regression function.

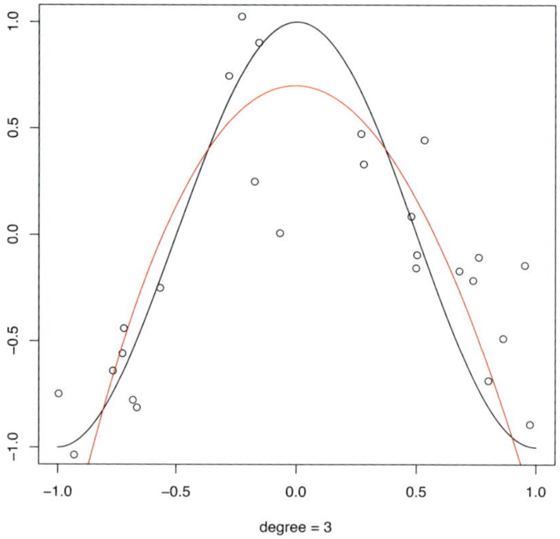

Figure 8.6 Fitted polynomial, $d = 3$

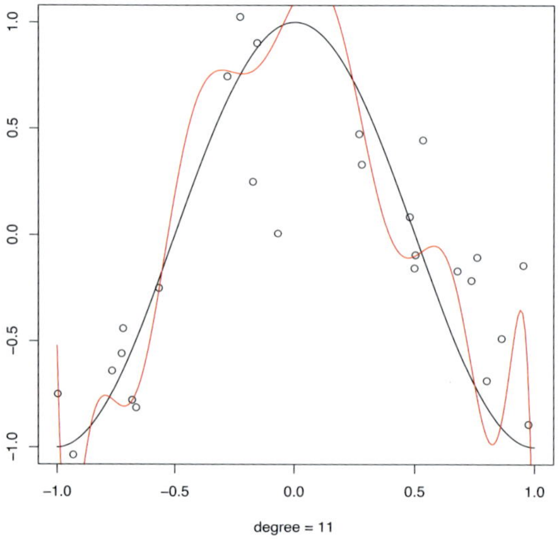

Figure 8.7 Fitted polynomial, $d = 11$

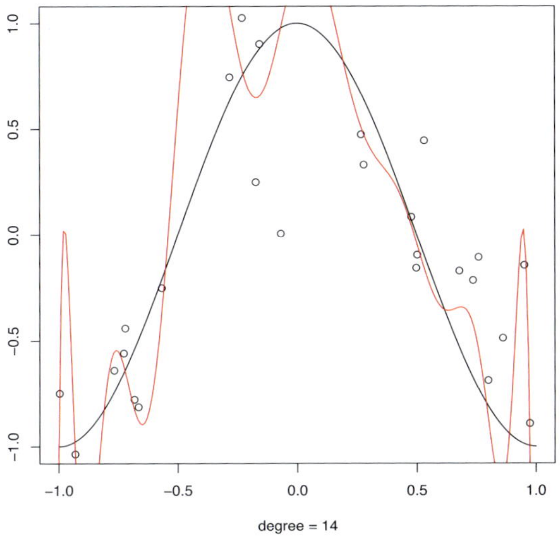

Figure 8.8 Fitted polynomial, $d = 14$

If this is so, the prediction risk cannot be made small regardless of the data. This can be seen directly from (8.17). Any estimate $\hat{f}$ in $\mathcal{H}$ must satisfy

$$R(\hat{f}) \geqslant R(f^*) + \min_{f \in \mathcal{H}} \mathbb{E}\left[(f^*(\mathbf{x}) - f(\mathbf{x}))^2\right]$$

Conversely, if $\mathcal{H}$ is too large, then we can attain low empirical risk but the prediction risk itself is large.

Of course, in statistical applications we do not have the luxury of knowing the true data-generating process when we choose $\mathcal{H}$. The best scenario is that we have firm theory that guides us to a suitable hypothesis space. The worst scenario is that we have no idea and choose blindly. Once again, the message is that statistical learning equals prior knowledge plus data.

8.3 Some Parametric Methods

In this section we review some standard parametric estimation methods, including maximum likelihood, Bayesian estimation, and the generalized method of moments.

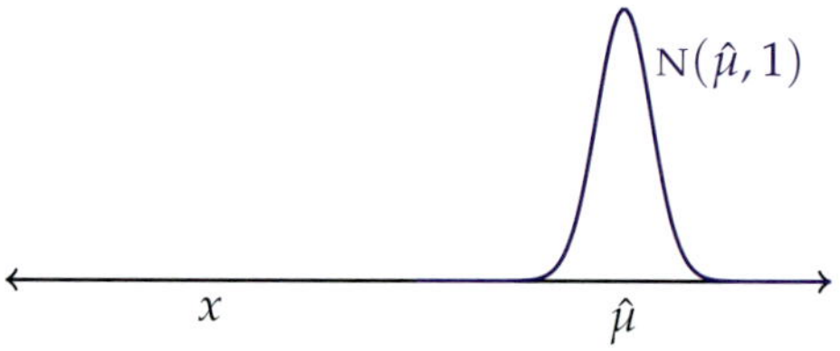

Figure 8.9 Maximizing the likelihood

8.3.1 Maximum Likelihood

One standard approach to deriving estimators in a parametric setting is the **principle of maximum likelihood**. Let's begin with a simple case and then progress to more complex applications.

Suppose that we observe a single draw x from distribution $\mathrm{N}(\mu, 1)$ where μ is unknown. The variance is known and set to 1 for simplicity. Our task is to guess the value of μ given the observation x. A guess $\hat{\mu}$ of μ also pins down the distribution $\mathrm{N}(\hat{\mu}, 1)$, so we could equivalently state that our job is to guess the distribution that generated x. In guessing this distribution, if we centered it around some number $\hat{\mu}$ much larger than x, say, then our observed data point x would be an "unlikely" outcome for this distribution. See figure 8.9. The same logic would apply if we centered the density at a point much smaller than x.[4]

In fact, in the absence of any additional information, the most obvious guess would be that the normal density is centered on x. To center the density on x, we just set $\hat{\mu} = x$.

Maximum likelihood formalizes these steps: The density of x is the density $p(s; \mu)$ of the distribution $\mathrm{N}(\mu, 1)$. Plugging the observed value x into this density gives

$$p(x; \mu) = (2\pi)^{-1/2} \exp\left\{-\frac{(x-\mu)^2}{2}\right\}$$

Think of $p(x; \mu)$ as representing the probability of realizing our sample point x. The principle of maximum likelihood suggests that we take as our guess $\hat{\mu}$ of μ the value that maximizes this probability. It's not hard to show that $\hat{\mu} = x$ is the maximizer. This coincides with our intuition from figure 8.9.

The same principle applies when the data are independent draws $x_1, \ldots, x_N$ from $\mathrm{N}(\mu, 1)$, where μ is unknown. The joint density of the sample is the product of the

4. The scare quotes on "unlikely" are just a reminder that our distribution is absolutely continuous and hence all individual outcomes $s \in \mathbb{R}$ have probability zero. When we say that an outcome x is unlikely, we mean that there is little probability mass in the neighborhood of x.

marginals. Plugging the sample values into the joint density, one then maximizes the joint density with respect to μ:

$$\hat{\mu} := \operatorname*{argmax}_{\mu \in \mathbb{R}} \frac{1}{(2\pi)^{N/2}} \prod_{n=1}^{N} \exp\left\{ -\frac{(x_n - \mu)^2}{2} \right\} \tag{8.28}$$

The maximizer $\hat{\mu}$ is precisely the sample mean of $x_1, \ldots, x_N$ (see ex. 8.5.4).

We can generalize these ideas in several ways. Let's suppose now that the data $x_1, \ldots, x_N$ has joint density p in the sense of (5.8) on page 132. We will assume that $p = p(\cdot\,; \boldsymbol{\theta})$ is a member of a parametric class $\mathscr{P}$ indexed by parameter vector $\boldsymbol{\theta} \in \Theta$. Each choice of $\boldsymbol{\theta}$ pins down a particular density $p = p(\cdot\,; \boldsymbol{\theta})$, but the value of $\boldsymbol{\theta}$ that generated the data is unknown.

In this setting, the **likelihood function** is p evaluated at the sample $x_1, \ldots, x_N$, and regarded as a function of $\boldsymbol{\theta}$:

$$L(\boldsymbol{\theta}) := p(x_1, \ldots, x_N; \boldsymbol{\theta}) \qquad (\boldsymbol{\theta} \in \Theta) \tag{8.29}$$

The principle of maximum likelihood tells us to estimate $\boldsymbol{\theta}$ by maximizing $L(\boldsymbol{\theta})$ over $\boldsymbol{\theta} \in \Theta$. A statistic $\hat{\boldsymbol{\theta}}$ is called a **maximum likelihood estimate** (MLE) of $\boldsymbol{\theta}$ if

$$\hat{\boldsymbol{\theta}} \in \operatorname*{argmax}_{\boldsymbol{\theta} \in \Theta} L(\boldsymbol{\theta}) \tag{8.30}$$

This is equivalent to maximizing the **log likelihood function**

$$\ell(\boldsymbol{\theta}) := \ln(L(\boldsymbol{\theta})) \qquad (\boldsymbol{\theta} \in \Theta)$$

The set of MLEs can in general be a singleton, contain multiple elements or be empty.

In the preceding discussion, p was a density function, but it can be a probability mass function as well. Examples are given below.

To implement maximum likelihood estimation, we need to compute the joint distribution of the data. As we saw in (8.28), when the data points are independent this is easy because the joint density p is the product of the marginals. More generally, if each x_n is drawn independently from fixed arbitrary (marginal) density $p_n(\cdot\,; \boldsymbol{\theta})$ on $\mathbb{R}$, then

$$L(\boldsymbol{\theta}) = \prod_{n=1}^{N} p_n(x_n; \boldsymbol{\theta}) \quad \text{and} \quad \ell(\boldsymbol{\theta}) = \sum_{n=1}^{N} \ln p_n(x_n; \boldsymbol{\theta}) \tag{8.31}$$

If each data point is multivariate, just replace x_n with $\mathbf{x}_n$.

Example 8.3.1 Suppose that $x_1, \ldots, x_N$ are IID draws from a normal distribution $\mathrm{N}(\mu, v)$

with $\boldsymbol{\theta} = (\mu, v)$ unknown. The log likelihood function is

$$\ell(\mu, v) = -\frac{N}{2} \ln(2\pi v) - \frac{1}{2} \sum_{n=1}^{N} \frac{(x_n - \mu)^2}{v} \tag{8.32}$$

Joint maximization over (μ, v) gives the maximum likelihood estimators

$$\hat{\mu} = \frac{1}{N} \sum_{n=1}^{N} x_n \quad \text{and} \quad \hat{v} = \frac{1}{N} \sum_{n=1}^{N} (x_n - \bar{x}_N)^2 \tag{8.33}$$

Thus, the MLEs of μ and v are the sample mean and sample variance respectively.

Maximum likelihood estimation is a much celebrated theory of estimation. MLE estimators typically have excellent asymptotic properties. But good finite sample properties are not guaranteed (more about this soon) and the attractive asymptotic theory is dependent on correct specification of the underlying parametric class. Indeed we need to bring a lot of knowledge to the table just to form the estimator. (To specify the likelihood function, we must specify the entire joint distribution of the sample.)

Example 8.3.2 Let $x_1, \ldots, x_N$ be IID observations from some unknown density on $\mathbb{R}$. If the class of candidate distributions is too large, maximum likelihood estimation will fail. For example, there is no solution to the problem

$$\max_p \prod_{n=1}^{N} p(x_n)$$

where the maximization is over all densities. We can make this expression arbitrarily large by choosing p to concentrate its mass in small neighborhoods around each sample point. The limit of this process is not a density.

8.3.1.1 Conditional Maximum Likelihood

As in §8.2.2, suppose that we observe inputs $\mathbf{x}_1, \ldots, \mathbf{x}_N$ to some system and corresponding outputs $y_1, \ldots, y_N$. The pairs $(\mathbf{x}_n, y_n)$ are assumed to be IID. Our aim is to estimate $\boldsymbol{\theta}$ in $p(y \,|\, \mathbf{x}; \boldsymbol{\theta})$ in order to pin down the conditional density of y given $\mathbf{x}$.

The principle of maximum likelihood tells us to maximize

$$\ell(\boldsymbol{\theta}) = \sum_{n=1}^{N} \ln p(\mathbf{x}_n, y_n; \boldsymbol{\theta}) \quad \text{where} \quad p := \text{ the joint density of } (\mathbf{x}_n, y_n)$$

Letting π be the marginal density of $\mathbf{x}$, we can use the decomposition (5.27) on page 142 to write

$$p(\mathbf{x}, y; \boldsymbol{\theta}) = p(y \mid \mathbf{x}; \boldsymbol{\theta}) \, \pi(\mathbf{x})$$

The density π is unknown but we have not parameterized it because we aren't trying to estimate it. We can now rewrite the log likelihood as

$$\ell(\boldsymbol{\theta}) = \sum_{n=1}^{N} \ln p(y_n \mid \mathbf{x}_n; \boldsymbol{\theta}) + \sum_{n=1}^{N} \ln \pi(\mathbf{x}_n)$$

The second term on the right-hand side is independent of $\boldsymbol{\theta}$ and as such it does not affect the maximizer. Hence the MLE is

$$\operatorname*{argmax}_{\boldsymbol{\theta} \in \Theta} \sum_{n=1}^{N} \ln p(y_n \mid \mathbf{x}_n; \boldsymbol{\theta})$$

The objective function here is called the **conditional log likelihood**. The preceding argument tells us that, when we want to estimate parameters in the conditional density of y given $\mathbf{x}$, we can maximize the conditional log likelihood directly, which is simpler and more direct than maximizing the full log likelihood.

Example 8.3.3 Consider a discrete response model with binary output y_n, where $y_n = 1$ indicates that the nth individual in a sample of women participates in the labor force. This decision is influenced by a vector $\mathbf{x}_n$ measuring characteristics such as income from the rest of the household. Let

$$q(\mathbf{s}) := \mathbb{P}\{y = 1 \mid \mathbf{x} = \mathbf{s}\} \qquad \left(\mathbf{s} \in \mathbb{R}^K\right)$$

One modeling approach is to take $q(\mathbf{s}) = F(\boldsymbol{\beta}^\top \mathbf{s})$, where $\boldsymbol{\beta}$ is a vector of parameters and F is a specified CDF. We can then write

$$\mathbb{P}\{y = i \mid \mathbf{x} = \mathbf{s}\} = F(\boldsymbol{\beta}^\top \mathbf{s})^i (1 - F(\boldsymbol{\beta}^\top \mathbf{s}))^{1-i} \quad \text{for } \mathbf{s} \in \mathbb{R}^K \text{ and } i \in \{0, 1\}$$

This is the conditional PMF of y given $\mathbf{x}$, so the conditional log likelihood of the sample is

$$\begin{aligned} \ell(\boldsymbol{\beta}) &= \sum_{n=1}^{N} \ln[F(\boldsymbol{\beta}^\top \mathbf{x}_n)^{y_n} (1 - F(\boldsymbol{\beta}^\top \mathbf{x}_n))^{1-y_n}] \\ &= \sum_{n=1}^{N} y_n \ln F(\boldsymbol{\beta}^\top \mathbf{x}_n) + \sum_{n=1}^{N} (1 - y_n) \ln(1 - F(\boldsymbol{\beta}^\top \mathbf{x}_n)) \end{aligned}$$

If F is the standard normal CDF Φ, then this model is called the **probit** model. If F is the logistic CDF $F(\mathbf{s}) = 1/(1+e^{-s})$, then it is called the **logit** model.

To find the MLE in this example, we can differentiate ℓ to obtain first order conditions, but this does not in general lead to an analytical solution. Instead, numerical optimization of the likelihood is required. Discussion of numerical optimization is given in §13.2.2.

8.3.2 Maximum Likelihood via ERM

Maximum likelihood is a special case of empirical risk minimization. To see this, suppose that we wish to learn unknown density q on the basis of observations from q. We take our loss function to be

$$L(p, x) := -\ln p(x)$$

The meaning is this: if our guess of q is p and the value x is realized, then our loss is $-\ln p(x)$. Thus we suffer large loss when p puts small probabilities near where x is realized. The corresponding risk function is

$$R(p) = \mathbb{E}_q[L(p, x)] = -\int \ln[p(s)]q(s)\,\mathrm{d}s$$

Now suppose that we observe IID draws $x_1, \ldots, x_N$ from q. To estimate q, the ERM principle indicates we should solve for

$$\hat{p} := \operatorname*{argmin}_{p \in \mathscr{P}} \left\{ \frac{1}{N} \sum_{n=1}^{N} -\ln p(x_n) \right\} = \operatorname*{argmax}_{p \in \mathscr{P}} \left\{ \sum_{n=1}^{N} \ln p(x_n) \right\}$$

where $\mathscr{P}$ is a hypothesis space of densities. To clarify the connection with maximum likelihood, take $\mathscr{P}$ to be a parametric class $\{p(\cdot\,;\boldsymbol{\theta})\}_{\boldsymbol{\theta}\in\Theta}$. Choosing our estimate $\hat{p}$ of q now reduces to choosing an estimate $\hat{\boldsymbol{\theta}}$ of $\boldsymbol{\theta}$. Rewriting our optimization problem for this case, we obtain

$$\hat{\boldsymbol{\theta}} = \operatorname*{argmax}_{\boldsymbol{\theta}} \left\{ \sum_{n=1}^{N} \ln p(x_n; \boldsymbol{\theta}) \right\} = \operatorname*{argmax}_{\boldsymbol{\theta}} \ell(\boldsymbol{\theta})$$

Here ℓ is the log-likelihood. It follows from this expression that the ERM estimator is precisely the maximum likelihood estimator.

Incidentally, the minimizer of the true risk $R(p)$ is the unknown density q. To see this, let us first transform our expression for the risk function to

$$R(p) = \int \ln \left[\frac{q(s)}{p(s)} \right] q(s) \, \mathrm{d}s - \int \ln[q(s)] q(s) \, \mathrm{d}s$$

The term on the far right is called the **entropy** of q, and does not involve p. Hence minimization of the risk comes down to minimization of

$$D(q, p) := \int \ln \left[\frac{q(s)}{p(s)} \right] q(s) \, \mathrm{d}s \tag{8.34}$$

This quantity is called the **Kullback–Leibler (KL) deviation** between q and p. The KL deviation is possibly infinite, always nonnegative, and zero if and only if $p = q$.[5] It follows that the unique minimizer of the risk is the true density q.

8.3.3 The Method of Moments and GMM

Suppose that we wish to estimate a vector $\boldsymbol{\theta}$ that solves an equation of the form

$$g(\boldsymbol{\theta}) = \mathbb{E} h(\mathbf{x}) \tag{8.35}$$

In this expression, g and h are observable vector-valued functions (taking values in $\mathbb{R}^K$, say). We cannot solve this expression because the distribution P of $\mathbf{x}$ is unknown, and hence the expectation cannot be evaluated. If, however, we have observations $\mathbf{x}_1, \ldots, \mathbf{x}_N$ from P then we can apply the sample analogue principle and replace the population expectation with the expectation under the empirical distribution. This yields the **method of moments estimator**, which is the solution $\hat{\boldsymbol{\theta}}$, if it exists, to the equation

$$g(\hat{\boldsymbol{\theta}}) = \frac{1}{N} \sum_{n=1}^{N} h(\mathbf{x}_n) \tag{8.36}$$

Example 8.3.4 The mean of the Pareto distribution with scale parameter $s_0 = 1$ and shape parameter α is $\alpha/(\alpha - 1)$. (The condition for existence of the mean is $\alpha > 1$.) Letting $g(\alpha) := \alpha/(\alpha - 1)$, we can write the same statement as

$$g(\alpha) = \mathbb{E} x \quad \text{where} \quad \mathcal{L}(x) = \text{Pareto}(\alpha, 1)$$

The first equation is a version of (8.35). To estimate α with observations $x_1, \ldots, x_N$ from a Pareto$(\alpha, 1)$ distribution, we can apply the method of moments, which tells us to solve $g(\hat{\alpha}) = \frac{1}{N} \sum_{n=1}^{N} x_n$ for $\hat{\alpha}$. The result is $\hat{\alpha} := \bar{x}_N / (\bar{x}_N - 1)$.

5. More precisely, $D(q, p) = 0$ if and only if $p = q$ almost everywhere. Densities are equal almost everywhere when the set of points at which they fail to be equal has Lebesgue measure zero.

Generalized method of moments (GMM) is a small step from method of moments. If we express (8.35) as $\mathbb{E}[g(\boldsymbol{\theta}) - h(\mathbf{x})] = \mathbf{0}$, then it becomes natural to consider the more general expression

$$\mathbb{E}\,G(\boldsymbol{\theta}, \mathbf{x}) = \mathbf{0} \tag{8.37}$$

This expression is called the **orthogonality condition**. The generalized method of moments estimator of $\boldsymbol{\theta}$ is the solution $\hat{\boldsymbol{\theta}}$ to the empirical counterpart, which is

$$\frac{1}{N}\sum_{n=1}^{N} G(\hat{\boldsymbol{\theta}}, \mathbf{x}_n) = \mathbf{0} \tag{8.38}$$

Of course, there is no guarantee that a solution will exist here, partly because the function G can be nonlinear and partly because the number of equations can be greater than the number of unknowns. If the number of equations is greater, then the estimation problem is said to be **overidentified**.

Our study of overdetermined systems of equations in §3.3.2 suggests a logical way to handle the overidentified case: Minimize the norm of the left-hand side of (8.38). This leads to the expression

$$\hat{\boldsymbol{\theta}} = \operatorname*{argmin}_{\boldsymbol{\theta} \in \Theta} \left\| \frac{1}{N}\sum_{n=1}^{N} G(\boldsymbol{\theta}, \mathbf{x}_n) \right\| \tag{8.39}$$

In practice, we usually make two adjustments to this expression. The first is trivial: we minimize the squared norm, instead of the norm, leaving the minimizer unchanged. The second is to replace the Euclidean norm $\|\cdot\|$ with a weighted norm $\|\cdot\|_W$ defined by $\|\mathbf{x}\|_W^2 = \mathbf{x}^\mathsf{T}\mathbf{W}\mathbf{x}$, where $\mathbf{W}$ is a positive definite **weighting matrix**. Positive definiteness is desired here because it shares with the Euclidean norm the property that led us to (8.39). That is, $\|\mathbf{x}\|_W = 0$ if and only if $\mathbf{x} = \mathbf{0}$. The estimation problem is then

$$\hat{\boldsymbol{\theta}} = \operatorname*{argmin}_{\boldsymbol{\theta} \in \Theta} \left[\frac{1}{N}\sum_{n=1}^{N} G(\boldsymbol{\theta}, \mathbf{x}_n) \right]^\mathsf{T} \hat{\mathbf{W}} \left[\frac{1}{N}\sum_{n=1}^{N} G(\boldsymbol{\theta}, \mathbf{x}_n) \right] \tag{8.40}$$

The weighting matrix has been written as $\hat{\mathbf{W}}$ because it is allowed to depend on the sample. Evidently the choice of $\hat{\mathbf{W}}$ affects the minimizer, and the objective in choosing this matrix is to produce an estimator that has small variance asymptotically.

Example 8.3.5 GMM is often used to estimate and test asset pricing models. Many asset pricing models lead to equations of the form

$$\mathbf{p}_t = \mathbb{E}\left[M_{t+1}\mathbf{x}_{t+1} \mid \mathcal{G}_t\right]$$

where $\mathbf{x}_{t+1}$ is a vector of payoffs on K assets at $t+1$, $\mathbf{p}_t$ is a corresponding vector of time t asset prices, M_{t+1} is a stochastic discount factor and $\mathcal{G}_t$ is the time t information set. See, for example, Hansen (2014b). If $\mathbf{Z}_t$ is a conformable matrix of observable variables adapted to the filtration $\mathcal{G}_t$, then we can postmultiply by $\mathbf{Z}_t$, pass through the conditional expectation and rearrange to obtain

$$\mathbb{E}\left[M_{t+1}\mathbf{x}_{t+1}\mathbf{Z}_t - \mathbf{p}_t\mathbf{Z}_t \,|\, \mathcal{G}_t\right] = \mathbf{0}$$

Taking the unconditional expectation and using the law of iterated expectations gives an expression in the form of (8.37). In Hansen and Singleton (1982), the variables in $\mathbf{Z}_t$ include lagged values of asset returns and aggregate consumption growth.

8.3.4 Bayesian Estimation

Bayesian inference adopts a rather different strategy from the methods discussed so far. The main idea is to treat parameters as unknown quantities for which we hold subjective beliefs regarding their values. These subjective beliefs are called **priors**. The Bayesian approach to estimation suggests that we take both data and prior knowledge into account when forming an estimate or prediction.

Example 8.3.6 Consider the expression "when you hear hooves, think horses, not zebras." Prior knowledge should be given some weighting when assessing evidence.

For the purposes of estimation, a prior can be thought of as a distribution over $\mathscr{P}$, the set of distributions in play. The standard Bayesian approach is parametric, so we can specialize this further to a density over parameter space. Thus the primitives in our analysis are:

- $\boldsymbol{\theta}$, the parameter vector, which takes values in $\Theta \subset \mathbb{R}^J$,
- π, the **prior distribution**, a density over Θ,
- $\mathbf{x}$, the data, and
- $p(\cdot \,|\, \boldsymbol{\theta})$, the joint density of the data given $\boldsymbol{\theta}$.

Note that $L(\boldsymbol{\theta}) := p(\mathbf{x} \,|\, \boldsymbol{\theta})$ is the likelihood function.

Priors are reassessed based on evidence in the data. This process leads to an updated density over parameter space called the **posterior distribution**, which we represent by $\pi(\boldsymbol{\theta} \,|\, \mathbf{x})$. The posterior is obtained via an application of Bayes' law (see page 142), which leads us to

$$\pi(\boldsymbol{\theta} \,|\, \mathbf{x}) = \frac{p(\mathbf{x} \,|\, \boldsymbol{\theta})\pi(\boldsymbol{\theta})}{p(\mathbf{x})} = \frac{p(\mathbf{x} \,|\, \boldsymbol{\theta})\pi(\boldsymbol{\theta})}{\int p(\mathbf{x} \,|\, \boldsymbol{\theta}')\pi(\boldsymbol{\theta}')\,\mathrm{d}\boldsymbol{\theta}'} \tag{8.41}$$

Here $p(\mathbf{x})$ represents the unconditional density of $\mathbf{x}$ evaluated at the outcome. The term on the far right shows why this unconditional density is not listed as a primitive: we can recover it from the other primitives using the law of total probability.

The same method can be applied when the densities are replaced with probability mass functions and the integral is replaced with a sum. Here's a standard example that mixes a density over priors with a binomial PMF for the likelihood:

Example 8.3.7 Consider a one-armed bandit (slot machine) with binary response v indicating a fixed payout ($v = 1$) or nothing ($v = 0$). We would like to know the probability θ of $v = 1$. Let $v_1, \ldots, v_N$ be a sequence of independent outcomes and let $x := \sum_{n=1}^{N} v_n$ be the total number of payouts. Recalling example 4.2.6 on page 104, the likelihood for x conditional on θ is

$$p(x \,|\, \theta) = \binom{N}{x} \theta^x (1-\theta)^{N-x}$$

For our prior we take a Beta(α, β) distribution, so

$$\pi(\theta) = \frac{\theta^{\alpha-1}(1-\theta)^{\beta-1}}{B(\alpha,\beta)} \tag{8.42}$$

for $0 < \theta < 1$. (Parameters like α and β that are used to define the prior density are called **hyperparameters**.) Applying (8.41) gives

$$\pi(\theta \,|\, x) = \frac{\theta^{x+\alpha-1}(1-\theta)^{N-x+\beta-1}}{c(x)} \tag{8.43}$$

where $c(x) := p(x)B(\alpha,\beta)/\binom{N}{x}$. We could try to calculate $c(x)$ directly but there's an easier way. We know that (8.43) is a density in θ given x. Hence $c(x)$ must be the normalizing constant at x. Moreover, in comparing (8.42) with (8.43), it's clear that $\pi(\theta \,|\, x)$ is a beta density. This leads us to the full form of the posterior, which is

$$\pi(\theta \,|\, x) = \frac{\theta^{\alpha+x-1}(1-\theta)^{N-x+\beta-1}}{B(x+\alpha, N-x+\beta)} \tag{8.44}$$

Figure 8.10 shows evolution of the posterior density (8.44) in a simulation. The prior is set to Beta$(3,5)$. The true payout probability is $\theta_0 = 0.7$. Despite the poor prior, the data shift probability mass towards θ_0. See `johnstachurski.net/emet.html` for code.

Point estimates are extracted from the posterior distribution based on some measure of central tendency, such as the mean, the median, or the **mode** of the posterior (i.e., the maximizer in the unimodal case).

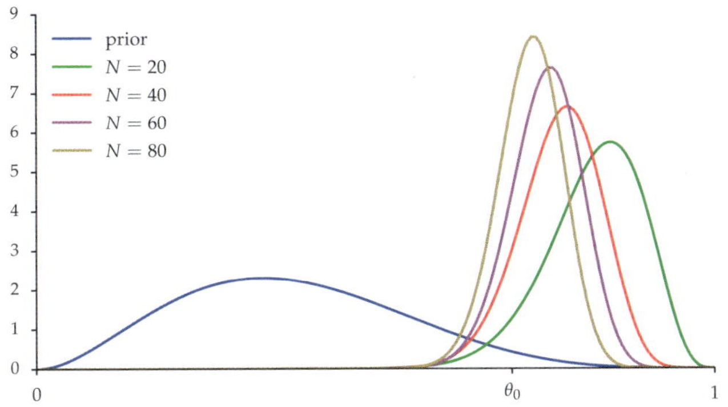

Figure 8.10 Evolution of the posterior from Beta$(3, 5)$ prior

Example 8.3.8 The mean of the posterior in (8.44) yields the estimator

$$\hat{\theta} := \frac{\alpha + x}{\alpha + \beta + N}$$

More payouts shift our estimator upwards. In the limit, $\hat{\theta}$ is near $\frac{x}{N}$, which is the MLE of θ. This illustrates a common theme: The difference between maximum likelihood and Bayesian estimates typically concerns finite sample properties.

The posterior we came up with in (8.44) belongs to the same parametric class as the prior. Priors where the parametric class is preserved under Bayesian updating for a specific likelihood function are called **conjugate**. Conjugacy makes application of Bayes' law particularly simple.

In applications, the existence of a closed-form solution for the posterior is rare, and the integration over the parameter space in (8.41) has to be carried out numerically. The standard technique is Markov chain Monte Carlo. An exposition of the Metropolis–Hastings algorithm was given in §7.4.2. If you return to (7.38), you will notice how implementation of this algorithm only requires us to evaluate ratios of of the posterior, which means that the integral term on the right-hand side of (8.41) cancels out. Because the integral can be very high dimensional, this often eliminates a huge amount of complexity.

Bayesian inference has experienced a surge of popularity in recent years. One reason is that in high dimensions, exploring the posterior via MCMC has proved to be more successful in practice than the numerical optimization required to obtain maximum likelihood estimates. Another is that Bayesian estimation provides a form of regularization that stabilizes and typically improves estimation of complex models. See §14.2.3. A third is that Bayesian estimation comes with an elegant, unified decision-theoretic approach to inference. Some discussion is given in §9.2.5.

8.4 Further Reading

The ERM principle is a very general principle for solving statistical problems and producing estimators. For such a general method it is difficult to give a set of strong results showing that ERM produces good estimators. Indeed, there will be instances when ERM produces poor estimators, as discussed in 8.2.3. Having said that, some rather general consistency results have been obtained. Additional discussion can be found in Vapnik (2000).

There are many good treatments of Bayesian estimation available in the literature, including Geweke (2005), Geweke et al. (2011), and Kroese and Chan (2014).

Chernozhukov and Fernández-Val (2011) discuss quantile regression of the τth quantile in cases where τ is close to zero or one.

8.5 Exercises

Ex. 8.5.1 Let x be a random variable with $\mu := \mathbb{E}[x]$ and finite second moment. Consider the risk function given by $R(\theta) = \mathbb{E}[(\theta - x)^2]$. Show that μ is the minimizer of $R(\theta)$ over all $\theta \in \mathbb{R}$.

Ex. 8.5.2 Confirm the solutions in (8.14) by differentiating (8.13).

Ex. 8.5.3 Show that the method of moments estimator $\hat{\alpha}$ in example 8.3.4 converges in probability to α whenever $\alpha > 1$. (Later we will call this property consistency.)

Ex. 8.5.4 Confirm that the maximizer of (8.28) is the sample mean of $x_1, \ldots, x_N$.

Ex. 8.5.5 Confirm the results in (8.33) by differentiating (8.32).

Ex. 8.5.6 Let F be a strictly increasing CDF on $\mathbb{R}$ and let $\tau \in (0,1)$ be given. Let y be a random variable with $\mathcal{L}(y) = F$. Adopting the notation of §8.2.2.1, show that the solution to the optimization problem $\min_{\xi \in \mathbb{R}} \mathbb{E}\, L_\tau(y, \xi)$ is the ξ that solves $F(\xi) = \tau$.

Ex. 8.5.7 Consider the one-armed bandit problem in example 8.3.7. Directly obtain the log likelihood function of θ given $v_1, \ldots, v_N$. Use the principle of maximum likelihood to show that the sample mean $\bar{v}_N$ is the MLE for θ.

Ex. 8.5.8 Let f and g be two fixed densities, let $x_1, \ldots, x_N$ be IID and consider the **likelihood ratio statistic**

$$y_n := \prod_{i=1}^{n} \frac{g(x_i)}{f(x_i)}$$

Show that if $\mathcal{L}(x_n) = f$ for all n, then $\{y_n\}$ is a martingale with respect to the filtration $\{\mathscr{F}_n\}$ defined by $\mathscr{F}_n := \{x_1, \ldots, x_n\}$.

Ex. 8.5.9 Let $D(p_1, p_2)$ be the KL deviation between normal densities p_1 and p_2 where $p_i = \mathrm{N}(\mu_i, \sigma_i^2)$ for $i = 1, 2$. Show that

$$D(p_1, p_2) = \ln \frac{\sigma_2}{\sigma_1} + \frac{\sigma_1^2 + (\mu_1 - \mu_2)^2}{2\sigma_2^2} - \frac{1}{2}$$

8.5.1 Solutions to Selected Exercises

Solution to Ex. 8.5.1. Adding and subtracting μ, we can express $R(\theta)$ as

$$R(\theta) = \mathbb{E}\{[(\theta - \mu) + (\mu - x)]^2\}$$

Expanding this out and using $\mathbb{E}[x] = \mu$, we obtain $R(\theta) = (\theta - \mu)^2 + \operatorname{var} x$. Evidently a minimum is obtained when $\theta = \mu$. □

Solution to Ex. 8.5.6. We can write the minimization problem as

$$\min_{\xi \in \mathbb{R}} \left\{ (\tau - 1) \int_{-\infty}^{\xi} (t - \xi)\, F(\mathrm{d}t) + \tau \int_{\xi}^{\infty} (t - \xi)\, F(\mathrm{d}t) \right\}$$

The first-order condition is $(1 - \tau)F(\xi) + \tau(F(\xi) - 1) = 0$. Simplifying gives $F(\xi) = \tau$, as was to be shown. □

Solution to Ex. 8.5.7. Each v_n is binary, with PMF given by $p(s; \theta) := \theta^s (1 - \theta)^{1-s}$ for $s \in \{0, 1\}$. By independence, the joint distribution is the product of the marginals, and hence the log likelihood is

$$\ell(\theta) = \sum_{n=1}^{N} \log p(v_n; \theta) = \sum_{n=1}^{N} [v_n \log \theta + (1 - v_n) \log(1 - \theta)]$$

Differentiating with respect to θ and setting the result equal to zero yields $\hat{\theta} = \bar{v}_N$ as claimed. □

Solution to Ex. 8.5.8. It is clear that y_n is $\mathscr{F}_n$-measurable, and hence $\{y_n\}$ is adapted to $\{\mathscr{F}_n\}$. In addition, we have

$$\mathbb{E}[y_{n+1} \mid \mathscr{F}_n] = \mathbb{E}\left[\prod_{i=1}^{n+1} \frac{g(x_i)}{f(x_i)} \mid \mathscr{F}_n\right] = \prod_{i=1}^{n} \frac{g(x_i)}{f(x_i)} \mathbb{E}\left[\frac{g(x_{n+1})}{f(x_{n+1})} \mid \mathscr{F}_n\right]$$

Since $\{x_n\}$ is IID, $\mathcal{L}(x_{n+1}) = f$ and g is a density, we have

$$\mathbb{E}\left[\frac{g(x_{n+1})}{f(x_{n+1})} \mid \mathscr{F}_n\right] = \mathbb{E}\left[\frac{g(x_{n+1})}{f(x_{n+1})}\right] = \int \frac{g(s)}{f(s)} f(s) \, ds = \int g(s) \, ds = 1$$

$$\therefore \quad \mathbb{E}[y_{n+1} \mid \mathscr{F}_n] = \prod_{i=1}^{n} \frac{g(x_i)}{f(x_i)} = y_n$$

□

Chapter 9

Properties of Estimators

When the concept of estimators was first introduced in §8.1.2 we mentioned that there is nothing in the definition that guarantees—or even alludes to—good performance. Let's now start to think about evaluating estimators.

9.1 Sampling Distributions

Our first step is to view estimators as random entities dependent on the data, and to consider their distributions under different specifications of the data-generating process. The notation below follows that set out in §8.1.1.

9.1.1 Estimators as Random Elements

By definition, a statistic T is a $\mathscr{B}$-measurable transformation of the sample space $Z_{\mathcal{D}}$ into some feature space S. As a function of the sample $\mathbf{z}_{\mathcal{D}} = (\mathbf{z}_1, \ldots, \mathbf{z}_N)$, it can be viewed as a random element mapping outcomes in the underlying space Ω to S via

$$\omega \mapsto T\left[\mathbf{z}_{\mathcal{D}}(\omega)\right] \in S$$

Here "random element" stands for either a random vector (or scalar), or something more general, such as the random distribution $\hat{P}_N$, or a density estimate, which is a random function of the sample.

Example 9.1.1 Consider a sample mean $\bar{x}_N := \frac{1}{N}\sum_{n=1}^{N} x_n$. The observations $x_1, \ldots, x_N$ are understood to be random variables on some probability space $(\Omega, \mathscr{F}, \mathbb{P})$. The sample mean inherits this property. Formally, it is the random variable

$$\bar{x}_N(\omega) := \frac{1}{N} \sum_{n=1}^{N} x_n(\omega) \qquad (\omega \in \Omega) \tag{9.1}$$

Example 9.1.2 A histogram is a random estimate of the density of the unknown distribution P, mapping sample realizations into step functions on the outcome space.

The idea that estimators are random can be counterintuitive. When we begin to study econometrics, we tend to think of data as fixed numbers determined by some prior historical outcome and statistics as deterministic functions of these numbers. Hence we only observe one value of any particular statistic—one sample mean, one sample variance, and so on. However, if we want to build a theory of estimators, then we need to consider their performance prior to observing the data. Each data set is viewed as a random draw from some unknown distribution. We seek estimators that perform well in the face of this uncertainty.

Once we agree that estimators are random, we know they must have distributions. These distributions determine how effective an estimator is at estimating the intended feature. Let's now turn to investigating these distributions.

9.1.2 Sampling Distributions

Suppose that T is a statistic mapping data $\mathbf{z}_\mathcal{D}$ into S. As just discussed, $T(\mathbf{z}_\mathcal{D})$ is a random element taking values in S. Its distribution $\mathcal{L}(T)$ on S can be expressed as

$$\mathcal{L}(T)(B) = \mathbb{P}\,\{\, T\,(\mathbf{z}_\mathcal{D}) \in B\,\} \tag{9.2}$$

$\mathcal{L}(T)$ is called the **sampling distribution** of T. Continuing to write $P_\mathcal{D}$ for the joint distribution of the sample $\mathbf{z}_\mathcal{D}$, we can also define the sampling distribution as

$$\mathcal{L}(T)(B) = P_\mathcal{D}\{\mathbf{s} \in Z_\mathcal{D} : T(\mathbf{s}) \in B\}$$

or even $P_\mathcal{D} \circ T^{-1}$ if you like that kind of notation. Note that the sampling distribution of T is fully determined by

(i) the statistic T that maps data to feature space,

(ii) the joint distribution $P_\mathcal{D}$ of the data.

Since $P_\mathcal{D}$ is unknown, the sampling distribution is likewise unknown. It can, however, be estimated, as we'll see below.

Mathematically, there is no difference between the "sampling distribution of T" and the "distribution of T." Nonetheless, the terminology is standard.

Example 9.1.3 Let $x_1, \ldots, x_N$ be IID on $\mathbb{R}$ with $P = \mathcal{L}(x_n) = \mathrm{N}(\mu, \sigma^2)$ for all n. Let T be the sample mean $\bar{x}_N$. By independence, the joint distribution $P_\mathcal{D}$ of $\mathbf{z}_\mathcal{D} = \mathbf{x} := (x_1, \ldots, x_N)$ is $\mathrm{N}(\mu\mathbf{1}, \sigma^2\mathbf{I})$. Applying fact 5.1.5 on page 133 gives

$$\mathcal{L}(\bar{x}_N) = \mathrm{N}\left(\mu, \frac{\sigma^2}{N}\right) \tag{9.3}$$

This is the sampling distribution of $\bar{x}_N$.

Sampling distributions are often complicated. Sometimes the best we can do is obtain the sampling distribution of some transformation of an estimator.

Example 9.1.4 Let $\mathbf{x} := (x_1, \ldots, x_N)$ have the same distribution as example 9.1.3. Let s_N^2 be the sample variance. If $\sigma > 0$, then

$$\mathcal{L}(q_N) = \chi^2(N-1) \quad \text{where} \quad q_N := \frac{N\, s_N^2}{\sigma^2} \tag{9.4}$$

To see why (9.4) holds, recall from example 2.2.3 on page 33 that if $S := \operatorname{span}\{\mathbf{1}\}$ and $\mathbf{P} = \operatorname{proj} S$, then the residual projection satisfies $\mathbf{Mx} = \mathbf{x} - \bar{x}\mathbf{1}$. Hence

$$N s_N^2 = \sum_{n=1}^{N} (x_n - \bar{x}_N)^2 = \|\mathbf{Mx}\|^2$$

Since $\mathbf{M1} = \mathbf{0}$ (see fact 2.2.8 on page 33) and $\mathbf{M}$ is idempotent and symmetric (fact 3.3.2), setting $\boldsymbol{\xi} := \sigma^{-1}(\mathbf{x} - \mu\mathbf{1})$ gives

$$q_N = \sigma^{-2}\|\mathbf{Mx}\|^2 = \left\|\mathbf{M}\sigma^{-1}(\mathbf{x} - \mu\mathbf{1})\right\|^2 = \|\mathbf{M}\boldsymbol{\xi}\|^2 = \boldsymbol{\xi}^\top \mathbf{M}\boldsymbol{\xi} \tag{9.5}$$

To see that the right-hand side has distribution $\chi^2(N-1)$, apply fact 3.3.4 on page 61 to obtain trace $\mathbf{M} = N - 1$, followed by fact 5.1.19 on page 141.

Fact 9.1.1 For an IID sample $x_1, \ldots, x_N$ with common distribution $\mathrm{N}(\mu, \sigma^2)$, the sample mean and sample variance are independent random variables.

Many long and involved proofs of fact 9.1.1 can be found in the literature, but a simple and informative proof can be obtained from fact 5.1.13 on page 137. See exercise 9.4.2 and its solution.

In the preceding examples we were able to obtain an analytical expression for the sampling distribution of our estimator (or a simple transformation of the estimator) from the underlying distribution of the data. In reality this case is the exception.

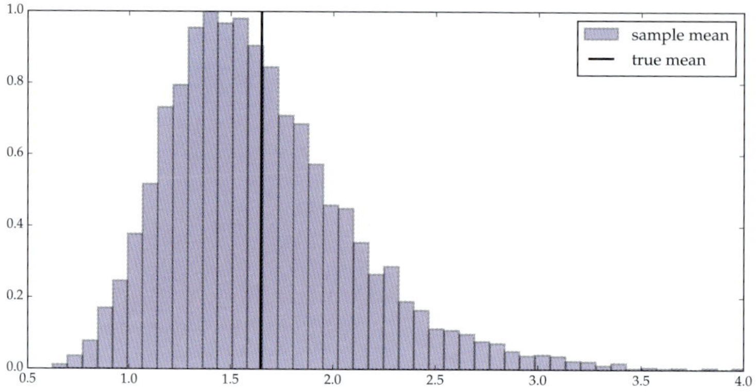

Figure 9.1 Sampling distribution of $\bar{x}_N$ when $N = 20$ and data are IID $\text{LN}(0, 1)$

Example 9.1.5 A random variable x is said to be **lognormally distributed** with parameters μ, σ if $\mathcal{L}(\ln x) = \text{N}(\mu, \sigma^2)$. We write $\mathcal{L}(x) = \text{LN}(\mu, \sigma^2)$. No neat expression exists for $\mathcal{L}(\bar{x}_N)$ when the data are IID lognormal.

When no closed-form exists, we can still approximate the sampling distribution using simulation, conditional on a specification of the joint distribution of the data. For example, figure 9.1 shows a histogram approximation to $\mathcal{L}(\bar{x}_N)$ when $N = 20$ and $x_1, \ldots, x_N$ is IID $\text{LN}(0, 1)$. The histogram is produced by generating 10,000 observations of $\bar{x}_N$. The loop that produced the observations is given in listing 5.

Listing 5 Generates 10,000 observations of the sample mean (Python)

```
import numpy as np

N = 20
num_reps = 10000
xbar_outcomes = np.empty(num_reps)  # Allocate memory

for i in range(num_reps):
    x = np.exp(np.random.randn(N))  # Generate N iid lognormal RVs
    xbar_outcomes[i] = x.mean()
```

9.1.2.1 Desirable Properties

The quality or performance of a given estimator is characterized by its sampling distribution. Let $\hat{\gamma}$ be an estimator of some feature γ based on a sample $\mathbf{z}_{\mathcal{D}}$. What would be an ideal sampling distribution for $\hat{\gamma}$? The answer is obvious: a point mass that puts probability one on the single point γ.

This scenario rarely arises because our sample is *random*. So here's a more realistic objective:

> It is desirable that the sampling distribution of an estimator of γ concentrate most of its probability mass in a small neighborhood around γ, regardless of the joint distribution $P_{\mathcal{D}}$ of the sample.

This statement considers only what is desirable, not what is possible. For example, if we look back at figure 9.1, we see that the sampling distribution of $\bar{x}_N$ does not cluster tightly around the mean. (The feature γ that we are estimating is the mean of the $\text{LN}(0,1)$ distribution, which is represented by the vertical black line.) But this is not unexpected, since the sample size is only 20. We simply don't have enough information to estimate the feature precisely.

Nonetheless, these ideas give us a way to start comparing different estimators of a given feature from a given amount of data. For example, suppose that we are estimating the mean of a distribution from a random sample of size 20. Suppose that each is drawn from the $\text{LN}(0,1)$ distribution, the mean of which is about 1.65. The sampling distributions of three estimators of the mean under the associated joint distribution have been approximated by simulation and represented as box plots in figure 9.2. The top sampling distribution is that of the mid-range estimator (see page 217), the second is that of a maximum likelihood estimator to be discussed later, and the third is that of the sample mean. The last two put more probability mass in the region around 1.65. Hence they outperform the mid-range estimator in this setting.

In what follows we will formalize the ideas presented above, including both finite sample and asymptotic theory. But first let's discuss a general way of estimating sampling distributions from the data.

9.1.3 The Bootstrap

While understanding sampling distributions is central to evaluating the precision of estimators, sampling distributions cannot be observed in the wild because they depend on $P_{\mathcal{D}}$. For example, suppose $x_1, \ldots, x_N$ are assumed to be IID $\text{N}(\mu, \sigma^2)$ with μ and σ unknown. By (9.3), the distribution of $\bar{x}_N$ is $\text{N}(\mu, \sigma^2/N)$. While this provides valuable information, it doesn't fully pin down the distribution because μ and σ are unknown.

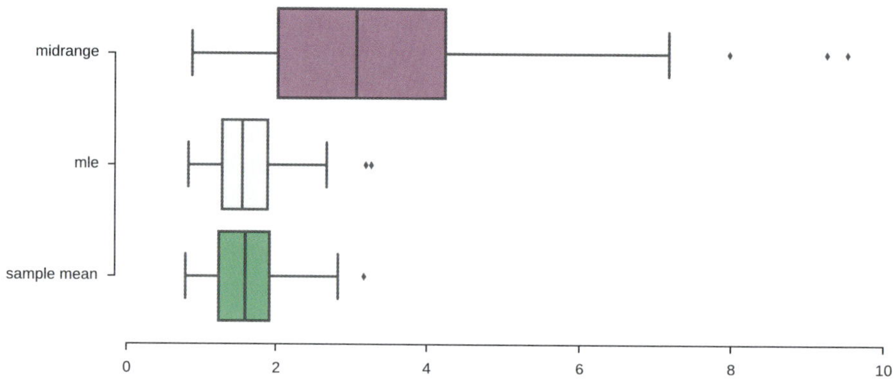

Figure 9.2 Sampling distributions of three estimators of a lognormal mean

Things are even more complicated for the sample mean of IID lognormals in example 9.1.5. There we can't easily write down the sampling distribution as a function of the parameters. Problems multiply further if we are not prepared to assume a parametric form for the distribution of the observations.

There is, however, a very general technique that allows us to approximate sampling distributions given data. We'll discuss the case of scalar data, although the vector case is similar. To begin, let T be any statistic and consider its sampling distribution

$$\mathcal{L}_P(T) := \text{ the distribution of } T(x_1, \ldots, x_N) \text{ when } x_1, \ldots, x_N \overset{\text{IID}}{\sim} P$$

The sampling distribution is unknown to us because P is unknown. Suppose, however, that we have access to a sample $x_1^o, \ldots, x_N^o$ of IID draws from P. We then have a good estimator of P given our sample: the empirical distribution $\hat{P}_N$ generated by $x_1^o, \ldots, x_N^o$. Given this empirical distribution, the **bootstrap distribution** of T is defined as

$$\mathcal{L}_{\hat{P}_N}(T) := \text{ the distribution of } T(x_1, \ldots, x_N) \text{ when } x_1, \ldots, x_N \overset{\text{IID}}{\sim} \hat{P}_N$$

Thus the bootstrap distribution is just the plug-in estimator of the sampling distribution.

Is $\mathcal{L}_{\hat{P}_N}(T)$ a good approximation to $\mathcal{L}_P(T)$? By the Glivenko–Cantelli theorem, $\hat{P}_N$ will be close to P when N is large. If $Q \mapsto \mathcal{L}_Q(T)$ is suitably continuous, then $\mathcal{L}_{\hat{P}_N}(T)$ will also be close to $\mathcal{L}_P(T)$. For details, see §29.2 of DasGupta (2008).

9.1.3.1 Simulation

One remaining problem with $\mathcal{L}_{\hat{P}_N}(T)$ is that it's not particularly tractable. We can, however, generate draws from this distribution easily on a computer. Here's an algorithm that returns M draws from $\mathcal{L}_{\hat{P}_N}(T)$:

1: set $\hat{P}_N$ = the empirical distribution of observed data $x_1^o, \ldots, x_N^o$
2: **for** m in $1, \ldots, M$ **do**
3: draw $x_1^b, \ldots, x_N^b$ independently from $\hat{P}_N$
4: set $T_m^b = T(x_1^b, \ldots, x_N^b)$
5: **end for**
6: return the sample $T_1^b, \ldots, T_M^b$

Using the definition of the empirical distribution, drawing samples from $\hat{P}_N$ is easy: we just make repeated draws from the set $x_1^o, \ldots, x_N^o$ with equal probability on each element. Listing 6 contains some Julia code implementing the whole algorithm as a function that returns M bootstrap samples. The other arguments to the function are `xo`, the array of observed data, and `stat`, which is a function representing T.

Listing 6 Function to generate bootstrap samples (Julia)

```
function bootstrap(xo, stat, M)
    N = length(xo)
    T_b = Array(Float64, M)
    x_b = Array(Float64, N)
    for m in 1:M
        for i in 1:N
            x_b[i] = xo[rand(1:N)]
        end
        T_b[m] = stat(x_b)
    end
    return T_b
end
```

Here's an example function call:

```
julia> bootstrap([1, 2, 3], mean, 3)
3-element Array{Float64,1}:
1.66667
1.0
1.66667
```

Here is the same routine in Python:

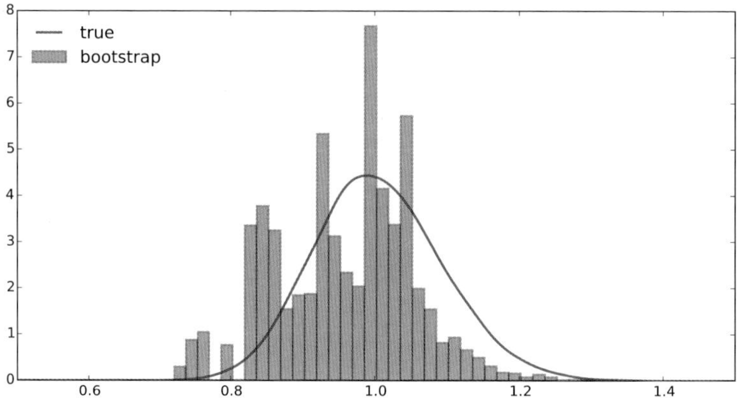

Figure 9.3 Bootstrap draws and sampling distribution for the median

```
def bootstrap(xo, stat, M):
    N = len(xo)
    T_b = np.empty(M)
    for m in range(M):
        x_b = np.random.choice(xo, size=N)
        T_b[m] = stat(x_b)
    return T_b
```

Figure 9.3 shows a histogram of observations from a bootstrap distribution generated using the Julia code above. The underlying sample $x_1^o, \ldots, x_N^o$ was created using $N = 200$ IID draws from the $\text{LN}(0,1)$ distribution. The statistic used was the sample median. The density shown in the same figure is a numerical approximation of the true sampling distribution of the median over 200 IID draws from the $\text{LN}(0,1)$ distribution. The (population) median of the $\text{LN}(0,1)$ distribution is 1. See `johnstachurski.net/emet.html` for the code.

9.1.3.2 Standard Errors

As discussed in 9.1.2.1, a good estimator is one that concentrates its probability mass close to the target feature. The extent to which probability mass concentrates is usually measured by the variance or standard deviation of the sampling distribution. The standard deviation is preferable because it comes in units that are easier to interpret.

Because the sampling distribution is typically unknown, so is its standard deviation. Hence we replace the true standard deviation with an estimate. An estimate of

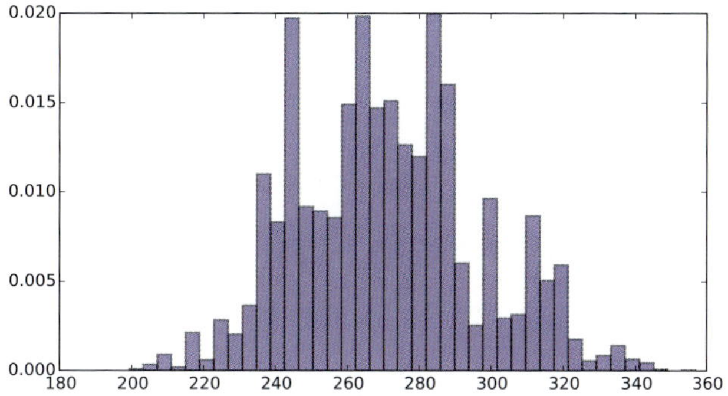

Figure 9.4 Bootstrapped draws for the median of firm sizes by sales

the standard deviation of a sampling distribution is usually referred to as the **standard error**. More generally,

$$\text{se}(\hat{\gamma}) := \text{ an estimate of the standard deviation of } \hat{\gamma}$$

This isn't a proper definition because we haven't specified *which* estimate of the standard deviation we are talking about, but nevertheless the terminology is common. One way to compute a standard error of an estimator is to take the sample standard deviation of the bootstrap draws.

Example 9.1.6 Figure 9.4 shows a histogram of draws from the bootstrap distribution of the median applied to 2,118 observations of US firm sizes by sales, as measured by 2013 Compustat data. Values are in millions of US dollars. The median of the sample itself is 269.9. The sample standard deviation of this particular set of bootstrap draws is 25.4. See `johnstachurski.net/emet.html` for the code.

9.2 Evaluating Estimators

As mentioned above, the standard definition of an estimator does not include any restrictions that imply sensible behavior (as opposed to, say, the definition of a probability on page 83). We now turn again to the problem of assessing estimators, following our informal discussion in §9.1.2.1. We'll begin with finite sample properties.

9.2.1 Bias

One common criterion for assessing estimators is bias, or lack thereof. Let $\hat{\gamma}$ be an estimator of a given feature $\gamma = \gamma(P)$. The **bias** of $\hat{\gamma}$ is defined as

$$\text{bias}_P(\hat{\gamma}, \gamma) = \mathbb{E}_P \hat{\gamma} - \gamma(P) \tag{9.6}$$

The estimator $\hat{\gamma}$ is called **unbiased** for γ over the class of distributions $\mathscr{P}$ if

$$\text{bias}_P(\hat{\gamma}, \gamma) = 0 \quad \text{for all } P \in \mathscr{P}$$

The definition is the same when the feature γ and estimator $\hat{\gamma}$ are vector-valued.

The notation $\mathbb{E}_P \hat{\gamma}$ indicates that expectation is taken under the assumption that the data points are IID with common distribution P. In general, the bias depends on P. For example, in the IID setting, the mid-range estimator (page 217) is unbiased as an estimator of the mean of a uniform distribution on $\mathbb{R}$ with unknown end points, but biased for many other distributions, including the lognormal.

Figure 9.2 already suggests bias of the mid-range estimator in the lognormal case. Here's a simulation in R that provides further confirmation.

```
> mr <- function(x) return((min(x) + max(x)) / 2)
> observations <- replicate(5000, mr(rlnorm(20)))
> mean(observations)   # Approximate sample mean of mid-range
[1] 3.800108
> exp(1/2)       # Mean of lognormal
[1] 1.648721
```

Fact 9.2.1 Let P be a distribution on $\mathbb{R}^K$, let $\{\mathbf{x}_n\}$ be a sample with $\mathcal{L}(\mathbf{x}_n) = P$ for all n, and let $\hat{P}_N$ be the empirical distribution. If

(i) $\gamma(P) = \int h(\mathbf{s})P(d\mathbf{s})$ for some integrable function h, and

(ii) $\hat{\gamma}$ is the plug-in estimator $\hat{\gamma} = \int h(\mathbf{s})\hat{P}_N(d\mathbf{s}) = \frac{1}{N}\sum_{n=1}^N h(\mathbf{x}_n)$,

then $\hat{\gamma}$ is unbiased for γ over the set of distributions such that $\int h(\mathbf{s})P(d\mathbf{s})$ exists.

Fact 9.2.1 is immediate from linearity of expectations, since

$$\mathbb{E}\hat{\gamma} = \mathbb{E}\left[\frac{1}{N}\sum_{n=1}^N h(\mathbf{x}_n)\right] = \frac{1}{N}\sum_{n=1}^N \mathbb{E}h(\mathbf{x}_n) = \int h(\mathbf{s})P(d\mathbf{s}) = \gamma(P)$$

Note that independence isn't used here. Fact 9.2.1 depends only on the existence of a common marginal P.

Example 9.2.1 For any identically distributed sample, the kth sample moment is an unbiased estimator of the kth moment, whenever the latter exists.

Example 9.2.2 Let $x_1, \ldots, x_N$ be an IID sample with finite variance σ^2. The sample variance s_N^2 is, in general, a biased estimator of σ^2, but not by much. In particular,

$$\mathbb{E} s_N^2 = \sigma^2 \frac{N-1}{N} \tag{9.7}$$

To obtain this expression, we can combine the definition of q_N in (9.4) and the expression in (9.5) to obtain

$$\mathbb{E} s_N^2 = \frac{1}{N} \sigma^2 \mathbb{E}\left[\boldsymbol{\xi}^\top \mathbf{M} \boldsymbol{\xi}\right] = \frac{1}{N} \sigma^2 \operatorname{trace} \mathbf{M}$$

Here $\mathbf{M}$ is the residual projection for the subspace $\operatorname{span}\{\mathbf{1}\}$ and the second equality is due to fact 5.1.3 (page 127). Now apply fact 3.3.4 on page 61.

9.2.2 Variance

The variance of a given estimator gives a measure of its dispersion. Sensible estimators almost always have the property that the variance goes to zero as $N \to \infty$.

Example 9.2.3 If $x_1, \ldots, x_N$ are uncorrelated with common finite variance σ^2, then

$$\operatorname{var} \bar{x}_N = \operatorname{var}\left[\frac{1}{N} \sum_{n=1}^{N} x_n\right] = \frac{\sigma^2}{N} \tag{9.8}$$

We saw this already in §6.1.2.

Example 9.2.4 Assume the IID Gaussian setting of example 9.1.4, where it was shown that the sample variance satisfies $\mathcal{L}(\sigma^{-2} N s_N^2) = \chi^2(N-1)$. The variance of a $\chi^2(k)$ distribution is $2k$. Using this fact and some algebra gives

$$\operatorname{var} s_N^2 = \frac{2\sigma^4}{N^2}(N-1)$$

Is small variance always desirable for an estimator? If the estimator is biased, then perhaps not, since probability mass might be concentrated in the wrong place. But for an unbiased estimator, low variance is good. It means that probability mass is concentrated around the feature that we wish to estimate.

Low variance is, of course, relative. For example, is the variance in (9.8) low or high? One way to approach this kind of question is to take the class of unbiased estimators of a given feature γ, and find the estimator in the class with the lowest variance. For given γ and given data $\mathbf{x}_1, \ldots, \mathbf{x}_N$, the estimator in the set of unbiased estimators

$$U_\gamma := \{\text{all statistics } \hat{\gamma} \text{ with } \mathbb{E}\,\hat{\gamma} = \gamma\}$$

that has the lowest variance within this class is called the **minimum variance unbiased estimator**.

Of course, it's quite possible that no minimizer exists. Even if it does, it might be hard to determine in practice, or require strong assumptions on the unknown distribution of the data. For these reasons it's common to focus on smaller classes than U_γ. For example, the estimator in the set of *linear* unbiased estimators

$$U_\gamma^\ell := \{\text{all linear statistics } \hat{\gamma} \text{ with } \mathbb{E}\,\hat{\gamma} = \gamma\}$$

with the lowest variance—if it exists—is called the **best linear unbiased estimator**.

Example 9.2.5 Let $x_1, \ldots, x_N$ be IID with common distribution P, where P has finite mean $\mu \neq 0$ and variance σ^2. The set of linear estimators of μ is given by

$$\left\{\text{all statistics of the form } \hat{\mu} = \sum_{n=1}^N \alpha_n x_n, \text{ where } \alpha_n \in \mathbb{R} \text{ for } n = 1, \ldots, N\right\}$$

Hence the set of linear unbiased estimators of μ is

$$U_\mu^\ell := \left\{\text{all } \hat{\mu} = \sum_{n=1}^N \alpha_n x_n \text{ with } \alpha_n \in \mathbb{R},\ \ n = 1, \ldots, N \text{ and } \mathbb{E}\left[\sum_{n=1}^N \alpha_n x_n\right] = \mu\right\}$$

Using linearity of expectations, this set can be rewritten as

$$U_\mu^\ell := \left\{\text{all } \hat{\mu} = \sum_{n=1}^N \alpha_n x_n \text{ with } \sum_{n=1}^N \alpha_n = 1\right\}$$

By independence and our rules for variance of sums (page 98), the variance of an element of this class is given by

$$\operatorname{var}\left[\sum_{n=1}^N \alpha_n x_n\right] = \sum_{n=1}^N \alpha_n^2 \operatorname{var} x_n = \sigma^2 \sum_{n=1}^N \alpha_n^2$$

To find the best linear unbiased estimator, we need to solve

$$\text{minimize } \sigma^2 \sum_{n=1}^{N} \alpha_n^2 \text{ over all } \alpha_1, \ldots, \alpha_N \text{ with } \sum_{n=1}^{N} \alpha_n = 1$$

To solve this constrained optimization problem, we can use the Lagrangian, setting

$$L(\alpha_1, \ldots, \alpha_N; \lambda) := \sigma^2 \sum_{n=1}^{N} \alpha_n^2 - \lambda \left[\sum_{n=1}^{N} \alpha_n - 1 \right]$$

where λ is the Lagrange multiplier. Differentiating with respect to α_n and setting the result equal to zero, the minimizer α_n^* satisfies $\alpha_n^* = \lambda(2\sigma^2)^{-1}$ for each n. In particular, each α_n^* takes the same value, and hence, from the constraint $\sum_n \alpha_n^* = 1$, we have $\alpha_n^* = 1/N$. Using these values, our estimator becomes

$$\sum_{n=1}^{N} \alpha_n^* x_n = \bar{x}_N$$

Thus, for IID data with finite variance, the sample mean is the best linear unbiased estimator of μ.

The theory of minimum variance unbiased estimators and best linear unbiased estimators is traditionally regarded as important. However, there's no convincing reason to restrict ourselves to unbiased estimators. In fact, as we'll see, there are good reasons not to.

9.2.3 Variance versus Bias

The mean squared error (MSE) of a given estimator $\hat{\gamma}$ of some feature $\gamma \in \mathbb{R}^K$ is

$$\text{mse}(\hat{\gamma}, \gamma) := \mathbb{E} \left\{ \|\hat{\gamma} - \gamma\|^2 \right\} \tag{9.9}$$

As for bias, $\text{mse}(\hat{\gamma}, \gamma)$ depends on the joint distribution of the data as well as the specification of $\hat{\gamma}$, although we haven't made that dependence explicit in the notation.

Mean squared error is an overall measure of the performance of an estimator that takes into account both bias and variance. In fact in the scalar case we can neatly decompose mean squared error into the sum of variance and squared bias:

$$\text{mse}(\hat{\gamma}, \gamma) = \text{var}\, \hat{\gamma} + \text{bias}(\hat{\gamma}, \gamma)^2 \tag{9.10}$$

This is just (6.3) on page 163 specialized to the current setting.

Example 9.2.6 Consider again the sample variance s_N^2 under the IID Gaussian setting of example 9.2.4. We saw there that $\operatorname{var} s_N^2 = 2\sigma^4 N^{-2}(N-1)$. Combining this result with (9.10) and (9.7), we have

$$\operatorname{mse}\left(s_N^2, \sigma^2\right) = \frac{2\sigma^4}{N^2}(N-1) + \left[\sigma^2 \frac{N-1}{N} - \sigma^2\right]^2 = \frac{\sigma^4}{N^2}(2N-1)$$

As can be seen from both (9.9) and (9.10), when $\operatorname{mse}(\hat{\gamma}, \gamma)$ is small for a given estimator $\hat{\gamma}$, the estimator concentrates probability mass around the target feature γ. Hence minimizing MSE is a natural and reasonable criterion. In doing so, we are making our subjective loss function explicit, while choosing a loss function that is simple and highly tractable.

When minimizing MSE, we typically find a trade-off between bias and variance: lower variance costs more bias and vice-versa. Moreover solutions usually turn out to be interior. In particular, we can often reduce variance significantly by accepting a small amount of bias.

Example 9.2.7 Let $\hat{\gamma}$ be any unbiased estimator of a feature $\gamma \in \mathbb{R}$. Let $v := \operatorname{var} \hat{\gamma}$. Consider the class of estimators $\{\lambda\hat{\gamma} : \lambda \in \mathbb{R}\}$. As exercise 9.4.3 asks you to verify, the value of λ that minimizes $\operatorname{mse}(\lambda\hat{\gamma}, \gamma)$ is

$$\lambda^* := \frac{\gamma^2}{\gamma^2 + v} \tag{9.11}$$

In other words, the unbiased estimator does not minimize MSE unless $v = 0$.

For most sensible estimators, v converges to zero as the sample size $\to \infty$. The message is that unbiased estimators only approach optimality when the data size is large. Here "large" should be understood as relative to model complexity. More complex models need more data to be estimated effectively.

9.2.3.1 Stein's Example

There is a famous example in the theory of statistics due to Stein (1956) that pertains to so-called admissible estimators. Here we'll borrow Stein's problem and proposed solution to illustrate several ideas, including the relationship between bias and mean squared error.

To make things concrete, consider the following application: In the field of public finance, one topic of interest is ability-based taxation, which has optimality properties in terms of welfare in certain models. Ability is not observable. Suppose, in particular, that we have a population of K individuals, where the kth individual has idiosyncratic ability $\mu_k \in [0, 1]$. For each agent, we get to observe N noisy signals of ability, each of the form $x_{kn} = \mu_k + \epsilon_{kn}$, $n = 1, \ldots, N$. The noise terms ϵ_{kn} are all independent $\text{N}(0, \sigma^2)$. Our task is to estimate the parameter vector $\boldsymbol{\mu} = (\mu_1, \ldots, \mu_K)$ given the data from the observations x_{nk}. To make things simpler we'll assume that only $\boldsymbol{\mu}$ is unknown.

A natural estimator of $\boldsymbol{\mu}$ is the vector sample mean

$$\bar{\mathbf{x}}_N = \begin{pmatrix} \frac{1}{N}\sum_{n=1}^N x_{1n} \\ \vdots \\ \frac{1}{N}\sum_{n=1}^N x_{Kn} \end{pmatrix}$$

This is the estimator produced by applying the sample analogue principle to our problem. It's also the maximum likelihood estimator and best linear unbiased.

What Stein showed is that, whenever $K > 2$, there exists an alternative estimator $\hat{\boldsymbol{\mu}}_N$ such that

$$\mathbb{E}\left\{ \|\hat{\boldsymbol{\mu}}_N - \boldsymbol{\mu}\|^2 \right\} < \mathbb{E}\left\{ \|\bar{\mathbf{x}}_N - \boldsymbol{\mu}\|^2 \right\} \quad \text{for all } \boldsymbol{\mu} \in \mathbb{R}^K \tag{9.12}$$

In other words, $\hat{\boldsymbol{\mu}}_N$ uniformly dominates $\bar{\mathbf{x}}_N$ in terms of MSE, for all possible values of $\boldsymbol{\mu}$! The estimator in question is what is now known as the **James–Stein estimator**. It is defined as

$$\hat{\boldsymbol{\mu}}_N = \kappa\, \bar{\mathbf{x}}_N \quad \text{where} \quad \kappa := 1 - \frac{K-2}{N} \frac{\sigma^2}{\|\bar{\mathbf{x}}_N\|^2}$$

This estimator is biased. It achieves lower mean squared error by reducing variance at the expense of a small amount of bias. A relatively simple proof of (9.12) can be found on p. 34 of Young and Smith (2005).

We can get some of the intuition from simulation. In our simulation we set $K = 200$, $N = 5$ and $\sigma = 1$. Thus we have 5 noisy observations on the ability of each of 200 agents. For each agent we choose their ability μ_k independently from a uniform distribution on $[0, 1]$ and next generate the disturbances ϵ_{kn} as independent standard normals. We then compute the estimators $\bar{\mathbf{x}}_N$ and $\hat{\boldsymbol{\mu}}_N$ and the corresponding error vectors.

Figure 9.5 shows a typical realization. The bars in the top panel are the elements of the vector $\bar{\mathbf{x}}_N - \boldsymbol{\mu}$, which records the errors for the sample mean estimator $\bar{\mathbf{x}}_N$. Those in the lower panel correspond to the errors of the James–Stein estimator. These are noticeably downward biased and also noticeably smaller than the errors of the sample mean estimator. This is reflected in the SSE values in the top left of each panel, which give the sum of squared errors (i.e., the squared norms of the error vectors). The SSE for the sample mean estimator is nearly twice as large.[1]

1. See `johnstachurski.net/emet.html` for the code that generates these results.

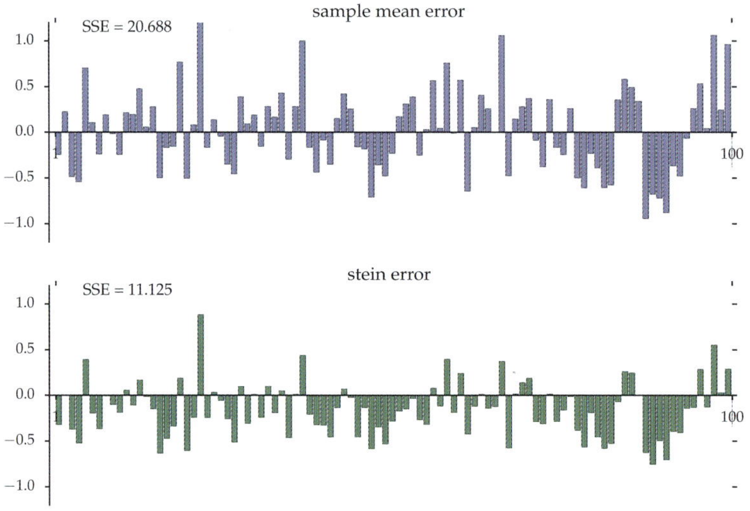

Figure 9.5 Error vectors for the two estimators

9.2.4 Asymptotic Properties

Let's now turn to asymptotic properties of estimators. Asymptotic theory concerns whether or not the sampling distribution of a given estimator increasingly concentrates around the feature we wish to estimate, the rate at which this occurs, and the shape of the sampling distribution in large samples.

A fundamental concept in asymptotic statistics is consistency. Let $\{\hat{\gamma}_N\}$ be a sequence of estimators of a given feature γ, based on a sample of size N. We say that $\hat{\gamma}_N$ is **consistent** for γ if

$$\hat{\gamma}_N \xrightarrow{p} \gamma \quad \text{as} \quad N \to \infty \tag{9.13}$$

The definition is the same whether the estimators are vector or scalar-valued. The statement that $\hat{\gamma}_N$ is consistent means more correctly that the sequence $\{\hat{\gamma}_N\}$ is consistent.

As for bias, whether consistency holds depends not just on $\hat{\gamma}_N$ but also on the joint distribution of the data. If we say that $\hat{\gamma}_N$ is consistent over a class of distributions $\mathscr{P}$, we mean that (9.13) holds true for any distribution in $\mathscr{P}$.

Example 9.2.8 The sample mean $\bar{x}_N$ of any IID sample is consistent for the mean over the class of distributions on $\mathbb{R}$ with finite first moment. Indeed, if P is such a distribution and $x_1, \ldots, x_N$ are IID draws from P, then the law of large numbers gives

$$\frac{1}{N}\sum_{n=1}^{N} x_n \xrightarrow{p} \int sP(ds) \quad \text{as} \quad N \to \infty$$

More generally, $\hat{\gamma}_N = \frac{1}{N}\sum_{n=1}^{N} h(\mathbf{x}_n)$ is consistent for $\gamma = \int h(\mathbf{s})P(d\mathbf{s})$ whenever

(i) $\mathbf{x}_1, \ldots, \mathbf{x}_N$ is an IID sample with $\mathcal{L}(\mathbf{x}_n) = P$ for all n and

(ii) $\int h(\mathbf{s})P(d\mathbf{s})$ exists.

(See (6.7) on page 164.) For example, the kth sample moment is consistent for the kth moment over the class of distributions with finite kth moment.

Here's an example of consistency that requires a bit more work.

Example 9.2.9 For any IID sample $x_1, \ldots, x_N$ with finite variance, the sample variance s_N^2 is consistent for the variance. This can be established from the expression

$$s_N^2 = \frac{1}{N}\sum_{n=1}^{N}(x_n - \mu)^2 - (\bar{x}_N - \mu)^2 \tag{9.14}$$

where μ is the common mean (see ex. 9.4.1 and its solution). Applying the law of large numbers to (9.14), the first term converges to σ^2, while $(\bar{x}_N - \mu) \xrightarrow{p} 0$, and hence $(\bar{x}_N - \mu)^2 \xrightarrow{p} 0$ by fact 6.1.1 on page 161. Consistency of s_N^2 follows.

Fact 9.2.2 If $\hat{\gamma}_N$ is consistent for γ and g is any continuous function, then $g(\hat{\gamma}_N)$ is consistent for $g(\gamma)$.

Fact 9.2.2 is immediate from fact 6.1.1 on page 161.

Example 9.2.10 The sample standard deviation $s_N = \sqrt{s_N^2}$ is consistent for the standard deviation whenever s_N^2 is consistent for the variance.

Reasonable estimators should be consistent, at least for the IID case. In fact, as we saw in theorem 8.1.1, the entire unknown distribution can be recovered asymptotically with repeated independent samples.

9.2.4.1 Asymptotic Distributions

In the IID Gaussian setting of example 9.1.3, the distribution of the sample mean is $\text{N}(\mu, \sigma^2/N)$. Beyond the information contained in the mean and variance, the fact that the sampling distribution is normal gives us important additional knowledge. We know that the distribution is symmetric, that it has thin tails, and that it puts around 95% of its mass within two standard deviations of the mean. We can determine probabilities of intervals or the expectation of any function of $\bar{x}_N$.

The only concern is our assumption that the observations are Gaussian. Economic theory rarely provides any convincing basis for this assumption. Fortunately, we have the central limit theorem to fall back on, which tells us (remarkably!) that the sample mean is always asymptotically Gaussian, provided that the underlying observations have finite second moment. Even better, the same approximation is valid for many estimators beyond the sample mean.

To clarify, let $\{\hat{\gamma}_N\}$ be a sequence of estimators for some feature γ. We say that $\hat{\gamma}_N$ is **asymptotically normal** if there exists a positive definite matrix Σ such that

$$\sqrt{N}(\hat{\gamma}_N - \gamma) \xrightarrow{d} \mathrm{N}(\mathbf{0}, \Sigma) \quad \text{as} \quad N \to \infty \tag{9.15}$$

When (9.15) holds, Σ is called the **asymptotic variance–covariance matrix** of $\hat{\gamma}_N$.

Example 9.2.11 Let $x_1, \ldots, x_N$ be IID with common mean μ and variance σ^2. If $\mathbb{E}[x_n^4] < \infty$, then the sample variance s_N^2 is asymptotically normal with

$$\sqrt{N}(s_N^2 - \sigma^2) \xrightarrow{d} \mathrm{N}(0, m_4 - \sigma^4) \quad \text{where} \quad m_4 := \mathbb{E}[(x_n - \mu)^4] \tag{9.16}$$

To show this, we can modify (9.14) to get

$$\sqrt{N}(s_N^2 - \sigma^2) = \sqrt{N}\left[\frac{1}{N}\sum_{n=1}^{N}(x_n - \mu)^2 - \sigma^2\right] - \sqrt{N}(\bar{x}_N - \mu)^2 \tag{9.17}$$

The last term on the right-hand side of (9.17) converges to zero in probability, since

$$\sqrt{N}(\bar{x}_N - \mu)^2 = a_N b_N \quad \text{where} \quad a_N := \sqrt{N}(\bar{x}_N - \mu),\ b_N := \bar{x}_N - \mu$$

By the CLT, the LLN and fact 6.1.8 on page 168, we have $a_N b_N \xrightarrow{p} 0$.

To complete the proof, let $Y_n := (x_n - \mu)^2$. The first term in (9.17) can then be written as $\sqrt{N}(\bar{Y}_N - \mathbb{E}[Y_n])$. Applying the CLT, this expression converges to a zero-mean normal with variance

$$\operatorname{var} Y_n = \mathbb{E}[(Y_n - \sigma^2)^2] = \mathbb{E}[(x_n - \mu)^4 - 2(x_n - \mu)^2\sigma^2 + \sigma^4]$$

The claim follows.

Example 9.2.12 Under the same assumptions as example 9.2.11, the sample standard deviation is also asymptotically normal, with

$$\sqrt{N}(s_N - \sigma) \xrightarrow{d} \mathrm{N}\left(0, \frac{m_4 - \sigma^4}{4\sigma^2}\right) \tag{9.18}$$

Exercise 9.4.10 asks you to confirm this.

Fact 9.2.3 Asymptotic normality implies consistency. In particular, if $\{\hat{\gamma}_N\}$ satisfies (9.15), then $\hat{\gamma}_N \xrightarrow{p} \gamma$ as $N \to \infty$ (see ex. 9.4.12).

Asymptotic normality also implies a rate at which $\hat{\gamma}_N$ converges to γ. Indeed, if $\hat{\gamma}_N$ is asymptotically normal, then $\sqrt{N}(\hat{\gamma}_N - \gamma)$ does not diverge. This means that $\hat{\gamma}_N - \gamma$ goes to zero fast enough to offset the diverging term $\sqrt{N}$. To emphasize this point, we say that an asymptotically normal estimator $\hat{\gamma}_N$ is **$\sqrt{N}$-consistent** for γ.

Still more significant is the fact that asymptotic normality gives us an approximation to the entire sampling distribution. This will provides us with a means of performing inference. Chapter 10 gives details.

9.2.5 Decision Theory

We've now reviewed the most common methods of assessing estimators. Next we'll look more deeply at the theory of estimation and decisions under uncertainty. Our focus will be on finite sample properties. This is the most interesting case, since it captures our need to generalize on the basis of limited information.

Despite the efforts of many brilliant statisticians and econometricians, we still lack a convincing general theory of optimality of estimators that rests on purely objective criteria. For example, while the theory of minimum variance unbiased estimators initially seems attractive because it can potentially yield estimators without any subjective judgment on the part of the statistician, there are simple settings where minimum variance unbiased estimators are *inadmissible*, which means that they fail a minimal requirement for what constitutes a sensible estimator (see below).

Without a fully objective theory of "good" estimators, there are competing notions of what good means, and we are forced to take a stand on what our criteria for assessing estimators are in different situations. This means that the estimation problem is not fully specified until we make our preferences explicit.

For economists it's natural to think of specifying preference in terms of utility or loss. To fit with modern statistical terminology, we will think in terms of loss. Thus a full description of an estimation problem includes specification of the loss incurred when an estimator performs poorly.

Let's frame these ideas in line with the seminal work of Wald (1939) and subsequent research on decision theory. A general decision problem consists of

(i) a sample space $\mathcal{X}$,

(ii) an action space $\mathcal{A}$,

(iii) a set $\mathscr{D}$ of decision rules, which are maps $d \colon \mathcal{X} \to \mathcal{A}$

(iv) a universe Θ of possible states of the world, with typical element θ,

(v) a set of probability distributions $\{P_\theta\}$ over the sample space $\mathcal{X}$, and

(vi) a loss function $L \colon \mathcal{A} \times \Theta \to \mathbb{R}$, with interpretation

$$L(a, \theta) = \text{loss incurred by choosing action } a \text{ when the state of the world is } \theta.$$

The state of the world is treated as unknown. The problem is to choose a decision rule $d \in \mathscr{D}$ that generates low loss in some sense to be made precise. Central to this discussion is the notion of **risk**, which is defined as

$$\mathcal{R}(d, \theta) := \int L[d(x), \theta] \, P_\theta(\mathrm{d}x) \tag{9.19}$$

The integral is over all $x \in \mathcal{X}$. The notation $\mathcal{R}$ is used to distinguish this decision-theoretic concept of risk from $R(f)$, the prediction risk of policy f as defined in (8.16).

Example 9.2.13 Let π be an inflation rate and let x be a noisy signal of inflation received by firms. Each firm responds by choosing a price $p = p(x)$ for their product. Let $\Pi(p, \pi)$ represent profits from choosing price p when the inflation rate is π, and let loss be negative profits (see Drenik and Perez (2015) for details and motivation). The risk is then

$$\mathcal{R}(p, \theta) = -\int \Pi(p(x), \pi) P_\theta(\mathrm{d}x, \mathrm{d}\pi)$$

If the distribution P_θ is known to the firm (think of $\{P_\theta\}$ as a singleton), then we have a standard problem of choosing price to maximize expected profits under known probabilities for outcomes. If, however, P_θ is not known, we have a problem of **Knightian uncertainty**. The risk is unknown because we have uncertainty over probabilities.

The problem of choosing estimators is a special case of the decision theory described above. Suppose that we observe data $\mathbf{z}_\mathcal{D}$ taking values in $Z_\mathcal{D}$ with joint distribution P_θ indexed by $\theta \in \Theta$. (The set Θ can be infinite dimensional and θ is just an index.) We wish to estimate some S-valued feature $\gamma_\theta = \gamma(P_\theta)$ using this data. An estimator in this context is a decision rule $\hat{\gamma}$ mapping $Z_\mathcal{D}$ to the action space $\mathcal{A} = S$. If we specify the loss $L(\hat{\gamma}, \theta)$ of choosing $\hat{\gamma}$ when the state of the world is θ, our risk becomes

$$\mathcal{R}(\hat{\gamma}, \theta) = \int_{Z_\mathcal{D}} L(\hat{\gamma}(\mathbf{z}), \gamma_\theta) P_\theta(\mathrm{d}\mathbf{z}) \tag{9.20}$$

Example 9.2.14 Suppose we want to estimate expected returns $\mu_\theta := \int s P_\theta(ds)$ to holding an asset based on IID observations $x_1, \ldots, x_N$ from P_θ. With quadratic loss for prediction error and the sample mean as our estimator, the risk is

$$\mathcal{R}(\bar{x}_N, \theta) = \mathbb{E}_\theta \left[(\bar{x}_N - \mu_\theta)^2 \right] \tag{9.21}$$

Since $\bar{x}_N$ is unbiased for μ_θ, this evaluates to the variance of $\bar{x}_N$ under P_θ. By (9.8), this is equal to $\sigma_\theta^2 / N = \int (s - \mu_\theta)^2 P_\theta(ds)/N$.

In the preceding example, the risk of the estimator is its MSE. More generally, if $\hat{\gamma}$ and γ in (9.20) are vectors and L measures squared vector deviation, then $\mathcal{R}(\hat{\gamma}, \theta) = \text{mse}(\hat{\gamma}, \gamma)$. Thus, risk gives us a generalization of the idea of evaluating estimators based on MSE, as described in §9.2.3. Since loss is subjective, there is no reason we should confine ourselves to quadratic loss.

Example 9.2.15 As an estimate of central tendency of housing prices in a given location, it's common to use the sample median rather the sample mean. This is because large upper tails distort the price faced by a "typical buyer." The choice of median over mean can be understood as minimization of a different loss function when estimating price given pricing data. See example 9.2.18.

9.2.5.1 Choosing Decision Rules

In the current setup, a natural idea for making optimal decisions—and for choosing optimal estimators, in particular—is to choose decision rules with low risk. The problem with this approach is that the risk depends, in general, on the unknown state of the world θ, and hence the risk-minimizing decision rule also depends on the unknown value θ. In other words, we face Knightian uncertainty. We can't evaluate risk because we don't know the probabilities.

Example 9.2.16 Let's return to the setting of example 9.2.14. The risk of the sample mean is equal to σ_θ^2 / N for every value of θ. Consider now a new estimator $\hat{\gamma}$ that is identically equal to 1. In other words, we are predicting 100% return on our investment. This is a great estimator when true mean returns are 1, since

$$\mu_\theta = 1 \quad \Longrightarrow \quad \mathcal{R}(\hat{\gamma}, \theta) = \mathbb{E}\left[(1 - \mu_\theta)^2 \right] = (1-1)^2 = 0$$

Compared with (9.21), we have $\mathcal{R}(\hat{\gamma}, \theta) < \mathcal{R}(\bar{x}_N, \theta)$ whenever $\sigma_\theta > 0$. But if μ_θ diverges sufficiently from 1, then

$$\mathcal{R}(\hat{\gamma}, \theta) = (1 - \mu_\theta)^2 > \frac{\sigma_\theta^2}{N} = \mathcal{R}(\bar{x}_N, \theta)$$

This example illustrates the fact that we cannot, in general, choose estimators based on lowest risk in a classical setting. One useful thing we can do, however, is exclude estimators that are always dominated in terms of risk. These are the so-called inadmissible estimators. In particular, a decision rule d is called **inadmissible** for the general decision problem if there exists a second rule e such that

(i) $\mathcal{R}(e,\theta) \leqslant \mathcal{R}(d,\theta)$ for all $\theta \in \Theta$ and

(ii) $\mathcal{R}(e,\theta) < \mathcal{R}(d,\theta)$ for at least one $\theta \in \Theta$.

A decision rule that is not inadmissible is called **admissible**

Example 9.2.17 Equation (9.12) tells us that the vector sample mean is inadmissible as an estimator of the mean when L is quadratic and the universe of distributions is the multivariate Gaussians.

Another idea that comes out of the desire to minimize risk is minimax. A decision rule d_m is called a **minimax** rule if

$$r(d_m) \leqslant r(d) \text{ for all } d \in \mathscr{D} \quad \text{where} \quad r(d) := \sup_{\theta \in \Theta} \mathcal{R}(d,\theta)$$

A minimax rule is one that performs well in the worst possible state of the world. Minimax decision rules are an important component of robust control and the study of policy under uncertainty. See, for example, Hansen and Sargent (2008). On the other hand, minimax decision rules can be inadmissible (see, e.g., Young and Smith 2005, p. 9).

9.2.5.2 Bayes Rules and Bayes Risk

The Bayesian approach to statistics leads naturally to a coherent and attractive decision theory. The horse race is not entirely fair, however, since we are granted additional information expressed as a prior. Let's review the main ideas.

Consider again the generic decision problem discussed above, but now with a prior distribution $\pi = \pi(\theta)$ over states of the world. In addition each P_θ is now restricted to be a density $p(x \mid \theta)$. As in §8.3.4, we obtain the posterior for θ from the prior given data x via Bayes' law:

$$\pi(\theta \mid x) = \frac{p(x \mid \theta)\pi(\theta)}{p(x)} \qquad (x \in \mathcal{X},\ \theta \in \Theta)$$

Given decision rule d with risk function $\mathcal{R}(d,\theta)$, the **posterior risk** or **Bayes risk** of d is

$$r_\pi(d) := \int \mathcal{R}(d,\theta)\pi(\theta)\,\mathrm{d}\theta$$

A decision rule d that minimizes the Bayes risk is called a **Bayes rule**. If d is an estimator, then a Bayes rule is called a **Bayes estimator**. Existence of such rules is not guaranteed, but in many practical instances they are well defined and unique. We give some simple examples below.

There are two particularly attractive features of Bayes rules, and Bayes estimators in particular. One is that Bayes rules are always admissible under mild regularity conditions. See, for example, theorem 10.4.2 of Casella and Berger (2002). A second is that Bayes rules can be computed as a function of observed data, meaning that we don't have to concern ourselves with how to act in situations that potentially never occur.

To understand the second point, note that we can write the joint density of (x, θ) as either $p(x \mid \theta)\pi(\theta)$ or $\pi(\theta \mid x)p(x)$. Using a change in order of integration followed by this identity, the Bayes risk can be expressed as

$$\begin{aligned} r_\pi(d) &= \int_\Theta \left\{ \int_\mathcal{X} L(d(x), \theta) p(x \mid \theta) \, \mathrm{d}x \right\} \pi(\theta) \, \mathrm{d}\theta \\ &= \int_\mathcal{X} \left\{ \int_\Theta L(d(x), \theta) p(x \mid \theta) \pi(\theta) \, \mathrm{d}\theta \right\} \mathrm{d}x \\ &= \int_\mathcal{X} \left\{ \int_\Theta L(d(x), \theta) \pi(\theta \mid x) \, \mathrm{d}\theta \right\} p(x) \, \mathrm{d}x \end{aligned}$$

It follows from this last expression that d will be a Bayes rule whenever

$$d(x) \in \operatorname*{argmin}_{a \in \mathcal{A}} \int_\Theta L(a, \theta) \pi(\theta \mid x) \, \mathrm{d}\theta \quad \text{for all } x \in \mathcal{X} \tag{9.22}$$

This is akin to the scenario encountered in dynamic programming after applying Bellman's principle of optimality: once we know the value function, we can choose the optimal action just by responding to any observed state.

Example 9.2.18 Let θ be scalar, let $L(a, \theta) = (a - \theta)^2$ and let $\pi(\theta \mid x)$ be the posterior distribution of θ given data x. The Bayes estimator of θ is, by (9.22), the solution to

$$\min_{a \in \mathbb{R}} \int (a - \theta)^2 \pi(\theta \mid x) \, \mathrm{d}\theta$$

As shown in a different context in exercise 8.5.1 on page 244, the minimizer is the mean of $\pi(\theta \mid x)$. In other words, with quadratic loss, the Bayes estimator is the mean of the posterior distribution.

Example 9.2.19 If we repeat the setting of example 9.2.18 but with the absolute loss function $L(a, \theta) = |a - \theta|$ instead of quadratic loss, the Bayes estimator of θ is

$$\operatorname*{argmin}_{a \in \mathbb{R}} \int |a - \theta| \pi(\theta \mid x) \, d\theta$$

As exercise 9.4.14 asks you to show, the solution is the median of $\pi(\theta \mid x)$.

9.3 Further Reading

There are many excellent general texts on statistical inference, including Casella and Berger (2002), Wasserman (2013), and Young and Smith (2005). For a discussion of estimation theory from the perspective of machine learning, see Friedman et al. (2009) or Abu-Mostafa et al. (2012).

9.4 Exercises

Ex. 9.4.1 Prove (9.14) in example 9.2.9.[2]

Ex. 9.4.2 Confirm fact 9.1.1 on page 249.[3]

Ex. 9.4.3 Verify the claim in (9.11) of example 9.2.7.

Ex. 9.4.4 Let $x_1, \ldots, x_N$ be IID random variables uniformly distributed on $[0, \theta]$. Consider the estimator of θ defined by $\hat{\theta}_N := \frac{2}{N} \sum_{n=1}^N x_n$.

(i) Calculate the bias of $\hat{\theta}_N$.

(ii) Calculate the mean squared error of $\hat{\theta}_N$.

(iii) Is $\hat{\theta}_N$ consistent? Why or why not?

Ex. 9.4.5 As in ex. 9.4.4, let $x_1, \ldots, x_N$ be IID draws from $U[0, \theta]$, where θ is an unknown positive parameter. Let $\mu := \mathbb{E}[x_n]$. Show that the estimator

$$\hat{\mu} := \frac{N+1}{2N} \cdot \max\{x_1, \ldots, x_N\}$$

is an unbiased estimator of μ.[4]

Ex. 9.4.6 Let $x_1, \ldots, x_N$ be IID and standard normal. Let $\bar{x}$ be the sample mean. Show that $\bar{x}$ and $x_i - \bar{x}$ are independent for $i = 1, \ldots, N$.

2. Hint: Review example 2.2.3 on page 33.
3. Hints: Look at fact 5.1.13 on page 137 and the proofs following example 9.1.4 on page 249.
4. Hint: If you're stuck, review ex. 5.4.6 and its solution.

Ex. 9.4.7 Following on from ex. 9.4.6, let $x_1, \ldots, x_N$ be IID and standard normal, let $\bar{x}$ be the sample mean, and s^2 be the sample variance. Show that $\bar{x}$ and s^2 are independent.

Ex. 9.4.8 Confirm (9.10): Show that, for any estimator $\hat{\gamma}$ of γ, we have $\text{mse}(\hat{\gamma}, \gamma) = \text{var}\,\hat{\gamma} + \text{bias}(\hat{\gamma}, \gamma)^2$.

Ex. 9.4.9 Let $\hat{\gamma}_N$ be an estimator of $\gamma \in \mathbb{R}$, based on a sample of size N.

(i) Is it true that if $\text{mse}(\hat{\gamma}_N, \gamma) \to 0$ as $N \to \infty$, then $\hat{\gamma}_N$ is consistent for γ? Why or why not?

(ii) Is it true that if $\hat{\gamma}_N$ is asymptotically unbiased and $\text{var}\,\hat{\gamma}_N \to 0$, then $\hat{\gamma}_N$ is consistent for γ? Why or why not?

Ex. 9.4.10 Assuming the conditions of examples 9.2.11–9.2.12, show that (9.18) on page 265 is valid.

Ex. 9.4.11 Let $x_1, \ldots, x_N$ be IID with mean μ and variance σ^2. Let $\bar{x}_N$ be the sample mean, and let σ_N be a consistent estimator of σ. What is the limiting distribution of

$$y_N := N \left(\frac{\bar{x}_N - \mu}{\sigma_N} \right)^2$$

Ex. 9.4.12 Let $\hat{\theta}_N$ be an estimator of θ. Show that if $\hat{\theta}_N$ is asymptotically normal, then $\hat{\theta}_N$ is consistent for θ. (You can restrict attention to the scalar case.)

Ex. 9.4.13 Consider the following estimation problem. Let $\{p_{\boldsymbol{\theta}}\}_{\boldsymbol{\theta} \in \Theta}$ be a parametric class of densities. Now let a particular $\boldsymbol{\theta}_0 \in \Theta$ be fixed, and suppose that an asymptotically normal sequence of estimators $\{\hat{\boldsymbol{\theta}}_N\}$ exists for it, in the sense that

$$\sqrt{N}(\hat{\boldsymbol{\theta}}_N - \boldsymbol{\theta}_0) \stackrel{d}{\to} \text{N}(\mathbf{0}, \Sigma)$$

for some positive definite Σ. Fix a point y and consider $p(y, \hat{\boldsymbol{\theta}}_N)$ as an estimator of $p(y, \boldsymbol{\theta}_0)$. State conditions under which this estimator is consistent and asymptotically normal. Derive the asymptotic distribution under these conditions.

Ex. 9.4.14 Confirm the claim in example 9.2.19 that the minimizer is the median of $\pi(\theta \,|\, x)$. In other words, it is the value $a \in \mathbb{R}$ that satisfies

$$\int_{-\infty}^{a} \pi(\theta \,|\, x) = \int_{a}^{\infty} \pi(\theta \,|\, x) = \frac{1}{2} \tag{9.23}$$

9.4.1 Solutions to Selected Exercises

Solution to Ex. 9.4.1. Let s_N^2, $\mathbf{x}$ and μ be as stated in the exercise. Here's one way to prove (9.14). Let $S = \operatorname{span}\{\mathbf{1}\}$, let $\mathbf{P} = \operatorname{proj} S$, and let $\mathbf{M}$ be the residual projection. Recalling example 2.2.3 on page 33, when $\mathbf{y} := \mathbf{x} - \mu\mathbf{1}$, we have $\mathbf{P}\mathbf{y} = \bar{y}\mathbf{1}$ and $\mathbf{M}\mathbf{y} = \mathbf{y} - \bar{y}\mathbf{1}$. Applying $\|\mathbf{y}\|^2 = \|\mathbf{P}\mathbf{y}\|^2 + \|\mathbf{M}\mathbf{y}\|^2$ now gives

$$\sum_{n=1}^N (x_n - \mu)^2 = N(\bar{x}_N - \mu)^2 + \sum_{n=1}^N (x_n - \bar{x}_N)^2$$

Some minor rearrangements give (9.14). □

Solution to Ex. 9.4.2. Let $\mathcal{L}(\mathbf{x}) = \mathrm{N}(\mu\mathbf{1}, \sigma^2\mathbf{I})$ and let $\boldsymbol{\xi} := \sigma^{-1}(\mathbf{x} - \mu\mathbf{1})$. Since the images of a standard normal random vector under a projection and its residual are independent (fact 5.1.13) and since arbitrary deterministic functions preserve independence (fact 5.1.10), it is enough to find functions f_1 and f_2 and a subspace S and its corresponding projection $\mathbf{P}$ and residual $\mathbf{M}$ such that

$$\bar{x}_N = f_1(\mathbf{P}\boldsymbol{\xi}) \quad \text{and} \quad s_N^2 = f_2(\mathbf{M}\boldsymbol{\xi}) \tag{9.24}$$

To this end, recall from example 2.2.3 (page 33) that if $S := \operatorname{span}\{\mathbf{1}\}$ and $\mathbf{P} = \operatorname{proj} S$, then $\mathbf{P}\mathbf{x} = \bar{x}_N\mathbf{1}$. In addition, $\mathbf{P}\mathbf{1} = \mathbf{1}$. From this you will be able to show that $\bar{x}_N = \sigma\mathbf{e}_1^\top\mathbf{P}\boldsymbol{\xi} + \mu$, where $\mathbf{e}_1$ is the first canonical basis vector. This confirms the first part of (9.24). For the second part, apply (9.5) on page 249 to get

$$s_N^2 = \frac{\sigma^2\boldsymbol{\xi}^\top\mathbf{M}\boldsymbol{\xi}}{N}$$

□

Solution to Ex. 9.4.5. Let $z := \max\{x_1, \ldots, x_N\}$. By the definition of the maximum, we have

$$z \leqslant s \quad \text{if and only if} \quad x_1 \leqslant s \text{ and } x_2 \leqslant s \text{ and } \cdots \text{ and } x_N \leqslant s$$

$$\therefore \quad \{z \leqslant s\} = \cap_{n=1}^N \{x_n \leqslant s\}$$

$$\therefore \quad \mathbb{P}\{z \leqslant s\} = \mathbb{P} \cap_{n=1}^N \{x_n \leqslant s\} = \prod_{n=1}^N \mathbb{P}\{x_n \leqslant s\}$$

For $s \in [0, \theta]$, the CDF of x_n is $F(s) = s/\theta$, and we obtain

$$\mathbb{P}\{z \leqslant s\} = \left(\frac{s}{\theta}\right)^N$$

Differentiating shows that density p of z on the interval $[0, \theta]$ is $p(s) = N \frac{s^{N-1}}{\theta^N}$. The expectation of z is therefore $\int_0^\theta s p(s) \, ds = \frac{N}{N+1} \theta$. We conclude that

$$\mathbb{E}[\hat{\mu}] = \frac{N+1}{2N} \mathbb{E}[z] = \frac{N+1}{2N} \frac{N}{N+1} \theta = \frac{\theta}{2} = \mu$$

In other words, the estimator is unbiased. □

Solution to Ex. 9.4.8. Adding and subtracting $\mathbb{E}[\hat{\gamma}]$, we get

$$\text{mse}(\hat{\gamma}, \gamma) := \mathbb{E}[(\hat{\gamma} - \gamma)^2] = \mathbb{E}[(\hat{\gamma} - \mathbb{E}[\hat{\gamma}] + \mathbb{E}[\hat{\gamma}] - \gamma)^2]$$

Expanding the square and minor manipulations yield the desired result. □

Solution to Ex. 9.4.10. The aim is to verify the claim

$$\sqrt{N}(s_N - \sigma) \xrightarrow{d} \text{N}\left(0, \frac{m_4 - \sigma^4}{4\sigma^2}\right)$$

under the conditions of example 9.2.12 on page 264. Letting $g(x) = \sqrt{x}$ and applying theorem 6.2.2 on page 173 along with (9.16), we have

$$\sqrt{N}(s_N - \sigma) = \sqrt{N}(g(s_N^2) - g(\sigma^2)) \xrightarrow{d} \text{N}\left(0, g'(\sigma^2)^2(m_4 - \sigma^4)\right)$$

The result follows. □

Solution to Ex. 9.4.11. Let

$$w_N := \sqrt{N}\frac{\bar{x}_N - \mu}{\sigma_N} = \frac{\sigma}{\sigma_N}\sqrt{N}\frac{\bar{x}_N - \mu}{\sigma}$$

Since $\sigma_N \xrightarrow{p} \sigma$ by assumption, fact 6.1.1 on page 161 yields $\sigma / \sigma_N \xrightarrow{p} \sigma / \sigma = 1$. Applying the central limit theorem and Slutsky's theorem (fact 6.1.7 on page 168) together, we then have $w_N \xrightarrow{d} z \sim \text{N}(0, 1)$. By the continuous mapping theorem (fact 6.1.6 on page 167), $y_N = w_N^2$ converges in distribution to z^2. As discussed in §5.1.6, the distribution of z^2 is $\chi^2(1)$. □

Solution to Ex. 9.4.12. Fix $\delta > 0$. It suffices to show that for any positive number ϵ we have

$$\lim_{N \to \infty} \mathbb{P}\{|\hat{\theta}_N - \theta| > \delta\} \leqslant \epsilon \tag{9.25}$$

(Note: If a is any nonnegative real number and $a \leqslant \epsilon$ for any $\epsilon > 0$, then $a = 0$.) To establish (9.25), fix $\epsilon > 0$. Let z be zero-mean Gaussian with variance equal to the asymptotic variance of $\hat{\theta}_N$. Choose M such that $\mathbb{P}\{|z| \geqslant M\} \leqslant \epsilon$. For N such that $\sqrt{N}\delta \geqslant M$ we have

$$\mathbb{P}\{|\hat{\theta}_N - \theta| > \delta\} = \mathbb{P}\{\sqrt{N}|\hat{\theta}_N - \theta| > \sqrt{N}\delta\} \leqslant \mathbb{P}\{\sqrt{N}|\hat{\theta}_N - \theta| > M\}$$

Taking $N \to \infty$, applying asymptotic normality, the continuous mapping theorem (fact 6.1.6 on page 167) and the definition of M gives (9.25). □

Solution to Ex. 9.4.13. First observe that, under the conditions of the exercise, $p(y, \hat{\boldsymbol{\theta}}_N)$ is consistent for $p(y, \boldsymbol{\theta}_0)$ whenever $\boldsymbol{\theta} \mapsto p(y, \boldsymbol{\theta})$ is continuous at $\boldsymbol{\theta}_0$. Indeed, since $\hat{\boldsymbol{\theta}}_N$ is asymptotically normal, it is also consistent. Under this continuity assumption, in probability convergence of $p(y, \hat{\boldsymbol{\theta}}_N)$ to $p(y, \boldsymbol{\theta}_0)$ now follows from fact 6.1.1 on page 161.

Regarding asymptotic normality, suppose that $\boldsymbol{\theta} \mapsto p(y, \boldsymbol{\theta})$ is differentiable at $\boldsymbol{\theta}_0$, and that the vector of partial derivatives $\nabla_{\boldsymbol{\theta}} p(y, \boldsymbol{\theta}_0)$ is not the zero vector. Applying (6.14) from page 173, we then have

$$\sqrt{n}\{p(y, \hat{\boldsymbol{\theta}}_N) - p(y, \boldsymbol{\theta}_0)\} \stackrel{d}{\to} \mathrm{N}(0, \nabla_{\boldsymbol{\theta}} p(y, \boldsymbol{\theta}_0)^{\mathsf{T}} \Sigma \nabla_{\boldsymbol{\theta}} p(y, \boldsymbol{\theta}_0))$$ □

Solution to Ex. 9.4.14. The minimization problem in example 9.2.19 can alternatively be written as

$$\operatorname*{argmin}_{a \in \mathbb{R}} \left\{ \int_{-\infty}^{a} (a - \theta)\pi(\theta \,|\, x) \, \mathrm{d}\theta + \int_{a}^{\infty} (\theta - a)\pi(\theta \,|\, x) \, \mathrm{d}\theta \right\}$$

Differentiating with respect to a, setting the result to zero, and using the fact that the posterior is a density gives (9.23). □

Chapter 10

Confidence Intervals and Tests

Until now we've focused primarily on point estimation. Since data are not infinite, point estimation involves uncertainty. We should not be overconfident in our claim to know the data-generating process. Rather, we should be only as confident as the data allows us to be.

We discussed uncertainty previously when we considered sampling distributions. In this chapter we further quantify estimation uncertainty using the language of confidence sets. We also cover hypothesis tests, which are a second key method of inference in classical statistics.

To tie in with standard presentations we'll switch to parametric language. The notation is as on page 214 except that

(i) the marginal distribution P of each observation $\mathbf{z}_n$ is written as P_θ,

(ii) the universe $\mathscr{P}$ of possible distributions is $\{P_\theta : \theta \in \Theta\}$, and

(iii) the joint distribution of the data $\mathbf{z}_\mathcal{D} = (\mathbf{z}_1, \ldots, \mathbf{z}_N)$ is written as $P_\theta^\mathcal{D}$.

However, we won't actually restrict ourselves to the case of finitely many parameters. Instead, θ can be thought of more generally as an index over the set of distributions.

10.1 Confidence Sets

Confidence sets are random subsets of model space that contain the true data generating process with high probability. Let's start with the key definitions and then move on to examples.

10.1.1 Finite Sample Confidence Sets

Fix $\alpha \in (0,1)$. A random set $C(\mathbf{z}_\mathcal{D}) \subset \Theta$ is called a $1 - \alpha$ **confidence set** for θ if $C(\mathbf{z}_\mathcal{D})$ is observable given the data and, for any $\theta \in \Theta$,

$$\mathbb{P}\{\theta \in C(\mathbf{z}_\mathcal{D})\} \geqslant 1 - \alpha \quad \text{whenever} \quad \mathcal{L}(\mathbf{z}_\mathcal{D}) = P_\theta^\mathcal{D} \tag{10.1}$$

Note that it's the set that's random here, not θ.

Confidence sets that are intervals are usually called **confidence intervals**.

Suppose, for example, that we want to estimate the mean of an unknown distribution based on a set of observations $\mathbf{z}_\mathcal{D}$. If we can come up with a 95% confidence set $C(\mathbf{z}_\mathcal{D})$ in the sense of (10.1), then we know that the set will contain the mean in about 95% of our experiments, regardless of the underlying distribution.

The last part of the sentence is essential: We don't know what θ is, and so the set *must be designed* such that the probability of containing θ exceeds $1 - \alpha$ regardless of which θ is generating the data. The difficulty is to actually construct a confidence set with this property for a reasonably large class of distributions. Here's a traditional approach that uses strong parametric assumptions.

Example 10.1.1 Let $\mathbf{z}_\mathcal{D} = \mathbf{x} = (x_1, \ldots, x_N)$ where each x_n is an independent draw from $\mathrm{N}(\mu, \sigma^2)$. Suppose for now that only $\mu \in \mathbb{R}$ is unknown. We wish to form a confidence interval for μ. By (9.3), we have

$$\mathcal{L}\left[\sqrt{N}\frac{(\bar{x}_N - \mu)}{\sigma}\right] = \mathrm{N}(0,1) \tag{10.2}$$

Notice that this statement is true regardless of the values of μ and σ. Applying (4.36) on page 115 now gives

$$\mathbb{P}\left\{\frac{\sqrt{N}}{\sigma}|\bar{x}_N - \mu| \leqslant z_{\alpha/2}\right\} = 1 - \alpha \quad \text{when} \quad z_{\alpha/2} := \Phi^{-1}\left(1 - \frac{\alpha}{2}\right)$$

Here Φ is the standard normal CDF. Some rearranging gives

$$\mathbb{P}\left\{\bar{x}_N - \frac{\sigma}{\sqrt{N}}z_{\alpha/2} \leqslant \mu \leqslant \bar{x}_N + \frac{\sigma}{\sqrt{N}}z_{\alpha/2}\right\} = 1 - \alpha$$

Since this argument is true regardless of the value of μ, we conclude that the interval

$$C(\mathbf{x}) := (\bar{x}_N - e_n,\ \bar{x}_N + e_n) \quad \text{with} \quad e_n := \frac{\sigma}{\sqrt{N}}z_{\alpha/2}$$

is a $1 - \alpha$ confidence interval for μ. (Note that $C(\mathbf{x})$ is indeed observable under our assumption that σ is known.)

In example 10.1.1, the assumption that σ is known is clearly unrealistic. If σ is unknown, a natural approach is to replace this term with the sample standard deviation s_N. In doing so, we will use the following fact, which exercise 10.4.1 asks you to prove.

Fact 10.1.1 If $x_1, \ldots, x_N$ are IID draws from $\mathrm{N}(\mu, \sigma^2)$, then

$$\sqrt{N-1}\frac{(\bar{x}_N - \mu)}{s_N} \tag{10.3}$$

has a Student's t-distribution with $N-1$ degrees of freedom.

The random variable (10.3) is called a **pivot**, which means that its distribution does not depend on the unknown parameters.

Example 10.1.2 Consider then the setting of example 10.1.1 but with σ also unknown. Let F_{N-1} be the CDF of the t-distribution with $N-1$ degrees of freedom. Using the same reasoning as example 10.1.1 with $z_{\alpha/2}$ replaced by $t_{\alpha/2} := F_{N-1}^{-1}(1-\alpha/2)$, we obtain

$$\mathbb{P}\left\{\bar{x}_N - \frac{s_N}{\sqrt{N-1}}t_{\alpha/2} \leqslant \mu \leqslant \bar{x}_N + \frac{s_N}{\sqrt{N-1}}t_{\alpha/2}\right\} = 1-\alpha$$

Recall that the standard deviation of $\bar{x}_N$ is $\sigma/\sqrt{N}$. The term $s_N/\sqrt{N-1}$ is a sample estimate of $\sigma/\sqrt{N}$. Following the discussion in §9.1.3.2, we call $s_N/\sqrt{N-1}$ the standard error of $\bar{x}_N$ and write it as $\mathrm{se}(\bar{x}_N)$. We can then write the confidence interval in example 10.1.2 as

$$C(\mathbf{x}) := (\bar{x}_N - \mathrm{se}(\bar{x}_N)t_{\alpha/2},\ \bar{x}_N + \mathrm{se}(\bar{x}_N)t_{\alpha/2}) \tag{10.4}$$

10.1.2 Asymptotic Methods

While strong parametric assumptions of the form used in examples 10.1.1 and 10.1.2 are difficult to justify in most econometric scenarios, there is another approach to forming confidence intervals that requires much less in terms of structure imposed on the underlying distributions, provided that the sample size is relatively large. Let's start with a definition: given $\alpha \in (0,1)$, a set $C_N(\mathbf{z}_{\mathcal{D}}) \subset \Theta$ is called an **asymptotic $1-\alpha$ confidence set** for θ if $C_N(\mathbf{z}_{\mathcal{D}})$ is observable given the data and

$$\lim_{N\to\infty} \mathbb{P}\{\theta \in C_N(\mathbf{z}_{\mathcal{D}})\} \geqslant 1-\alpha \tag{10.5}$$

for all $\theta \in \Theta$. Note that $C_N(\mathbf{z}_{\mathcal{D}})$ is really a sequence of sets and the definition concerns this sequence.

How can we create asymptotic confidence sets? Let's consider first the case of scalar θ. Suppose that we have an estimator $\hat{\theta}_N$ of θ that is asymptotically normal for all $\theta \in \Theta$. Specializing the results in §9.2.4.1 to the scalar case, this means that, for all $\theta \in \Theta$, there exists a positive constant $v(\theta)$ such that

$$\sqrt{N}(\hat{\theta}_N - \theta) \stackrel{d}{\to} \mathrm{N}(0, v(\theta)) \quad \text{as} \quad N \to \infty \tag{10.6}$$

The constant $v(\theta)$ is called the asymptotic variance of $\hat{\theta}_N$. Suppose we have a sequence of statistics $\mathrm{se}(\hat{\theta}_N)$ such that

$$\sqrt{N}\,\mathrm{se}(\hat{\theta}_N) \stackrel{p}{\to} \sqrt{v(\theta)} \quad \text{as} \quad N \to \infty \tag{10.7}$$

As exercise 10.4.2 asks you to show, (10.6) and (10.7) imply that

$$\frac{\hat{\theta}_N - \theta}{\mathrm{se}(\hat{\theta}_N)} \stackrel{d}{\to} \mathrm{N}(0, 1) \quad \text{as} \quad N \to \infty \tag{10.8}$$

We can now create our asymptotic confidence intervals as

$$C_N := (\hat{\theta}_N - \mathrm{se}(\hat{\theta}_N) z_{\alpha/2}, \hat{\theta}_N + \mathrm{se}(\hat{\theta}_N) z_{\alpha/2}) \tag{10.9}$$

To see this, take the limit and apply (10.8) to get

$$\begin{aligned}
\lim_{N \to \infty} \mathbb{P}\{\theta \in C_N(\mathbf{z}_{\mathcal{D}})\} &= \lim_{N \to \infty} \mathbb{P}\left\{\hat{\theta}_N - \mathrm{se}(\hat{\theta}_N) z_{\alpha/2} \leqslant \theta \leqslant \hat{\theta}_N + \mathrm{se}(\hat{\theta}_N) z_{\alpha/2}\right\} \\
&= \lim_{N \to \infty} \mathbb{P}\left\{-z_{\alpha/2} \leqslant \frac{\hat{\theta}_N - \theta}{\mathrm{se}(\hat{\theta}_N)} \leqslant z_{\alpha/2}\right\} \\
&= 1 - \alpha
\end{aligned}$$

Example 10.1.3 Let $\bar{x}_N$ be the sample mean of IID data $\{x_n\}$. Suppose that these data come from some distribution with finite second moment. Let μ denote the common mean and let σ^2 denote the variance. Let s_N be the sample standard deviation. Combining the central limit theorem and consistency of s_N for σ (see page 263), we have

$$\sqrt{N}(\bar{x}_N - \mu) \stackrel{d}{\to} \mathrm{N}(0, \sigma^2) \text{ and } \sqrt{N}\,\mathrm{se}(\bar{x}_N) \stackrel{p}{\to} \sigma \quad \text{for} \quad \mathrm{se}(\bar{x}_N) := \frac{s_N}{\sqrt{N}} \tag{10.10}$$

It follows that, with this definition of $\mathrm{se}(\bar{x}_N)$, the set

$$(\bar{x}_N - \mathrm{se}(\bar{x}_N) z_{\alpha/2}, \bar{x}_N + \mathrm{se}(\bar{x}_N) z_{\alpha/2})$$

is an asymptotic $1 - \alpha$ confidence interval for $\bar{x}_N$.

10.1.3 A Nonparametric Example

Here's an example of a nonparametric confidence set. In §8.1.3 we learned that if $\mathbf{x} = (x_1, \ldots, x_N)$ is a vector of IID draws from some CDF F and $\hat{F}_N$ is the corresponding ECDF, then $\|F - \hat{F}_N\|_\infty$ converges in probability to 0. In 1933, A. N. Kolmogorov used an extension of the central limit theorem to obtain an asymptotic distribution for this term. In particular, he showed that when F is continuous,

$$\sqrt{N} \sup_{s \in \mathbb{R}} |\hat{F}_N(s) - F(s)| \stackrel{d}{\to} K \tag{10.11}$$

where K is the **Kolmogorov** CDF

$$K(s) := \frac{\sqrt{2\pi}}{s} \sum_{i=1}^{\infty} \exp\left[-\frac{(2i-1)^2\pi^2}{8s^2}\right] \qquad (s \geqslant 0) \tag{10.12}$$

As in the CLT, the limiting distribution K is independent of the CDF F that generates the data.

We can use (10.11) to produce an asymptotic $1 - \alpha$ confidence set for F. To do so, let $\mathfrak{F}$ be the set of all CDFs on $\mathbb{R}$, let $x_1, \ldots, x_N$ be IID draws from $F \in \mathfrak{F}$, let $k_{1-\alpha} := K^{-1}(1 - \alpha)$, and let

$$C_N(\mathbf{x}) := \left\{ G \in \mathfrak{F} \,:\, \hat{F}_N(s) - \frac{k_{1-\alpha}}{\sqrt{N}} \leqslant G(s) \leqslant \hat{F}_N(s) + \frac{k_{1-\alpha}}{\sqrt{N}} \text{ for all } s \in \mathbb{R} \right\}$$

The set $C_N(\mathbf{x}) \subset \mathfrak{F}$ is an asymptotic $1 - \alpha$ confidence set for F. Indeed, after rearranging the expression, we get

$$\begin{aligned} F \in C_N(\mathbf{x}) &\iff -k_{1-\alpha} \leqslant \sqrt{N}(\hat{F}_N(s) - F(s)) \leqslant k_{1-\alpha} \text{ for all } s \\ &\iff \sqrt{N}|\hat{F}_N(s) - F(s)| \leqslant k_{1-\alpha} \text{ for all } s \\ &\iff \sup_s \sqrt{N}|\hat{F}_N(s) - F(s)| \leqslant k_{1-\alpha} \end{aligned}$$

Applying (10.11) now confirms our claim:

$$\lim_{N\to\infty} \mathbb{P}\{F \in C_N(\mathbf{x})\} = \lim_{N\to\infty} \mathbb{P}\left\{\sup_s \sqrt{N}|\hat{F}_N(s) - F(s)| \leqslant k_{1-\alpha}\right\} = 1 - \alpha$$

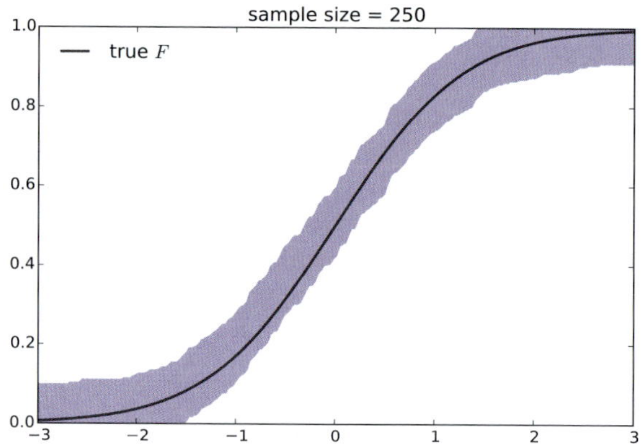

Figure 10.1 Confidence set for the ECDF with 250 observations

Given our data $x_1, \ldots, x_N$ and the corresponding ECDF $\hat{F}_N$, we can present the confidence set $C_N(\mathbf{x})$ visually by highlighting the area between the lower bound $\hat{F}_N(s) - k_{1-\alpha}/\sqrt{N}$ and the upper bound $\hat{F}_N(s) + k_{1-\alpha}/\sqrt{N}$ over s. This is done in figures 10.1 and 10.2. The data are drawn from a t-distribution F with 10 degrees of freedom and α is set to 0.05. The values of N are 250 for figure 10.1 and 1,000 for figure 10.2.

10.2 Hypothesis Tests

This section considers problems of inference where we

(i) hold a belief or theory concerning the probabilities generating the data and

(ii) consider whether the data provides evidence for or against that theory.

Example 10.2.1 While asset price returns data tend to have heavier tails than the normal distribution, for certain assets normality might still be a reasonable and convenient approximation. Let's look at whether or not normality provides a reasonable fit in the case of daily returns on the Nikkei 225. Figure 10.3 shows a comparison of the empirical distribution of standardized returns from January 2014 until July 2015 with the CDF of the standard normal distribution.[1] While the ECDF of the data and the CDF are not identical, we wouldn't expect this even if the hypothesis of normality is completely true. After all, we are only observing a sample, and a sample is subject to

1. Returns are standardized by subtracting the sample mean and dividing by the sample standard deviation. Data are sourced from the Federal Reserve of St. Louis FRED data set.

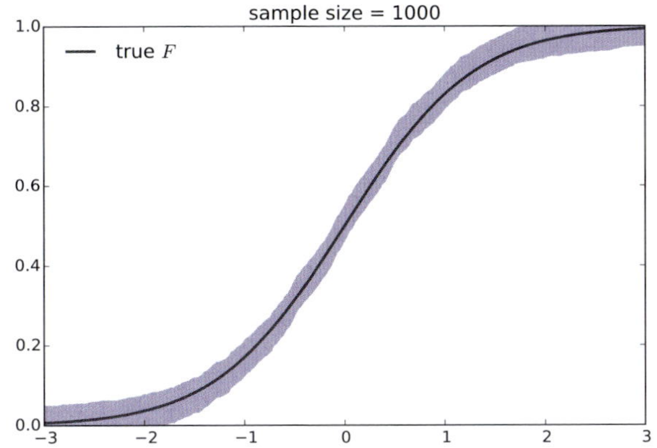

Figure 10.2 Confidence set for the ECDF with 1,000 observations

randomness. So the question becomes, is the sample "unlikely" given the hypothesis of normality?

To take the next steps, we must formalize the process of setting up a hypothesis and quantifying the extent to which the data points in this or some other direction.

Hypothesis testing begins with the specification of a **null hypothesis**, which is a statement that the observed data are being generated by a certain model, or one of a certain class of models. One might imagine that the standard procedure in statistics is to show the validity of the null hypothesis but it is not. Rather, a hypothesis test is an attempt to reject the null.

To see why, let's recall a famous example due to Karl Popper (1902–1994). Consider the claim that all swans are white. It is futile to attempt to prove correctness of this hypothesis: No quantity of white swan sightings can confirm the claim that *all* swans on planet earth are white. Yet a single black swan can show the claim to be false. In this sense, attempting to falsify a theory on the basis of observation is more constructive than attempting to confirm it.

Although we attempt to reject the null hypothesis, we do so only if strong evidence against it is observed. The rationale is this: Suppose that we have a collection of theories about how the economy works. The procedure would then be to step through the theories, at each stage taking correctness of the theory as the null hypothesis and attempting to reject. If the theory is rejected, then we can discard it. This is a useful process of elimination. However, we don't want to mistakenly discard a good theory. Hence we only reject when there is strong evidence against the null hypothesis.

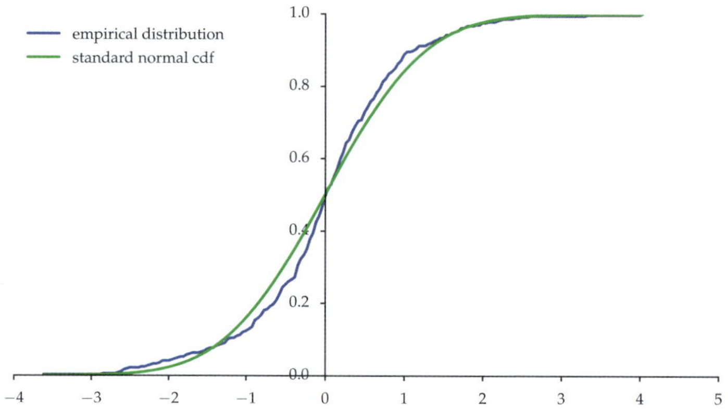

Figure 10.3 ECDF for standardized returns versus the standard normal CDF

10.2.1 Constructing Tests

We adopt the setting and notation used in §10.1.1. A null hypothesis is a specification of a set of models that we believe the data-generating process belongs to. This amounts to specifying a subset Θ_0 of Θ. The null hypothesis is often written as

$$H_0 \colon \theta \in \Theta_0$$

If Θ_0 is a singleton, then the null hypothesis is called a **simple hypothesis**. If not, then the null hypothesis is called a **composite hypothesis**. A test of the null hypothesis is a test of whether or not the observed data were generated by P_θ for some $\theta \in \Theta_0$.

Example 10.2.2 The hypothesis of purchasing power parity is tested by considering models such as

$$p = a + \beta e p^* + \sigma u \tag{10.13}$$

where p is a price or index of domestic prices, e is an exchange rate, p^* is a corresponding foreign price, u is a disturbance term and a, β, σ are parameters. The null hypothesis for absolute purchasing power parity is that (10.13) holds with $a = 0$ and $\beta = 1$. Since σ is not pinned down by the null, this is a composite null hypothesis.

Formally, a **test** of H_0 is a binary function ϕ mapping the observed data $\mathbf{z}_\mathcal{D}$ into $\{0, 1\}$. The decision rule is

$$\begin{aligned} &\text{if } \phi(\mathbf{z}_\mathcal{D}) = 1, \text{ then reject } H_0 \\ &\text{if } \phi(\mathbf{z}_\mathcal{D}) = 0, \text{ then do not reject } H_0 \end{aligned}$$

(Failing to reject H_0 should not be confused with accepting H_0. More on this below.) Our aim will be to design ϕ such that it takes the value 1 when the data present strong evidence against H_0.

Example 10.2.3 Let $\mathbf{z}_{\mathcal{D}}$ be a set of pairs $\mathbf{z}_n = (x_n, y_n)$ from some unknown bivariate distribution P_θ. If H_0 is the hypothesis that the correlation between x and y is negative, then a large positive sample correlation would constitute evidence against H_0. Hence our test might take the form $\phi(\mathbf{z}_{\mathcal{D}}) = \mathbb{1}\{\hat{\varrho} > c\}$, where $\hat{\varrho}$ is the sample correlation. An appropriate value of c remains to be determined.

The outcome of our test depends on the random sample $\mathbf{z}_{\mathcal{D}}$, and being random, its realization can be misleading. There are two different ways in which the realization can mislead us. First, we can mistakenly reject the null hypothesis when it is in fact true. This is called **type I error**. Second, we can fail to reject the null hypothesis when it is false. This is called **type II error**.

The **power function** associated with the test ϕ is the function

$$\beta(\theta) := \mathbb{P}_\theta\{\phi(\mathbf{z}_{\mathcal{D}}) = 1\} \qquad (\theta \in \Theta)$$

Here and below, the symbol $\mathbb{P}_\theta$ indicates that we are computing probabilities under the assumption that $\mathcal{L}(\mathbf{z}_{\mathcal{D}}) = P_\theta^{\mathcal{D}}$. Thus, $\beta(\theta)$ is the probability that the test rejects when the data are generated by the probabilistic model identified by θ.

Ideally, we would like $\beta(\theta) = 0$ when $\theta \in \Theta_0$, and $\beta(\theta) = 1$ when $\theta \notin \Theta_0$. In practice, this is difficult to achieve.

As discussed above, we tend to be conservative in rejecting the null because we don't want to discard good theories. For this reason it is traditional to keep the probability of type I error small. Then, if our test tells us to reject the null, it's unlikely the null is true. Because of this, the standard procedure is to choose a small number α such as 0.05 or 0.01, and then adjust the test such that

$$\beta(\theta) \leqslant \alpha \quad \text{for all } \theta \in \Theta_0 \tag{10.14}$$

If (10.14) holds, then the test is said to be of **size α**. Similarly the **size** of any test with power function β is

$$\alpha := \sup_{\theta \in \Theta_0} \beta(\theta) \tag{10.15}$$

This is the maximal rejection probability when the null hypothesis is true.

In constructing tests, a common (but not universal) setup is to define a real-valued **test statistic** T and a **critical value** c, and then set

$$\phi(\mathbf{z}_{\mathcal{D}}) := \mathbb{1}\{T(\mathbf{z}_{\mathcal{D}}) > c\} \tag{10.16}$$

The pair (T, c) then defines the test, and the rule becomes:

$$\text{reject } H_0 \text{ if and only if } T(\mathbf{z}_{\mathcal{D}}) > c$$

Example 10.2.4 Suppose that $x_1, \ldots, x_N$ are independent draws from $\mathrm{N}(\mu, 1)$ where the value of μ is unknown. The null hypothesis is $\mu \leqslant 0$, or $\Theta_0 = (-\infty, 0]$. Since we want to make inference about the mean, a natural choice for our test statistic is the sample mean. Thus

$$T(\mathbf{z}_{\mathcal{D}}) =: T(x_1, \ldots, x_N) := \bar{x}_N$$

Each $c \in \mathbb{R}$ now gives us a test via (10.16), with power function $\beta(\mu) = \mathbb{P}_\mu\{\bar{x}_N > c\}$. To evaluate β, recall that $\mathcal{L}(\bar{x}_N) = \mathrm{N}(\mu, 1/N)$. As a result, if Φ is the CDF of the standard normal distribution and $\mathcal{L}(z) = \Phi$, then

$$\mathbb{P}_\mu\{\bar{x}_N \leqslant c\} = \mathbb{P}\{\mu + N^{-1/2} z \leqslant c\} = \mathbb{P}\{z \leqslant N^{1/2}(c - \mu)\} = \Phi[N^{1/2}(c - \mu)]$$

$$\therefore \quad \beta(\mu) = 1 - \Phi[N^{1/2}(c - \mu)] \tag{10.17}$$

Given c, the power function is increasing in μ because higher μ pushes up the mean of $\bar{x}_N$, making the event $\{\bar{x}_N > c\}$ more likely. Given μ, the function is decreasing in c, because higher c makes the event $\{\bar{x}_N > c\}$ less likely.

Plots of the power function β in (10.17) are presented in figure 10.4 for two different values of c. Here N is fixed at 10. Since $\Theta_0 = (-\infty, 0]$, the size of the test in each case is $\sup_{\mu \leqslant 0} \beta(\mu)$. Since the power curves are increasing, this is just $\beta(0)$.

Figure 10.4 illustrates a typical trade-off between type I and type II error. If we increase c, we make rejection less likely for all values of μ. This pushes down type I error, but it also increases the probability that we fail to reject a false null.

10.2.2 Choosing Critical Values

Let's think a bit more about the test in (10.16). Typically, the choice of T is suggested by the problem. For example, if our hypothesis is a statement about the second moment of a random variable, then we might take T to be the sample second moment. Once T is fixed, we need to adjust c such that (T, c) attains the appropriate size. Thus the standard procedure is to

(i) choose a desired size α according to our tolerance for type I error,

(ii) identify a suitable test statistic T, and

(iii) choose a critical value c so that (T, c) is of size α.

In performing the last step, we can balance our desire to minimize type II error while maintaining a size α test by choosing c such that (10.14) holds with equality. In

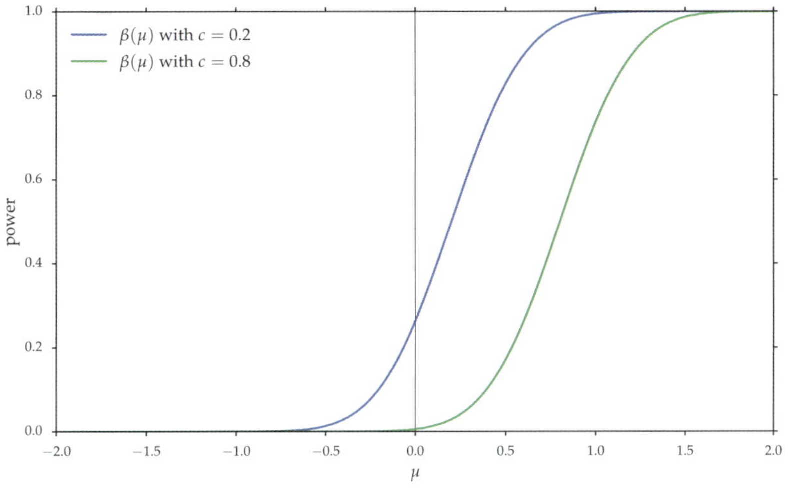

Figure 10.4 Power function β

this case, the problem is to choose c to solve

$$\alpha = \sup_{\theta \in \Theta_0} \mathbb{P}_\theta\{T(\mathbf{z}_\mathcal{D}) > c\} \tag{10.18}$$

Figure 10.5 gives an illustration. In the figure, we've taken Θ_0 to be the two element set $\{\theta_a, \theta_b\}$. The blue line gives an imaginary distribution of $T(\mathbf{z}_\mathcal{D})$, represented as a density, when $\mathbf{z}_\mathcal{D}$ is generated by θ_a. The black line gives the same for θ_b. Assuming that a value of α is prescribed, our next step is to determine the c such that (10.18) holds. Here we choose c such that the largest of the two shaded areas is equal to α.

Example 10.2.5 Let's look again at example 10.2.4, where $x_1, \ldots, x_N \overset{\text{IID}}{\sim} \mathrm{N}(\mu, 1)$ for μ unknown, and our null hypothesis is $\mu \leqslant 0$. Given α, our task is to find the appropriate critical value c so that the test (T, c) is of size α. To solve for c given α, we use (10.18). Applying the expression for the power function in (10.17), this becomes

$$\alpha = \sup_{\mu \leqslant 0} \{1 - \Phi[N^{1/2}(c - \mu)]\}$$

The right-hand side is increasing in μ, so the supremum is obtained by setting $\mu = 0$.

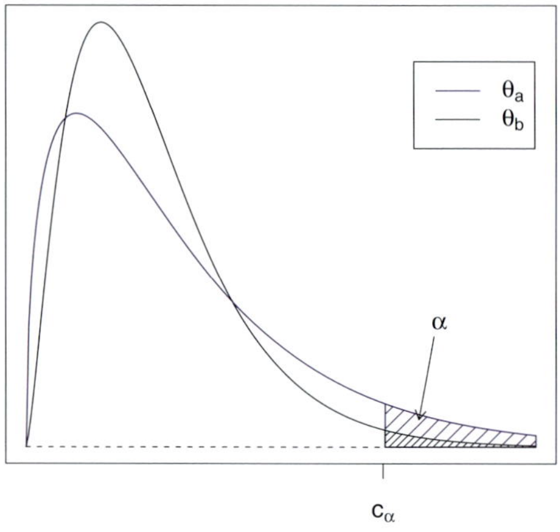

Figure 10.5 Determining the critical value

Setting $\mu = 0$ and solving for c, we obtain

$$c(\alpha) := N^{-1/2}\Phi^{-1}(1 - \alpha)$$

where Φ^{-1} is the quantile function of the standard normal distribution. In R, this function can be evaluated using `qnorm`. For example,

```
> alpha = 0.05
> qnorm(1 - alpha)
[1] 1.644854
```

Since Φ^{-1} is increasing, we see that smaller α corresponds to larger $c(\alpha)$—we reduce the probability of type I error by increasing the critical value that the mean $\bar{x}_N$ must obtain for rejection to occur. Also higher N brings down $c(\alpha)$: more data allows us to reduce the critical value without increasing the probability of rejecting a true null.

10.2.3 Asymptotic Tests

In general, constructing a test of a given size requires some knowledge of the distribution of the test statistic under the null hypothesis. In many cases, however, we know relatively little about the distribution of the test statistic. Fortunately, we still have options. One approach is to bootstrap. Another is to try to determine the asymptotic distribution of the test statistic. As we've learned from the central limit theory, asymptotics hold out the possibility that we can pin down distributions without actually assuming a parametric structure *a priori*.

To proceed, we need to switch to a notion of asymptotic size for tests, rather than finite sample size. Writing β_N instead of β to emphasize the fact that the power function typically depends on sample size, a test is called **asymptotically of size α** if

$$\lim_{N\to\infty} \beta_N(\theta) \leqslant \alpha \quad \text{for all } \theta \in \Theta_0 \tag{10.19}$$

Example 10.2.6 Let $x_1, \ldots, x_N$ be an IID sample with mean θ and variance σ^2. Assume that both θ and σ are unknown. We wish to test the hypothesis $H_0\colon \theta = \theta_0$. Consider the statistic

$$t_N := \sqrt{N}\left\{\frac{\bar{x}_N - \theta_0}{s_N}\right\} = \frac{\bar{x}_N - \theta_0}{\text{se}(\bar{x}_N)} \tag{10.20}$$

where $\text{se}(\bar{x}_N) := \frac{s_N}{\sqrt{N}}$ as in (10.10). As discussed in example 10.1.3, this expression converges in distribution to a standard normal. Hence

$$\phi_N(\mathbf{x}) := \mathbb{1}\{|t_N| > z_{\alpha/2}\} \tag{10.21}$$

is asymptotically of size α (see ex. 10.4.3).

10.2.3.1 A Test for the Empirical Distribution

As another example of how to construct tests which are asymptotically of size α, let's return to the standardized daily returns data presented in figure 10.3. Let Φ be the standard normal CDF as before, and let H_0 be that standardized returns are IID draws from Φ. Let α be given, and let $k_{1-\alpha} = K^{-1}(1-\alpha)$ be the $1-\alpha$ quantile of the Kolmogorov distribution K, as defined in (10.12). Finally, let $\hat{F}_N$ be the ECDF of the data. If the null hypothesis is true, then, by (10.11) on page 279, we have

$$\sqrt{N} \sup_{s\in\mathbb{R}} |\hat{F}_N(s) - \Phi(s)| \xrightarrow{d} K \tag{10.22}$$

For the test

$$\phi_N(\mathbf{x}) := \mathbb{1}\left\{\sqrt{N} \sup_{s\in\mathbb{R}} |\hat{F}_N(s) - \Phi(s)| > k_{1-\alpha}\right\}$$

let $\beta_N(\Phi)$ be the value of the power function when the null hypothesis is true. By (10.22), we have

$$\lim_{N\to\infty} \beta_N(\Phi) = \lim_{N\to\infty} \mathbb{P}\left\{\sqrt{N} \sup_{s\in\mathbb{R}} |\hat{F}_N(s) - \Phi(s)| > k_{1-\alpha}\right\} = \alpha$$

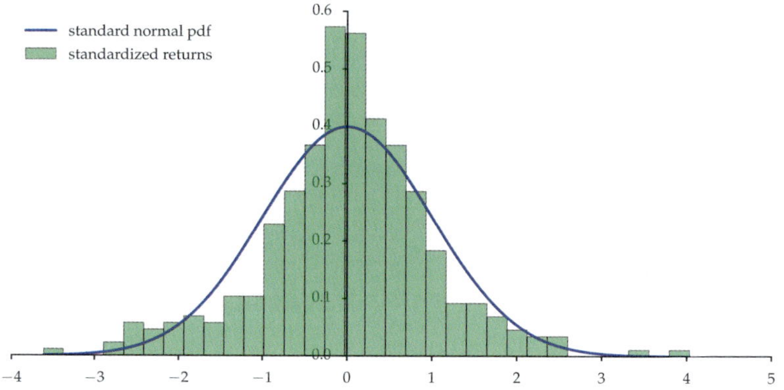

Figure 10.6 Standardized daily returns for the Nikkei 225

Hence (10.19) is verified, and the test is asymptotically of size α. Notice how the construction of the test inverts the confidence set in §10.1.3.

The Nikkei data set used here has 364 observations. The value of the test statistic $\sqrt{N} \sup_{s \in \mathbb{R}} |\hat{F}_N(s) - \Phi(s)|$ is 1.548. If $\alpha = 0.05$, then, as shown in §10.1.3, the critical value $k_{1-\alpha}$ is 1.36. Hence the test statistic exceeds the critical value, and the null hypothesis is rejected. See `johnstachurski.net/emet.html` for the code.

While the departure from normality is not easy to see in figure 10.3, it can be seen more clearly in a comparison of the histogram and density, as in figure 10.6. The data are noticeably more peaked and there is evidence of heavy tails.

This application also illustrates how tests often depend on a range of assumptions beyond those that are the focus of a particular hypothesis. Here, for example, a full description of H_0 is that standardized returns are IID draws from the standard normal density. The rejection suggests this null is false, but it may be the IID assumption rather than the normality assumption that makes our null a poor fit to the data.[2]

10.2.3.2 p-Values

Typically, a test that rejects at size 0.05 will also reject at size 0.1, but may not reject at size 0.01. Lower α means less tolerance for type I error, and forces the critical value to become larger. Hence, for a fixed value of the test statistic, the result of the test may switch from reject to don't reject. A natural question then is: What is the smallest

2. The test we've implemented can be modified to tackle the case of dependent data. See Negri and Nishiyama (2010) for one such test and more references.

value of α at which we can still reject a given test statistic? This value is called the p-value.

To state this more precisely, consider again the setting of §10.2. The null hypothesis is $H_0 : \theta \in \Theta_0$ and, for each $\alpha \in (0,1)$, a test $(T, c(\alpha))$ of size α. We assume here that $c(\alpha)$ is determined via the relationship in (10.18). In this setting, the p-value of the test is defined as

$$p(\mathbf{z}_{\mathcal{D}}) := \inf\{\alpha \in (0,1) \, : \, c(\alpha) < T(\mathbf{z}_{\mathcal{D}})\}$$

Roughly speaking, this is the α at which the test switches from reject to don't reject. Typically, $\alpha \mapsto c(\alpha)$ is continuous, and in this case the expression for $p(\mathbf{z}_{\mathcal{D}})$ reduces to

$$p(\mathbf{z}_{\mathcal{D}}) := \text{ the } \alpha \text{ such that } c(\alpha) = T(\mathbf{z}_{\mathcal{D}}) \tag{10.23}$$

Example 10.2.7 Recall the test (10.21). Here $c(\alpha) := \Phi^{-1}(1 - \alpha/2)$, and $c(\alpha)$ is continuous in α, so we can apply the definition of $p(\mathbf{z}_{\mathcal{D}})$ in (10.23). To solve for $p(\mathbf{z}_{\mathcal{D}})$, then, we need to solve for α in the expression $\Phi^{-1}(1 - \alpha/2) = |t_N(\mathbf{z}_{\mathcal{D}})|$. With a bit of rearranging and an application of symmetry, we obtain

$$p(\mathbf{z}_{\mathcal{D}}) = 2\Phi(-|t_N(\mathbf{z}_{\mathcal{D}})|) \tag{10.24}$$

10.2.4 Accepting the Null?

Sometimes failure to reject a null hypothesis comes to be seen as presenting evidence in favor of that hypothesis. This is a slippery slope. Here's one illustration.

In the 1980s econometricians found a new set of toys called unit root tests. First it was discovered that a newly developed test due to Dickey and Fuller (1979) did not reject the null hypothesis of a unit root when applied to a variety of economic time series (Nelson and Plosser 1982). It was argued that this finding called into question a range of earlier time series methods that assumed trend stationarity, as well as a variety of business cycle studies that assumed stationary innovations around a trend. A raft of new unit root tests appeared. The idea that innovations to major economic time series contain a permanent component became something like a stylized fact.

Let's think about this carefully. For the sake of concreteness, suppose that we are considering unemployment rate data, where the unit root hypothesis was associated with the concept of hysteresis (see, e.g., Mitchell 1993). In this setting the unit root null can be expressed most simply as the hypothesis that $a = 1$ in the AR(1) process

$$u_{t+1} = a u_t + b + \epsilon_{t+1} \tag{10.25}$$

Here $\{u_t\}$ is unemployment, a and b are parameters and $\{\epsilon_t\}$ is a zero-mean innovation (see eq. (5) of Mitchell 1993). Letting T be the length of the sample, the standard one-sided Dickey–Fuller test of the unit root null is to

(i) estimate the parameters as $\hat{a}$ and $\hat{b}$ by least squares (see page 224) and

(ii) reject the null if $T(\hat{a} - 1) < c$, where c is a critical value.

Intuitively, when $a < 1$, the test statistic will evaluate to a negative number in large samples. While we omit the derivation, Dickey and Fuller (1979) showed that the test statistic converges in distribution under the null and tabulated critical values for different test sizes.

A number of studies have been unable to reject a unit root null for unemployment rate data (see Mitchell 1993 for an earlier study or Cheng et al. 2012 for a study using a newer set of tests). How should we interpret failure to reject the null in this setting? One possibility is that (10.25) is a good model for the data with $a = 1$. This is not the only possibility, however. Another possibility is that the data are being generated by some other process against which this test has little power.

The second possibility seems more plausible than the first. Indeed, if $a = 1$ in (10.25), then $\mathbb{P}\{u_t \in B\} \to 0$ as $t \to \infty$ for every bounded $\mathscr{B}$-measurable $B \subset \mathbb{R}$. But employment rates don't diverge. A more likely story is that while unemployment rates are highly persistent for some range of values, there are equilibrium forces that become increasingly stronger outside this band. For example, the further the unemployment rate falls, the more tightness in the labor market boosts wages, encouraging employers to substitute toward other factors of production and putting upward pressure on the unemployment rate.

We can easily reconcile these equilibrium forces with the idea that the unemployment rate is highly persistent at commonly observed values by adopting a nonlinear model. For example, consider the following simple variation on a random walk:

$$u_{t+1} = h(u_t) + \epsilon_{t+1} \tag{10.26}$$

where h is the generalized logistic function depicted in figure 10.7, along with the 45 degree line. For unemployment rates in a band between about 5 and 15, the function has a slope close to one, and the process exhibits strong persistence, just like a random walk. For values above and below this number the shape of h causes drift back to the band.

Listing 7 gives code for a simulation when this model generates the data. The shocks $\{\epsilon_t\}$ are independent Gaussian. In each loop a time series of length 100 is drawn and the Dickey–Fuller test statistic is calculated. The size of the test is set to 0.05, in which case the critical value for the test is -13.7 (see, e.g., Hayashi 2000, p. 576). If you run the code you will see that for this random seed, the rejection frequency over 5,000 repetitions is around 0.05. This is the same rejection frequency as when the null is true. For this data size, the great majority of tests would fail to reject

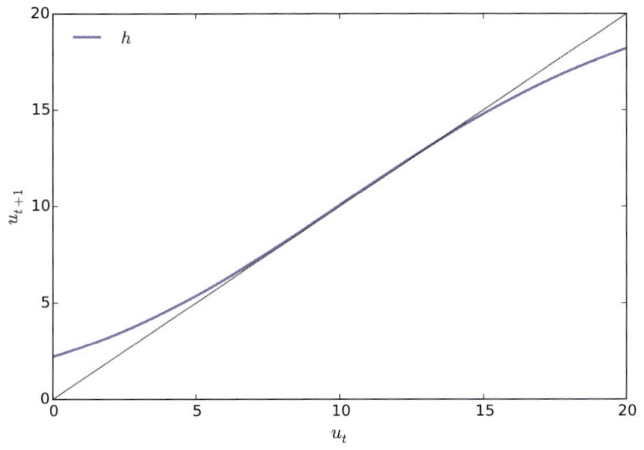

Figure 10.7 A nonlinear process for unemployment dynamics

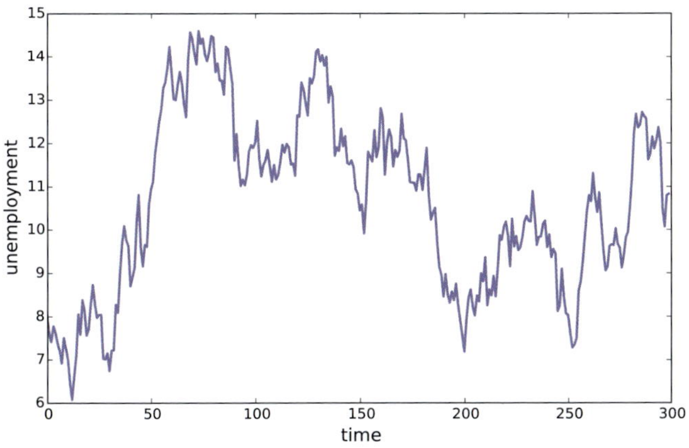

Figure 10.8 Simulated unemployment dynamics

the unit root model, even though the data-generating process is (10.26).

Listing 7 DF test applied to a nonlinear time series (Julia)

```
N = 100             # Length of time series
alpha = 0.05        # Size of test
critical = -13.7    # Critical value for DF test of size 0.05
srand(123)          # Set random seed

function h(x, a=0.0, k=22, b=.16, q=0.6, m=10)
    return a + (k - a) / ((1 + q * exp(-b * (x - m)))^(1/q))
end

function dickey_fuller_stat(y)
    y1 = y[1:end-1]
    y2 = y[2:end]
    z2 = y2 - mean(y2)
    z1 = y1 - mean(y1)
    rho = dot(z1, z2) / dot(z1, z1)
    return length(y1) * (rho - 1)
end

function sim_dgp(N)
    y = Array(Float64, N)
    y[1] = 8  # Initial value of unemployment rate
    for i in 1:N-1
        y[i+1] = h(y[i]) + 0.5 * randn()
    end
    return y
end

M = 5000
rejections = 0
for m in 1:M
    y = sim_dgp(N)
    rejections += (dickey_fuller_stat(y) < critical)
end
println("Fraction under critical value: ", rejections / M)
```

The interesting thing about this experiment is that the nonlinear data-generating process has very different properties from the null. Not only is it stationary, it is uniformly ergodic, as can be seen by checking the conditions of theorem 16.0.2 of Meyn and Tweedie (2009). This is the strongest possible form of stationarity after the IID property. It means that the effect of initial conditions dies out at a geometric rate that is bounded away from one uniformly over the state space. There is no "permanent component."

10.2.5 Statistical Tests in Economics

While the mechanics of hypothesis testing are relatively straightforward, the scientific paradigm based around hypothesis testing is the subject of continual debate. Macroeconomics is an interesting case in point. In the 1970s the rational expectations revolution ushered in a new class of macroeconomic models. One of the first things the proponents of rational expectations did was to test these models against data. Thomas Sargent's account runs as follows (Evans and Honkapohja 2005):

> My recollection is that Bob Lucas and Ed Prescott were initially very enthusiastic about rational expectations econometrics. After all, it simply involved imposing on ourselves the same high standards we had criticized the Keynesians for failing to live up to. But after about five years of doing likelihood ratio tests on rational expectations models, I recall Bob Lucas and Ed Prescott telling me that those tests were rejecting too many good models.

In the following years, many macroeconomists moved away from formal hypothesis testing. A standard response to classical testing was: "I already know that my model is wrong. Rejection of my model using standard inference tells me nothing new." For example, Kydland and Prescott (1991) define econometrics as a process without tests:

> The main steps in econometric analysis are as follows: defining the question; setting up the model; calibrating the model; and reporting the findings.

How does this line of thinking compare with the standard statistical paradigm? The standard paradigm certainly recognizes that all models are wrong. All sensible models are wrong along some dimensions because they are, by definition, simplified representations of reality. Rejection of models is intended to facilitate survival of the fittest: Those models that explain observed phenomena effectively, and, at the same time, are most difficult to reject, will survive.[3]

3. Incidentally, given this description of model selection, it might appear there is an easy way to produce

At the same time, it's reasonable to feel sympathy for the frustration with classical hypothesis testing expressed by some economists. While the hypothesis that water boils at 100 degrees C will never be refuted (at least at sea level), in economics even the best models capture only some phenomena of interest. Inevitably they fail to match with reality when viewed in other ways. With enough data almost all sensible economic models can be rejected. But should we discard them? Perhaps some of these models are still useful in guiding our thinking.

Example 10.2.8 The consumption-based asset pricing model of Lucas (1978) fails to provide a good fit for returns on most classes of assets. But the key pricing equation still provides an important benchmark, as well as a way for econometricians to organize their thoughts on asset prices in a quantitative manner.

How to resolve these different points of view? Some researchers argue that calibration and matching of moments are sufficient as a means of validating their models. But this form of validation imposes little discipline on model builders. Clever economists can find multiple ways to replicate most interesting phenomena observed in the data, each with their own distinct policy implications. More important, the objective of matching moments is largely an in-sample criterion. The dangers of such an approach were illustrated in figure 8.4 on page 230.

One middle ground is testing of partially specified models, where tests are only concerned with a specific restriction implied by theory. A second path forward is more emphasis on out-of-sample performance in economic studies, which provides a much stricter test of true understanding. A third is offered by the Bayesian approach to model selection, where the emphasis is on comparing and improving models rather than rejection. A fourth is improvements in economic theory, to better match our models to the data.

10.3 Further Reading

For a technical discussion of the results surrounding the convergence to the Kolmogorov distribution in (10.12), see section 19.4 of Van der Vaart (2000).

For a discussions of statistical testing in econometrics see, for example, McCloskey and Ziliak (1996) and Freedman (2009). Discussions of calibration in relation to estimation and hypothesis testing can be found in Kydland and Prescott (1991), Kim and Pagan (1999), and many other places. Hansen (2014b) presents the main arguments

a model that survives forever in the pool of currently acceptable theories, without ever being culled via rejection: just make sure that the model has no testable implications. However, this strategy does not work because a model with no testable implications cannot be considered as a theory of anything. The *definition* of a scientific theory, as proposed by Karl Popper, is that the theory has one or more testable implications. In other words, the theory can be *falsified*.

in favor of tests of restrictions in partially specified models. Silver (2012) provides an interesting read on estimation and uncertainty with applications in forecasting.

An excellent summary of unit root tests is given in Hayashi (2000). For a critical overview of unit root testing, see Cochrane (1991).

10.4 Exercises

Ex. 10.4.1 Confirm fact 10.1.1 on page 277.

Ex. 10.4.2 Show that (10.8) is valid when (10.6) and (10.7) hold.

Ex. 10.4.3 Let $\alpha \in (0,1)$ and set $z_{\alpha/2} := \Phi^{-1}(1-\alpha/2)$. Show that if $t_N(\mathbf{x}) \xrightarrow{d} \mathrm{N}(0,1)$ whenever H_0 is true, and $T_N(\mathbf{x}) = |t_N(\mathbf{x})|$, the sequence of tests $\phi_N(\mathbf{x}) := \mathbb{1}\{T_N(\mathbf{x}) > z_{\alpha/2}\}$ is asymptotically of size α.

Ex. 10.4.4 If a test is well-designed, then the rejection probability will converge to one as $N \to \infty$ whenever H_0 is false:

$$\beta_N(\theta) \to 1 \text{ as } N \to \infty \quad \text{whenever} \quad \theta \notin \Theta_0$$

Such a test is said to be **consistent**. Show that the test in example 10.2.6 is consistent whenever $\alpha \in (0,1)$.[4]

Ex. 10.4.5 (Computational) The chi-squared goodness of fit test is used to test whether or not a given data set was generated from a particular discrete distribution, described by a PMF $p_1, \ldots, p_J$ over values $1, \ldots, J$. More precisely, let $x_1, \ldots, x_N$ be N random variables, each x_n taking integer values between 1 and J. The null hypothesis of the test is that the sample is IID with $\mathbb{P}\{x_n = j\} = p_j$ for $n \in \{1, \ldots, N\}$ and $j \in \{1, \ldots, J\}$. The test statistic is given by

$$X := N \sum_{j=1}^{J} \frac{(q_j - p_j)^2}{p_j} \tag{10.27}$$

where q_j is the fraction of the sample $x_1, \ldots, x_N$ taking the value j. Write a function called `chsqts` that takes arguments `observations` and `p`, where `observations` is a vector storing the sample $x_1, \ldots, x_N$ and `p` is a vector storing the values $p_1, \ldots, p_J$. The function call `chsqts(observations, p)` should return the value X in equation (10.27).[5]

4. Hint: In essence, you need to show that the absolute value of the test statistic $|t_N|$ in (10.20) diverges to infinity when $\theta \neq \theta_0$. Try the add and subtract strategy, replacing the expression $\bar{x}_N - \theta_0$ in (10.20) with $(\bar{x}_N - \theta) + (\theta - \theta_0)$.

5. `R` has a built-in function called `chisq.test` that you can use to test your results.

Ex. 10.4.6 (Computational) This exercise continues on from ex. 10.4.5. Under the null hypothesis, X in (10.27) is asymptotically chi-squared with $J-1$ degrees of freedom. Let $J=3$ with $p_1=0.2$, $p_2=0.2$ and $p_3=0.6$. Let $N=20$. By repeatedly simulating 20 IID observations $x_1,\ldots,x_{20}$ from this PMF,[6] generate 5,000 independent observations of the statistic X, and store them in a vector called `obsX`. Plot the ECDF of `obsX`. In the same figure, plot the chi-squared CDF with 2 degrees of freedom. The functions should be close. (You can improve the fit further by taking N larger.)

10.4.1 Solutions to Selected Exercises

Solution to Ex. 10.4.1. Assume the conditions of fact 10.1.1. Let s_N^2 be the sample variance. Combining fact 5.1.16 on page 140, example 9.1.4 on page 249, fact 9.1.1 on page 249 and equation (10.2), the distribution of

$$\sqrt{N}\frac{(\bar{x}_N-\mu)}{\sigma}\sqrt{\frac{N-1}{Ns_N^2/\sigma^2}}$$

has a t distribution with $N-1$ degrees of freedom. Some algebra gives (10.3). □

Solution to Ex. 10.4.2. We aim to show that $(\hat{\theta}_N-\theta)/\operatorname{se}(\hat{\theta}_N)$ converges in distribution to a standard normal when $\sqrt{N}(\hat{\theta}_N-\theta)\xrightarrow{d}\mathrm{N}(0,v(\theta))$ and $\sqrt{N}\operatorname{se}(\hat{\theta}_N)\xrightarrow{p}\sqrt{v(\theta)}$. To see this, observe that

$$\frac{\hat{\theta}_N-\theta}{\operatorname{se}(\hat{\theta}_N)}=\xi_N\eta_N \quad\text{where}\quad \xi_N:=\frac{\sqrt{N}(\hat{\theta}_N-\theta)}{\sqrt{v(\theta)}} \quad\text{and}\quad \eta_N:=\frac{\sqrt{v(\theta)}}{\sqrt{N}\operatorname{se}(\hat{\theta}_N)}$$

Using the various rules for convergence in probability and distribution (check them carefully—see facts 6.1.1 and 6.1.6) we obtain $\xi_N\xrightarrow{d}Z\sim\mathrm{N}(0,1)$ and $\eta_N\xrightarrow{p}1$. Applying Slutsky's theorem (page 168) now gives $\xi_N\eta_N\xrightarrow{d}Z$, as was to be shown. □

Solution to Ex. 10.4.3. Fix $\alpha\in(0,1)$, and let $z\sim\mathrm{N}(0,1)$. In view of (4.36) on page 115, we have $\mathbb{P}\{|z|>z_{\alpha/2}\}=\alpha$. If H_0 is true, then $t_N(\mathbf{x})\xrightarrow{d}z$ by assumption. Since $g(s):=|s|$ is continuous, fact 6.1.6 on page 167 implies that $|t_N(\mathbf{x})|\xrightarrow{d}|z|$. As a result we have

$$\lim_{N\to\infty}\beta_N(\theta)=\lim_{N\to\infty}\mathbb{P}_\theta\{|t_N(\mathbf{x})|>z_{\alpha/2}\}=\mathbb{P}\{|z|>z_{\alpha/2}\}=\alpha$$

This confirms (10.19), and the exercise is done. □

6. In particular, draw each x_n such that $\mathbb{P}\{x_n=j\}=p_j$ for $j=1,2,3$.

Part III

Econometric Models

Chapter 11

Regression

11.1 Linear Regression

Linear regression is one of the core topics of statistics. It is even more central to econometrics, where a shortage of controlled experiments often leaves econometricians trying to factor heterogeneity out ex post. We begin with a nontraditional view of linear regression based on minimal assumptions.

11.1.1 The Setup

Let's start with the kind of prediction problem discussed in §8.2.2. We study a system with vector input $\mathbf{x}_n \in \mathbb{R}^K$ followed by scalar output y_n. For example,

- $\mathbf{x}_n$ is a description of a lottery (probabilities, possible outcomes, etc.) in a controlled experiment and y_n is willingness to pay in order to participate (see, e.g., Peysakhovich and Naecker 2015).
- $\mathbf{x}_n$ is a set of household characteristics (ethnicity, age, location, etc.) and y_n is household wealth at some later date (see, e.g., McKernan et al. 2014).
- $\mathbf{x}_n$ is price of electricity, prices of alternatives, temperature, household income, and measurements of the regional income distribution, while y_n is regional electricity consumption (see, e.g., Auffhammer and Wolfram 2014).

Although we don't exclude the possibility that y is categorical (i.e., discrete), our loss function will be oriented toward regression (where y takes values in $\mathbb{R}$).

Suppose that we have N observations $\mathbf{z}_n := (\mathbf{x}_n, y_n)$, all of which are draws from some fixed joint distribution P. Since P is fixed, we are assuming that the system is stationary across the set of draws. Our aim is to predict new output values from input values on the basis of this data. In particular, our problem is to

$$\text{choose a function } f\colon \mathbb{R}^K \to \mathbb{R} \text{ such that } f(\mathbf{x}) \text{ is a good predictor of } y \tag{11.1}$$

To define "good predictor" mathematically, we need a loss function. Throughout this chapter we will be using quadratic loss. Thus, in the language of §8.2.2, our aim is to minimize the prediction risk

$$R(f) := \mathbb{E}_P (y - f(\mathbf{x}))^2 \tag{11.2}$$

As we saw in §5.2.5, the minimizer of (11.2) over the set of all $\mathscr{B}$-measurable functions is the regression function $f^*(\mathbf{x}) := \mathbb{E}_P [y \,|\, \mathbf{x}]$. If we could compute this, then all our problems would be solved. But we cannot compute it because P is not known. Instead we apply the principle of empirical risk minimization (see §8.2.2), which leads to the problem

$$\min_{f \in \mathcal{H}} R_{\text{emp}}(f) \quad \text{where} \quad R_{\text{emp}}(f) := \frac{1}{N} \sum_{n=1}^{N} (y_n - f(\mathbf{x}_n))^2 \tag{11.3}$$

Here $\mathcal{H}$ is the hypothesis space, a set of candidate functions mapping $\mathbb{R}^K$ into $\mathbb{R}$. For obvious reasons, the problem (11.3) is called a **least squares** problem.

If we take $\mathcal{H}$ to be the set of all functions from $\mathbb{R}^K$ to $\mathbb{R}$, then, provided the input vectors are all distinct, we can set the empirical risk $R_{\text{emp}}(f)$ to zero by choosing any function f satisfying $y_n = f(\mathbf{x}_n)$ for all n. However, as discussed at length in §8.2.3, minimizing empirical risk is different from minimizing the prediction risk $R(f)$. The latter is what we actually want to minimize. Thus $\mathcal{H}$ must be restricted.

In this chapter we consider the case $\mathcal{H} = \mathcal{H}_\ell$, where $\mathcal{H}_\ell$ is all linear functions from $\mathbb{R}^K$ to $\mathbb{R}$. Recalling theorem 3.1.1 on page 48, we can write

$$\mathcal{H}_\ell = \left\{ \text{all } f\colon \mathbb{R}^K \to \mathbb{R} \text{ such that } f(\mathbf{x}) = \mathbf{x}^\top \mathbf{b} \text{ for some } \mathbf{b} \in \mathbb{R}^K \right\} \tag{11.4}$$

The problem (11.3) then reduces to

$$\min_{\mathbf{b} \in \mathbb{R}^K} \sum_{n=1}^{N} (y_n - \mathbf{x}_n^\top \mathbf{b})^2 \tag{11.5}$$

The term $\frac{1}{N}$ has been dropped because it does not affect the minimizer. This is the multivariate version of (8.22) on page 227.

The idea of choosing $\mathbf{b}$ to minimize (11.5) is intuitive: We are choosing a "line of best fit" to minimize in-sample prediction error. This optimization problem has a long tradition. It dates back at least as far as Carl Gauss's work on the orbital position of Ceres, published in 1801.

You might be wondering whether the choice $\mathcal{H} = \mathcal{H}_\ell$ is a suitable one. This is an excellent question. It might not be. However, there are good reasons to start with $\mathcal{H}_\ell$, even in this setting where no linearity assumptions are imposed. First, $\mathcal{H}_\ell$ is a natural starting point when seeking a class of simple, well-behaved functions. Second, as we'll see, setting $\mathcal{H} = \mathcal{H}_\ell$ allows us to obtain an analytical expression for the minimizer, which simplifies both analysis and computation. Third, the technique has an extension from $\mathcal{H}_\ell$ to broader classes of functions, as described in §11.2.1.

11.1.2 The Least Squares Estimator

Now let's solve (11.5). With our knowledge of overdetermined systems (see §3.3.2), we already have all the necessary tools. This will be more obvious after we switch to matrix notation. To do this, let

$$\mathbf{y} := \begin{pmatrix} y_1 \\ y_2 \\ \vdots \\ y_N \end{pmatrix}, \quad \mathbf{x}_n := \begin{pmatrix} x_{n1} \\ x_{n2} \\ \vdots \\ x_{nK} \end{pmatrix} = n\text{th observation of all regressors} \tag{11.6}$$

and

$$\mathbf{X} := \begin{pmatrix} \mathbf{x}_1^\top \\ \mathbf{x}_2^\top \\ \vdots \\ \mathbf{x}_N^\top \end{pmatrix} =: \begin{pmatrix} x_{11} & x_{12} & \cdots & x_{1K} \\ x_{21} & x_{22} & \cdots & x_{2K} \\ \vdots & \vdots & & \vdots \\ x_{N1} & x_{N2} & \cdots & x_{NK} \end{pmatrix} \tag{11.7}$$

Sometimes $\mathbf{X}$ is called the **design matrix**. By construction, $\text{col}_k \mathbf{X} =$ all observations on the kth regressor. Also, for any $\mathbf{b} \in \mathbb{R}^K$, we have

$$\mathbf{X}\mathbf{b} = \begin{pmatrix} \mathbf{x}_1^\top \mathbf{b} \\ \mathbf{x}_2^\top \mathbf{b} \\ \vdots \\ \mathbf{x}_N^\top \mathbf{b} \end{pmatrix}$$

It follows that the objective function in (11.5) can be written as

$$\sum_{n=1}^{N} (y_n - \mathbf{x}_n^\top \mathbf{b})^2 = \|\mathbf{y} - \mathbf{X}\mathbf{b}\|^2$$

Since strictly increasing transforms preserve the set of minimizers (see §15.4),

$$\operatorname*{argmin}_{\mathbf{b}\in\mathbb{R}^K} \|\mathbf{y} - \mathbf{X}\mathbf{b}\|^2 = \operatorname*{argmin}_{\mathbf{b}\in\mathbb{R}^K} \|\mathbf{y} - \mathbf{X}\mathbf{b}\| \tag{11.8}$$

We already know how to solve for the minimizer on the right-hand side of (11.8). By theorem 3.3.2 (page 63), the solution is

$$\hat{\beta} := (\mathbf{X}^\mathsf{T}\mathbf{X})^{-1}\mathbf{X}^\mathsf{T}\mathbf{y} \tag{11.9}$$

Traditionally, this random vector $\hat{\beta}$ is called the **least squares estimator**. Once we move to more classical assumptions it will be an estimator of a particular parameter vector. At this stage it just defines our answer to the problem posed in (11.1). That is,

$$\text{given } \mathbf{x} \in \mathbb{R}^K, \text{ our prediction of } y \text{ is } f(\mathbf{x}) = \mathbf{x}^\mathsf{T}\hat{\beta}$$

In terms of geometric interpretation, since $\mathbf{X}\hat{\beta}$ solves (11.8), it is the closest point in colspace $\mathbf{X}$ to $\mathbf{y}$. In particular,

$$\mathbf{P}\mathbf{y} = \mathbf{X}\hat{\beta} \quad \text{when} \quad \mathbf{P} := \operatorname{proj}(\operatorname{colspace}\mathbf{X})$$

(See (3.13) on page 63.) In what follows, $\mathbf{M}$ is the residual projection, as defined in (2.11) on page 32.

11.1.2.1 Assumptions

Theorem 3.3.2 and our definition of $\hat{\beta}$ in 11.9 require that $\mathbf{X}$ has full column rank (or, equivalently, that the columns of $\mathbf{X}$ are linearly independent—see page 50).

Assumption 11.1.1 $\mathbf{X}$ has full column rank with probability one.

By theorem 2.1.3 on page 20, $N \geqslant K$ is a necessary condition for assumption 11.1.1 to hold. (If $N < K$, then $\mathbb{R}^N$, which is necessarily spanned by N vectors, cannot contain K linearly independent vectors.)

If assumption 11.1.1 fails, then a minimizer of (11.8) still exists but is no longer unique (see ex. 3.5.34). While we can treat this case, it rarely occurs in well-designed regression problems.

Let's also put some mild regularity conditions on the common joint distribution P of each data point $\mathbf{z}_n := (\mathbf{x}_n, y_n)$.

Assumption 11.1.2 P is such that all elements of $\mathbb{E}_P[\mathbf{z}_n\mathbf{z}_n^\mathsf{T}]$ are finite. Moreover

$$\Sigma_{\mathbf{x}} := \mathbb{E}_P[\mathbf{x}_n\mathbf{x}_n^\mathsf{T}] \text{ is finite and positive definite} \tag{11.10}$$

Finite second moments are imposed because we want to evaluate expected squared errors. This assumption cannot be weakened unless we are willing to work with a different loss function. Positive definiteness of $\Sigma_\mathbf{x}$ ensures that the asymptotic limit of our estimator is well defined.[1]

11.1.2.2 Notation

There's a range of standard notation associated with linear least squares estimation. Let's collect it in one place. First, the projection

$$\hat{\mathbf{y}} := \mathbf{X}\hat{\beta} = \mathbf{P}\mathbf{y}$$

is called the **vector of fitted values**. The nth fitted value $\hat{y}_n$ is the prediction $\mathbf{x}_n^\top \hat{\beta}$ associated with least squares estimate and the nth observation $\mathbf{x}_n$ of the input vector. The vector $\mathbf{My}$ is often denoted $\hat{\mathbf{u}}$, and called the **vector of residuals**:

$$\hat{\mathbf{u}} := \mathbf{My} = \mathbf{y} - \hat{\mathbf{y}}$$

The vector of residuals corresponds to the error that occurs when $\mathbf{y}$ is approximated by $\mathbf{Py}$. From fact 2.2.8 on page 33 we have

$$\mathbf{My} \perp \mathbf{Py} \quad \text{and} \quad \mathbf{y} = \mathbf{Py} + \mathbf{My} \tag{11.11}$$

In other words, $\mathbf{y}$ can be decomposed into two orthogonal vectors $\mathbf{Py}$ and $\mathbf{My}$, where the first represents the best approximation to $\mathbf{y}$ in colspace $\mathbf{X}$, and the second represents the residual.

Related to the fitted values and residuals, we have some standard definitions:

- **Total sum of squares** := TSS := $\|\mathbf{y}\|^2$.
- **Residual sum of squares** := RSS := $\|\mathbf{My}\|^2$.
- **Explained sum of squares** := ESS := $\|\mathbf{Py}\|^2$.

By (11.11) and the Pythagorean law (page 27),

$$\text{TSS} = \text{ESS} + \text{RSS} \tag{11.12}$$

When running regressions it is conventional to report the **coefficient of determination**, or R^2. The plain vanilla definition of R^2 is

$$R^2 := \frac{\text{ESS}}{\text{TSS}} \tag{11.13}$$

1. In essence, positive definiteness of $\Sigma_\mathbf{x}$ requires that no random variable in $\mathbf{x}$ can be written as a linear combination of other variables in $\mathbf{x}$. See exercise 11.4.1.

Many regression packages report an alternative definition of R^2. See §11.2.3 below.

11.1.3 Out-of-Sample Fit

We have stressed a number of times that learning from data (statistics) means generalization from current observations to new ones. As such, the most important measure of success for a statistical procedure is out-of-sample fit. So how does linear least squares perform out-of-sample? We start with a general observation about linear predictors.

Theorem 11.1.1 *If ℓ is the linear function $\ell(\mathbf{x}) = \mathbf{x}^\mathsf{T}\mathbf{b}$, then*

$$R(\ell) = \mathbb{E}\,(y - f^*(\mathbf{x}))^2 + \mathbb{E}\,(f^*(\mathbf{x}) - \mathbf{x}^\mathsf{T}\mathbf{b}^*)^2 + (\mathbf{b}^* - \mathbf{b})^\mathsf{T}\boldsymbol{\Sigma}_\mathbf{x}(\mathbf{b}^* - \mathbf{b})$$

Here f^* is the regression function and $\mathbf{b}^* = \boldsymbol{\Sigma}_\mathbf{x}{}^{-1}\,\mathbb{E}\,[\mathbf{x}\,y]$ is the vector of coefficients in the best linear predictor (see page 147). $R(f)$ is the prediction risk of f and expectations are taken under the unknown joint distribution P of the pairs $(\mathbf{x}, y)$.

The proof of theorem 11.1.1 is given in §11.1.3.1. For now let's look at interpretation. The general question is how well we can generalize (i.e., reduce prediction risk) using linear functions. Theorem 11.1.1 decomposes the prediction risk of an arbitrary linear predictor $\ell(\mathbf{x}) = \mathbf{x}^\mathsf{T}\mathbf{b}$ into three terms:

(i) The **intrinsic risk** $\mathbb{E}\,(y - f^*(\mathbf{x}))^2$.

(ii) The **approximation error** $\mathbb{E}\,(f^*(\mathbf{x}) - \mathbf{x}^\mathsf{T}\mathbf{b}^*)^2$.

(iii) The **estimation error** $(\mathbf{b}^* - \mathbf{b})^\mathsf{T}\boldsymbol{\Sigma}_\mathbf{x}(\mathbf{b}^* - \mathbf{b})$.

The intrinsic risk is also called Bayes risk (see example 8.2.3 on page 226). It is the residual error after y is approximated with the best possible predictor (i.e., the regression function). It is large to the extent that y is hard to predict using $\mathbf{x}$.

The approximation error or *bias* is the deviation between the best predictor and the best linear predictor. It reflects the cost of our decision to approximate the regression function using a linear architecture. If this architecture is held fixed, the approximation error is also fixed and cannot be reduced in the estimation process.

The estimation error is caused by the deviation of our estimator from the best linear predictor $\mathbf{b}^*$. This deviation occurs because we are predicting using finite sample information on the joint distribution of $(\mathbf{x}, y)$.

Theorem 11.1.1 tells us that once $\mathcal{H}$ is set to the class of linear functions, the best we can do is find an estimation method (a learning algorithm) that produces an estimate that is close to $\mathbf{b}^*$ on average when the sample size is sufficiently large. The next result states that the least squares estimator $\hat{\beta}$ has this property.

Theorem 11.1.2 *Let assumptions 11.1.2–11.1.1 hold and let $\hat{\beta}_N$ be the least squares estimator given sample size N. If the observations $\{\mathbf{z}_n\}$ are independent, then*

$$\hat{\beta}_N \xrightarrow{p} \mathbf{b}^* \quad as \quad N \to \infty \tag{11.14}$$

The proof is below. Independence is required only for the LLN to function. We could weaken this to ergodicity (see §7.1.1) and obtain the same conclusion.[2]

On one level, theorems 11.1.1 and 11.1.2 are reassuring. They tell us that if the underlying process is relatively linear, then we will attain small risk asymptotically. On the other hand, the Glivenko–Cantelli theorem tells us that we can learn everything about the underlying distribution in the limit. Here we are bounded away from this kind of consistency whenever the approximation error is positive.

As will be discussed in chapter 14, a general principle of induction is that we should introduce bias in finite samples to avoid overfitting, while at the same time reducing bias asymptotically, as the empirical distribution converges to the true distribution. By comparison, in standard linear regression the bias is held fixed by the linearity assumption.

11.1.3.1 Proofs

Proof of theorem 11.1.1. Fix $\mathbf{b} \in \mathbb{R}^K$ and let $\ell(\mathbf{x}) = \mathbf{x}^\top \mathbf{b}$. In view of (8.17) on page 226, we have the prediction risk

$$R(\ell) = \mathbb{E}\,[(y - f^*(\mathbf{x}))^2] + \mathbb{E}\,[(f^*(\mathbf{x}) - \mathbf{x}^\top \mathbf{b})^2]$$

Hence the result will established if we can show that

$$\mathbb{E}\,[(f^*(\mathbf{x}) - \mathbf{x}^\top \mathbf{b})^2] = \mathbb{E}\,[(f^*(\mathbf{x}) - \mathbf{x}^\top \mathbf{b}^*)^2] + \mathbb{E}\,[(\mathbf{b}^* - \mathbf{b})^\top \mathbf{x}\mathbf{x}^\top (\mathbf{b}^* - \mathbf{b})] \tag{11.15}$$

To see that (11.15) holds, observe that

$$f^*(\mathbf{x}) - \mathbf{x}^\top \mathbf{b} = f^*(\mathbf{x}) - \mathbf{x}^\top \mathbf{b}^* + \mathbf{x}^\top (\mathbf{b}^* - \mathbf{b}) \tag{11.16}$$

The terms $f^*(\mathbf{x}) - \mathbf{x}^\top \mathbf{b}^*$ and $\mathbf{x}^\top (\mathbf{b}^* - \mathbf{b})$ are orthogonal. The reason is that $\mathbf{x}^\top \mathbf{b}^*$ is the orthogonal projection of $f^*(\mathbf{x})$ onto $S = \text{span}\{\mathbf{x}\}$, the linear subspace of L_2 spanned by all linear combinations of the form $\mathbf{a}^\top \mathbf{x}$. (See ex. 5.4.18 on page 156.) As such, $f^*(\mathbf{x}) - \mathbf{x}^\top \mathbf{b}^*$ is orthogonal to every element of the target subspace $\text{span}\{\mathbf{x}\}$. This includes $\mathbf{x}^\top (\mathbf{b}^* - \mathbf{b})$.

For any orthogonal elements u and v of L_2 we have $\mathbb{E}\,[(u+v)^2] = \mathbb{E}\,[u^2] + \mathbb{E}\,[v^2]$.

2. Later, in §13.1, we'll do something similar (i.e., weaken independence to ergodicity) in a setting with some additional structure.

(This is the Pythagorean law in L_2.) Squaring both sides of (11.16), taking expectations and applying this law gives (11.15). The proof of theorem 11.1.1 is done. □

Proof of theorem 11.1.2. The proof of theorem 11.1.2 is not hard if we express $\hat{\boldsymbol{\beta}}_N$ in a slightly different way. Multiplying and dividing by N in the definition of $\hat{\boldsymbol{\beta}}_N$ and then expanding out the matrix products (see ex. 11.4.9) gives

$$\hat{\boldsymbol{\beta}}_N = \left[\frac{1}{N}\mathbf{X}^\top\mathbf{X}\right]^{-1} \cdot \frac{1}{N}\mathbf{X}^\top\mathbf{y} = \left[\frac{1}{N}\sum_{n=1}^{N}\mathbf{x}_n\mathbf{x}_n^\top\right]^{-1} \cdot \frac{1}{N}\sum_{n=1}^{N}\mathbf{x}_n y_n \tag{11.17}$$

By the matrix LLN in fact 6.2.3 (page 173), we have

$$\frac{1}{N}\sum_{n=1}^{N}\mathbf{x}_n\mathbf{x}_n^\top \xrightarrow{p} \boldsymbol{\Sigma}_\mathbf{x} \quad \text{and} \quad \frac{1}{N}\sum_{n=1}^{N}\mathbf{x}_n y_n \xrightarrow{p} \mathbb{E}\,[\mathbf{x}y] \quad \text{as} \quad N \to \infty$$

By fact 6.2.1 on page 170, convergence in probability is preserved over the taking of inverses and products. Hence $\hat{\boldsymbol{\beta}}_N \xrightarrow{p} \boldsymbol{\Sigma}_\mathbf{x}{}^{-1}\mathbb{E}\,[\mathbf{x}\,y] = \mathbf{b}^*$, as was to be shown. □

11.1.4 In-Sample Fit

In-sample fit measures how well a given model fits the same data set that it was estimated on. The difference between in-sample fit (empirical risk) and out-of-sample fit (risk) was discussed in §8.2.3. In-sample fit of a regression is often measured with R^2 (see (11.13)). Let's make some further comments on R^2 and then discuss how R^2 relates to in-sample fit.

Fact 11.1.1 $0 \leqslant R^2 \leqslant 1$ with $R^2 = 1$ if and only if $\mathbf{y} \in \operatorname{colspace}\mathbf{X}$.

That $R^2 \leqslant 1$ is immediate from $\|\mathbf{P}\mathbf{y}\| \leqslant \|\mathbf{y}\|$ (cf. theorem 2.2.2 on page 31). Exercise 11.4.17 asks you to prove the second claim. More generally, a high R^2 indicates $\mathbf{y}$ is relatively close to colspace $\mathbf{X}$. This fact suggests that we can increase R^2 at least weakly by adding regressors. As we do so the column space of $\mathbf{X}$ expands, pushing out towards $\mathbf{y}$. Here's a formal statement:

Fact 11.1.2 Let $\mathbf{X}_a$ and $\mathbf{X}_b$ be two design matrices. If R_a^2 and R_b^2 are the respective coefficients of determination, then

$$\operatorname{colspace}\mathbf{X}_a \subset \operatorname{colspace}\mathbf{X}_b \implies R_a^2 \leqslant R_b^2$$

For a proof, see exercise 11.4.8 and its solution.

High R^2 is sometimes equated with successful regression. This is a misunderstanding of the aim of statistics. The correct definition of statistical learning is effective generalization from existing data. In the present context this means that the linear predictor produced by regression attains low risk.

So how does R^2 relate to risk? What R^2 actually measures is the degree to which empirical risk is minimized. To see this, note that

$$R^2 = 1 - \frac{\text{RSS}}{\text{TSS}} = 1 - N\frac{R_{\text{emp}}(\hat{f})}{\text{TSS}}$$

where R_{emp} is as defined in (11.3) and $\hat{f}$ is our linear predictor $\hat{f}(\mathbf{x}) = \mathbf{x}^\top \hat{\boldsymbol{\beta}}$. Thus high R^2 means low empirical risk and good in-sample fit. But low empirical risk is no guarantee of low prediction risk, as was emphasized in §8.2.3.

Here's a simulation that shows how we can produce high R^2 without estimating anything meaningful. We take x_n and y_n as independent draws from a uniform distribution on $[0, 1]$. By construction, there is no relationship between these two variables. For the regressors we take the powers $1, x, x^2, \ldots, x^K$, where K is a positive integer. The R code below runs these regressions for different values of K. At $K = 25$ the value of R^2 is around 0.95. This is despite the fact that no relationship exists between x and y.

```
set.seed(1234)
N <- 25
y <- runif(N)
x <- runif(N)
X <- rep(1, N)

Kmax <- 25
for (K in 1:Kmax) {
    X <- cbind(X, x^K)
    results <- lm(y ~ 0 + X)
    Py2 <- sum(results$fitted.values^2)
    y2 <- sum(y^2)
    cat("K =", K, "R^2 =", Py2 / y2, "\n")
}
```

(You can obtain all code from the text at `johnstachurski.net/emet.html`.)

To finish this section, let's draw a connection between fact 11.1.2, which says that the value of R^2 is at least weakly increasing in the number of right-hand side variables, and fact 8.2.1 on page 229. Suppose that $\mathbf{x}$ lists a large number of possible regressors.

Let the hypothesis space be

$$\mathcal{H}_j := \left\{ \text{all } f\colon \mathbb{R}^j \to \mathbb{R} \text{ s.t. } f(\mathbf{x}) = \mathbf{x}^\top \mathbf{b} \text{ for some } \mathbf{b} \in \mathbb{R}^j \right\} \tag{11.18}$$

Here $1 \leqslant j \leqslant K$. Empirical risk minimization over $\mathcal{H}_j$ is equivalent to linear regression over the first j regressors. Empirical risk falls as j increases by fact 8.2.1 on page 229. Hence R^2 increases. This is the same conclusion as fact 11.1.2.

11.2 The Geometry of Least Squares

In this section we cover transformations of the data and an important theorem on subsets of the least squares estimator.

11.2.1 Transformations and Basis Functions

In discussing the decision to set $\mathcal{H} = \mathcal{H}_\ell$ in §11.1.1, we mentioned that we can use many of the same ideas when extending $\mathcal{H}$ to a broader class of functions. The idea is to first transform the data using some arbitrary function $\boldsymbol{\phi}\colon \mathbb{R}^K \to \mathbb{R}^J$. The action of $\boldsymbol{\phi}$ on $\mathbf{x} \in \mathbb{R}^K$ is

$$\mathbf{x} \mapsto \boldsymbol{\phi}(\mathbf{x}) = \begin{pmatrix} \phi_1(\mathbf{x}) \\ \phi_2(\mathbf{x}) \\ \vdots \\ \phi_J(\mathbf{x}) \end{pmatrix} \in \mathbb{R}^J$$

The individual functions $\phi_1, \ldots, \phi_J$ mapping $\mathbb{R}^K$ into $\mathbb{R}$ are sometimes called **basis functions**. In machine learning texts, the range of $\boldsymbol{\phi}$ is called **feature space**. Linear least squares is now applied in feature space. That is, we solve the empirical risk minimization problem when the hypothesis space is

$$\mathcal{H}_{\boldsymbol{\phi}} := \{\text{all functions } \ell \circ \boldsymbol{\phi}, \text{ where } \ell \text{ is a linear function from } \mathbb{R}^J \text{ to } \mathbb{R}\}$$

The empirical risk minimization problem is then

$$\min_{\ell} \sum_{n=1}^{N} \{y_n - \ell(\boldsymbol{\phi}(\mathbf{x}_n))\}^2 = \min_{\gamma \in \mathbb{R}^J} \sum_{n=1}^{N} (y_n - \gamma^\top \boldsymbol{\phi}(\mathbf{x}_n))^2 \tag{11.19}$$

Switching to matrix notation, if

$$\mathbf{\Phi} := \begin{pmatrix} \phi_1(\mathbf{x}_1) & \cdots & \phi_J(\mathbf{x}_1) \\ \phi_1(\mathbf{x}_2) & \cdots & \phi_J(\mathbf{x}_2) \\ \vdots & \cdots & \vdots \\ \phi_1(\mathbf{x}_N) & \cdots & \phi_J(\mathbf{x}_N) \end{pmatrix} \in \mathbb{R}^{N \times J} \tag{11.20}$$

then the objective in (11.19) can be expressed as $\|\mathbf{y} - \mathbf{\Phi}\gamma\|^2$. Since increasing functions don't affect minimizers, the problem becomes

$$\underset{\gamma \in \mathbb{R}^J}{\operatorname{argmin}} \|\mathbf{y} - \mathbf{\Phi}\gamma\| \tag{11.21}$$

Assuming that $\mathbf{\Phi}$ is full column rank, the solution is

$$\hat{\gamma} := (\mathbf{\Phi}^\top \mathbf{\Phi})^{-1} \mathbf{\Phi}^\top \mathbf{y}$$

Example 11.2.1 Adding an intercept to a regression can be regarded as a transformation of the data. Indeed adding an intercept is equivalent to applying the transformation

$$\boldsymbol{\phi}(\mathbf{x}) = \begin{pmatrix} 1 \\ \mathbf{x} \end{pmatrix} = \begin{pmatrix} 1 \\ x_1 \\ \vdots \\ x_K \end{pmatrix}$$

In practice, adding an intercept means fitting an extra parameter, and this extra degree of freedom allows a more flexible fit in our regression.

Example 11.2.2 Let $K = 1$, so that $x_n \in \mathbb{R}$. Consider the mononomial basis functions $\phi_j(x) := x^{j-1}$, so that

$$\gamma^\top \boldsymbol{\phi}(x_n) = \gamma^\top \begin{pmatrix} x_n^0 \\ x_n^1 \\ \vdots \\ x_n^{J-1} \end{pmatrix} = \sum_{j=1}^{J} \gamma_j x_n^{j-1} \tag{11.22}$$

The mononomial basis transformation applied to scalar x corresponds to univariate polynomial regression, as discussed in §8.2.3. Under this transformation, the matrix $\mathbf{\Phi}$ in (11.20) is called the **Vandermonde matrix**. By the Weierstrass approximation theorem, polynomials of sufficiently high order can effectively approximate any one-dimensional continuous nonlinear relationship.

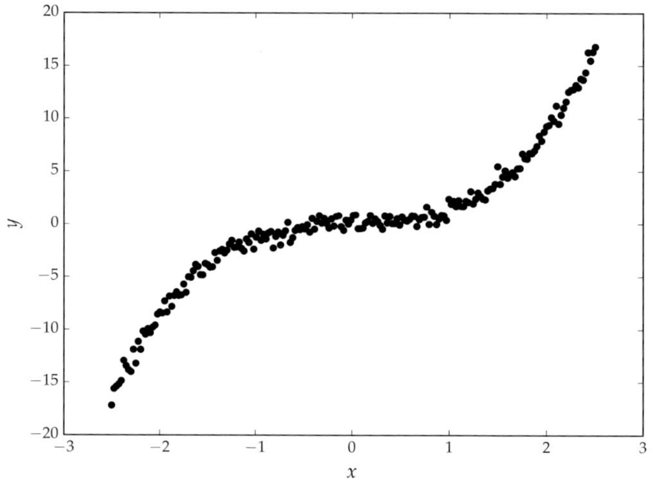

Figure 11.1 Nonlinear relationship between x and y

Example 11.2.3 Example 11.2.2 uses mononomials as the basis functions. A common alternative is to use orthogonal polynomials such as Chebychev polynomials or Hermite polynomials. Other alternatives include wavelets and splines. In econometrics this procedure is often referred to as nonparametric series regression. A key topic is the optimal number of basis functions.[3]

Figures 11.1 and 11.2 help illustrate how transformations can reduce approximation error. In figure 11.1 it is clear that no linear function mapping x to y can produce small approximation error. Figure 11.2 shows the data after applying the transformation $\mathbb{R} \ni x \mapsto \boldsymbol{\phi}(x) := (x, x^3)^\top \in \mathbb{R}^2$. The plane drawn in figure 11.2 represents a linear function $\ell\colon \mathbb{R}^2 \to \mathbb{R}$. The composition $\ell \circ \boldsymbol{\phi}$ has low approximation error. The two figures illustrate how nonlinear data can become linear when projected into higher dimensions.

Below, when y is regressed on $\mathbf{x}$, we can imagine that the data have already been transformed, and $\mathbf{x}$ is the result. Hence we use $\mathbf{X}$ to denote the design matrix instead of Φ without loss of generality.

3. See, for example, Hong and White (1995), Sun (2011), or Chen and Christensen (2015).

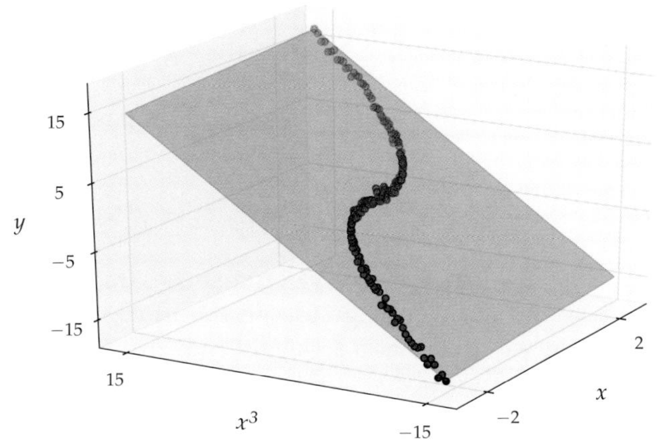

Figure 11.2 Approximate linearity after projecting the data to $\mathbb{R}^2$

11.2.2 The Frisch–Waugh–Lovell Theorem

The Frisch–Waugh–Lovell (FWL) theorem yields an expression for an arbitrary subvector of the least squares estimator $\hat{\boldsymbol{\beta}}$ obtained by regressing $\mathbf{y}$ on $\mathbf{X}$. In stating the theorem, we continue with the assumptions of §11.1. Let $\mathbf{y}$ and $\mathbf{X}$ be given and let $\hat{\boldsymbol{\beta}}$ be as in (11.9). In addition, let K_1 be an integer with $1 \leqslant K_1 < K$, and let

- $\mathbf{X}_1$ be a matrix consisting of the first K_1 columns of $\mathbf{X}$,
- $\mathbf{X}_2$ be a matrix consisting of the remaining $K_2 := K - K_1$ columns,
- $\hat{\boldsymbol{\beta}}_1$ be the $K_1 \times 1$ vector consisting of the first K_1 elements of $\hat{\boldsymbol{\beta}}$.
- $\hat{\boldsymbol{\beta}}_2$ be the $K_2 \times 1$ vector consisting of the remaining K_2 elements of $\hat{\boldsymbol{\beta}}$,
- $\mathbf{P}_1 := \operatorname{proj}(\operatorname{colspace} \mathbf{X}_1)$, and
- $\mathbf{M}_1 := \mathbf{I} - \mathbf{P}_1 =$ the corresponding residual projection (see page 32).

Theorem 11.2.1 (FWL theorem) *The vector $\hat{\boldsymbol{\beta}}_2$ satisfies*

$$\hat{\boldsymbol{\beta}}_2 = (\mathbf{X}_2^\top \mathbf{M}_1 \mathbf{X}_2)^{-1} \mathbf{X}_2^\top \mathbf{M}_1 \mathbf{y} \tag{11.23}$$

Proof. From (11.11) and the definitions above we have

$$\mathbf{y} = \mathbf{X}\hat{\boldsymbol{\beta}} + \mathbf{M}\mathbf{y} = \mathbf{X}_1\hat{\boldsymbol{\beta}}_1 + \mathbf{X}_2\hat{\boldsymbol{\beta}}_2 + \mathbf{M}\mathbf{y}$$

Premultiplying both sides of this expression by $\mathbf{X}_2^\top \mathbf{M}_1$, we obtain

$$\mathbf{X}_2^\top \mathbf{M}_1 \mathbf{y} = \mathbf{X}_2^\top \mathbf{M}_1 \mathbf{X}_1 \hat{\boldsymbol{\beta}}_1 + \mathbf{X}_2^\top \mathbf{M}_1 \mathbf{X}_2 \hat{\boldsymbol{\beta}}_2 + \mathbf{X}_2^\top \mathbf{M}_1 \mathbf{M} \mathbf{y} \tag{11.24}$$

The first term on the right-hand side is zero by fact 3.3.1 on page 61. The last term is also zero because

$$(\mathbf{X}_2^\top \mathbf{M}_1 \mathbf{M} \mathbf{y})^\top = \mathbf{y}^\top \mathbf{M}^\top \mathbf{M}_1^\top \mathbf{X}_2 = \mathbf{y}^\top \mathbf{M} \mathbf{M}_1 \mathbf{X}_2 = \mathbf{y}^\top \mathbf{M} \mathbf{X}_2 = \mathbf{0}$$

In the first equality, we used the usual property of transposes (fact 3.2.4); in the second, we used symmetry of $\mathbf{M}$ and $\mathbf{M}_1$ (see page 61); in the third, we used fact 2.2.9 on page 34; and in the fourth, we used fact 3.3.1 again (which tells us that $\mathbf{M}$ maps all columns of $\mathbf{X}$, and hence all columns of $\mathbf{X}_2$, to the zero vector).

In light of the above, (11.24) becomes $\mathbf{X}_2^\top \mathbf{M}_1 \mathbf{y} = \mathbf{X}_2^\top \mathbf{M}_1 \mathbf{X}_2 \hat{\boldsymbol{\beta}}_2$. To go from this equation to (11.23), we just need to check that the matrix premultiplying $\hat{\boldsymbol{\beta}}_2$ is nonsingular. The proof is left as an exercise (ex. 11.4.23). □

As exercise 11.4.22 asks you to show, the expression for $\hat{\boldsymbol{\beta}}_2$ in theorem 11.2.1 can be rewritten as

$$\hat{\boldsymbol{\beta}}_2 = [(\mathbf{M}_1 \mathbf{X}_2)^\top \mathbf{M}_1 \mathbf{X}_2]^{-1} (\mathbf{M}_1 \mathbf{X}_2)^\top \mathbf{M}_1 \mathbf{y} \tag{11.25}$$

Close inspection of this formula confirms the following claim: There is another way to obtain $\hat{\boldsymbol{\beta}}_2$ besides just regressing $\mathbf{y}$ on $\mathbf{X}$ and then extracting the last K_2 elements: we can also regress $\mathbf{M}_1 \mathbf{y}$ on $\mathbf{M}_1 \mathbf{X}_2$ to produce the same result.

To get some feeling for what this means, let's look at a special case, where $\mathbf{X}_2$ is the single column $\operatorname{col}_K \mathbf{X}$, containing the observations on the Kth regressor. To tie into this notation let's write $\mathbf{X}_1$ as $\mathbf{X}_{-K}$ to remind us that it stands for all columns of $\mathbf{X}$ expect the Kth one, and similarly for $\mathbf{M}_1$. In view of the preceding discussion, the least squares estimate $\hat{\beta}_K$ can be found by regressing

$$\tilde{\mathbf{y}} := \mathbf{M}_{-K} \mathbf{y} = \text{residuals of regressing } \mathbf{y} \text{ on } \mathbf{X}_{-K} \tag{11.26}$$

on

$$\tilde{\mathbf{x}}_K := \mathbf{M}_{-K} \operatorname{col}_K \mathbf{X} = \text{residuals of regressing } \operatorname{col}_K \mathbf{X} \text{ on } \mathbf{X}_{-K} \tag{11.27}$$

Loosely speaking, these two residual terms $\tilde{\mathbf{y}}$ and $\tilde{\mathbf{x}}_K$ can be thought of as the parts of $\mathbf{y}$ and $\operatorname{col}_K \mathbf{X}$ that are "not explained by" $\mathbf{X}_{-K}$. Thus, on an intuitive level, the process for obtaining the least squares estimate $\hat{\beta}_K$ is as follows:

(i) Remove effects of all other regressors from $\mathbf{y}$ and $\operatorname{col}_K \mathbf{X}$, producing $\tilde{\mathbf{y}}$ and $\tilde{\mathbf{x}}_K$.

(ii) Regress $\tilde{\mathbf{y}}$ on $\tilde{\mathbf{x}}_K$.

This is obviously different from the process for obtaining the coefficient of the vector

$\text{col}_K \mathbf{X}$ in a simple univariate regression, the latter being just

(i) Regress $\mathbf{y}$ on $\text{col}_K \mathbf{X}$.

In words, the difference between the univariate least squares estimated coefficient of the Kth regressor and the multiple regression least squares coefficient is that the multiple regression coefficient $\hat{\beta}_K$ measures the *isolated relationship* between x_K and y, without taking into account indirect channels involving other variables.

We can illustrate this idea further with a small simulation. Suppose that

$$y = x_1 + x_2 + u \quad \text{where} \quad u \overset{\text{IID}}{\sim} \text{N}(0, 1)$$

If we generate N independent observations from this model and regress y on the observations of (x_1, x_2), then, provided that N is sufficiently large, the coefficients for x_1 and x_2 will both be close to unity (see theorem 11.1.2). However, if we regress y on x_1 alone, then the coefficient for x_1 will depend on the relationship between x_1 and x_2. For example:

```
> N <- 1000
> x1 <- runif(N)
> x2 = 10 * exp(x1) + rnorm(N)
> y <- x1 + x2 + rnorm(N)
> results <- lm(y ~ 0 + x1)
> results$coefficients
        x1
        30.83076
```

Here the coefficient for x_1 is much larger than unity, because an increase in x_1 tends to have a large positive effect on x_2, which in turn increases y. The coefficient in the univariate regression reflects this total effect.

11.2.2.1 Application: Simple Regression

Here's an easy application of the FWL theorem: deriving the familiar expression for the slope coefficient in simple linear regression (see §8.2.1.1) from the multivariate expression. Simple linear regression is a special case of multivariate regression when $\mathbf{1}$ is the first column of $\mathbf{X}$ and $K = 2$. In this section, the second column of $\mathbf{X}$ will be denoted by $\mathbf{x}$. As we saw in (8.14) on page 224, the least squares estimates are

$$\hat{\beta}_2 = \frac{\sum_{n=1}^N (x_n - \bar{x})(y_n - \bar{y})}{\sum_{n=1}^N (x_n - \bar{x})^2} \quad \text{and} \quad \hat{\beta}_1 = \bar{y} - \hat{\beta}_2 \bar{x}$$

where $\bar{x}$ is the sample mean of $\mathbf{x}$ and $\bar{y}$ is the sample mean of $\mathbf{y}$. We can rewrite the slope coefficient $\hat{\beta}_2$ more succinctly as

$$\hat{\beta}_2 = [(\mathbf{x} - \bar{x}\mathbf{1})^\top (\mathbf{x} - \bar{x}\mathbf{1})]^{-1} (\mathbf{x} - \bar{x}\mathbf{1})^\top (\mathbf{y} - \bar{y}\mathbf{1}) \tag{11.28}$$

By the FWL theorem (equation 11.25), we also have

$$\hat{\beta}_2 = [(\mathbf{M}_c\mathbf{x})^\top \mathbf{M}_c\mathbf{x}]^{-1} (\mathbf{M}_c\mathbf{x})^\top \mathbf{M}_c\mathbf{y} \tag{11.29}$$

where $\mathbf{M}_c$ is the residual projection associated with the linear subspace $S = \text{span}\{\mathbf{1}\}$, as defined in (3.10) on page 61. For this residual projection $\mathbf{M}_c$ and any $\mathbf{z}$, we have $\mathbf{M}_c\mathbf{z} = \mathbf{z} - \bar{z}\mathbf{1}$. Hence the right-hand sides of (11.28) and (11.29) coincide.

11.2.3 Centered Observations

Let's generalize the preceding discussion to the case where there are multiple nonconstant regressors. The only difference is that instead of one column $\mathbf{x}$ of observations on a single nonconstant regressor, we have a matrix $\mathbf{X}_2$ containing multiple columns, each a vector of observations on a nonconstant regressor. If the least squares estimate $\hat{\boldsymbol{\beta}}$ is partitioned into $(\hat{\beta}_1, \hat{\boldsymbol{\beta}}_2)$, then we can write

$$\mathbf{X}\hat{\boldsymbol{\beta}} = \mathbf{1}\beta_1 + \mathbf{X}_2\hat{\boldsymbol{\beta}}_2$$

Applying the FWL theorem (equation 11.25) once more, we can write $\hat{\boldsymbol{\beta}}_2$ as

$$\hat{\beta}_2 = [(\mathbf{M}_c\mathbf{X}_2)^\top \mathbf{M}_c\mathbf{X}_2]^{-1} (\mathbf{M}_c\mathbf{X}_2)^\top \mathbf{M}_c\mathbf{y}$$

where $\mathbf{M}_c$ is the residual projection in (3.10). As we saw in the last section, $\mathbf{M}_c\mathbf{y}$ is $\mathbf{y}$ centered around its mean. Similarly, $\mathbf{M}_c\mathbf{X}_2$ is a matrix formed by taking each column of $\mathbf{X}_2$ and centering it around its mean. It follows that in a least squares regression with an intercept, the estimated coefficients of the nonconstant regressors are equal to the estimated coefficients of a zero-intercept regression performed after all variables have been centered around their mean.

Let's use some related ideas to discuss an alternative to the coefficient of determination introduced in (11.13). There are several versions of R^2 reported in common regression packages. One of these is so called centered R^2. The version in (11.13) will henceforth be called the uncentered R^2 for clarity.

One motivation for introducing an alternative to uncentered R^2 is that it fails to be invariant to certain changes of units. While it is invariant to changes of units that involve rescaling of the regressand $\mathbf{y}$ (see ex. 11.4.2), it is not invariant to changes of units that involve addition or subtraction (actual inflation versus inflation in excess of a certain level, income versus income over a certain threshold, etc.) whenever $\mathbf{X}$ contains an intercept. Exercise 11.4.3 asks you to prove this.

This is one reason many econometricians use the **centered** R^2 rather than R^2, at least when the regression contains an intercept. For the purposes of this section, let's assume that this is the case (or, more generally, that $\mathbf{1} \in \operatorname{colspace} \mathbf{X}$). Centered R^2 is defined as

$$R_c^2 := \frac{\|\mathbf{P}\mathbf{M}_c\mathbf{y}\|^2}{\|\mathbf{M}_c\mathbf{y}\|^2} = \frac{\|\mathbf{M}_c\mathbf{P}\mathbf{y}\|^2}{\|\mathbf{M}_c\mathbf{y}\|^2} \tag{11.30}$$

$\mathbf{M}_c$ is as defined in (3.10) on page 61. The equality of the two expressions for R_c^2 is left as an exercise (ex. 11.4.6). Adding a constant to each element of $\mathbf{y}$ will have no effect on R_c^2 because $\mathbf{M}_c$ maps constant vectors to $\mathbf{0}$ (see example 3.3.1).

Centered R^2 can be rewritten (ex. 11.4.7) as

$$R_c^2 = \frac{\sum_{n=1}^N (\hat{y}_n - \bar{y})^2}{\sum_{n=1}^N (y_n - \bar{y})^2} \tag{11.31}$$

It is a further exercise (ex. 11.4.5) to show that, in the case of the simple regression, the R_c^2 is equal to the square of the sample correlation between the regressor and regressand, as defined in (8.5) on page 218. Thus R_c^2 is a measure of correlation.

11.3 Further Reading

For additional references on the material covered in this chapter see, for example, Friedman et al. (2009), Ruud (2000), Cameron and Trivedi (2005), or Davidson and MacKinnon (2004).

11.4 Exercises

Ex. 11.4.1 Let $\mathbf{x} := (z, az)^\top$, where $a \in \mathbb{R}$ and z is any scalar random variable. Show that $\mathbb{E}\,\mathbf{x}\mathbf{x}^\top$ is nonnegative definite but fails to be positive definite.

Ex. 11.4.2 Show that uncentered R^2 is invariant to changes of units that involve rescaling of the regressand $\mathbf{y}$ (dollars versus cents, kilometers versus miles, etc.)

Ex. 11.4.3 Fix $\mathbf{X}, \mathbf{y}$ and consider regressing $\mathbf{y}$ on $\mathbf{X}$. Suppose that $\mathbf{X}$ contains the intercept, in the sense that $\mathbf{1} \in \operatorname{colspace} \mathbf{X}$. Let R^2 represent the uncentered coefficient of determination. Let R_α^2 represent the same when $\mathbf{y}$ is replaced by $\mathbf{y} + \alpha\mathbf{1}$. Show that $R_\alpha^2 \to 1$ as $\alpha \to \infty$.

Ex. 11.4.4 Show that R^2 is invariant to a rescaling of the regressors.

Ex. 11.4.5 Show that, in the case of the simple regression model in §11.2.2.1, R_c^2 is equal to the square of the sample correlation between $\mathbf{x}$ and $\mathbf{y}$.

Ex. 11.4.6 Confirm the equality of the two alternative expressions for R_c^2 in (11.30).

Ex. 11.4.7 Verify the expression for R_c^2 in (11.31).

Ex. 11.4.8 Prove fact 11.1.2 on page 306.

Ex. 11.4.9 Verify expression (11.17).

Ex. 11.4.10 Let's show that $\hat{\boldsymbol{\beta}}$ solves the least squares problem in a slightly different way: Let $\mathbf{b}$ be any $K \times 1$ vector, and let $\hat{\boldsymbol{\beta}} := (\mathbf{X}^\top \mathbf{X})^{-1} \mathbf{X}^\top \mathbf{y}$.

(i) Show that $\|\mathbf{y} - \mathbf{X}\mathbf{b}\|^2 = \|\mathbf{y} - \mathbf{X}\hat{\boldsymbol{\beta}}\|^2 + \|\mathbf{X}(\hat{\boldsymbol{\beta}} - \mathbf{b})\|^2$.

(ii) Using (i), argue that $\hat{\boldsymbol{\beta}}$ is the minimizer of $\|\mathbf{y} - \mathbf{X}\mathbf{b}\|^2$ over all $K \times 1$ vectors $\mathbf{b}$.

Ex. 11.4.11 Verify that $\sum_{n=1}^{N} (y_n - \mathbf{b}^\top \mathbf{x}_n)^2 = \|\mathbf{y} - \mathbf{X}\mathbf{b}\|^2$.

Ex. 11.4.12 Show carefully that any solution to $\min_{\mathbf{b} \in \mathbb{R}^K} \|\mathbf{y} - \mathbf{X}\mathbf{b}\|^2$ is also a solution to $\min_{\mathbf{b} \in \mathbb{R}^K} \|\mathbf{y} - \mathbf{X}\mathbf{b}\|$, and vice versa.

Ex. 11.4.13 Confirm that $\mathbf{P}\mathbf{1} = \mathbf{1}$ whenever $\mathbf{1} \in \operatorname{colspace} \mathbf{X}$.

Ex. 11.4.14 Show that, for any regression containing the intercept, the vector of residuals must sum to zero.

Ex. 11.4.15 Show that, for any regression containing the intercept, the mean of the fitted values $\hat{\mathbf{y}} = \mathbf{P}\mathbf{y}$ is equal to the mean of $\mathbf{y}$.

Ex. 11.4.16 Show that $\mathbf{PM} = \mathbf{MP} = \mathbf{0}$. Using this fact (instead of the orthogonal projection theorem), show that the vector of fitted values and the vector of residuals are orthogonal.

Ex. 11.4.17 Show that if $R^2 = 1$, then the vector of residuals is identically zero, $\mathbf{P}\mathbf{y} = \mathbf{y}$, and $\mathbf{y} \in \operatorname{colspace} \mathbf{X}$.

Ex. 11.4.18 Suppose that the regression contains an intercept. Let $\bar{y}$ be the sample mean of $\mathbf{y}$, and let $\bar{\mathbf{x}}$ be a $1 \times K$ row vector such that the kth element of $\bar{\mathbf{x}}$ is the sample mean of the kth column of $\mathbf{X}$. Show that $\bar{y} = \bar{\mathbf{x}}\hat{\boldsymbol{\beta}}$.

Ex. 11.4.19 Suppose the regression contains an intercept. Let $\mathbf{M}_c$ be as defined in (3.10). Show that the following identity always holds:

$$\|\mathbf{M}\mathbf{y}\|^2 = \|\mathbf{M}_c\mathbf{y}\|^2 - \|\mathbf{P}\mathbf{M}_c\mathbf{y}\|^2 \tag{11.32}$$

Ex. 11.4.20 Let $\mathbf{X}_a$ and $\mathbf{X}_b$ be $N \times K_a$ and $N \times K_b$ respectively. Suppose that every column of $\mathbf{X}_a$ is also a column of $\mathbf{X}_b$. Show that colspace $\mathbf{X}_a \subset$ colspace $\mathbf{X}_b$.

Ex. 11.4.21 Let $\mathbf{x} := (x_1, \ldots, x_N)$ and $\mathbf{y} := (y_1, \ldots, y_N)$ be sequences of scalar random variables. Show that the sample correlation $\hat{\varrho}$ between $\mathbf{x}$ and $\mathbf{y}$ (defined in (8.5) on page 218) can be written as

$$\hat{\varrho} = \frac{(\mathbf{M}_c \mathbf{x})^\top (\mathbf{M}_c \mathbf{y})}{\|\mathbf{M}_c \mathbf{x}\| \|\mathbf{M}_c \mathbf{y}\|}$$

Ex. 11.4.22 Show that the two expressions for $\hat{\boldsymbol{\beta}}_2$ in (11.23) and (11.25) are equal.[4]

Ex. 11.4.23 At the end of the proof of theorem 11.2.1, it was claimed that the matrix $\mathbf{X}_2^\top \mathbf{M}_1 \mathbf{X}_2$ is nonsingular. Verify this claim.

Ex. 11.4.24 (Computational) Build an arbitrary data set $\mathbf{X}$, $\mathbf{y}$ by simulation. Run a regression with the intercept, and record the values of the estimated coefficients of the nonconstant (i.e., $k \geqslant 2$) regressors. Confirm that these values are equal to the estimated coefficients of the no-intercept regression after all variables have been centered around their mean.

11.4.1 Solutions to Selected Exercises

Solution to Ex. 11.4.1. The expression $\mathbb{E}\,\mathbf{x}\mathbf{x}^\top$ is nonnegative definite for any $\mathbf{x}$ because, given $\mathbf{c} \in \mathbb{R}^K$, we have

$$\mathbf{c}^\top \mathbb{E}\,\mathbf{x}\mathbf{x}^\top \mathbf{c} = \mathbb{E}\,(\mathbf{c}^\top \mathbf{x})(\mathbf{x}^\top \mathbf{c}) = \mathbb{E}\,(\mathbf{x}^\top \mathbf{c})^2 \geqslant 0$$

Here we used the fact that the transpose of a scalar is equal to the scalar. However, if $\mathbf{x} := (z, az)^\top$, then

$$\mathbb{E}\,\mathbf{x}\mathbf{x}^\top = \mathbb{E}\,z^2 \begin{pmatrix} 1 & a \\ a & a^2 \end{pmatrix}$$

The second column is a multiple of the first, so the matrix is singular and the determinant is zero. As such it cannot be positive definite (see fact 3.2.9 on page 60). □

Solution to Ex. 11.4.2. If $\mathbf{y}$ is scaled by $\alpha \in \mathbb{R}$, then

$$\frac{\|\mathbf{P}\alpha\mathbf{y}\|^2}{\|\alpha\mathbf{y}\|^2} = \frac{\|\alpha\mathbf{P}\mathbf{y}\|^2}{\|\alpha\mathbf{y}\|^2} = \frac{\alpha^2\|\mathbf{P}\mathbf{y}\|^2}{\alpha^2\|\mathbf{y}\|^2} = \frac{\|\mathbf{P}\mathbf{y}\|^2}{\|\mathbf{y}\|^2}$$

Hence the uncentered R^2 is unchanged. □

4. Hint: Use the symmetry and idempotence of the matrix $\mathbf{M}_1$.

Solution to Ex. 11.4.3. Fix $\alpha \in \mathbb{R}$. By definition, R^2_α is

$$\frac{\|\mathbf{P}(\mathbf{y}+\alpha\mathbf{1})\|^2}{\|\mathbf{y}+\alpha\mathbf{1}\|^2} = \frac{\|\mathbf{P}\mathbf{y}+\alpha\mathbf{P}\mathbf{1}\|^2}{\|\mathbf{y}+\alpha\mathbf{1}\|^2} = \frac{\|\mathbf{P}\mathbf{y}+\alpha\mathbf{1}\|^2}{\|\mathbf{y}+\alpha\mathbf{1}\|^2} = \frac{\alpha^2\|\mathbf{P}\mathbf{y}/\alpha+\mathbf{1}\|^2}{\alpha^2\|\mathbf{y}/\alpha+\mathbf{1}\|^2} = \frac{\|\mathbf{P}\mathbf{y}/\alpha+\mathbf{1}\|^2}{\|\mathbf{y}/\alpha+\mathbf{1}\|^2}$$

where the second inequality follows from the fact that $\mathbf{1} \in \operatorname{colspace} \mathbf{X}$. Taking the limit as $\alpha \to \infty$, we find that $R^2_\alpha \to 1$ as $\alpha \to \infty$. □

Solution to Ex. 11.4.4. This follows immediately from the definition of R^2, and the fact that, for any $\alpha \neq 0$,

$$\mathbf{P} = \mathbf{X}(\mathbf{X}^\top\mathbf{X})^{-1}\mathbf{X}^\top = \frac{\alpha^2}{\alpha^2}\mathbf{X}(\mathbf{X}^\top\mathbf{X})^{-1}\mathbf{X}^\top = (\alpha\mathbf{X})((\alpha\mathbf{X})^\top(\alpha\mathbf{X}))^{-1}(\alpha\mathbf{X}^\top) \qquad \square$$

Solution to Ex. 11.4.5. From exercise 11.4.21, the squared sample correlation between $\mathbf{x}$ and $\mathbf{y}$ can be written as

$$\hat{\varrho}^2 = \frac{[(\mathbf{M}_c\mathbf{x})^\top(\mathbf{M}_c\mathbf{y})]^2}{\|\mathbf{M}_c\mathbf{x}\|^2\|\mathbf{M}_c\mathbf{y}\|^2}$$

Also, $R^2_c = \|\mathbf{M}_c\mathbf{P}\mathbf{y}\|^2/\|\mathbf{M}_c\mathbf{y}\|^2$. Hence it suffices to show that, for the simple linear regression model in §11.2.2.1, we have

$$\|\mathbf{M}_c\mathbf{P}\mathbf{y}\| = \frac{|(\mathbf{M}_c\mathbf{x})^\top(\mathbf{M}_c\mathbf{y})|}{\|\mathbf{M}_c\mathbf{x}\|} \tag{11.33}$$

Let $\mathbf{X} = (\mathbf{1}, \mathbf{x})$ be the design matrix, where the first column is $\mathbf{1}$ and the second column is $\mathbf{x}$. Let

$$\hat{\beta}_1 := \bar{y} - \hat{\beta}_2\bar{x} \quad \text{and} \quad \hat{\beta}_2 := \frac{(\mathbf{M}_c\mathbf{x})^\top(\mathbf{M}_c\mathbf{y})}{\|\mathbf{M}_c\mathbf{x}\|^2}$$

be the least squares estimators of β_1 and β_2 respectively (see §11.2.2.1). We then have

$$\mathbf{P}\mathbf{y} = \mathbf{X}\hat{\boldsymbol{\beta}} = \mathbf{1}\hat{\beta}_1 + \mathbf{x}\hat{\beta}_2$$

$$\therefore \quad \mathbf{M}_c\mathbf{P}\mathbf{y} = \mathbf{M}_c\mathbf{X}\hat{\boldsymbol{\beta}} = \mathbf{M}_c\mathbf{x}\hat{\beta}_2$$

$$\therefore \quad \|\mathbf{M}_c\mathbf{P}\mathbf{y}\| = \|\mathbf{M}_c\mathbf{x}\hat{\beta}_2\| = |\hat{\beta}_2|\|\mathbf{M}_c\mathbf{x}\| = \frac{|(\mathbf{M}_c\mathbf{x})^\top(\mathbf{M}_c\mathbf{y})|}{\|\mathbf{M}_c\mathbf{x}\|^2}\|\mathbf{M}_c\mathbf{x}\|$$

Canceling $\|\mathbf{M}_c\mathbf{x}\|$ we get (11.33). This completes the proof. □

Solution to Ex. 11.4.6. It is sufficient to show that $\mathbf{P}\mathbf{M}_c = \mathbf{M}_c\mathbf{P}$. Since $\mathbf{1} \in \operatorname{colspace} \mathbf{X}$ by assumption, we have $\mathbf{P}\mathbf{1} = \mathbf{1}$, and $\mathbf{1}^\top\mathbf{P} = (\mathbf{P}^\top\mathbf{1})^\top = (\mathbf{P}\mathbf{1})^\top = \mathbf{1}^\top$. Therefore $\mathbf{P}\mathbf{1}\mathbf{1}^\top =$

$\mathbf{1}\mathbf{1}^\top \mathbf{P}$, and

$$\mathbf{P}\mathbf{M}_c = \mathbf{P} - \frac{1}{N}\mathbf{P}\mathbf{1}\mathbf{1}^\top = \mathbf{P} - \frac{1}{N}\mathbf{1}\mathbf{1}^\top \mathbf{P} = \mathbf{M}_c\mathbf{P} \qquad \square$$

Solution to Ex. 11.4.7. It suffices to show that $\|\mathbf{P}\mathbf{M}_c\mathbf{y}\|^2 = \sum_{n=1}^N (\hat{y}_n - \bar{y})^2$. This holds because

$$\sum_{n=1}^N (\hat{y}_n - \bar{y})^2 = \|\mathbf{P}\mathbf{y} - \mathbf{1}\bar{y}\|^2 = \|\mathbf{P}\mathbf{y} - \mathbf{P}\mathbf{1}\bar{y}\|^2 = \|\mathbf{P}(\mathbf{y} - \mathbf{1}\bar{y})\|^2 = \|\mathbf{P}\mathbf{M}_c\mathbf{y}\|^2 \qquad \square$$

Solution to Solution 11.4.8. Adopt the notation and assumptions of fact 11.1.2 on page 306. Let $\mathbf{y}$ be given. Let $\mathbf{P}_a$ and $\mathbf{P}_b$ be the projections onto the column spaces of $\mathbf{X}_a$ and $\mathbf{X}_b$ respectively, so that $R_i^2 = \|\mathbf{P}_i\mathbf{y}\|^2 / \|\mathbf{y}\|^2$ for $i \in \{a, b\}$. From fact 2.2.7 on page 32 we have $\mathbf{P}_a\mathbf{P}_b\mathbf{y} = \mathbf{P}_a\mathbf{y}$. Using this fact, and setting $\mathbf{y}_b := \mathbf{P}_b\mathbf{y}$, gives

$$\frac{R_a^2}{R_b^2} = \left(\frac{\|\mathbf{P}_a\mathbf{y}\|}{\|\mathbf{P}_b\mathbf{y}\|}\right)^2 = \left(\frac{\|\mathbf{P}_a\mathbf{P}_b\mathbf{y}\|}{\|\mathbf{P}_b\mathbf{y}\|}\right)^2 = \left(\frac{\|\mathbf{P}_a\mathbf{y}_b\|}{\|\mathbf{y}_b\|}\right)^2 \leqslant 1$$

where the final inequality follows from theorem 2.2.2 on page 31. Hence $R_b^2 \geqslant R_a^2$, and regressing with $\mathbf{X}_b$ produces (weakly) larger R^2. $\square$

Solution to Ex. 11.4.10. Part (ii) follows immediately from part (i). Regarding part (i), observe that

$$\|\mathbf{y} - \mathbf{X}\mathbf{b}\|^2 = \|\mathbf{y} - \mathbf{X}\hat{\boldsymbol{\beta}} + \mathbf{X}(\hat{\boldsymbol{\beta}} - \mathbf{b})\|^2$$

By the Pythagorean law, the claim

$$\|\mathbf{y} - \mathbf{X}\mathbf{b}\|^2 = \|\mathbf{y} - \mathbf{X}\hat{\boldsymbol{\beta}}\|^2 + \|\mathbf{X}(\hat{\boldsymbol{\beta}} - \mathbf{b})\|^2$$

will be confirmed if $\mathbf{y} - \mathbf{X}\hat{\boldsymbol{\beta}} \perp \mathbf{X}(\hat{\boldsymbol{\beta}} - \mathbf{b})$. This follows from the definition of $\hat{\boldsymbol{\beta}}$, because for arbitrary $\mathbf{a} \in \mathbb{R}^K$ we have

$$(\mathbf{X}\mathbf{a})^\top(\mathbf{y} - \mathbf{X}\hat{\boldsymbol{\beta}}) = \mathbf{a}^\top(\mathbf{X}^\top\mathbf{y} - \mathbf{X}^\top\mathbf{X}(\mathbf{X}^\top\mathbf{X})^{-1}\mathbf{X}^\top\mathbf{y}) = \mathbf{a}^\top(\mathbf{X}^\top\mathbf{y} - \mathbf{X}^\top\mathbf{y}) = 0 \qquad \square$$

Solution to Ex. 11.4.12. Let $\hat{\boldsymbol{\beta}}$ be a solution to $\min_{\mathbf{b} \in \mathbb{R}^K} \|\mathbf{y} - \mathbf{X}\mathbf{b}\|^2$, which is to say that

$$\|\mathbf{y} - \mathbf{X}\hat{\boldsymbol{\beta}}\|^2 \leqslant \|\mathbf{y} - \mathbf{X}\mathbf{b}\|^2 \quad \text{for any } \mathbf{b} \in \mathbb{R}^K$$

If a and b are nonnegative constants with $a \leqslant b$, then $\sqrt{a} \leqslant \sqrt{b}$, and hence

$$\|\mathbf{y} - \mathbf{X}\hat{\boldsymbol{\beta}}\| \leqslant \|\mathbf{y} - \mathbf{X}\mathbf{b}\| \quad \text{for any } \mathbf{b} \in \mathbb{R}^K$$

In other words, $\hat{\boldsymbol{\beta}}$ is a solution to $\min_{\mathbf{b} \in \mathbb{R}^K} \|\mathbf{y} - \mathbf{X}\mathbf{b}\|$. The "vice versa" argument follows along similar lines. □

Solution to Ex. 11.4.14. To see why the vector of residuals sums to zero, observe that

$$\mathbf{1}^\top \mathbf{M}\mathbf{y} = \mathbf{1}^\top \mathbf{y} - \mathbf{1}^\top \mathbf{P}\mathbf{y} = \mathbf{1}^\top \mathbf{y} - (\mathbf{P}^\top \mathbf{1})^\top \mathbf{y} = \mathbf{1}^\top \mathbf{y} - (\mathbf{P}\mathbf{1})^\top \mathbf{y}$$

where the last equality uses the fact the $\mathbf{P}$ is symmetric. Moreover, by exercise 11.4.13, we have $\mathbf{P}\mathbf{1} = \mathbf{1}$ whenever $\mathbf{1}$ is a column of $\mathbf{X}$. Therefore

$$\mathbf{1}^\top \mathbf{M}\mathbf{y} = \mathbf{1}^\top \mathbf{y} - (\mathbf{P}\mathbf{1})^\top \mathbf{y} = \mathbf{1}^\top \mathbf{y} - \mathbf{1}^\top \mathbf{y} = 0$$

□

Solution to Ex. 11.4.15. Since $\mathbf{1} \in \operatorname{colspace} \mathbf{X}$, we have $\mathbf{P}\mathbf{1} = \mathbf{1}$. It follows that

$$\frac{1}{N}\sum_{n=1}^{N} \hat{y}_n = \frac{1}{N}\mathbf{1}^\top \hat{\mathbf{y}} = \frac{1}{N}\mathbf{1}^\top \mathbf{P}\mathbf{y} = \frac{1}{N}\mathbf{1}^\top \mathbf{y} = \frac{1}{N}\sum_{n=1}^{N} y_n$$

□

Solution to Ex. 11.4.17. If $R^2 = 1$, then, by (11.12) on page 303, we have $\|\mathbf{M}\mathbf{y}\|^2 = 0$, and hence have $\hat{\mathbf{u}} = \mathbf{M}\mathbf{y} = \mathbf{0}$. Since $\mathbf{M}\mathbf{y} + \mathbf{P}\mathbf{y} = \mathbf{y}$, this implies that $\mathbf{P}\mathbf{y} = \mathbf{y}$. But then $\mathbf{y} \in \operatorname{colspace} \mathbf{X}$ by (vi) of theorem 2.2.2. □

Solution to Ex. 11.4.19. Fact 2.2.8 tells us that for any conformable vector $\mathbf{z}$ we have $\mathbf{z} = \mathbf{P}\mathbf{z} + \mathbf{M}\mathbf{z}$, where the two vectors on the right-hand side are orthogonal. Letting $\mathbf{z} = \mathbf{M}_c\mathbf{y}$, we obtain

$$\mathbf{M}_c\mathbf{y} = \mathbf{P}\mathbf{M}_c\mathbf{y} + \mathbf{M}\mathbf{M}_c\mathbf{y}$$

From fact 2.2.9 we have $\mathbf{M}\mathbf{M}_c\mathbf{y} = \mathbf{M}\mathbf{y}$. Using this result, orthogonality, and the Pythagorean law, we obtain

$$\|\mathbf{M}_c\mathbf{y}\|^2 = \|\mathbf{P}\mathbf{M}_c\mathbf{y}\|^2 + \|\mathbf{M}\mathbf{y}\|^2$$

Rearranging gives (11.32) □

Solution to Ex. 11.4.20. This is just fact 2.1.3 on page 16. □

Solution to Ex. 11.4.23. By fact 3.2.9, to show that $\mathbf{X}_2^\top \mathbf{M}_1 \mathbf{X}_2$ is nonsingular, it suffices to show that the matrix is positive definite. By idempotence and symmetry of $\mathbf{M}_1$,

$$\mathbf{X}_2^\top \mathbf{M}_1 \mathbf{X}_2 = \mathbf{X}_2^\top \mathbf{M}_1 \mathbf{M}_1 \mathbf{X}_2 = \mathbf{X}_2^\top \mathbf{M}_1^\top \mathbf{M}_1 \mathbf{X}_2 = (\mathbf{M}_1 \mathbf{X}_2)^\top \mathbf{M}_1 \mathbf{X}_2$$

Take any $\mathbf{a} \neq \mathbf{0}$. We need to show that

$$\mathbf{a}^\top (\mathbf{M}_1 \mathbf{X}_2)^\top \mathbf{M}_1 \mathbf{X}_2 \mathbf{a} = (\mathbf{M}_1 \mathbf{X}_2 \mathbf{a})^\top \mathbf{M}_1 \mathbf{X}_2 \mathbf{a} = \|\mathbf{M}_1 \mathbf{X}_2 \mathbf{a}\|^2 > 0$$

Since the only vector with zero norm is the zero vector, it now suffices to show that $\mathbf{M}_1\mathbf{X}_2\mathbf{a}$ is nonzero. From fact 2.2.8 on page 33, we see that $\mathbf{M}_1\mathbf{X}_2\mathbf{a} = \mathbf{0}$ only when $\mathbf{X}_2\mathbf{a}$ is in the column span of $\mathbf{X}_1$. Thus, the proof will be complete if we can show that $\mathbf{X}_2\mathbf{a}$ is not in the column span of $\mathbf{X}_1$.

Indeed, $\mathbf{X}_2\mathbf{a}$ is not in the column span of $\mathbf{X}_1$. If it were, then we could write $\mathbf{X}_1\mathbf{b} = \mathbf{X}_2\mathbf{a}$ for some $\mathbf{b} \in \mathbb{R}^{K_1}$. Rearranging, we get $\mathbf{X}\mathbf{c} = \mathbf{0}$ for some nonzero $\mathbf{c}$ (recall $\mathbf{a} \neq \mathbf{0}$). This contradicts linear independence of the columns of $\mathbf{X}$. $\square$

Chapter 12

Ordinary Least Squares

In chapter 11 we imposed only mild regularity conditions on the data. To further investigate linear least squares estimation and provide additional interpretation of the estimated coefficients, we need to make more assumptions. The purpose of this chapter is to describe the properties of linear least squares estimation under the classical OLS assumptions, where OLS stands for **ordinary least squares**.

12.1 Estimation under OLS

In this section we introduce the OLS assumptions and study the finite sample properties of the OLS estimators under these assumptions.

12.1.1 Assumptions

Let $\mathbf{X}$ and $\mathbf{y}$ be as defined in §11.1. The OLS assumptions are as follows:

Assumption 12.1.1 (Full rank) $\mathbf{X}$ has full column rank with probability one.

Assumption 12.1.2 (Linearity) The observations satisfy $\mathbf{y} = \mathbf{X}\boldsymbol{\beta} + \mathbf{u}$ for some unknown K-vector of parameters $\boldsymbol{\beta}$ and unobservable vector of shocks $\mathbf{u}$.

Assumption 12.1.3 (Orthogonal regressors) $\mathbb{E}[\mathbf{u} \mid \mathbf{X}] = \mathbf{0}$.

Assumption 12.1.4 (Spherical errors) $\mathbb{E}[\mathbf{u}\mathbf{u}^\top \mid \mathbf{X}] = \sigma^2\mathbf{I}$ for some unknown $\sigma > 0$.

Let's break these assumptions down and see what they imply.

Assumption 12.1.1 is just a repetition of assumption 11.1.1 from chapter 11. Assumption 12.1.2 can be decomposed into the separate equations

$$y_n = \mathbf{x}_n^\top \boldsymbol{\beta} + u_n, \qquad n = 1, \ldots, N \tag{12.1}$$

Here are some examples of models that produce relationships in the form of (12.1).

Example 12.1.1 The **Cobb–Douglas production function** relates capital and labor inputs with output via $y = Ak^a \ell^\delta$, where A is a random, firm-specific productivity term and a and δ are parameters. Taking logs yields the linear regression model

$$\ln y = \gamma + a \ln k + \delta \ln \ell + u$$

where the random term $\ln A$ is represented by $\gamma + u$.

Example 12.1.2 The **gravity model** relates international trade flows between country ℓ and country n via the equation $T_{\ell n} = \lambda \xi_{\ell n} G_\ell^\alpha G_n^\beta / D_{\ell n}^\gamma$. Here $T_{\ell n}$ is exports from country ℓ to country n, λ is a constant term, $\xi_{\ell n}$ is a shock, G_ℓ and G_n are GDP in country ℓ and n respectively, and $D_{\ell n}$ is distance between them. Taking logs gives

$$\ln T_{\ell n} = \ln \lambda + \alpha \ln G_\ell + \beta \ln G_n - \gamma \ln D_{\ell n} + \ln \xi_{\ell n} \tag{12.2}$$

For motivation and discussion, see, for example, Bergeijk and Brakman (2010).

Fact 12.1.1 If the linearity assumption 12.1.2 holds, then

(i) $\mathbf{My} = \mathbf{Mu}$.

(ii) $\mathbf{Py} = \mathbf{X}\boldsymbol{\beta} + \mathbf{Pu}$.

(iii) $\text{RSS} = \mathbf{u}^\top \mathbf{Mu}$.

The notation in fact 12.1.1 follows §11.1.2.2. Exercise 12.4.2 requests a proof.

Fact 12.1.2 If assumption 12.1.3 holds, then

(i) $\mathbb{E}[\mathbf{u}] = \mathbf{0}$,

(ii) $\mathbb{E}[u_m \mid x_{nk}] = 0$ for any m, n, k,

(iii) $\mathbb{E}[u_m x_{nk}] = 0$ for any m, n, k (orthogonality), and

(iv) $\text{cov}[u_m, x_{nk}] = 0$ for any m, n, k.

Exercise 12.4.3 asks you to give proofs.

Fact 12.1.3 If assumption 12.1.4 holds, then

(i) $\text{var}[\mathbf{u}] = \mathbb{E}[\mathbf{u}\mathbf{u}^\top] = \sigma^2 \mathbf{I}$,

(ii) $\mathbb{E}[u_i^2 \mid \mathbf{X}] = \mathbb{E}[u_j^2 \mid \mathbf{X}] = \sigma^2$ for any i, j in $1, \ldots, N$, and

(iii) $\mathbb{E}[u_i u_j \mid \mathbf{X}] = 0$ whenever $i \neq j$.

Parts (ii) and (iii) are called **homoskedasticity** and zero correlation respectively. Combining assumptions 12.1.3 and 12.1.4 gives

$$\operatorname{var}[\mathbf{u} \mid \mathbf{X}] := \mathbb{E}[\mathbf{u}\mathbf{u}^\top \mid \mathbf{X}] - \mathbb{E}[\mathbf{u} \mid \mathbf{X}]\mathbb{E}[\mathbf{u}^\top \mid \mathbf{X}] = \mathbb{E}[\mathbf{u}\mathbf{u}^\top \mid \mathbf{X}]$$

Thus the conditional variance–covariance matrix is the diagonal matrix $\sigma^2 \mathbf{I}$.

12.1.2 The OLS Estimators

The standard estimator of $\boldsymbol{\beta}$ in (12.1) is the least squares estimator $\hat{\boldsymbol{\beta}}$ defined in (11.9). That is,

$$\hat{\boldsymbol{\beta}} := (\mathbf{X}^\top \mathbf{X})^{-1} \mathbf{X}^\top \mathbf{y} \tag{12.3}$$

Unlike chapter 11, it's now understood as an estimator of the unknown parameter vector $\boldsymbol{\beta}$. In this context, $\hat{\boldsymbol{\beta}}$ is also called the **OLS estimator** of $\boldsymbol{\beta}$. Substituting $\mathbf{y} = \mathbf{X}\boldsymbol{\beta} + \mathbf{u}$ into (12.3) and cancel terms gives the useful comparison

$$\hat{\boldsymbol{\beta}} = \boldsymbol{\beta} + (\mathbf{X}^\top \mathbf{X})^{-1} \mathbf{X}^\top \mathbf{u} \tag{12.4}$$

The usual OLS estimator of the parameter σ^2 introduced in assumption 12.1.4 is

$$\hat{\sigma}^2 := \frac{\text{RSS}}{N - K} \tag{12.5}$$

While we can compute $\hat{\boldsymbol{\beta}}$ and $\hat{\sigma}^2$ directly using the expressions in (12.3) and (12.5), in practice it's more common to pass them to a routine in a regression package. Here's an example that runs the gravity model regression (12.2) on world trade data using Python. Like other worked examples, the full set of code and data for replicating these results can be found at `johnstachurski.net/emet.html`, along with references, details on the data source and the definitions of the variables.

First we import some Python libraries often used for statistics:

```
import pandas as pd
import statsmodels.formula.api as smf
```

Then we read in the data to a pandas `DataFrame` from a local CSV file:

```
data = pd.read_csv("./data/gravity_dataset_2013.csv")
```

Next we build a model using a formula to indicate the regression we want to run symbolically (similar to `R`).

```
formula = "log(value) ~ log(egdp) + log(igdp) + log(dist)"
model = smf.ols(formula, data)
```

The formula used above is analogous to (12.2). We omit the shock (the last term in (12.2)) because it is not part of the data set, as well as the constant term, which is included automatically. The names egdp and igdp represent exporter and importer GDP respectively.

Now we can perform the estimation and print a table summarizing results:

```
result = model.fit(cov_type='HC1')
print(result.summary())
```

The output is as follows:

```
                            OLS Regression Results
==============================================================================
Dep. Variable:             log(value)   R-squared:                       0.652
Model:                            OLS   Adj. R-squared:                  0.652
Method:                 Least Squares   F-statistic:                 1.203e+04
Date:                Wed, 04 Nov 2015   Prob (F-statistic):               0.00
Time:                        16:02:42   Log-Likelihood:                -47185.
No. Observations:               19655   AIC:                         9.438e+04
Df Residuals:                   19651   BIC:                         9.441e+04
Df Model:                           3
Covariance Type:                  HC1
==============================================================================
                 coef    std err          z      P>|z|      [95.0% Conf. Int.]
------------------------------------------------------------------------------
Intercept    -30.2350      0.394    -76.773      0.000       -31.007   -29.463
log(egdp)      1.2783      0.008    153.772      0.000         1.262     1.295
log(igdp)      1.0287      0.009    118.885      0.000         1.012     1.046
log(dist)     -1.3483      0.023    -58.113      0.000        -1.394    -1.303
==============================================================================
Omnibus:                     1819.031   Durbin-Watson:                   1.798
Prob(Omnibus):                  0.000   Jarque-Bera (JB):             3361.159
Skew:                          -0.639   Prob(JB):                         0.00
Kurtosis:                       4.571   Cond. No.                         708.
==============================================================================
```

The value of the OLS estimate $\hat{\beta}$ is the column under coef. Objects such as standard errors are discussed below. The argument cov_type='HC1' to the model.fit call that produced this table requests heteroskedasticity-consistent or "robust" standard errors, which will be discussed in §12.2.1.

Let's check that the values for $\hat{\beta}$ reported under `coef` coincide with the expression for $\hat{\beta}$ given in (12.3). First we build the design matrix $\mathbf{X}$ (see the URL given above for details) and then compute as follows:

```
betahat = inv(X.T @ X) @ X.T @ y
```

When we print the result the output agrees with the output in the table

```
[-30.23498073   1.27825004   1.02865139  -1.34830012]
```

The expression for the R^2 in the table above is for R_c^2, as given in (11.31). A verification is provided in the code available at `johnstachurski.net/emet.html`.

Figure 12.1 shows a **partial regression plot** for the linear model just described. It is produced from the `result` object generated above via the commands

```
import matplotlib.pyplot as plt
import statsmodels.api as sm
fig = plt.figure()
fig = sm.graphics.plot_partregress_grid(result, fig=fig)
```

To understand the figure, consider, for example, the bottom left subplot, which shows the relationship between `log(igdp)` and the dependent variable. The data points in the plot correspond to the residuals in (11.26) and (11.27). In particular, the values on the horizontal axis are the residuals from regressing `log(igdp)` on all other columns in $\mathbf{X}$, while those on the vertical axis are the residuals from regressing the dependent variable `log(value)` on all other columns in $\mathbf{X}$.

The relationship between these residuals measures the change in `log(value)` associated with changing `log(igdp)` while holding all other variables fixed. The slope of the regression line running through the plot is exactly the coefficient estimate on `log(igdp)`. For clarification see the discussion surrounding (11.26) and (11.27).

The partial regression plot can be useful both for interpretation and diagnostics. For now, however, let's look at some general theory concerning properties of the OLS estimators.

12.1.3 Finite Sample Properties

Let's start with classical results on finite sample properties under the OLS assumptions. These are elegant results, although you should also read §14.2 if you want to view them with proper perspective. Our first result shows that, under the OLS assumptions, the OLS estimators are unbiased.

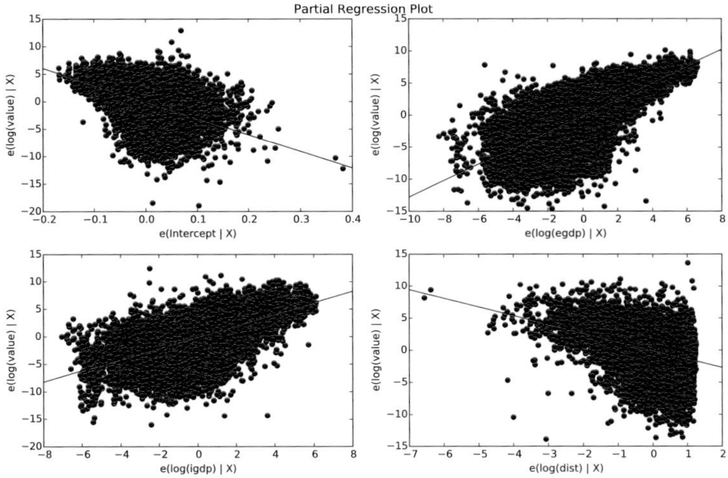

Figure 12.1 Partial regression plot for the gravity model

Theorem 12.1.1 *If assumptions 12.1.1–12.1.3 hold, then*

$$\mathbb{E}\,\hat{\boldsymbol{\beta}} = \mathbb{E}\,[\hat{\boldsymbol{\beta}} \,|\, \mathbf{X}] = \boldsymbol{\beta} \tag{12.6}$$

If assumption 12.1.4 also holds, then

$$\mathbb{E}\,\hat{\sigma}^2 = \mathbb{E}\,[\hat{\sigma}^2 \,|\, \mathbf{X}] = \sigma^2 \tag{12.7}$$

Proof. By (12.4) and assumption 12.1.3, we have $\mathbb{E}\,[\hat{\boldsymbol{\beta}} \,|\, \mathbf{X}] = \boldsymbol{\beta} + (\mathbf{X}^\top \mathbf{X})^{-1} \mathbf{X}^\top \mathbb{E}\,[\mathbf{u} \,|\, \mathbf{X}] = \boldsymbol{\beta}$. Taking the unconditional expectation gives (12.6).

Regarding (12.7), if we use the expression for RSS in fact 12.1.1, we get

$$\mathbb{E}\,[\text{RSS} \,|\, \mathbf{X}] = \mathbb{E}\,[\mathbf{u}^\top \mathbf{M} \mathbf{u} \,|\, \mathbf{X}] = \sigma^2 \mathbb{E}\,[\boldsymbol{\xi}^\top \mathbf{M} \boldsymbol{\xi} \,|\, \mathbf{X}] \quad \text{where} \quad \boldsymbol{\xi} := \sigma^{-1} \mathbf{u}$$

It follows now from fact 5.1.3 on page 127 that $\mathbb{E}\,[\text{RSS} \,|\, \mathbf{X}] = \sigma^2 \operatorname{trace} \mathbf{M}$. Hence

$$\mathbb{E}\,[\hat{\sigma}^2 \,|\, \mathbf{X}] = \frac{\sigma^2 \operatorname{trace}(\mathbf{M})}{N - K}$$

By fact 3.3.4 on page 61 we have $\operatorname{trace} \mathbf{M} = N - K$. Inserting this into the preceding equation and taking unconditional expectations gives (12.7). □

Now that we know $\hat{\boldsymbol{\beta}}$ is unbiased, let's consider the variance.

Theorem 12.1.2 *If assumptions 12.1.1–12.1.4 hold, then*

$$\text{var}[\hat{\boldsymbol{\beta}} \mid \mathbf{X}] = \sigma^2 (\mathbf{X}^\top \mathbf{X})^{-1} \tag{12.8}$$

For a proof, see exercise 12.4.5 and its solution.

Is the value on the right-hand side of (12.8) small or large? A famous result in OLS theory is that under the stated conditions, the OLS estimator $\hat{\boldsymbol{\beta}}$ is best linear unbiased. That is, in the class of linear unbiased estimators of $\boldsymbol{\beta}$, the OLS estimator has the lowest variance.

Theorem 12.1.3 (Gauss–Markov) *Let assumptions 12.1.1–12.1.4 hold and let* $\mathbf{b}$ *be an estimator of* $\boldsymbol{\beta}$. *If* $\mathbf{b}$ *is linear and unbiased, then*

$$\text{var}[\hat{\boldsymbol{\beta}} \mid \mathbf{X}] \leqslant \text{var}[\mathbf{b} \mid \mathbf{X}]$$

Here $\text{var}[\hat{\boldsymbol{\beta}} \mid \mathbf{X}] \leqslant \text{var}[\mathbf{b} \mid \mathbf{X}]$ means that $\text{var}[\mathbf{b} \mid \mathbf{X}] - \text{var}[\hat{\boldsymbol{\beta}} \mid \mathbf{X}]$ is nonnegative definite. Since matrices have no standard ordering, this is one way to assert that $\text{var}[\mathbf{b} \mid \mathbf{X}]$ is "larger." One implication is that $\text{var}[b_k \mid \mathbf{X}] \geqslant \text{var}[\hat{\beta}_k \mid \mathbf{X}]$ for all k. (Why?)

Also, linearity of $\mathbf{b}$ means that $\mathbf{b}$ is linear as a function of $\mathbf{y}$, taking $\mathbf{X}$ as fixed. In view of theorem 3.1.1 on page 48, this is equivalent to requiring that $\mathbf{b} = \mathbf{C}\mathbf{y}$ for some matrix $\mathbf{C}$. The matrix $\mathbf{C}$ is allowed to depend on $\mathbf{X}$ but not $\mathbf{y}$.

The statement that $\mathbf{b}$ is unbiased means $\mathbb{E}[\mathbf{b} \mid \mathbf{X}] = \mathbb{E}[\mathbf{C}\mathbf{y} \mid \mathbf{X}] = \boldsymbol{\beta}$ for all $\boldsymbol{\beta} \in \mathbb{R}^K$.

Proof of theorem 12.1.3. Let $\mathbf{b} = \mathbf{C}\mathbf{y}$, as described above, and let $\mathbf{D} := \mathbf{C} - \mathbf{A}$, where $\mathbf{A} := (\mathbf{X}^\top\mathbf{X})^{-1}\mathbf{X}^\top$. Then

$$\mathbf{b} = \mathbf{C}\mathbf{y} = \mathbf{D}\mathbf{y} + \mathbf{A}\mathbf{y} = \mathbf{D}(\mathbf{X}\boldsymbol{\beta} + \mathbf{u}) + \hat{\boldsymbol{\beta}} = \mathbf{D}\mathbf{X}\boldsymbol{\beta} + \mathbf{D}\mathbf{u} + \hat{\boldsymbol{\beta}} \tag{12.9}$$

Taking conditional expectations and using the fact that $\mathbf{D}$ is a function of $\mathbf{X}$, we obtain

$$\begin{aligned}
\mathbb{E}[\mathbf{b} \mid \mathbf{X}] &= \mathbb{E}[\mathbf{D}\mathbf{X}\boldsymbol{\beta} \mid \mathbf{X}] + \mathbb{E}[\mathbf{D}\mathbf{u} \mid \mathbf{X}] + \mathbb{E}[\hat{\boldsymbol{\beta}} \mid \mathbf{X}] \\
&= \mathbf{D}\mathbf{X}\,\mathbb{E}[\boldsymbol{\beta} \mid \mathbf{X}] + \mathbf{D}\,\mathbb{E}[\mathbf{u} \mid \mathbf{X}] + \mathbb{E}[\hat{\boldsymbol{\beta}} \mid \mathbf{X}] \\
&= \mathbf{D}\mathbf{X}\boldsymbol{\beta} + \mathbf{0} + \boldsymbol{\beta}
\end{aligned}$$

Since $\mathbf{b}$ is unbiased and, in particular, $\mathbb{E}[\mathbf{b} \mid \mathbf{X}] = \boldsymbol{\beta}$ for any given $\boldsymbol{\beta}$, we have

$$\boldsymbol{\beta} = \mathbf{D}\mathbf{X}\boldsymbol{\beta} + \boldsymbol{\beta} \quad \text{for all } \boldsymbol{\beta} \in \mathbb{R}^K$$

$$\therefore \quad \mathbf{0} = \mathbf{D}\mathbf{X}\boldsymbol{\beta} \quad \text{for all } \boldsymbol{\beta} \in \mathbb{R}^K$$

In light of exercise 3.5.13 on page 71, we conclude that $\mathbf{D}\mathbf{X} = \mathbf{0}$. Combining this result with (12.9), we obtain $\mathbf{b} = \mathbf{D}\mathbf{u} + \hat{\boldsymbol{\beta}}$. Hence $\mathbf{b}$ is equal to the OLS estimator plus zero-mean noise.

To complete the proof, observe that

$$\operatorname{var}[\mathbf{b} \mid \mathbf{X}] = \operatorname{var}[\mathbf{D}\mathbf{u} + \hat{\boldsymbol{\beta}} \mid \mathbf{X}] = \operatorname{var}[(\mathbf{D} + \mathbf{A})\mathbf{u} \mid \mathbf{X}] = (\mathbf{D} + \mathbf{A}) \operatorname{var}[\mathbf{u} \mid \mathbf{X}](\mathbf{D} + \mathbf{A})^{\top}$$

Using assumption 12.1.4 and fact 3.2.4, the right-hand side of this expression becomes

$$\sigma^2(\mathbf{D} + \mathbf{A})(\mathbf{D}^{\top} + \mathbf{A}^{\top}) = \sigma^2(\mathbf{D}\mathbf{D}^{\top} + \mathbf{D}\mathbf{A}^{\top} + \mathbf{A}\mathbf{D}^{\top} + \mathbf{A}\mathbf{A}^{\top})$$

Since

$$\mathbf{D}\mathbf{A}^{\top} = \mathbf{D}\mathbf{X}(\mathbf{X}^{\top}\mathbf{X})^{-1} = \mathbf{0}(\mathbf{X}^{\top}\mathbf{X})^{-1} = \mathbf{0}$$

and

$$\mathbf{A}\mathbf{A}^{\top} = (\mathbf{X}^{\top}\mathbf{X})^{-1}\mathbf{X}^{\top}\mathbf{X}(\mathbf{X}^{\top}\mathbf{X})^{-1} = (\mathbf{X}^{\top}\mathbf{X})^{-1}$$

we conclude that

$$\operatorname{var}[\mathbf{b} \mid \mathbf{X}] = \sigma^2[\mathbf{D}\mathbf{D}^{\top} + (\mathbf{X}^{\top}\mathbf{X})^{-1}] = \sigma^2\mathbf{D}\mathbf{D}^{\top} + \operatorname{var}[\hat{\boldsymbol{\beta}} \mid \mathbf{X}]$$

The matrix $\sigma^2\mathbf{D}\mathbf{D}^{\top}$ is nonnegative definite, so the proof is now done. □

12.1.3.1 Precision of the Estimates

Theorem 12.1.2 shows that the variance–covariance matrix of $\hat{\boldsymbol{\beta}}$ given $\mathbf{X}$ is $\sigma^2(\mathbf{X}^{\top}\mathbf{X})^{-1}$. The scalar variances of the individual OLS coefficient estimates $\hat{\beta}_1, \ldots, \hat{\beta}_K$ are given by the principal diagonal of this matrix. Since each $\hat{\beta}_k$ is unbiased (theorem 12.1.1), small variance means probability mass concentrated around the true parameter β_k. In this case, we say that the estimator has high **precision**.

The Gauss–Markov theorem states that, as far as unbiased linear estimators go, the OLS estimates will have highest precision. But what if we hold the estimation technique fixed, as well as the sample size, and vary the application? Which problems will have high precision estimates, and which will have low precision estimates?

To answer this question, let's focus on the variance of a fixed coefficient β_k. We can write $\mathbf{y} = \mathbf{X}\boldsymbol{\beta} + \mathbf{u}$ as

$$\mathbf{y} = \mathbf{X}_1\boldsymbol{\beta}_1 + \operatorname{col}_k(\mathbf{X})\beta_k + \mathbf{u} \tag{12.10}$$

where $\operatorname{col}_k(\mathbf{X})$ is the vector of observations of the kth regressor, $\mathbf{X}_1$ contains as its columns the observations of the other regressors, and $\hat{\boldsymbol{\beta}}_1$ is the OLS estimates of the corresponding coefficients. By the FWL theorem,

$$\hat{\beta}_k = (\operatorname{col}_k(\mathbf{X})^{\top}\mathbf{M}_1 \operatorname{col}_k(\mathbf{X}))^{-1} \operatorname{col}_k(\mathbf{X})^{\top}\mathbf{M}_1\mathbf{y} \tag{12.11}$$

where $\mathbf{M}_1$ is the residual projection $\mathbf{M}_1 := \mathbf{I} - \mathbf{P}_1$ and $\mathbf{P}_1 := \mathbf{X}_1(\mathbf{X}_1^{\top}\mathbf{X}_1)^{-1}\mathbf{X}_1^{\top}$ projects onto colspace $\mathbf{X}_1$. Applying $\mathbf{M}_1$ to both sides of (12.10) yields

$$\mathbf{M}_1 \mathbf{y} = \mathbf{M}_1 \operatorname{col}_k(\mathbf{X})\beta_k + \mathbf{M}_1 \mathbf{u}$$

Substituting into (12.11) gives

$$\hat{\beta}_k = \beta_k + (\operatorname{col}_k(\mathbf{X})^\top \mathbf{M}_1 \operatorname{col}_k(\mathbf{X}))^{-1} \operatorname{col}_k(\mathbf{X})^\top \mathbf{M}_1 \mathbf{u} \tag{12.12}$$

Some calculations then show (ex. 12.4.11) that

$$\operatorname{var}[\hat{\beta}_k \,|\, \mathbf{X}] = \sigma^2 (\operatorname{col}_k(\mathbf{X})^\top \mathbf{M}_1 \operatorname{col}_k(\mathbf{X}))^{-1} = \sigma^2 \|\mathbf{M}_1 \operatorname{col}_k(\mathbf{X})\|^{-2} \tag{12.13}$$

Thus the variance of $\hat{\beta}_k$ depends on two components, the variance σ^2 of the shock u and the norm of the vector $\mathbf{M}_1 \operatorname{col}_k \mathbf{X}$.

The variance in σ^2 is unavoidable: some data are noisier than others. The larger the variance in the unobservable shock, the harder it will be to estimate β_k with good precession.

The other term is more interesting. $\mathbf{M}_1 \operatorname{col}_k \mathbf{X}$ is the residuals from regressing $\operatorname{col}_k \mathbf{X}$ on $\mathbf{X}_1$, and $\|\mathbf{M}_1 \operatorname{col}_k \mathbf{X}\|$ is the norm of this vector. If this norm is small, then the variance of $\hat{\beta}_k$ will be large.

When will this norm be small? It will be so when $\operatorname{col}_k \mathbf{X}$ is "almost" a linear combination of the other regressors and hence close to colspace $\mathbf{X}_1$. Then

$$\|\mathbf{M}_1 \operatorname{col}_k \mathbf{X}\| = \|\operatorname{col}_k \mathbf{X} - \mathbf{P}_1 \operatorname{col}_k \mathbf{X}\| \approx 0$$

This situation is sometimes referred to as **multicollinearity**.

Figure 12.2 gives an illustration of the effect of multicollinearity on the variance of OLS estimate $\hat{\beta}_2$. In this example $\mathbf{X}$ has two columns. They are related by $\operatorname{col}_2 \mathbf{X} = \delta \operatorname{col}_1 \mathbf{X} + (1 - \delta)\mathbf{z}$, where $\mathbf{z}$ is a vector of N independent draws from the standard normal distribution. Larger δ means more dependence between $\operatorname{col}_1 \mathbf{X}$ and $\operatorname{col}_2 \mathbf{X}$. The true parameter is $\beta_2 = 1$. The figure shows the distribution of $\hat{\beta}_2$ for different values of δ. The estimator $\hat{\beta}_2$ is unbiased but its variance increases with δ. Further details on the simulation can be found at `johnstachurski.net/emet.html`. (The normal shape of the distribution is explained in the next section.)

12.1.4 Inference with Normal Errors

If we want to compute confidence intervals or test hypotheses about the coefficients in finite samples (i.e., without appealing to asymptotics), we need to strengthen our OLS assumptions even further, by specifying the parametric class of the error vector $\mathbf{u}$. Because of its many attractive properties, the normal distribution is the default.

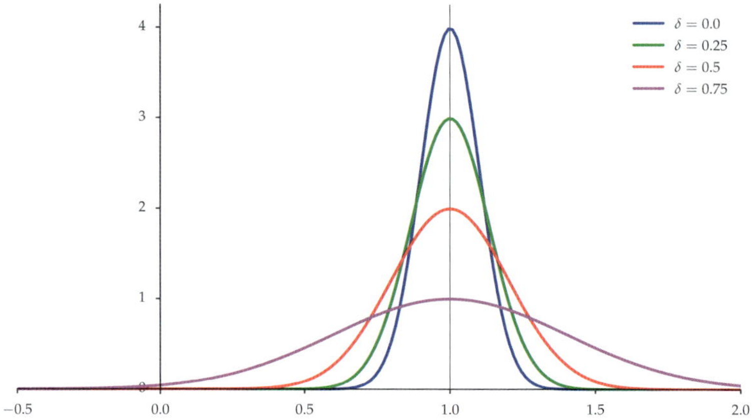

Figure 12.2 Distribution of $\hat{\beta}_2$ when $\operatorname{col}_2 \mathbf{X} = \delta \operatorname{col}_1 \mathbf{X} + (1-\delta)\mathbf{z}$

Assumption 12.1.5 $\mathbf{X}$ and $\mathbf{u}$ are independent and $\mathcal{L}(\mathbf{u}) = \mathrm{N}(\mathbf{0}, \sigma^2 \mathbf{I})$.

Assumption 12.1.5 implies both assumption 12.1.3 and assumption 12.1.4. It also implies that the conditional distribution of $\hat{\boldsymbol{\beta}}$ given $\mathbf{X}$ is normal, as can be seen from (12.4) and fact 5.1.5 on page 133. The next theorem records this result.

Theorem 12.1.4 *If assumptions 12.1.1–12.1.2 and 12.1.5 hold, then*

$$\mathcal{L}\left[\hat{\boldsymbol{\beta}} \,|\, \mathbf{X}\right] = \mathrm{N}(\boldsymbol{\beta}, \sigma^2 (\mathbf{X}^\top \mathbf{X})^{-1})$$

It follows from theorem 12.1.4 and (5.12) on page 133 that the distribution of individual coefficient $\hat{\beta}_k$ given $\mathbf{X}$ is also normal, with

$$\mathcal{L}\left[\hat{\beta}_k \,|\, \mathbf{X}\right] = \mathcal{L}\left[\mathbf{e}_k^\top \hat{\boldsymbol{\beta}} \,|\, \mathbf{X}\right] = \mathrm{N}(\beta_k, \sigma^2 v_k(\mathbf{X})) \tag{12.14}$$

Here $v_k(\mathbf{X}) :=$ the (k,k)th element of $(\mathbf{X}^\top \mathbf{X})^{-1}$.

Theorem 12.1.4 and the normality of the marginal distributions along the individual coefficients is illustrated in figure 12.3. The central plot shows the contours of a density estimate that can be understood as a smoothed histogram based on simulated observations of $\hat{\boldsymbol{\beta}}$ (see §14.1 for details on these density estimates). Each observation $\hat{\boldsymbol{\beta}} = (\hat{\beta}_1, \hat{\beta}_2)$ is obtained by fitting the regression model $y_n = \beta_1 + \beta_2 x_n + u_n$, where $\beta_1 = 0.5$, $\beta_2 = 1$ and u_n is standard normal. The sample size for each fit is $N = 250$. The univariate distributions on the top and right are univariate density

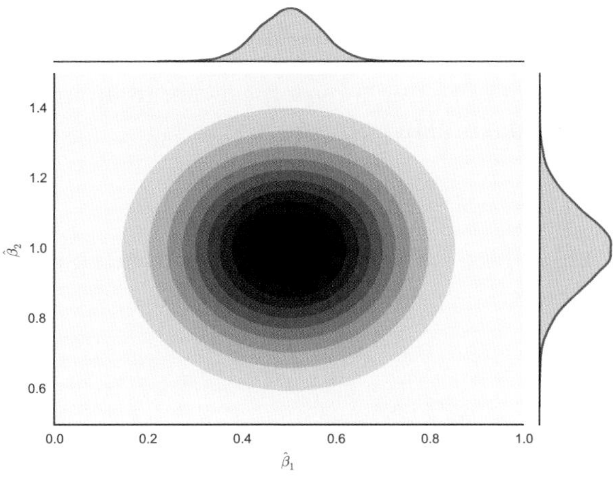

Figure 12.3 Simulated observations of $\hat{\boldsymbol{\beta}}$ and its marginals

estimates based on the observations of $\hat{\beta}_1$ and $\hat{\beta}_2$ respectively.[1]

We also want to know the distribution of $\hat{\sigma}^2$, as defined in (12.5). It turns out to be more convenient to work with a transformation of $\hat{\sigma}^2$ defined as

$$Q := \frac{\text{RSS}}{\sigma^2} = (N-K)\frac{\hat{\sigma}^2}{\sigma^2} \tag{12.15}$$

Theorem 12.1.5 *If assumptions 12.1.1–12.1.2 and 12.1.5 hold, then*

$$\mathcal{L}\,[\,Q\,|\,\mathbf{X}\,] = \chi^2(N-K)$$

Proof. Recalling fact 12.1.1 on page 324, we have

$$Q = \frac{\mathbf{u}^\top \mathbf{M} \mathbf{u}}{\sigma^2} = (\sigma^{-1}\mathbf{u})^\top \mathbf{M} (\sigma^{-1}\mathbf{u})$$

The claim now follows from fact 5.1.19 on page 141 and the fact that trace $\mathbf{M} = N - K$. (The last equality was discussed in the proof of theorem 12.1.1.) □

Fact 12.1.4 If assumptions 12.1.1–12.1.2 and 12.1.5 hold, then the random elements $\hat{\sigma}^2$ and $\hat{\boldsymbol{\beta}}$ are independent given $\mathbf{X}$ (see ex. 12.4.6).

1. The code for the simulation can be found at `johnstachurski.net/emet.html`.

12.1.4.1 The t-Test

Let's consider the problem of testing a hypothesis about an individual coefficient β_k. Specifically, we consider the null hypothesis

$$H_0\colon \beta_k = \beta_k^0$$

where β_k^0 is any number. If we knew σ^2, we could construct a test of H_0 based around the following observation:

$$z_k := \frac{\hat{\beta}_k - \beta_k}{\sigma\sqrt{v_k(\mathbf{X})}} \implies \mathcal{L}[\, z_k \,|\, \mathbf{X}\,] = \mathrm{N}(0,1) \tag{12.16}$$

(The implication follows from (12.14).) Since we don't, the standard methodology is to replace σ^2 with its estimator $\hat{\sigma}^2$, and determine the distribution of the resulting test statistic. Our next result implements this idea. In doing so, we will make use of the following notation:

$$\mathrm{se}(\hat{\beta}_k) := \sqrt{\hat{\sigma}^2 v_k(\mathbf{X})}$$

The term $\mathrm{se}(\hat{\beta}_k)$ is called the **standard error** of $\hat{\beta}_k$. It can be regarded as the sample estimate of the standard deviation of $\hat{\beta}_k$. Replacing this standard deviation with its sample estimate $\mathrm{se}(\hat{\beta}_k)$ and β_k with β_k^0 in (12.16), we obtain the **t-statistic**

$$t_k := \frac{\hat{\beta}_k - \beta_k^0}{\mathrm{se}(\hat{\beta}_k)} \tag{12.17}$$

associated with the hypothesis H_0. The distribution of this statistic under the null is described in the next theorem.

Theorem 12.1.6 *Let assumptions 12.1.1–12.1.2 and 12.1.5 hold. If H_0 is true, then*

$$\mathcal{L}\,[\, t_k \,|\, \mathbf{X}\,] = \textit{Student's } t \textit{ with } N-K \textit{ degrees of freedom}$$

Proof. Taking $\mathbf{X}$ as fixed, we need to show that t_k can be written as

$$t_k = z_k \sqrt{\frac{N-K}{Q}} \tag{12.18}$$

where z_k is standard normal, Q is $\chi^2(N-K)$ and z_k and Q are independent. The desired result then follows from fact 5.1.16 on page 140.

To establish these properties, observe that, under H_0,

$$t_k = \frac{\hat{\beta}_k - \beta_k^0}{\sqrt{\hat{\sigma}^2 v_k(\mathbf{X})}} = \frac{\hat{\beta}_k - \beta_k}{\sqrt{\sigma^2 v_k(\mathbf{X})}} \sqrt{\frac{\sigma^2}{\hat{\sigma}^2}}$$

In view of the definition of z_k in (12.16), the definition of Q in (12.15) and theorem 12.1.5, it remains only to show that z_k and Q are independent given $\mathbf{X}$. Since we can write z_k as a function of $\hat{\boldsymbol{\beta}}$ and Q as a function of $\hat{\sigma}^2$, this follows from fact 12.1.4. □

Let $T := |t_k|$ and let a desired size α for our test of H_0 be given. In view of (10.18) on page 285, to generate a test of size α, we choose $c = c_\alpha$ to solve $\alpha = \mathbb{P}_\theta\{T > c\}$, or

$$1 - \alpha = \mathbb{P}_\theta\{|t_k| \leqslant c\}$$

From (4.36) on page 115, the solution is $c_\alpha = F^{-1}(1 - \alpha/2)$, where F is the Student's t CDF with $N - K$ degrees of freedom. In view of example 10.2.7, the corresponding p-value is $2F(-|t_k|)$.

Example 12.1.3 A common implementation of the t-test is the test that a given coefficient is equal to zero. For the kth coefficient β_k, this leads to the statistic

$$t_k := \frac{\hat{\beta}_k}{\text{se}(\hat{\beta}_k)}$$

This statistic is sometimes called the **Z-score**. An application with simulated data is given in listing 8. Running the code shows that the Z-scores calculated by the `zscore` function agree with the "t value" column of the summary table produced by R's **`summary`** function (the last line of listing 8, output not shown). It is left as an exercise to check that the p-values in the same table agree with the formula $2F(-|t_k|)$ given above.

12.1.4.2 The F-Test

The t-test is used to test hypotheses about individual regressors. For hypotheses concerning multiple regressors, the most common test is the F-test. The F-test can test quite general hypotheses. For simplicity we will focus on null hypotheses that restrict a subset of the coefficients to be zero.

Let $\mathbf{X}_1$, $\mathbf{X}_2$, $\hat{\boldsymbol{\beta}}_1$, $\hat{\boldsymbol{\beta}}_2$, $\mathbf{P}_1$, and $\mathbf{M}_1$ be as defined in §11.2.2. As our null hypothesis we take

$$H_0 \colon \boldsymbol{\beta}_2 = \mathbf{0}$$

Listing 8 Calculating Z-scores (R)

```
set.seed(1234)
N <- 50; K <- 3
beta <- rep(1, K)
X <- cbind(runif(N), runif(N), runif(N))
u <- rnorm(N)
y <- X %*% beta + u

betahat <- solve(t(X) %*% X) %*% t(X) %*% y
residuals <- y - X %*% betahat
sigmahat <- sqrt(sum(residuals^2) / (N - K))

# Compute t-stat (Z-score) for k-th regressor
zscore <- function(k) {
    se <- sigmahat * sqrt(solve(t(X) %*% X)[k, k])
    return(betahat[k] / se)
}
# Print t-stats
for (k in 1:3) {
    cat("t-stat, k =", k, ":", zscore(k), "\n")
}
# For comparison:
print(summary(lm(y ~ X - 1)))
```

Since

$$\mathbf{y} = \mathbf{X}\boldsymbol{\beta} + \mathbf{u} = \mathbf{X}_1\boldsymbol{\beta}_1 + \mathbf{X}_2\boldsymbol{\beta}_2 + \mathbf{u} \tag{12.19}$$

it follows that under the null hypothesis we have

$$\mathbf{y} = \mathbf{X}_1\boldsymbol{\beta}_1 + \mathbf{u} \tag{12.20}$$

Letting

$$\text{USSR} := \|\mathbf{M}\mathbf{y}\|^2 \quad \text{and} \quad \text{RSSR} := \|\mathbf{M}_1\mathbf{y}\|^2$$

be the residual sums of squares for the unrestricted regression (12.19) and restricted regression (12.20) respectively, the standard test statistic for our null hypothesis is

$$F := \frac{(\text{RSSR} - \text{USSR})/K_2}{\text{USSR}/(N-K)} \tag{12.21}$$

Large residuals in the restricted regression (12.20) relative to those in (12.19) result in large values for F, which translates to evidence against the null hypothesis.

Theorem 12.1.7 *Let assumptions 12.1.1–12.1.2 and 12.1.5 hold. If H_0 is true, then, given $\mathbf{X}$, the statistic F defined in* (12.21) *has the F distribution with parameters $(K_2, N-K)$.*

Proof. Let $Q_1 := (\text{RSSR} - \text{USSR})/\sigma^2$ and let $Q_2 := \text{USSR}/\sigma^2$, so that

$$F = \frac{Q_1/K_2}{Q_2/(N-K)}$$

In view of fact 5.1.17 on page 140, it now suffices to show that, under the null hypothesis,

(a) Q_1 is chi-squared with K_2 degrees of freedom,

(b) Q_2 is chi-squared with $N-K$ degrees of freedom, and

(c) Q_1 and Q_2 are independent.

Part (b) was established in theorem 12.1.5. Regarding part (a), observe that, under the null hypothesis,

- $\text{USSR} = \|\mathbf{My}\|^2 = \|\mathbf{M}(\mathbf{X}_1\boldsymbol{\beta}_1 + \mathbf{u})\|^2 = \|\mathbf{Mu}\|^2 = \mathbf{u}^\top\mathbf{Mu}$ and
- $\text{RSSR} = \|\mathbf{M}_1\mathbf{y}\|^2 = \|\mathbf{M}_1(\mathbf{X}_1\boldsymbol{\beta}_1 + \mathbf{u})\|^2 = \|\mathbf{M}_1\mathbf{u}\|^2 = \mathbf{u}^\top\mathbf{M}_1\mathbf{u}$.

It follows that

$$\text{RSSR} - \text{USSR} = \mathbf{u}^\top\mathbf{M}_1\mathbf{u} - \mathbf{u}^\top\mathbf{Mu} = \mathbf{u}^\top(\mathbf{M}_1 - \mathbf{M})\mathbf{u}$$

Using the definitions of $\mathbf{M}$ and $\mathbf{M}_1$, we obtain

$$Q_1 = \frac{\text{RSSR} - \text{USSR}}{\sigma^2} = \frac{\mathbf{u}^\top(\mathbf{I} - \mathbf{P}_1 - \mathbf{I} + \mathbf{P})\mathbf{u}}{\sigma^2} = (\sigma^{-1}\mathbf{u})^\top(\mathbf{P} - \mathbf{P}_1)(\sigma^{-1}\mathbf{u})$$

It is an exercise to show that $(\mathbf{P} - \mathbf{P}_1)$ is symmetric and idempotent.[2] Hence

$$\operatorname{rank}(\mathbf{P} - \mathbf{P}_1) = \operatorname{trace}(\mathbf{P} - \mathbf{P}_1) = \operatorname{trace}\mathbf{P} - \operatorname{trace}\mathbf{P}_1 = K - K_1 = K_2$$

Via fact 5.1.19, we conclude that $\mathcal{L}(Q_1) = \chi^2(K_2)$, as was to be shown.

To complete the proof, it remains to show that, under the null hypothesis and taking $\mathbf{X}$ as given, Q_1 and Q_2 are independent. To see this, observe that Q_1 is a function of $(\mathbf{P} - \mathbf{P}_1)\mathbf{u}$, while Q_2 is a function of $\mathbf{Mu}$. Hence it suffices to show that $(\mathbf{P} - \mathbf{P}_1)\mathbf{u}$ and $\mathbf{Mu}$ are independent given $\mathbf{X}$. By fact 5.1.12 on page 137, it suffices to show that

2. Hint: See fact 2.2.7 on page 32.

their covariance is zero. To verify this, observe that

$$\operatorname{cov}[(\mathbf{P}-\mathbf{P}_1)\mathbf{u}, \mathbf{M}\mathbf{u} \mid \mathbf{X}] = \mathbb{E}[(\mathbf{P}-\mathbf{P}_1)\mathbf{u}(\mathbf{M}\mathbf{u})^\top \mid \mathbf{X}] = \mathbb{E}[(\mathbf{P}-\mathbf{P}_1)\mathbf{u}\mathbf{u}^\top\mathbf{M} \mid \mathbf{X}]$$

Since $\mathbf{P}$, $\mathbf{P}_1$, and $\mathbf{M}$ are just functions of $\mathbf{X}$, this becomes

$$(\mathbf{P}-\mathbf{P}_1)\mathbb{E}[\mathbf{u}\mathbf{u}^\top \mid \mathbf{X}]\mathbf{M} = \sigma^2(\mathbf{P}-\mathbf{P}_1)\mathbf{M} = \sigma^2(\mathbf{P}-\mathbf{P}_1)(\mathbf{I}-\mathbf{P})$$

Using idempotence and fact 2.2.7, the matrix product on the right is

$$(\mathbf{P}-\mathbf{P}_1)(\mathbf{I}-\mathbf{P}) = \mathbf{P}-\mathbf{P}^2-\mathbf{P}_1+\mathbf{P}_1\mathbf{P} = \mathbf{P}-\mathbf{P}-\mathbf{P}_1+\mathbf{P}_1 = \mathbf{0}$$

This completes the proof of independence, and hence of theorem 12.1.7. □

The most common implementation of the F-test is the test that all coefficients of nonconstant regressors are zero. In this case (12.19) becomes

$$\mathbf{y} = \mathbf{1}\beta_1 + \mathbf{X}_2\boldsymbol{\beta}_2 + \mathbf{u} \tag{12.22}$$

where $\boldsymbol{\beta}_2$ is the vector of coefficients corresponding to the nonconstant regressors. Since $\mathbf{X}_1 = \mathbf{1}$, we then have $\mathbf{M}_1 = \mathbf{M}_c$, where the latter is defined in (3.10) on page 61, and hence RSSR is the squared norm of $\mathbf{y} - \bar{y}\mathbf{1}$. An application with simulated data is given in listing 9. If you run the program, you will find that the F statistic calculated by the theoretical formula agrees with the F statistic produced by R's `summary` function.

It is an exercise to show that in the case of (12.22), the F statistic in (12.21) can be rewritten as

$$F = \frac{R_c^2}{1-R_c^2}\frac{N-K}{K_2} \tag{12.23}$$

where R_c^2 is the centered R squared defined in §11.2.3. Can you provide some intuition as to why large F is evidence against the null?

12.2 Problems and Extensions

The standard OLS assumptions are strict and the results we have obtained are sensitive to their failure. Let's discuss some situations where the OLS assumptions fail and investigate the implications.

12.2.1 Nonspherical Errors

Heteroskedasticity occurs when the variance of the error term is not constant across observations, in contradiction to assumption 12.1.4. In particular, the errors are called

Listing 9 Calculating the F statistic (R)

```
set.seed(1234)
N <- 50; K <- 3
beta <- rep(1, K)
x2 <- runif(N); x3 <- runif(N)
X <- cbind(rep(1, N), x2, x3)
u <- rnorm(N)
y <- X %*% beta + u

betahat <- solve(t(X) %*% X) %*% t(X) %*% y
residuals <- y - X %*% betahat
ussr <- sum(residuals^2)
rssr <- sum((y - mean(y))^2)

Fa <- (rssr - ussr) / 2
Fb <- ussr / (N - K)

cat("F =", Fa / Fb, "\n")          # Print result
print(summary(lm(y ~ x2 + x3)))  # For comparison
```

heteroskedastic if the diagonal terms of $\mathbb{E}[\mathbf{u}\mathbf{u}^\top \mid \mathbf{X}]$ are not constant. If the off-diagonal terms are nonzero, then the errors are said to have **serial correlation**.

Failure of assumption 12.1.4 does not alone cause bias in the OLS estimator $\hat{\boldsymbol{\beta}}$. This is easily verified by reading the proof of the first part of theorem 12.1.1. Indeed, the proof that $\hat{\boldsymbol{\beta}}$ is unbiased for $\boldsymbol{\beta}$ does not require assumption 12.1.4. At the same time, the claim that $\hat{\sigma}^2$ is unbiased for σ in the second part of theorem 12.1.1 does not make sense without assumption 12.1.4, and the expression $\text{var}[\hat{\boldsymbol{\beta}} \mid \mathbf{X}] = \sigma^2(\mathbf{X}^\top\mathbf{X})^{-1}$ from (12.8) is no longer valid. The Gauss–Markov theorem also breaks down. The most important practical consequence is that the results on inference in §12.1.4, which depend on the expression for the variance given above, are no longer valid.

What happens if we replace the assumption $\mathbb{E}[\mathbf{u}\mathbf{u}^\top \mid \mathbf{X}] = \sigma^2\mathbf{I}$ with the more general assumption

$$\mathbb{E}[\mathbf{u}\mathbf{u}^\top \mid \mathbf{X}] = \boldsymbol{\Omega} \tag{12.24}$$

for some positive definite matrix $\boldsymbol{\Omega}$? (Assumptions 12.1.1–12.1.3 are maintained.) Using (12.4) on page 325, we can write the variance of the OLS estimator $\hat{\boldsymbol{\beta}}$ under these conditions as

$$\text{var}[\hat{\boldsymbol{\beta}} \mid \mathbf{X}] = \mathbb{E}[(\hat{\boldsymbol{\beta}} - \boldsymbol{\beta})(\hat{\boldsymbol{\beta}} - \boldsymbol{\beta})^\top \mid \mathbf{X}] = (\mathbf{X}^\top\mathbf{X})^{-1}\mathbf{X}^\top\boldsymbol{\Omega}\mathbf{X}(\mathbf{X}^\top\mathbf{X})^{-1} \tag{12.25}$$

If $\mathbf{\Omega}$ is known, then we can estimate under assumptions 12.1.1–12.1.3 and (12.24) using **generalized least squares**. The idea is as follows: In view of fact 3.3.10 on page 67, there exists a nonsingular matrix $\mathbf{C}$ such that $\mathbf{C}^\top \mathbf{C} = \mathbf{\Omega}^{-1}$. Using $\mathbf{C}$, we transform the regression model by multiplying both sides of $\mathbf{y} = \mathbf{X}\boldsymbol{\beta} + \mathbf{u}$ by $\mathbf{C}$. This gives

$$\mathbf{y}_c = \mathbf{X}_c \boldsymbol{\beta} + \mathbf{u}_c \quad \text{where} \quad \mathbf{y}_c := \mathbf{C}\mathbf{y},\, \mathbf{X}_c := \mathbf{C}\mathbf{X} \text{ and } \mathbf{u}_c := \mathbf{C}\mathbf{u}$$

Exercise 12.4.17 asks you to show that

$$\mathbb{E}\left[\mathbf{u}_c \,|\, \mathbf{X}_c\right] = \mathbf{0} \quad \text{and} \quad \mathbb{E}\left[\mathbf{u}_c \mathbf{u}_c^\top \,|\, \mathbf{X}_c\right] = \mathbf{I} \tag{12.26}$$

Hence the full set of OLS assumptions 12.1.1–12.1.4 is satisfied for the transformed data. If we use the transformed data to estimate $\boldsymbol{\beta}$ via $(\mathbf{X}_c^\top \mathbf{X}_c)^{-1} \mathbf{X}_c^\top \mathbf{y}_c$, we recover the best linear unbiased property. Expanding out the definitions of $\mathbf{X}_c$ and $\mathbf{y}_c$ and using $\mathbf{C}^\top \mathbf{C} = \mathbf{\Omega}^{-1}$, we can show the new estimator to be

$$\hat{\boldsymbol{\beta}}_{\text{GLS}} := (\mathbf{X}^\top \mathbf{\Omega}^{-1} \mathbf{X})^{-1} \mathbf{X}^\top \mathbf{\Omega}^{-1} \mathbf{y} \tag{12.27}$$

This estimator is called the **generalized least squares (GLS) estimator** of $\boldsymbol{\beta}$.

In practice, $\mathbf{\Omega}$ is rarely known. While we can estimate it, estimation is difficult unless additional structure is imposed. This is because $\mathbf{\Omega}$ is $N \times N$, implying that, absent further restrictions, the number of parameters contained in $\mathbf{\Omega}$ grows *faster* than the sample. Our estimation problem gets harder the more data that we have.

A common way of adding structure is to assume that $\mathbf{\Omega}$ is diagonal. That is, $\mathbf{\Omega} = \operatorname{diag}(\sigma_1^2, \ldots, \sigma_N^2)$, where each σ_n is strictly positive and unknown. The diagonal assumption rules out correlation but maintains the possibility of heteroskedasticity. One estimator of $\mathbf{\Omega}$ is

$$\hat{\mathbf{\Omega}} := \operatorname{diag}(\hat{u}_1^2, \ldots, \hat{u}_N^2) \quad \text{where} \quad \hat{\mathbf{u}} := \mathbf{M}\mathbf{y}$$

Replacing $\mathbf{\Omega}$ with $\hat{\mathbf{\Omega}}$ in (12.25) leads to the estimate of $\operatorname{var}[\hat{\boldsymbol{\beta}} \,|\, \mathbf{X}]$ given by

$$\hat{\mathbf{V}} := (\mathbf{X}^\top \mathbf{X})^{-1} \mathbf{X}^\top \hat{\mathbf{\Omega}} \mathbf{X} (\mathbf{X}^\top \mathbf{X})^{-1} \tag{12.28}$$

If we use this expression in place of the usual variance estimate $\hat{\sigma}^2 (\mathbf{X}^\top \mathbf{X})^{-1}$ when we form our standard errors, we get the **heteroskedasticity-consistent standard errors** proposed by White (1980).

12.2.2 Bias

In §12.2.1 we considered what happens when assumption 12.1.4 (spherical errors) fails. What about the other OLS assumptions? Assumption 12.1.1 (full rank) is fairly benign. Assumptions 12.1.2 and 12.1.3 (linearity and exogeneity) are more problematic. Let's have a look at how they might fail and the consequences.

The linearity assumption $y_n = \mathbf{x}_n^\top \boldsymbol{\beta} + u_n$ is fundamental. If we replace it with a more general assumption such as $y_n = f(\mathbf{x}_n) + u_n$ for some arbitrary function f, then OLS theory falls apart. For example, we cannot even *ask* if the OLS estimator is unbiased because $\boldsymbol{\beta}$ has vanished. There is no parameter vector for $\hat{\boldsymbol{\beta}}$ to estimate.[3]

The remaining assumption we need to consider is exogenous regressors. What happens if all other OLS assumptions hold but assumption 12.1.3 fails?

Observe that, by (12.4) on page 325,

$$\mathbb{E}\,[\hat{\boldsymbol{\beta}} \,|\, \mathbf{X}] - \boldsymbol{\beta} = (\mathbf{X}^\top \mathbf{X})^{-1} \mathbf{X}^\top \mathbb{E}\,[\mathbf{u} \,|\, \mathbf{X}] \tag{12.29}$$

Without $\mathbb{E}\,[\mathbf{u} \,|\, \mathbf{X}] = \mathbf{0}$, we cannot assert that the right-hand side is zero. Hence $\hat{\boldsymbol{\beta}}$ is biased. Bias due to failure of assumption 12.1.3 is called **endogeneity bias**.

As discussed in several parts of this text, striving for unbiasedness is somewhat misguided. Better estimators can usually be constructed by admitting some degree of bias in order to penalize complexity (thereby acknowledging that the empirical distribution is not the true distribution). However, there is an important difference with the bias in (12.29). Good estimators reduce bias as the sample size increases, so that the object they aim to compute can be recovered asymptotically. This is not true for the OLS estimator when exogeneity fails.

To see this, recall from theorem 11.1.2 on page 304 that $\hat{\boldsymbol{\beta}} \xrightarrow{p} \mathbb{E}\,[\mathbf{x}\mathbf{x}^\top]^{-1}\,\mathbb{E}\,[\mathbf{x}\,y]$ as $N \to \infty$. The right-hand side is the vector of coefficients in the best linear predictor (see page 147). If $y = \mathbf{x}^\top \boldsymbol{\beta} + u$, then this becomes

$$\hat{\boldsymbol{\beta}} \xrightarrow{p} \mathbb{E}\,[\mathbf{x}\mathbf{x}^\top]^{-1}\,\mathbb{E}\,[\mathbf{x}\,(\mathbf{x}^\top \boldsymbol{\beta} + u)] = \boldsymbol{\beta} + \mathbb{E}\,[\mathbf{x}\mathbf{x}^\top]^{-1}\,\mathbb{E}\,[\mathbf{x}\,u]$$

With exogeneity we get $\mathbb{E}\,[\mathbf{x}\,u] = \mathbb{E}\,[\mathbf{x}\,\mathbb{E}\,[u \,|\, \mathbf{x}]] = 0$ and the OLS estimator is consistent. Without exogeneity we cannot assert the same.

12.2.2.1 Examples of Endogeneity Bias

Let's look at some applications where assumption 12.1.3 fails. First up, consider again the Cobb–Douglas example on page 324, which yields the regression model

$$\ln y_n = \gamma + a \ln k_n + \delta \ln \ell_n + u_n$$

3. It is an interesting habit of economists to quibble endlessly about whether someone's estimators are biased, even when their models are wildly speculative in terms of specific functional forms. (For example, do we really believe that log GDP per capita is a linear function of various measures of institutional quality and an Africa dummy, say, or even that this is a close depiction of reality? If not, what exactly does it mean to say that $\hat{\boldsymbol{\beta}}$ is biased?)

Here y is output, k is capital, ℓ is labor, and subscript n indicates observation on the nth firm. The term u_n is a firm specific productivity shock. A likely problem here is that the firm will choose higher levels of both capital and labor when it anticipates high productivity in the current period. This will lead to endogeneity bias.

To illustrate, suppose that $u_{n,-1}$ is the productivity shock received by firm n last period and this value is observable to the firm. Suppose further that productivity follows a random walk, with $u_n = u_{n,-1} + \eta_n$, where η_n is zero-mean white noise. As a result the firm forecasts period n productivity as $\mathbb{E}[u_n \mid u_{n,-1}] = u_{n,-1}$. Finally, suppose that the firm increases labor input when productivity is anticipated to be high, with the specific relationship $\ell_n = a + b\mathbb{E}[u_n \mid u_{n,-1}]$ for $b > 0$. When all shocks are zero-mean, we then have

$$\mathbb{E}[\ell_n u_n] = \mathbb{E}[(a + bu_{n,-1})(u_{n,-1} + \eta_n)] = \mathbb{E}[bu^2_{n,-1}]$$

This term will be strictly positive whenever $u_{n,-1}$ has positive variance. Thus the conditions of fact 12.1.2 (page 324) fail, and therefore assumption 12.1.3 does not hold (because assumption 12.1.3 implies fact 12.1.2).

This source of endogeneity bias in estimating production functions has been discussed many times in the literature. The best solution is better modeling. For one illustration of careful modeling, see Olley and Pakes (1996).

As a second example of endogeneity bias, suppose next that we have in hand data generated according to the simple AR(1) model

$$x_0 = 0 \quad \text{and} \quad x_n = \beta x_{n-1} + u_n \quad \text{for } n = 1, \ldots, N \tag{12.30}$$

Let $\{u_n\}_{n=1}^N$ be IID with distribution $\text{N}(0, \sigma^2)$. The unknown parameters are β and σ^2. Letting $\mathbf{y} := (x_1, \ldots, x_N)$, $\mathbf{x} := (x_0, \ldots, x_{N-1})$, and $\mathbf{u} := (u_1, \ldots, u_N)$, we can write the N equations in (12.30) as $\mathbf{y} = \beta\mathbf{x} + \mathbf{u}$. The OLS estimate of β is $\hat{\beta} := (\mathbf{x}^\top\mathbf{x})^{-1}\mathbf{x}^\top\mathbf{y}$.

By fact 12.1.2, if assumption 12.1.3 holds, then $\mathbb{E}[u_m x_{n+1}] = 0$ for any m and n. In the current setup this equality fails. For example, if $n \geqslant m$, then we can (ex. 12.4.15) write x_n as

$$x_n = \sum_{j=0}^{n-1} \beta^j u_{n-j} \tag{12.31}$$

Hence $\mathbb{E}[x_n u_m] = \sum_{j=0}^{n-1} \beta^j \mathbb{E}[u_{n-j} u_m] = \beta^{n-m}\sigma^2$. In particular, assumption 12.1.3 fails whenever $\beta \neq 0$.

To illustrate the bias in $\hat{\beta}$, listing 10 generates the data 10,000 times, computes $\hat{\beta}$ on each occasion and histograms the result. The parameters are $N = 25$ and $\beta = 0.9$. The output is figure 12.4. If you modify the code to print the sample mean, it gives around 0.82. Since the number of replications is large, this is close to $\mathbb{E}[\hat{\beta}]$. An asymptotic

95% confidence interval for our estimate is around (0.818, 0.824).

Listing 10 Generates and histograms observations of $\hat{\beta}$ (Python)

```
import numpy as np
import matplotlib.pyplot as plt

N = 25
x = np.zeros(N)
beta = 0.9
num_reps = 10000
betahat_obs = np.empty(num_reps)

for j in range(num_reps):
    u = np.random.randn(N)
    for t in range(N-1):
        x[t+1] = beta * x[t] + u[t+1]
    y = x[1:]       # x_1 ,..., x_N
    x_vec = x[:-1]  # x_0, ..., x_{N-1}
    betahat_obs[j]  = np.sum(x_vec * y) / np.sum(x_vec**2)

plt.hist(betahat_obs, bins=50, alpha=0.6, normed=True)
plt.show()
```

12.2.3 Instrumental Variables

The discussion in §12.2.2 shows that the OLS estimator is biased and inconsistent when regressors are endogenous. Here we show that a consistent estimator of $\boldsymbol{\beta}$ can be found when extra information is available in the form of "exogenous" variables called **instruments**. These instruments will be collected into a $N \times J$ matrix $\mathbf{Z}$, where each column is observations on one exogenous variable. We connect $\mathbf{Z}$ and the other variables via the following assumptions:

(i) $\mathbf{y} = \mathbf{X}\boldsymbol{\beta} + \mathbf{u}$.

(ii) $\mathbb{E}[\mathbf{u} \mid \mathbf{Z}] = \mathbf{0}$.

(iii) $\mathbb{E}[\mathbf{u}\mathbf{u}^\top \mid \mathbf{Z}] = \sigma^2 \mathbf{I}$ for some positive constant σ.

(iv) $\mathbf{Z}^\top \mathbf{X}$ has full column rank.

As exercise 12.4.18 asks you to show, assumption (iv) implies that $J \geqslant K$, which is to say that we have at least as many instruments as regressors. If $J > K$, the model

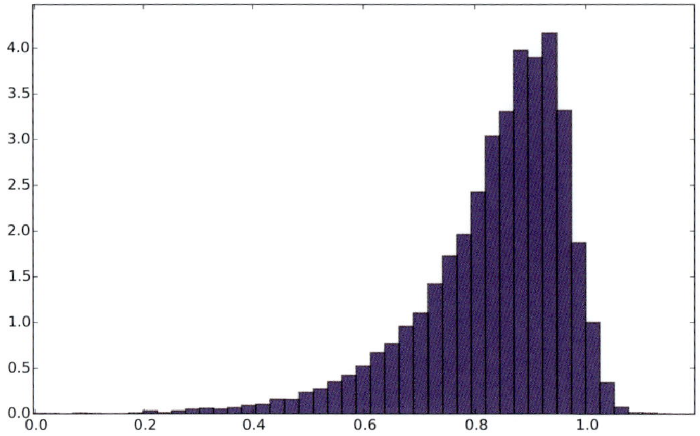

Figure 12.4 Observations of $\hat{\beta}$ when $\beta = 0.9$

is said to be **overidentified**. If $J = K$, the model is called **exactly identified**. (When $J < K$, the model is called **underidentified**.)

The idea of instrumental variables least squares is to multiply $\mathbf{y} = \mathbf{X}\boldsymbol{\beta} + \mathbf{u}$ by $\mathbf{Z}^\top$ to produce

$$\mathbf{Z}^\top \mathbf{y} = \mathbf{Z}^\top \mathbf{X}\boldsymbol{\beta} + \mathbf{w} \quad \text{where} \quad \mathbf{w} := \mathbf{Z}^\top \mathbf{u} \tag{12.32}$$

Applying (ii) and (iii) from the IV assumptions gives $\mathbb{E}[\mathbf{w} \,|\, \mathbf{Z}] = \mathbf{0}$ and $\mathbb{E}[\mathbf{w}\mathbf{w}^\top \,|\, \mathbf{Z}] = \sigma^2 \mathbf{Z}^\top \mathbf{Z}$. This suggests that we might apply generalized least squares estimation to the linear equation in (12.32). We can use the expression for the GLS estimator from (12.27) after substituting $\mathbf{X}$ for $\mathbf{Z}^\top\mathbf{X}$, $\mathbf{y}$ for $\mathbf{Z}^\top\mathbf{y}$, and $\boldsymbol{\Omega}$ for $\sigma^2\mathbf{Z}^\top\mathbf{Z}$. This leads to the **instrumental variable least squares (IVLS) estimator**

$$\hat{\beta}_{\text{IVLS}} := (\mathbf{X}^\top \mathbf{Z}(\mathbf{Z}^\top \mathbf{Z})^{-1}\mathbf{Z}^\top \mathbf{X})^{-1}\mathbf{X}^\top \mathbf{Z}(\mathbf{Z}^\top \mathbf{Z})^{-1}\mathbf{Z}^\top \mathbf{y} \tag{12.33}$$

In the case where $J = K$, this reduces to the simpler expression

$$\hat{\beta}_{\text{IVLS}} := (\mathbf{Z}^\top \mathbf{X})^{-1}\mathbf{Z}^\top \mathbf{y} \tag{12.34}$$

In the preceding discussion, the analogy with GLS was not exact. (Direct application of GLS to (12.32) would require that $\mathbb{E}[\mathbf{w} \,|\, \mathbf{Z}^\top\mathbf{X}] = \mathbf{0}$ rather than $\mathbb{E}[\mathbf{w} \,|\, \mathbf{Z}] = \mathbf{0}$.) As a consequence we cannot claim unbiasedness and other properties by appealing to the GLS theory. Indeed $\hat{\beta}_{\text{IVLS}}$ is, in general, biased (see ex. 12.4.20).

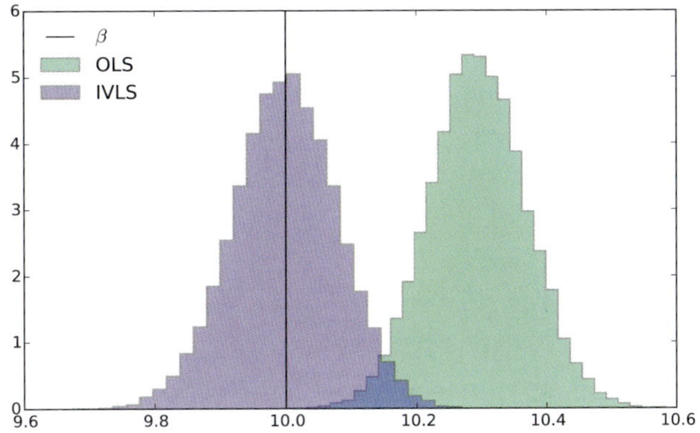

Figure 12.5 Simulated draws of OLS and IVLS estimators of β

At the same time, the bias is typically smaller than OLS and vanishes asymptotically (see, e.g., §8.3 of Davidson and MacKinnon 2004). Figure 12.5 gives an illustration. This figure corresponds to OLS and IVLS estimates of β in $y = x\beta + u$ when $\beta = 10$, z is drawn independently of u, and x is set equal to $\alpha z + (1 - \alpha)u$. Thus z is exogenous and x is a mixture of z and u. The value α is a constant. In the simulation, α is set to 0.8, so z is a relatively strong instrument. The histograms are observations of the two estimators over 25,000 repetitions, each one having a sample size of 250. IV provides a much better estimator of β in this case.[4]

There is another way to derive the expression given for $\hat{\boldsymbol{\beta}}_{\text{IVLS}}$ on the right-hand side of (12.33). It involves a method called **two-stage least squares**. The key idea is to project the endogenous regressors onto the column space of the exogenous instruments before running the regression. Exercise 12.4.21 walks you through the details.

12.2.4 Causality

Causality is a slippery concept. Let's touch on some basic points, particularly concerning the connection between causality and regression. (References to more detailed treatments are given in §12.3.)

You might have heard R^2 interpreted as measuring the "explanatory power" of the regressors in a particular econometric problem. The idea is that regression amounts to decomposing $\mathbf{y}$ into the sum of two orthogonal parts, the fitted values $\mathbf{Py}$ and the residuals $\mathbf{My}$. As in (11.12), the squared norm $\|\mathbf{y}\|^2 =: \text{TSS}$ can then be decomposed

4. For code and full details of the simulation, see `johnstachurski.net/emet.html`.

as $\|\mathbf{Py}\|^2 =:$ ESS plus $\|\mathbf{My}\|^2 =:$ RSS. This is sometimes paraphrased as "the total variation in **y** is the sum of explained and unexplained variation." The value of R^2 is then claimed to be the fraction of the variation in **y** "explained" by the regressors.

This terminology is problematic because the notion that the regressors "explain" variation in **y** suggests causation, and R^2 says nothing about causation *per se*. Instead, R^2 is better thought of as a measure of correlation (see §11.2.3). As has been observed on many occasions, correlation and causation are not the same thing. Two informal examples are as follows:

- We often see car crashes and ambulances together (correlation). This does not imply that ambulances cause crashes.
- Say we observe that people sleeping with their shoes on often wake up with sore heads. One possible explanation is that wearing shoes to bed causes headaches. Another is that both phenomena are caused by too many pints at the pub the night before.

Identifying causality in observational data can be very challenging. Here's another example, which, although it falls in the realm of traffic safety, is nonetheless interesting because it involves choices and human behavior: It has been observed that motorcycles fitted with ABS brakes have much lower crash rates than those without anti-lock brakes (see, e.g., Teoh 2011). Does that mean fitting ABS to a given motorcycle will reduce the probability that the bike is involved in an accident by a similar amount? If so, should traffic authorities mandate the use of ABS brakes?

There's an obvious problem in jumping to this conclusion: selection bias in the sample. Cautious motorcyclists are more likely to choose bikes with safety features such as ABS. Lower crash rates for ABS bikes might therefore be caused primarily by more careful riding.

We can eliminate the selection bias by randomly assigning bikes of both types to a large group of riders and observing the results. One might expect that such randomization would reduce the observed effect, although perhaps not eliminate it entirely. In fact such a study has already been conducted for the case of passenger vehicles. In Munich, half of a large fleet of taxis were fitted with anti-lock brakes and half were fitted with conventional brakes (Aschenbrenner and Biehl 1994). The study lasted three years and drivers were randomly assigned across vehicles. A total of 747 accidents were observed. The authors found that accidents rates where slightly *higher* for taxis fitted with ABS.

The conclusion of the authors is that, while anti-lock brakes do improve braking performance, drivers compensate by driving faster, making shaper turns, poorer lane changes, and so forth. (This altered behavior is called "risk compensation.") The net effect is roughly zero: mandatory ABS brakes will cause no appreciable drop in accident rates.

In general, understanding causality requires either good experiments or good theory. There is no magic econometric procedure that can reliably extract causality from observational data without a good model.

12.3 Further Reading

General econometrics texts treating OLS and its extensions include Hayashi (2000), Kennedy (2008), Greene (2011), Davidson and MacKinnon (2004), Wooldridge (2010), and Cameron and Trivedi (2005). A comprehensive treatment of theory can be found in Ruud (2000).

Regarding robust standard errors, asymptotics of the estimator in (12.28) are provided in White (1980). Closely related is the covariance matrix estimator proposed in Newey and West (1987). See Hayashi (2000), Hansen (2015), and Cameron and Trivedi (2005) for textbook treatments.

Measurement errors form another source of bias in OLS estimators. There is a standard approach to so-called errors-in-variables models based around instrumental variables. See, for example, chapter 8 of Davidson and MacKinnon (2004). For a treatment of nonlinear errors-in-variables, see Chen et al. (2011).

For more discussion of causality, see Freedman (2009), Angrist and Pischke (2009), Pearl (2009), or Imbens and Rubin (2015). An important notion of causality in time series models is the ability of one time series to predict another. A seminal contribution is Granger (1969). See Dufour and Taamouti (2010) for a more recent discussion. Chernozhukov et al. (2013) consider how to perform inference on counterfactual distributions. Belloni et al. (2014) discuss treatment effects in high dimensional settings.

12.4 Exercises

Ex. 12.4.1 Argue that the sample mean of a random sample $y_1, \ldots, y_N$ from a given distribution F can be viewed as a least squares estimator of the mean of F.

Ex. 12.4.2 Prove the claims in fact 12.1.1 on page 324.

Ex. 12.4.3 Prove the claims in fact 12.1.2.

Ex. 12.4.4 Confirm part (i) of fact 12.1.3.

Ex. 12.4.5 Prove theorem 12.1.2 on page 328.

Ex. 12.4.6 Prove fact 12.1.4 on page 333.[5]

5. Hint: Use fact 5.1.13 on page 137.

Ex. 12.4.7 Show by direct calculation that $\text{cov}[\mathbf{Py}, \mathbf{My} \mid \mathbf{X}] = \mathbf{0}$.

Ex. 12.4.8 Show that under assumptions 12.1.1–12.1.4, we have $\text{cov}[\hat{\boldsymbol{\beta}}, \mathbf{Mu} \mid \mathbf{X}] = \mathbf{0}$.

Ex. 12.4.9 Show that $\mathbb{E}[\mathbf{Py} \mid \mathbf{X}] = \mathbf{X}\boldsymbol{\beta}$ and $\text{var}[\mathbf{Py} \mid \mathbf{X}] = \sigma^2 \mathbf{P}$.

Ex. 12.4.10 Show that $\mathbb{E}[\mathbf{My} \mid \mathbf{X}] = \mathbf{0}$ and $\text{var}[\mathbf{My} \mid \mathbf{X}] = \sigma^2 \mathbf{M}$.

Ex. 12.4.11 Confirm (12.13) on page 331.

Ex. 12.4.12 Using (12.13), show that for the simple OLS model $\mathbf{y} = \beta_1 \mathbf{1} + \beta_2 \mathbf{x} + \mathbf{u}$, the variance of $\hat{\beta}_2$ given $\mathbf{x}$ is $\sigma^2 / \sum_{n=1}^{N} (x_n - \bar{x})^2$.

Ex. 12.4.13 Show that in the case of (12.22), the F statistic in (12.21) can be rewritten as (12.23).

Ex. 12.4.14 Suppose that assumption 12.1.5 holds, so that $\mathbf{X}$ and $\mathbf{u}$ are independent and $\mathcal{L}(\mathbf{u}) = \text{N}(\mathbf{0}, \sigma^2 \mathbf{I})$. Show that, conditional on $\mathbf{X}$,

(i) $\mathbf{Py}$ and $\mathbf{My}$ are normally distributed, and

(ii) $\mathbf{Py}$ and $\mathbf{My}$ are independent.

Ex. 12.4.15 Verify the expression for x_n in (12.31).

Ex. 12.4.16 Obtain fact 10.1.1 on page 277 as a special case of theorem 12.1.6.[6]

Ex. 12.4.17 Prove the claims $\mathbb{E}[\mathbf{u}_c \mid \mathbf{X}_c] = \mathbf{0}$ and $\mathbb{E}[\mathbf{u}_c \mathbf{u}_c^\top \mid \mathbf{X}_c] = \mathbf{I}$ from (12.26).

Ex. 12.4.18 In connection with the theory of instrumental variables in §12.2.3, show that if $\mathbf{Z}$ is $N \times J$, $\mathbf{X}$ is $N \times K$ and $\mathbf{Z}^\top \mathbf{X}$ has full column rank, then $J \geqslant K$.

Ex. 12.4.19 Let all OLS assumptions hold except 12.1.2 (page 323). Suppose that the data-generating process is

$$\mathbf{y} = \mathbf{X}\boldsymbol{\beta} + \mathbf{Z}\boldsymbol{\theta} + \mathbf{u} \tag{12.35}$$

with $\boldsymbol{\theta} \neq \mathbf{0}$ and $\mathbb{E}[\mathbf{u} \mid \mathbf{X}, \mathbf{Z}] = \mathbf{0}$. Suppose further that we mistakenly ignore $\mathbf{Z}$, and simply regress $\mathbf{y}$ on $\mathbf{X}$. Show that the OLS estimator is biased whenever $\mathbf{X}^\top \mathbf{Z} = \mathbf{0}$.

Ex. 12.4.20 Show that the assumptions of §12.2.3 are not sufficient for unbiasedness of the IVLS estimator of $\boldsymbol{\beta}$.

Ex. 12.4.21 This exercise asks you to construct $\hat{\boldsymbol{\beta}}_{\text{IVLS}}$ in (12.33) via an alternative approach called two-stage least squares. Your task is to show that the estimator produced by the following two steps is identical to the expression given in the right-hand side of (12.33).

(i) Construct $\hat{\mathbf{X}}$ by projecting each column of $\mathbf{X}$ onto colspace $\mathbf{Z}$.

(ii) Regress $\mathbf{y}$ on $\hat{\mathbf{X}}$ using OLS.

6. Hint: Consider the regression model $\mathbf{y} = \mathbf{1}\beta + \mathbf{u}$.

12.4.1 Solutions to Selected Exercises

Solution to Ex. 12.4.1. Letting $\mu := \mathbb{E}[y_n]$ we can write $y_n = \mu + u_n$ when $u_n := y_n - \mu$. In other words, $\mathbf{y} = \mathbf{1}\mu + \mathbf{u}$. The OLS estimate of μ is

$$\hat{\mu} := (\mathbf{1}^\top \mathbf{1})^{-1}\mathbf{1}^\top \mathbf{y} = \frac{1}{N}\mathbf{1}^\top \mathbf{y} = \frac{1}{N}\sum_{n=1}^{N} y_n = \bar{y}_N$$

Reading right to left, the sample mean of $\mathbf{y}$ is the OLS estimate of the mean. □

Solution to Ex. 12.4.2. From fact 3.3.1 on page 61 we have $\mathbf{MX} = \mathbf{0}$ and $\mathbf{PX} = \mathbf{X}$. From this (i) and (ii) follow easily. For example,

$$\mathbf{My} = \mathbf{M}(\mathbf{X}\boldsymbol{\beta} + \mathbf{u}) = \mathbf{Mu}$$

Regarding (iii), since $\mathbf{M}$ is symmetric and idempotent (page 61), we have

$$\text{RSS} := \|\mathbf{My}\|^2 = \|\mathbf{Mu}\|^2 = (\mathbf{Mu})^\top(\mathbf{Mu}) = \mathbf{u}^\top\mathbf{M}^\top\mathbf{Mu} = \mathbf{u}^\top\mathbf{Mu}$$ □

Solution to Ex. 12.4.3. The respective proofs for claims 1–4 are as follows:

(i) $\mathbb{E}[\mathbf{u}] = \mathbb{E}[\mathbb{E}[\mathbf{u} \,|\, \mathbf{X}]] = \mathbb{E}[\mathbf{0}] = \mathbf{0}$

(ii) $\mathbb{E}[u_m \,|\, x_{nk}] = \mathbb{E}[\mathbb{E}[u_m \,|\, \mathbf{X}] \,|\, x_{nk}] = \mathbb{E}[0 \,|\, x_{nk}] = 0$

(iii) $\mathbb{E}[u_m x_{nk}] = \mathbb{E}[\mathbb{E}[u_m x_{nk} \,|\, x_{nk}]] = \mathbb{E}[x_{nk}\mathbb{E}[u_m \,|\, x_{nk}]] = 0$

(iv) $\text{cov}[u_m, x_{nk}] = \mathbb{E}[u_m x_{nk}] - \mathbb{E}[u_m]\mathbb{E}[x_{nk}] = 0$

□

Solution to Ex. 12.4.4. By definition, $\text{var}\,\mathbf{u} = \mathbb{E}[\mathbf{u}\mathbf{u}^\top] - \mathbb{E}[\mathbf{u}]\mathbb{E}[\mathbf{u}^\top]$. Since $\mathbb{E}[\mathbf{u}] = \mathbb{E}[\mathbb{E}[\mathbf{u} \,|\, \mathbf{X}]] = \mathbf{0}$, this reduces to $\text{var}\,\mathbf{u} = \mathbb{E}[\mathbf{u}\mathbf{u}^\top]$. Moreover

$$\mathbb{E}[\mathbf{u}\mathbf{u}^\top] = \mathbb{E}[\mathbb{E}[\mathbf{u}\mathbf{u}^\top \,|\, \mathbf{X}]] = \mathbb{E}[\sigma^2\mathbf{I}] = \sigma^2\mathbf{I}$$ □

Solution to Ex. 12.4.5. If $\mathbf{A} := (\mathbf{X}^\top\mathbf{X})^{-1}\mathbf{X}^\top$, then by (12.4) we have $\hat{\boldsymbol{\beta}} = \boldsymbol{\beta} + \mathbf{Au}$, and

$$\text{var}[\hat{\boldsymbol{\beta}} \,|\, \mathbf{X}] = \text{var}[\boldsymbol{\beta} + \mathbf{Au} \,|\, \mathbf{X}] = \text{var}[\mathbf{Au} \,|\, \mathbf{X}]$$

Treating $\mathbf{A}$ as nonrandom given $\mathbf{X}$ and applying fact 5.1.2 on page 127, we have

$$\text{var}[\mathbf{Au} \,|\, \mathbf{X}] = \mathbf{A}\,\text{var}[\mathbf{u} \,|\, \mathbf{X}]\mathbf{A}^\top = \mathbf{A}(\sigma^2\mathbf{I})\mathbf{A}^\top$$

Moreover, $\mathbf{A}(\sigma^2\mathbf{I})\mathbf{A}^\top = \sigma^2\mathbf{A}\mathbf{A}^\top = \sigma^2(\mathbf{X}^\top\mathbf{X})^{-1}\mathbf{X}^\top\mathbf{X}(\mathbf{X}^\top\mathbf{X})^{-1} = \sigma^2(\mathbf{X}^\top\mathbf{X})^{-1}$. Hence

$$\text{var}[\hat{\boldsymbol{\beta}} \,|\, \mathbf{X}] = \text{var}[\mathbf{Au} \,|\, \mathbf{X}] = \sigma^2(\mathbf{X}^\top\mathbf{X})^{-1}$$ □

Solution to Ex. 12.4.6. Note first that $\mathbf{Pu}$ and $\mathbf{Mu}$ are independent by fact 5.1.13 on page 137. By fact 5.1.10 on page 137, functions of independent random vectors are likewise independent. Hence it suffices to show that $\hat{\boldsymbol{\beta}}$ and $\hat{\sigma}^2$ are functions of $\mathbf{Pu}$ and $\mathbf{Mu}$ respectively. The case of $\hat{\sigma}^2$ is straightforward. For $\hat{\boldsymbol{\beta}}$ we have

$$\hat{\boldsymbol{\beta}} = \boldsymbol{\beta} + (\mathbf{X}^\top \mathbf{X})^{-1} \mathbf{X}^\top \mathbf{Pu}$$

as can be seen by writing out $\mathbf{P}$ in terms of $\mathbf{X}$ and canceling to get (12.4). □

Solution to Ex. 12.4.7. Note that

$$\mathbb{E}[\mathbf{My} \,|\, \mathbf{X}] = \mathbb{E}[\mathbf{Mu} \,|\, \mathbf{X}] = \mathbf{M}\mathbb{E}[\mathbf{u} \,|\, \mathbf{X}] = \mathbf{0}$$

Using these facts, we obtain

$$\operatorname{cov}[\mathbf{Py}, \mathbf{My} \,|\, \mathbf{X}] = \operatorname{cov}[\mathbf{X}\boldsymbol{\beta} + \mathbf{Pu}, \mathbf{Mu} \,|\, \mathbf{X}] = \mathbb{E}[(\mathbf{X}\boldsymbol{\beta} + \mathbf{Pu})(\mathbf{Mu})^\top \,|\, \mathbf{X}]$$

By linearity of expectations and symmetry of $\mathbf{M}$, this becomes

$$\operatorname{cov}[\mathbf{Py}, \mathbf{My} \,|\, \mathbf{X}] = \mathbb{E}[\mathbf{X}\boldsymbol{\beta}\mathbf{u}^\top \mathbf{M} \,|\, \mathbf{X}] + \mathbb{E}[\mathbf{Puu}^\top \mathbf{M} \,|\, \mathbf{X}]$$

Regarding the first term on the right-hand side, we have

$$\mathbb{E}[\mathbf{X}\boldsymbol{\beta}\mathbf{u}^\top \mathbf{M} \,|\, \mathbf{X}] = \mathbf{X}\boldsymbol{\beta}\mathbb{E}[\mathbf{u}^\top \,|\, \mathbf{X}]\mathbf{M} = \mathbf{0}$$

Regarding the second term on the right-hand side, we have

$$\mathbb{E}[\mathbf{Puu}^\top \mathbf{M} \,|\, \mathbf{X}] = \mathbf{P}\mathbb{E}[\mathbf{uu}^\top \,|\, \mathbf{X}]\mathbf{M} = \mathbf{P}\sigma^2\mathbf{IM} = \sigma^2\mathbf{PM} = \mathbf{0}$$

$$\therefore \quad \operatorname{cov}[\mathbf{Py}, \mathbf{My} \,|\, \mathbf{X}] = \mathbf{0}$$ □

Solution to Ex. 12.4.8. Since $\mathbf{M}$ is a function of $\mathbf{X}$, we have $\mathbb{E}[\mathbf{Mu} \,|\, \mathbf{X}] = \mathbf{M}\mathbb{E}[\mathbf{u} \,|\, \mathbf{X}] = \mathbf{0}$. As a result

$$\begin{aligned}
\operatorname{cov}[\hat{\boldsymbol{\beta}}, \mathbf{Mu} \,|\, \mathbf{X}] &= \mathbb{E}[\hat{\boldsymbol{\beta}}\,(\mathbf{Mu})^\top \,|\, \mathbf{X}] \\
&= \mathbb{E}[\boldsymbol{\beta}(\mathbf{Mu})^\top + (\mathbf{X}^\top\mathbf{X})^{-1}\mathbf{X}^\top\mathbf{u}\,(\mathbf{Mu})^\top \,|\, \mathbf{X}] \\
&= \mathbb{E}[(\mathbf{X}^\top\mathbf{X})^{-1}\mathbf{X}^\top\mathbf{u}\,(\mathbf{Mu})^\top \,|\, \mathbf{X}] \\
&= \mathbb{E}[(\mathbf{X}^\top\mathbf{X})^{-1}\mathbf{X}^\top\mathbf{uu}^\top\mathbf{M} \,|\, \mathbf{X}] = \sigma^2(\mathbf{X}^\top\mathbf{X})^{-1}\mathbf{X}^\top\mathbf{M}
\end{aligned}$$

The claim now follows from $\mathbf{X}^\top\mathbf{M} = (\mathbf{MX})^\top = \mathbf{0}$. □

Solution to Ex. 12.4.9. Regarding the claim that $\mathbb{E}[\mathbf{Py} \,|\, \mathbf{X}] = \mathbf{X}\boldsymbol{\beta}$, our previous results and linearity of expectations gives

$$\mathbb{E}[\mathbf{Py} \mid \mathbf{X}] = \mathbb{E}[\mathbf{X}\boldsymbol{\beta} + \mathbf{Pu} \mid \mathbf{X}] = \mathbf{X}\boldsymbol{\beta} + \mathbf{P}\mathbb{E}[\mathbf{u} \mid \mathbf{X}] = \mathbf{X}\boldsymbol{\beta}$$

Regarding the claim that $\text{var}[\mathbf{Py} \mid \mathbf{X}] = \sigma^2\mathbf{P}$, our rules for manipulating variances yield

$$\text{var}[\mathbf{Py} \mid \mathbf{X}] = \text{var}[\mathbf{X}\boldsymbol{\beta} + \mathbf{Pu} \mid \mathbf{X}] = \text{var}[\mathbf{Pu} \mid \mathbf{X}] = \mathbf{P}\,\text{var}[\mathbf{u} \mid \mathbf{X}]\mathbf{P}^\top = \mathbf{P}\sigma^2\mathbf{I}\mathbf{P}^\top$$

Using symmetry and idempotence of $\mathbf{P}$, we obtain $\text{var}[\mathbf{Py} \mid \mathbf{X}] = \sigma^2\mathbf{P}$. □

Solution to Ex. 12.4.10. Similar to the solution of exercise 12.4.9. □

Solution to Ex. 12.4.11. Repeating (12.12) we have

$$\hat{\beta}_k = \beta_k + (\text{col}_k(\mathbf{X})^\top \mathbf{M}_1 \,\text{col}_k(\mathbf{X}))^{-1} \text{col}_k(\mathbf{X})^\top \mathbf{M}_1 \mathbf{u} \tag{12.36}$$

Since β_k is constant, taking the variance of (12.36) conditional on $\mathbf{X}$, we obtain

$$\text{var}[\hat{\beta}_k \mid \mathbf{X}] = \text{var}[\mathbf{Au} \mid \mathbf{X}] \quad \text{where } \mathbf{A} := (\text{col}_k(\mathbf{X})^\top \mathbf{M}_1 \,\text{col}_k(\mathbf{X}))^{-1} \text{col}_k(\mathbf{X})^\top \mathbf{M}_1$$

Since $\mathbf{A}$ is a function of $\mathbf{X}$, we can treat it as constant given $\mathbf{X}$, and we obtain

$$\text{var}[\hat{\beta}_k \mid \mathbf{X}] = \mathbf{A}\,\text{var}[\mathbf{u} \mid \mathbf{X}]\mathbf{A}^\top = \mathbf{A}\sigma^2\mathbf{I}\mathbf{A}^\top = \sigma^2\mathbf{A}\mathbf{A}^\top$$

To complete the proof, we just observe that

$$\begin{aligned}\mathbf{A}\mathbf{A}^\top &= (\text{col}_k(\mathbf{X})^\top \mathbf{M}_1 \,\text{col}_k(\mathbf{X}))^{-1} \text{col}_k(\mathbf{X})^\top \mathbf{M}_1 \mathbf{M}_1^\top \,\text{col}_k(\mathbf{X}) (\text{col}_k(\mathbf{X})^\top \mathbf{M}_1 \,\text{col}_k(\mathbf{X}))^{-1} \\ &= (\text{col}_k(\mathbf{X})^\top \mathbf{M}_1 \,\text{col}_k(\mathbf{X}))^{-1}\end{aligned}$$

where the last equality is due to symmetry and idempotence of $\mathbf{M}_1$. We conclude that (12.13) is valid. □

Solution to Ex. 12.4.12. We will apply (12.13). For the model $\mathbf{y} = \beta_1\mathbf{1} + \beta_2\mathbf{x} + \mathbf{u}$, the matrix $\mathbf{M}_1$ is the residual projection $\mathbf{M}_c$ associated with $\mathbf{1}$, and $\text{col}_k \mathbf{X}$ is just $\mathbf{x}$. Hence, from (12.13), we have

$$\text{var}[\hat{\beta}_2 \mid \mathbf{X}] = \sigma^2(\mathbf{x}^\top \mathbf{M}_c \mathbf{x})^{-1}$$

Using symmetry and idempotence of $\mathbf{M}_c$, this becomes

$$\text{var}[\hat{\beta}_2 \mid \mathbf{X}] = \sigma^2[(\mathbf{M}_c\mathbf{x})^\top \mathbf{M}_c\mathbf{x}]^{-1} = \sigma^2 / \sum_{n=1}^{N} (x_n - \bar{x})^2$$

Finally, since the only random variables in $\mathbf{X}$ are the random variables in $\mathbf{x}$, we obtain the solution

$$\text{var}[\hat{\beta}_2 \,|\, \mathbf{x}] = \sigma^2 / \sum_{n=1}^{N} (x_n - \bar{x})^2 \qquad \square$$

Solution to Ex. 12.4.13. We need to show that in the special case (12.22) we have

$$\frac{(\text{RSSR} - \text{USSR})/K_2}{\text{USSR}/(N-K)} = \frac{R_c^2}{1 - R_c^2} \frac{N-K}{K_2}$$

or, equivalently,

$$\frac{\text{RSSR} - \text{USSR}}{\text{USSR}} = \frac{R_c^2}{1 - R_c^2} \tag{12.37}$$

Consider first the left-hand side of (12.37). In the case of (12.22), this becomes

$$\frac{\text{RSSR} - \text{USSR}}{\text{USSR}} = \frac{\|\mathbf{M}_c\mathbf{y}\|^2 - \|\mathbf{M}\mathbf{y}\|^2}{\|\mathbf{M}\mathbf{y}\|^2}$$

On the other hand, regarding the right-hand side of (12.37), the definition of R_c^2 and some minor manipulation gives

$$\frac{R_c^2}{1 - R_c^2} = \frac{\|\mathbf{P}\mathbf{M}_c\mathbf{y}\|^2}{\|\mathbf{M}_c\mathbf{y}\|^2 - \|\mathbf{P}\mathbf{M}_c\mathbf{y}\|^2}$$

Hence, to establish (12.37), we need to show that

$$\frac{\|\mathbf{M}_c\mathbf{y}\|^2 - \|\mathbf{M}\mathbf{y}\|^2}{\|\mathbf{M}\mathbf{y}\|^2} = \frac{\|\mathbf{P}\mathbf{M}_c\mathbf{y}\|^2}{\|\mathbf{M}_c\mathbf{y}\|^2 - \|\mathbf{P}\mathbf{M}_c\mathbf{y}\|^2}$$

This is can be established using (11.32). □

Solution to Ex. 12.4.14. We have shown previously that $\mathbf{M}\mathbf{y} = \mathbf{M}\mathbf{u}$ and $\mathbf{P}\mathbf{y} = \mathbf{X}\boldsymbol{\beta} + \mathbf{P}\mathbf{u}$. Since we are conditioning on $\mathbf{X}$, we can treat it as constant. When $\mathbf{X}$ is constant, $\mathbf{P}$, $\mathbf{M}$ and $\mathbf{X}\boldsymbol{\beta}$ are all constant. Since linear (or affine) transformations of normal random vectors are normal, $\mathbf{M}\mathbf{u}$ and $\mathbf{X}\boldsymbol{\beta} + \mathbf{P}\mathbf{u}$ are both normally distributed.

It remains to show that $\mathbf{P}\mathbf{y}$ and $\mathbf{M}\mathbf{y}$ are independent given $\mathbf{X}$. Since they are normally distributed given $\mathbf{X}$, we need only show that they are uncorrelated given $\mathbf{X}$. This was already proved in exercise 12.4.7. □

Solution to Ex. 12.4.17. The proof of $\mathbb{E}[\mathbf{u}_c \,|\, \mathbf{X}_c] = \mathbf{0}$ is easy. Regarding the second claim, recall that $\mathbf{C}$ is a nonsingular matrix chosen to satisfy $\mathbf{C}^\top \mathbf{C} = \boldsymbol{\Omega}^{-1}$. (Existence is from the Cholesky decomposition; see page 67.) From $\mathbf{u}_c = \mathbf{C}\mathbf{u}$ we have

$$\mathbb{E}[\mathbf{u}_c\mathbf{u}_c^\top \mid \mathbf{X}_c] = \mathbf{C}\,\mathbb{E}[\mathbf{u}\mathbf{u}^\top \mid \mathbf{X}_c]\mathbf{C}^\top = \mathbf{C}\boldsymbol{\Omega}\mathbf{C}^\top$$

Since $\mathbf{C}$ is nonsingular, we have

$$\mathbf{C}\boldsymbol{\Omega}\mathbf{C}^\top = \mathbf{C}(\mathbf{C}^\top\mathbf{C})^{-1}\mathbf{C}^\top = \mathbf{C}\mathbf{C}^{-1}(\mathbf{C}^\top)^{-1}\mathbf{C}^\top = \mathbf{I} \qquad \square$$

Solution to Ex. 12.4.18. If not then $\mathbf{Z}^\top\mathbf{X}$ has fewer rows than columns, and hence its columns cannot be linearly independent. See theorem 2.1.3 on page 20. □

Solution to Ex. 12.4.19. The OLS estimator is $\hat{\boldsymbol{\beta}} = (\mathbf{X}^\top\mathbf{X})^{-1}\mathbf{X}^\top\mathbf{y}$. Substituting into (12.35) gives

$$\hat{\boldsymbol{\beta}} = (\mathbf{X}^\top\mathbf{X})^{-1}\mathbf{X}^\top(\mathbf{X}\boldsymbol{\beta} + \mathbf{Z}\boldsymbol{\theta} + \mathbf{u}) = \boldsymbol{\beta} + (\mathbf{X}^\top\mathbf{X})^{-1}\mathbf{X}^\top\mathbf{Z}\boldsymbol{\theta} + (\mathbf{X}^\top\mathbf{X})^{-1}\mathbf{X}^\top\mathbf{u}$$

Therefore

$$\mathbb{E}[\hat{\boldsymbol{\beta}}] = \mathbb{E}[\mathbb{E}[\hat{\boldsymbol{\beta}} \mid \mathbf{X}, \mathbf{Z}]] = \boldsymbol{\beta} + \mathbb{E}[(\mathbf{X}^\top\mathbf{X})^{-1}\mathbf{X}^\top\mathbf{Z}]\boldsymbol{\theta}$$

If $\mathbf{X}^\top\mathbf{Z} = \mathbf{0}$ then the last term on the right-hand side drops out, and $\hat{\boldsymbol{\beta}}$ is unbiased. Otherwise $\hat{\boldsymbol{\beta}}$ is biased. □

Solution to Ex. 12.4.20. To solve this exercise it suffices to give an example of a model that satisfies the assumptions of §12.2.3 and yet produces a biased IV estimator. To this end, suppose that we have only one observation, and let all variables be scalar. Let z and u be independent random variables with $\mathcal{L}(u) = \mathrm{N}(0, \sigma^2)$ and let $x = u$. Let $y = x\beta + u$. While the IV assumptions of §12.2.3 are satisfied, the IVLS estimator is biased. Indeed, the expression (12.34) combined with $y = x\beta + u$ gives us

$$\hat{\beta}_{\mathrm{IVLS}} = (zx)^{-1}zy = \beta + (zx)^{-1}zu = \beta + \frac{u}{x}$$

Using $x = u$ gives $\mathbb{E}[\hat{\beta}_{\mathrm{IVLS}}] = \hat{\beta}_{\mathrm{IVLS}} = \beta + 1$. □

Solution to Ex. 12.4.21. By theorem 3.3.1 on page 60, the matrix that implements orthogonal projection onto colspace $\mathbf{Z}$ is $\mathbf{P}_Z := \mathbf{Z}(\mathbf{Z}^\top\mathbf{Z})^{-1}\mathbf{Z}^\top$. Applying this operation to each column of $\mathbf{X}$ is equivalent to premultiplying $\mathbf{X}$ by $\mathbf{P}_Z$. Regressing $\mathbf{y}$ on $\mathbf{P}_Z\mathbf{X}$ using OLS produces the estimator

$$\hat{\beta}_{\mathrm{2SLS}} = [(\mathbf{P}_Z\mathbf{X})^\top(\mathbf{P}_Z\mathbf{X})]^{-1}(\mathbf{P}_Z\mathbf{X})^\top\mathbf{y} = [\mathbf{X}^\top\mathbf{P}_Z\mathbf{X}]^{-1}\mathbf{X}^\top\mathbf{P}_Z\mathbf{y}$$

(The second equality uses symmetry and idempotence of $\mathbf{P}_Z$. See fact 3.3.2 on page 61.) Using the definition of $\mathbf{P}_Z$ gives (12.33). □

Chapter 13

Large Samples and Dependence

With IID data, the joint distribution of the sample is pinned down by the common marginal of the observations. The statistical learning problem becomes one of learning the marginal. With dependent data the joint distribution is more complex. The fundamental statistical problem from page 213 has to be extended as follows:

Problem 13.0.1 We observe a draw $\mathbf{z}_{\mathcal{D}}$ from some joint distribution $P_{\mathcal{D}}$, which is assumed to belong to a given class of distributions $\mathscr{P}$ but is otherwise unknown. We wish to infer some features of $P_{\mathcal{D}}$ from the observation $\mathbf{z}_{\mathcal{D}}$.

Let's look at how we might tackle this problem, starting with least squares.

13.1 Large Sample Least Squares

Our treatment of least squares in this chapter permits dependent data but at the same time requires that the sample size is large. Large samples allow us to drop some of the strict parametric assumptions on the error term we made when we considered finite sample inference (see, e.g., assumption 12.1.5 on page 332). In this sense, the theory developed below is also useful for cross-sectional environments with no correlation between observations.

13.1.1 Setup and Assumptions

Let's go back to the linear model assumption of chapter 12. That is, we assume that our data $(y_1, \mathbf{x}_1), \ldots, (y_T, \mathbf{x}_T)$ are generated by the linear model

$$y_t = \mathbf{x}_t^{\top} \boldsymbol{\beta} + u_t, \qquad t = 1, \ldots, T, \tag{13.1}$$

where $\boldsymbol{\beta}$ is a K-vector of unknown coefficients, and u_t is an unobservable shock. Observations are indexed by t rather than n to remind us that observations are dependent. The sample size will be denoted by T.

We let $\mathbf{y}$ be the $T \times 1$ vector of observed outputs, so that y_t is the tth element of $\mathbf{y}$, and $\mathbf{u}$ be the vector of shocks, so that u_t is the tth element of $\mathbf{u}$. We let $\mathbf{X}$ be the $T \times K$ matrix $\mathbf{X} := (x_{tk})$, where $1 \leqslant t \leqslant T$ and $1 \leqslant k \leqslant K$.

We will estimate the parameter vector $\boldsymbol{\beta}$ via least squares. The OLS estimate is therefore unchanged at

$$\hat{\boldsymbol{\beta}}_T = \left[\frac{1}{T} \sum_{t=1}^{T} \mathbf{x}_t \mathbf{x}_t^\top \right]^{-1} \cdot \frac{1}{T} \sum_{t=1}^{T} \mathbf{x}_t y_t$$

(Recall (11.17) on page 306.) The expression for the sampling error in (12.4) can be expanded into sums to obtain

$$\hat{\boldsymbol{\beta}}_T - \boldsymbol{\beta} = \left[\frac{1}{T} \sum_{t=1}^{T} \mathbf{x}_t \mathbf{x}_t^\top \right]^{-1} \cdot \frac{1}{T} \sum_{t=1}^{T} \mathbf{x}_t u_t \tag{13.2}$$

In this section we drop the exogeneity assumption $\mathbb{E}[\mathbf{u} \mid \mathbf{X}] = \mathbf{0}$ (assumption 12.1.3) because it excludes too many dynamic models. For example, we know from §12.2.2 that exogeneity fails when we try to estimate the simple AR(1) model $y_{t+1} = \beta y_t + u_{t+1}$ by setting $x_t = y_{t-1}$, thereby producing the regression model

$$y_t = \beta x_t + u_t, \qquad t = 1, \ldots, T \tag{13.3}$$

For this specification of (13.1), the regressor is correlated with lagged values of the shock.

Assumption 13.1.1 The matrix $\mathbf{X}$ is full column rank with probability one and the sequence $\{\mathbf{x}_t\}$ is stationary. Moreover

(i) $\boldsymbol{\Sigma}_{\mathbf{x}} := \mathbb{E}[\mathbf{x}_t \mathbf{x}_t^\top]$ exists and is positive definite, and

(ii) the sequence $\{\mathbf{x}_t\}$ satisfies $\frac{1}{T} \sum_{t=1}^{T} \mathbf{x}_t \mathbf{x}_t^\top \stackrel{p}{\to} \boldsymbol{\Sigma}_{\mathbf{x}}$ as $T \to \infty$.

The full column rank condition is the same as assumption 11.1.1 on page 302 and ensures that expressions like the matrix inverse in (13.2) make sense. Condition (i) is borrowed from the identical condition given in (11.10) on page 302 and ensures that the limit in (13.2) exists. Condition (ii) gives convergence.

Example 13.1.1 Let $\{x_t\}$ be the Markov process in example 7.2.11 on page 195. To repeat,

$$x_{t+1} = a|x_t| + (1-a^2)^{1/2} w_{t+1} \quad \text{with} \quad -1 < a < 1 \quad \text{and} \quad \{w_t\} \overset{\text{IID}}{\sim} \text{N}(0,1)$$

As discussed in example 7.2.11, the model has a unique, globally stable stationary distribution π_∞. If $\mathcal{L}(x_0) = \pi_\infty$, then the process $\{x_t\}$ is stationary (see fact 7.2.5 on page 191) and all of the conditions in assumption 13.1.1 are satisfied (see ex. 13.4.3).

Assumption 13.1.2 (Weak exogeneity) The shocks $\{u_t\}$ are IID. Moreover

(i) $\mathbb{E}[u_t] = 0$ and $\mathbb{E}[u_t^2] = \sigma^2$ for all t, and

(ii) u_t is independent of $\mathbf{x}_1, \mathbf{x}_2, \ldots, \mathbf{x}_t$ for all t.

Assumption 13.1.2 permits dependence between current shocks and future regressors. This is desirable in a time series setting, since current shocks usually feed into future state variables.

Example 13.1.2 In the AR(1) regression (13.3), assumption 13.1.2 holds whenever the shock process $\{u_t\}$ is IID, because the contemporaneous and lagged regressors $x_1, \ldots, x_t$ are equal to the lagged state variables $y_0, \ldots, y_{t-1}$, which in turn are functions of only y_0 and $u_1, \ldots, u_{t-1}$, and therefore independent of u_t.

One consequence of assumption 13.1.2 is that

$$\mathbb{E}[u_s u_t \mid \mathbf{x}_1, \ldots, \mathbf{x}_t] = \begin{cases} \sigma^2 & \text{if} \quad s = t \\ 0 & \text{if} \quad s < t \end{cases} \tag{13.4}$$

The proof is an exercise (ex. 13.4.4).

A useful implication of assumptions 13.1.1 and 13.1.2 is that linear functions of $\{\mathbf{x}_t u_t\}$ form a martingale difference sequence (MDS). This will allow us to apply the sample path results in theorem 7.3.1.

Lemma 13.1.1 *If assumptions 13.1.1 and 13.1.2 both hold, then, for any constant vector* $\mathbf{a} \in \mathbb{R}^K$*, the sequence* $\{m_t\}$ *defined by* $m_t = \mathbf{a}^\top \mathbf{x}_t u_t$ *is*

(i) stationary with $\mathbb{E}[m_t^2] = \sigma^2 \mathbf{a}^\top \boldsymbol{\Sigma}_{\mathbf{x}} \mathbf{a}$ *for all* t*, and*

(ii) an MDS *with respect to the filtration defined by*

$$\mathscr{F}_t := \{\mathbf{x}_1, \ldots, \mathbf{x}_t, \mathbf{x}_{t+1}, u_1, \ldots, u_t\} \tag{13.5}$$

Proof. First let's check part (i). That $\{m_t\}$ is stationary follows from the assumption that $\{u_t\}$ and $\{\mathbf{x}_t\}$ are stationary. Regarding the second moment $\mathbb{E}[m_1^2]$, we have

$$\mathbb{E}[m_1^2] = \mathbb{E}[\mathbb{E}[u_1^2(\mathbf{a}^\top \mathbf{x}_1)^2 \mid \mathbf{x}_1]] = \mathbb{E}[(\mathbf{a}^\top \mathbf{x}_1)^2 \mathbb{E}[u_1^2 \mid \mathbf{x}_1]]$$

From independence of u_1 and $\mathbf{x}_1$, the inner expectation is σ^2. Moreover

$$(\mathbf{a}^\top \mathbf{x}_1)^2 = \mathbf{a}^\top \mathbf{x}_1 \mathbf{a}^\top \mathbf{x}_1 = \mathbf{a}^\top \mathbf{x}_1 \mathbf{x}_1^\top \mathbf{a}$$

$$\therefore \quad \mathbb{E}[m_1^2] = \mathbb{E}[\mathbf{a}^\top \mathbf{x}_1 \mathbf{x}_1^\top \mathbf{a}\, \sigma^2] = \sigma^2 \mathbf{a}^\top \mathbb{E}[\mathbf{x}_1 \mathbf{x}_1^\top]\mathbf{a} = \sigma^2 \mathbf{a}^\top \boldsymbol{\Sigma}_{\mathbf{x}} \mathbf{a}$$

To check part (ii), note that $\{m_t\}$ is adapted to $\{\mathscr{F}_t\}$, since $m_t := u_t \mathbf{a}^\top \mathbf{x}_t$ is a function of variables in $\mathscr{F}_t$. Moreover we have

$$\mathbb{E}[m_{t+1} \,|\, \mathscr{F}_t] = \mathbb{E}[u_{t+1}\mathbf{a}^\top \mathbf{x}_{t+1} \,|\, \mathscr{F}_t] = \mathbf{a}^\top \mathbf{x}_{t+1}\mathbb{E}[u_{t+1} \,|\, \mathscr{F}_t] = \mathbf{a}^\top \mathbf{x}_{t+1}\mathbb{E}[u_{t+1}] = 0$$

(Here the second equality follows from the fact that $\mathbf{x}_{t+1} \in \mathscr{F}_t$, while the third follows from the independence in assumption 13.1.2.) This confirms that $\{m_t\}$ is an MDS with respect to $\{\mathscr{F}_t\}$. □

13.1.2 Consistency

Under the conditions of §13.1.1, the OLS estimator $\hat{\boldsymbol{\beta}}_T$ is consistent for $\boldsymbol{\beta}$:

Theorem 13.1.1 *If assumptions 13.1.1 and 13.1.2 hold, then*

$$\hat{\boldsymbol{\beta}}_T \xrightarrow{p} \boldsymbol{\beta} \quad \textit{as} \quad T \to \infty$$

Proof. It suffices to show that the expression on the right-hand side of (13.2) converges in probability to $\mathbf{0}$. As a first step, let's show that $\frac{1}{T}\sum_{t=1}^T \mathbf{x}_t u_t \xrightarrow{p} \mathbf{0}$. In view of fact 6.1.1 on page 161, it suffices to show that, for any $\mathbf{a} \in \mathbb{R}^K$, we have

$$\mathbf{a}^\top \left[\frac{1}{T} \sum_{t=1}^T \mathbf{x}_t u_t \right] \xrightarrow{p} \mathbf{a}^\top \mathbf{0} = 0 \tag{13.6}$$

If we define $m_t := \mathbf{a}^\top \mathbf{x}_t u_t$, then the left-hand side of (13.6) can be written as $T^{-1}\sum_{t=1}^T m_t$. Since $\{m_t\}$ is a stationary MDS (lemma 13.1.1), the convergence $T^{-1}\sum_{t=1}^T m_t \xrightarrow{p} 0$ follows from theorem 7.3.1 (page 200).

Now let's return to the expression on the right-hand side of (13.2). By assumption 13.1.1 and fact 6.2.1, we see that

$$\left[\frac{1}{T} \sum_{t=1}^T \mathbf{x}_t \mathbf{x}_t^\top \right]^{-1} \xrightarrow{p} \boldsymbol{\Sigma}_{\mathbf{x}}{}^{-1} \quad \text{as} \quad T \to \infty \tag{13.7}$$

Appealing to fact 6.2.1 once more, we obtain

$$\hat{\beta}_T - \beta = \left[\frac{1}{T}\sum_{t=1}^{T} \mathbf{x}_t \mathbf{x}_t^\top\right]^{-1} \cdot \frac{1}{T}\sum_{t=1}^{T} u_t \mathbf{x}_t \xrightarrow{p} \boldsymbol{\Sigma}_{\mathbf{x}}{}^{-1}\mathbf{0} = \mathbf{0} \qquad \square$$

13.1.2.1 Consistency of $\hat{\sigma}_T^2$

In (12.5) we estimated the error variance σ^2 using $\hat{\sigma}^2 := \text{RSS}/(N-K)$, with N being the sample size. Here the sample size is T, and since T is assumed to be large relative to K, we have $1/(T-K) \approx 1/T$. Hence in this chapter we set $\hat{\sigma}_T^2 = \text{RSS}/T$ instead. (None of the following theory is affected if we use $\text{RSS}/(T-K)$, however.)

Theorem 13.1.2 *If assumptions 13.1.1 and 13.1.2 hold, then*

$$\hat{\sigma}_T^2 \xrightarrow{p} \sigma^2 \quad \textit{as} \quad T \to \infty$$

Proof. By the definition of $\hat{\sigma}_T^2$ and the linear model assumption (13.1),

$$\hat{\sigma}_T^2 = \frac{1}{T}\sum_{t=1}^{T}(y_t - \mathbf{x}_t^\top \hat{\beta}_T)^2 = \frac{1}{T}\sum_{t=1}^{T}\left[u_t + \mathbf{x}_t^\top(\beta - \hat{\beta}_T)\right]^2 \tag{13.8}$$

Expanding out the square gives

$$\hat{\sigma}_T^2 = \frac{1}{T}\sum_{t=1}^{T} u_t^2 + 2(\beta - \hat{\beta}_T)^\top \frac{1}{T}\sum_{t=1}^{T}\mathbf{x}_t u_t + (\beta - \hat{\beta}_T)^\top \left[\frac{1}{T}\sum_{t=1}^{T}\mathbf{x}_t\mathbf{x}_t^\top\right](\beta - \hat{\beta}_T)$$

By assumption 13.1.2 and the law of large numbers, the first term on the right-hand side converges in probability to σ^2. Hence it suffices to show that the second and third term converge in probability to zero as $T \to \infty$. These results follow from repeated applications of fact 6.2.1 on page 170 and convergence results we have already established. The details are left as an exercise. $\square$

13.1.3 Asymptotic Normality of $\hat{\beta}$

Next we show that $\sqrt{T}(\hat{\beta}_T - \beta)$ is asymptotically normal. From this information we can develop asymptotic tests and confidence intervals.

Theorem 13.1.3 *If assumptions 13.1.1 and 13.1.2 hold, then*

$$\sqrt{T}(\hat{\beta}_T - \beta) \xrightarrow{d} \text{N}\left(\mathbf{0}, \sigma^2 \boldsymbol{\Sigma}_{\mathbf{x}}^{-1}\right) \quad \textit{as} \quad T \to \infty$$

Proof. Expression (13.2) gives

$$\sqrt{T}(\hat{\boldsymbol{\beta}}_T - \boldsymbol{\beta}) = \left[\frac{1}{T}\sum_{t=1}^{T}\mathbf{x}_t\mathbf{x}_t^\top\right]^{-1} \cdot T^{-1/2}\sum_{t=1}^{T}u_t\mathbf{x}_t \tag{13.9}$$

Let $\mathbf{z}$ be a random variable satisfying $\mathcal{L}(\mathbf{z}) = \mathrm{N}(\mathbf{0}, \sigma^2\boldsymbol{\Sigma}_{\mathbf{x}})$. Suppose we can show that

$$T^{-1/2}\sum_{t=1}^{T}u_t\mathbf{x}_t \stackrel{d}{\to} \mathbf{z} \quad \text{as} \quad T \to \infty \tag{13.10}$$

If (13.10) is valid, then, applying assumption 13.1.1 along with fact 6.2.2, we obtain

$$\sqrt{T}(\hat{\boldsymbol{\beta}}_T - \boldsymbol{\beta}) = \left[\frac{1}{T}\sum_{t=1}^{T}\mathbf{x}_t\mathbf{x}_t^\top\right]^{-1} \cdot T^{-1/2}\sum_{t=1}^{T}u_t\mathbf{x}_t \stackrel{d}{\to} \boldsymbol{\Sigma}_{\mathbf{x}}^{-1}\mathbf{z}$$

Clearly $\boldsymbol{\Sigma}_{\mathbf{x}}^{-1}\mathbf{z}$ is Gaussian with zero mean. By symmetry of $\boldsymbol{\Sigma}_{\mathbf{x}}^{-1}$ (since $\boldsymbol{\Sigma}_{\mathbf{x}}$ is symmetric) the variance of $\boldsymbol{\Sigma}_{\mathbf{x}}^{-1}\mathbf{z}$ is

$$\boldsymbol{\Sigma}_{\mathbf{x}}^{-1}\,\mathrm{var}[\mathbf{z}]\,\boldsymbol{\Sigma}_{\mathbf{x}}^{-1} = \boldsymbol{\Sigma}_{\mathbf{x}}^{-1}\,\sigma^2\,\boldsymbol{\Sigma}_{\mathbf{x}}\,\boldsymbol{\Sigma}_{\mathbf{x}}^{-1} = \sigma^2\boldsymbol{\Sigma}_{\mathbf{x}}^{-1}$$

This completes the proof of theorem 13.1.3, conditional on (13.10). Let's now check that (13.10) is valid.

By the Cramér–Wold device (fact 6.1.6 on page 167), it suffices to show that for any $\mathbf{a} \in \mathbb{R}^K$ we have

$$\mathbf{a}^\top\left[T^{-1/2}\sum_{t=1}^{T}u_t\mathbf{x}_t\right] \stackrel{d}{\to} \mathbf{a}^\top\mathbf{z} \tag{13.11}$$

Fixing $\mathbf{a}$ and letting $m_t := u_t\mathbf{a}^\top\mathbf{x}_t$, the expression on the left of (13.11) can be rewritten as $T^{-1/2}\sum_{t=1}^{T}m_t$. Since $\mathcal{L}(\mathbf{z}) = \mathrm{N}(\mathbf{0}, \sigma^2\boldsymbol{\Sigma}_{\mathbf{x}})$, to establish (13.11) we need to show that

$$T^{-1/2}\sum_{t=1}^{T}m_t \stackrel{d}{\to} \mathrm{N}(0, \sigma^2\mathbf{a}^\top\boldsymbol{\Sigma}_{\mathbf{x}}\mathbf{a}) \tag{13.12}$$

From lemma 13.1.1 we know that $\{m_t\}$ is stationary with $\mathbb{E}[m_t^2] = \sigma^2\mathbf{a}^\top\boldsymbol{\Sigma}_{\mathbf{x}}\mathbf{a}$ and an MDS with respect to the filtration given in (13.5). By the martingale difference CLT on page 200, the result in (13.12) holds whenever

$$\frac{1}{T}\sum_{t=1}^{T}\mathbb{E}[m_t^2 \mid \mathscr{F}_{t-1}] \stackrel{p}{\to} \sigma^2\mathbf{a}^\top\boldsymbol{\Sigma}_{\mathbf{x}}\mathbf{a} \quad \text{as } T \to \infty \tag{13.13}$$

Since $\mathbf{x}_t \in \mathscr{F}_{t-1}$, we have

$$\mathbb{E}\,[m_t^2 \mid \mathscr{F}_{t-1}] = \mathbb{E}\,[u_t^2(\mathbf{a}^\top \mathbf{x}_t)^2 \mid \mathscr{F}_{t-1}] = (\mathbf{a}^\top \mathbf{x}_t)^2 \mathbb{E}\,[u_t^2 \mid \mathscr{F}_{t-1}] = \sigma^2(\mathbf{a}^\top \mathbf{x}_t)^2$$

Another way to write the last expression is $\sigma^2 \mathbf{a}^\top \mathbf{x}_t \mathbf{x}_t^\top \mathbf{a}$. The left-hand side of (13.13) is therefore

$$\frac{1}{T}\sum_{t=1}^{T} \mathbb{E}\,[m_t^2 \mid \mathscr{F}_{t-1}] = \frac{1}{T}\sum_{t=1}^{T} (\sigma^2 \mathbf{a}^\top \mathbf{x}_t \mathbf{x}_t^\top \mathbf{a}) = \sigma^2 \mathbf{a}^\top \left[\frac{1}{T}\sum_{t=1}^{T} \mathbf{x}_t \mathbf{x}_t^\top \right] \mathbf{a}$$

which converges in probability to $\sigma^2 \mathbf{a}^\top \boldsymbol{\Sigma}_{\mathbf{x}} \mathbf{a}$ by assumption 13.1.1 and fact 6.2.1. This verifies (13.13), completing the proof of theorem 13.1.3. □

Example 13.1.3 Consider again the scalar linear Gaussian AR(1) model $x_{t+1} = a x_t + w_{t+1}$ with $|a| < 1$ and $\{w_t\}$ IID and standard normal. Let $\{x_t\}$ be stationary. As discussed in §12.2.2, the OLS estimator of a is

$$\hat{a}_T := \frac{\mathbf{x}^\top \mathbf{y}}{\mathbf{x}^\top \mathbf{x}} \quad \text{where} \quad \mathbf{y} := (x_1, \ldots, x_T) \text{ and } \mathbf{x} := (x_0, \ldots, x_{T-1})$$

Both assumption 13.1.1 and assumption 13.1.2 are satisfied, so $\sqrt{T}(\hat{a}_T - a)$ converges in distribution to $\mathrm{N}(0, \sigma^2 \boldsymbol{\Sigma}_{\mathbf{x}}^{-1})$. In this case, $\sigma^2 = 1$ because the shocks are standard normal. Furthermore $\boldsymbol{\Sigma}_{\mathbf{x}}^{-1}$ reduces to $1/\mathbb{E}\,[x_1^2]$, where the expectation is under the stationary distribution. By (7.18) on page 190, we see that the stationary distribution is $\mathrm{N}(0, 1/(1-a^2))$. Hence the inverse of $\mathbb{E}\,[x_1^2]$ is $1 - a^2$, and

$$\sqrt{T}(\hat{a}_T - a) \xrightarrow{d} \mathrm{N}(0, 1 - a^2) \tag{13.14}$$

13.1.4 Large Sample Tests

In §12.1.4.1 we considered the problem of testing a hypothesis about an individual coefficient β_k. Let's consider this problem again in the large sample setting. The hypothesis to be tested is

$$H_0 \colon \beta_k = \beta_k^0$$

In §12.1.4.1 we showed that if the error terms are normally distributed, then the expression $(\hat{\beta}_k - \beta_k)/\operatorname{se}(\hat{\beta}_k)$ is t-distributed with $N - K$ degrees of freedom. In the large sample case, we can use the CLT to show that the same statistic is asymptotically normal.[1] The next theorem gives details.

1. This isn't surprising because the t-distribution converges to the standard normal distribution as the degrees of freedom converges to infinity. However, we can't use this result directly because our model assumptions are different.

Theorem 13.1.4 *Let assumptions 13.1.1 and 13.1.2 hold, and let*

$$\operatorname{se}(\hat{\beta}_k^T) := \sqrt{\hat{\sigma}_T^2 v_k(\mathbf{X})}$$

Under the null hypothesis H_0, we have

$$z_k^T := \frac{\hat{\beta}_k^T - \beta_k^0}{\operatorname{se}(\hat{\beta}_k^T)} \stackrel{d}{\to} \mathrm{N}(0,1) \quad \textit{as} \quad T \to \infty \tag{13.15}$$

In the theorem, $\hat{\sigma}_T$ is as defined in (13.8) on page 359 and $v_k(\mathbf{X})$ is the (k,k)th element of $(\mathbf{X}^\mathsf{T}\mathbf{X})^{-1}$.

Proof. Recall from theorem 13.1.3 that $\sqrt{T}(\hat{\boldsymbol{\beta}}_T - \boldsymbol{\beta}) \stackrel{d}{\to} \mathbf{z}$, where $\mathbf{z}$ is a random vector with distribution $\mathrm{N}(\mathbf{0}, \sigma^2 \boldsymbol{\Sigma}_\mathbf{x}^{-1})$ and $\boldsymbol{\beta}$ is the true parameter vector. It follows that

$$\sqrt{T}(\hat{\beta}_k^T - \beta_k) = \mathbf{e}_k^\mathsf{T}[\sqrt{T}(\hat{\boldsymbol{\beta}}_T - \boldsymbol{\beta})] \stackrel{d}{\to} \mathbf{e}_k^\mathsf{T}\mathbf{z}$$

The distribution of $\mathbf{e}_k^\mathsf{T}\mathbf{z}$ is $\mathrm{N}(0, \mathbf{e}_k^\mathsf{T} \operatorname{var}[\mathbf{z}]\mathbf{e}_k) = \mathrm{N}(0, \sigma^2 \mathbf{e}_k^\mathsf{T} \boldsymbol{\Sigma}_\mathbf{x}^{-1} \mathbf{e}_k)$, so

$$\frac{\sqrt{T}(\hat{\beta}_k^T - \beta_k)}{\sqrt{\sigma^2 \mathbf{e}_k^\mathsf{T} \boldsymbol{\Sigma}_\mathbf{x}^{-1} \mathbf{e}_k}} \stackrel{d}{\to} \mathrm{N}(0,1) \tag{13.16}$$

Applying (13.7) and (v) of fact 6.2.1 on page 170,

$$T v_k(\mathbf{X}) = T \mathbf{e}_k^\mathsf{T} (\mathbf{X}^\mathsf{T}\mathbf{X})^{-1} \mathbf{e}_k = \mathbf{e}_k^\mathsf{T} \left[\frac{1}{T} \sum_{t=1}^T \mathbf{x}_t \mathbf{x}_t^\mathsf{T} \right]^{-1} \mathbf{e}_k \stackrel{p}{\to} \mathbf{e}_k^\mathsf{T} \boldsymbol{\Sigma}_\mathbf{x}{}^{-1} \mathbf{e}_k$$

By theorem 13.1.2 we have $\hat{\sigma}_T^2 \stackrel{p}{\to} \sigma^2$, and hence

$$\sqrt{\hat{\sigma}_T^2 \, T v_k(\mathbf{X})} \stackrel{p}{\to} \sqrt{\sigma^2 \mathbf{e}_k^\mathsf{T} \boldsymbol{\Sigma}_\mathbf{x}{}^{-1} \mathbf{e}_k}$$

Combining this with (13.16) yields

$$\frac{\sqrt{T}(\hat{\beta}_k^T - \beta_k)}{\sqrt{\hat{\sigma}_T^2 \, T v_k(\mathbf{X})}} \stackrel{d}{\to} \mathrm{N}(0,1)$$

Assuming H_0 and canceling $\sqrt{T}$ gives (13.15). □

13.2 MLE for Markov Processes

Let's now turn to nonlinear estimation in a time series setting, using maximum likelihood. We will cover just the foundations of building and maximizing the likelihood.

13.2.1 The Likelihood Function

If we have IID observations from some common density, then, as we saw in §8.3.1, the likelihood function for that data is the product of the marginals evaluated at the sample. If, instead, the data contains dependence, the likelihood is more complex.

One intermediate case is Markov processes, the joint distribution of which was given in (7.17) on page 189. Suppose that the transition density $p_{\boldsymbol{\theta}}$ depends on some unknown parameter vector $\boldsymbol{\theta} \in \Theta$. Suppose further that the process has a unique stationary density $\pi_\infty^{\boldsymbol{\theta}}$ for all $\boldsymbol{\theta}$, and that $\mathbf{x}_1$ is a draw from this stationary density. Then the log-likelihood function is given by

$$\ell(\boldsymbol{\theta}) = \ln \pi_\infty^{\boldsymbol{\theta}}(\mathbf{x}_1) + \sum_{t=1}^{T-1} \ln p_{\boldsymbol{\theta}}(\mathbf{x}_{t+1} \,|\, \mathbf{x}_t)$$

In practice, it is usual to drop the first term in this expression, particularly when the data size is large, since the influence of a single element is likely to be negligible. In addition, even though the stationary density is formally defined by (7.19), for many processes, there is no known analytical expression for this density.[2] Here we'll follow this convention and, abusing notation slightly, write

$$\ell(\boldsymbol{\theta}) = \sum_{t=1}^{T-1} \ln p_{\boldsymbol{\theta}}(\mathbf{x}_{t+1} \,|\, \mathbf{x}_t) \tag{13.17}$$

13.2.1.1 Example: The ARCH Case

Let's look at a relatively simple case: the ARCH model from (7.5) on page 183. By (13.17), the log-likelihood function is

$$\ell(a, b) = \sum_{t=1}^{T-1} \left\{ -\frac{1}{2} \ln(2\pi(a + bx_t^2)) - \frac{x_{t+1}^2}{2(a + bx_t^2)} \right\} \tag{13.18}$$

2. It is still possible to compute the density numerically. See, for example, Stachurski and Martin (2008).

Rearranging, dropping terms that don't depend on a or b, and multiplying by 2 (an increasing transformation), we can rewrite this (abusing notation again) as

$$\ell(a,b) = -\sum_{t=1}^{T-1} \left\{ \ln z_t + \frac{x_{t+1}^2}{z_t} \right\} \quad \text{where} \quad z_t := a + bx_t^2 \tag{13.19}$$

Let's run some simulations to see what this function looks like. In the simulations we will set $T = 500$ and $a = b = 0.5$. Thus, we imagine the situation where, unbeknown to us, the true parameter values are $a = b = 0.5$, and we observe a time series $x_1, \ldots, x_{500}$ generated by these parameters. In order to estimate a and b, we form the likelihood function (13.19), and obtain the MLEs $\hat{a}$ and $\hat{b}$ as the vector $(\hat{a}, \hat{b})$ that maximizes $\ell(a, b)$.

Four different simulations of ℓ are given in figure 13.1. In each figure, a separate data set $x_1, \ldots, x_{500}$ is generated using the true parameter values $a = b = 0.5$ and the function ℓ in (13.19) is then plotted using contour lines and a color map. Lighter colors refer to larger values. The horizontal axis is a values, and the vertical axis is b values. The code for producing one of these figures (modulo randomness) is given in listing 11. The function `arch_like(theta, data)` represents ℓ in (13.19), with `theta` corresponding to (a, b) and `data` corresponding to the time series $x_1, \ldots, x_T$.

In each of the four simulations, a rough guess of the MLEs can be obtained just by looking for maximizers in the figures. For example, in simulation (a), the MLEs look to be around $\hat{a} = 0.44$ and $\hat{b} = 0.61$. To get more accurate estimates, we can use some form of analytical or numerical optimization. For this problem we don't have any analytical expressions for the MLEs because setting the two partial derivatives of ℓ in (13.19) to zero does not yield neat expressions for $\hat{a}$ and $\hat{b}$. However, there are many numerical routines we can use to obtain the MLEs for a given data set.

The simplest approach is to use one of `R`'s inbuilt optimization routines. For example, given the definition of `arch_like` in listing 11 and a sequence of observations $x_1, \ldots, x_T$ stored in a vector `xdata`, the function `arch_like` can be optimized numerically via the commands

```
start_theta <- c(0.65, 0.35)  # An initial guess of (a,b)
neg_like <- function(theta) {
    return(-arch_like(theta, xdata))  # xdata is the data
}
opt <- optim(start_theta, neg_like, method="BFGS")
```

Here `optim` is an built-in `R` function for numerical optimization of multivariate functions. Most built-in functions perform minimization rather than maximization and `optim` is no exception. For this reason the function that we pass to `optim` is `neg_like`, which is -1 times ℓ. The first argument to `optim` is a vector of starting values (a guess of the MLEs). The last argument tells `optim` to use the BFGS routine, which is variation on the Newton–Raphson algorithm. The return value of `optim` is a list, and the approximate minimizing vector is one element of this list (called `par`).

In this particular setup, for most realizations of the data and starting values, you will find that the algorithm converges to a good approximation to the global optimizer. However, there's no guarantee that it will. In case of problems, it's useful to know how these kinds of algorithms work, and how to code up simple implementations on your own. The next section will get you started.

13.2.2 The Newton–Raphson Algorithm

The Newton–Raphson algorithm is a *root-finding* algorithm. In other words, given a function $g\colon \mathbb{R} \to \mathbb{R}$, the algorithm searches for points $\bar{s} \in \mathbb{R}$ such that $g(\bar{s}) = 0$. Any root-finding algorithm can be used to optimize differentiable functions because, for differentiable functions, interior optimizers are always roots of the objective function's first derivative.

To describe the algorithm, let's begin with the root-finding problem and then specialize to optimization. To begin, let $g\colon \mathbb{R} \to \mathbb{R}$, and let s_0 be some initial point in $\mathbb{R}$ that we think (hope) is somewhere near a root. We don't know how to jump from s_0 straight to a root of g (otherwise, there would be no problem to solve), but what we can do is move to the root of the function that forms the *tangent line* to g at s_0. In other words, we replace g with its linear approximation around s_0, which is given by

$$\tilde{g}(s) := g(s_0) + g'(s_0)(s - s_0) \qquad (s \in \mathbb{R})$$

and solve for the root of $\tilde{g}$. This point is represented as s_1 in figure 13.2, and the value is easily seen to be $s_1 := s_0 - g(s_0)/g'(s_0)$. The point s_1 is taken as our next guess of the root, and the procedure is repeated, taking the tangent of g at s_1, solving for the root, and so on. This generates a sequence of points $\{s_k\}$ satisfying

$$s_{k+1} = s_k - \frac{g(s_k)}{g'(s_k)}$$

There are various results telling us that when g is suitably well-behaved and s_0 is sufficiently close to a given root $\bar{s}$, then sequence $\{s_k\}$ will converge to $\bar{s}$.[3]

To move from general root-finding to the specific problem of optimization, suppose now that $g\colon \mathbb{R} \to \mathbb{R}$ is a twice differentiable function we wish to maximize. We know that if s^* is a maximizer of g, then $g'(s^*) = 0$. Hence it is natural to begin

3. In practical situations we often have no way of knowing whether the conditions are satisfied, and there have been many attempts to make the procedure more robust. The R optimization routine described above is a child of this process.

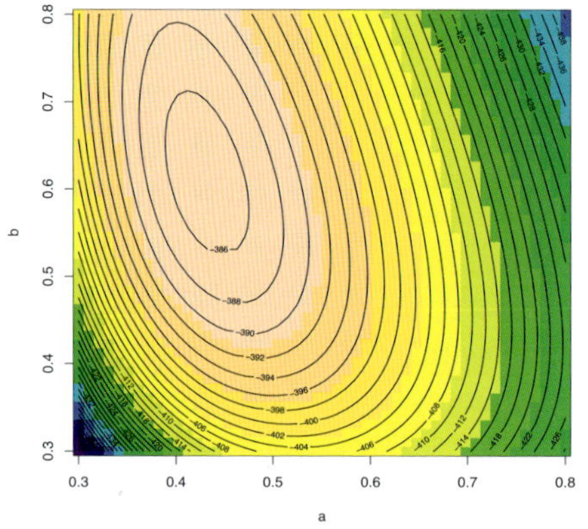

(a) Simulation 1

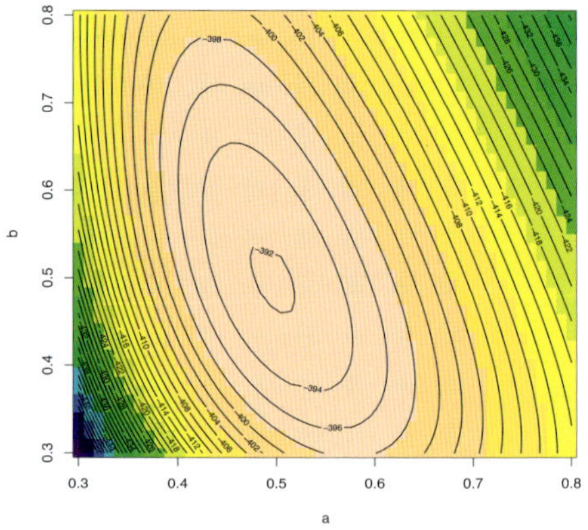

(b) Simulation 2

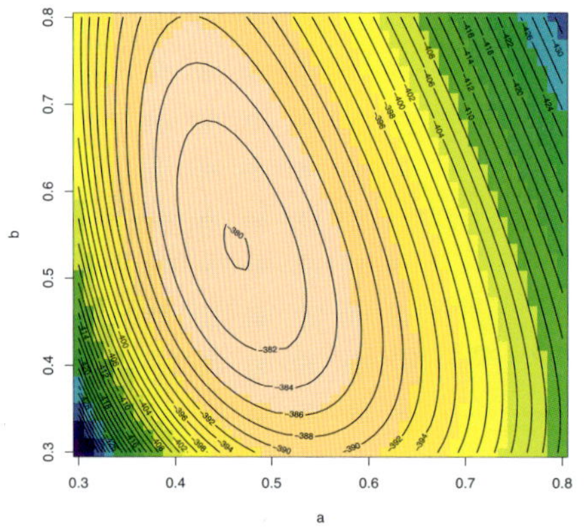

(c) Simulation 3

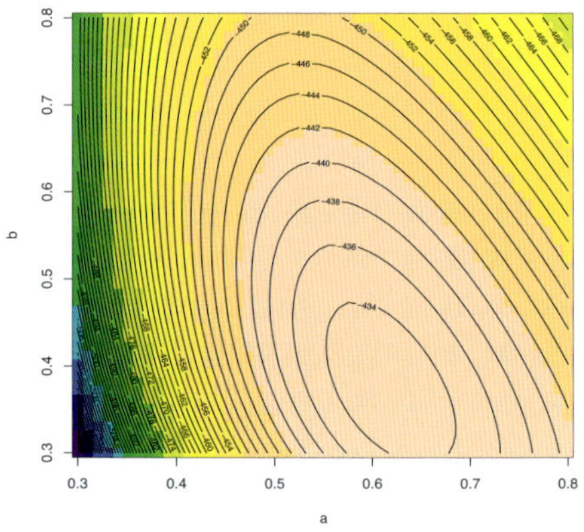

(d) Simulation 4

Figure 13.1 Simulations of the function (13.19) with $T = 500$

Listing 11 Code for figure 13.1 (R)

```
arch_like <- function(theta, data) {
    Y <- data[-1]              #  All but first element
    X <- data[-length(data)]   #  All but last element
    Z <- theta[1] + theta[2] * X^2
    return(-sum(log(Z) + Y^2 / Z))
}

sim_data <- function(a, b, n=500) {
    x <- numeric(n)
    x[1] = 0
    w = rnorm(n)
    for (t in 1:(n-1)) {
        x[t+1] = sqrt(a + b * x[t]^2) * w[t]
    }
    return(x)
}

xdata <- sim_data(0.5, 0.5)  #  True parameters

K <- 50
a <- seq(0.3, 0.8, length=K)
b <- seq(0.3, 0.8, length=K)
M <- matrix(nrow=K, ncol=K)
for (i in 1:K) {
    for (j in 1:K) {
        theta <- c(a[i], b[j])
        M[i,j] <- arch_like(theta, xdata)
    }
}
image(a, b, M, col=topo.colors(12))
contour(a, b, M, nlevels=40, add=T)
```

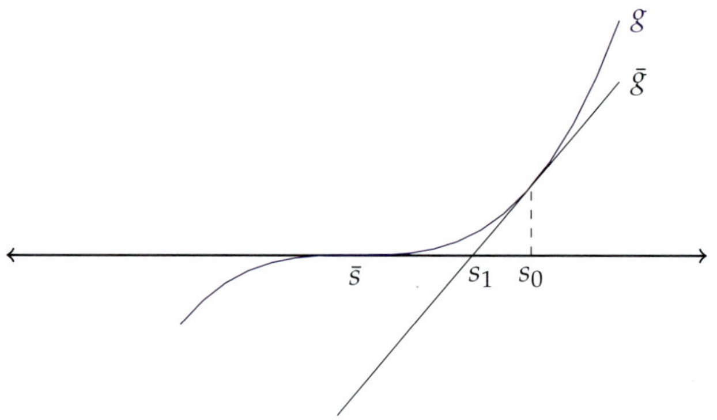

Figure 13.2 First step of the Newton–Raphson algorithm

our search for maximizers by looking for roots to this equation. This can be done by applying the Newton–Raphson algorithm to g', which yields the sequence

$$s_{k+1} = s_k - \frac{g'(s_k)}{g''(s_k)} \tag{13.20}$$

We can extend this algorithm to the multivariate case as well. Let's suppose that g is a function of two arguments. In particular, suppose that g is twice differentiable and $g \colon \mathbb{R}^2 \to \mathbb{R}$. The **gradient vector** and **Hessian** of g at $(x, y) \in \mathbb{R}^2$ are defined as

$$\nabla g(x,y) := \begin{pmatrix} g_1'(x,y) \\ g_2'(x,y) \end{pmatrix} \quad \text{and} \quad \nabla^2 g(x,y) := \begin{pmatrix} g_{11}''(x,y) & g_{12}''(x,y) \\ g_{21}''(x,y) & g_{22}''(x,y) \end{pmatrix}$$

Here g_i' is the first partial of g with respect to its ith argument, g_{ij}'' is the second cross-partial, and so on.

By analogy with (13.20), the Newton–Raphson algorithm for this two dimensional case is the algorithm that generates the sequence $\{(x_k, y_k)\}$ defined by

$$(x_{k+1}, y_{k+1}) = (x_k, y_k) - [\nabla^2 g(x_k, y_k)]^{-1} \nabla g(x_k, y_k) \tag{13.21}$$

from some initial guess (x_0, y_0).[4]

For the sake of the exercise, let's apply this to maximization of (13.19). Let z_t be as

4. We are assuming that the Hessian matrix is nonsingular.

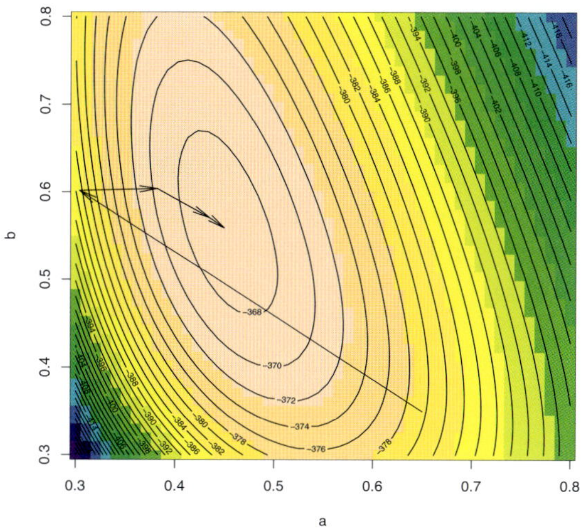

Figure 13.3 Newton–Raphson iterates

defined in (13.19). The first partials are then

$$\frac{\partial \ell}{\partial a}(a,b) = \sum_{t=1}^{T-1} \left[\frac{x_{t+1}^2}{z_t^2} - \frac{1}{z_t} \right], \quad \frac{\partial \ell}{\partial b}(a,b) = \sum_{t=1}^{T-1} x_t^2 \left[\frac{x_{t+1}^2}{z_t^2} - \frac{1}{z_t} \right]$$

while the second partials are

$$\frac{\partial^2 \ell}{\partial a^2}(a,b) = \sum_{t=1}^{T-1} \left[\frac{1}{z_t^2} - 2\frac{x_{t+1}^2}{z_t^3} \right], \quad \frac{\partial^2 \ell}{\partial b^2}(a,b) = \sum_{t=1}^{T-1} x_t^4 \left[\frac{1}{z_t^2} - 2\frac{x_{t+1}^2}{z_t^3} \right]$$

The cross-partial is

$$\frac{\partial^2 \ell}{\partial a \partial b}(a,b) = \sum_{t=1}^{T-1} x_t^2 \left[\frac{1}{z_t^2} - 2\frac{x_{t+1}^2}{z_t^3} \right]$$

From these expressions we can form the gradient vector and the Hessian, pick an initial guess, and iterate according to (13.21). Figure 13.3 shows four iterations of this procedure, starting from $(a_0, b_0) = (0.65, 0.35)$.[5] In this case the convergence is quick, and we are already close to the global optimum.

Replication of this figure (modulo randomness) is left as an exercise.

5. As before, the simulation uses $a = b = 0.5$ and $T = 500$.

13.3 Further Reading

Suitable topics for study after reading this chapter include GARCH models, hidden Markov models, Markov switching models, stochastic volatility models, factor models, and cointegration. High-quality textbook treatments of these and other topics in time series econometrics include Martin et al. (2012) and Hamilton (1994). Useful chapters on time series econometrics can be found in Hansen (2015) and Hayashi (2000). For a recent survey, see Diebold et al. (2009). For financial applications, see, for example, Ruppert (2011).

13.4 Exercises

Ex. 13.4.1 Let $\{x_t\}$ be the scalar AR(1) process $x_{t+1} = ax_t + w_{t+1}$, where $|a| < 1$ and $\{w_t\}$ is IID and standard normal. Let x_0 be drawn from the stationary distribution $\pi_\infty = \mathrm{N}(0, 1/(1-a^2))$. Show that

$$\frac{1}{\sqrt{T}} \sum_{t=1}^{T} x_t \xrightarrow{d} \mathrm{N}(0, v) \quad \text{where} \quad v := \frac{1}{(1-a)^2} \tag{13.22}$$

(Note how v increases in a, meaning that greater correlation makes it harder to estimate the mean of x_t via the sample mean. The intuition is that dependent data are less informative than independent data.)

Ex. 13.4.2 Recall that the sample variance is a consistent and asymptotically normal estimator of the variance of a distribution when the data are IID. A proof was given in example 9.2.11 on page 264. Now assume the conditions of exercise 13.4.1. While the data sequence $\{x_t\}$ is no longer IID, it is a stable Markov process. Using the proof in example 9.2.11 as a starting point, prove that asymptotic normality still holds. In particular, show that

$$\sqrt{T}\left\{s_T^2 - \mathrm{var}[x_t]\right\} \xrightarrow{d} \mathrm{N}(0, \gamma^2) \quad \text{where} \quad \gamma^2 := 2\frac{1+a^2}{(1-a^2)^3}$$

Note that this exercise involves substantial calculation.

Ex. 13.4.3 In example 13.1.1 it was claimed that the threshold process studied in that example satisfies all of the conditions of assumption 13.1.1. Verify that this is the case.

Ex. 13.4.4 Verify the claim that (13.4) holds when assumption 13.1.2 is valid.

Ex. 13.4.5 Let $K \times 1$ random vector $\hat{\boldsymbol{\theta}}_T$ be an estimator of $\boldsymbol{\theta}$. Suppose that this estimator is asymptotically normal, in the sense that

$$\sqrt{T}(\hat{\boldsymbol{\theta}}_T - \boldsymbol{\theta}) \stackrel{d}{\to} \mathrm{N}(\mathbf{0}, \mathbf{C})$$

where $\mathbf{C}$ is positive definite. By exercise 3.5.36, for such a $\mathbf{C}$ there exists a symmetric $K \times K$ matrix $\mathbf{D}$ such that $\mathbf{DCD} = \mathbf{I}$. Let $\hat{\mathbf{D}}_T$ be a consistent estimator of $\mathbf{D}$. Show that

$$T \| \hat{\mathbf{D}}_T(\hat{\boldsymbol{\theta}}_T - \boldsymbol{\theta}) \|^2 \stackrel{d}{\to} \chi^2(K) \tag{13.23}$$

Incidentally, (13.23) can be used to test the null hypothesis that $\boldsymbol{\theta} = \boldsymbol{\theta}_0$. Under the null hypothesis, we have

$$T \| \hat{\mathbf{D}}_T(\hat{\boldsymbol{\theta}}_T - \boldsymbol{\theta}_0) \|^2 \stackrel{d}{\to} \chi^2(K)$$

Fixing α and letting c be the $1 - \alpha$ quantile of the $\chi^2(K)$ distribution, we reject the null if $T \| \hat{\mathbf{D}}_T(\hat{\boldsymbol{\theta}}_T - \boldsymbol{\theta}_0) \|^2 > c$. This test is asymptotically of size α.

Ex. 13.4.6 Consider once more the scalar linear Gaussian AR(1) model $x_{t+1} = a x_t + w_{t+1}$ with $|a| < 1$ and $\{w_t\}$ IID and standard normal. In example 13.1.3 we saw that the OLS estimator $\hat{a}_T$ is a consistent and asymptotically normal estimator of a, with asymptotic variance $1 - a^2$. Let's now look at another consistent and asymptotically normal estimate of a and compare its performance with the OLS estimator in terms of asymptotic variance (with small variance being better).

For this second estimator, we can exploit the fact that the sample variance converges to the stationary variance of x_t, which in this case is $1/(1 - a^2)$. Once we estimate the variance with the sample variance, we can solve for the value of a. The exercise is to formalize this idea, and show that

$$\sqrt{T}(a_T^* - a) \stackrel{d}{\to} \mathrm{N}\left(0, (1 - a^2)\left(1 + \frac{1 - a^2}{2a^2}\right)\right) \tag{13.24}$$

where a_T^* is the estimator just described. Comments:

- The exercise shows that the OLS estimator has lower asymptotic variance than a_T^* (cf. (13.14) on page 361). We say that the OLS estimator is **relatively more efficient**.

- In attempting the exercise, you should first consult exercise 13.4.2 on page 370.

13.4.1 Solutions to Selected Exercises

Solution to Ex. 13.4.1. Let $\{x_t\}$ be as in the statement of the problem. The claim is that (13.22) holds. To see this, apply (7.27) on page 194. (All the relevant conditions are satisfied; see, in particular, example 7.2.10 on page 195. Observe also that the stationary distribution $\pi_\infty = \mathrm{N}(0, 1/(1-a^2))$ has finite moments of all orders.) This gives

$$\frac{1}{\sqrt{T}} \sum_{t=1}^{T} x_t = \sqrt{T} \left[\frac{1}{T} \sum_{t=1}^{T} x_t \right] = \sqrt{T} \left[\frac{1}{T} \sum_{t=1}^{T} x_t - \int s \pi_\infty(s) \, \mathrm{d}s \right] \stackrel{d}{\to} \mathrm{N}(0, v)$$

where, from (7.28),

$$v = \mathrm{var}[x_0] + 2 \sum_{t=1}^{\infty} \mathrm{cov}[x_0, x_t]$$

Recall here that $\mathcal{L}(x_0) = \mathrm{N}(0, 1/(1-a^2))$, so this becomes

$$v = \frac{1}{1-a^2} + 2 \sum_{t=1}^{\infty} a^t \mathbb{E}[x_0^2] = \frac{1}{1-a^2} + \frac{2}{1-a^2} \sum_{t=1}^{\infty} a^t = \frac{1}{1-a^2} + \frac{2a}{(1-a)(1-a^2)}$$

Here the first equality follows from the discussion of correlation in §7.2.4. Simplifying the right-hand side gives $v = 1/(1-a)^2$ as claimed. □

Solution to Ex. 13.4.2. In this exercise we are assuming that $x_{t+1} = a x_t + w_{t+1}$ where $|a| < 1$, $\{w_t\}$ is IID and standard normal, and $\mathcal{L}(x_0) = \pi_\infty = \mathrm{N}(0, 1/(1-a^2))$. (The stationary distribution was obtained on page 193.) The aim is to show that

$$\sqrt{T} \left\{ s_T^2 - \frac{1}{1-a^2} \right\} \stackrel{d}{\to} \mathrm{N}(0, \gamma^2) \quad \text{where} \quad \gamma^2 := 2 \frac{1+a^2}{(1-a^2)^3} \tag{13.25}$$

Letting $v := 1/(1-a^2)$, note from the manipulations in example 9.2.11 that it suffices to prove that

$$\sqrt{T} \left\{ \frac{1}{T} \sum_{t=1}^{T} x_t^2 - v \right\} \stackrel{d}{\to} \mathrm{N}(0, \gamma^2) \tag{13.26}$$

All of the conditions of theorem 7.2.2 on page 193 are satisfied, and we apply the resulting CLT in (7.27) with $h(x) = x^2$ to get (13.26) with

$$\gamma^2 := \mathbb{E}[(x_0^2 - v)^2] + 2 \sum_{t=1}^{\infty} \mathbb{E}[(x_0^2 - v)(x_t^2 - v)] \tag{13.27}$$

To check (13.25) it only remains to show that this expression for γ^2 matches that in

(13.25). To see this, consider the first term on the right-hand side of (13.27). We have

$$\mathbb{E}\left[(x_0^2 - v)^2\right] = \mathbb{E}\left[x_0^4\right] - 2v\mathbb{E}\left[x_0^2\right] + v^2 = 2v^2$$

(The fourth moment of the distribution $N(0, \sigma^2)$ is $3\sigma^4$.) For the second term on the right-hand side of (13.27), we have

$$\mathbb{E}\left[(x_0^2 - v)(x_t^2 - v)\right] = \mathbb{E}\left[x_0^2 x_t^2\right] - v^2 = \mathbb{E}\left\{x_0^2[a^t x_0 + s(w)]^2\right\} - v^2$$

for $s(w) := \sum_{i=1}^t a^{t-i} w_i$. Note that $s(w)$ and x_0 is independent. (For a Markov process, the initial condition is always assumed to be independent of the shocks.) Working through all the algebra, we get

$$\mathbb{E}\left[(x_0^2 - v)(x_t^2 - v)\right] = 2a^{2t}v^2$$

Returning to (13.27) we have

$$\gamma^2 = 2v^2 + 2\sum_{t=1}^{\infty} 2a^{2t}v^2 = 2v^2 + 4\frac{a^2}{1-a^2}v^2 \tag{13.28}$$

Using $v = 1/(1-a^2)$ and working through the remaining algebra will get you to the expression for γ^2 in (13.25). □

Solution to Ex. 13.4.3. Let $\pi_\infty(s) = 2\phi(s)\Phi(qs)$, where $q := a(1-a^2)^{-1/2}$, ϕ is the standard normal density and Φ is the standard normal CDF. The process $\{x_t\}$ studied in example 13.4.3 is identically distributed as a result of our assumption that $\mathcal{L}(x_0) = \pi_\infty$ (see fact 7.2.5 on page 191). It remains to check the conditions on $\boldsymbol{\Sigma}_{\mathbf{x}}$. In the present case,

$$\boldsymbol{\Sigma}_{\mathbf{x}} = \mathbb{E}\left[x_t^2\right] = \int_{-\infty}^{\infty} s^2 \pi_\infty(s)\,ds = \int_{-\infty}^{\infty} s^2 2\phi(s)\Phi(qs)\,ds$$

To verify that $\boldsymbol{\Sigma}_{\mathbf{x}}$ is positive definite, we need to check that the term on the right-hand side is strictly positive. This is clearly true, because the function inside the integral is strictly positive everywhere but zero. To be careful, we should also check that $\boldsymbol{\Sigma}_{\mathbf{x}}$ is finite, and this is also true because $\Phi(qs) \leqslant 1$, and hence

$$\int_{-\infty}^{\infty} s^2 2\phi(s)\Phi(qs)\,ds \leqslant \int_{-\infty}^{\infty} s^2 2\phi(s)\,ds = 2\int_{-\infty}^{\infty} s^2\phi(s)\,ds = 2$$

Last, we need to show that

$$\frac{1}{T}\sum_{t=1}^{T} x_t^2 \xrightarrow{p} \mathbf{\Sigma}_{\mathbf{x}} = \mathbb{E}\left[x_t^2\right] \tag{13.29}$$

Since the conditions of theorem 7.2.2 (page 193) are satisfied, the convergence in (13.29) is valid. □

Solution to Ex. 13.4.4. Suppose that assumption 13.1.2 (page 357) is valid. We need to show that

$$\mathbb{E}\left[u_s u_t \,|\, \mathbf{x}_1, \ldots, \mathbf{x}_t\right] = \begin{cases} \sigma^2 & \text{if} \quad s = t \\ 0 & \text{if} \quad s < t \end{cases}$$

On one hand, if $s = t$, then $\mathbb{E}\left[u_t^2 \,|\, \mathbf{x}_1, \ldots, \mathbf{x}_t\right] = \mathbb{E}\left[u_t^2\right] = \sigma^2$ by independence. On the other hand, if $s < t$, then

$$\begin{aligned} \mathbb{E}\left[u_s u_t \,|\, \mathbf{x}_1, \ldots, \mathbf{x}_t\right] &= \mathbb{E}\left[\mathbb{E}\left[u_s u_t \,|\, \mathbf{x}_1, \ldots, \mathbf{x}_t, u_s\right] \,|\, \mathbf{x}_1, \ldots, \mathbf{x}_t\right] \\ &= \mathbb{E}\left[u_s \mathbb{E}\left[u_t \,|\, \mathbf{x}_1, \ldots, \mathbf{x}_t, u_s\right] \,|\, \mathbf{x}_1, \ldots, \mathbf{x}_t\right] \\ &= \mathbb{E}\left[u_s \mathbb{E}\left[u_t\right] \,|\, \mathbf{x}_1, \ldots, \mathbf{x}_t\right] \\ &= \mathbb{E}\left[u_s 0 \,|\, \mathbf{x}_1, \ldots, \mathbf{x}_t\right] = 0 \end{aligned}$$

□

Solution to Ex. 13.4.5. By assumption we have $\hat{\mathbf{D}}_T \xrightarrow{p} \mathbf{D}$ and $\sqrt{T}(\hat{\boldsymbol{\theta}}_T - \boldsymbol{\theta}) \xrightarrow{d} \mathbf{z}$, where $\mathcal{L}(\mathbf{z}) = \text{N}(\mathbf{0}, \mathbf{C})$. Applying Slutsky's theorem, we obtain

$$\hat{\mathbf{D}}_T \sqrt{T}(\hat{\boldsymbol{\theta}}_T - \boldsymbol{\theta}) \xrightarrow{d} \mathbf{Dz} \tag{13.30}$$

Clearly $\mathbf{Dz}$ is normally distributed with mean $\mathbf{0}$. Moreover

$$\text{var}[\mathbf{Dz}] = \mathbf{D}\,\text{var}[\mathbf{z}]\mathbf{D}^\top = \mathbf{DCD} = \mathbf{I}$$

In other words, $\mathbf{Dz}$ is standard normal. As a result, $\|\mathbf{Dz}\|^2 \sim \chi^2(K)$. Applying the continuous mapping theorem to (13.30), we obtain

$$\|\hat{\mathbf{D}}_T \sqrt{T}(\hat{\boldsymbol{\theta}}_T - \boldsymbol{\theta})\|^2 \xrightarrow{d} \|\mathbf{Dz}\|^2 \sim \chi^2(K)$$

This is equivalent to (13.23). □

Solution to Ex. 13.4.6. Let $v := 1/(1 - a^2)$, the asymptotic variance of x_t. We can solve this for a to get

$$a = g(v) \quad \text{for} \quad g(v) := \sqrt{1 - \frac{1}{v}}$$

We take as our estimator a_T^* the statistic $g(s_T^2)$, where s_T^2 is the sample variance. We then have

$$\sqrt{T}(a_T^* - a) = \sqrt{T}\{g(s_T^2) - g(v)\}$$

Applying the delta method (see page 173) combined with the result in exercise 13.4.2 we have

$$\sqrt{T}(a_T^* - a) \stackrel{d}{\to} \mathrm{N}(0, g'(v)^2\gamma^2) \quad \text{where} \quad \gamma^2 := 2\frac{1+a^2}{(1-a^2)^3}$$

Using the definition of v and a bit of algebra leads to the expression on the right-hand side of (13.24). □

Chapter 14

Regularization

In several sections of this book we touched on the topic of regularization (see, e.g., §8.2.1.2 and §8.2.3). A variety of statistical procedures and machine learning algorithms employ regularization (under different names) to improve out-of-sample fit. Good out-of-sample fit means generalization from observed data, which, as we've stressed before, is the key problem of statistics. This chapter introduces a number of methods that use regularization and discusses their statistical properties.

14.1 Nonparametric Density Estimation

Nonparametric density estimation is an application of regularization to the problem of recovering distributions from data. It combines the data with a prior belief that probability mass most likely falls in places other than just the sample points observed so far. As well as being of interest from a theoretical perspective, nonparametric density estimation is used in a great variety of applied studies. We begin our analysis with a review of parametric density estimation and then proceed to nonparametric methods.

14.1.1 Introduction

Suppose our data consist of IID observations $\mathbf{x}_1, \ldots, \mathbf{x}_N$ from unknown distribution P on $\mathbb{R}^d$. We assume throughout this section that P is absolutely continuous. Our aim is to estimate the density of P, denoted below by f.

We know how to do this in a parametric setting. For example, let's add the assumption that f belongs to the class of normal densities on $\mathbb{R}$, so that $f = f(\cdot\,; \mu, \sigma) =$ the normal density for distribution $\mathrm{N}(\mu, \sigma^2)$. The MLEs of the parameters are $\hat{\mu}_N :=$

$\bar{x}_N$ and $\hat{\sigma}_N := s_N$ (see page 235). Plugging these back into f gives density estimate $f(\cdot\,; \bar{x}_N, s_N)$. Since $\bar{x}_N$ and s_N are consistent (see §9.2.4), the random density $f(\cdot\,; \bar{x}_N, s_N)$ will be close to $f(\cdot\,; \mu, \sigma)$ with high probability for large N.

We can clarify convergence of the densities themselves if we extend the notion of consistency from vectors to densities. To extend consistency to densities we need a notion of global deviation between densities. Perhaps the most important measures of global distance are the L_p distances. Let's now define and discuss them.

For any $\mathscr{B}$-measurable function $f\colon \mathbb{R}^d \to \mathbb{R}$ and $p \geqslant 1$, we set

$$\|f\|_p := \left\{ \int |f|^p \right\}^{1/p} := \left\{ \int |f(\mathbf{s})|^p \, \mathrm{d}\mathbf{s} \right\}^{1/p} \tag{14.1}$$

where integration is over all of $\mathbb{R}^d$. If this expression is finite, then we write $f \in L_p$. For densities f and g on $\mathbb{R}^d$ the L_p distance between these densities is then defined as

$$d_p(f, g) := \|f - g\|_p \tag{14.2}$$

The norm $\|\cdot\|_p$ satisfies most of the properties of the norms we've met so far. For example, we have the triangle inequality

$$\|f - g\|_p \leqslant \|f - h\|_p + \|h - g\|_p \tag{14.3}$$

for all $p \geqslant 1$ and $f, g, h \in L_p$. See, for example, theorem 5.1.5 of Dudley (2002).

Specializing to $p = 1$ gives the L_1 distance, which sums over absolute deviation. Specializing to $p = 2$ gives the popular L_2 distance, which is a variation of the L_2 distance we used in §5.2.2. See, in particular, (5.28) on page 142, where distance between random variables is evaluated based on expected deviation.

The L_2 distance is popular largely because it's so tractable, and because it's similarity to Euclidean vector distance means that we have L_2 analogies for a variety of fundamental results on vector space. Nevertheless, the L_1 distance is arguably a better choice for studying deviation between densities. For example, the L_1 distance between densities is always well-defined (see ex. 14.4.1), which is essential if one hopes to provide universal consistency results.

Fact 14.1.1 **Scheffés lemma**: If $\{f_n\}$ and f are densities on $\mathbb{R}^d$, then

$$f_n(\mathbf{s}) \to f(\mathbf{s}) \text{ for all } \mathbf{s} \text{ in } \mathbb{R}^d \quad \Longrightarrow \quad \|f_n - f\|_1 \to 0$$

Fact 14.1.2 For any densities f, g and h on $\mathbb{R}^d$ we have

(i) $\|f - g\|_1 \leqslant \sqrt{2D(f, g)}$, where $D(f, g)$ is the KL deviation defined in (8.34), and

(ii) $\|f - g\|_1 = 2 \sup_{B \in \mathscr{B}(\mathbb{R}^d)} \left| \int_B f - \int_B g \right|$.

The bound in (i) is called **Pinsker's inequality**, while (ii) is called **Scheffé's identity**. Scheffé's identity tells us that L_1 distance measures something that we directly care about: when L_1 deviation is small, so is the maximal deviation between probabilities assigned to events.[1]

In what follows, we will say that a sequence $\{\hat{f}_N\}$ of random densities on $\mathbb{R}^d$ is **L_p-consistent** for a density f on $\mathbb{R}^d$ if

$$\|\hat{f}_N - f\|_p \xrightarrow{p} 0 \quad \text{as} \quad N \to \infty$$

Example 14.1.1 Let $\hat{f}_N = f(\cdot\,; \bar{x}_N, s_N)$ be the Nth element of the sequence of normal densities described above, where $x_1, \ldots, x_N$ are independent draws from a normal density $f = f(\cdot\,; \mu, \sigma)$ and $\bar{x}_N$ and s_N the sample mean and standard deviation respectively. This sequence of densities is L_1-consistent for f. See exercise 14.4.3.

14.1.1.1 Failure of Consistency

The risk with the parametric approach is that the parametric assumption is incorrect, in the sense that the parametric class doesn't contain the density generating the data or any good approximation. If this is the case, a parametric approach is typically not consistent. More precisely, if we estimate f with parametric class $\{f_\theta\}_{\theta \in \Theta}$, then the L_p deviation between our estimate and f is bounded below by

$$\delta(f) := \inf_{\theta \in \Theta} \|f - f_\theta\|_p \tag{14.4}$$

This value will be zero only when f can be attained as the limit of elements of $\{f_\theta\}_{\theta \in \Theta}$.

Example 14.1.2 Consider again the setting of 14.1.1 but now suppose that the true density f is not Gaussian. Then either the sequence $\hat{f}_N$ is not L_1-consistent for any density, or, if it is L_1-consistent for some density, then that density is not f. The reason is that $\delta(f)$ in (14.4) is always positive when the parametric class is Gaussian and f is not, since the set of normal densities is closed under the taking of limits in L_1.

14.1.2 Kernel Density Estimation

Sometimes we can make good choices for parametric classes by using descriptive statistics or by appealing to some theory with sharp quantitative implications. At other times this is difficult. In such settings it is best to use a nonparametric approach that is consistent under weaker assumptions.

1. For a proof, see p. 39 of Devroye and Lugosi (2001).

Let's start with an intuitive discussion and then turn to theory. Suppose that we have IID data $\mathbf{x}_1, \ldots, \mathbf{x}_N$ generated from unknown density f on $\mathbb{R}^d$. To estimate f using the data we will employ a **kernel density estimator** (KDE), which takes the form

$$\hat{f}_N(\mathbf{s}) := \frac{1}{Nh^d} \sum_{n=1}^{N} K\left(\frac{\mathbf{s} - \mathbf{x}_n}{h}\right) \tag{14.5}$$

Here K is called the **kernel function** of the estimator, and h is called the **bandwidth**. The kernel function K is required to be a density on $\mathbb{R}^d$ but is otherwise unrestricted. The bandwidth h is any positive number. Exercise 14.4.4 asks you to confirm that $\hat{f}_N$ is always a density.

To get a feeling for the estimate $\hat{f}_N$ in (14.5), let's look at a simple instance created from just three data points x_1, x_2, x_3 on $\mathbb{R}$. For K we take the standard normal density. Since $N = 3$, the function $\hat{f}_N$ is the sum of three individual functions, the nth of which can be written as

$$g_n(s) = \frac{1}{Nh} K\left(\frac{s - x_n}{h}\right) = \frac{1}{Nh} \frac{1}{\sqrt{2\pi}} \exp\left\{-\frac{(s - x_n)^2}{2h^2}\right\}$$

This is $\frac{1}{N}$ times the density of a $\mathrm{N}(x_n, h^2)$ random variable. So the three functions g_n are smooth bumps, each centered on one of the data points and with the degree of concentration around x_n governed by h. The top panel of figure 14.1 shows these three functions along with the data points for when $h = 1$. The black line is the pointwise sum of these functions, which is the density estimate $\hat{f}_N$. By construction, it is large near the data points and small away from data points.

The lower panel of figure 14.1 shows the same functions when the bandwidth is increased to 1.4. Each g_n becomes more spread out, and the sum $\hat{f}_N$ is smoother.

As discussed in more detail below, the role of the bandwidth is to add smoothing to the empirical distribution, so we can generalize from a finite sample. But what is the right amount of smoothing? Figure 14.2 illustrates the trade-off associated with smoothing. The shaded distribution is the density f, which we imagine to be unknown. 40 observations are drawn from this distribution and represented as dots. The black line in each panel is the KDE $\hat{f}_N$ built from these observations. The kernel is the standard normal density again, while the bandwidth varies across the panels.

As the bandwidth goes to zero, the kernel density becomes similar to the empirical distribution, with all probability mass in very small regions around the sample points. Hence, when we use a very small bandwidth , we make the mistake of treating the empirical distribution as the true distribution. This is overfitting. At the same time, excessive smoothing adds too much bias, hiding the features of the true distribution.[2]

2. Figure 14.2 is produced using `scikit-learn`. See `johnstachurski.net/emet.html` for code. In R, KDEs

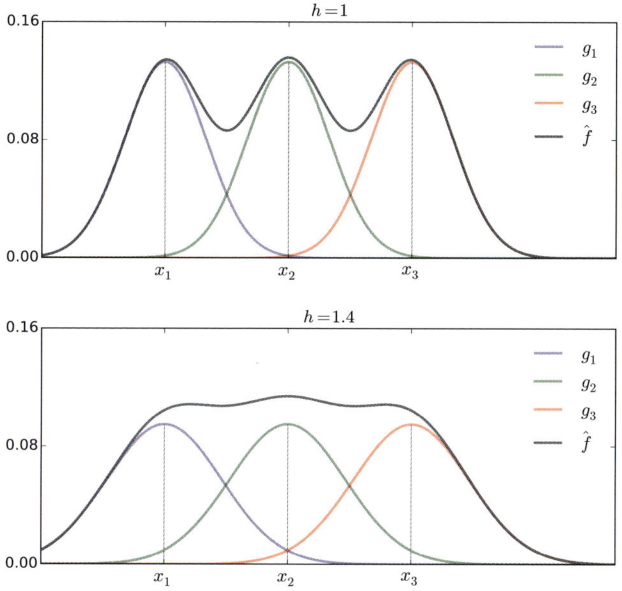

Figure 14.1 Nonparametric KDE, different bandwidths

The optimal bandwidth in terms of minimizing L_p deviation depends on the the unknown density f. For example, if f is smooth, then a relatively large bandwidth should be used. Of course f is unknown. As such there are two standard approaches. One is to make assumptions on f and choose the bandwidth accordingly. Another is to use cross-validation. For a review of both procedures see Scott (2015). We'll say more about cross-validation in the context of ridge regression below.

14.1.3 Theory

A natural way to study kernel density estimates is via the notion of convolutions. The convolution of an arbitrary distribution Q and a density K on $\mathbb{R}^d$ is the density on $\mathbb{R}^d$ defined by

$$(K \star Q)(\mathbf{s}') = \int K(\mathbf{s}' - \mathbf{s})Q(d\mathbf{s}) \qquad (\mathbf{s}' \in \mathbb{R}^d) \tag{14.6}$$

We already encountered this concept in the discrete case in exercise 5.4.10 on page 155, where you were asked to prove a version of

---

can be constructed from the `density` function. Try, for example, `plot(density(runif(200)))`.

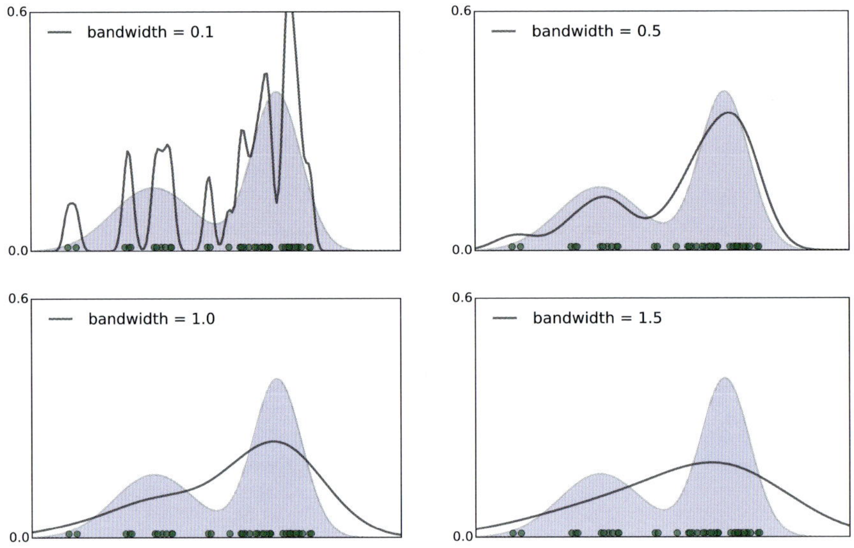

Figure 14.2 Effect of changing the bandwidth

Fact 14.1.3 For any density K and arbitrary distribution Q on $\mathbb{R}^d$, the density $K \star Q$ equals $\mathcal{L}(\mathbf{x} + \mathbf{y})$ when $\mathbf{x}$ and $\mathbf{y}$ are independent with $\mathcal{L}(\mathbf{x}) = K$ and $\mathcal{L}(\mathbf{y}) = Q$.

Example 14.1.3 If $K = \mathrm{N}(0, \sigma^2)$ for some $\sigma > 0$ and Q is a distribution on $\mathbb{R}$ that puts mass q_n on points $s_1, \ldots, s_N$, then by (14.6) and the rule for integrating over discrete distributions (see (5.14) on page 134),

$$(K \star Q)(s') = \sum_{n=1}^{N} K(s' - s_n) q_n \tag{14.7}$$

This distribution is a mixture of normals. Exercise 14.4.5 illustrates the connection between (14.7) and fact 14.1.3.

We will be particularly interested in a certain class of convolutions, induced by densities of the form

$$K_h(\mathbf{s}) := \frac{1}{h^d} K\left(\frac{\mathbf{s}}{h}\right) \tag{14.8}$$

where K is any density and $h > 0$ is a parameter. The density K_h in (14.8) is the density of $h\mathbf{x}$ when $\mathbf{x}$ is a random vector on $\mathbb{R}^d$ with density K. (See ex. 14.4.6.)

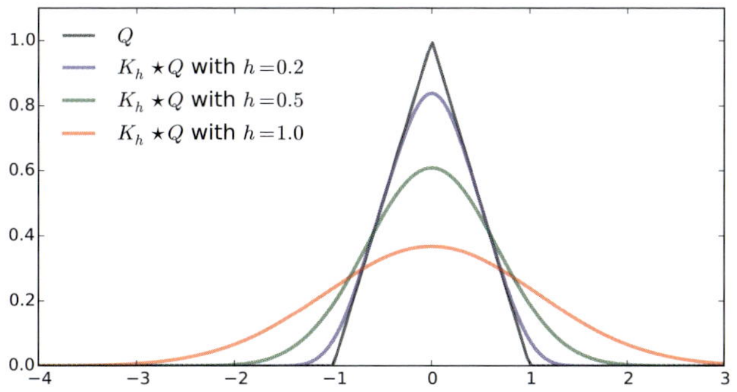

Figure 14.3 Smoothing induced by convolutions

Example 14.1.4 Figure 14.3 shows the convolution of a tent-shaped distribution Q and K_h when K is the standard normal density and h takes different values.

Note how in figure 14.3 the distribution of $K_h \star Q$ is close to Q when h is near zero. This makes sense, since $K_h \star Q$ is the distribution of $x + hy$ where x is drawn from Q and y is standard normal. As we take $h \downarrow 0$, the distribution of $x + hy$ converges to the distribution of x. In fact this is always true:

Fact 14.1.4 Let f and K be any densities on $\mathbb{R}^d$, and let K_h be defined from K via (14.8). If $f \in L_p$, then $K_h \star f \in L_p$, and

$$\lim_{h \downarrow 0} \|K_h \star f - f\|_p = 0$$

For a proof, see theorem 9.1 of Devroye and Lugosi (2001).

14.1.3.1 Convolution and KDEs

Let h be a positive number and let K_h be as defined in (14.8). Using this notation, we can rewrite the KDE in (14.5) as $\hat{f}_N(\mathbf{s}) = \frac{1}{N} \sum_{n=1}^{N} K_h(\mathbf{s} - \mathbf{x}_n)$. Letting $\hat{P}_N$ denote the empirical distribution of the sample and recalling the expression for integrals with respect to $\hat{P}_N$ (see page 219), we can also write this as $\hat{f}_N(\mathbf{s}') = \int K_h(\mathbf{s}' - \mathbf{s}) \hat{P}_N(d\mathbf{s})$, or, more simply,

$$\hat{f}_N = K_h \star \hat{P}_N \tag{14.9}$$

This equation says something interesting. In §8.2.1.2 we first tried to estimate the density by a naive application of the sample analogue principle. The method failed. In (14.9) we have an alternative method that employs smoothing, or regularization.

We apply the "smoothing operator" $K_h\star$ in addition to replacing the target distribution with the empirical distribution. As the next section shows, this method can be successful under very mild assumptions.

14.1.3.2 Consistency

It can be proved that, for *any* density f and kernel K, the nonparametric kernel density estimator $\hat{f}_N$ is L_1-consistent for f. See theorem 9.2 of Devroye and Lugosi (2001). The L_1 proof involves a large amount of measure-theoretic machinery. Here we'll state and prove the corresponding L_2 result instead.

Theorem 14.1.1 *Let f and K be densities on $\mathbb{R}^d$ and elements of L_2. If*

(i) $\{\mathbf{x}_n\}_{n\geqslant 1}$ is an IID *sequence of draws from f, and*

(ii) the bandwidth sequence $\{h_N\}$ satisfies $h_N \to 0$ and $Nh_N^d \to \infty$ as $N \to \infty$,

then the sequence of density estimates $\{\hat{f}_N\}$ defined in (14.5) *is L_2-consistent for f.*

Let's break this claim down into smaller pieces. For the remainder of this section, $\|\cdot\|$ is the L_2 norm and $h := h_N$. Using the expression for $\hat{f}_N$ in (14.9) and the triangle inequality in (14.3), we have

$$\|\hat{f}_N - f\| \leqslant \|K_h \star \hat{P}_N - K_h \star f\| + \|K_h \star f - f\| \tag{14.10}$$

The first term is called the **estimation error**, and the second is called the **approximation error** or **bias**. The first error is caused by the fact that we only observe the empirical distribution $\hat{P}_N$ rather than the true distribution f. The second error is caused by the smoothing we deliberately added to control the estimation error. (Compare with the error decomposition on page 304.)

The fact that $h_N \to 0$ in condition (ii) of theorem 14.1.1 means that we shrink the amount of smoothing as the sample size increases, thereby reducing the approximation error. The requirement $Nh_N^d \to \infty$ ensures that smoothing is not reduced too quickly, allowing us to control estimation error.

One way to think about the relationship between inference and the sample is that, when viewed as a "generalized density" with all its mass on data points, the empirical distribution is too rough. To generalize we need to add smoothing. At the same time, the need for smoothing decreases as the sample size gets large.

Proof of theorem 14.1.1. By fact 14.1.4, the approximation error converges to zero under the conditions of theorem 14.1.1. Hence it suffices to show that the estimation error converges in probability to zero. Fix $\delta > 0$. By Chebyshev's inequality (see page 96), we have

$$\mathbb{P}\left\{\|K_h \star \hat{P}_N - K_h \star f\| \geqslant \delta\right\} = \mathbb{P}\left\{\|K_h \star \hat{P}_N - K_h \star f\|^2 \geqslant \delta^2\right\} \leqslant \frac{\xi_N}{\delta^2}$$

where

$$\xi_N := \mathbb{E}\left\{\|K_h \star \hat{P}_N - K_h \star f\|^2\right\}$$

To complete the proof, we need only show that ξ_N converges to zero. Let

$$\bar{K}_N(\mathbf{s}) := (K_h \star \hat{P}_N)(\mathbf{s}) - (K_h \star f)(\mathbf{s}) = \frac{1}{N}\sum_{n=1}^{N}\{K_h(\mathbf{s}-\mathbf{x}_n) - \mathbb{E}[K_h(\mathbf{s}-\mathbf{x}_n)]\}$$

We can then write

$$\xi_N = \mathbb{E}\left\{\int [\bar{K}_N(\mathbf{s})]^2\,\mathrm{d}\mathbf{s}\right\} = \int \mathbb{E}\left\{[\bar{K}_N(\mathbf{s})]^2\right\}\mathrm{d}\mathbf{s} \tag{14.11}$$

(The interchange of order of expectation and integration is valid for nonnegative integrands—see theorem 4.4.5 of Dudley (2002).) Since $\bar{K}_N(\mathbf{s})$ is the sample mean of N IID zero-mean random variables, we have

$$\mathbb{E}\left\{[\bar{K}_N(\mathbf{s})]^2\right\} = \mathrm{var}\left[\bar{K}_N(\mathbf{s})\right] = \frac{1}{N}\mathrm{var}[K_h(\mathbf{s}-\mathbf{x}_n)]$$

Moreover

$$\mathrm{var}[K_h(\mathbf{s}-\mathbf{x}_n)] = \mathbb{E}\left\{[K_h(\mathbf{s}-\mathbf{x}_n)]^2\right\} - \{\mathbb{E}[K_h(\mathbf{s}-\mathbf{x}_n)]\}^2 \leqslant \mathbb{E}\left\{[K_h(\mathbf{s}-\mathbf{x}_n)]^2\right\}$$

In summary,

$$\xi_N \leqslant \frac{1}{N}\int \mathbb{E}\left\{[K_h(\mathbf{s}-\mathbf{x}_n)]^2\right\}\mathrm{d}\mathbf{s} \tag{14.12}$$

Now observe that, switching the order of integration once more,

$$\int \mathbb{E}\left\{[K_h(\mathbf{s}-\mathbf{x}_n)]^2\right\}\mathrm{d}\mathbf{s} = \int\left\{\int [K_h(\mathbf{s}-\mathbf{s}')]^2\,\mathrm{d}\mathbf{s}\right\} f(\mathbf{s}')\,\mathrm{d}\mathbf{s}'$$

From the definition of K_h and a change of variable argument,

$$\int [K_h(\mathbf{s}-\mathbf{s}')]^2\,\mathrm{d}\mathbf{s} = \frac{1}{h^{2d}}\int\left[K\left(\frac{\mathbf{s}-\mathbf{s}'}{h}\right)\right]^2\mathrm{d}\mathbf{s} = \frac{1}{h^d}\int [K(\mathbf{u})]^2\,\mathrm{d}\mathbf{u}$$

Putting this together with (14.12) gives the bound

$$\xi_N \leqslant \int \frac{1}{Nh^d} \|K\|^2 f(\mathbf{s}') \, \mathrm{d}\mathbf{s}' = \frac{1}{Nh^d} \|K\|^2$$

The term $\|K\|^2 := \|K\|_2^2$ is finite by assumption. Recalling that $Nh^d = Nh_N^d \to \infty$, we see that $\xi_N \to 0$ as required. □

14.1.4 Commentary

In some fields of science, researchers have considerable knowledge about parametric classes and specific functional forms. For example, the theory of Brownian motion describes how the location of a tiny particle in liquid is approximately normally distributed. Thus the underlying theory provides an exact parametric class. In this kind of setting the parametric approach excels. It allows us to generalize by combining data with information we have on functional forms.

Unfortunately, the quantitative foundations of economics and other social sciences are looser and more prone to shifting over time. Econometricians usually come to the table with less knowledge of parametric classes and functional forms. These facts make nonparametric techniques attractive.

At the same time, nonparametric methods do not solve all our problems. The theoretical results presented above are purely asymptotic. Finite sample results are available, but it isn't possible to obtain strong results in this direction without correspondingly strict assumptions on the target density. There is no uniform rate of convergence for all target densities (Devroye and Lugosi 2001, p. 85). This is because nonparametric methods have relatively little structure in the form of prior knowledge and hence require abundant data.

14.2 Controlling Complexity

In the last section we discussed flexible estimation methods that perform well asymptotically. In this section we turn our attention to finite sample properties. A common thread will be ridge regression, which is a popular method of estimation in both econometrics and machine learning (see, e.g., Peysakhovich and Naecker 2015, Kim and Swanson 2014, or Varian 2014). Ridge regression also connects to some deep ideas at the heart of finite sample theory, including complexity, prior knowledge and the bias–variance trade-off.

14.2.1 Ridge Regression

Let's start off in the classical OLS setting of §12.1.1, with assumptions 12.1.2–12.1.4 all in force. The usual OLS estimator is $\hat{\boldsymbol{\beta}}$ as given in (12.3). It can also be expressed as

$$\hat{\boldsymbol{\beta}} = \operatorname*{argmin}_{\mathbf{b} \in \mathbb{R}^K} \sum_{n=1}^{N} (y_n - \mathbf{x}_n^\top \mathbf{b})^2$$

As shown in §11.1.2, the OLS estimator minimizes the empirical risk under quadratic loss when the hypothesis space is the set of linear functions. Under our current assumptions, it is also unbiased for $\boldsymbol{\beta}$ (theorem 12.1.1) and, by the Gauss–Markov theorem, it has the lowest variance among all linear unbiased estimators of $\boldsymbol{\beta}$ (theorem 12.1.3).

While the Gauss–Markov theorem has historical importance, a more natural way to evaluate estimators is to consider their mean squared error, which tells us directly how much probability mass the estimator puts around the object it is trying to estimate (see §9.2.3). Recalling (9.9) on page 259, the MSE of an estimator $\hat{\mathbf{b}}$ of $\boldsymbol{\beta}$ is defined as

$$\operatorname{mse}(\hat{\mathbf{b}}, \boldsymbol{\beta}) := \mathbb{E}\left\{ \|\hat{\mathbf{b}} - \boldsymbol{\beta}\|^2 \right\}$$

As exercise 14.4.8 asks you to show, the following representation is also valid:

$$\operatorname{mse}(\hat{\mathbf{b}}, \boldsymbol{\beta}) = \mathbb{E}\left\{ \| \hat{\mathbf{b}} - \mathbb{E}[\hat{\mathbf{b}}] \|^2 \right\} + \| \mathbb{E}[\hat{\mathbf{b}}] - \boldsymbol{\beta} \|^2 \tag{14.13}$$

This equation extends (9.10) on page 259, and tells us that MSE is the sum of a variance and a bias term. Minimization of MSE involves a trade-off between these two terms. Typically, the optimal choice is not at either extreme: MSE is minimized when some amount of bias is admitted.

Applying this idea to the OLS setting, Hoerl and Kennard (1970) showed that there exists a biased linear estimator that has lower mean squared error than $\hat{\boldsymbol{\beta}}$. The estimator is defined as the solution to the modified least squares problem

$$\min_{\mathbf{b} \in \mathbb{R}_K} \left\{ \sum_{n=1}^{N} (y_n - \mathbf{x}_n^\top \mathbf{b})^2 + \lambda \|\mathbf{b}\|^2 \right\} \tag{14.14}$$

where $\lambda \geqslant 0$ is called the **regularization parameter**. In solving (14.14), we are minimizing the empirical risk plus a term that penalizes large values of $\|\mathbf{b}\|$. The effect is to "shrink" the solution relative to the unpenalized solution $\hat{\boldsymbol{\beta}}$. Some calculus shows that the solution to (14.14) is

$$\hat{\boldsymbol{\beta}}_\lambda := (\mathbf{X}^\top \mathbf{X} + \lambda \mathbf{I})^{-1} \mathbf{X}^\top \mathbf{y} \tag{14.15}$$

The estimator $\hat{\boldsymbol{\beta}}_\lambda$ is called the **ridge regression estimator**. Note that

(i) $\hat{\boldsymbol{\beta}}_\lambda$ is the OLS estimator when $\lambda = 0$ and

(ii) $\hat{\boldsymbol{\beta}}_\lambda$ is biased whenever $\lambda > 0$ (ex. 14.4.9).

The following result is proved in Hoerl and Kennard (1970).

Theorem 14.2.1 *Under the OLS assumptions 12.1.2–12.1.4, there exists a $\lambda > 0$ such that*

$$\operatorname{mse}\left(\hat{\boldsymbol{\beta}}_\lambda, \boldsymbol{\beta}\right) < \operatorname{mse}\left(\hat{\boldsymbol{\beta}}, \boldsymbol{\beta}\right)$$

The reduction in MSE over the least squares estimator occurs because, for some intermediate value of λ, the variance of $\hat{\boldsymbol{\beta}}_\lambda$ falls by more than enough to offset the bias induced by regularization.

Note that, for suitable choice of λ, the ridge regression estimator $\hat{\boldsymbol{\beta}}_\lambda$ outperforms $\hat{\boldsymbol{\beta}}$ even though all of the classical OLS assumptions are valid. At the same time the right choice of λ is a nontrivial problem. This problem falls under the heading of model selection, which is the topic treated in the next few sections.

14.2.1.1 Interpretation

The traditional view of ridge regression runs as follows: The standard OLS assumptions are treated as valid. There may, however, be instances where $\mathbf{X}^\top \mathbf{X}$ is almost singular due to strong correlation between regressors. In this case the process of inverting $\mathbf{X}^\top \mathbf{X}$ is numerically unstable. We can stabilize the inversion by adding some positive value of λ in (14.15).

Here's another view: The standard OLS assumptions are implausible. Since our loss function is quadratic, we would ideally like to obtain the regression function f^* but recovering this infinite dimensional object with a finite amount of data is ill-posed. We need to control the complexity of the candidate functions we use to approximate the regression function. The regularization term in ridge regression provides a means of managing complexity.

14.2.1.2 Tikhonov Regularization

Let's build some more intuition for the result in theorem 14.2.1 by running simulations. We'll frame the simulations in a general setting, of which ridge regression is a special case.

We know that the least squares estimator is the solution to an overdetermined system of equations. There is an existing theory for solving ill-posed linear systems in high dimensions. The basic idea is that any attempt to back out or infer a complex object by solving a system about which we have limited information requires a degree of regularization.

To illustrate, suppose that

(i) $\mathbf{A}\mathbf{b} = \mathbf{c}$ is an overdetermined system, where $\mathbf{A}$ is $N \times K$ with $N > K$.

(ii) Due to measurement error, we only observe an approximation $\mathbf{c}_0$ of $\mathbf{c}$.

(iii) $\mathbf{b}^*$ is the (unobservable) least squares solution $\operatorname{argmin}_{\mathbf{b}} \|\mathbf{A}\mathbf{b} - \mathbf{c}\|^2$.

In the absence of additional information, a natural approach to approximating $\mathbf{b}^*$ is to solve $\mathbf{A}\mathbf{b} = \mathbf{c}_0$ by least squares. An alternative, less obvious approach, is to minimize

$$m(\lambda) := \|\mathbf{A}\mathbf{b} - \mathbf{c}_0\|^2 + \lambda \|\mathbf{b}\|^2 \tag{14.16}$$

for some small but positive λ. This second approach is called **Tikhonov regularization**. We are minimizing least squares plus a penalty term.

Let's look at a simulation where $\mathbf{A}$ is chosen stochastically but with a tendency towards multicollinearity.[3] To aid clarity, we first set $\mathbf{b}^* := (10, 10, \ldots, 10)^\top$, and then set $\mathbf{c} := \mathbf{A}\mathbf{b}^*$. By construction, $\mathbf{b}^*$ is a solution to the system $\mathbf{A}\mathbf{b}^* = \mathbf{c}$, and also the least squares solution.

Measurement of $\mathbf{c}$ is corrupted with a Gaussian shock. In particular, $\mathbf{c}_0$ is drawn from $\mathrm{N}(\mathbf{c}, \sigma^2 \mathbf{I})$ where σ is a small positive number. We then plot the OLS solution based on $\mathbf{c}_0$, which minimizes $\|\mathbf{A}\mathbf{b} - \mathbf{c}_0\|^2$, and the regularized solution, which minimizes $m(\lambda)$ in (14.16). The former are plotted against their index in green, while the latter are plotted in blue. The true solution $\mathbf{b}^*$ is plotted in black. The result is figure 14.4.

The figure shows 10 solutions each for the ordinary and regularized solutions, corresponding to 10 draws of $\mathbf{c}_0$. The regularized solutions are much closer to the true solution on average.

Note that this result is dependent on a reasonable choice for λ. If you experiment with the code on the text website, you will see that for very small values of λ, the regularized solutions are almost the same as the unregularized solutions. Conversely, very large values of λ pull the regularized solutions too close to the zero vector.

14.2.2 Subset Selection and Ridge Regression

One problem frequently faced in regression problems is which variables to include. For example, if we are comparing crime rates across different cites, we can think of

3. Full details on the choice of $\mathbf{A}$ are given in the code for this chapter at `johnstachurski.net/emet.html`.

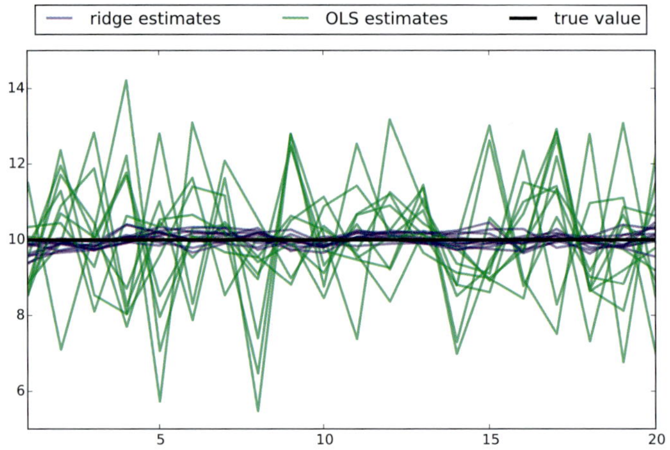

Figure 14.4 Effect of Tikhonov regularization, $\lambda = 1$

any number of variables that might be relevant (median wage, unemployment, police density, etc.). The same is true if we are trying to model credit default rates for some group of individuals, or educational attainment across schools. A similar problem arises in time series models, where we want to know how many lags of the state variables to include. The general problem is known as **subset selection**, since we are trying to choose the right subset of all candidate regressors.

Further dimensions appear when we consider basis functions. Given a set of covariates $\mathbf{x}$, we have the option to map this into a larger vector $\boldsymbol{\phi}(\mathbf{x})$ using basis functions, as discussed in §11.2.1. For example, given a single covariate x, we may consider mapping it into $\boldsymbol{\phi}(x) = (1, x, x^2, \ldots, x^d)$ and regressing y on $\boldsymbol{\phi}(x)$. As we saw in figures 8.5–8.8 (page 231), a good choice of d is crucial. Choosing d is another example of the subset selection problem because we are trying to decide whether to include the regressor x^j for some given j.

Subset selection is a version of the empirical risk minimization problem. Suppose that we have output y and inputs $\mathbf{x} \in \mathbb{R}^K$, in the sense that $\mathbf{x}$ contains K candidate regressors. If we want to include all regressors, then we can minimize empirical risk over $\mathcal{H}_\ell$ in (11.4), the hypothesis space of linear functions from $\mathbb{R}^K$ to $\mathbb{R}$. If we wish to exclude some subset of regressors, we can set $I \subset \{1, \ldots, K\}$ to be the set of indices of the regressors we want to exclude and regress y on the remainder, which is equivalent to minimizing the empirical risk over the hypothesis space

$$\mathcal{H}_{-I} := \{ \text{ all functions } f(\mathbf{x}) = \mathbf{b}^\top \mathbf{x} \text{ with } b_k = 0 \text{ for all } k \in I \}$$

We are back to the problem of choosing a suitable hypothesis space over which to minimize empirical risk.

The subset selection problem has been tackled by many researchers. Well-known approaches include the Akaike Information Criterion (AIC), the Bayesian Information Criterion (BIC), and Mallow's C_p statistic. For example, Mallow's C_p statistic consists of two terms, one increasing in the size of the empirical risk, and the other increasing in $|I|$, the size of the subset selected. The objective is to minimize the statistic, which involves trading off poor fit (large empirical risk) against excess complexity of the hypothesis space (large $|I|$).

One of the problems with subset selection is that K regressors means 2^K subsets to step through.[4] To avoid this computational problem, one alternative is to use ridge regression. With ridge regression, the regularization term leads us to choose an estimate with smaller norm. What this means, in practice, is that the coefficients of less helpful regressors are driven towards zero, thereby "almost excluding" those regressors. While the model selection problem is not solved, it has been reduced to tuning a single parameter.

We can illustrate the idea by reconsidering the regression problem discussed in §8.2.3. Figures 8.5–8.8 (see page 231) showed the fit we obtained by minimizing empirical risk over larger and larger hypothesis spaces. The hypothesis spaces were the sets $\mathscr{P}_d$ of degree d polynomials for different values of d. For each d we minimized the empirical risk over $\mathscr{P}_d$, which translates into solving

$$\min_{\mathbf{b}} \sum_{n=1}^{N} \left[y_n - \mathbf{b}^\top \boldsymbol{\phi}(x_n)\right]^2 \quad \text{where} \quad \boldsymbol{\phi}(x) = (x^0, x^1, \ldots, x^d)$$

As discussed above, choosing the right d is isomorphic to subset selection, since we are deciding what powers of x to include as regressors. Figure 8.4 (page 230) showed that intermediate values of d did best at minimizing risk.

We can do a similar thing using ridge regression. First, let's take $\mathscr{P}_{14}$ as our hypothesis space. This space is certainly large enough to provide a good fit to the data, but with empirical risk minimization the result is overfitting (see figure 8.8 on page 233). Here, instead of using empirical risk minimization, we solve the regularized problem

$$\min_{\mathbf{b}} \sum_{n=1}^{N} \left\{ \left[y_n - \mathbf{b}^\top \boldsymbol{\phi}(x_n)\right]^2 + \lambda \|\mathbf{b}\|^2 \right\}$$

for different values of λ. The data used here are exactly the same data used in the original figures 8.5–8.8 from §8.2.3. The solution for each λ we denote by $\hat{\boldsymbol{\beta}}_\lambda$, which is the ridge regression estimator, and the resulting prediction function we denote by $\hat{f}_\lambda$,

4. Remember Sala-i-Martin (1997) and his two million growth regressions?

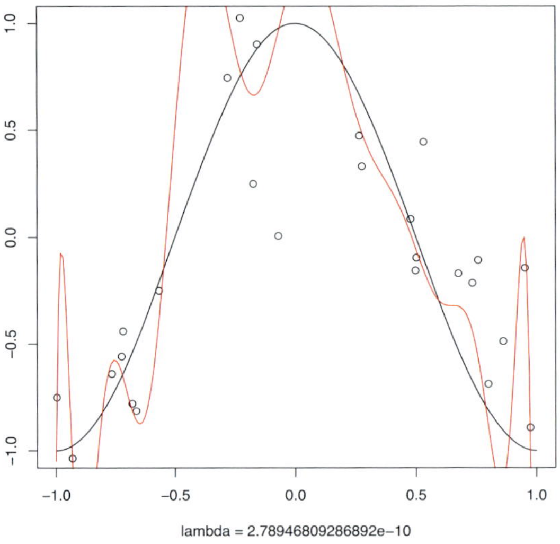

Figure 14.5 Fitted polynomial, $\lambda \approx 0$

so that $\hat{f}_\lambda(x) = \hat{\boldsymbol{\beta}}_\lambda^\top \boldsymbol{\phi}(x)$.

The function $\hat{f}_\lambda$ is plotted in red for increasingly larger values of λ over figures 14.5–14.7. The black line is the risk-minimizing function. In figure 14.5, the value of λ is too small to impose any real restriction, and the procedure overfits. In figure 14.6, the value of λ is larger and the fit is good. In figure 14.7 the value of λ is too large and the estimate is poor.

As in §8.2.3, we can compute the risk of each function $\hat{f}_\lambda$, since we know the underlying model (see (8.25) on page 229). The risk is plotted against λ in figure 14.8. The x-axis is on log-scale. The risk is smallest for small but nonzero values of λ.

14.2.3 Bayesian Methods and Regularization

The ideal case with model selection is that we have clear guidance from economic theory on which regressors to include, which functional forms to use, which values of our regularization parameter to choose, and so on. If theory or prior knowledge provides this information, then every effort should be made to exploit it. One technique for injecting prior information into statistical estimation is via Bayesian analysis. Let's now look at Bayesian linear regression and how it compares to ridge regression.

Suppose that our regression data take the linear form $\mathbf{y} = \mathbf{X}\boldsymbol{\beta} + \mathbf{u}$. To simplify the

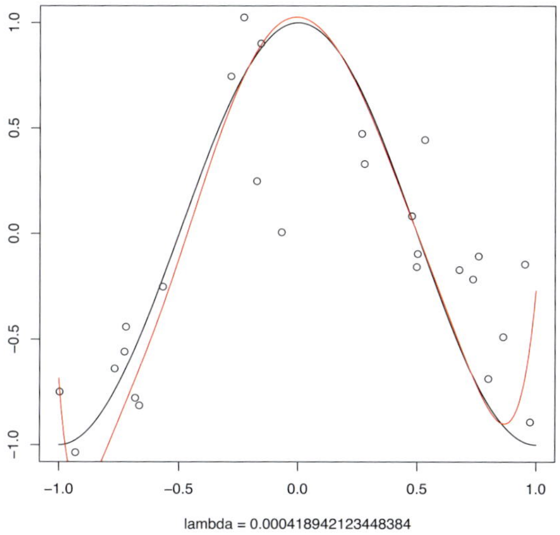

Figure 14.6 Fitted polynomial, $\lambda \approx 0.0004$

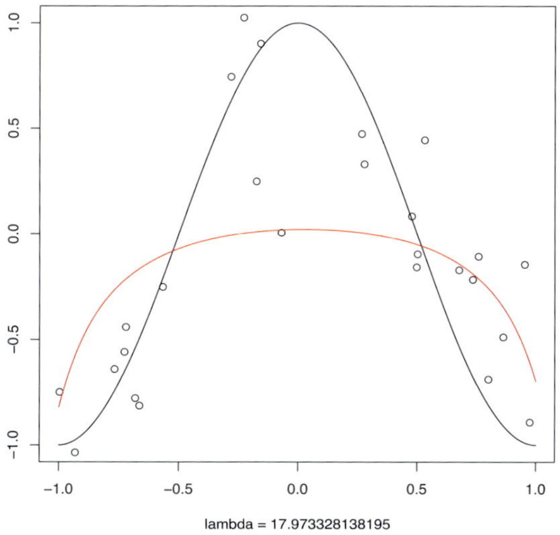

Figure 14.7 Fitted polynomial, $\lambda \approx 18$

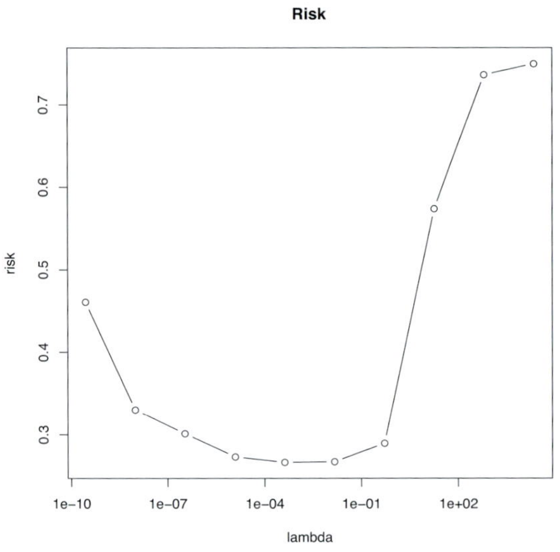

Figure 14.8 Risk of $\hat{f}_\lambda$ plotted against λ

presentation we will assume that $\mathbf{X}$ is nonrandom. (Taking $\mathbf{X}$ to be random leads to the same conclusions but with a longer derivation). As before, $\mathbf{u}$ is random and unobservable. The new feature provided by the Bayesian perspective is that we take $\boldsymbol{\beta}$ to be random and unobservable as well. In addition we are assumed to have subjective prior beliefs regarding likely values for these variates, expressed in the form of probability distributions. Here we take the priors to be $\mathcal{L}(\mathbf{u}) = \mathrm{N}(\mathbf{0}, \sigma^2\mathbf{I})$ and $\mathcal{L}(\boldsymbol{\beta}) = \mathrm{N}(\mathbf{0}, \tau^2\mathbf{I})$.

Given our model $\mathbf{y} = \mathbf{X}\boldsymbol{\beta} + \mathbf{u}$, our prior on $\mathbf{u}$ implies that the density of $\mathbf{y}$ given $\boldsymbol{\beta}$ is $\mathrm{N}(\mathbf{X}\boldsymbol{\beta}, \sigma^2\mathbf{I})$. In generic notation, we can write our distributions as

$$p(\mathbf{y} \,|\, \boldsymbol{\beta}) = \mathrm{N}(\mathbf{X}\boldsymbol{\beta}, \sigma^2\mathbf{I}) \quad \text{and} \quad p(\boldsymbol{\beta}) = \mathrm{N}(\mathbf{0}, \tau^2\mathbf{I}) \tag{14.17}$$

Applying Bayes' law (see (5.25)) to the pair $(\mathbf{y}, \boldsymbol{\beta})$, we obtain

$$p(\boldsymbol{\beta} \,|\, \mathbf{y}) = \frac{p(\mathbf{y} \,|\, \boldsymbol{\beta}) p(\boldsymbol{\beta})}{p(\mathbf{y})} \tag{14.18}$$

The left-hand side is the posterior density of $\boldsymbol{\beta}$ given the data $\mathbf{y}$, and represents our new beliefs updated from the prior on the basis of the data $\mathbf{y}$.

One way to summarize the information contained in the posterior is by examining its maximum value. The maximizer of the posterior is called the **maximum a poste-**

riori (MAP) probability estimate. Taking logs of (14.18) and dropping the term that does not contain $\boldsymbol{\beta}$, it can be expressed as

$$\hat{\boldsymbol{\beta}}_M := \underset{\boldsymbol{\beta}}{\operatorname{argmax}} \{\ln p(\mathbf{y} \mid \boldsymbol{\beta}) + \ln p(\boldsymbol{\beta})\} \tag{14.19}$$

Inserting our functional forms into (14.17), dropping constant terms and multiplying by -1, we obtain the expression

$$\hat{\boldsymbol{\beta}}_M = \underset{\boldsymbol{\beta}}{\operatorname{argmin}} \left\{ \sum_{n=1}^{N} (y_n - \mathbf{x}_n^\top \boldsymbol{\beta})^2 + \frac{\sigma^2}{\tau^2} \|\boldsymbol{\beta}\|^2 \right\} \tag{14.20}$$

This is precisely the penalized least squares problem (14.14) on page 387, where the regularization parameter λ is equal to $(\sigma/\tau)^2$. In view of (14.15), the solution is

$$\hat{\boldsymbol{\beta}}_M := (\mathbf{X}^\top \mathbf{X} + (\sigma/\tau)^2 \mathbf{I})^{-1} \mathbf{X}^\top \mathbf{y}$$

Thus Bayesian estimation provides a principled derivation of the penalized objective function from ridge regression. Bayesian analysis provides the same effect as Tikhonov regularization, but now regularization arises out of combining prior knowledge with the data. Moreover, at least in principle, the value $(\sigma/\tau)^2$ is part of our prior knowledge, and hence there is no model selection problem.

In practice, one could of course question the assertion that we have so much prior knowledge that the regularization parameter $\lambda := (\sigma/\tau)^2$ is pinned down. If such knowledge is lacking, then we are back at the model selection problem. In the next section we forgo the assumption that this strong prior knowledge is available, and consider a more automated approach to choosing λ.

14.2.4 Cross-Validation

A natural way to think about model selection is to think about minimizing risk. Recall that, given loss function L and a system producing input–output pairs $(\mathbf{x}, y) \in \mathbb{R}^{K+1}$ with joint distribution P, the prediction risk of a function $f : \mathbb{R}^K \to \mathbb{R}$ is the expected loss

$$R(f) := \mathbb{E}[L(y, f(\mathbf{x}))] = \int \int L(t, f(\mathbf{s})) P(\mathrm{d}t, \mathrm{d}\mathbf{s})$$

that occurs when we use $f(\mathbf{x})$ to predict y. Now suppose that we observe N IID input–output pairs $\mathbf{z}_{\mathcal{D}} := \{(\mathbf{x}_1, y_1), \ldots (\mathbf{x}_N, y_N)\}$. Given a selection of models, we would like to find the one that takes this data set and returns a predictor $\hat{f}$ such that $\hat{f}$ has lower prediction risk than the predictors returned by the other models.

We have to be precise in defining risk because, if we define it as $\mathbb{E}[L(y, \hat{f}(\mathbf{x}))]$, then we are taking expectation over all randomness, including that in $\hat{f}$, which depends on the data set $\mathbf{z}_{\mathcal{D}}$. What we want to do now is take the data set as given, and see how well we can do in terms of predicting new values as evaluated by expected loss. Hence we define the prediction risk of $\hat{f}$ to be the expected loss taking $\mathbf{z}_{\mathcal{D}}$ (and hence $\hat{f}$) as given:

$$R(\hat{f} \mid \mathcal{D}) := \mathbb{E}[L(y, \hat{f}(\mathbf{x})) \mid \mathcal{D}] = \int \int L(t, \hat{f}(\mathbf{s}))P(\mathrm{d}t, \mathrm{d}\mathbf{s})$$

If we have a collection of models M indexed by m, and $\hat{f}_m$ is the predictor produced by fitting model m with data $\mathcal{D}$, then we would like to find the model m^* such that

$$R(\hat{f}_{m^*} \mid \mathcal{D}) \leqslant R(\hat{f}_m \mid \mathcal{D}) \quad \text{for all } m \in M$$

The obvious problem with this idea is that risk is unobservable. If we knew the joint distribution P then we could calculate it; but then again, if we knew P there would be no need to estimate anything in the first place.

Looking at this problem, you might have the following idea: Although we don't know P, we do have the data $\mathbf{z}_{\mathcal{D}}$, which consists of IID draws from P. From the law of large numbers, we know that expectations can be approximated by averages over IID draws, so we could approximate $R(\hat{f} \mid \mathcal{D})$ by

$$\frac{1}{N} \sum_{n=1}^{N} L(y_n, \hat{f}(\mathbf{x}_n))$$

where the pairs $(\mathbf{x}_n, y_n)$ are from the data set $\mathbf{z}_{\mathcal{D}}$.

However, this is just the empirical risk, and the empirical risk is a highly biased estimator of the risk. This point was discussed extensively in §8.2.3. See, in particular, figure 8.4 on page 230. The point that figure made was that complex models tend to overfit, producing low empirical risk, but high risk. In essence, the problem is that we are using the data $\mathbf{z}_{\mathcal{D}}$ twice, for conflicting objectives. First, we are using it to fit the model, producing $\hat{f}$. Second, we are using it to evaluate the predictive ability of $\hat{f}$ on new observations.

So what we really need is fresh data. New data will tell us how $\hat{f}$ performs out-of-sample. If we had J new observations $(y_j^v, \mathbf{x}_j^v)$, then we could estimate the risk by

$$\frac{1}{J} \sum_{j=1}^{J} L(y_j^v, \hat{f}(\mathbf{x}_j^v))$$

Of course, this isn't a genuine solution because we don't have any new data in general. One way to work around this problem is to take $\mathbf{z}_{\mathcal{D}}$ and split it into two disjoint subsets, called the **training set** and the **validation set**. The training set is used to fit

$\hat{f}$ and the validation set is used to estimate the risk of $\hat{f}$. We then repeat this for all models and choose the one with lowest estimated risk.

Since data are scarce, a more common procedure is **cross-validation**, which attempts to use the whole data set for both fitting the model and estimating the risk. To illustrate the idea, suppose that we partition the data set into two subsets $\mathcal{D}_1$ and $\mathcal{D}_2$. First, we use $\mathcal{D}_1$ as the training set and $\mathcal{D}_2$ as the validation set. Next we use $\mathcal{D}_2$ as the training set, and $\mathcal{D}_1$ as the validation set. The estimate of the risk is the average of the estimates of the risk produced in these two steps.

Of course, we could divide the data into more than two sets. The extreme is to partition the data into N subsets. This procedure is called **leave-one-out cross-validation**. Letting $\mathcal{D}_{-n} := \mathbf{z}_{\mathcal{D}} \setminus \{(\mathbf{x}_n, y_n)\}$, the data set with just the nth data point $(\mathbf{x}_n, y_n)$ omitted, the leave-one-out cross validation algorithm can be expressed as follows:

```
for n = 1, ..., N do
    fit f̂_{-n} using data D_{-n}
    set r_n := L(y_n, f̂_{-n}(x_n))
end for
return the risk estimate r := (1/N) Σ_{n=1}^N r_n
```

At each step inside the loop, we fit the model using all but the nth data point, and then predict the nth data point using the fitted model. The prediction quality is evaluated in terms of loss. Repeating this n times, we produces estimate of the risk using average loss. On an intuitive level, the procedure is attractive because we are using the available data intensively but still evaluating based on out-of-sample error.

In terms of model selection, the idea is to run each model through the cross-validation procedure, and then select the one that produces the lowest value of r, the estimated risk. Let's illustrate this idea, by considering again the ridge regression procedure used in §14.2.2. In this problem the set of models is indexed by λ, the regularization parameter in the ridge regression. The data set $\mathbf{z}_{\mathcal{D}}$ is the set of points shown in figures 14.5–14.7. For each λ, the fitted function $\hat{f}_\lambda$ is

$$\hat{f}_\lambda(x) = \hat{\boldsymbol{\beta}}_\lambda^\top \boldsymbol{\phi}(x) \quad \text{where} \quad \hat{\boldsymbol{\beta}}_\lambda := \operatorname*{argmin}_{\mathbf{b}} \sum_{n=1}^{N} \left\{ (y_n - \mathbf{b}^\top \boldsymbol{\phi}(x_n))^2 + \lambda \|\mathbf{b}\|^2 \right\}$$

Recall here that $\boldsymbol{\phi}(x) = (x^0, x^1, \ldots, x^d)$ with d fixed at 14, so we are fitting a polynomial of degree 14 to the data by minimizing regularized least squares error. The amount of regularization is increasing in λ. The resulting functions $\hat{f}_\lambda$ were shown for different values of λ in figures 14.5–14.7. Intermediate values of λ produced the best fit in terms of minimizing risk (see figures 14.6 and 14.8).

In that discussion, we used the fact that we knew the underlying model to evaluate the risk, and hence the values of λ that produce low risk (figure 14.8). In real

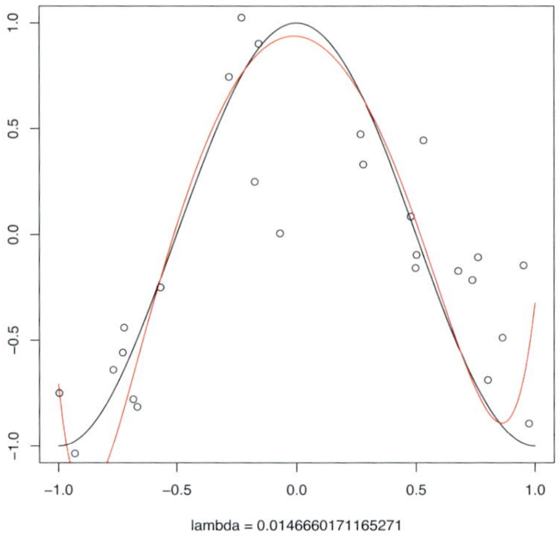

Figure 14.9 Fitted polynomial, $\lambda \approx 0.015$

estimation problems, risk is unobservable, and we need to choose λ on the basis of the data alone (assuming we don't have prior knowledge, as in the Bayesian case—see §14.2.3). Let's see how a data-based procedure such as cross-validation performs in terms of selecting a good value of λ.

In this experiment, for each λ in the grid `exp(seq(-22, 10, length=10))` we perform leave-one-out cross-validation. The fit at each step within the loop is via ridge regression, omitting the nth data point, and the resulting polynomial is used to predict y_n from x_n. The prediction error is measured by squared loss. In other words, for each λ in the grid, we use the following algorithm to estimate the risk:

for $n = 1, \ldots, N$ **do**
  set $\hat{\boldsymbol{\beta}}_{\lambda,-n} := \operatorname{argmin}_{\mathbf{b}} \sum_{i \neq n} \{(y_i - \mathbf{b}^\top \boldsymbol{\phi}(x_i))^2 + \lambda \|\mathbf{b}\|^2\}$
  set $r_{\lambda,n} := (y_n - \hat{\boldsymbol{\beta}}_{\lambda,-n}^\top \boldsymbol{\phi}(x_n))^2$
end for
return $r_\lambda := \frac{1}{N} \sum_{n=1}^N r_{\lambda,n}$

The value of λ producing the smallest estimated risk r_λ is around 0.015. This is in fact very close to the value that minimizes the actual risk (see figure 14.8 on page 394). The associated function $\hat{f}_\lambda$ is plotted in red in figure 14.9, and indeed the fit is close. In this instance, our fully automated procedure is successful.[5]

5. The code to run this experiment can be found at `johnstachurski.net/emet.html`.

14.3 Further Reading

Textbook treatments of nonparametric methods in econometrics can be found in Pagan and Ullah (1999), Li and Racine (2006), Ullah (1989), Henderson and Parmeter (2015) and Hansen (2015). Bosq (1996) covers nonparametrics for time series models. Recent studies in the econometrics literature using nonparametric or semiparametric methods include Chen and Hong (2012), Jeong et al. (2012), Henderson et al. (2012), Christensen (2014), Canay et al. (2013), Su and Ullah (2013), Bajari et al. (2013), Newey (2013), Hansen (2014a), Mastromarco and Simar (2015), Hickman and Hubbard (2015), Matzkin (2015), Bhattacharya (2015), and Du and Escanciano (2015). A beautiful overview of nonparametrics and the method of sieves can be found in Geman and Hwang (1982).

Good discussions of ridge regression and cross-validation can be found in Friedman et al. (2009) and Abu-Mostafa et al. (2012). One alternative to ridge regression is the LASSO method (Tibshirani 1996), where the term $\lambda \sum_{k=1}^{K} b_k^2$ in (14.14) is replaced with an absolute deviation penalty $\lambda \sum_{k=1}^{K} |b_k|$. Also related is penalized maximum likelihood estimation. A recent application can be found in Gentzkow et al. (2015).

An important contribution to the literature on subset selection is the least angle regression of Efron et al. (2004). A discussion of this method in relation to other subset techniques can be found in Hesterberg et al. (2008).

Recent papers treating regularization and related topics within the econometrics literature include Florens (2003), Carrasco et al. (2007), Chen and Reiss (2011), Florens and Simoni (2014), Darolles et al. (2011), Hoderlein and Holzmann (2011), Horowitz (2014), Hautsch et al. (2012), Li et al. (2015), Lunde et al. (forthcoming), Chernozhukov et al. (2015), and Ando and Bai (forthcoming).

Regarding implementations, one powerful and increasingly popular package for Bayesian learning is Stan. See `http://mc-stan.org/`. A popular and high-quality routine for cross validation in the context of ridge regression can be found in the `sklearn.linear_model.RidgeCV` method in Python's `scikit-learn` package.

14.4 Exercises

Ex. 14.4.1 Let $\| \cdot \|_1$ denote the L_1 norm as defined in (14.2). Show that $\|f - g\|_1$ is bounded over the set of all densities.[6]

Ex. 14.4.2 Prove the triangle inequality in the case of L_1 (see (14.3)).

Ex. 14.4.3 Prove the claim in example 14.1.1 on page 379.[7]

6. Hint: It is a basic property of integration that $g \leqslant h$ pointwise implies $\int g \leqslant \int h$.
7. Hint: Use fact 14.1.2 and exercise 8.5.9 on page 245.

Ex. 14.4.4 For the case $d = 1$, show that $\hat{f}$ in (14.5) is a density for every N, every $h > 0$ and every realization of the sample.[8]

Ex. 14.4.5 Let x be a finite random variable taking value s_n in $\{s_n\}_{n=1}^N$ with probability p_n. Let y be independent of x with density g on $\mathbb{R}$. Show that $z = x + y$ has density $f(s') = \sum_{n=1}^N g(s' - s_n)p_n$.

Ex. 14.4.6 Let $\mathbf{x}$ be multivariate Gaussian, with distribution $\text{N}(\boldsymbol{\mu}, \boldsymbol{\Sigma})$ and let $h > 0$. Suppose that $\boldsymbol{\Sigma}$ is nonsingular. Let K be the density of $\mathbf{x}$ (see page 130) and let K_h be the density of $h\mathbf{x}$. Show that K and K_h satisfy the relationship shown in (14.8). (The result is true more generally but the Gaussian case is a nice exercise.)

Ex. 14.4.7 Let $x_1, \ldots, x_N$ be IID scalar random variables with common density f and let $\hat{f}$ be as defined in (14.5). Show that if $K(t) = \mathbb{1}\{-1/2 < t < 1/2\}$, then, for any number s, we have

$$\mathbb{E}[\hat{f}(s)] = \frac{1}{h}\int_{s-h/2}^{s+h/2} f(t)\,\mathrm{d}t$$

Ex. 14.4.8 Verify the claim in (14.13).

Ex. 14.4.9 By taking derivatives in (14.14) to find stationary points, derive the expression for the ridge regression estimator $\hat{\boldsymbol{\beta}}_\lambda$. Show that $\hat{\boldsymbol{\beta}}_\lambda$ is a biased estimator of $\boldsymbol{\beta}$ whenever $\lambda > 0$.

Ex. 14.4.10 In deriving $\hat{\boldsymbol{\beta}}_\lambda$ in (14.15), we do not require the full rank assumption (see assumption 11.1.1 on page 302) whenever $\lambda > 0$. Explain why.

Ex. 14.4.11 Verify (14.20) on page 395 using (14.17) and (14.19).

14.4.1 Solutions to Selected Exercises

Solution to Ex. 14.4.1. Let f and g be any two densities on $\mathbb{R}^J$. By the triangle inequality, for any given $\mathbf{s} \in \mathbb{R}^J$, we have

$$|f(\mathbf{s}) - g(\mathbf{s})| \leqslant |f(\mathbf{s})| + |g(\mathbf{s})| = f(\mathbf{s}) + g(\mathbf{s})$$

Integrating both sides of this inequality gives $\|f - g\|_1 \leqslant 2$. □

Solution to Ex. 14.4.2. Fix densities f, g and h on $\mathbb{R}^d$. Pick any $\mathbf{s} \in \mathbb{R}^d$. By the scalar triangle inequality, we have $|f(\mathbf{s}) - g(\mathbf{s})| \leqslant |f(\mathbf{s}) - h(\mathbf{s})| + |h(\mathbf{s}) - g(\mathbf{s})|$. As per the hint in exercise 14.4.1, integration preserves this bound. This gives the triangle inequality in L_1. □

8. Hint: Try a change-of-variables argument.

Solution to Ex. 14.4.3. By Pinsker's inequality and exercise 8.5.9, we have

$$\|f(\cdot\,;\mu,\sigma) - f(\cdot\,;\bar{x}_N, s_N)\|_1 \leqslant \sqrt{\frac{\delta_N}{2}} \quad \text{where } \delta_N := \ln\frac{s_N}{\sigma} + \frac{\sigma^2 + (\mu - \bar{x}_N)^2}{2s_N^2} - \frac{1}{2}$$

Since $\bar{x}_N \stackrel{p}{\to} \mu$ and $s_N \stackrel{p}{\to} \sigma$ (see §9.2.4), applying the rules in fact 6.1.1 on page 161, we have $\delta_N \stackrel{p}{\to} 0$. The claim follows. □

Solution to Ex. 14.4.4. The nonnegativity of $\hat{f}$ is obvious. To show that $\int \hat{f}(s)\,\mathrm{d}s = 1$, it is enough to show that $\int K\left(\frac{s-a}{h}\right)\mathrm{d}s = h$ for any given number a. This equality can be obtained by the change of variable $u := (s-a)/h$, which leads to

$$\int K\left(\frac{s-a}{h}\right)\mathrm{d}s = \int K(u)h\,\mathrm{d}u = h\int K(u)\,\mathrm{d}u$$

Since K is a density, the proof is done. □

Solution to Ex. 14.4.5. Fix $s' \in \mathbb{R}$. By the law of total probability we have

$$\mathbb{P}\{z \leqslant s'\} = \sum_{n=1}^{N} \mathbb{P}\{x + y \leqslant s' \mid x = s_n\}\mathbb{P}\{x = s_n\} = \sum_{n=1}^{N} \mathbb{P}\{y \leqslant s' - s_n\}p_n$$

Differentiating with respect to s' gives the stated form for the density of z. □

Solution to Ex. 14.4.6. Adopting the setting and notation of ex. 14.4.6, our aim is to show that K and K_h satisfy (14.8). By our rules for linear transforms of Gaussians (see page 133), the distribution of $h\mathbf{x}$ is $\mathrm{N}(h\boldsymbol{\mu}, h^2\boldsymbol{\Sigma})$. That is,

$$K_h(\mathbf{s}) = (2\pi)^{-d/2}\det(h^2\boldsymbol{\Sigma})^{-1/2}\exp\left\{-\frac{1}{2}(\mathbf{s} - h\boldsymbol{\mu})^\top(h^2\boldsymbol{\Sigma})^{-1}(\mathbf{s} - h\boldsymbol{\mu})\right\}$$

Applying scalar multiple rules for inverses and determinants (see page 52 and page 52), we can also write this as

$$K_h(\mathbf{s}) = \frac{1}{h^d}(2\pi)^{-d/2}\det(\boldsymbol{\Sigma})^{-1/2}\exp\left\{-\frac{1}{2}(\mathbf{s}/h - \boldsymbol{\mu})^\top\boldsymbol{\Sigma}^{-1}(\mathbf{s}/h - \boldsymbol{\mu})\right\}$$

That is, $K_h(\mathbf{s}) := \frac{1}{h^d}K(\frac{\mathbf{s}}{h})$, where K is the density of $\mathrm{N}(\boldsymbol{\mu}, \boldsymbol{\Sigma})$. □

Solution to Ex. 14.4.10. The full rank assumption is not necessary because the matrix $\mathbf{Z} := \mathbf{X}^\top\mathbf{X} + \lambda\mathbf{I}$ is always invertible. To show this it suffices to show that $\mathbf{Z}$ is positive definite. This is not difficult to verify using the definition. □

Part IV

Appendix

Chapter 15

Appendix

15.1 Sets

In the text we often refer to the **real numbers**. This set is denoted by $\mathbb{R}$, and we understand it to contain "all the numbers." $\mathbb{R}$ can be visualized as the "continuous" real line:

The term "real" sounds odd but it means "not imaginary."

$\mathbb{R}$ is an example of a **set**. A set is a collection of distinct objects viewed as a whole. In the case of $\mathbb{R}$, the objects are numbers. Other examples of sets are the set of all rectangles in the plane, or the set of all monkeys in Japan.

If A is a set, then the statement $x \in A$ means that x is contained in (alternatively, is an element of) A. If B is another set, then $A \subset B$ means that any element of A is also an element of B, and we say that A is a **subset** of B. The statement $A = B$ means that A and B contain the same elements (or, equivalently, $A \subset B$ and $B \subset A$). For example, if $\mathbb{I}$ is the irrational numbers,[1] then $\mathbb{I} \subset \mathbb{R}$. Also, $0 \in \mathbb{R}$, $\pi \in \mathbb{R}$, $-3 \in \mathbb{R}$, $e \in \mathbb{R}$, and so on.

Commonly used subsets of $\mathbb{R}$ include the intervals. For arbitrary a and b in $\mathbb{R}$, the

1. The **irrationals** are those numbers such as π and $\sqrt{2}$ that cannot be expressed as fractions of whole numbers.

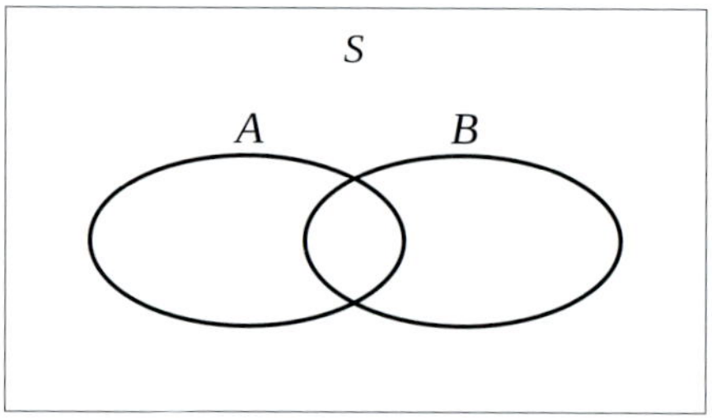

Figure 15.1 Sets A and B in S

open interval (a, b) is defined as

$$(a, b) := \{x \in \mathbb{R} : a < x < b\}$$

while the **closed interval** $[a, b]$ is defined as

$$[a, b] := \{x \in \mathbb{R} : a \leqslant x \leqslant b\}$$

We also use half open intervals such as $[a, b) := \{x \in \mathbb{R} : a \leqslant x < b\}$, half lines such as $(-\infty, b) = \{x \in \mathbb{R} : x < b\}$, and so on.

Let S be a set and let A and B be two subsets of S, as illustrated in figure 15.1. The **union** of A and B is the set of elements of S that are in A or B or both:

$$A \cup B := \{x \in S : x \in A \text{ or } x \in B\}$$

Here and elsewhere, "or" is used in the mathematical sense. It means "and/or". The **intersection** of A and B is the set of all elements of S that are in both A and B:

$$A \cap B := \{x \in S : x \in A \text{ and } x \in B\}$$

The set $A \setminus B$ is all points in A that are not points in B:

$$A \setminus B := \{x \in S : x \in A \text{ and } x \notin B\}$$

The **complement** of A is the set of elements of S that are not contained in A:

$$A^c := S \setminus A := \{x \in S : x \notin A\}$$

Figure 15.2 illustrate these definitions.

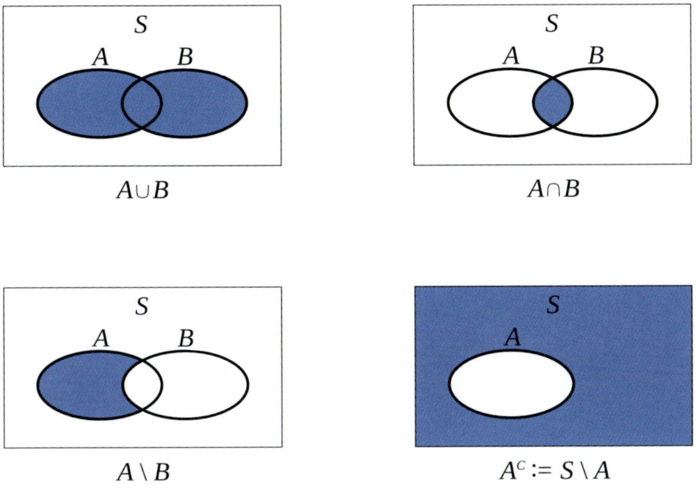

Figure 15.2 Union, intersection, and complement

For example, since $\mathbb{R}$ consists of the irrationals $\mathbb{I}$ and the rationals $\mathbb{Q}$, we have

$$\mathbb{Q} \subset \mathbb{R}, \; \mathbb{I} \subset \mathbb{R}, \; \mathbb{Q} \cup \mathbb{I} = \mathbb{R}, \; \mathbb{Q}^c = \mathbb{I}, \text{ etc.}$$

Also

$$\mathbb{N} := \{1, 2, 3, \ldots\} \subset \mathbb{Q} \subset \mathbb{R}$$

The **empty set** is the set containing no elements. It is denoted by $\emptyset$. If the intersection of A and B equals $\emptyset$, then A and B are said to be **disjoint**.

The next fact lists some well-known rules for set-theoretic operations.

Fact 15.1.1 Let A and B be subsets of S. The following statements are true:

(i) $A \cup B = B \cup A$ and $A \cap B = B \cap A$.

(ii) $(A \cup B)^c = B^c \cap A^c$ and $(A \cap B)^c = B^c \cup A^c$.

(iii) $A \setminus B = A \cap B^c$.

(iv) $(A^c)^c = A$.

If $\{A_\alpha\}_{\alpha \in \Lambda}$ is an infinite collection of subsets of S, the union $\cup_{\alpha \in \Lambda} A_\alpha$ is defined as all $x \in S$ such that $x \in A_\alpha$ for some $\alpha \in \Lambda$. The intersection $\cap_{\alpha \in \Lambda} A_\alpha$ is all $x \in S$ that lie in A_α for all $\alpha \in \Lambda$.

Example 15.1.1 If $A_n = (-n, n)$ for each $n \in \mathbb{N}$, then $\cup_{n \in \mathbb{N}} A_n = \mathbb{R}$.

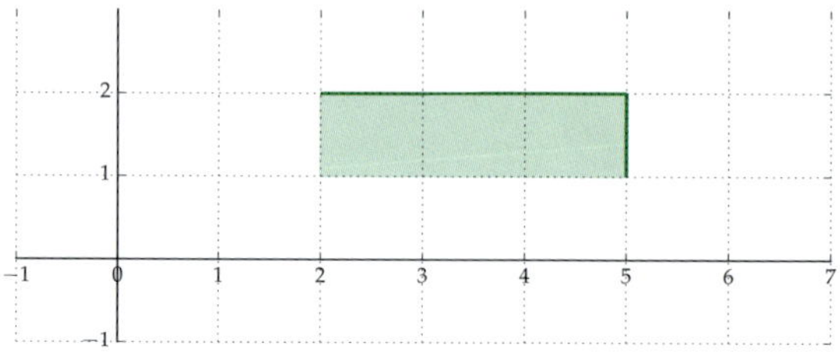

Figure 15.3 Rectangle $(2, 5] \times (1, 2]$ in $\mathbb{R}^2$

15.1.1 Cartesian Products

Collections with natural order are frequently written as **tuples**. These are finite sequences of terms, usually denoted using notation such as (a_1, a_2) or (x_1, x_2, x_3). Collections of tuples arise naturally in Cartesian products. The **Cartesian product** of set $A_1, \ldots, A_N$ is the set

$$A_1 \times \cdots \times A_N := \{(a_1, \ldots, a_N) : a_n \in A_n \text{ for } n = 1, \ldots, N\}$$

The **vector space** $\mathbb{R}^N$ is one example of a Cartesian product, defined as

$$\mathbb{R}^N = \mathbb{R} \times \cdots \times \mathbb{R} \quad (N \text{ times})$$

Thus $\mathbb{R}^N$ is all tuples $(x_1, \ldots, x_N)$ with $x_n \in \mathbb{R}$ for each n.

A useful class of subsets of $\mathbb{R}^N$ is those that are formed as Cartesian products of intervals. These are called **rectangles**. An example is

$$I = \times_{n=1}^{N} (a_n, b_n] := \{(x_1, \ldots, x_N) \in \mathbb{R}^N : a_n < x_n \leqslant b_n \text{ for } n = 1, \ldots, N\}$$

where $a_1, b_1, \ldots, a_N, b_N$ are given numbers. The rectangle $(2, 5] \times (1, 2]$ is shown in figure 15.3.

15.2 Functions

There are two fundamental primitives in mathematics: sets and functions.[2] A **function** f from set A to set B is a rule that associates to each element of A a unique element

2. Actually functions can be represented as a special type of set containing ordered pairs, and hence in pure mathematics cannot claim to be as foundational as sets. However, for our purposes, it will be fine to think of a function as a primitive in its own right.

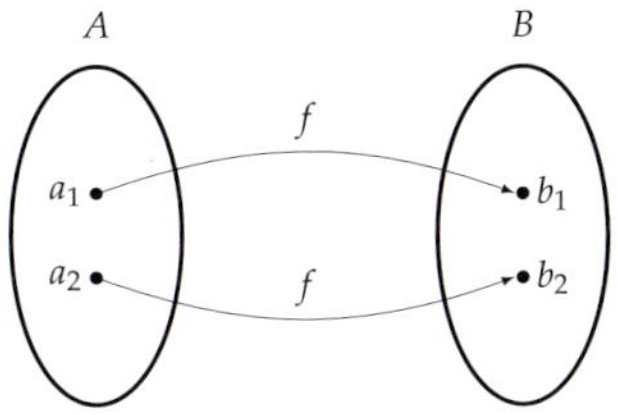

Figure 15.4 A function from A to B

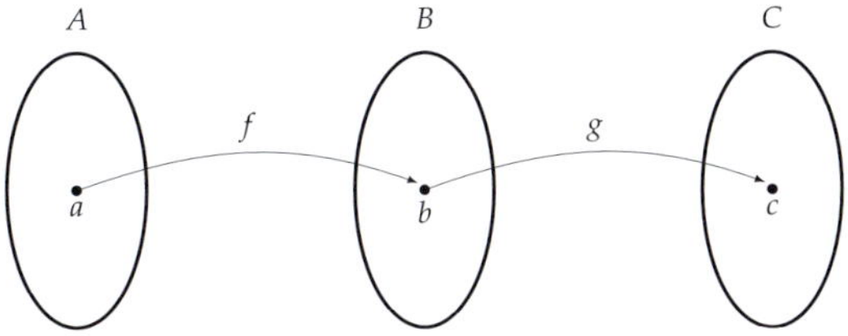

Figure 15.5 The composition $g \circ f$

of B. The symbols $f\colon A \to B$ means that f is a function from A to B. The set A is called the **domain** of f, while B is called the **codomain**. Figure 15.4 illustrates.

If $f\colon A \to B$ and $g\colon B \to C$ then the function $h\colon A \to C$ defined by $h(a) = g(f(a))$ is called the **composition** of g and f, and written as $g \circ f$.

Example 15.2.1 If $f\colon \mathbb{R} \to \mathbb{R}$ is defined by $f(x) = e^x =: \exp(x)$ and $g\colon \mathbb{R} \to \mathbb{R}$ is defined by $g(x) = x^2$, then

$$(g \circ f)(x) = g(f(x)) = \exp(2x)$$

If a and b are points such that $f(a) = b$, then a is called a **preimage** of b. The set of preimages of b can be empty, a singleton or contain multiple values. The set of points

$$\{b \in B : f(a) = b \text{ for some } a \in A\}$$

is called the **range** of f, and written as $\operatorname{rng} f$. Thus b is in the range of f if it has at least one preimage. Figure 15.6 depicts the range of a given function $f\colon A \to B$.

A function $f\colon A \to B$ is called **one-to-one** if distinct elements of A are always mapped into distinct elements of B. That is, if

$$a \in A,\ a' \in A, \text{ and } a \neq a' \implies f(a) \neq f(a')$$

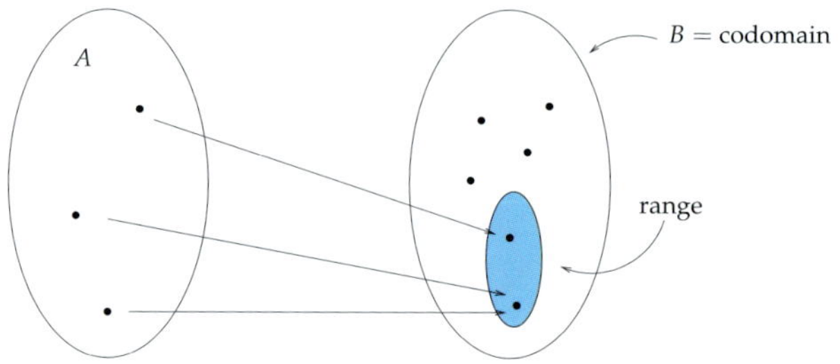

Figure 15.6 Range of $f\colon A \to B$

or, equivalently, if $f(a) = f(a') \implies a = a'$. Evidently $f\colon A \to B$ is one-to-one if and only if each element of B has at most one preimage under f. If a function $f\colon A \to B$ and f is one-to-one, then the equation $f(x) = b$ has at most one solution.

A function $f\colon A \to B$ is called **onto** if $\operatorname{rng} f = B$; this is if every $b \in B$ has at least one preimage. If $f\colon A \to B$ and f is onto, then the equation $f(x) = b$ has at least one solution.

Finally, $f\colon A \to B$ is called a **bijection** if it is both one-to-one and onto. Bijections are sometimes called one-to-one correspondences.

Example 15.2.2 The function $f(x) = 2x$ is a bijection from $\mathbb{R}$ to $\mathbb{R}$.

If f is a bijection, then the equation $f(x) = b$ always has exactly one solution. We can therefore define the **inverse function** to f, denoted by f^{-1}, as the map from $B \to A$ such that $f^{-1}(b)$ is the unique a with $f(a) = b$.

Example 15.2.3 The function $f\colon A \to B$ in figure 15.4 is a bijection, with $f^{-1}\colon B \to A$ mapping b_1 to a_1 and b_2 to a_2.

Example 15.2.4 If $f\colon \mathbb{R} \to (0, \infty)$ is defined by $f(x) = \exp(x) := e^x$ and $\phi\colon (0, \infty) \to \mathbb{R}$ is defined by $\phi(x) = \log(x)$, then $\phi = f^{-1}$ because, for any $a \in \mathbb{R}$, we have $\phi(f(a)) = \log(\exp(a)) = a$.

Fact 15.2.1 Let $f\colon A \to B$ and $g\colon B \to C$ be bijections.

(i) f^{-1} is a bijection and its inverse is f.

(ii) $f^{-1}(f(a)) = a$ for all $a \in A$.

(iii) $f(f^{-1}(b)) = b$ for all $b \in B$.

(iv) $g \circ f$ is a bijection from A to C and $(g \circ f)^{-1} = f^{-1} \circ g^{-1}$.

Part (iv) of fact 15.2.1 is illustrated in figure 15.7.

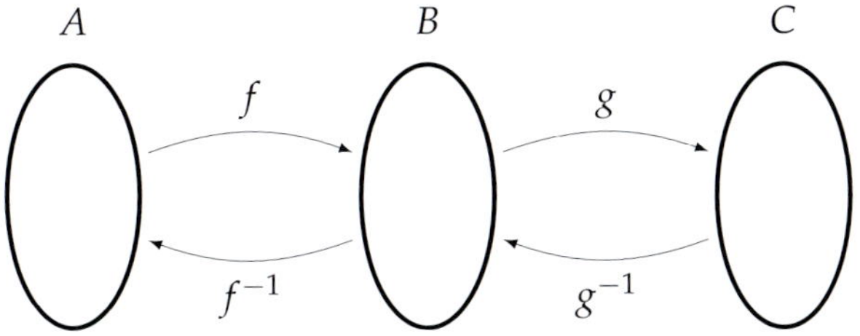

Figure 15.7 The inverse of $g \circ f$ is $f^{-1} \circ g^{-1}$

15.2.1 Preimage of Sets

Given any function f from A to B and any subset E of B, the symbol $f^{-1}(E)$ denotes the set of points that are mapped into E under f. That is,

$$f^{-1}(E) := \{x \in A : f(x) \in E\}$$

The set $f^{-1}(E)$ is called the **preimage** of E under f.

Example 15.2.5 If $f(x) = x^2$ and $E = [0,1]$, then $f^{-1}(E) = [-1,1]$.

Preimages of sets interact nicely with set-theoretic operations. For example, given any $E, F \subset B$, we have

(i) $f^{-1}(E \cup F) = f^{-1}(E) \cup f^{-1}(F)$,
(ii) $f^{-1}(E \cap F) = f^{-1}(E) \cap f^{-1}(F)$, and
(iii) $f^{-1}(E^c) = [f^{-1}(E)]^c$.

The equalities in (i) and (ii) also extend to infinite intersections and unions.

15.3 Cardinality and Measure

For finite sets we have a fairly clear idea of what "the same size" means. For infinite sets things get tricker. It is nonetheless valuable to distinguish infinite sets according to size. To this end, when a bijection exists between sets A and B, they are said to have the **same cardinality**, and we write $|A| = |B|$.

Example 15.3.1 If $A = \{a_1, \ldots, a_n\}$ and $B = \{b_1, \ldots, b_n\}$ then $|A| = |B|$ because $f(a_n) = b_n$ is a bijection. (Remember that elements of a set are by definition distinct.)

More generally, we have the following result:

Fact 15.3.1 If A and B are finite then $|A| = |B|$ if and only if A and B have the same number of elements.

This fact tells us that classifying sets by cardinality generalizes the notion of classifying sets by number of elements.

Fact 15.3.2 For any sets A, B, C we have $|A| = |B|$ and $|B| = |C| \implies |A| = |C|$.

In other words, cardinality is transitive. This follows from the fact that compositions of bijections are bijections (fact 15.2.1).

A nonempty set A is called **finite** if $|A| = |\{1, 2, \ldots, n\}|$ for some $n \in \mathbb{N}$. Otherwise, A is called **infinite**.

Sets that either are finite or have the same cardinality as $\mathbb{N}$ are called **countable**.

Example 15.3.2 $E := \{2, 4, \ldots\}$ is countable because it can be put in one-to-one correspondence with $\mathbb{N}$ via $f : E \ni m \mapsto m/2 \in \mathbb{N}$.

In essence, sets formed by sequences are countable.

Uncountable sets are sets that are not countable. For example, $\mathbb{R}$ is uncountable, as is any set that contains a nonempty open interval (a, b). Put simply, you cannot write down a sequence that will exhaust the elements of these sets. The story is similar for $\mathbb{R}^N$. (Such sets are said to have **the power of the continuum**.) For a beautiful proof that $\mathbb{R}$ is uncountable, look up the diagonalization argument of Georg Cantor.

15.3.1 Lebesgue Measure and Sets of Measure Zero

A set $B \subset \mathbb{R}$ is said to have **Lebesgue measure zero** in $\mathbb{R}$ if, given any $\epsilon > 0$, there exists a sequence of intervals $I_n = (a_n, b_n)$ such that B is contained in the union of these intervals and $\sum_{n=1}^{\infty}(b_n - a_n) \leqslant \epsilon$. The definition extends to $\mathbb{R}^N$ by replacing intervals with rectangles (see page 408 for a definition of the latter).

For example, any countable set has measure zero. To see this in $\mathbb{R}$, let $C := \cup_{n=1}^{\infty}\{x_n\}$ with $x_n \in \mathbb{R}$. Fix $\epsilon > 0$. To each x_n we assign an interval (a_n, b_n) containing x_n and satisfying $b_n - a_n < \epsilon 2^{-n}$. The union of intervals contains C, and, in addition, the sum of their lengths is $\epsilon \sum_{n=1}^{\infty} 2^{-n} = \epsilon$.

Uncountable sets can have measure zero too. For example, every linear subspace S with $\dim S < N$ has measure zero in $\mathbb{R}^N$. A more classical example of an uncountable set with measure zero is the Cantor set. Details can be found in many texts on analysis.

The concept of measure zero sets forms part of a branch of mathematics called **measure theory**. We have used aspects of measure theory in this text—for example, in our discussion of σ-algebras in §4.1.1.2 and probabilities in §4.1.2. The basic problem of measure theory is how to provide a well-defined notion of "measure" or "size" to sets. This is easy if we just want to assign area to a circle (area $= \pi r^2$) or rectangle, or volume to a sphere. But what about an arbitrary subset of $\mathbb{R}^N$? Is there a well-defined and widely accepted notion of size for such a set?

The answer to this question is affirmative. The so-called **Lebesgue outer measure** is a map, typically denoted λ^*, that gives a natural notion of size to any set. It works by approximating arbitrary sets by simpler sets, like rectangles, and agrees with standard notions of area or volume for common geometric objects. The only problem is that it isn't always additive, in the sense that

$$\lambda^*(A \cup B) = \lambda^*(A) + \lambda^*(B) \tag{15.1}$$

can fail. To get around this problem, we exclude any sets that cause (15.1) to fail. That is, we define the **Lebesgue measurable sets** to be those set on which additivity holds. This causes no difficulty since the discarded sets never come up in day-to-day analysis. In fact we usually focus on a smaller class of well-behaved sets, called the **Borel sets**. These were introduced in §4.1.1.2.

15.4 Real-Valued Functions

For any set A, if $f\colon A \to \mathbb{R}$ then f is called a **real-valued function**. If f and g are real-valued functions, then $f + g$ is defined by $(f+g)(x) = f(x) + g(x)$, while αf is defined by $(\alpha f)(x) = \alpha f(x)$. A **maximizer** of f on A is a point $a^* \in A$ such that $f(a^*) \geqslant f(a)$ for all $a \in A$. The value $f(a^*)$ is called the **maximum** of f on A. A **minimizer** of f on A is a point $b^* \in A$ such that $f(b^*) \leqslant f(a)$ for all $a \in A$. The value $f(b^*)$ is called the **minimum** of f on A.

Monotone increasing transformations of functions do not affect maximizers. To see this, let $f\colon \mathbb{R} \to \mathbb{R}$ and let h be **monotone increasing**, in the sense that if $x \leqslant x'$, then $h(x) \leqslant h(x')$, and let g be the function defined by $g(a) = h(f(a))$. Any maximizer of f on A is also a maximizer of g on A. To see why, let $a \in A$. Since a^* is a maximizer of f, it must be the case that $f(a) \leqslant f(a^*)$. Since h is monotone increasing, this implies that $h(f(a)) \leqslant h(f(a^*))$. Given that a was chosen arbitrarily, we have now shown that $g(a^*) \geqslant g(a)$ for all $a \in A$. In other words, a^* is a maximizer of g on A.

15.4.1 Sup and Inf

Maximizers and minimizers don't always exist. To illustrate, consider $f\colon (0,1) \to (0,1)$ defined by $f(x) = x$. The function f has neither maximizer nor minimizer on $(0,1)$. For example, no $a \in (0,1)$ is a minimizer because $b := a/2$ is in $(0,1)$ and $f(b) < f(a)$.

To negotiate this kind of problem, we can use the notion of supremum instead. If A is a set, then the **supremum** $s := \sup A$ is the unique $s \in \mathbb{R}$ such that (i) $a \leqslant s$ for

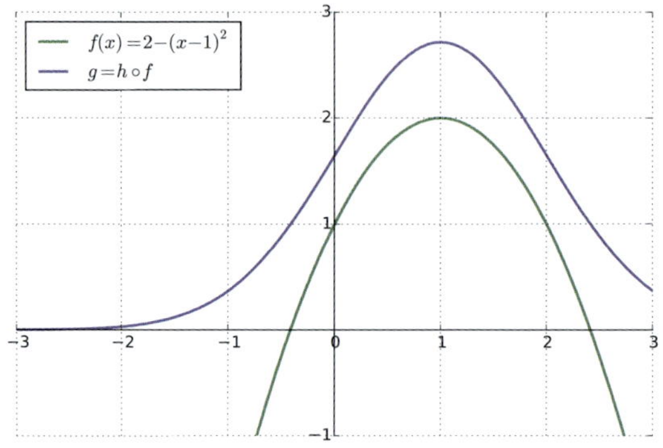

Figure 15.8 Increasing transform $h(x) = \exp(x/2)$ preserves the maximizer

every $a \in A$ and (ii) there exists a sequence $\{x_n\} \subset A$ such that $x_n \to s$. For example, 1 is the supremum of both $(0,1)$ and $[0,1]$. The **infimum** $i := \inf A$ is the unique $i \in \mathbb{R}$ such that (i) $a \geqslant i$ for every $a \in A$ and (ii) there exists a sequence $\{x_n\} \subset A$ such that $x_n \to i$. For example, 0 is the infimum of both $(0,1)$ and $[0,1]$.

One can show that the supremum and infimum of any bounded set A exist. The boundedness requirement can be dropped when the values $-\infty$ and ∞ are admitted as a possible infima and suprema.

Returning to our original example with $f(x) = x$, while $\max_{x \in (0,1)} f(x)$ is not well-defined, $\sup_{x \in (0,1)} f(x) := \sup\{f(x) : x \in (0,1)\} = \sup(0,1) = 1$.

Bibliography

Abu-Mostafa, Y. S., M. Magdon-Ismail, and H.-T. Lin. 2012. *Learning from Data.* AML-Book.com.

Ando, T., and J. Bai. Forthcoming. Selecting the regularization parameters in high-dimensional panel data models: consistency and efficiency. *Econometric Reviews.*

Angrist, J. D., and J.-S. Pischke. 2009. *Mostly Harmless Econometrics: An Empiricist's Companion.* Princeton: Princeton University Press.

Aschenbrenner, K., and B. Biehl. 1994. "Improved safety through improved technical measures?" In *Challenges to Accident Prevention. The Issue of Risk Compensation Behaviour,* edited by R. M. Trimpop and G. J. S. Wilde, 81–89.

Athey, S. 2015. Machine Learning and Causal Inference for Policy Evaluation. In *Proceedings of the 21th ACM SIGKDD International Conference on Knowledge Discovery and Data Mining,* 5–6. ACM.

Athey, S., and S. Wager. 2015. *Estimation and Inference of Heterogeneous Treatment Effects using Random Forests.* Technical report. arXiv preprint arXiv:1510.04342.

Auffhammer, M., and C. D. Wolfram. 2014. Powering up China: income distributions and residential electricity consumption. *American Economic Review* 104 (5): 575–580.

Axler, S. 2015. *Linear Algebra Done Right.* New York: Springer.

Bajari, P., H. Hong, and D. Nekipelov. 2013. Econometrics for game theory. In *Advances in Economics and Econometrics: Theory and Applications, 10th World Congress,* 3:3–52.

Belloni, A., V. Chernozhukov, and C. Hansen. 2014. High-dimensional methods and inference on structural and treatment effects. *Journal of Economic Perspectives* 28:29–50.

Benhabib, J., A. Bisin, and S. Zhu. 2015. The wealth distribution in Bewley economies with capital income risk. *Journal of Economic Theory* 159:489–515.

Bergeijk, P. A. van, and S. Brakman. 2010. *The Gravity Model in International Trade: Advances and Applications.* Cambridge, UK: Cambridge University Press.

Bhattacharya, D. 2015. Nonparametric welfare analysis for discrete choice. *Econometrica* 83 (2): 617–649.

Bishop, C. M. 2006. *Pattern Recognition and Machine Learning.* New York: Springer.

Bonhomme, S., and J.-M. Robin. 2009. Assessing the equalizing force of mobility using short panels: France, 1990–2000. *The Review of Economic Studies* 76 (1): 63–92.

Bosq, D. 1996. *Nonparametric Statistics for Stochastic Processes: Estimation and Prediction.* Vol. 110. New York: Springer.

Brooks, S., A. Gelman, G. Jones, and X.-L. Meng. 2011. *Handbook of Markov Chain Monte Carlo.* Boca Raton: CRC Press.

Bru, B., and M. Yor. 2002. Comments on the life and mathematical legacy of Wolfgang Doeblin. *Finance and Stochastics* 6 (1): 3–47.

Cameron, A. C., and P. K. Trivedi. 2005. *Microeconometrics: Methods and Applications.* Cambridge, UK: Cambridge University Press.

Canay, I. A., A. Santos, and A. M. Shaikh. 2013. On the testability of identification in some nonparametric models with endogeneity. *Econometrica* 81 (6): 2535–2559.

Carrasco, M., J.-P. Florens, and E. Renault. 2007. "Linear inverse problems in structural econometrics estimation based on spectral decomposition and regularization." In *Handbook of Econometrics,* edited by J. J. Heckman and E. E. Leamer, 6:5633–5751. Elsevier.

Casella, G., and R. L. Berger. 2002. *Statistical Inference.* 2nd ed. Pacific Grove CA: Duxbury.

Chen, B., and Y. Hong. 2012. Testing for smooth structural changes in time series models via nonparametric regression. *Econometrica* 80 (3): 1157–1183.

Chen, X., and T. M. Christensen. 2015. Optimal uniform convergence rates and asymptotic normality for series estimators under weak dependence and weak conditions. *Journal of Econometrics* 188:447–465.

Chen, X., H. Hong, and D. Nekipelov. 2011. Nonlinear models of measurement errors. *Journal of Economic Literature* 49 (4): 901–937.

Chen, X., and M. Reiss. 2011. On rate optimality for ill-posed inverse problems in econometrics. *Econometric Theory* 27 (3): 497–521.

Cheney, W. 2001. *Analysis for Applied Mathematics.* New York: Springer.

Cheng, K. M., N. Durmaz, H. Kim, and M. L. Stern. 2012. Hysteresis vs. natural rate of US unemployment. *Economic Modelling* 29 (2): 428–434.

Chernozhukov, V., and I. Fernández-Val. 2011. Inference for extremal conditional quantile models, with an application to market and birthweight risks. *Review of Economic Studies* 78 (2): 559–589.

Chernozhukov, V., I. Fernández-Val, and B. Melly. 2013. Inference on counterfactual distributions. *Econometrica* 81 (6): 2205–2268.

Chernozhukov, V., C. B. Hansen, and M. Spindler. 2015. *Post-selection and post-regularization inference: linear models with very many controls and instruments.* Technical report. No. 15-02. MIT Department of Economics.

Christensen, T. M. 2014. Nonparametric identification of positive eigenfunctions. *Econometric Theory* 31 (06): 1310–1330.

Çinlar, E. 2011. *Probability and Stochastics.* New York: Springer.

Çinlar, E., and R. J. Vanderbei. 2013. *Real and Convex Analysis.* New York: Springer.

Cochrane, J. H. 1991. A critique of the application of unit root tests. *Journal of Economic Dynamics and Control* 15 (2): 275–284.

Darolles, S., Y. Fan, J.-P. Florens, and E. Renault. 2011. Nonparametric instrumental regression. *Econometrica* 79 (5): 1541–1565.

DasGupta, A. 2008. *Asymptotic Theory of Statistics and Probability.* New York: Springer.

Davidson, R., and J. G. MacKinnon. 2004. *Econometric Theory and Methods.* Oxford: Oxford University Press.

Devroye, L., and G. Lugosi. 2001. *Combinatorial Methods in Density Estimation.* New York: Springer.

Diaconis, P. 2009. The Markov chain Monte Carlo revolution. *Bulletin of the American Mathematical Society* 46 (2): 179–205.

Dickey, D. A., and W. A. Fuller. 1979. Distribution of the estimators for autoregressive time series with a unit root. *Journal of the American Statistical Association* 74 (366a): 427–431.

Diebold, F. X., L. Kilian, and M. Nerlove. 2009. "Time series analysis." In *The New Palgrave Dictionary of Economics*, edited by L. E. Blume and S. N. Durlauf. New York: Palgrave Macmillan.

Drenik, A., and D. J. Perez. 2015. *Price setting under uncertainty about inflation*. Technical report. New York University.

Du, Z., and J. C. Escanciano. 2015. A nonparametric distribution-free test for serial independence of errors. *Econometric Reviews* 34 (6-10): 1011–1034.

Dudley, R. M. 2002. *Real Analysis and Probability*. 2nd ed. Cambridge, UK: Cambridge University Press.

Dufour, J.-M., and A. Taamouti. 2010. Short and long run causality measures: Theory and inference. *Journal of Econometrics* 154 (1): 42–58.

Durrett, R. 2010. *Probability: Theory and Examples*. 4th ed. Cambridge, UK: Cambridge University Press.

Efron, B., T. Hastie, I. Johnstone, and R. Tibshirani. 2004. Least angle regression. *Annals of Statistics* 32 (2): 407–451.

Einav, L., and J. D. Levin. 2014. The data revolution and economic analysis. *Innovation Policy and the Economy* 14:1–24.

Evans, G. W., and S. Honkapohja. 2005. An interview with Thomas J. Sargent. *Macroeconomic Dynamics* 9 (4): 561–583.

Florens, J.-P. 2003. Inverse problems and structural econometrics. In *Advances in Economics and Econometrics: Theory and Applications, Eighth World Congress*, 2:46–85. Cambridge, UK: Cambridge University Press.

Florens, J.-P., and A. Simoni. 2014. Regularizing priors for linear inverse problems. *Econometric Theory* FirstView:1–51.

Freedman, D. A. 2009. *Statistical Models: Theory and Practice*. 2nd ed. Cambridge, UK: Cambridge University Press.

Friedman, J., T. Hastie, and R. Tibshirani. 2009. *The Elements of Statistical Learning*. 2nd ed. New York: Springer.

Geman, S., and C.-R. Hwang. 1982. Nonparametric maximum likelihood estimation by the method of sieves. *Annals of Statistics* 10 (2): 401–414.

Gentzkow, M., J. M. Shapiro, and M. Taddy. 2015. *Measuring polarization in high-dimensional data: method and application to congressional speech*. Technical report. National Bureau of Economic Research.

Geweke, J. 1996. "Monte Carlo simulation and numerical integration." In *Handbook of Computational Economics,* edited by Z. Griliches, R. F. Engle, and M. D. Intriligator, 1:731–800. Elsevier.

———. 2005. *Contemporary Bayesian Econometrics and Statistics.* Hoboken, NJ: Wiley.

Geweke, J., J. L. Horowitz, and M. Pesaran. 2006. *Econometrics: a bird's eye view.* Technical report. CESifo Working Paper Series. CESifo Group Munich.

Geweke, J., G. Koop, and H. Van Dijk. 2011. *The Oxford Handbook of Bayesian Econometrics.* Oxford: Oxford University Press.

Granger, C. W. 1969. Investigating causal relations by econometric models and cross-spectral methods. *Econometrica* 37 (3): 424–438.

Greene, W. 2011. *Econometric Analysis.* 7th ed. New York: Prentice Hall.

Gut, A. 2009. *An Intermediate Course in Probability.* 2nd ed. New York: Springer.

Hall, R. E. 1978. Stochastic implications of the life cycle-permanent income hypothesis: theory and evidence. *Journal of Political Economy* 86 (6): 971–987.

Hamilton, J. D. 1994. *Time Series Analysis.* Princeton: Princeton University Press.

Hansen, B. E. 2014a. "Nonparametric sieve regression: Least squares, averaging least squares, and cross-validation." In *The Oxford Handbook of Applied Nonparametric and Semiparametric Econometrics and Statistics,* edited by J. Racine, L. Su, and A. Ullah. Oxford: Oxford University Press.

———. 2015. *Econometrics.* Textbook in preparation. http://www.ssc.wisc%20edu/~bhansen/econometrics.

Hansen, L. P. 2014b. Nobel lecture: Uncertainty outside and inside economic models. *Journal of Political Economy* 122 (5): 945–987.

Hansen, L. P., and T. J. Sargent. 2008. *Robustness.* Princeton: Princeton University Press.

Hansen, L. P., and K. J. Singleton. 1982. Generalized instrumental variables estimation of nonlinear rational expectations models. *Econometrica* 50 (5): 1269–1286.

Hautsch, N., L. M. Kyj, and R. C. Oomen. 2012. A blocking and regularization approach to high-dimensional realized covariance estimation. *Journal of Applied Econometrics* 27 (4): 625–645.

Hayashi, F. 2000. *Econometrics.* Princeton: Princeton University Press.

Heckman, J. J. 1992. Haavelmo and the birth of modern econometrics: A review of the history of econometric ideas by Mary Morgan. *Journal of Economic Literature* 30 (2): 876–886.

Henderson, D. J., J. A. List, D. L. Millimet, C. F. Parmeter, and M. K. Price. 2012. Empirical implementation of nonparametric first-price auction models. *Journal of Econometrics* 168 (1): 17–28.

Henderson, D. J., and C. F. Parmeter. 2015. *Applied Nonparametric Econometrics.* Cambridge, UK: Cambridge University Press.

Hesterberg, T., N. H. Choi, L. Meier, and C. Fraley. 2008. Least angle and ℓ_1 penalized regression: A review. *Statistics Surveys* 2:61–93.

Hickman, B. R., and T. P. Hubbard. 2015. Replacing sample trimming with boundary correction in nonparametric estimation of first-price auctions. *Journal of Applied Econometrics* 30:739–762.

Hill, R. C., W. E. Griffiths, and G. C. Lim. 2008. *Principles of Econometrics.* Vol. 5. Hoboken, NJ: Wiley.

Hoderlein, S., and H. Holzmann. 2011. Demand analysis as an ill-posed inverse problem with semiparametric specification. *Econometric Theory* 27 (03): 609–638.

Hoerl, A. E., and R. W. Kennard. 1970. Ridge regression: biased estimation for nonorthogonal problems. *Technometrics* 12 (1): 55–67.

Hong, Y., and H. White. 1995. Consistent specification testing via nonparametric series regression. *Econometrica* 63 (5): 1133–1159.

Horowitz, J. L. 2014. Adaptive nonparametric instrumental variables estimation: Empirical choice of the regularization parameter. *Journal of Econometrics* 180 (2): 158–173.

Imbens, G. W., and D. B. Rubin. 2015. *Causal Inference in Statistics, Social, and Biomedical Sciences: An Introduction.* Cambridge, UK: Cambridge University Press.

Izenman, A. J. 2008. *Modern Multivariate Statistical Techniques: Regression, Classification, and Manifold Learning.* Vol. 1. New York: Springer.

Jänich, K. 1994. *Linear Algebra.* New York: Springer.

Jeong, K., W. K. Härdle, and S. Song. 2012. A consistent nonparametric test for causality in quantile. *Econometric Theory* 28 (04): 861–887.

Joe, H. 1997. *Multivariate Models and Multivariate Dependence Concepts.* Vol. 73. Boca Raton: CRC Press.

Jones, G. L. 2004. On the Markov chain central limit theorem. *Probability Surveys* 1:299–320.

Kendall, D., G. Batchelor, N. Bingham, W. Hayman, J. Hyland, G. Lorentz, H. Moffatt, W. Parry, A. Razborov, and C. Robinson. 1990. Andrei Nikolaevich Kolmogorov (1903–1987). *Bulletin of the London Mathematical Society* 22 (1): 31–100.

Kennedy, P. 2008. *A Guide to Econometrics.* 6th ed. Hoboken, NJ: Wiley Blackwell.

Kim, H. H., and N. R. Swanson. 2014. Forecasting financial and macroeconomic variables using data reduction methods: New empirical evidence. *Journal of Econometrics* 178:352–367.

Kim, K., and A. R. Pagan. 1999. "The econometric analysis of calibrated macroeconomic models." In *Handbook of Applied Econometrics in Macroeconomics,* edited by M. H. Pesaran and M. R. Wickens, 356–390. Oxford: Blackwell.

Koenker, R., and K. Hallock. 2001. Quantile regression: an introduction. *Journal of Economic Perspectives* 15 (4): 43–56.

Kroese, D. P., and J. C. Chan. 2014. *Statistical Modeling and Computation.* New York: Springer.

Kydland, F. E., and E. C. Prescott. 1991. The econometrics of the general equilibrium approach to business cycles. *Scandinavian Journal of Economics* 93 (2): 161–178.

Lasota, A., and M. C. Mackey. 1994. *Chaos, Fractals, and Noise: Stochastic Aspects of Dynamics.* Vol. 97. New York: Springer.

Li, J., V. Todorov, and G. Tauchen. 2015. Estimating the volatility occupation time via regularized Laplace inversion. *Econometric Theory:* 1–36.

Li, Q., and J. S. Racine. 2006. *Nonparametric Econometrics: Theory and Practice.* Princeton: Princeton University Press.

Lucas, R. E. 1978. Asset prices in an exchange economy. *Econometrica* 46 (6): 1429–1445.

Lunde, A., N. Shephard, and K. Sheppard. Forthcoming. Econometric analysis of vast covariance matrices using composite realized kernels and their application to portfolio choice. *Journal of Business and Economic Statistics.*

Manski, C. F. 1986. "Analog estimation of econometric models." In *Handbook of Econometrics,* edited by R. F. Engle and D. McFadden, 4:2559–2582. Elsevier.

Marcus, M., and H. Minc. 1988. *Introduction to Linear Algebra.* Mineola, NY: Dover Publications.

Martin, V., S. Hurn, and D. Harris. 2012. *Econometric Modelling with Time Series: Specification, Estimation and Testing.* Cambridge, UK: Cambridge University Press.

Mastromarco, C., and L. Simar. 2015. Effect of FDI and time on catching up: new insights from a conditional nonparametric frontier analysis. *Journal of Applied Econometrics* 30:826–847.

Matzkin, R. L. 2015. Estimation of nonparametric models with simultaneity. *Econometrica* 83 (1): 1–66.

McCloskey, D. N., and S. T. Ziliak. 1996. The standard error of regressions. *Journal of Economic Literature* 34 (1): 97–114.

McKernan, S.-M., C. Ratcliffe, E. Steuerle, and S. Zhang. 2014. Disparities in wealth accumulation and loss from the great recession and beyond. *American Economic Review* 104 (5): 240–244.

Meyn, S. P., and R. L. Tweedie. 2009. *Markov Chains and Stochastic Stability.* 2nd ed. Cambridge, UK: Cambridge University Press.

Mitchell, W. F. 1993. Testing for unit roots and persistence in OECD unemployment rates. *Applied Economics* 25 (12): 1489–1501.

Negri, I., and Y. Nishiyama. 2010. Review on goodness of fit tests for ergodic diffusion processes by different sampling schemes. *Economic Notes* 39 (1-2): 91–106.

Nelson, C. R., and C. R. Plosser. 1982. Trends and random walks in macroeconmic time series: some evidence and implications. *Journal of Monetary Economics* 10 (82): 139–162.

Newey, W. K. 2013. Nonparametric instrumental variables estimation. *American Economic Review* 103 (3): 550–556.

Newey, W. K., and K. D. West. 1987. A simple, positive semi-definite, heteroskedasticity and autocorrelation consistent covariance matrix. *Econometrica* 55 (3): 703–708.

Olley, G. S., and A. Pakes. 1996. The dynamics of productivity in the telecommunications equipment industry. *Econometrica* 64 (6): 1263–1297.

Pagan, A., and A. Ullah. 1999. *Nonparametric Econometrics.* Cambridge, UK: Cambridge University Press.

Pearl, J. 2009. *Causality.* 2nd ed. Cambridge, UK: Cambridge University Press.

Peysakhovich, A., and J. Naecker. 2015. *Machine learning and behavioral economics: evaluating models of choice under risk and ambiguity.* Technical report. SSRN 2548564.

Pollard, D. 2002. *A User's Guide to Measure Theoretic Probability*. Vol. 8. Cambridge, UK: Cambridge University Press.

Richey, M. 2010. The evolution of Markov chain Monte Carlo methods. *American Mathematical Monthly* 117 (5): 383–413.

Roberts, G. O., J. S. Rosenthal, et al. 2004. General state space Markov chains and MCMC algorithms. *Probability Surveys* 1:20–71.

Rosenthal, J. S. 2006. *A first Look at Rigorous Probability Theory*. 2nd ed. New Jersey: World Scientific.

Ruppert, D. 2011. *Statistics and Data Analysis for Financial Engineering*. Springer.

Ruud, P. A. 2000. *An Introduction to Classical Econometric Theory*. Oxford: Oxford University Press.

Sala-i-Martin, X. X. 1997. I just ran two million regressions. *American Economic Review* 87 (2): 178–183.

Schilling, R. L. 2005. *Measures, Integrals and Martingales*. Cambridge, UK: Cambridge University Press.

Scott, D. W. 2015. *Multivariate Density Estimation: Theory, Practice, and Visualization*. 2nd ed. Hoboken, NJ: Wiley.

Silver, N. 2012. *The Signal and the Noise: Why So Many Predictions Fail–But Some Don't*. London: Penguin Press.

Sklar, M. 1959. Fonctions de répartition à n dimensions et leurs marges. *Publications of the Institute of Statistics*: 229–231.

Stachurski, J. 2009. *Economic Dynamics: Theory and Computation*. Cambridge: MIT Press.

Stachurski, J., and V. Martin. 2008. Computing the distributions of economic models via simulation. *Econometrica* 76 (2): 443–450.

Stein, C. 1956. Inadmissibility of the usual estimator for the mean of a multivariate normal distribution. In *Proceedings of the Third Berkeley Symposium on Mathematical Statistics and Probability*, 1:197–206. 399.

Su, L., and A. Ullah. 2013. A nonparametric goodness-of-fit-based test for conditional heteroskedasticity. *Econometric Theory* 29 (01): 187–212.

Sun, Y. 2011. Robust trend inference with series variance estimator and testing-optimal smoothing parameter. *Journal of Econometrics* 164 (2): 345–366.

Taylor, J. C. 1997. *An Introduction to Measure and Probability*. New York: Springer.

Teoh, E. R. 2011. Effectiveness of antilock braking systems in reducing motorcycle fatal crash rates. *Traffic Injury Prevention* 12 (2): 169–173.

Tibshirani, R. 1996. Regression shrinkage and selection via the lasso. *Journal of the Royal Statistical Society. Series B (Methodological)* 58:267–288.

Tierney, L. 1994. Markov chains for exploring posterior distributions. *The Annals of Statistics* 22 (4): 1701–1728.

Ullah, A. 1989. *Semiparametric and Nonparametric Econometrics.* Heidelberg: Physica.

Van der Vaart, A. W. 2000. *Asymptotic Statistics.* Cambridge, UK: Cambridge University Press.

Vapnik, V. N. 2000. *The Nature of Statistical Learning Theory.* 2nd ed. New York: Springer.

———. 2006. *Estimation of Dependences Based on Empirical Data.* New York: Springer.

Varian, H. R. 2014. Big data: New tricks for econometrics. *The Journal of Economic Perspectives* 28:3–27.

Wald, A. 1939. Contributions to the theory of statistical estimation and testing hypotheses. *The Annals of Mathematical Statistics* 10 (1): 299–326.

Wasserman, L. 2013. *All of Statistics: A Concise Course in Statistical Inference.* New York: Springer.

White, H. 1980. A heteroskedasticity-consistent covariance matrix estimator and a direct test for heteroskedasticity. *Econometrica* 48 (4): 817–838.

Williams, D. 1991. *Probability with Martingales.* Cambridge, UK: Cambridge University Press.

Wooldridge, J. M. 2010. *Econometric Analysis of Cross Section and Panel Data.* 2nd ed. Cambridge: MIT Press.

Young, G. A., and R. L. Smith. 2005. *Essentials of Statistical Inference.* Cambridge, UK: Cambridge University Press.

Index